A CHILD'S HISTORY OF THE WORLD

美国学生世界历史

（英汉对照）

〔美〕希利尔⊙著

欧阳瑾⊙译

台海出版社

图书在版编目(CIP)数据

美国学生世界历史：英汉对照 / (美) 希利尔著；
欧阳瑾译 . -- 北京：台海出版社，2018.3
ISBN 978-7-5168-1779-7

Ⅰ.①美… Ⅱ.①希… ②欧… Ⅲ.①英语—汉语—
对照读物②世界史—青少年读物 Ⅳ.① H319.4：K

中国版本图书馆CIP数据核字(2018)第037456号

美国学生世界历史：英汉对照

著　　者：〔美〕希利尔	译　　者：欧阳瑾	
责任编辑：刘　峰	装帧设计：同人内文化传媒 · 书装设计	
版式设计：同人内文化传媒 · 书装设计	责任印制：蔡　旭	

出版发行：台海出版社

地　　址：北京市东城区景山东街 20 号　　邮政编码：100009

电　　话：010 — 64041652（发行，邮购）

传　　真：010 — 84045799（总编室）

网　　址：www.taimeng.org.cn/thcbs/default.htm

E-mail：thcbs@126.com

经　　销：全国各地新华书店

印　　刷：香河利华文化发展有限公司

本书如有破损、缺页、装订错误，请与本社联系调换

开　　本：710mm×1000mm　　　　1/16

字　　数：629 千字　　　　　　　印　　张：28.25

版　　次：2018年5月第1版　　　印　　次：2018年5月第1次印刷

书　　号：ISBN 978-7-5168-1779-7

定　　价：49.80 元

目录
Contents

PREFACE / 引 言 ··· 1

INTRODUCTION / 导 言 ··· 2

1 How Things Started / 万物起源 ····························· 10

2 People Who Lived in Caves / 生活在洞穴里的人 ············· 15

3 Fire! Fire!! Fire!!! / 火!火!!火!!! ··························· 20

4 From an Airplane / 从飞机上向下看 ······················· 24

5 Real History Begins / 真正的历史由此开始 ················· 28

6 The Puzzle Writers in Egypt / 埃及谜语 ··················· 33

7 The Tomb Builders / 修建坟墓的人 ······················· 38

8 A Rich Land Where There Was No Money / 没有钱的富庶之地······ 43

9 The Jews Search for a Home / 犹太人寻找家园 ············· 48

10 Fairy-Tale Gods / 神话传说中的神灵 ····················· 53

11 A Fairy-Tale War / 一场传说中的战争 ····················· 59

12 The Kings of the Jews / 犹太诸王 ························· 63

13 The People Who Made Our A B C's / 发明文字的人 ········· 67

14 Hard as Nails / 铁石心肠 ······························· 71

15 The Crown of Leaves / 桂冠 ····························· 76

16 A Bad Beginning / 邪恶的开端 ··························· 80

17 Kings with Corkscrew Curls / 一头卷发的国王 ················ 84

18 A City of Wonders and Wickedness / 奇迹和邪恶并存的城市 ·········· 87

19 A Surprise Party / 宴会奇袭 ·································· 90

20 The Other Side of the World: India / 世界的另一边：印度 ·········· 94

21 All the Way Around the World in China / 概说中国 ·············· 97

22 Rich Man, Poor Man / 富人、穷人 ·························· 100

23 Rome Kicks Out Her Kings / 罗马废除国王 ·················· 104

24 Greece vs. Persia / 希腊对波斯 ····························· 108

25 Fighting Mad / 战争狂人 ································· 114

26 One Against a Thousand / 以一敌千 ····················· 118

27 The Golden Age / 黄金时代 ····························· 123

28 When Greek Meets Greek / 当希腊人遇上希腊人 ············· 129

29 Wise Men and Otherwise / 智者与庸人 ················· 133

30 A Boy King / 少年国王 ································· 138

31 Picking a Fight / 挑起争端 ·························· 143

32 The Boot Kicks and Stamps / "靴子"左右出击 ············· 147

33 The New Champion of the World / 新的世界霸主 ············· 150

34 The Noblest Roman of Them All / 最高贵的罗马人 ············ 156

35 An Emperor Who Was Made a God / 被奉为神灵的皇帝 ·········· 162

36 "Thine Is the Kingdom, the Power, and the Glory" / "国度、权柄和
   荣耀，全是你的" ································· 167

37 Blood and Thunder / 鲜血与雷霆 ···················· 172

38 A Good Emperor and a Bad Son / 好皇帝，坏儿子 ·········· 178

39 I_H__S____V_____ / I_H_S___V____ ················· 182

40 Barbarian Invaders / 野蛮的侵略者 ·················· 186

41 Barbarians Meet the Champions of the World / 野蛮人碰上了世界霸主 ········ 191

42 New Places — New Heroes / 新的地方，新的英雄 ············· 196

43 Being Good / 为善 ································· 199

44 A Christian Kingdom in Africa / 非洲的基督教王国 ················ 204

45 Muhammad and the Early Years of Islam / 穆罕默德和早期的伊斯兰教 ········ 208

46 Arabian Days / 阿拉伯时代 ······················· 214

47 Two Empires, Two Emperors / 两个帝国，两位皇帝 ·········· 219

48 Getting a Start / 刚刚起步 ······················· 224

49 The End of the World / 世界末日 ··················· 228

50 Real Castles / 真正的城堡 ······················· 231

51 Knights and Days of Chivalry / 骑士和骑士时代 ··········· 236

52 A Pirate's Great Grandson / 了不起的海盗后裔 ··········· 241

53 A Great Adventure / 一场伟大的探险 ··············· 247

54 Tick-Tack-Toe; Three Kings in a Row / 井字过三关；连续三王 ····· 251

55 Three Kingdoms in West Africa / 西非三王国 ··········· 257

56 Bibles Made of Stone and Glass / 石头与玻璃制成的《圣经》 ······· 262

57 John, Whom Nobody Loved / 没人喜欢的约翰 ··········· 267

58 A Great Story Teller / 了不起的故事先生 ············· 271

59 "Thing-a-ma-jigger" and "What-cher-may-call-it" or a Magic Needle and a
   Magic Powder / "小小装置"和"无名之物"，或者魔针和魔粉 ·········· 275

60 Thelon Gest Wart Hate Verwas / 史上最久的战争 ········· 278

61 Print and Powder or Off with the Old, On with the New / 印刷术和火药——
   弃旧迎新 ······························· 283

62 A Sailor Who Found a New World / 发现新大陆的水手 ······· 286

63 Fortune Hunters / 淘金的人 ····················· 293

64 The Land of Enchantment or the Search for Gold and Adventure / 魅力之地：
   寻宝与冒险 ····························· 300

65 Along the Coast of East Africa / 东非沿海 ············ 304

66 Rebirth / 重生 ····························· 310

67 Christians Quarrel / 基督徒反目 ·················· 315

68 Queen Elizabeth / 伊丽莎白女王 ·················· 320

69 The Age of Elizabeth / 伊丽莎白时代·······································325

70 James the Servant or What's in a Name? / 公仆詹姆斯·············329

71 A King Who Lost His Head / 掉了脑袋的国王······················334

72 Red Cap and Red Heels / 红帽子、红鞋跟·························338

73 A Self-Made Man / 白手起家的人·······································343

74 A Prince Who Ran Away / 离家出走的王子·························347

75 America Gets Rid of Her King / 美国摆脱了国王·················351

76 Upside Down / 天翻地覆···357

77 A Little Giant / 小个子巨人··363

78 Latin America and the Caribbean Islands / 拉丁美洲和加勒比群岛·············369

79 From Pan and His Pipes to the Phonograph / 从潘及其排笛到留声机···········378

80 The Daily Papers of 1854—1865 / 1854—1865年间的日报·········384

81 Three New Postage Stamps / 三枚新邮票·····························389

82 The Age of Miracles / 奇迹时代··393

83 A Different Kind of Revolution / 另类革命·························398

84 A World at War / 战火蔓延的世界·······································404

85 A Short Twenty Years / 二十年，弹指一挥间·····················408

86 Modern Barbarians / 现代"蛮子"···415

87 Fighting the Dictators / 对抗独裁者·····································421

88 A New Spirit in the World / 全球新精神·······························427

89 A New BIG POWER in the World / 一个新的世界大国·········432

90 Yesterday, Today, and Tomorrow / 昨天、今天和明天·············437

This page is not for you, boys and girls. It is for that old man or woman — twenty, thirty, or forty years old, who may peek into this book; and is what they would call the

小朋友们，这一页不是写给你们看的，而是给大人看的，是给那些已经有20岁、30岁或者40岁，可能会偷偷地来翻一翻这本书的人看的；他们把这一页叫——

PREFACE

引 言

To give the child some idea of what has gone on in the world before he arrived;

To take him out of his little self-centered, shut-in life, which looms so large because it is so close to his eyes;

To extend his horizon, broaden his view, and open up the vista down the ages past;

To acquaint him with some of the big events and great names and fix these in time and space as a basis for detailed study in the future;

To give him a chronological file with main guides, into which he can fit in its proper place all his further historical study —

Is the purpose of this first Survey of the World's History.

让孩子初步了解他/她出生之前世界上发生的一些事情；

让孩子摆脱他/她那种小小的、以自我为中心的封闭生活，他/她也许认为自己所处的那种生活与世界就是他/她的一切；

让孩子开阔视野、拓宽眼界，并且在他/她面前展开一幅从古至今的历史长卷；

让孩子熟悉一些重大事件和重要人物，并且将它们与特定的时间和空间联系起来，以便为孩子将来的全面学习打好基础；

让孩子以时间为主线熟悉世界历史，从而能够对自己将来的历史学习进行准确定位；

这些方面，就是这本书的目的。

This part is not for you, either. It is for your father, mother, or teacher, and is what they would call the

小朋友们，这一部分也不是写给你们看的。这一部分，是写给你们的父亲、母亲或者老师看的，他们会把这一部分叫——

INTRODUCTION
导　言

In common with all children of my age, I was brought up on American History and given no other history but American, year in and year out, year after year for eight or more years.

So far as I knew 1492 was the beginning of the world. Any events or characters before that time, reference to which I encountered by any chance, were put down in my mind in the same category with fairy-tales. Christ and His times, of which I heard only in Sunday-school, were to me mere fiction without reality. They were not mentioned in any history that I knew and therefore, so I thought, must belong not to a realm in time and space, but to a spiritual realm.

To give an American child only American History is as provincial as to teach a Texas child only Texas History. Patriotism is usually given as the reason for such history teaching. It only promotes a narrow-mindedness and an absurd conceit, based on utter ignorance of any other peoples and any other times — an intolerant egotism without foundation in fact. Since World War I it has become increasingly more and more important that American children should have a knowledge of other countries and other peoples in order that their attitude may be intelligent and unprejudiced.

小的时候，我与所有同龄的孩子一样，学的都是美国历史，并且只学美国历史，一年接一年地学了八年多的时间。

在我看来，整个世界是在1492年诞生的。那一年之前的任何事件或者人物，凡是在偶然当中碰到的，我都会在心里将它们归入"神话故事"一类中去。基督和他生活的那个时代，我只在教会学校里听说过；它们对我而言，不过都是一些虚构出来的故事罢了，一点儿也不真实。在我所知的历史中，根本就没有提到过这些事情；因此，我觉得它们一定不是属于真实世界中的，而是属于一种精神领域里的东西。

让美国孩子只了解美国历史的这种做法，与只让得克萨斯州的孩子学习该州的历史一样，都狭隘得很。人们常常将爱国主义当成是实行这种历史教学法的理由。但这种做法，只会让孩子们在完全无视其他民族、无视其他时代的基础上，形成一种狭隘的荒唐观念，即一种没有事实依据的、褊狭的唯我主义。从第一次世界大战以来，下面这一点已经变得越来越重要了：美国的儿童，应当去了解其他国家、其他民族的情况，从而形成一种更加明智、更加公允的态度。

As young as nine years of age, a child is eagerly inquisitive as to what has taken place in the ages past and readily grasps a concept of World History. Therefore, for many years Calvert School nine-year-old pupils have been taught World History in spite of academic and parental skepticism and antagonism. But I have watched the gradual drift toward adoption of this plan of history teaching, and with it an ever-increasing demand for a text-book of general history for young children. I have found, however, that all existing text-books have to be largely abridged and also supplemented by a running explanation and comment, to make them intelligible to the young child.

The recent momentous studies into the native intelligence of children show us what the average child at different ages can understand and what he cannot understand — what dates, figures of speech, vocabulary, generalities, and abstractions he can comprehend and what he cannot comprehend — and in the future all text-books will have to be written with constant regard for these intelligence norms. Otherwise, such texts are very likely to be "over the child's head." They will be trying to teach him some things at least that, in the nature of the case, are beyond him.

In spite of the fact that the writer has been in constant contact with the child mind for a great many years, he has found that whatever was written in his study had to be revised and rewritten each time after the lesson had been tried out in the class-room. Even though the first writing was in what he considered the simplest language, he has found that each and every word and expression has had to be subjected again and again to this class-

一个孩子，虽然只有九岁，但他也会对过去历朝历代发生的事情产生极大的好奇心，并且很容易领会这个世界的历史概念。因此，尽管学术界和家长们都持有疑虑和反对意见，但多年以来，卡尔弗特学校一直都在给九岁的学生讲授世界历史。不过我也注意到，学术界和家长们都已经逐渐开始接受了此种历史教学计划；且随之而来的，便是人们对一般性幼儿用的历史教材的需求也增加了。然而我却发现，目前的所有教材都必须进行大幅的删减才行，同时还需要补充必要的解释和说明，才能让幼儿理解并接受。

近来针对美国儿童智力而进行的一些重大研究，向我们说明了不同年龄段的孩子能够理解些什么，又不能理解些什么，比如他能够理解哪些年代、修辞手法、词汇、概括表述和抽象概念，又不能理解哪些年代、哪些修辞手法、词汇、哪些概括表述和抽象概念；因此，将来的所有教材，在编写时都必须始终考虑到这些标准。否则的话，编写出来的教材就会是"超出儿童智力范围"的教材。它们试图教授给孩子的，必然会是孩子难以理解的一些东西。

尽管本书作者多年来一直与孩子们打交道，但他已经发现，自己关起门来写下的任何东西，在每次上完课、进行了课堂检验之后，都必须进行修改、重新写过才行。就算是认为初稿所用的语言已经极为简单，但之后他也发现，每个词语都必须一次又一次地进行推敲，才能适应此种课堂的检验，才能确定它们所传达的意思。哪怕是最小的反向修辞和可能出现的歧义，也经常会引起孩子们的误解，或者让孩子们觉得困惑。比方说，"罗马在台伯河上"这句话，孩子们通常都会理解为，它

room test to determine what meaning is conveyed. The slightest inverted phraseology or possibility of double meaning has oftentimes been misconstrued or found confusing. For instance, the statement that "Rome was on the Tiber River" has quite commonly been taken to mean that the city was literally built on top of the river, and the child has had some sort of fantastic vision of houses built on piles in the river. A child of nine is still very young — he may still believe in Santa Claus — younger in ideas, in vocabulary and in understanding than most adults appreciate — even though they be parents or teachers — and new information can hardly be put too simply.

So the topics selected have not always been the most important — but the most important that can be understood and appreciated by a child. Most political, sociological, economic, or religious generalities are beyond a child's comprehension, no matter how simply told. After all, this History is only a preliminary story.

Excellent biographies and stories from general history have been written. But biographies from history do not give an historic outline. They do not give any outline at all for future filling in; and, indeed, unless they themselves are fitted into such a general historical scheme, they are nothing more than so many disconnected tales floating about in the child's mind with no associations of time or space.

The treatment of the subject in this book is, therefore, chronological — telling the story of what has happened century by century and epoch by epoch, not by nations. The story of one nation is interrupted to take up that of another as different plots in a novel are brought forward simultaneously. This is in line with the purpose, which is to give the pupil

指的是罗马这个城市全然建造在台伯河的正上方；因此，孩子们就会产生一种怪异的想法，认为房子都是建造在立于河中的柱子上面的。一个九岁的孩子，年纪还很小，可能仍然相信世界上有圣诞老人，并且在思想、词汇和理解能力上，都要比绝大多数成年人所认为的更为幼稚，哪怕这些成年人是孩子的父母或者老师；所以，向孩子们传授新的知识也不是一件非常容易的事。

因此，对历史主题的选择一向都不是最重要的；而最重要的，则是选择孩子能够了解和理解的主题。政治学、社会学、经济学或者宗教方面的绝大部分概义，无论用多么简单的方式进行讲授，孩子都是理解不了的。毕竟，此种历史课程不过是一种初步的背景知识教学罢了。

人们已经根据通史，写出了许多优秀的传记作品和小说。不过，根据历史写就的传记作品，并不能让我们把握历史的轮廓。它们根本没有给孩子提供在未来的学习过程中能够加以填充的任何历史框架；而事实上，除非这些传记本身融入了此种普通历史的结构中去，否则的话，它们就只是在孩子的脑海中游离不定、互不相关并且与时空毫无联系的诸多故事和传说罢了。

因此，本书的办法便是以年代为主线，即逐个世纪、逐个年代地讲述历史上发生的事件，而不是按照国别来进行讲述。我们会中断对某个国家历史的叙述，从而开始叙述另一个国家的历史，就像是一部小说中同时展开不同的情节那样。这种方法与本书的目的是一致的，因为本书旨在让学生能够连贯把握整个世界历史，或者

a continuous view or panorama of the ages, rather than Greek History from start to finish, then, retracing the steps of time, Roman History, and so on. The object is to sketch the whole picture in outline, leaving the details to be gradually filled in by later study, as the artist sketches the general scheme of his picture before filling in the details. Such a scheme is as necessary to orderly classification of historical knowledge as is a filing system in any office that can function properly or even at all.

The Staircase of Time is to give a visual idea of the extent of time and the progressive steps in the History of the World. Each "flight" represents a thousand years, and each "step" a hundred — a century. If you have a spare wall, either in the play-room, attic, or barn such a Staircase of Time on a large scale may be drawn upon it from floor to reaching height and made a feature if elaborated with pictures or drawings of people and events. If the wall faces the child's bed so much the better, for when lying awake in the morning or at any other time, instead of imagining fantastic designs on the wallpaper, he may picture the crowded events on the Staircase of Time. At any rate, the child should constantly refer either to such a Staircase of Time or to the Time Table as each event is studied, until he has a mental image of the Ages past.

At first a child does not appreciate time values represented by numbers or the relative position of dates on a time line and will wildly say twenty-five hundred B.C. or twenty-five thousand B.C. or twenty-five million B.C. indiscriminately. Only by constantly referring dates to position on the Staircase of Time or the Time Table can a child come to visualize dates. You may be amused, but do not be amazed, if a child gives 776 thousand

说能够一窥历史全貌，而不是从头到尾地学完希腊历史，然后再重新按照时间顺序去学习罗马历史，并依此类推。本书的目标，就是给学生描绘出一个整体轮廓，进而让他们在日后的学习中去逐渐填补其中的细节，就像一位画家先是打好草图，然后再去填充细节一样。这种方法，不但是有条有理地去整理历史知识所必需的，也是任何一个办公室里的文件归档系统要想正常而平稳地运作所必需的。

本书中的"时间阶梯图"，旨在让学生对时间以及世界历史的各个发展阶段有个视觉概念。阶梯上的每一"段"，都代表了一千年的时间；而其中的每一"级"，则代表着一百年，即一个世纪。假如您的家里有一面空墙，无论这面空墙是在儿童游戏室里、阁楼上还是谷仓里，您都可以在这面墙上绘制出一张大大的"时间阶梯图"来，从地板一直画到屋顶；并且，倘若再仔细地加上人物与事件的图片，就很有特色了。如果这堵墙壁正对着孩子的卧床，那就更好；因为这样一来，孩子早上醒来或者其他时间躺在床上的时候，可能就不会去想象墙纸上有着各种稀奇古怪的图案，而是去想象"时间阶梯图"上那些诸多的事件了。不管怎么说，学习了每一桩历史事件之后，孩子都应当经常性地去参考参考这样一张"时间阶梯图"或者"时间表"，直到脑子里形成一幅历史时代图才是。

一开始的时候，孩子并不会理解数字或者时间轴线上某个相对位置所代表的时间值，因此会不加区别，公元前2500年、公元前25000年或者公元前2500万年地乱说一通。只有经常性地将日期与"时间阶梯图"或者"时间表"上的位置对应起

years A.D. as the date for the First Olympiad, or says that Italy is located in Athens, or that Abraham was a hero of the Trojan War.

If you have ever been introduced to a roomful of strangers at one time, you know how futile it is to attempt even to remember their names to say nothing of connecting names and faces. It is necessary to hear something interesting about each one before you can begin to recall names and faces. Likewise an introduction to World History, the characters and places in which are utterly unknown strangers to the child, must be something more than a mere name introduction, and there must be very few introductions given at a time or both names and faces will be instantly forgotten. It is also necessary to repeat new names constantly in order that the pupil may gradually become familiarized with them, for so many strange people and places are bewildering.

In order to serve the purpose of a basal out-line, which in the future is to be filled in, it is necessary that the Time Table be made a permanent possession of the pupil. This Time Table, therefore, should be studied like the multiplication tables until it is known one hundred per cent and for "keeps", and until the topic connected with each date can be elaborated as much as desired. The aim should be to have the pupil able to start with Primitive Man and give a summary of World History to the present time, with dates and chief events without prompting, questioning, hesitation, or mistake. Does this seem too much to expect? It is not as difficult as it may sound, if suggestions given in the text for connecting the various events into a sequence and for passing names and events in a

来，孩子才能开始将日期具体化。倘若一个孩子说第一届奥运会是在公元776000年举行的，或者说意大利位于雅典境内，或者说亚伯拉罕是特洛伊战争中的一位英雄，您可以觉得有趣，但可不要吃惊。

如果您曾经有过被介绍给一屋子陌生人的经历，那么您就会明白，要想记住这些陌生人的名字是多么的困难，更别说将名字与每个人的长相一一联系起来了。您必须听到每个陌生人某种有意思的事情，才能开始回忆起他们的名字和长相来。同样，在一本世界历史的入门教材中，有许多的人物和地点，它们对于孩子来说都不亚于完全没有见过面的陌生人，因此学习这一教材的难度，必定不只是像介绍名字那样简单，而且一次也不能介绍太多，否则的话，名字和长相马上就会被孩子忘掉。经常性地反复提及新的名称，以便让学生逐渐熟悉它们也很有必要，因为那么多陌生的人物和地点，也确实会让人眼花缭乱。

为了实现让学生掌握基本轮廓、以便日后填充细节的目的，学生必须始终都拥有这样一份"时间表"才行。因此，这份"时间表"应当像"九九乘法表"那样去学习，直到学生百分之百地熟悉和"完全掌握"，并且能够做到对每个日期相关联的主题尽可能详细地进行阐述为止。而教学目标，则应当是让学生能够从原始人开始，概述出迄今为止的世界历史，并且不用启发、不用提问、毫不支吾、毫无差错地用日期和主要事件来加以说明。这一目标，看起来是不是期望值太高呢？不过，倘若遵循本教材中给出的建议，将各种不同的事件连成一串，对过去的人物和事件进行扼要回顾，那么这一目标实现起来就不会有听起来那么困难了。在卡尔弗特学

condensed review are followed. Hundreds of Calvert children each year are successfully required to do this very thing.

The attitude, however, usually assumed by teachers, that "even if the pupil forgets it all, there will be left a valuable impression," is too often an apology for superficial teaching and superficial learning. History may be made just as much a "mental discipline" as some other studies, but only if difficulties of dates and other abstractions are squarely met and overcome by hard study and learned to be remembered, not merely to be forgotten after the recitation. The story part the child will easily remember, but it is the "who and when and where and why" that are important, and this part is the serious study. Instead of, "A man, once upon a time," he should say, "King John in 1215 at Runnymede because —"

This book, therefore, is not a supplementary reader but a basal history study. Just enough narrative is told to give the skeleton flesh and blood and make it living. The idea is not how much but how little can be told; to cut down one thousand pages to less than half of that number without leaving only dry bones.

No matter how the subject is presented it is necessary that the child do his part and put his own brain to work; and for this purpose he should be required to retell each story after he has read it and should be repeatedly questioned on names and dates as well as stories, to make sure he is retaining and assimilating what he hears.

I recall how once upon a time a young chap, just out of college, taught his first class in history. With all the enthusiasm of a full-back who has just kicked a goal from field,

校，我们每年都是要求成百上千的孩子这样去做的，而他们做得也都很成功。

然而，老师们通常都会持有这样一种态度，那就是：即便学生全都忘光，也会留下一种可贵的印象。并且，这种态度也经常被老师们当成肤浅教学和学生们不求甚解的学习做法的借口。我们虽然也可以把历史当成一种与其他学习一样的"智力训练"，但只有在学生通过努力学习，完全掌握和攻克了日期与其他抽象概念的问题，并且学会记住这些日期和抽象概念，而不只是背过就忘的情况下，才能这样。孩子很容易记住其中的故事部分，但真正重要的，却是"谁、何时、何地与为何"等方面，因为这一部分才是真正严肃的学习。学生不能说："从前，有个人……"而应当这样说："1215年，英王约翰于兰尼米德[1]，因为……"

因此，本书并不是一个辅助读本，而是一种学习历史基础知识的教材。其中的故事，恰好足以让历史这具"骨架"中有了血肉，使之变得栩栩如生起来。本书的主旨，并不在于其中讲述的内容可以有多庞大，而在于其中讲述的内容可以有多微小，在于将一千页的内容缩减至一半以下，同时不至于让整个历史只剩下一具干巴巴的骨架。

无论这门课程是如何讲授的，孩子们都必须尽自己的力量，开动脑筋、努力学习才行；为此，阅读完每一个故事之后，都应当要求孩子进行复述，并且反复就人

---

[1] 兰尼米德（Runnymede），英国伦敦以西、泰晤士河南岸的一处草地，距温莎城堡不远。据说英王约翰于1215年在此地签署了《大宪章》（拉丁文为the Magna Carta，英文为the Great Charter）。

he talked, he sang; he drew maps on the blackboard, on the floor, on the field; he drew pictures, he vaulted desks, and even stood on his head to illustrate points. His pupils attended spellbound, with their eyes wide open, their ears wide open, and their mouths wide open. They missed nothing. They drank in his flow of words with thirst unquenched; but, like Baron Munchausen, he had failed to look at the other end of the drinking horse that had been cut in half. At the end of a month his kindly principal suggested a test, and he gave it with perfect confidence.

There were only three questions:

(1)Tell all you can about Columbus.

(2) "   "   "   "   " Jamestown.

(3) "   "   "   "   " Plymouth.

And here are the three answers of one of the most interested pupils:

(1)He was a grate man.

(2) "   "   "   "

(3) "   "   "   "   " to.

名、日期以及故事内容向孩子提问，以确保孩子记住并吸收所学的知识。

　　我还记得，有一位年轻人大学刚刚毕业后去教第一堂历史课时的情形。他带着激情，犹如一名刚刚在球场上踢进了球的后卫，滔滔不绝地讲啊、唱啊，在黑板、地板、操场上画地图啊，还跳上课桌，甚至倒立起来，想方设法地去说明要点。他的那些学生有如被施了魔法一般，一个个都瞪大眼睛、竖着耳朵、张着嘴巴地听着。他们可以说毫厘不漏。他们如饥似渴，聆听着他的话语；可是，就像孟豪森男爵[1]那样，他却没有去看一看那匹饮水的马儿被劈成两半之后另一半的情况。一个月之后，那位和蔼可亲的校长提出测试一下其教学效果；于是，这位老师便自信满满地对学生进行了测试。

　　试卷上，总共只有三个问题：

　　（1）请尽量介绍一下哥伦布。

　　（2）请尽量介绍一下詹姆斯敦。

　　（3）请尽量介绍一下普利茅斯。

　　而对这门课程最感兴趣的一名学生，给出的三个答案竟然如下：

　　（1）他是个了不起[2]的人。

　　（2）他是个了不起的人。

　　（3）他也[3]是个了不起的人。

---

　　[1]　孟豪森男爵（Baron Munchausen），18世纪德国的一位旅行家，他所讲述的传奇故事被作家埃·拉斯佩和戈·奥·毕尔格集结成《孟豪森男爵旅俄奇侠记》（the Adventures of Baron Munchausen），亦译为《吹牛大王历险记》。"半匹马"的故事见于该书中的《自述》，说的是孟豪森男爵在俄罗斯跟着俄军对付土耳其人时，坐骑后半部分被敌人铡断后却仍能驮着他作战，而在喝水过程中由于喝进去的水都从身体后面流出去了，因此坐骑喝个不停的故事。

　　[2]　在原著中，此处应是学生拼写错误，所以作者将 great（了不起）写成了 grate（格栅，壁炉）。

　　[3]　此处在原著中也应是学生拼写错误，将 too（也）写成了 to。

Here is the 下面就是

STAIRCASE OF TIME 时间阶梯图

It starts far, far, below the bottom of the pages and rises up, Up, UP to where we are NOW — each step a hundred years,

each flight of steps a thousand. It will keep on up until it reaches high heaven. From where we are NOW let us look down the flights below us and listen to the Story of what has happened in the long years gone by.

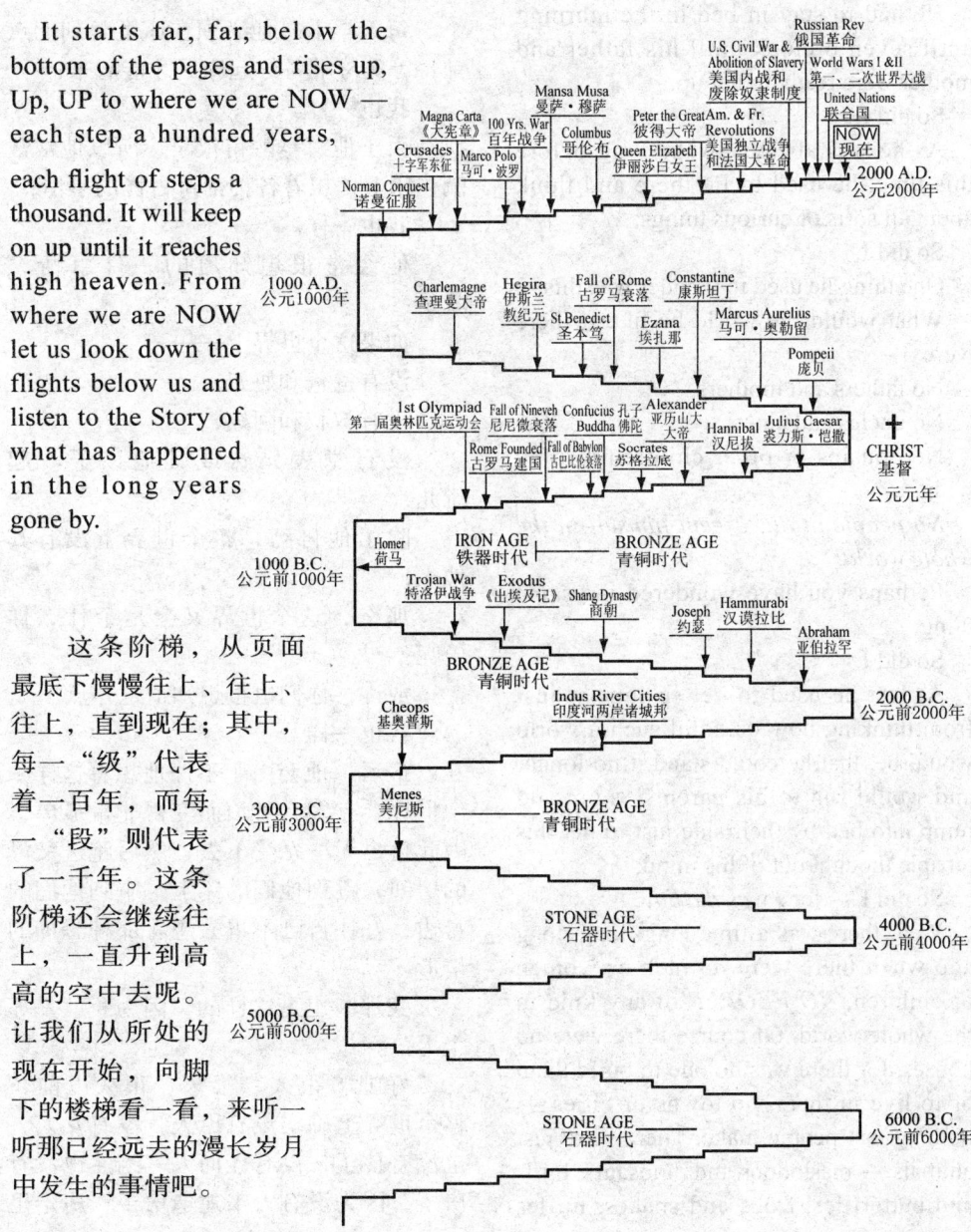

这条阶梯，从页面最底下慢慢往上、往上、往上，直到现在；其中，每一"级"代表着一百年，而每一"段"则代表了一千年。这条阶梯还会继续往上，一直升到高高的空中去呢。让我们从所处的现在开始，向脚下的楼梯看一看，来听一听那已经远去的漫长岁月中发生的事情吧。

1 How Things Started

Once upon a time there was a boy —
Just like me.
He had to stay in bed in the morning until seven o'clock until his father and mother were ready to get up;
So did I.
As he was always awake long before this time, he used to lie there and think about all sorts of curious things;
So did I.
One thing he used to wonder was this:
What would the world be like if there were —
No fathers and mothers,
No uncles and aunts,
No cousins or other children to play with,
No people at all, except himself in the whole world!
Perhaps you have wondered the same thing;
So did I.
At last he used to get so lonely, just from thinking how dreadful such a world would be, that he could stand it no longer and would run to his parents' room and jump into bed by their side just to get this terrible thought out of his mind;
So did I — for *I was the boy.*
Well, there was a time long, long, long ago when there were no men or women or children, *NO PEOPLE* of any kind in the whole world. Of course there were no houses, for there was no one to build them or to live in them, no towns or cities — nothing that people make. There were just animals — mastodons and dinosaurs, birds and butterflies, frogs and snakes, turtles

1 万物起源

从前，有一个小男孩，
就像我一样。
每天早上，他必须在床上睡到七点钟，等父母准备好起床后才能起来；
我也一样。
由于他总是醒得很早，所以他常常躺在床上，想着各种稀奇古怪的事情；
我也一样。
他经常很想知道的一件事情，就是：
如果这个世界上——
没有爸爸和妈妈，
没有叔叔和阿姨，
没有堂表兄妹或其他孩子一起玩儿，
除了他自己，整个世界上没有其他人，
那么，这个世界又会是个什么样子呢？
或许，你们也很想知道这一点。
我也一样。
最后，他会由于不停地想着这样一个世界会有多么可怕而变得非常孤单，因此再也无法忍受下去，然后跑进父母的房间，跳到他们的床上，躺到他们的身边，好让自己不再去想着那种恐怖的情形。
我那时也是这样的，因为我就是那个男孩。
好吧，很久、很久、很久以前，整个世界上确实没有男人，没有女人，也没有孩子，没有任何人。当然也没有房子，因为没有人来建造房子，房子里

and fish. Can you think of such a world as that?

Then,

　　　　long, long, long

before that, there was a time when there were *NO PEOPLE* and *NO ANIMALS* of any sort in the whole world; there were just growing plants. Can you think of such a world as that?

Then,

　　　　long, long, long,
　　　　long, long, long

before that, there was a time when there were NO PEOPLE, NO ANIMALS, NO PLANTS, in the whole world; there was just bare rock and water every where. Can you think of such a world as that?

Then,

　　　　long, long, long
　　　　long, long, long — you might
　　　　keep on saying —
　　　　"long, long, long," all day, and
　　　　tomorrow, and all next week,
　　　　and next month, and next
　　　　year, and it would not be long
　　　　enough —

before this, there was a time when there was *NO WORLD AT ALL*!

No world at all! Only the stars, and God, who made the stars.

Now, real stars are not things with points like those in the corner of a flag or the gold ones you put on a Christmas tree. The real stars in the sky have no points. They are huge burning balls of fire — balls of fire. Each star, however, is so huge that there is nothing in the world now anywhere nearly as big. One little bit, one little scrap of a star is bigger than our whole world — than our whole world.

One of these stars is our sun — yes, our sun. The other stars would look the same as the sun if we could get as

也没有人去住；当时还没有城镇，也没有任何人造的东西。整个世界上只有动物，比如乳齿象啊，恐龙啊，鸟儿啊，蝴蝶啊，青蛙啊，蛇类啊，乌龟啊，鱼类啊。你能想象得出这样一个世界的样子吗？

而且，那时的

　　　　很久、很久、很久

以前，还有过一个时期，当时整个世界上既没有人，也没有动物，只是生长着植物。你能想象得出这样一个世界的样子吗？

而且，那时的

　　　　很久、很久、很久
　　　　很久、很久、很久

以前，还有过一个时期，当时整个世界上既没有人、没有动物，也没有任何植物；到处都只有光秃秃的石头和水。你能想象得出这样一个世界的样子吗？

而且，那时的

　　　　很久、很久、很久
　　　　很久、很久、很久……

（你可以一直说下去，"很久、很久、很久"地说上一整天，直到明天，直到下个星期，直到明年，可这样也还是不够久）以前，还有过一个时期，当时整个世界根本就不存在！

当时根本就没有世界！整个宇宙之中，只有星星，以及这些星星的创造者。

注意，真正的星星可不是旗帜一角上的五角星，也不是你们挂在圣诞树上的那种金灿灿的东西。天空中真正的星星是没有尖角的。它们都是非常巨大的球体，如今的世界上根本就没有什么东西有星星那么大呢。有些星星的一小点儿、一小块儿，就比我们的整个世界都

close to them. But at that time, so long, long ago, our sun was not just a big, round, white, hot ball as we see it in the sky today. It was then more like the fireworks you may have seen on the Fourth of July. It was whirling and sputtering and throwing off sparks.

One of these sparks which the Sun threw far off got cool just as a spark from the crackling log in the fireplace gets cool, and this cooled off spark was —

What do you suppose?

See if you can guess —

It was our world! — yes, the world
on which we now live.

The sun sputtering and throwing off sparks
太阳向四周喷溅火花

At first, however, our World, or Earth, was nothing but a ball of rock. This ball of rock was wrapped around with steam, like a heavy fog.

Then the steam turned to rain and it rained on the world,

a a a
n n n
d d d

要大——就比我们所处的整个世界都要大哩。

在这些星星当中，有一颗便是我们的太阳；是的，就是我们的太阳。如果我们与其他星星的距离跟与太阳的距离一样近的话，其他星星看上去就会跟太阳没什么两样。不过那个时候，就是很久、很久以前，太阳可不像今天我们看到的这样，它并不是天空中一个又大又圆的白色火球。当时的太阳，更像是你们可能在7月4日美国国庆日里看到的焰火那样。它旋转着，噼里啪啦，火花四溅。

太阳喷溅出来的、甩得远远的那些火花当中，有一颗冷却下来了，就像壁炉里噼啪作响的木头上溅出的一颗火花熄灭之后那样；于是，这颗冷却了的火花，就变成了——

你们觉得会变成什么呢？

看看你们能不能猜到——

它就变成了我们的世界！是的，就是现在我们生活的这个世界。

然而一开始的时候，我们的这个世界，或者说地球，不过是一个圆圆的石球罢了。这个石球，被一层像浓雾似的水汽包裹着。

接着，这层水汽变成了雨，于是整个世界便开始下起雨来，

并

```
i     i     i
t     t     t

r     r     r
a     a     a
i     i     i
n     n     n
e     e     e
d     d     d
```

until it had filled up the hollows and made enormously big puddles. These puddles were the oceans. The dry places were bare *rock*.

Then, after this, came the first living things — tiny plants that you could only have seen under a microscope. At first they grew only in the water, then along the water's edge, then out on the rock.

Then dirt or soil, as people call it, formed all over the rock and made the rock into land, and the plants grew larger and spread farther over the land.

Then, after this, came the first tiny animals in the water. They were wee specks too small, like the first plants, to be seen without the help of a microscope.

Then, after this, in the water came larger animals like *Jellyfish* and clams and horseshoe crabs.

Then, after this, came *Insects*, some that live *in* the water, some on the water, some on the land, like cockroaches, and some *in* the air.

Then, after this, came *Fish*, that live only in the water.

Then, after this, came animals like frogs called *Amphibians* that live in the water and also on the land.

Then, after this, came *Reptiles*, like snakes, turtles, lizards, and huge dinosaurs.

Then, after this, came *Birds* that lay eggs and *Mammals*, like foxes and monkeys and cows, that nurse their babies

且
一
直
下
个
不
停，

直到雨水填满地球上的凹处，形成了一个个巨大无比的水坑。这些水坑，就是如今的海洋。而没有水的地方，则是光秃秃的岩石。

在这之后，世界上接着便出现了最初的生物；它们就是微生植物，只有用一台显微镜，你们才能看得到。起初，它们只是生长在水里，但接下来它们却慢慢地沿着水边生长，然后从水里出来，长到了岩石上。

接下来，岩石上面便形成了一层泥土，也就是人们所称的"土壤"，从而让岩石变成了土地；而那些植物也越长越大，蔓延到了整个陆地之上。

在这之后，接着水中又出现了最初的微型动物。它们都非常非常微小，就像最初的植物一样，不用显微镜是看不到的。

在这之后，接着水中又出现了大一点儿的动物，比如水母、蛤蜊和鲨。

在这之后，世界上接着又出现了昆虫；它们有的生活在水里，有的生活在水面，有的生活在陆地上，比如蟑螂，还有的则生活在空中。

在这之后，世界上接着又出现了鱼类，它们只能生活在水中。

在这之后，世界上接着又出现了像青蛙这样的动物；它们叫作"两栖动物"，既可以生活在水中，也可生活在陆地上。

在这之后，世界上接着又出现了爬

when they are born.

Then, last of all, came — what do you suppose? Yes — *People* — men, women, and children. Here are the steps; see if you can take them:

STARS,
  SUN,
    SPARK,
      WORLD,
        STEAM,
          RAIN,
            OCEANS,
              PLANTS,
ANIMALS,
  JELLYFISH,
    INSECTS,
      FISH,
        AMPHIBIANS,
          REPTILES,
            BIRDS,
              MAMMALS,
PEOPLE.
  And here we are!

What do you suppose will be next?

行动物，比如蛇类、海龟、蜥蜴和巨型恐龙。

在这之后，世界上接着出现了会下蛋的鸟类，以及像狐狸、猴子和母牛这样的哺乳动物，它们都会照料自己刚生下来的幼崽。

最后，世界上就出现了——你们觉得会是什么呢？是的，最后就出现了人类，出现了男人、女人和小孩。下面就是上述万物出现的各个阶段，看你们能不能记住吧：

星星，
  太阳，
    火花，
      世界，
        水汽，
          雨水，
            海洋，
植物，
  动物，
    水母，
      昆虫，
        鱼类，
          两栖动物，
            爬行动物，
              鸟类，
                哺乳动物
人类。
  最后就有了我们！

你们觉得，接下来世界上又会出现什么呢？

2 People Who Lived in Caves

How do you suppose I know about all these things that took place so long ago? I don't. I'm only guessing about them.

But there are different kinds of guesses. If I hold out my two closed hands and ask you to guess which one has the penny in it, that is one kind of a guess. Your guess might be right or it might be wrong. It would be just luck.

But there is another kind of guess. When there is snow on the ground and I see tracks of a boot in the snow, I guess that a person must have passed by, for boots don't usually walk without someone in them. That kind of guess is not just luck but common sense.

So we can guess about a great many things that have taken place long ago, even though there was no one there at the time to see them or tell about them.

We have dug down deep under the ground in different parts of the world and have found there — what do you suppose?

I don't believe you would ever guess.

We have found the heads of arrows and spears and hatchets.

The peculiar thing about these arrows and spears and hatchets is that they are not made

2　生活在洞穴里的人

你们想一想，发生在那么久以前的这些事情，我又是怎么知道的呢？

其实我不知道。

我只是猜测罢了。

不过，猜测可有不同的种类。我伸出两个握着的拳头来，让你们猜一猜哪个拳头里有硬币，这是一种猜测。你们可能猜得对，也有可能猜得不对。这种猜测，完全是靠运气。

但还有另外一种猜测。假如地上有雪，我又看到雪上有一行靴子印，那我就会猜测，肯定有人刚刚走过，因为靴子要是没人穿着的话，是不可能自己会走路的。这种猜测，靠的不只是运气，而是常识。

因此，我们就能猜测出很久以前发生的许多事情，即便是当时并没有人在现场看到这些事情，或者并没人把这些事情告诉别人。

人们已经在世界上的不同地区深入向地下挖掘，发现了——你们认为，他们会发现些什么呢？

我觉得，你们可能永远都猜不到。

人们发现了箭头、矛头和斧头。

这些箭头、矛头和斧头的奇特之处，就在于它们并不像你们料想的那样，是用

of iron or steel, as you might expect, but of stone.

Now, we are sure that only human beings could have made and used such things, for birds and fish or other animals do not use hatchets or spears. We are also sure that these people must have lived long, long years ago before iron and steel were known, because it must have taken long, long years for these things to have become covered up so deep by dust and dirt. We have also found the bones of the people themselves, who died several million years ago, long before anyone began to write down history. The oldest bones we have ever found were in East Africa. We know that people long ago were working and playing, eating and fighting — doing many of the same things we are today — especially the fighting.

This time in the prehistory of the world, when people used such things made of stone, is therefore called the Stone Age.

Life was hard for Stone Age people. They didn't have all the things we are used to having today.

Some wild animals make houses. Foxes dig holes, beavers make houses of sticks and mud. These first people probably had no houses of any sort in which to live. They simply found any shelter they could. They found caves in the rocks or in the hillsides where they could get away from the cold and storms and wild animals. So men, women, and children of this time were called *Cave People*.

They spent their days hunting some animals and running and hiding from others. They

铁或者钢做成的，而是用石头做成的。

如今我们已经确信，只有人类才有可能制造和使用这些东西，因为鸟类、鱼类或者其他动物都不会使用斧头或者长矛。我们还确信，这些人一定生活在人类知道用铁或者知道用钢之前很久、很久的时候，因为将这些东西用厚厚的泥土覆盖起来埋在地下如此之深的地方，必定花了好多、好多年的时间。我们还发现了这些人的骸骨；他们死去的时间，必定是在成千上万年以前，那时还没有人记载历史呢。年代最久远的尸骨，我们是在东非地区发现的。因此，我们便可以得知，很久以前的人也会工作、玩耍、吃喝和打仗；他们所做的许多事情，都跟我们今天一样，尤其是打仗。

史前世界的这一时期，由于人们使用的都是一些石制的工具，故被称为石器时代。

石器时代的人们，生活非常艰难。他们并没有如今我们已经习以为常的东西可用。

有些野生动物也会建造住所。比如说，狐狸会打洞，海狸会用木棍和泥巴筑穴。那些最初的人类，很可能没有任何房屋可住。他们只是能找到什么地方，就在什么地方栖身。他们在岩石中或者山坡上找到了一些洞穴；住在这些洞穴里，可以让他们不受寒冷的侵扰、不受风吹雨打和野兽的袭击。于是，这一时期的人类，包括男人、女人和儿童，都被称为穴居人。

他们每天所做的事情，便是猎杀其他一些动物，并且跑来跑去，躲避其他动

caught animals by trapping them in a pit covered over with bushes, or they killed them with a club or a rock if they had a chance, or with stone-headed arrows or hatchets. They even painted or cut pictures of these animals on the walls of their caves. Some of these pictures we can still see today.

They lived on berries and nuts and seeds. They robbed the nests of birds for the eggs, which they ate raw, for at first they had no fire with which to cook. They liked to drink the warm blood of animals they killed, as you would a glass of milk.

They talked to each other by some sort of grunts or very simple words. They made clothes of skins of animals they killed, for there was no such thing as cloth.

These early people must have spent most of their time hunting for food or trying to get away from animals hunting *them* for food. They had no thick hide like an elephant to protect them; they did not grow a coat of fur like a bear to keep them warm; they could not run very fast, like a deer to escape their enemies; they were no match for an animal with sharp teeth and claws and strong muscles like a lion. It's a wonder any of them lived to grow up.

Stone Age people had two things that helped them more than sharp claws, or strong muscles, or tough skins. They had better brains than the animals. And they had hands instead of front feet. With their brains they could *think*. They could *think* of ways of doing things better.

With their brains they could *think* of using tools. With their hands they could make

物的猎杀。他们挖出陷阱，然后在上面盖上树叶来捕捉动物；如果有机会，他们还会用木棍或者石头击杀猎物，或者用石箭和石斧杀死猎物。他们甚至还把这些动物的样子画或刻在自己居住的洞穴墙壁上。这些图画当中，有一些我们如今还看得到呢。

他们以浆果、坚果和草籽为生。他们从鸟窝里掏出鸟蛋来生吃，因为起初他们并没有火来煮熟食物。他们残忍嗜杀，喜欢喝下所杀的动物体内暖和的鲜血，就像你们喝下一杯牛奶似的。

他们之间，是用某种低沉嘟囔的声音或者简单的词语进行交流的。他们用所杀野兽的兽皮做衣服，因为当时还没有"布匹"这种东西呢。

这些早期的人类，必定整天都是在猎杀动物来吃，或者尽力躲开那些想猎杀他们来吃的动物。他们不像大象，身上并没有那种厚厚的兽皮来保护自己；他们不像熊，身上并没有长出一层兽毛来保暖；他们并不像小鹿逃离天敌那样跑得很快；他们也不是像狮子这种有着獠牙利爪、强壮肌肉的野兽的对手。在这样的环境下，他们能够长大成人，可真是一种奇迹啊。

生活在石器时代的人类，有两个方面胜过了獠牙利爪、肌肉强壮或是厚重兽皮。他们的大脑比动物聪明。并且，他们拥有灵巧的双手，而不是两只前脚。有了大脑，他们就能思考。他们能够想出更好的做事方法。

有了大脑，他们就能够想到利用工具。有了双手，他们就能够制造工具和使用工具。人类可以利用长矛，而不是利用尖锐的牙齿。人类能够利用兽皮来保暖，而

tools and use them. Instead of sharp teeth, men could use spears. In place of a furry skin to keep them warm, men could use the skins of animals.

Suppose you had been a boy or a girl in the Stone Age. I wonder how you would have liked the life.

When you woke up in the morning, you would not have bathed or even washed your hands and face or brushed your teeth or combed your hair.

You ate with your fingers, for there were no knives or forks or spoons or cups or saucers, only one bowl — which your mother had made out of mud and dried in the sun to hold water to drink — no dishes to wash and put away, no chairs, no tables, no table manners.

There were no books, no paper, no pencils.

There was no Saturday or Sunday, January or July. Except that one day was warm and sunny or another cold and rainy, they were all alike. There was no school to go to.

There was nothing to do all day long but make mud pies or pick berries or play tag with your brothers and sisters.

I wonder how you would like that kind of life!

"Fine!" do you think? — "a great life — just like camping out"?

But I have only told you part of the story.

The cave would have been cold and damp and dark, with only the bare ground or a pile of leaves for a bed. There would probably have been bats and big spiders sharing the cave with you.

You might have had on the skin of some animal your father had killed, but as this only

不是用长满长毛的皮肤来保暖。

假设你们是生活在石器时代的一个男孩或女孩。我可不知道，你们会不会喜欢那种生活呢。

早上醒来之后，你们不会去冲澡，甚至不会洗手、洗脸、刷牙或者梳头。

你们会用手指抓起东西来吃，因为那时还没有刀叉、汤匙、杯子、碟子，只有一个碗（这是你们的妈妈用泥巴做成的，晒干后用来舀水喝）；还没有碗碟要清洗或者收拾，还没有椅子、桌子，因此也就没有什么就餐礼仪。

那时还没有书，也没有纸和笔。

那时还没有星期六或者星期天，也没有一月或者七月。除了暖和、晴朗和寒冷、下雨这种差别，所有日子都差不多。你们没有学校可上。

整日里，除了做泥巴团、捡浆果或者与兄弟姐妹捉捉迷藏之外，你们便无事可做了。

我可不知道你们会不会喜欢那种生活！

"太好了！"你们这样觉得吗？还是说，"这种生活太棒了，就像是在野营"？

可是，我的话才说了一半呢。

你们所住的洞穴会很寒冷，既潮湿又阴暗；至于床嘛，只是光秃秃的地面，或者是一堆树叶。洞里很可能还会有蝙蝠和巨大的蜘蛛和你们住在一起。

你们身上可能穿着父亲猎杀的某头野兽的兽皮；但是，由于这种兽皮只能盖住

covered part of your body and as there was no fire, you would have felt cold in winter, and when it got very cold you might have frozen to death.

For breakfast you might have had some dried berries or grass seed or a piece of raw meat, for lunch the same thing, for dinner still the same thing.

You would never have had any bread or cheese or griddlecakes with syrup, or oatmeal with sugar on it, or apple pie or ice cream.

There was nothing to do all day long but watch out for wild animals — bears and tigers; for there was no door with lock and key, and a tiger, if he found you out, could go wherever you went and "get you" even in your cave.

And then some day your father or brother, who had left the cave in the morning to go hunting, would not return, and you would know he had been torn to pieces by some wild beast, and you would wonder how long before your turn would come.

Do you think you would like to have lived then?

你们身体的一部分，洞里又没有生火，因此你们在冬天会觉得很冷，而在天气变得极其寒冷的时候，你们可能还会冻死哩。

你们的早饭，可能是某种风干了的浆果、草籽或者一片生肉；中餐吃的也是一样，而晚餐呢，仍然还是这些东西。

你们永远也吃不到面包、奶酪、糖煎饼、甜麦片、苹果派或者冰淇淋这些东西。

一整天，你们什么也干不了，只能提防着不被熊啊、虎啊等野兽袭击，因为洞穴既没有门，也没有锁；一只老虎要是发现了你们，就可以追着你们到处跑，甚至到你们的洞穴里"逮住你"。

然后，你们的父亲或者哥哥有一天早上离开洞穴去打猎之后，就不会再回来了；你们会明白，他已经被某头野兽撕成了碎片；而你们也不知道，这种事情多久之后便会轮到你们的头上。

你们还觉得自己很愿意生活在那个时候吗？

3 Fire! Fire!! Fire!!!

The first things are usually the most interesting — the first baby, the first tooth, the first step, the first word, the first spanking. This book will be chiefly the story of first things; those that came second or third or fourth or fifth you can read about and study later.

Primitive people did not at first know what fire was. They had no matches nor any way of making a light or a fire. They had no light at night. They had no fire to warm themselves by. They had no fire with which to cook their food. Somewhere and sometime, we do not know exactly when or how, they found out how to make and use fire.

If you rub your hands together rapidly, they become warm. Try it. If you rub them together still more rapidly, they become hot. If you rub two sticks together rapidly, they become warm. If you rub them together still more rapidly, they become hot. If you rub two sticks together very, very, very rapidly, they become hot and at last, if you keep it up long enough and fast enough, are set on fire. Native Americans and Boy Scouts and Girl Scouts do this and make a fire by twisting one stick against another.

This was one of the first inventions, and this invention was as remarkable for them at that time as the invention of electric light in our own times.

3　火!火!!火!!!

凡属"第一"的东西，通常都是最有意思的，比如第一个宝宝、第一颗牙齿、迈出的第一步、第一次说话、第一次打屁股，等等。这本书，主要讲述的就是这种属于"第一"的事物的历史。至于那些属于第二、第三、第四或者第五位的东西，你们可以日后再去阅读和学习。

原始人起初并不知道火是什么东西。他们没有火柴，也没有其他什么办法点灯或者生火。他们晚上没有灯火。他们没有火来给自己取暖。他们没有火来烧饭。但在某个地点、在某个时间，虽说我们并不确切地知道究竟是什么时候、用的是什么方式，他们还是发现了生火和用火的办法。

假如你们合拢双掌，迅速摩擦，双手就会暖和起来。试一试吧。假如摩擦得更快，你们的双手便会变热。同样，如果将两根棍子挨在一起迅速摩擦的话，它们也会变暖。如果将两根棍子摩擦得更快的话，它们就会变热。倘若你们将两根棍子摩擦得非常、非常、非常快，它们就会变得很热；而倘若摩擦的时间够久、速度够快的话，它们最终便会着火。美洲的印第安人和童子军就是这样，用一根棍子对着另一根棍子旋转来生火的。

这就是人类最初的发明之一，并且这一发明对当时的人类意义极其重大，就像发明电灯对我们这个时代意义非凡那样。

People of the Stone Age had hair and beards that were never cut, because they had nothing to cut them with, even had they wanted them short, which they probably didn't.

They had no clothes made of cloth, for they had no cloth and nothing with which to cut and sew cloth if they had.

They had no saws to cut boards, no hammer or nails to fasten them together to make houses or furniture.

They had no forks nor spoons; no pots nor pans; no buckets nor shovels, no needles nor pins.

The people of the Stone Age had never seen or heard of such a thing as iron or steel or tin or brass or anything made of these metals. For thousands and thousands of years primitive people got along without any of the things that are made of metal.

Then one day a Stone Age man found out something by accident; a *discovery* we call it.

He was making a fire; and a fire, which is to us such a common, everyday thing, was still to him very wonderful. Round his fire he placed some rocks to make a sort of campfire stove. Now, it happened that this particular rock was not ordinary rock but what we now call "ore",

A cave man discovering copper
一名穴居人发现了铜

石器时代的人类，头发和胡须从来都是不剃的；因为即便是想要剃短一点儿，他们也没有理发工具，更何况他们很可能也并不想将头发和胡须剃短呢。

他们没有用布料制成的衣物，因为他们根本就没有布料；而就算有了布料，他们也没有裁剪和缝纫布料的工具啊。

他们没有锯子来锯开木板，没有锤子或钉子将木板钉合在一起来建造房屋或者制作家具。

他们没有叉子和汤匙之类的餐具，没有壶、锅等炊具，没有水桶、铲子，也没有针线或者别针这样的东西。

石器时代的人类，根本就没有见过或者听说过铁、钢、锡、黄铜之类的东西，也没有见过或听说过由这些金属制成的物品。几千年里，原始人一直都过着没有任何金属制品的生活。

接下来，有一天，一名石器时代的男子无意中找到了某种东西；我们将这种过程称之为"发现"。

当时，这名男子正在生火；对于我们来说，火已经是一种司空见惯、每天都会见到的东西，但对他来说，却仍然显得非常神奇。他在火堆周围堆了一些石头，想做成一个有点儿像是营火那样的炉灶。注意，他所用的那种石头，恰巧并不是普通

for it had copper in it. The heat of the fire melted some of the copper out of the rock, and it ran out on the ground.

What were those bright, shining drops?

He examined them.

How pretty they were!

He heated some more of the same rock and got some more copper.

Thus was the first metal discovered.

At first people used the copper for beads and ornaments, for it was so bright and shiny. But they soon found out that copper could be pounded into sharp blades and points, which were much better than the stone knives and arrow-heads they had used before.

Notice that it was not iron they discovered first; it was copper.

We think people next discovered tin in somewhat the same way. Then, after that, they found out that tin when mixed with copper made a still harder and better metal than either alone. This metal, made of tin and copper together, we now call bronze; and for two or three thousand years people made their tools and weapons out of bronze. We call the time when men used bronze tools, and bronze weapons for hunting and fighting the Bronze Age.

At last somebody discovered iron, and soon people saw that iron was better for most useful things than either copper or bronze. The Iron Age lasted three thousand years.

People who lived in the Bronze and Iron Ages were able, after the discovery of metal,

的石头，而是我们所称的"矿石"，因为其中含有铜。火堆的温度很高，让石头中的一部分铜熔化出来，流淌到了地上。

那些亮晶晶、一滴一滴地闪烁着光泽的东西是什么呢？

他仔细地研究了一会儿。

它们看上去是多么的漂亮啊！

他又多烧了一些这样的石头，得到了更多的熔化的铜。

这样，人类就发现了第一种金属。

起初，人们用铜来做小珠子和装饰品，因为铜亮晶晶的，闪闪发光。不过，他们很快就发现，铜可以被锤打成锋利的刀片和箭头，比他们原来所用的石刀和石制箭头要好得多呢。

但我们要注意，他们首先发现的不是铁，而是铜。

我们认为，人类接着又用差不多相同的方式发现了锡。此后他们又发现，将锡和铜混合起来制成的金属，要比单用锡或者单用铜制成的金属更硬，质量也更好。由锡和铜混合而成的这种金属，我们如今称之为"青铜"；在两三千年的时间里，人类都是用这种青铜来制造工具和武器的。因此，我们将人类用青铜工具和青铜武器来狩猎、打仗的这一时期，称为青铜器时代。

最后，又有人发现了铁；而人们很快就发现，铁比铜或青铜都要更适合于制造大部分用具。这个铁器时代，持续了三千年的时间。

发现金属之后，生活在青铜器时代和铁器时代里的人类，便能够做到以前只用

to do many things they could not possibly have done before with only stone.

You may have heard in your mythology or fairy tales of a *Golden Age* also, but by this is meant something quite different. The Golden Age means a time when everything was beautiful and lovely and everybody wise and good. There have been times in the world's history which have been called the Golden Age for this reason.

But I am afraid there never has been really a Golden Age — only in fairy tales.

石器时不可能做到的许多事情了。

你们可能在神话故事中还听到过"黄金时代"的说法；但这种说法的意思却与字面完全不同。所谓的"黄金时代"，是指一切事物都非常美好、可爱，所有的人都很聪明且心地善良的一个时期。正是出于这个原因，世界历史上才有多个被称为"黄金时代"的时期。

可我却觉得，历史上恐怕并没有什么真正的"黄金时代"，只是神话故事里才有哩。

4 From an Airplane

People of the Bronze and Iron Ages thought the world was flat, and they knew only a little bit of the world, the small part where they lived; and they thought that if you went too far the world came to an end where you would

TU
M
B
L
E

O
F
F

If we should go up in an airplane and look down on the world at the place where the first civilized people once lived, we should see several rivers, seas, and a gulf, and from so high up in the air they would look something like this:

Now, you probably have never even heard of these rivers and seas, and yet they have been known longer than any other places in the world. One of these rivers is the Tigris River, and another is the Euphrates. They run along getting closer and closer together until at last they join each other and flow into what is called the Persian Gulf.

You might make these two rivers in the ground of your yard or garden or draw them on the floor if your mother will let you. Just for fun you might name your drinking cup *Tigris* and your glass *Euphrates*. Then you might call your mouth, into which they both empty, the Persian Gulf, for you will hear a great

4 从飞机上向下看

生活在青铜器时代和铁器时代的人，都认为世界是平的，并且他们只了解整个世界的一点点儿，那就是他们生活的那一小块地方；所以，他们认为，如果走得太远，他们就会来到世界的尽头，就会在那里

掉
下
去。

假如坐上一架飞机，在第一批文明的人类曾经生活的那个地方向下俯瞰世界，我们就会看到数条河流、几个海洋和一个海湾；而从空中那么高的地方往下看去，它们就像是这样：

注意，你们很可能从来没有听说过这些河流和海洋的名字，但其实它们为人们所知的时间，比世界上其他任何地方都更加悠久呢。其中，有一条河流叫作底格里斯河，另一条则叫作幼发拉底河。它们在流经的途中，彼此之间的距离变得越来越近，最终汇集到了一起，流入了那个叫作波斯湾的海湾当中。

你们可以在自家院子、花园的地上画出这两条河流来；要是妈妈允许的话，你们也可以在家里的地板上将它们画出来。为了好玩一点儿，你们完全可以把自己的水杯叫作"底格里斯"，将自己的牛奶杯子叫作"幼发拉底"。这样一来，你们就可以把自己的嘴巴叫作"波斯湾"了，因为水和牛奶都是喝到嘴里去的呀。由于日后会听到越来越多的新名称，所以，

many new names by and by, and as grown-up people give names to their houses and boats, to their horses and dogs, why shouldn't you give names to things that belong to you? For instance, you might call your chair, your bed, your table, your comb and brush, even your hat and shoes, after these strange names.

Then, if we flew in our airplane to the west, we should in the northeast corner of Africa see a country called Egypt, a river called the Nile, and a sea now named the Mediterranean. Mediterranean simply means *between the land*, for this sea is surrounded by land. It is, indeed, almost like a big lake. It is supposed that long, long ago in the Stone Age, there was no water at all where this sea now is, only a dry valley, and that people once lived there.

Along the Nile in what is now Egypt, and along the Tigris and Euphrates in what was then Babylon, Assyria, and Syria, lived people who were recording their activities in writing and pictures that have survived to this day.

Certainly there were cave men and other primitive peoples who were drawing pictures of their way of life. But because travel was not easy in those days, people in one

Map of Mesopotamia and Mediterranean
美索不达米亚和地中海地区示意图

你们为什么就不能像大人给他们的房子、船只、马儿、小狗都起个名字那样，给那些属于你们自己的东西也起个名字呢？比如说，你们完全可以用这些陌生的名称，来给自己的椅子、床、桌子、梳子和牙刷，甚至是帽子和鞋子起名。

接下来，如果乘坐飞机往西飞去，我们就会看到，非洲的东北角有一个叫作埃及的国家，有一条叫作尼罗河的河流，以及如今称作地中海的一个海域。顾名思义，"地中"就是指"陆地之间"，因为这个大海的四周都是陆地。事实上，地中海差不多就像是一个巨大的湖泊。人们认为，在很久、很久以前的石器时代，如今这个海洋所在的地方根本就没有水，只是一个干涸的谷地，还有人类曾经在这里生活过呢。

沿着如今埃及境内的尼罗河两岸和沿着当时的古巴比伦、亚述和叙利亚境内的底格里斯河与幼发拉底河两岸生活着的人类，都用文字和图画记录下了他们的活动；这些文字和图画，一直保存到了今天。

当然，还有穴居人和其他一些原始人类也用图画描绘出了他们的生活方式。但是，由于当时交通不便，生活在一个地方的人，对生活在另一个地方的人并不是很

region didn't know a great deal about people in another part of the world. This was soon to change.

Many different groups of people lived in the country of the Tigris and Euphrates and along the Nile, and all of them wanted to own the best land. There were many battles. People moved around a lot — because they lost a battle and had to move or just because they were looking for a better place to live.

One group or family of people called Semites lived in the land that today we call the Middle East, near the Mediterranean Sea and the Tigris and Euphrates. Modern Arabs and Jews are Semites. They speak Semitic languages that are part of one language family and sound very similar. Here's an example. In Hebrew, the word for peace is shalom. In Arabic, the word for peace is *salaam*.

Another group of people lived along the Nile. In Egypt and other parts of North Africa, Egyptians and people called Berbers were related to the Middle Eastern Semites. Nubians who came from the part of Africa south of Egypt belonged to a group of people called Nilo-Saharans. If you look at a map, you can see how they got this name. They lived along the Nile River and near the Sahara Desert. These Nubians traveled northward along the Nile Valley into Egypt. And sometimes Egyptians traveled south into Nubia.

Another group of people came from the area that is now Iran. They are called Indo-Europeans, and they spread eastward into northern India and westward into Europe. Today, people in Europe, Iran, and India are descended from these early Indo-Europeans. Just like

了解。不过，这种情况很快就会改变了。

在底格里斯河与幼发拉底河所在的那个国度，以及尼罗河两岸，生活着许多不同的人群，并且他们都想拥有最好的土地。他们之间，进行了许多次战争。因为打输了一场战争而不得不迁徙，或者仅仅是因为他们正在寻找更好的生活之地，所以那时的人们经常迁徙。

有一群人，或者说一个氏族，叫作闪米特人，他们生活在如今我们所称的"中东"地区；这里靠近地中海，以及底格里斯河与幼发拉底河。现代的阿拉伯人和犹太人，都属于闪族人。他们都说属于同一语系的并且听上去很相似的闪族语。给你们举个例子吧。在希伯来语中，表示"和平"的词语是"萨洛姆"（shalom）。而在阿拉伯语中，表示"和平"的词语则是"萨拉姆"（salaam）。

还有一群人则生活在尼罗河两岸。在埃及和北非的其他地区，埃及人以及那些叫作"柏柏尔人"的人，都与生活在中东地区的闪族人有关。来自埃及以南的非洲地区的努比亚人，属于一个叫作"尼罗河—撒哈拉人"的族群。如果从地图上来看，你们就会明白，他们为什么会叫这个名字。那是因为他们生活在尼罗河沿岸，距撒哈拉沙漠不远。这些努比亚人沿着尼罗河河谷向北迁徙，从而进入了埃及。有的时候，埃及人也会向南迁徙到努比亚去。

还有一个族群，来自如今伊朗所在的那个地区。他们被称为"印欧人"；他们向东扩张，进入印度北部，向西扩张，则进入了欧洲。如今，居住在欧洲、伊朗和印度的人，都是这些早期印欧人的后裔。与闪米特人一样，他们所说的语言，相互

the Semites, they speak languages that are related to each other.

We know now that these ancient peoples moved around a lot more than we used to think they did. They taught each other to grow different kinds of food. They exchanged goods with each other. And sometimes people settled down in the new land and stayed there. Just as the United States has seen many nationalities of people move here and become Americans, people in ancient times also migrated and settled down in a new land.

之间也有关联。

如今我们知道，这些古代人经常迁徙，并且迁徙得比我们过去所认为的更加频繁。他们相互传授不同粮食作物的种植方法。他们彼此交换物品。有的时候，人们迁徙到一个新的地方之后，就在那里永久定居下来。就像有许多不同的民族迁徙到美利坚合众国，从而变成了美国人一样，古代人也会四处迁徙，然后在一个新的地方定居下来。

5 Real History Begins

You can remember the big things that have happened in your own lifetime.

Perhaps you may have heard your grand-parents or your parents tell about things that happened in their own lives — things like World War II or the wars in Korea or Vietnam.

And your grandparents, of course, had parents and grandparents and great grandparents, just like you.

Perhaps your
 great,
  great,
   great,
    grandparents
may have been living when Washington was President, and his
 great
  great,
   great,
    great,
     great,
      grandparents
were living in the days of Julius Caesar.

Although these ancestors, as they are called, are dead long since, the story of what did happen in all their lifetimes 'way, 'way back has been written down in books and this story is history — *his story* one boy named it.

Christ was living in the Year 1 — no, not the first year of the world, of course.

Do you know how many years ago that was?

You can tell if you know what year this is now.

If Christ were living today, how old would He be?

5　真正的历史由此开始

你们都能够记住自己生活中发生的一些重大事件吧。

或许你们曾听到爷爷奶奶或者爸爸妈妈说起过他们一生中发生的一些事情，比如第二次世界大战、朝鲜战争或者越南战争。

而你们的爷爷奶奶，自然也像你们一样，也有他们的爸爸妈妈、爷爷奶奶和曾祖父曾祖母。

或许，你们的
 爷爷的
  爷爷的
   爷爷的
    爷爷
可能生活在华盛顿当美国总统的那个时代，而他的
 爷爷的
  爷爷的
   爷爷的
    爷爷的
     爷爷的
      爷爷
则可能生活在裘力斯·恺撒的那个年代呢。

虽然被我们所称的这些"祖先"很久以前就已经去世了，但他们老早、老早以前的一生中所发生的故事，却被人们用书本记载下来了，而这种记载，就是历史；有个男孩，还称之为"他的故事"[1]呢。

---

[1] 他的故事（his story），这两个单词合在一起并去掉中间的一个 s 之后，便是"历史"（history）。

Two thousand years may seem a long time. But perhaps you have seen or heard of a man or a woman who was a hundred years old. Have you?

Well, in two thousand years only twenty people, each a hundred years old, might have lived one after the other — twenty people one after the other since the time of Christ — and that doesn't seem so long after all!

Everything that happened *before* Christ was born is called B.C., which you can guess are the initials of Before Christ, so B.C. stands for Before Christ. So much is easy.

Everything that has happened in the world since the time of Christ is called A.D. This is not so easy, for though A. might stand for After, we know D. is not the initial of Christ.

As a matter of fact, A.D. are the initials of two Latin words, *Anno Domini*. Anno means *in the year*, Domini *of the Lord*, which in ordinary, everyday language means of course *since the time of Christ*.

I have told you about things I have had to guess at. We call these things *before-history*, or *pre-history*, which means the same thing. But the things that have happened in the lifetime of people who wrote them down — the stories I don't have to guess at — we call history. The first history that we feel fairly sure is true begins with the people in North Africa and the Middle East.

Some people began writing down their stories thousands of years ago. What's

基督诞生于公元1年[1]；当然，公元1年可不是世界诞生的那一年。

你们知道从公元1年到现在已经过去了多少年吗？

假如你们知道今年是公元多少年，那就能说出公元1年是多少年以前了。

如果基督活到今天，他又会有多大年纪了呢？

两千多年，看上去可是很长的一段时间。不过，你们可能看见过，或者听说过百岁老人吧，有没有呢？

那么，两千年就只是二十个百岁老人一个接一个地活着的这段时间，即从公元1年起，一个接一个地活到一百岁所经历的那一段时间；这样来看，就一点儿也不长了吧！

基督降生之前发生的一切事情，都被称为发生在"公元前（B.C.）"多少年；你们可以猜到，B.C.就是"基督之前（Before Christ）"的英文首字母的缩写，因此"公元前"代表的就是"基督降生之前"。多么简单啊。

而自从基督降生以来，世间所发生的一切事情，就都被称为发生在"公元（A.D.）"多少年了。但这个词猜起来，就没有那么容易了；因为尽管"A."可能代表"之后（After）"，但我们知道，"D."并不是"基督（Christ）"这个英文单词的首字母。

事实上，"公元（A.D.）"是"Anno Domini"这两个拉丁语单词的首字母。"Anno"指的是"在那一年"，"Domini"指的是"神的"，因此，用普通的日常

---

[1] 译者注：基督诞生的正确年份应为公元前4年，后文（第36章）有对其诞生的时间进行解释。

interesting is that different peoples in parts of the world that were really far apart figured out all by themselves how to write, and they did this at different times. Ancient people in the Middle East invented a written language called cuneiform. Ancient people in Egypt wrote in hieroglyphics. Centuries ago, people in India were writing in Sanskrit. People as far away as China, Nubia, and Central America invented their own writing. So did people on the island of Crete in the Mediterranean Sea, halfway between Egypt and Greece.

Today, we know how to read some of these languages from several thousand years ago. But other languages are like an unsolved puzzle. We see the writing, but we don't have any idea what it means.

If you think about all these early civilizations, which ones do you suppose we know the most about? The ones whose writing we can read, or the others? Well, I'll bet you all guessed the right answer to that question! Of course, we know the most about places whose stories *we can read*.

Four places whose early stories we can read about are Egypt, Mesopotamia, India, and China. We can read their writing, so we know what people were there during all those long years ago. We're not as good on the writing of Nubia or Central America or Crete, so we don't know as much about what was happening in those places long, long ago.

What's really interesting is what we *do* know about the places whose history we can read. We know that all four of those ancient civilizations grew up along river valleys.

语言来说，"Anno Domini" 当然就是指 "自基督降生以来" 了。

前面我已经跟你们说过了我只能去猜测的一些事情。这些事情，我们称之为 "有史以前" 或 "史前" 时期发生的事情；这两种说法，意思是一样的。但是，对于人们记录下来的、他们自己一生当中所发生的事情，也就是我不用去猜测的那些事情，我们则称之为 "历史"。大部分人认为属于真实的第一段历史，就是从生活在北非和中东地区的人类开始的。

有些人在几千年前便开始将自己的经历记录下来了。有意思的是，尽管不同民族生活在世界各地，彼此天各一方，但他们都是自行发明出了书写方法，只是发明的时间不同罢了。中东地区的古人发明了一种被称作 "楔形文字" 的书写语言。埃及的古代人则用 "象形文字" 来书写。几百年之前，印度人还在用梵文书写呢。远至像中国、努比亚和中美洲地区的人，全都发明了各自的书写文字。而地处埃及和希腊之间的克里特岛上的人，也发明了自己的文字。

这些几千年前写下的语言文字，如今我们已经理解了一些。但还有一些语言文字，却像是一个个没有破解的谜语那样。我们看得见这些文字，却根本不知道它们的意思。

想一想所有这些早期文明的话，你们觉得，我们最了解的应该是哪一种呢？是我们能够读懂其文字的文明呢，还是其他的文明？好吧，我敢打赌，你们都会猜中这个问题的正确答案！我们最了解的，当然是我们能够读懂其历史的那些地方。

有四个地方的早期历史，我们都能够读懂；它们就是：埃及、美索不达米亚、印度和中国。我们能够读懂这些地方的文字，因此知道在如此漫长的过去居住在这

Egypt was built along the Nile River valley. And Mesopotamia grew along the valleys of two rivers — the Tigris and the Euphrates. But you already know about those rivers.

Now here are two new rivers for you. India's first history took place along the valley of the Indus River and China's along the Huang River. The Huang River is sometimes called the Yellow River because the river's bottom is thick yellow mud.

Even though they lived far apart, the peoples who lived along these rivers did a lot of the same things. This isn't too surprising when you think about it. You may never have visited Africa or India or China today, but you can guess that girls and boys there play games, and that mothers cook, and so on. Even in ancient times, people around the world did many of the same things.

The river valleys were a good place to live because food was plentiful. There was lots of water for animals to drink, and to use to water plants. So men and women and boys and girls all settled down next to the rivers — in Egypt, in Mesopotamia, in India and in China.

Soon enough people were living so close together that they were living in what we call a town. Then people in these towns began to build little boats, then bigger boats. Soon the boats were sailing up and down the river to the next town and to towns farther away. The towns began to trade with each other. And sometimes the towns began to fight with each other.

One of the best ways to stop the towns from having little wars was to put them all under

些地方的都是些什么样的民族。而对于努比亚、中美洲或克里特岛等地的文字，我们则不那么了解，因而对很久、很久以前这些地方发生的情况，也就了解不多。

真正有意思的，便是对能够读懂其历史的这些地方，我们已经切实了解到的那些情况。我们知道，这四大古代文明，都是沿着河流流域发展起来的。

埃及是沿着尼罗河流域发展起来的。美索不达米亚是沿着两河流域，即底格里斯河流域和幼发拉底河流域发展起来的。而对这几条河流，你们都已经有所了解了。

在这里，你们又会接触到两条新的河流。古印度的历史，发源于印度河流域，而中国的历史则发源于黄河流域。"黄河"有时又被叫作"黄色之河"，因为这条河流的河底，全是厚厚的黄色泥沙。

尽管相距遥远，但生活在这些河流两岸的不同民族，所作所为却有很多相同的地方。仔细想一想，你们就会明白，这没什么可惊讶的。如今，虽说你们可能从来没有到非洲、印度或者中国去旅游过，但你们完全猜想得出，那里的小朋友们也在做游戏，那里的妈妈们也在做饭，等等。就算是在古代，世界各地人们的所作所为，也有很多是相同的呢。

河流两岸是适合人类生活的地方，因为那里的食物会很充足。那里有充沛的河水可供动物饮用和浇灌植物。于是，埃及、美索不达米亚、印度和中国等地的男女老少，便全都是临河而居。

不久之后，一些地方生活的人越来越多、越来越密集，便形成了我们所称的市镇。接下来，生活在这些市镇里的人开始建造一些小型的船只，然后又开始建造较大的船只。很快，船只便开始在河流里面上下航行，往来于附近市镇和更远的市镇

the rule of one

person. So, in place after place, a *government* grew up. Sometimes the towns agreed to get together. Other times they were united when one strong man conquered his neighbors. Either way, a king, or emperor, or pharaoh was in charge of the government and was ruler of what we now call a nation.

So, if you look back at these river civilizations, you can see a piece of history that is really quite remarkable. At a time when many people were still hunters and gatherers, maybe even living in caves, something new and exciting was happening first in Egypt and Mesopotamia and soon afterwards in India and China. People settled down and farmed, then built towns, then traded with each other, and then built nations. And, sometime during all this, they figured out that it would be a great thing to write — and so they wrote down their history for us to read today.

Trading boat of river valley town
河流两岸市镇间进行贸易的船只

之间了。于是，市镇之间便开始进行相互贸易。有的时候，市镇之间也会彼此征战。

阻止市镇之间爆发小规模战争的最佳办法之一，就是将这些市镇全都掌控在一个人的统治之下。于是，各地便一个接一个地出现了政府。有的时候，是各个市镇一致同意团结起来。其他时候，则是由一个强有力的人物征服邻近市镇而将它们统一起来。但不论是哪种方式，都是由一个国王、皇帝或者法老来掌控政府，这个掌控政府的人便成为我们如今所称的一国之君。

所以，假如回顾一下这些流域文明的历史，你们便会明白，这一段历史的确是非比寻常的。在许多民族仍然只会狩猎和采集果实、甚至仍然居住在洞穴之中的时候，某种新的、令人激动的东西率先在古埃及和美索不达米亚地区出现了，不久后在古印度和中国也开始出现。人们定居下来，开始耕作，然后又建立市镇，彼此贸易，然后又建立了国家。并且，在这一过程中的某个时候，他们又认识到，书写是一件很了不起的事情，于是他们便将自己的历史记录下来，供我们如今来阅读。

6 The Puzzle Writers in Egypt

Egypt was one of the first places where people began to write. The Egyptians did not write with letters like ours, but with signs that looked like little pictures — a lion, a spear, a bird, a whip. This picture-writing was called hieroglyphics — see if you can say *hi-er-o-glyph-ics*. Perhaps you have seen, in the puzzle sections of a newspaper, stories written in pictures for you to guess the meaning. Well, hieroglyphics were something like that.

Here is the name of an Egyptian queen written in hieroglyphics. You would never guess her name from this funny writing. Her name was Hatshepsut. Can you say it? It's not as hard as it looks at first. *Hat SHEP sut*. She was the first woman ruler known to history.

A king's or queen's name always had a line drawn around it, like the one you see around the name of Hatshepsut, in order to mark it more

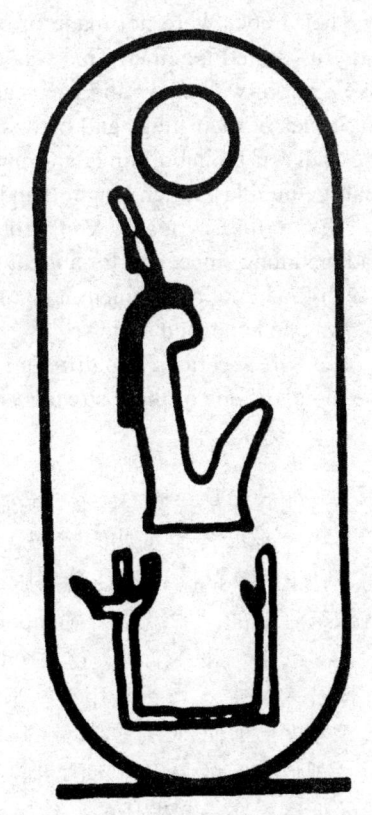

Hatshepsut in hieroglyphic writing
用象形文字书写的 "哈特谢普苏特"

6 埃及谜语

埃及是人类最早开始用文字进行书写的地区之一。但埃及人并不像如今的我们，并不是用字母来书写，而是用有点儿像是图画的符号，比如一头狮子、一支长矛、一只小鸟或者一根鞭子来书写的。这种用图画书写出来的文字，就叫作"象形文字"；你们不妨将这个词多读几遍：象—形—文—字。或许，你们在报纸的谜语版里已经看到过用图画写成的、让你们去猜测意思的故事。是的，象形文字正像是这种故事。

上面这位埃及王后的名字，便是用象形文字写出来的。这种文字很是滑稽古怪，你们永远都猜不出她叫什么的。她叫"哈特谢普苏特"。你们能一口气读出来吗？它并没有乍一看的那么难吧。哈特—谢普—苏特。她可是人类历史上的第一位女性统治者哩。

国王或者王后的名字，四周通常都会画有线条，就像你们看到"哈特谢普苏特"这个名字周围有线条框住一样，其目的就是突出这个名字，使它显得更加重

prominently and give it more importance. It was something like the frame that we put around a fine picture to make it Hatshepsut in look better where it hangs on the wall.

There was no paper in those days and so the Egyptians wrote on the stalks of a plant called papyrus that grew in the water. They pressed the thick stalks until they were thin and flat and looked like paper. It is from this name *papyrus* that we get the name *paper*. Can you see that *paper* and *papyrus* look and sound something alike? The Egyptians' books were written by hand, of course, but they had no pencils nor pens nor ink with which to write. For a pen they used a reed, split at the end, and for ink a mixture of water and soot.

Their books were not made of separate pages like our books, but from long sheets of papyrus pasted together. This was rolled up to form what was called a scroll, something like a roll of wallpaper, and was read as it was unrolled.

Stories of their kings and battles and great events in their history they used to write on the walls of their buildings and monuments. This writing they carved into the stone, so that it would last much longer than that on the papyrus leaves.

All the old Egyptians, who wrote in hieroglyphics and knew how to read this writing, had died long since, and for a great many years no one knew what such writing meant. But a man found out by accident how to read and understand hieroglyphics once again. This is the way he happened to do so.

The Nile separates into different streams before it flows into the Mediterranean Sea. At the mouth of one of these streams is a port called Rosetta.

要。这就好像是我们会给一幅好画裱上边框，从而使得画作挂上墙后更好看那样。

由于那时没有纸张，所以古埃及人是在一种生长于水中、叫作"纸草"的植物茎秆上写字的。他们使劲按压纸草，直到厚厚的纸草茎秆变得又薄又平，看上去就像纸张似的。"纸张"（paper）一词，正是从"纸草"（papyrus）这个词而来的。"纸张"和"纸草"这两个词看起来、听上去都有点儿相似，你们发现了吗？古埃及人的书，当然是用手写成的；可他们却并没有写字所用的铅笔、钢笔和墨水。原来，他们是把芦苇的一头劈开做成钢笔，并用水和烟灰和起来当墨水的。

他们所写的书，可不像我们的图书那样分成一页一页，而是将长长的、一片一片的纸草粘在一起做成的。然后，他们将这种用纸草写成的书卷起来，形成我们所称的"卷轴"；它有点儿像是一卷墙纸，要看的时候就展开来。

他们常常把国王的经历、战争等重大的历史事件写在建筑物的墙壁或者纪念碑上。他们将这些文字刻在石头上，从而使之能够比纸草片上的文字更加长久地保存下去。

那些能够书写并阅读象形文字的古埃及人，很久、很久以前就全都死了，因此在很长一段时间里，都没有人明白这种文字的意思。不过，有个人却在无意当中发现了再次阅读和理解象形文字的方法。下面就来说一说这个人碰巧发现的办法。

尼罗河一路上分成了数条不同的支流，然后才流入地中海。在这些支流当中的一条河的入海口，有个叫作罗塞塔的港口。

One day some soldiers were digging near Rosetta when they found a stone, something like a tombstone with three kinds of writing on it. The top writing was in pictures, which we now call hieroglyphics, and no one understood what it meant. Below this was written what was supposed to be the same story in the Greek language, and a great many people do understand Greek. All one had to do, therefore, to find out the meaning of the hieroglyphics, was to compare the two writings. It was like reading secret writing when we know what the letters stand for. You may have tried to solve a puzzle in the back of your magazine, and this was just such an interesting puzzle, only there was no one to tell the answers.

The puzzle was not as easy as it sounds, however, for it took a clever man almost twenty years to solve it. That is a long time for anyone to spend in trying to solve a puzzle, isn't it? But after this *key* to the puzzle was found, men were able to read all of the hieroglyphics in Egypt and so to find out what happened in that country long ago.

This stone is called the Rosetta Stone. It is now in the great British Museum in London and is very famous, because from it we were able to learn so much history that we otherwise would not have known.

We know that Egypt was a fine place to live. It was chiefly on account of a habit of the river Nile — a bad habit you might at first think it — a habit of flooding the country once a year.

It rained so hard that the water filled up the river Nile, overflowed its banks, and spread water and mud far out over the land, but not very deep.

The people knew when the overflow was coming. They invented a calendar to keep

有一天，一些士兵正在罗塞塔附近一个地方进行挖掘的时候，发现了一块石头；这块石头有点儿像是墓碑，上面写着三种文字。最上面的那种文字是图画，即如今我们所称的象形文字，可没有人理解它的意思。图画之下，应当是用希腊语叙述了同一个故事，而很多人都懂得希腊语。因此，要想理解那些象形文字的意思，我们需要做的就是把两种文字进行比较。这就好比是我们在懂得了每个字所代表的意思后，再去阅读一封密信一样。你们可能都试过解出杂志背面的谜语，而这正像是一个有趣的谜语，只是没有人来告诉你们正确的答案是什么罢了。

然而，这个谜语可不像听上去那么容易，因为它让一个聪明人花了差不多二十年的时间才解答出来。对于任何一个试图解开谜语的人来说，这段时间都花得够久的，不是吗？不过，解开谜语的这把钥匙找到之后，人们就可以读懂古埃及的所有象形文字，从而了解那个国家很久以前的情况了。

这块石头，被人们称为"罗塞塔碑"。如今，它保存在伦敦的大英博物馆内，非常有名；因为从这块石头上，我们能够了解到大量的历史，而倘若没有这块石头，我们便无从得知这些历史。

我们知道，古埃及是个适合于人类生活的好地方。而这主要是由于尼罗河有一个习惯，那就是它每年都要让该国发一次洪水；乍一想来，你们可能会觉得这可不是个好习惯呢。

大雨滂沱之后，雨水便会注满尼罗河、漫过河堤，将河水和泥沙泛滥到陆地深

track of it. After most of the water dried up, it left a layer of rich, dark, moist earth over the whole valley. This was a natural fertilizer, like compost that some of your families may use in your own gardens. This fertile soil made it easy to grow dates, wheat, and other good things to eat.

We know also that Egypt was ruled by a king who was called a pharaoh. The first Egyptian king whose name we know was Menes. He came from southern Egypt and conquered the north. He united the country under his rule. He also declared that he was a god. So Egyptians believed that they should obey him both because he was king and because he was a god. Menes lived around 3100 B.C.

People in Egypt were divided into classes. Children in each class usually became what their parents had been. Only a very few ever got to move up.

The highest class of people were called priests. They were not like priests or ministers of a church nowadays, however, for there was no church at that time. The priests made the religion and rules, which everyone had to obey as everybody does the laws of our land.

The priests were not only priests; they were doctors and lawyers and engineers, as well. They were the best-educated class, and they were the only people who knew how to read and write, for it was very difficult, as you

Menes, 3100 B.C.
公元前3100年的美尼斯

处；不过，洪水和泥沙淹没得并不是很深。

那里的人们知道河水何时泛滥。他们发明了一种日历，来记录河水泛滥的时间。大部分洪水退去之后，便会在整个河谷里留下一层肥沃而湿润的黑土。这是一种天然的肥料，就像你们当中有些家庭会在自家花园里施用的粪肥一样。这种肥沃的土壤，使得人们很容易种植枣椰、小麦以及其他好吃的粮食作物。

我们还知道，古埃及是由一个被称作"法老"的国王统治着。我们所知的第一任埃及国王，名叫美尼斯。他来自古埃及南部，然后又征服了古埃及的北部。他将整个国家统一起来，置于自己的统治之下。他还宣称自己是神。由于他既是国王、又是神，所以古埃及人便都觉得，他们理应服从他的统治才是。美尼斯生活的时代，大约是在公元前3100年。

古埃及人被划分成了不同的等级。每个等级中的孩子，长大以后通常也属于父母所在的那个等级。只有极少数人，才会上升到较高的等级中去。

其中最高的那个等级，被称为"祭司"。然而，他们与如今教会里的神父或者牧师可不一样，因为那时还没有什么教会。祭司们负责制定宗教教义和教规教条，并且人人都得服从这些教义和规定，就像如今人人都得遵守国家的法律一样。

祭司们并非仅仅是祭司；他们还是医生、律师和工程技术人员。他们是受教育程度最高的一个等级，也只有他们才能读会写，因为正如你们可能认为的那样，学

might suppose, to learn how to read and write hieroglyphics.

The next highest class to the priests were the soldiers, and below these were the lower classes — farmers, shepherds, shopkeepers, merchants, mechanics, and last of all the swineherds.

The Egyptians did not worship one God as we do. They believed in hundreds of gods and goddesses, and they had a special god for every sort of thing, who ruled over and had charge of that thing — a god of the farms, a god of the home, and so on. Some of their gods were good and some were bad, but the Egyptians prayed to them all.

Osiris was the chief god, and Isis was his wife. Osiris was the god of farming and judge of the dead. Their son, Honrs, had the head of a falcon.

Many of their gods had bodies of men with heads of animals, animals they thought sacred. The dog and the cat were sacred animals. The ibis, which is a bird like a stork, was another. Then there was the beetle, which was called a scarab. If anyone killed a sacred animal he was put to death, for the Egyptians thought it much worse to kill a sacred and holy creature than to kill even a human being.

会阅读和书写象形文字是非常困难的。

次于祭司的第二个等级，便是武士了。祭司、武士这两个等级之下，是较低的等级，其中包括农民、牧民、店主、商人、手艺人；而最卑贱的一个等级，则是猪倌。

古埃及人不像我们这样只崇拜一个神。他们崇拜着数百位神灵，男神女神都有，并且每种东西都有一个特定的、主宰和掌管这种东西的神，比如农场有农神，家中有家神，如此等等。虽说他们崇拜的神灵中，既有善良之神，也有邪恶之神，但古埃及人都一视同仁地向这些神进行祈祷。

奥西里斯是古埃及人的主神，他的妻子是伊西斯。奥西里斯是农神和阴间的判官。他们的儿子荷鲁斯还长着一个鹰头呢。

古埃及人所崇拜的许多神灵，都有着人的身体、动物的脑袋，因为他们认为那些动物都很神圣。狗和猫都是圣兽。长得像鹳的朱鹭也是一种圣兽。还有金龟子，他们称之为圣甲虫。如果有人胆敢杀死一头圣兽，他就会被处死；因为古埃及人认为，杀死一种神圣生物的罪过，甚至要比杀死一个人的罪过更大。

7 The Tomb Builders

The Egyptians believed that when they died, their souls stayed near by their bodies. So when a person died, they put in the tomb with him all sorts of things that he had used in daily life — things to eat and drink, furniture and dishes, toys and games. They thought the soul would return to its own body at the day of judgment. They wanted their bodies to be kept from decaying until judgment day, in

order that the soul might then have a body to return to. So they pickled the bodies of the dead by soaking them in a mineral called natron and wrapping them round and round and round with a cloth like a bandage. A dead body pickled in this way is called a *mummy*, and after thousands of years the mummies of the Egyptians may still be seen. Most of them are not, however, in the tombs where they were at first placed. They have been moved away and put in museums, and we may see them there now. Although they are yellow and dried up, they still look like

Little old men
All skin and bones.

7 修建坟墓的人

古埃及人相信，他们死后，灵魂还会留在自己的尸体附近。所以一个人死后，人们就会把他生前所用的东西全都放进他的墓穴里，比如吃的、喝的、家具、碗碟、玩具、器物，等等。他们认为，在最后审判日，灵魂还会回到自己的躯体里。他们希望自己的尸体不会腐烂，直到审判日来临，以便届时灵魂能够回到自己的躯体之中。因此，他们会将死者的尸体浸泡在一种叫作"泡碱"的矿物质里，然后用一根绑带似的长布将尸体一圈又一圈地包裹起来进行保存。用这种方法处理过的一具尸体，就叫作"木乃伊"。几千年之后，我们还看得到古埃及人制作的这些木乃伊呢。然而，其中的大部分木乃伊，都不再待在它们最初下葬的坟墓里了。它们已经被搬到了博物馆里；如果我们去博物馆的话，可能就会看到。它们尽管如今已经发黄变干，但看上去却仍然像是

一个个皮包骨头
的矮小老头

At first only kings or important people of the highest classes were made mummies, but after a while all the classes, except perhaps the lowest, were treated in the same way. Sacred animals from beetles to cows were also made into mummies.

When an Egyptian died, his friends heaped up a few stones over his body just to cover it up decently and keep it from being stolen or destroyed by those wild animals that fed on dead bodies. But a king or a rich man wanted a bigger pile of stones over his body than just ordinary people had. To make sure that his pile would be big enough, a king built it for himself before he died. Each king tried to make his pile larger than anyone else's until at last the pile of stones became so big it was a hill of rocks and called a *pyramid*. The pyramids therefore were tombs of the kings, who built them while they were alive, to be monuments to themselves when they were dead. In fact a king was much more interested in building a home for his dead body than he was in a home for his live body. So, instead of palaces, kings built pyramids. There are many of these pyramids built along the bank of the Nile, and most of them were built, we think, just after 3000 B.C.

In Nubia, up the Nile farther south in Africa, in what is now the modern nation of Sudan, kings also built pyramids for themselves. This is not surprising since Egyptians and Nubians shared many of the same religious beliefs.

Tutankhamen's tomb showing foods preserved
图坦卡蒙[1]的墓穴中储存着食物

　　一开始的时候，只有国王和上等阶层的重要人物死后才会被制成木乃伊；但过了一段时间之后，所有等级的人（或许最低等级的人除外）死后便都开始这样处理了。而从金龟子到母牛之类的圣兽，也都被制成了木乃伊。

　　一名古埃及人死后，亲友们只会用不多的石块将他的尸体草草掩埋起来，目的只是防止尸体被盗或者被食尸动物咬坏。可国王或者富人们却希望，自己死后尸体上会有比普通人更大的一堆石头。为了确保掩埋自己尸体的石堆足够大，一位国王会在生前就开始为自己建造坟墓。每位国王都尽力让自己的坟堆比其他人的大；最后，这种由石头堆砌而成的坟堆便变得大如一座石山了，人们则称之为"金字塔"。因此，金字塔其实就是国王的坟墓；它们都由国王生前所建，而这些国王死后，它们就成了他们的纪念碑。事实上，相比于给生前的自己建造房子，古埃及的国王们更热衷于给自己的尸体建造容身之所。因此，他们建的不是宫殿，而是金字塔。尼罗河沿岸有许多这样的金字塔；我们认为，其中绝大多数都建于公元前3000年以后。

　　[1] 图坦卡蒙（Tutankhamen，约公元前1341年—公元前1323年），古埃及新王国时期第十八王朝的法老，九岁时登上王位，但在十九岁时却神秘地死了。只是因为他的坟墓（即金字塔）在1922年被完整地发现，才为世人所知。

When a building is being put up nowadays, men use derricks and cranes and engines to haul and raise heavy stones and beams. But the Egyptians had no such machinery, and though they used huge stones to build the pyramids, they had to drag these stones for many miles and raise them into place simply by pushing and pulling them. The three biggest of all the pyramids are near the city of Cairo. The largest one of them, which is called the Great Pyramid, was built by a king named Cheops. That name is pronounced just like KEY ops. Here is his date:

Cheops...................................2900 B.C.

It is said that one hundred thousand men worked twenty years to build his pyramid. It is one of the largest buildings in the world, and some of the blocks of stone themselves are as big as a small house. I have been to the top if it, and it is like climbing a steep mountain with rocky sides. I have also been far inside to the cavelike room in the center where Cheops's mummy was placed. There is nothing in there now, however, except bats that fly about in the darkness, for the mummy has disappeared — been stolen, perhaps.

Near the Pyramid of Cheops is the Sphinx. It is a huge statue of a lion with a man's head. Although it is big, it was carved out of one single rock. The Sphinx is a statue of the god of the morning, and the head is that of one of the Egyptian pharaohs who built a pyramid near that of Cheops. The desert sand has covered the paws and most of the body. Though the sand has been dug away from time to time, the wind quickly covers the body with sand again.

在努比亚，沿着尼罗河上游深入非洲南部后，在现代的苏丹这个国家境内，古时的国王们也给自己建造了许多的金字塔。这并不奇怪，因为埃及人和努比亚人有着许多共同的宗教信仰。

如今在建造房屋时，人们会利用起重机、吊车和发动机来拖拉并吊起大石和梁柱。可古埃及人并没有这样的机械设备，因此，尽管他们是用巨石来建造金字塔的，但他们必须仅凭人力推拉，从数英里[1]外将这些巨石拖过来，然后再将它们安放就位。在所有的金字塔中，最大的三座都距开罗[2]不远。其中最大的一座，被称为"大金字塔"；它是由一个叫作基奥普斯[3]的国王建造起来的。这个名字，读音就像"鸡—阿普斯"。他所处的年代是：

基奥普斯……………公元前2900年

据说，他的这座金字塔，是十万人用了二十年的时间才建成的呢。它是世界上最大的建筑之一，其中一些巨石本身就有一小座房子那么大。我曾经到过这座金字塔的塔顶，感觉就像是在爬一座两侧都是崖壁的陡峭山峰一样。我还去过金字塔的里面，到达了中心那个像是洞穴一般、摆放基奥普斯那具木乃伊的房间。然而，如今那个房间里什么也没有了，只有在黑暗中飞来飞去的蝙蝠；因为基奥普斯的木乃伊已经不见了，没准是被人偷走了呢。

[1] 英里（mile），英制长度单位。1 英里 =1.609 千米。
[2] 开罗（Cairo），今埃及的首都。
[3] 基奥普斯（Cheops），公元前三到四世纪古埃及第四王朝的法老，又名"胡夫（Khufu）"。他所建造的大金字塔，又称"胡夫金字塔"。

The Egyptians carved other large statues of men and women out of rock. These figures are usually many times bigger than life-size, and sit or stand stiffly erect with both feet flat on the ground and hands close to the body in the position some children take when they *sit* for their photograph.

They built huge houses for their gods. These were called temples. These temples had gigantic — that's the way it is spelled, though it means *giant-ic* — columns and pillars. Ordinary people standing beside them look like dwarfs.

Here is one of these temples, and you can see how different it is from a church.

They decorated their temples and pyramids, and the cases in which the mummies were put, with paintings. They did not try to make these paintings look real, however. For example, when they wanted to make a picture of water, they simply made zigzag lines to represent waves and colored them blue-green. When they wanted to draw a row of men behind a row in front, they put those in back *on top* of those in front. To show that a man

Cheops building his pyramid
基奥普斯正在建造他的金字塔

基奥普斯金字塔的附近，就是"斯芬克斯"。这是一座巨大的狮身人面雕像。尽管硕大无比，它却是用一整块石头雕刻出来的。斯芬克斯是黎明之神的雕像；而它的头部，却是一位埃及法老[1]的形象，这位法老在基奥普斯金字塔的不远处也建了一座金字塔。大漠里的滚滚黄沙，已经掩埋了斯芬克斯的脚爪和身体的大部分。尽管人们不断地将沙土刨走，但大风很快又裹携着黄沙，将狮身人面像的身体再次掩埋起来了。

古埃及人还用岩石雕刻出了其他一些大型的男女雕像。这些雕像通常都要比真人大上好多倍；它们或坐或站，都是呆板生硬地立着，双脚平踩在地上，两手则紧贴着身体，就像一些小朋友坐着拍照时的那种姿势。

他们还为诸神建造了一座座巨大的房子。这些房子，被称为神庙。在这些神庙里，都有许多硕大的圆柱和梁墩；注意"硕大"一词的英文就是这样写的：gigantic，尽管它指的是"巨人一般"（giant-ic）。一般的人站在这些柱子旁边，看上去就像侏儒那样矮小呢。

下页图就是这些神庙当中的一座；你们都看得出，它与一座教堂完全不同呢。

古埃及人会在神庙、金字塔以及放置木乃伊的棺木上画画。然而，他们并没有尽量让这些画看上去像真的一样。比如说，假如想要画的是水，他们只会用数根参差不齐的曲线来代表波浪，然后再把这些曲线描成青绿色。倘若想要画的是一排人在前、另一排人在后，那他们就会把后排的人画在前排人的头顶上。如果要表明一

---

[1] 指古埃及第四王朝的哈夫拉（Khafre）法老。

Egyptian Temple
古埃及的神庙

was a king, they made him larger than the other men in the picture.

The Egyptians used bright colors in their pictures. They used a lot of red, yellow, and brown. You can see in their pictures that some people had dark skin and some had light tan skin. At first people from southern Egypt had darker skin, and people from near the Mediterranean had lighter skin. Over the years, people moved all over Egypt and then you could no longer tell where a person came from by the color of his or her skin.

个人是国王的话，他们就会将国王画得比画面上其他的人都要大。

古埃及人绘画时，用的都是很亮丽的颜色。他们大量使用红色、黄色和褐色。你们可以看到，他们的图画中有些人皮肤黝黑，有些人的肤色则是浅褐色。起初的时候，来自埃及以南的人皮肤较黑，而来自地中海附近的人则肤色较浅。而随着岁月流逝，由于人们在整个埃及境内四处迁徙，所以后来我们就无法再根据肤色来判断出一个人来自何处了。

8 A Rich Land Where There Was No Money

You have read in fairy tales of a land where cakes and candy and sugarplums grow on trees, where everything you want to eat or to play with can be had just by picking it. Well, long, long ago people used to think there had been really such a country, and where do you suppose they said it was? Somewhere near the Tigris and Euphrates Rivers — those rivers with the strange names I asked you to learn — and they called this spot the Garden of Eden. We do not know exactly where it was, for there is no such place now quite as wonderful as the Garden of Eden was supposed to be.

Egypt was a land of one river, the Nile. The land of the Two Rivers had several names.

Let us suppose we are flying over the country in an airplane and looking down at the land between these two rivers. It is called Mesopotamia, which is two Greek words simply meaning *between the rivers*.

See the land over there by the upper Tigris. It is called Assyria.

See the land near where the rivers join each other. That is called Babylonia.

See the land near where they empty. That is called Chaldea.

And see over there is Mount Ararat, where it is supposed Noah's Ark rested after the flood.

8 没有钱的富庶之地

你们一定在童话故事里看到过这样的地方：在那里，糕点、糖果和棒棒糖都是长在树上，你们想要吃的、玩的，伸手便可以摘到。是的，很久、很久以前，人们曾经认为，世界上确实有过这样的一个国家；你们觉得，人们说的这个国家位于哪儿呢？就在底格里斯河与幼发拉底河附近的一个地方，他们将这个地方称作"伊甸园"；这两条名字古怪的河流，我曾经要你们记住，你们还记得吗？我们并不知道这个国家的准确位置，因为如今没有哪个地方再有人们所认为的"伊甸园"那样奇妙了。

古埃及这个国度只有一条河流，即尼罗河。而两河流域这片土地，却有着种种不同的名称。

假设我们坐在一架飞机上飞过这个国家，并且往下俯瞰这两条河流之间的那片大地。这片土地叫作美索不达米亚；"美索不达米亚"其实是由两个希腊语单词组成的，只是指"位于河流之间"罢了。

看一看底格里斯河上游的那个地方，那里叫亚述。

看一看两河交汇之处附近的那个地方，那里叫巴比伦尼亚。

看一看两河入海口的附近，那里叫迦勒底。

再看一看，那里还有亚拉拉特山脉；传说大洪水过后，诺亚的方舟就停在那儿呢。

Here are a lot of new names. A young friend of mine had a train of toy cars. He had noticed that the cars on which he had ridden had names, and so he gave his toy cars names also. He called them:

Assyria	Mesopotamia
Babylonia	Ararat
Chaldea	Euphrates

Babylonia was a very rich country, for the two rivers brought down and dropped great quantities of earth just as the Nile did in Egypt, and this made very rich soil. Wheat, from which we make bread, is called the staff of life. It is the most valuable of all foods which grow. It is supposed that wheat first grew in Babylonia. Dates in that part of the world are almost as important a food as wheat. Dates, too, grow there very plentifully. Now, you may think dates are something to be eaten almost like candy, but in Babylonia dates took

The ancient Mediterranean world
古代的地中海地区示意图

这里又出现了一大堆的新名称。我认识的一位小朋友有许多辆玩具汽车。他注意到，自己坐过的许多汽车都有名字，于是他也给自己的玩具汽车一一取了名字。他把自己那些玩具汽车分别叫作：

亚述	美索不达米亚
巴比伦尼亚	亚拉拉特
迦勒底	幼发拉底河

巴比伦尼亚是个非常富庶的国家，因为底格里斯和与幼发拉底两条河流携带并沉积下来大量的泥沙，就像埃及境内的尼罗河那样，而这些泥沙又形成了非常肥沃的土壤。我们用来做面包的小麦，被称为"生命支柱"。在人类种植的所有粮食作物当中，小麦是最重要的一种。人们认为，小麦是在巴比伦尼亚最先种植出来的。这个地方种植的枣椰，也是与小麦差不多同样重要的一种粮食。该地的枣椰也种植得非常多。注意，你们可能会以为，枣椰是与糖果差不多相似的一种零食；可是在巴比伦尼亚，枣椰却是用来代替燕麦的主食呢。这两条河流当中盛产优质鱼类；由于当时

the place of oatmeal. In the rivers there were quantities of good fish, and as fishing was just fun, you see that the people who lived in Babylonia — the Babylonians, as they were called — had plenty of good food. No one had any money in those days; people had pigs and sheep and goats, and a man was rich who had much of these goods. Early on, if a man wanted to buy or sell, he had to buy or sell by trading something he had for something he wanted.

Somewhere in Babylonia the people built a great tower called the *Tower of Babel*, which you have probably heard about. It was more like a mountain than a tower. They built other towers, too. Some say the Tower of Babel and towers like it were built so that the people might have a high place to which they could climb in case of another flood. Others give a different reason. They say that the people who built these towers came to Babylonia from farther north where there were mountains. In this northern land they had always placed their altars on the top of a mountain, to be close to heaven. So when they moved to a flat country like Mesopotamia and Babylonia, where there were not mountains, they built mountains in order to have a high place for the altar on top. To reach the top of these mountains or towers, they made, instead of a staircase on the inside, a slanting roadway that wound around the outside in somewhat the way a road winds around a mountain.

There was hardly any stone either in or near Babylonia as there was in Egypt, and so the Babylonians built their buildings of bricks, which were made of mud formed into blocks and dried in the sun. In the course of time, bricks of this sort crumble and turn back into dust again, just as mud pies that you might make would do. This is the reason why

捕鱼只是一种消遣，所以你们便看得出，那些生活在巴比伦尼亚的人（他们被称为巴比伦人）有多么丰富的美食了。那时的人并没有钱；人们有的只是绵羊、山羊，因此饲养了许多这类家畜的人，就是富人。在早期的时候，一个人倘若想要买卖什么东西，他就只能用自己已有的东西去交换想要的东西。

在巴比伦尼亚的一个地方，人们还建造了一座叫作"通天塔"的高塔；你们很可能听说过它的故事呢。它更像是一座山峰，而不像是一座塔。人们还建造了其他的一些高塔。有人说，古巴比伦人之所以建造通天塔和其他类似的高塔，是为了再发洪水时人们有高处可爬。其他人却给出了不同的解释。他们说，建造这些高塔的人，都是从遥远的、有着高山的北方来到巴比伦尼亚的。在北方，这些人往往将祭坛建在山顶上，以便更靠近天堂。因此，当他们迁徙到像美索不达米亚和巴比伦尼亚这样没有高山的平原地带之后，为了有一个可以将祭坛放置上去的高地，他们便建造出了一座座高山。为了到达这些高山或者高塔顶上，他们可不是在高塔内部修建楼梯，而是在塔身外面修筑了一条斜路，绕着塔身蜿蜒而上，有点儿像是如今的盘山公路呢。

与古埃及不同，古巴比伦王国境内和附近地区并没有石头，因此古巴比伦人都是用砖块来建造房屋的；这些砖块，都是先用湿泥做成块状，然后晒干形成的。随着时光流逝，这种砖块会破碎、重新变成了泥土，就像你们玩的泥巴团干了后就会碎裂一样。很久以前用砖块建造的这些高塔和其他建筑，如今之所以全都只剩下了

all that is left of the towers and the other buildings that were put up so long ago are now simply hills of clay into which the brick has turned.

The Egyptians wrote on papyrus or carved their history in stone, but the Babylonians had neither papyrus nor stone. All they had were bricks. So they wrote on bricks before they were dried, while they were still soft clay. This writing was made by punching marks into the clay with the end of a stick. It was called *cuneiform*, which means wedge-shaped, for it looked like little groups of wedge-shaped marks, like chicken-tracks, made in the mud. I have seen boys' writing that looked more like cuneiform than it did like English.

As the Babylonians watched their flocks by day and night, they watched also the sun and the moon and the stars moving across the sky. So they came to know a great deal about these heavenly bodies.

Did you ever see the moon in the daytime?

Oh, yes, you can.

Well, every once in a great while the moon as it moves across the sky gets in front of the sun and shuts out its light — just as, if you should put a plate in front of an electric lamp, the plate would block the light from the lamp. It may be ten o'clock in the morning and broad daylight, when suddenly the sun is covered up by the moon, and it becomes night and the stars shine out, and chickens, thinking it is night, go to roost. But in a few moments the moon passes by and the sun shines out once again. This is called an *eclipse* of the sun.

Now you may never have seen an eclipse of the sun, but some day you may. If you do, I hope you do not think the way ignorant people always have: they think that something

一座座土堆，原因就在这里。

古埃及人在纸草上记录或者在石头上刻下他们的历史，可古巴比伦人却既无纸草，又没有石头。他们有的，只是砖块。于是，他们便趁着砖块还没有晒干、还是很湿软的黏土之时，在砖块上写字。这种写法，就是用棍子的一头，把符号压进黏土里。这种文字被称为"楔形文字"；所谓楔形，指的是像楔子一样，因为这种文字看起来全都是小小的楔形符号，就像小鸡在泥地里留下的爪印那样。我可看到过，有些小朋友写出来的字更像是楔形文字，而不像是英语呢。

在古巴比伦人日夜照料家畜的过程中，他们也注意到了天空中的太阳、月亮及星辰的运行情况。于是，他们便开始了解到了这些天体的许多知识。

你们在白天有没有看到过月亮呢？

哦，是的，你们可能都看到过。

没错，每隔很久一段时间，在天空中移动的月亮便会运行到太阳的前面，挡住太阳的光线；就像是你把一个盘子放到一盏电灯前面，盘子便会挡住灯光那样。此时可能是上午十点，正是大白天。突然之间，太阳便被月亮遮挡住了，白天一下子变成了黑夜，而小鸡们则以为到了晚上，纷纷进窝去了。但不一会儿，月亮移走之后，到处便又是阳光普照。这种现象，就叫作"日食"。

尽管你们现在可能从来没有看到过日食，但总有一日你们都会看到的。如果的确看到了日食，那我希望，你们可不要像一些愚昧的人往往所想的那样；只是因为他们以前从来没有见过这种奇观，不知道那是一种经常出现的自然现象，不知道这

dreadful is going to happen — the end of the world, perhaps, just because they have never seen such a strange sight before and do not know that it is a thing that happens regularly and that no harm comes from it.

Well, nearly twenty-three hundred years before Christ, in 2300 B.C., the Babylonians told beforehand just when there was going to be an eclipse of the sun. They had watched the moon moving across the sky and they had figured out how long it would be before it would catch up with the sun and cross directly over it. You see how much the old Babylonians knew about such things. Men who study the stars and other heavenly bodies are called *astronomers*, and the Babylonians, therefore, were famous astronomers. The Babylonians worshiped these wonderful heavenly bodies the sun, moon, and stars — that they knew so well.

The first king of Babylonia whom we know much about — and that much is very little — was Sargon I, who may have lived about the same time that the pyramids were built in Egypt.

About 1770 B.C. Babylonia had a king known far and wide for the laws he made. His name was Hammurabi, and we still have the code of laws he made though we no longer obey them. They were carved into a stone in cuneiform, and we have the stone. Sargon and Hammurabi are strange names like no one's name you ever heard before, yet they are real names of real kings who ruled over real people.

Babylonians watching eclipse
古巴比伦人观察日食

种现象并无危害，所以那些愚昧者便认为，日食意味着世上即将发生什么可怕的事情，或许还是世界末日即将到来了哩。

在基督降生以前的2300年左右，即在公元前2300年左右，古巴比伦人便已经预测出了日食发生的时间。他们已经观察到月亮横过天空，已经算出月亮多久后会赶上太阳并径直横过太阳。你们都看得出，古巴比伦人在这些方面的知识有多么丰富了吧。那些研究星星和其他天体的人，被称为"天文学家"；因此，古巴比伦人可都是著名的天文学家呢。古巴比伦人崇拜日、月、星辰这些奇妙的天体，并且对它们都了如指掌。

我们了解较多的、古代阿卡德王国的第一位国王，就是萨尔贡一世；这种所谓"较多"的了解，其实还是非常微小的。萨尔贡一世所在的时代，差不多就是埃及修建金字塔的那一时期。

在公元前1700年左右，古巴比伦出了一位国王，并且因为他颁布了一部律法而变得远近闻名了。这位国王叫作汉谟拉比；我们如今仍然看得到他制定的那部法典，只是我们如今不再遵守这部法典了。这部法典，用楔形文字刻在一块石头上，而我们也将这块石头保存下来了。尽管"萨尔贡"和"汉谟拉比"这两个名字很古怪，你们以前从来没有听说过这样的人名，可它们确实是这两位国王的真名；而这两位真正的国王，统治的也是真正的人民呢。

9 The Jews Search for a Home

You are spells *Ur*. It is one of the shortest names I know. It is the name of a little place in that part of Babylonia called Chaldea. In this place — about nineteen hundred years B.C. — there lived a man named Abraham. Abraham had a very large family and though he had no money, he was rich. He had large herds of sheep and goats, and these were the chief riches in those days. Now Abraham believed in one God, as we do, while his neighbors, the Babylonians, worshiped many gods and the heavenly bodies, such as the sun, moon, and stars, as I have just said. Abraham did not agree with his neighbors for this reason; and his neighbors didn't agree with him, either, for they thought his ideas were peculiar or even crazy. So, about nineteen hundred years before Christ, Abraham took his large family, his flocks, and his herds and moved to a land called Canaan, far away near the Mediterranean Sea.

Abraham lived to be a very old man, and he had a large family. One of his grandsons named Jacob, who was also known by the name of Israel, had a son Joseph. You probably remember the Bible story of Jacob's favorite son Joseph with the coat of many colors. Joseph's brothers were jealous of him, as children and even dogs are apt to be jealous of

9 犹太人寻找家园

"乌尔"（Ur）一词，由U和r这两个英文字母所组成。这是我所知的最短的英语单词之一。它是叫作迦勒底的这个小地方的一个地名。公元前1900年左右，这个地方住着一个名叫亚伯拉罕的人。亚伯拉罕有一大家子，并且虽说没有钱，可他却很富裕。他家里养着大群大群的绵羊和山羊；而在那个时候，这可是两种主要的财产呢。当时，亚伯拉罕和我们一样，只信仰一个神；可他的那些邻居，即古巴比伦人，却崇拜许多的神灵和天体，比如我上一节已经提到过的太阳啊，月亮啊，星辰啊。由于这个原因，亚伯拉罕与邻居们的关系并不好；而他的邻居们也不喜欢他，因为邻居们都觉得亚伯拉罕的想法很古怪，甚至还很愚蠢。于是，在公元前1900年左右，亚伯拉罕便带上他的那一大家子人，连同他家的牲口牛羊，都搬到地中海附近一个叫作哈兰的遥远之地去了。

亚伯拉罕活到很老才死，因此膝下儿孙众多。他有个孙子叫雅各，而雅各还有一个更著名的名字，那就是"以色列"；雅各又有一个叫作约瑟的儿子。你们很可能还记得，《圣经》故事中曾经说到，约瑟是雅各最喜欢的一个儿子，他还有一件五彩斑斓的衣服。约瑟的哥哥们都很嫉妒他，因为小孩子都很容易嫉妒比自己更招人喜欢的孩子，甚至小狗也会这样呢。于是，他们便把约瑟推到一口井里，后来又

anyone who is liked better than they are. So they put Joseph into a well and then sold him as a slave to some Egyptians who were passing by. Then they told their father Jacob that Joseph had been killed by wild animals. The Egyptians took Joseph to far-off Egypt — far away from Canaan.

As I told you, it was very difficult for anyone to work his way up out of his class to a higher class. Nevertheless, Joseph was a slave in Egypt, and he was so bright that at last he became one of the rulers in Egypt.

At that time when he was ruler, there came a famine in Canaan and there was no food. In Egypt, however, there was plenty of food stored up. So Joseph's wicked brothers went down to Egypt to beg the rulers for bread. They probably thought by that time their brother was dead. They did not know that he had become such a great man and that he was now the ruler from whom they were begging food. You can imagine how surprised they were and how ashamed they must have felt when they found out that the great ruler was their own brother, whom they had planned to kill and then had sold as a slave.

Joseph might have let his brothers starve to death or put them in prison, or sent them back to Canaan without anything, if he had wanted to revenge himself on them. Instead of doing any of these things, he gave them not only all the food they wanted and more to

Abraham leaving Ur, 1900 B.C.
公元前1900年，亚伯拉罕离开乌尔城

把他卖给过路的埃及人做奴隶。然后，他们便对父亲雅各说，约瑟被野兽吃掉了。那些埃及人则把约瑟带往了远方，带往了距哈兰十分遥远的埃及。

我在前面已经告诉过你们，在古埃及，一个人是很难跳出本身所属的等级而上升到较高等级的。但尽管如此，尽管约瑟起初只是埃及的一个奴隶，但由于他非常聪明，所以最终变成了埃及的统治者之一。

他当上了统治者之后，哈兰发生了饥荒，没有了粮食。然而在埃及，人们却储存了大量的粮食。因此，约瑟那些恶毒的哥哥们便南下前往埃及，乞求埃及的统治者给他们施舍面包。他们很可能认为，那时他们的弟弟约瑟早就已经死了。可他们并不知道，约瑟已经变成了大人物，变成了如今他们要去乞求其施舍食物的统治者。你们可以想见，当他们发现那位伟大的统治者就是自己的弟弟，就是他们曾经计划谋害、然后又把他当成奴隶卖掉的弟弟之后，他们是多么的惊讶和羞愧啊。

假如约瑟想要报仇的话，他本来是可以让自己的哥哥们饿死、将他们关进监狱或者什么也不给就打发他们回哈兰的。可他并没有这样做；他不但给了他们想要的粮食，并且多给了许多粮食让他们带回去，还送给了他们很多贵重的礼物。然

take back home, but made them rich presents besides. Then he told them to go back and get the rest of his family and return with them to Egypt, and he promised to give them a piece of land called Goshen where there would be no famines and they might live happily. They did as they were told, and Israel and his sons and all their families came down and settled in Goshen about 1700 B.C. They were called Israelites, which means of course the children of Israel. These are the people we now call the Jews.

After Joseph, who was of course an Israelite himself, died, the kings or Pharaohs of Egypt did not like these foreign people and treated them very badly, as other peoples have often treated the Jews badly ever since. Though the Jews and their children and children's children lived in Egypt for about four hundred years, they were enslaved by the Egyptians.

Now about four hundred years from the time the Jews first came into Egypt — 400 from 1700 is 1300 B.C. — there was a ruler of Egypt called Rameses the Great.

Rameses so feared the growing number of Jews that finally he gave orders to have every Jewish boy baby killed. In this way he thought to control these people. One little Jewish boy named Moses, however, was saved, and when he grew up he became the greatest leader of his people. Moses wanted to get the Jews out of this hostile country where the people worshiped false gods. At last he led all his people out of Egypt across the Red Sea. This was called the *Exodus*, and

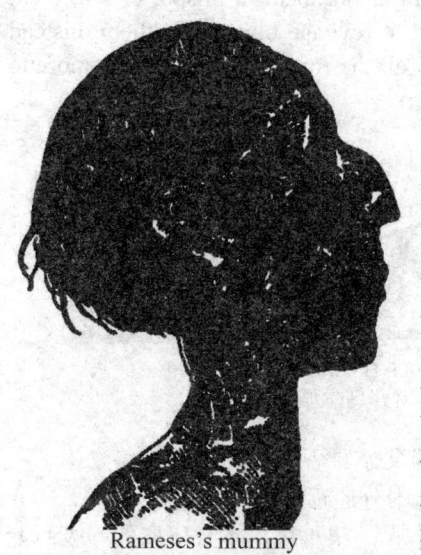

Rameses's mummy
拉美西斯大帝的木乃伊

后，他让哥哥们回去，带上其他的家人回到埃及来，并且还承诺赐给他们一处叫作歌珊地的土地，那里不会有饥荒，他们可以生活得很幸福。他们遵照弟弟的吩咐去做了；于是，公元前1700年左右，以色列和他的所有儿子和家人便全都南下而去，在歌珊地定居下来。他们被称作"以色列人"，这当然是指他们都是以色列的后裔。这个民族，就是如今我们所称的犹太人。

本身当然也是以色列人的约瑟死后，古埃及的国王或者法老都很不喜欢这些外国人，对他们很不好；而自那以后，其他民族也开始欺负犹太人了。尽管犹太人祖祖辈辈在埃及生活了大约四百年的时间，但他们一直都受到埃及人的奴役。

从犹太人最初踏入埃及之时过了大约四百年后（1700减去400，就是公元前1300年），埃及出了一个统治者，叫作拉美西斯大帝。

由于拉美西斯对犹太人数量的日益增加极为担心，所以最终他下令，将所有的犹太男婴全都杀掉。他认为，这样就可以牢牢控制住犹太民族了。然而，有一个叫作摩西的犹太小男孩却被救了下来，并且长大后成了犹太民族最伟大的领袖。摩西想要带领犹太人离开这个对他们充满敌意、民众又崇拜邪教神灵的国度。最后，他率领族人横渡红海，离开了埃及。这一事件，被称为"出埃及记"，发生在公元前

it took place about 1300 B.C.

After the Jews had left Egypt, they first stopped at the foot of a mountain called Mount Sinai, while Moses went up to the top where he could be by himself and learn what God wanted him and the Jews to do. Moses spent forty days praying on top of the mountain. When he came down from the mountain-top, he brought with him the Ten Commandments, the same Ten Commandments you may have learned in Sunday school. But Moses had been gone so long that when he came back again to his people, he found them worshiping a golden calf as the Egyptians had done. They had lived in Egypt until they had come to think it was all right to worship idols.

Moses was very angry. It was high time, he thought, that they should get rid of the bad influence of their old Egyptian neighbors. At last he succeeded in making them worship God again and gave them the Ten Commandments for their rule of life. So Moses is called a lawgiver and the first teacher of the Jewish religion. The Jews wandered from place to place for a great many years before Moses died. Then Joshua, their new leader, led them into Canaan.

The Jews had no kings. They were ruled by men called judges, but the judges lived very simply, just like everyone else and not

Rameses the Great
拉美西斯大帝

1300年左右。

犹太人离开埃及之后，他们先是在一座叫作西奈山的山脚下停了下来，而摩西则爬上了山顶；在那里，他独自一人，聆听着上帝对于他和犹太人行动的启示。他在西奈山顶上祷告了四十天。从山顶下来之后，他带来了十条戒律，这就是你们在主日学校可能已经学习过的《十诫》。但由于摩西在山上祷告的时间太久，所以他下山回到族人当中后，却发现族人竟然像埃及人那样，在崇拜一头金牛犊。他们在埃及生活得太久，竟然开始认为崇拜多个神灵也是正确的了。

摩西非常生气。他认为，此时已经到了摆脱原来埃及对他们的坏影响的时候了。最后，他成功地让族人重新开始礼拜上帝，并且将《十诫》授予他们，让他们奉行为生活准则。于是，摩西便被称为犹太教的立法者和第一位导师。摩西死前，犹太人四处漂泊流浪了许多年。后来，新的领袖约书亚带领他们回到了哈兰。

犹太人没有国王。他们由那些叫作"士师"的人统治着，而这些士师生活得非常简朴，就像其他人一样，而不是像在皇宫里的国王那样，仆役成群，穿着精美的

like kings in palaces with servants and fine robes and rich jewels. But the Jews thought it would be better to have a real king like their neighbors had.

At last a judge who was named Samuel said they should have a king, and Saul was chosen. Then Samuel poured olive-oil over Saul's head. To us this seems a strange thing to do, but it took the place of putting a crown on his head and was a sign that he was to be king. Samuel, therefore, was the last one of their judges, and Saul was their first king.

All other nations at that time believed as the Egyptians and Chaldeans did, in many different gods. The Jews alone believed in one God and lived by laws they believed God had given them. They had a holy book that contained these laws and recorded their early history. This book is also known as the Old Testament and has been made a part of the Christian Bible. Many Old Testament stories also appear in the Koran, the Muslims' holy book.

This is the story of the Jews, who gave us the Old Testament and the Ten Commandments, and here is the way they wandered:

From Ur to Canaan — 1900 B.C.

From Canaan to Egypt — 1700 B.C.

From Egypt back to Canaan — 1300 B.C. You can see that they finally settled down in Canaan, and then they called that land their home.

袍子、戴着贵重的珠宝。不过，犹太人认为，像别的国家那样有一个真正的国王，可能会更好一些。

最后，一名叫作撒母耳的士师说，他们应当有一个国王；于是，他们便选举扫罗来当国王。接着，撒母耳又把橄榄油浇到扫罗的头上。在我们看来，这是一件很奇怪的事情；但在当时，这跟将一顶王冠戴到他头上是一样的，是他成为国王的标志。因此，撒母耳便成了犹太人的最后一位士师，而扫罗则成了犹太人的第一任国王。

当时，所有的民族都像古埃及人和迦勒底人一样，信仰许多不同的神灵。只有犹太人信仰一个上帝，并且遵照戒律生活；他们认为，这些戒律都是上帝授予他们的。他们有一本圣书，里面记载着这些戒律，并且记录着他们早期的历史。这本书，也被称作《旧约全书》，如今已经成为基督教《圣经》中的一个组成部分。《旧约全书》中的许多故事，也出现在《古兰经》里。

这就是犹太人的历史；他们给我们带来了《旧约全书》和《十诫》。下面就是他们漂泊流浪的路线：

从乌尔城到哈兰——公元前1900年；

从哈兰到埃及——公元前1700年；

从埃及返回哈兰——公元前1300年。你们能够看出，他们最终是在哈兰定居下来了，因而后来他们把这个地方叫作自己的故乡。

10 Fairy-Tale Gods

There was once a man named Hellen — strange-sounding name for a man, isn't it? He had a great many children and children's children, and they called themselves Hellenes. They lived in a little scrap of a country that juts into the Mediterranean Sea, and they called their land Hellas. I once upset a bottle of ink on my desk, and the ink ran out into a wriggly spot that looked exactly as Hellas does on the map. Though Hellas is hardly any bigger than one of our states, its history is more famous than that of any other country of its size in the world. We call Hellas Greece and the people who lived there Greeks.

About the same time, the Jews were leaving Egypt, about the time when people were beginning to use iron instead of bronze, that is, about 1300 B.C., we first begin to hear of Hellas and the Hellenes, of Greece and the Greeks.

The Greeks believed in many gods, not in one God, as we do and as the Jews do, and their gods were more like people in fairy tales than like divine beings. Many beautiful statues have been made of their different gods, and poems and stories have been written about them.

There were twelve — just a dozen — chief gods. Six of these were female gods, known

10 神话传说中的神灵

曾经有一个叫赫楞的男子；男人叫这个名字，听起来怪得很，对不对？他有一大群子孙后代，这些人都自称是赫楞人。他们生活在伸进地中海中的一小片土地上，并且将这个地方称作赫拉斯。我曾经把书桌上的一瓶墨水打翻了，墨水淌出来后，弯弯曲曲地形成的一片，看上去正是赫拉斯在地图上的样子。虽然赫拉斯的面积并不比美国的任何一个州大，但它的名气却比世界上其他任何一个面积与之相同的国家都要大。我们将赫拉斯叫作"希腊"，而将生活在那里的人称作"希腊人"。

几乎就在犹太人正离开埃及，差不多正是人类开始使用铁器而不再用青铜器的那个时候，也就是说公元前1300年左右，我们第一次开始得知了赫拉斯和赫楞人的存在，得知了希腊和希腊人的存在。

古希腊人信仰诸多神灵，而不是像我们和犹太人一样只信仰一个上帝。而且，在神话传说中，他们崇拜的神灵更像是凡人，而非神祇。他们为不同的神灵雕刻出了许多美丽的塑像，并且写出了许多关于这些神灵的诗歌和故事。

古希腊人信仰的主神有十二位，刚好是一打[1]。其中有六位是女性神灵，即人

---

[1] 打（dozen），西方人所用的数量单位，一打=12个。"打"是美国对 dozen 这个词的音译。

as goddesses. They were supposed to live on Mount Olympus, which was the highest mountain in Greece. These gods were not always good, but often quarreled and cheated and did even worse things. The gods lived on a kind of food that was much more delicious than what we eat. It was called nectar and ambrosia, and the Greeks thought it made those who ate it immortal; that is, so that they would never die.

Let me introduce you to the family of the gods. I know you will be pleased to meet them. Most of them are known by two names; the first name is Greek, the second is Roman.

Zeus or *Jupiter* is the father of the gods and the king who rules over all human beings. He sits on a throne and holds a zigzag flash of lightning called a thunderbolt in his hand. An eagle, the king of birds, is usually by his side.

Hera or *Juno* is his wife and the queen of the gods. She carries a scepter, and her pet bird, the peacock, is often with her.

Poseidon or *Neptune* is one of the brothers of Zeus. He rules over the sea. He rides in a chariot drawn by sea-horses and carries in his hand a trident, which looks like a pitchfork with three points. He can make a storm at sea or quiet the waves simply by striking them with his trident.

Hephaestus or *Vulcan* is the god of fire. He is a lame blacksmith and works at a forge. His forge is said to be in the cave of a mountain, and as smoke and fire come forth from some mountains they are called volcanoes after the god Vulcan inside.

们所称的女神。他们认为，这些神灵都住在希腊境内海拔最高的奥林匹斯山上。这些主神并不是始终善良的，他们之间经常会发生争执、相互欺骗，甚至干出更坏的事情来。神灵们所吃的东西，比我们所吃的东西要美味得多。他们的食物叫作"甘露"和"仙果"，而古希腊人认为，吃了这些东西便会长生不老；也就是说，神灵们都是永远不会死的。

我来给你们简单地介绍一下古希腊人崇拜的这些神灵吧。我知道，你们肯定都会很乐意认识认识这些神仙的。他们中的大多数都有两个名字，其中第一个是他们在古希腊神话中的名称，而第二个则是他们在古罗马神话里的名字。

宙斯（朱庇特）既是众神之父，也是世界之王，统治着所有人类。他坐在宝座上，手中擎着一道之字形的闪电，称作"霹雳"。一只属于百鸟之王的鹰隼，常常陪伴在他的身边。

赫拉（朱诺）既是宙斯的妻子，也是神界的王后。她手执权杖，而她的爱鸟孔雀也经常不离她的左右。

波塞冬（尼普顿）是宙斯的一位哥哥。他统治着海洋。他驾驶着一辆由海马拉着的两轮战车，手持三叉戟；三叉戟的样子就像是一把有着三个尖齿的铁叉。他既能在海上掀起暴风雨，而且只要用三叉戟一击，就能平息海上的巨浪。

赫菲斯托斯（伏尔甘）是火神。他是一个瘸了腿的铁匠，在铁匠铺里打铁。据说他的铁匠铺建造在一个山洞里；因此，看到一些大山冒出浓烟和火焰后，人们便根据火神伏尔甘（Vulcan）这个名字，将那些大山叫作火山（volcano）。

Apollo is the most beautiful of all the gods; his name is the same to both Greeks and Romans. Apollo is the god of the sun and of song and music. Every morning — so the Greeks said — he drives his sun-chariot across the sky from the east to the west, and this makes the sunlighted day.

Artemis or *Diana* is the twin sister of Apollo. She is the goddess of the moon and of hunting.

Ares or *Mars* is the terrible god of war, who is only happy when a war is going on — so that he is happy most of the time.

Hermes or *Mercury* is the messenger of the gods. He has wings on his cap and on his sandals, and he carries in his hand a wonderful winged stick or wand, which, if placed between two people who are quarreling, will immediately make them friends. One day Hermes saw two snakes fighting and he put his wand between them, whereupon they twined around it as if in a loving hug, and ever since the snakes have remained entwined around it. This wand is called a *caduceus*.

Athena or *Minerva* is the goddess of wisdom. She was born in a very strange way. One day Zeus had a terrible headache — what we call a splitting headache. It got worse and worse, until at last he could stand it no longer, but he took a very strange way to cure it. He called Hephaestus, the lame blacksmith, and told him to hit him on the head with his hammer. Though Hephaestus must have thought this a funny request, of course he had to obey the father god. So he struck Zeus a terrible blow on the head, whereupon there

阿波罗是众神当中长得最英俊的一位；他的名字，在古希腊神话和古罗马神话中相同。阿波罗既是太阳神，又是音乐之神。据希腊人说，每天清晨，阿波罗都会驾驶着自己的那辆太阳战车，从东向西越过整个天空，从而开启阳光普照的白天。

阿耳忒弥斯（狄安娜）是阿波罗的孪生姐姐。她既是月亮女神，也是狩猎女神。

阿瑞斯（玛尔斯）是令人生畏的战神，他只有在爆发战争的时候才感到快乐；由于世界上经常爆发战争，因此他大多数时候都是快乐的。

赫耳墨斯（墨丘利）是众神的信使。他的帽子和鞋子上都长有翅膀，并且手里持着的也是一根长着翅膀的奇妙棍子，称为"魔杖"；要是有人吵架的话，他只要把魔杖往两人中间一放，两人马上就会化敌为友。有一天，赫耳墨斯看到两条蛇在打架，便把魔杖往它们中间一放，它们马上便在魔杖上缠到了一起，就像是在亲切地拥抱那样；从那以后，这两条蛇便一直缠在魔杖上了。这根魔杖，人称"节杖"。

雅典娜（密涅瓦）是智慧女神。她出生时的情形，实在是古怪得很。有一天，宙斯得到了一个神谕，赫拉生下的第三个孩子将会推翻并取缔他。宙斯害怕预言成真，遂将赫拉生下的第三个孩子吞入腹中。此后宙斯的头疼得厉害，就是我们所说的那种"头疼欲裂"。他的头越来越疼，最后实在难以忍受了；可他却采用了一种奇怪的方式来治疗自己的头疼。宙斯把那个瘸腿的铁匠赫菲斯托斯叫过来，命令后者用铁锤击打他的脑袋。尽管赫菲斯托斯一定觉得这是一个很奇怪的要求，但他当然必须服从众神之父的命令。于是，他在宙斯的脑袋上狠狠地敲了一记，然后雅典娜便全身披挂着盔甲，从宙斯的脑袋里跳了出来；而由她所引发的头疼，也就此消

sprang forth Athena in all her armor, and the headache, of which she had been the cause, had gone. So she was born from his brain; that is why Athena is the goddess of wisdom. She founded a great city in Greece and named it Athens, after herself. She is supposed to look out for this city as a mother does for her child.

Aphrodite or *Venus* is the goddess of love and beauty. She is the most beautiful of the goddesses, as Apollo is the most beautiful of the gods. She is said to have been born from the sea foam. Eros or Cupid, her son, is a chubby boy with a quiver of arrows on his back. He goes about shooting his invisible arrows into the hearts of human beings, but instead of dying when they are hit, they at once fall in love with someone. That is why we put hearts with arrows through them on valentines.

Hestia or *Vesta* is the goddess of the home and fireside, who looks out for the family.

Demeter or *Ceres* is the goddess of the farmer.

These are the twelve gods and goddesses of the Olympian family.

Hades or *Pluto* is a brother of Zeus. He rules the world underground and lives down there.

There are many other less important gods and goddesses as well as some gods that are half human, such as the three Fates, the three Graces, and the nine Muses.

Some of the planets in the sky that look like stars are still called by the names of these gods. Jupiter is the name of the largest planet. Mars is the name of one that is reddish — the color of blood. Venus is the name of one that is very beautiful. There is also a Mercury,

失了。所以，雅典娜是从宙斯的脑袋里生出来的；雅典娜之所以是智慧女神，原因就在于此。她在希腊建立了一座伟大的城市，并且根据自己的名字，将这座城市命名为"雅典"。人们认为，她在守护着这座城市，就像一位妈妈守护着自己的孩子那样。

阿弗洛狄忒（维纳斯）是掌管爱与美的女神。她是所有女神中最美丽的一位，就像阿波罗是所有男神中最英俊的一位那样。据说，她是从大海的泡沫中出生的。她的儿子厄洛斯（丘比特）是个胖乎乎的小男孩，背上背着一袋箭矢。他到处闲逛，将自己那种看不见的箭射到人类的心上；但被射中的人不会死去，而是会立马爱上某个人。我们在情人节的时候，常常用一支箭穿过两颗心的图形来表示相爱，原因就在于此。

赫斯提亚（维斯塔）是掌管家庭和炉灶、守护家人的女神。

得墨忒耳（克瑞斯）是农神。

他们就是奥林匹斯山上那个神族中的十二位男神和女神。

哈得斯（普路托）是宙斯的一位哥哥。他掌管着地下的冥界，并且住在地下。

古希腊神话里，还有其他许多不那么重要的男神和女神，以及一些属于半人半神的神灵，比如命运三女神、美惠三女神和九位掌管文艺的缪斯女神等。

如今，天空中一些看上去像是恒星的行星，仍然是用这些神灵的名字来命名的。朱庇特就是最大的行星，即木星。玛尔斯是一颗颜色像血一样红的行星，即火星。维纳斯是一颗非常美丽的行星的名字，即金星。太阳系中，还有三颗叫作墨丘

a Neptune, and a Pluto.

The Greeks' prayers to their gods were not like ours. Instead of kneeling and closing their eyes as we do, they stood up and stretched their arms straight out before them. They did not pray to be forgiven for their sins and to be made better. They prayed for victory over their enemies or to be protected from harm.

When they prayed, they often made the gods an offering of animals, fruit, honey, or wine in order to please them so that the gods or goddesses would grant their prayer. The wine they poured out on the ground, thinking the gods would like to have them do this. The animals they killed and then burned by building a fire under them on an altar. This was called a *sacrifice*. Their idea seemed to be that even though the gods could not eat the meat of the animals nor drink the wine themselves, they liked to have something *given up* for them. Even today we say a person makes a sacrifice when he *gives up* something for another person.

When the Greeks were sacrificing, they usually looked for some sign to tell whether the gods were pleased with the sacrifice and whether they would answer the prayer and do what was asked. A flock of birds flying overhead, a flash of lightning, or any unusual happening they thought was a sign which meant something. Such signs were called *omens*. Some omens were good and showed that the god would do what he was asked, and some omens were very much like some of the signs that people believe in even today when they say it is a good sign or good luck if you see the new moon over the right shoulder, or a bad

利、尼普顿和普路托的行星，它们分别对应于水星、海王星和冥王星。

古希腊人对神灵的祷告方法，与我们的不一样。他们不像我们那样双膝下跪、闭上眼睛，而是站在那里，双臂径直向前张开。他们既不祈祷神灵宽恕自己的罪过，也不祈祷神灵让自己变得更加幸福。他们祈祷的，都是让神灵保佑自己胜过敌人，或者免于受到敌人的伤害。

在祷告的时候，他们通常都会用牲畜、水果、蜂蜜或者葡萄酒做祭品，献给神灵，来讨好神灵，从而让众神答应他们的祈祷、实现他们的愿望。他们把葡萄酒泼在地上，认为这样做是遵从神灵的意愿。他们宰杀牲畜，然后在祭坛上燃起一堆火来烧烤。这一过程，便叫作"献祭"。他们似乎认为，就算是众神无法亲自前来吃肉喝酒，有人向他们献出某种东西，众神也是很高兴的。即便到了今天，倘若有人为他人放弃了某种东西，我们仍会说这个人是做出了牺牲。

古希腊人在献祭的时候，通常都会寻找某种迹象，看众神是否对祭品感到满意，看众神会不会满足他们的愿望，会不会按照他们所祈祷的那样去做。他们认为，一群飞过头顶的鸟儿、一道划过天际的闪电，或者任何不同寻常的事情，都是一种迹象，都具有某种意义。这样的迹象，叫作"征兆"。其中有些迹象是好兆头，表明众神会满足他们所祈祷的事情。还有一些迹象，则跟如今人们所相信的情况很相似：即便是到了今天，倘若你们看到一轮新月位于右肩上方，人们就会说这是个好兆头，或者说你们会交上好运；可若是将盐撒到了地上，人们就会说那是个不好的兆头，或者说会倒霉呢。

sign or bad luck if you spill the salt.

Not so very far from Athens is a mountain called Mount Parnassus. On the side of Mount Parnassus was a town called Delphi. In the town of Delphi there was a crack in the ground, from which gas came forth, somewhat as it does from cracks in a volcano. This gas was supposed to be the breath of the god Apollo, and there was a woman priest called a priestess, who sat on a three-legged stool or tripod over the crack so as to breathe the gas. She would become delirious, as some people do when they are sick with fever and we say they are *out of their heads*, and when people asked her questions she would mutter strange things and a priest would tell what she meant. This place was called the Delphic Oracle, and people would go long distances to ask the oracle questions, for they thought Apollo was answering them.

The Greeks went to the oracle whenever they wanted to know what to do or what was going to happen, and they firmly believed in what the oracle told them. Usually, however, the answers of the oracle were like a riddle, so that they could be understood in more than one way. For instance, a king who was about to go to war with another king asked the oracle who would win. The oracle replied, "A great kingdom will fall." What do you suppose the oracle meant? Such an answer, which you can understand in two or three ways, is still called *oracular.*

离雅典不远的地方，有一座山峰，叫作帕纳塞斯山。在帕纳塞斯山的一侧，有一个叫作特尔斐的城市。特尔斐市的地面上有一条裂缝，从中不断地冒出气体，有点儿像是火山裂缝中冒出烟气那样。古希腊人认为，这种气体是太阳神阿波罗呼出的；曾经有一个女祭司，她坐在裂缝上方一把只有三条腿的凳子（即三脚凳）上，吸入气体。然后，她便变得胡言乱语起来，就像有些人生病发烧时那样，我们说这样的人是"神志不清"；而当人们问她问题的时候，她就会喃喃地说出一些稀奇古怪的话语，另一位祭司则会解释她说的是什么意思。这个地方，便叫作"特尔斐神谕之地"；人们会不远万里地来到这里问神，因为他们觉得，是太阳神阿波罗在回答他们的问题。

无论何时，只要不知道怎么去做或者想知道将来会发生什么，古希腊人都会去求助于神，并且坚定不移地相信神所给出的启示。然而，神谕通常都有点儿像是谜语，因此可以有不止一种解释。比如说，一位国王即将与另一位国王开战，他便去问神，看哪一方会获胜。神的回答是："一个伟大的王国将被征服。"你们觉得，这一神谕的意思是什么呢？这种回答可以有两种或三种解释，所以人们至今仍称之为"玄妙"哩。

11 A Fairy-Tale War

The history of countries usually begins — and also ends — with war. The first great happening in the history of Greece was a war. It was called the Trojan War and was supposed to have taken place about twelve hundred years before Christ, or not long after the beginning of the Iron Age. But we are not only unsure of the date; we are not even sure that there ever was such a war, for a great deal of it, we know is simply fairy tale. This is the way the tale goes.

Once there was a wedding feast of the gods and goddesses on Mount Olympus, when suddenly a goddess who had not been invited threw a golden apple on the table. On the apple were written these words:

To the fairest.

The goddess who had thrown the apple was the goddess of quarreling; and true to her name she *did* start a quarrel, for each of the goddesses, like vain human beings, thought she was the fairest and should have the apple. At last they called in a shepherd boy named Paris to decide who was the fairest.

Each goddess offered Paris a present if he would choose her. Hera, the queen of the gods, offered to make him a king; Athena, the goddess of wisdom, offered to make him

11   一场传说中的战争

各个国家的历史，通常都是以战争开始，最终也以战争结束的。古希腊历史上的第一桩重大事件，正是一场战争。这场战争被称为"特洛伊战争"。人们认为，它发生在公元前1193年左右，即铁器时代开始之后不久。不过，我们既不知道此次战争的确切日期，甚至也不确定究竟有没有爆发过这样一场战争；因为这场战争的很多情况，我们所知的不过都是神话故事罢了。故事的发生经过是这样的。

奥林匹斯山上的男女众神，曾经举行了一场盛大的婚宴；其间，一位不请自来的女神突然将一个金苹果扔到了桌子上。金苹果上写着这样一句话：

送给最美丽的人。

扔出那个金苹果的女神，就是"不和女神"；而她的这一举动，也的确恰如其名地引发了一场争执，因为每位女神都像自负的凡人那样，认为自己最美丽，因而觉得自己应当得到那个金苹果。最后，她们叫来了一个叫作帕里斯的牧童，要他来评判到底是哪位女神最美丽。

每位女神都对帕里斯说，如果选她的话，她就会送给帕里斯一份礼物。神界王后赫拉说，她会让帕里斯当上国王；智慧女神雅典娜说，她会让帕里斯变得聪颖、有智慧；而美丽女神阿弗洛狄忒则说，她会让帕里斯娶世界上最美丽的女子为妻。

wise; but Aphrodite, the goddess of beauty, offered to give him the most beautiful girl in the world for his wife.

Now, Paris was not really a shepherd boy but the son of Priam, the king of Troy, which was a city on the seashore opposite Greece. When he was a baby, Paris had been left on a mountain to die, but he had been found by a shepherd and was brought up by him as his own child.

Paris didn't care about being wise; he didn't care about being king; what he did want was to have the most beautiful woman in the world for his wife, and so he gave the apple to Aphrodite.

Now the most beautiful woman in the world was named Helen, and she was already married to Menelaus, the king of Sparta. In spite of that fact, Aphrodite told Paris to go to Sparta in Greece, where he would find Helen, and then run away with her. So Paris went to Sparta to visit King Menelaus and was royally entertained by him. And then Paris, although he had been treated so kindly and had been trusted, one night stole Helen away and carried her off across the sea to Troy.

Menelaus and the Greeks were naturally very angry and immediately prepared for war and sailed off for Troy to get Helen back. Now, in ancient times all cities had walls built around them to protect them from the enemy. As there were no cannons nor guns nor deadly weapons such as are used in war nowadays, it was very hard to get into a walled city or capture it. Troy was protected in this way by walls; and though the Greeks tried for ten years to capture it, at the end of the ten years Troy was still unconquered.

　　注意，帕里斯其实并不是牧童，而是特洛伊国王普里阿摩斯的儿子。帕里斯还在襁褓之中的时候，就被人丢弃到了一座山上去等死；但一个牧羊人发现了他，便把他当成自己的亲生儿子那样抚养成人了。

　　帕里斯并不在意自己聪不聪明，也不喜欢成为国王；他想要的，是娶世界上最美丽的女子为妻，所以便把金苹果给了阿弗洛狄忒。

　　当时，世界上最美丽的女子名叫海伦，已经嫁给了斯巴达的国王墨涅拉俄斯为王后。可阿弗洛狄忒却不管这个事实，让帕里斯前往斯巴达，在那里找到海伦，然后带着她私奔。于是，帕里斯便前往斯巴达谒见墨涅拉俄斯国王，并且受到了后者的盛情招待。尽管受到了这种礼遇，尽管得到了墨涅拉俄斯国王的信任，但接下来，帕里斯还是在一天晚上带走了海伦，并且带着她渡海前往特洛伊去了。

　　墨涅拉俄斯国王和希腊人自然十分震怒，因此马上准备开战，出海前往特洛伊去夺回海伦。注意，古时候的所有城市四周，都筑有防御敌人的城墙。由于那时没有如今战争中所用的大炮、机枪和致命性武器，因此要攻入或者攻陷一座四周都有城墙的城市是很困难的。特洛伊的四周，正是筑有这样的城墙；所以，尽管希腊人花了十年的时间想要攻破它，但十年过去之后，特洛伊城却依然没有陷落。

　　最后，希腊人决定要个花招，攻入特洛伊城。他们制造了一匹巨大的木马，并让士兵们埋伏在木马的肚子里。他们将木马放到特洛伊城墙前面之后，便驾船离去，假装他们最终停战了。他们还派了一个间谍去对特洛伊人说，这匹木马是众神

At last the Greeks decided to try a trick to get into the city. They built a huge horse of wood, and inside this wooden horse they put soldiers. They placed the horse in front of the city walls and then sailed away as if at last they were giving up the war. The Trojans were told by a spy that the horse was a gift of the gods and that they ought to take it into the city. A Trojan priest named Laocoon, however, told his people not to have anything to do with the horse, for he suspected a trick. But people seldom take advice when told not to do what they want to do.

Just then some huge snakes came out of the sea and attacked Laocoon and his two sons and, twining around them, strangled them to death. The Trojans thought this was a sign from the gods, or an omen as they would have said, that they should not believe Laocoon; so they determined to take the horse into the city against his advice. The horse was so big, however, that it would not go through the gates, and in order to get it inside the walls they had to tear down part of the wall itself. When night fell, the Greek soldiers came out of the horse and opened the gates of the city. The other Greeks, who had been waiting just out of sight, returned and entered through the gates and the hole the Trojans had made in the wall. Troy was easily conquered then, and the city was burned to the ground, and Helen's husband carried her back to Greece. Because of this horse trick, we still have a saying, "Beware of Greeks bearing gifts," which is as much as to say, "Look out for an enemy who brings you a present."

The story of the Trojan War was told in two long poems. Some people think they are the finest poems that were ever written. One of these poems is called the *Iliad*, from the

送给特洛伊人的礼物，因此他们应当把木马拖进城里去。然而，特洛伊一位名叫拉奥孔的祭司却对民众说，千万不要去动那匹木马，因为他怀疑那是一种诡计。可是，人们在一心想要做什么事情，却有人来劝他们不要去做的时候，都是很少听得进劝告的。

就在那时，海里游出了几条大蛇，袭击了拉奥孔和他的两个儿子，紧紧地缠在他们身上，并将他们勒死了。特洛伊人都认为这是一种神谕，或者是他们所称的预兆，要他们不要相信拉奥孔的话；于是，他们决定不听拉奥孔的劝告，把木马拖进城去。然而，那匹木马太大，进不了城门；为了把木马拖进城去，他们还拆毁了一段城墙呢。夜幕降临后，希腊士兵们从藏身的木马中出来，打开了城门。其余那些希腊人一直都待在看不见的地方等候着，此时便返回来，通过城门和特洛伊人在城墙上拆开的口子进了城。这样一来，特洛伊城便被轻而易举地攻破了，整个城市都被烧成了一堆焦土，而海伦的丈夫也带着她回到了希腊。由于这个木马计，我们如今仍然有一句谚语，即"提防带着礼物的希腊人"呢。它相当于是说："提防送给你礼物的敌人。"

有两首长诗，叙述了特洛伊战争的经过。有些人认为，它们是历史上写得最好的两首诗歌。其中一首叫作《伊利亚特》，诗名源自特洛伊城的名字，因为特洛伊又名"伊利昂"。《伊利亚特》描述的是特洛伊战争本身的经过。另一首诗叫作《奥德赛》，描述的是希腊人中的一位英雄在特洛伊战争结束后回家途中的冒险故

name of the city of Troy, which was also known as Ilium. The *Iliad* describes the Trojan War itself. The other poem is called the *Odyssey* and describes the adventures of one of the Greek heroes on his way home after the war was over. The Greek hero's name was Odysseus, which gives the name Odyssey to the book, but he was also called Ulysses. These poems, the *Iliad* and the *Odyssey*, were composed by a Greek poet named Homer, who is supposed to have lived at some time before 700 B.C.

Homer may have been a bard; that is, a singing poet who went about from place to place and sang his songs to the people. He probably collected old legends and made his poems from them. Usually a bard played on a lyre as he sang, and the people gave him something to eat or a place to sleep to pay him for his songs.

People enjoyed hearing Homer's songs. They learned them by heart, and mothers taught them to their children after Homer had died. The poems are written down in Greek, and you may some day read them in Greek, if you study that language, or at least in an English translation.

I have told you that Homer probably made his songs out of old legends. There were many legends, too, about Homer himself, and we don't know which are true. He was said to have been blind. Seven different cities each proudly claimed that Homer had been born in their city, so you can count six or seven legends right there!

事。这位希腊英雄叫作奥德修斯，《奥德赛》这一诗名，便是由他的名字而来；但他还有一个名字，叫作尤利西斯[1]。《伊利亚特》和《奥德赛》这两首诗，都是由一位名叫荷马的希腊诗人所作；人们认为，荷马生活在公元前700年以前的某个时期。

荷马可能是一位吟游诗人；也就是说，他可能是一位在各地游历并对人们吟诵自己所写诗歌的吟唱诗人。他很可能是搜集到了一些古老的传说，然后以此为基础来写作诗歌的。通常来说，吟游诗人会边吟唱边弹竖琴，而作为对他吟唱诗歌的回报，人们则会给他一些吃的，或者为他提供住处。

人们都喜欢聆听荷马的诗歌。他们将这些诗歌用心记住，而在荷马去世后，就由母亲们把这些诗歌教给孩子们。这两首诗是用希腊文写成的；倘若学习希腊语的话，你们有朝一日可能会读到它们，或者起码也会看到它们的英译版的。

前面我已经说过，荷马很可能是根据古老的传说而创作出这两首诗歌的。对于荷马本身，世间也有很多的传说；因此，究竟哪一种是真的，我们无从得知。据说他还是一位盲人。曾经有七座城市都骄傲地宣称它们是荷马的出生地；由此你们可以想见，关于荷马的传说就有六七个了！

[1] 尤利西斯（Ulysses），是奥德修斯（Odysseus）的拉丁名。前面说特洛伊（Troy）又名"伊利昂"（Ilium），也是指特洛伊的拉丁名。奥德修斯和特洛伊都是希腊名。

12 The Kings of the Jews

A few centuries before Homer was singing his wonderful songs through the streets of Greece, a great king of the Jews was singing other wonderful songs in Canaan. This king was named David, and he wasn't born a king. He was only a shepherd boy in King Saul's army. This is the way he happened to become king.

At first, as you remember, the Jews had no kings; but they had asked for kings, and at last they were given one by the name of Saul.

David had killed the giant Goliath. We all love this Bible story because we are always glad when the skillful little chap beats the great, big, bragging bully.

Well, King Saul had a daughter, and she fell in love with this brave and athletic young David the Giant-Killer, and at last they were married.

After Saul died, David became king, and he was the greatest king the Jews had ever had. Although Saul had been king, he had lived in a tent, not in a palace, and he didn't even have a capital city.

David eventually conquered a city in Canaan called Jerusalem and made this city the capital of the Jews.

12　犹太诸王

就在荷马沿着希腊的大街小巷吟唱着他那些美妙诗歌的几个世纪之前，犹太人中也有一位伟大的国王，正在哈兰吟唱着另外的奇妙诗歌。这位国王叫作大卫，可他并不是出生于帝王世家。他原来只是扫罗王手下军队里的一名牧童。下面说的，就是他无意之中当上了国王的过程。

你们应当都还记得，起初犹太人是没有国王的；但他们希望拥立一位国王，于是最后便有了国王扫罗。

大卫曾经杀死了巨人哥利亚。我们之所以都很喜欢《圣经》上的这个故事，是因为看到小个子巧妙地打败那些赫赫有名的、恃强凌弱的大块头恶棍，我们都会觉得很高兴。

此时，扫罗王有个女儿，她爱上了这个勇敢、健壮、年轻且杀死了哥利亚的大卫。于是，最后两人便结成了夫妇。

扫罗死后，大卫便成了国王；他也是犹太人历史上最伟大的一位国王。尽管扫罗当了国王，但他还是住在帐篷里，而不是住在宫殿里；而且，他甚至也没有建造一座属于自己的都城。

最后，大卫征服了哈兰一座叫作耶路撒冷的城市，并让此地成了犹太人的首都。

David was not only a brave warrior and a great king; he wrote beautiful songs as well. The blind poet Homer sang of his fairy-tale gods. The great King David sang of his one God. These songs are the *Psalms*, which are still read and sung in churches and synagogues.

Nowadays even a popular song is popular for only a few months, but the songs that David wrote almost three thousand years ago are still popular today! The Twenty-third Psalm, which starts, "The Lord is my shepherd," is one of the most beautiful and a good one to learn by heart. David likens himself to a sheep and his Lord to a good shepherd, who tenderly looks out for the comfort and safety of his sheep.

David's son was named Solomon, and when David died Solomon became king.

If a good fairy had asked you what you would rather have than anything in the world, I wonder what you would have chosen. When Solomon became king, God is said to have appeared to him in a dream and asked him what he would rather have than anything else in the world. Instead of saying he wanted to be made rich or powerful, Solomon asked to be made wise, and God said He would make him the wisest man that ever lived. Here is a story that shows how wise he was.

Once upon a time two women came to Solomon with a baby, and each woman said the baby was her own child. Solomon called for a sword and said, "Cut the baby in two, and give each a half." One of the women cried out to give the baby to the other rather than do this, and Solomon then knew who was the real mother and ordered the baby to be given to her.

    大卫不仅是一位勇敢的武士、一位伟大的国王，而且还写出了许多美妙的诗篇哩。

    盲人诗人荷马歌颂的，都是神话传说中的众神。而伟大的大卫王所歌颂的，却是他那个唯一的上帝。

    这些诗篇，被称为"赞美诗"；如今，人们在教堂和犹太会堂里仍然会诵读和吟唱它们。

    现在，即便是一首流行歌曲，也只会流行几个月之久；而大卫在差不多三千年前所作的这些颂歌，却一直流行到了今天呢！第二十三首赞美诗开篇即写道："耶和华是我的牧者。"它是最优美、最好的赞美诗之一，值得我们用心去铭记。大卫把自己比作一只绵羊，而把他的上帝比作一位好的牧羊人，在细心地守护着自己所牧羊群的舒适与安全。

    大卫的儿子叫作所罗门；大卫死后，所罗门便继承了王位。

    假如有位好心的仙女问你们，在这个世界上你们最想要的是什么，我可不知道你们究竟会选择什么东西。所罗门当上国王之后，据说他梦见了上帝，上帝问他在这个世界上最想要的是什么。所罗门没有请求上帝让他变得富有或者变得有权有势，而是希望上帝让他变得聪明而有智慧；于是，上帝说，他会让所罗门变成世界上最聪明的人。下面这个故事，便说明了所罗门究竟有多聪明。

    有一次，两位妇女带着一个小宝宝来到所罗门面前，两人都说这个小宝宝是自己的孩子。所罗门叫人拿来了一把剑，说："把小宝宝劈成两半，一人各得一

Solomon built a magnificent temple made of cedar-wood, from the famous forest of Lebanon, and of marble and gold and studded with jewels. Then he built himself a wonderful palace, which was so gorgeous and splendid that people came from all over the world to see it. The Bible tells us just how large this temple and palace were, not in feet but in cubits. A cubit was the distance from a man's elbow to the end of his middle finger, which is about one foot and a half.

The queen of Sheba, among others, came a long distance across Arabia to hear the wise sayings of Solomon and see his palace and the temple he had built.

Although the palace and temple were considered extraordinarily magnificent at that time, you must remember that this was a thousand years before Christ.

Solomon's temple and palace have disappeared long since. But his wise sayings are preserved in many languages and read by many people all around the world. There are thousands of buildings now in the world that would make his palace, if still standing, look like a child's toy house. But no one has ever been able to say any better the things he said. Do you think you could? Suppose you try. Here are some of them. They are called proverbs.

A soft answer turneth away wrath;
but grievous words stir up anger.

What's that mean?

A good name is rather to be chosen than great

半。"其中一名妇女大哭起来，宁愿把孩子给另一名妇女，也不愿把孩子劈死；于是，所罗门便明白了谁才是孩子的亲生母亲，下令把孩子交给了她。

所罗门用从著名的黎巴嫩森林中采伐来的香柏木、大理石、黄金和宝石，建造了一座宏伟壮丽的神庙。然后，他又给自己建造了一所神奇的宫殿；这座宫殿金碧辉煌，蔚为壮观，世界各地的人都纷纷前来一睹风采。《圣经》中说到那座神庙和那所宫殿有多大时，用的度量单位竟然不是英尺[1]，而是肘尺呢。一肘尺就是从一个人的肘部到其中指指尖的距离，相当于一点五英尺左右。

在前来参观的人当中，有一位是示巴[2]女王；她不远千里，穿过了阿拉伯半岛[3]，为的就是去聆听所罗门的至理名言，并且一睹他所建造的神庙和宫殿。

尽管所罗门的宫殿和神庙在当时被世人认为辉煌无比，但你们必须记住，那时毕竟还是公元前1000年啊。

所罗门建造的神庙和宫殿，很久以前就已经不复存在了。不过他说的那些至理名言却被译成了多种语言保存至今，并被世界各地的许多人所诵读。假如他的那座宫殿依然存在的话，那么如今世界上的成千上万座高楼大厦，都会让他的宫殿看上

---

[1] 英尺（foot），英制长度单位。1 英尺 =30.48 厘米 =12 英寸。因此后面面所说的肘尺，换算后就是：1 肘尺≈45.72 厘米。

[2] 示巴（Sheba），阿拉伯半岛南部的一个古国，以富庶著称。

[3] 阿拉伯半岛（Arabia），亚洲西南部的一个地区，是世界上最大的半岛。如今的沙特阿拉伯、也门、阿曼、阿拉伯联合酋长国、伊拉克、以色列等国都位于这个半岛上。亦译"阿拉比亚"。

riches and loving favor rather than silver and gold.

What's that mean?

Let another man praise thee and not thine own mouth.

What's that mean?

Solomon was the last great king the Jews ever had. After he died the Jewish nation gradually broke up and then came back together again. Then, six hundred years later it finally went to pieces and, for about two thousand years, the Jewish people were without a king, without a capital, and without a country of their own, though they are found in many other countries of the world. Then at last they formed a new country, a country called Israel. Israel is in the land that used to be called Canaan.

去像是小朋友用玩具搭成的房屋似的。可是，迄今为止却没有人能够说出比他更有智慧的话语呢。你们觉得，自己能够说出比所罗门的至理名言更有智慧的话语吗？你们不妨来试一试。下面就是所罗门说过的一些话。这些话语，叫作"箴言"。

回答柔和，使怒消退；
言语暴戾，触动怒气。

这句话是什么意思呢？

美名胜过大财，
恩宠强如金银。

这句话是什么意思呢？

要别人夸奖你，不可用口自夸。

这句话又是什么意思呢？

所罗门是犹太人历史上最后一位伟大的国王。他死后，犹太民族逐渐开始了合久又分、分久又合的过程。接下来，六百年之后，犹太民族最终分崩离析了。并且，在差不多两千年的时间里，虽说犹太民族遍布世界各地，但他们既无国王和首都，也没有自己的国家。最后，他们才建立了一个新的国家，一个叫作"以色列"的国家。如今的以色列，就处于过去被称作"哈兰"的那片土地上。

13 The People Who Made Our A B C's

Long before people knew how to write, there lived a carpenter named Cadmus. One day he was at work on a house when he wanted a tool that he had left at home. Picking up a chip of wood, he wrote something on it and, handing it to his slave, told him to go to his home and give the chip to his wife, saying that it would tell her what he wanted. The slave, wondering, did as he was told. Cadmus's wife looked at the chip, and without a word handed the tool to the amazed slave, who thought the chip in some mysterious way had spoken the message. When he returned to Cadmus with the tool, he begged for the remarkable chip, and when it was given him, hung it around his neck for a charm. This is the story the Greeks told of the man they say invented the alphabet. We believe, however, that Cadmus was a mythical person, for the Greeks liked to make up such stories, and we think no *one* person made the alphabet. But Cadmus was a Phoenician and we do know that the

Cadmus's slave and the chip
卡德摩斯的奴隶和木片

13 发明文字的人

在人类懂得如何写字的很久以前，希腊曾经有一个叫作卡德摩斯的木匠。有一天，他在建造房屋时，想要用到一件落在家里了的工具。他捡起一块薄木片，在上面写了点东西，递给自己手下的奴隶，让奴隶到他家去，把木片交给他的妻子，说她看到木片就会明白他要的是什么工具。那名奴隶虽然觉得很奇怪，但还是遵命行事。卡德摩斯的妻子看了看木片，不发一言便把工具交给了奴隶；那名奴隶惊讶不已，以为卡德摩斯必定是用某种神秘的方法传达出了信息。带着工具回到卡德摩斯那里之后，他便请主人将那片神奇的木片赐给他；而得到主人赐予之后，他便把木片挂到脖子上，把它当成了护身符。

这就是希腊人关于发明了字母的那个人的传说。然而，我们却认为，卡德摩斯是一个虚构出来的人物，因为希腊人很喜欢虚构这类故事；故我们觉得，发明字母的并不是哪一个人。但卡德摩斯是一个腓尼基人，而我们也确实知道，是腓尼基人发明了最初的字母；我们如今所用的字母，便是在这一基础之上发展而来的。你

Phoenician people invented the alphabet on which ours is based. You probably call it your A B C's, but the Greeks had much harder names for the letters. They called A *alpha*, B *beta*, and so on. So the Greek boy spoke of learning his *alpha beta*, and that is why we call it the *alphabet*.

You may never have heard of Phoenicia or the Phoenician people. Yet, if there had been no such country as Phoenicia, you might now be learning at school to read and write in hieroglyphics or in cuneiform.

Up to this time, you know, people had very clumsy ways of writing. The Egyptians had to draw pictures, and the Babylonians made writing like chicken tracks. The alphabet that the Phoenicians invented had twenty-two letters, and from it we get the alphabet we use today.

Of course, we do not use just the same alphabet now that the Phoenicians did, but some of the letters are almost, if not quite, like those we now have after three thousand years. For instance the

Phoenician A was written on its side — ⊲
E " "   backward — Ǝ
Z " "   just the same — Z
O " " " " " "   — O

The Phoenicians lived next door to the Jews; like the Jews, they were Semites. Their

们很可能称之为A、B、C的字母，希腊人给这些字母所起的名称，却要复杂得多。他们称A为"阿尔法"（alpha），称B为"贝它"（beta），诸如此类。因此，希腊孩子说识字就是学习"阿尔法（alpha）-贝它（beta）"，而这也正是我们称之为"字母表"（alphabet）的原因。

你们以前可能从来没有听说过什么腓尼基或者腓尼基人。尽管如此，要是历史上没有腓尼基的话，你们现在可能就是在学校里学习象形文字或者楔形文字的读写呢。

到了如今，你们都知道了，人类曾经有过许多笨拙的书写方法。古埃及人只能画画，古巴比伦人写的字就像是鸡爪印。而腓尼基人发明的字母表，却包括二十二个字母，由此我们才有了今天所用的字母表。

当然，今天我们所用的字母表，与腓尼基人当初所用的字母表并不相同；但腓尼基人的字母表中，有些字母就算不是完全相同，也与三千年后如今我们所用的那些字母差不多是一样的。例如：

腓尼基人的字母A，是侧着写的，即 ⊲
腓尼基人的字母E，是反过来写的，即Ǝ
腓尼基人的字母Z，写法与我们的相同，即Z
腓尼基人的字母O，写法与我们的相同，即O

腓尼基人与犹太人比邻而居；与犹太人一样，他们也是闪米特人。他们建立的

country was just north of the kingdom of the Jews; that is, above it on the map and lying along the shore of the Mediterranean Sea.

The Phoenicians had a great king named Hiram who lived at the same time as Solomon. In fact, Hiram was a friend of Solomon and sent him some of his best workmen to help build a temple at Jerusalem. Yet Hiram himself and the Phoenicians did not believe in the Jewish God.

The Phoenicians worshiped idols named Baal and Moloch, which they called gods of the sun. They also believed in a goddess of the moon named Astarte and made sacrifices of live children to her idol, Fe-Fi-Fo-Fum; this is a real story and not a fairy tale. Just suppose you had been a child then!

The Phoenicians were great business people. They made many things to sell, such as objects carved from ivory, engraved gold and silver items, and beautiful glassware. They knew how to weave woolen and linen cloth, and were well known for the dyed cloth and robes that they manufactured.

They knew the secret of making a wonderful purple dye from the body of a little shell-fish that lived in the water near the city of Tyre. This dye was known as Tyrian purple from the name of that city, and it was so beautiful that kings' robes were colored with it.

Tyre and Sidon were the two chief cities of Phoenicia, and once upon a time they were two of the busiest cities in the world.

In order to find people to sell to, the Phoenicians traveled in boats all over the

国家，就在犹太王国的北面；也就是说，在地图上，腓尼基在犹太王国的上面，位于地中海沿岸。

腓尼基人曾经有过一位伟大的国王，叫作希兰，他与所罗门生活在同一时代。事实上，希兰还是所罗门的朋友，并且曾经派遣了一些最能干的工匠去协助所罗门在耶路撒冷建造一座神庙哩。不过，希兰和腓尼基人都不信仰犹太人所信仰的上帝。

腓尼基人信仰的神灵，有巴力神和摩洛神，他们称这两个神灵为太阳神。他们还信仰一个叫作阿斯塔蒂的月亮女神，并且用童男童女来向她那座叫作"爱情-生育女神"的神像献祭；这可是真实的历史，并不是神话传说。想想看，如果你们是那个时候的小朋友，该是多么可怕的一件事情啊！

腓尼基人都是些了不起的生意人。他们制造出了许许多多的东西来卖，比如象牙制品、金银雕饰和漂亮的玻璃制品等。他们懂得如何编织羊毛和麻布，并且因为制作出来的印染布匹和长袍而闻名遐迩。

他们还掌握了一种秘诀，能够用一种小贝类制造出一种奇妙的紫色染料来；这种小贝类，生在蒂尔城附近的海域里。于是，这种染料便以该城为名，称为"蒂尔紫"；由于蒂尔紫非常漂亮，因此国王的王袍都是染成这种颜色。

蒂尔和西顿，是腓尼基的两个主要城市，并且它们一度也是世界上商业最为繁忙的两个城市呢。

为了找到买家，腓尼基人驾着小船，走遍了地中海各地，甚至驶出了地中海海域，进入了大西洋。从地中海进入大西洋的那条水道，如今叫作直布罗陀海峡；

Mediterranean Sea and even went outside this sea into the Great Ocean. This opening is now called the Strait of Gibraltar, but was then known as the Pillars of Hercules. They went as far as the British Isles and along the coast of Africa. Many other people in those days had not dared to go so far in boats; they thought they would come to the edge of the ocean and tumble off. But the Phoenicians had no such fear, and so they were the greatest sailors as well as the greatest traders of their times. Their ships were built from the cedar trees that grew on the slopes of their hills. The trees were called the cedars of Lebanon.

In one way, the Phoenicians were very shortsighted. They cut down all their wonderful cedar trees until almost none were left. Then no more ships — or anything else — could be made with the strong wood. Do you think we would ever do anything as foolish as that?

When the Phoenicians found good harbors for their boats, they often started little towns where they traded with the local people. Often they drove a hard bargain, trading purple cloth worth very little for gold or silver or other things worth a great deal. On the coast of north Africa, one of these towns they started was called Carthage. Carthage later grew to be very strong and wealthy — but you will have to wait a while until I come to that story.

但在当时，人们却称之为"赫拉克勒斯[1]之柱"。他们的足迹，远至大不列颠群岛以及非洲海岸。当时，其他许多民族都不敢驾驶船只走这么远；他们认为，走得太远的话，就会来到大洋的边缘，一不小心就会掉下去呢。可腓尼基人却没有这种担忧；因此，他们既是当时最伟大的航海家，又是最了不起的商人。他们驾驶的船只，是用生长在本国山坡上的柏木制成的。这种柏木，被称为黎巴嫩香柏。

从某种意义上来说，腓尼基人的眼光是非常短浅的。他们将那些神奇的香柏木砍伐得几乎一棵不剩了。这样一来，他们就再也没有这样一种牢固的木材去建造船只或者其他东西了。你们觉得，我们会不会像他们一样，再干这种蠢事呢？

腓尼基人一旦发现有适于船只停靠的港口，通常便会在港口建立一个小城镇，开始与当地人进行贸易。他们往往会精打细算，用成本不高的紫色布料，换得金银或者其他贵重物品。他们在非洲北部沿海建立的这种城镇中，有一座叫作迦太基。后来，迦太基还变得非常强大、非常富庶了；不过，你们还得等一等，我等会说到那段历史。

---

[1] 赫拉克勒斯(Hercules)，古希腊神话中的英雄和大力士，是宙斯和阿尔克墨涅所生的儿子。他力大无比，因为完成了天后赫拉所要求的十二项任务而获得永生。这些任务中，有一项便是到西方去牵回巨人革律翁的牛群；这是赫拉克勒斯往西出行最远的一次，终点就是人们所称的"赫拉克勒斯之柱"，即直布罗陀海峡两侧对峙的两座峭壁。因此，人们后来就用"赫拉克勒斯之柱"指代直布罗陀海峡。

14 Hard as Nails

Our story goes back again to Greece, the land of Homer and the fairytale gods, and to Sparta, where Helen once lived.

About nine hundred years before Christ was born, there lived in Sparta a man named Lycurgus. That is a hard name, and when you hear about this man you may think he was hard, too. Lycurgus wanted his city to be the greatest in the world.

First he had to find out what it was that made a city and a people great.

He started off and traveled for years and years, visiting all the chief countries of the world to see if he could learn what it was that made them great. And this is what he learned.

Wherever the people thought chiefly of fun and pleasure, of amusing themselves and having a good time — he found they were not good for much, not of much account — not great.

Wherever the people thought chiefly of hard work and did what they ought, whether it was pleasant or not, he found they were usually good for something — of some account — great.

14 铁石心肠

我们的故事，又回到了属于荷马的故乡、属于神话传说中众神之地的希腊，回到了美女海伦曾经生活过的斯巴达。

公元前900年左右的时候，斯巴达曾经有一个叫作莱克格斯的人。这可是个很硬气的名字，而你们在听完他的故事之后，可能也会认为他是条硬汉子的。莱克格斯希望，让自己所在的斯巴达成为世界上最强大的一座城市。

首先，他必须弄清楚，什么因素能够让一座城市和一个民族变得强大起来。

于是，他开始动身四处游历，并且在多年里走访了当时世界上所有的主要国家，以便弄清楚究竟是什么东西让这些国家变得强大。而他发现的就是：

无论是哪里，倘若人们心中所想的主要是享乐，是让他们自己过得开心、快乐，那么这些地方的人就不会有什么擅长的，威望也不高，因而该地就不会很强大。

他还发现，无论是哪里，倘若人们心中所想的主要是努力工作和尽职尽责，而不管自己所做的工作舒不舒适，那么这些地方的人通常在某个方面都很出色和具有某种威望，因而该地通常都很强大。

于是，莱克格斯便回到故乡斯巴达，开始着手制定出一系列的法律法规；他认

So Lycurgus came back to his home Sparta and set to work to make a set of rules that he thought would make his people greater than all other people in the world. These rules were called a Code of Laws, and I think you'll agree they were very hard, and they made the Spartans hard, too — as *hard as nails*. We shall see whether they made the Spartans really great, also.

To begin with, babies, as soon as they were born, were examined to see that they were strong and perfect. Whenever one was found who did not seem to be so, he or she was put out on the mountainside and left to die. Lycurgus wanted no weaklings in Sparta.

When boys were seven years old, they were taken from their mothers and put in a school, which was more like a soldiers' camp than a school, and they never lived anywhere else until they were sixty years old.

In this school they were not taught the things you are, but only the things that trained them to be good soldiers.

There were no such things as schoolbooks then.

There were no spelling books.

There were no arithmetics.

There were no geographies. No one knew enough about the world to write a geography.

There were no histories. No one knew much about things that had happened in the world before that time, and of course none of the history since then that you now study had taken place.

为，这些法律法规将会让斯巴达这个民族变得比世界上其他所有的民族都要强大。这些法律法规统称为"法典"，它们极其严厉，让斯巴达人也变得非常冷酷无情，简直变得铁石心肠；我觉得，你们也会这样认为的。当然，我们也应当来看一看，它们是不是真的让斯巴达人变得强大了。

首先，斯巴达人在婴儿刚刚出生后，就会对婴儿进行体检，看他们的身体是不是强壮、是不是有缺陷。假如发现哪个婴儿看上去身体不好或者是生理上有缺陷，他或她就会被扔到山坡上去自生自灭。莱克格斯可不希望斯巴达有体弱多病的人。

男孩长到七岁时，就会被带离母亲身边，到学校里去。这种学校，更像是军营；而从此时开始，男孩子们就会一直在这里生活，直到六十岁为止。

在这个学校里，他们学习的并不是像你们如今所学的这种知识，而是只学习能够将他们一个个都训练成优秀战士的知识。

那时，他们还没有课本之类的东西。

他们还没有拼写课本。

他们还没有算术课。

他们还没有地理课。这是因为，当时人们对整个世界的了解不多，还不足以让人编写出一本地理书来。

他们也没有历史课。这是因为，当时人们对世界上以前所发生的事情还不怎么了解；而你们如今所学的、从那时以来的历史，当然也还没有发生。

在某些时候，斯巴达的男孩都会接受鞭打；这并不是因为他们做错了什么事

At certain times, the Spartan boy was whipped, not because he had done anything wrong, but just to teach him to suffer pain without whimpering. He would have been disgraced forever if he had cried, no matter how badly he was hurt.

He was exercised and drilled and worked until he was ready to drop. Still he was obliged to keep on, no matter how tired or hungry or sleepy or aching he might be, and he must never show by any sign how he felt.

He was made to eat the worst kind of food, to go hungry and thirsty for long periods of time, to go out in the bitter cold with little or no clothing, just to get used to such hardships and able to bear all sorts of discomforts. This kind of training, this kind of hardening, is therefore called *Spartan discipline*. How do you think you would have liked it?

The Spartans' food, clothing, and lodging were all furnished them, though it was very poor food and poor clothing and poor lodging. They were not allowed good things to eat, soft beds to lie on, or fine clothing to wear. Such things were called luxuries, and luxuries, Lycurgus thought, would make people soft and weak, and he wanted his people hard and strong.

The Spartans were even taught to speak in a short and blunt manner; they were taught not to waste words; they must say what they had to say in as few words as possible. This manner of speaking we call *laconic* from the name Laconia, the state in which Sparta was located.

Once a king wrote to the Spartans a threatening letter, saying that they had better do

情，而是为了教会他们咬紧牙关、一声不吭地承受痛苦。无论受了多重的伤，只要哭一声，他以后就会永远都抬不起头来。

他会一直接受锻炼、一直进行训练和工作，直到快要累趴下才作罢。但无论身体有多累、多饿、多困或者多疼，他仍然必须坚持下去，并且绝不能表现出一丝痛苦。

他必须吃最不好的食物，必须长时间地忍受饥饿和口渴，必须在衣着单薄或者甚至不穿衣服的情况下出去忍受刺骨的寒冷；这样做，都是为了让他们习惯这些磨难，从而能够忍受各种各样的艰苦环境。因此，这种训练和磨炼，便被人们称作是"斯巴达式的训练"。你们觉得，你们会不会喜欢这样的训练呢？

斯巴达人的食物、衣服和住所都是免费供应的，但他们的食物都极其糟糕，衣物都极其粗糙，住所都极其简陋。他们不允许吃美味可口的食物，不能睡柔软舒适的床铺，也不准穿华美精制的衣服。他们把这些东西称作奢侈品；莱克格斯认为，奢侈品会让人们变得软弱无能，而他则希望自己的人民一个个都坚强健壮。

甚至在说话方式上，斯巴达人也被训练得说话非常简短而直率；他们被训练得毫无废话，只能用尽量简短的语句说出必须要说的话语。因此，我们便根据斯巴达人所在的"拉科尼亚"这个国家的名称，将这种方式叫作"拉科尼亚式"[1]的说话方式。

有一次，一位国王给斯巴达人写了一封恐吓信，要他们最好遵照他的命令行

---

[1] 拉科尼亚式（laconic），如今多意译为"简洁的，言简意赅的"。

what he told them to, for if he came and took their country, he would destroy their city and make them slaves.

The Spartans sent a messenger back with their answer, and when the letter was opened, it contained only one word:

"IF!"

Even today, we call such an answer, short but to the point, a laconic answer.

Did all this hard training and hard work make the Spartans the greatest people in the world?

Lycurgus did make the Spartans the strongest and best fighters in the world — but —

The Spartans conquered all the peoples around about them, though there were ten times as many — but —

They made these people their slaves, who did all their farming and other work — but —

We shall see later whether Lycurgus's idea was right.

North of Sparta was another great city of Greece called Athens. There were, of course, many other towns in Greece, but Sparta and Athens were the most important. In Athens the people lived and thought quite differently from those in Sparta.

The Athenians were just as fond of everything beautiful as the Spartans were of discipline and of everything military.

The Athenians loved athletic games of all sorts just as the Spartans did, but they also

事；如果胆敢不服从，逼得他前来征服斯巴达的话，他就会摧毁斯巴达城，让斯巴达人都做奴隶。

斯巴达人派了一名信使前去回复；国王拆开回信后，却发现里面只有一个词：

"胆敢！"

就算是到了今天，我们还会把这样一种简洁却又切中要害的回答，称作拉科尼亚式的回答呢。

这种种艰苦的训练和辛勤的劳作，有没有让斯巴达人变成世界上最强大的一个民族呢？

莱克格斯的确让斯巴达人变成了世界上最强大和最优秀的战士，但是——

斯巴达人征服了周边地区所有的民族，尽管这些民族的人数有斯巴达人的十倍之多，但是——

他们让这些民族的人全都变成了自己的奴隶，替他们干农活和其他的工作，但是——

我们日后就会看出，莱克格斯的想法究竟对不对？

斯巴达的北面，是古希腊另一个伟大的城市，叫作雅典。当然，古希腊还有其他许多的城镇，但斯巴达和雅典是其中最重要的两座。在雅典，人们的生活方式和思维方式都与斯巴达人大不一样。

雅典人热爱一切美丽的事物，就像斯巴达人热爱纪律和军事一样。

尽管雅典人像斯巴达人一样热爱各种各样的体育竞赛，但他们还热爱音乐和诗

loved music and poetry and beautiful statues, paintings, vases, buildings, and such things that are known as the arts.

The Athenians believed in training the mind *as well* as the body. The Spartans believed the training of the body was the all-important thing. Which do you like better, the Athenians' idea or the Spartans' idea?

Once at a big game a very old man was looking for a seat on the Athenians' side. There was no seat empty, and no Athenian offered to give him one. Whereupon the Spartans called to the old man and gave him the best seat on their side. The Athenians cheered the Spartans to show how fine they thought this act. At this the Spartans said:

"The Athenians *know* what is right but they don't do it."

歌，热爱美丽的雕塑、油画、花瓶、建筑物等我们称为艺术品的事物。

雅典人认为，既要锻炼身体，同时也应锻炼心智。可斯巴达人却认为，锻炼身体才是最重要的事情。那么，你们是赞同雅典人的观点呢，还是赞同斯巴达人的观点呢？

有一次，雅典和斯巴达之间举行了一场重大的比赛。一位老年人想在雅典人那边找个座位，可那边已经没有空座位了，也没有一个雅典人给他让座。于是，斯巴达人把老人叫到了他们那一边，给他让出了最好的一个座位。雅典人都纷纷为斯巴达人喝彩，表示他们都认为这一举动非常好。对此，斯巴达人评价说：

"雅典人明白什么事情是对的，可他们却不去行动。"

15 The Crown of Leaves

Greek boys and young men and even girls loved all sorts of outdoor sports.

They didn't play football or baseball or basketball, but they ran and jumped and wrestled and boxed and threw the discus — a thing like a big, heavy dinner plate of iron.

From time to time matches were held in different parts of Greece to see who was the best in these sports.

The Big Meet, however, took place only once every four years at a place called Olympia in southern Greece, for all the winners from different parts of the country were here matched against each other to see who should be the champion of all Greece.

The time when the games were held was a great national holiday, for the games were in honor of the head god, Zeus, as the Greeks called him. People came from far and wide to see the games, much as they do now when a World's Fair is held or a modern Olympics.

Only Greeks could enter this contest, and only those who had never committed a crime or broken any laws — as a boy or girl nowadays must have a clean record in order to be allowed to play on a college or school team. In ancient Greece, only men and boys competed in the Olympics.

15 桂冠

古希腊的男孩子、小伙子，甚至是姑娘们，都很喜欢进行各种各样的户外运动。

可他们并不是去踢足球、打棒球或者打篮球，而是跑步、跳高、摔跤、拳击和掷铁饼；铁饼就是一块像盘子那样的大铁盘。

古希腊的各地经常举办比赛，看谁在这些体育项目上表现得最优秀。

然而，大型比赛每四年才举行一次，举办地点是希腊南部一个叫作奥林匹亚的地方；全国各地的获胜者纷纷来到这里，相互进行较量，以便角逐出整个希腊的冠军。

举办比赛的日期，就是一个全国性的盛大假日；因为举办比赛，是为了向古希腊人所称的宙斯这位众神之王致敬。人们从四面八方赶来观看比赛，很像是如今人们赶去参加世界博览会或者观看现代奥运会那样。

只有希腊人才能参加比赛，并且只有那些从来没有犯过罪或者违过法的人才能参加；这就好比是如今的青少年必须没有不良记录，才能加入大学或学校里的球队一样。在古希腊，奥林匹克运动会只有男人和男孩子参加。

举办比赛的时候，倘若城邦之间恰巧在打仗（这种情况很常见），由于这个节

If there happened to be a war going on at the time, and there usually was, so important was this holiday that a truce was declared, and everybody went off to the games. Nothing could be allowed to interfere with the games, and even war was not as important. "Business before pleasure!" When the games were finished, they started fighting again!

The Greek boys and young men would train for four years getting ready for this big event, and then nine months before the great day they would go to Olympia to train at an openair gymnasium near the field.

The games lasted five days and began and ended with a parade and prayers and sacrifices to the Greek gods, beautiful statues to whom were placed all about the field, for this was not only sport, but a religious service in honor of Zeus and the other gods.

There were all sorts of matches — in running, jumping, wrestling, boxing, chariot-racing, and throwing the discus.

Anyone who cheated would have been put out and never again allowed to take part. The Greeks believed in what we call being a good sport. A Greek didn't brag if he won. He didn't make excuses if he lost; he didn't cry out that the decision was unfair.

The athlete who won one or more of these games was the hero of all Greece, and in particular of the town from which he came. The winner received no money prize but was crowned with a wreath made of laurel leaves. This he valued much more than an athlete nowadays does the silver cup or gold medal he may win. Besides receiving the laurel wreath, the winner had songs written to him by poets, and often statues were made of him by sculptors.

日如此重大，因此交战双方都会休战，然后大家都去参加比赛。希腊人不允许任何事情干扰到比赛，所以哪怕是战争，也没有比赛重要。"干正事要紧！"比赛结束后，他们便会再次开始战斗！

古希腊的男孩和小伙子们都会进行四年的训练，来为这场盛大的比赛做好准备；然后，在比赛开幕日的九个月之前，他们便会来到奥林匹亚，在比赛场地附近的一个露天体育场进行训练。

比赛会持续进行五天，并且在比赛开幕和闭幕时都会组织游行，都会进行祷告并向古希腊的众神献祭，向摆放在比赛场地四周的、众神的美丽雕塑献祭；因为这并非仅仅是一场体育竞赛，还是一场祭祀宙斯及其他众神的宗教仪式。

比赛项目各种各样，有跑步、跳高、摔跤、拳击、战车赛和掷铁饼。

作弊的选手将被驱逐出场，并且再也不准参加比赛。古希腊人崇尚我们如今所说的堂堂正正。倘若赢了，希腊人不会自夸；倘若输了，他们也不会找什么借口。他们才不会大喊大叫，说裁判不公正呢。

在一项或多项比赛里夺冠的运动员，就是全希腊的英雄，尤其会成为他出生的那个城镇的英雄。获胜者并没有奖金可得，人们会把一个用桂树叶子编成的花环戴到他的头上。在他看来，这项桂冠可比如今的运动员可能获得的什么银牌或者金牌重要得多。除了这项桂冠，诗人们还会写诗对获胜者进行歌颂，而雕塑家通常也会给获胜者制作雕像。

古希腊不仅有体育比赛，也有诗人和音乐家之间的竞赛，即看谁能够写出最

There were not only athletic matches but contests between poets and musicians to see who could write the best poetry or compose and play the sweetest music on a kind of small harp called the lyre. The winners of these contests did not receive a laurel wreath, but they were carried in triumph on the shoulders of the throng, as you may have seen the captain of a winning team picked up and raised aloft by his fellow-players after he has won.

Now, in Greek history the first event that we can be absolutely sure is true is the record of the winner of a footrace in these Olympic Games 776 years before Christ was born. From this event the Greeks began to count their history dates, as we do now from the birth of Christ. It was their Year 1.

The four years' time between the Olympic Games was called an Olympiad. Up to this time, they had no calendar that gave the year or date, so 776 is the date of the first Olympiad. Greek history before that time may have been partly true, but we know much of it was mythical. Beginning with 776, however, Greek history is pretty much all true.

After a long while they stopped having the games, but in 1896 it was thought it would be a good thing to start them again. For the first time in over two thousand years, new Olympic Games were again held in 1896 A.D., not in Olympia,

Greek runner
古希腊的赛跑运动员

好的诗歌，或者谁能创作出最美妙的音乐，创作出的乐曲用一种叫作七弦琴的小型竖琴来弹奏。虽说这些比赛的获胜者不会得到桂冠，但他们会被人们抬到肩上欢呼游行；就像你们可能看到过的那样，在比赛获胜后，获胜球队的队长会被队员们抬起来，高高地抛向空中。

注意，在希腊历史上，我们能够完全肯定情况属实的第一场比赛记录，就是公元前776年奥林匹克运动会上一位赛跑获胜者的记录。自这场比赛以后，希腊人开始计算自己的历史年代，就像我们如今是从基督降生开始计算历史年代一样。所以，那一年，就是希腊人的公元元年。

两届奥林匹克运动会之间的那四年时间，被称为一个奥林匹克周期。由于直到此时，古希腊人都没有日历来记录年份和日期，因此公元前776年便是第一个奥林匹克周期开始的时间。那一年之前的希腊历史，可能有一部分是真实的；但我们也知道，其中大部分都属于神话传说。然而，自公元前776年开始，希腊历史中的大部分却都是真实的了。

奥林匹克运动会停办了很长时间之后，到了1896年的时候，人们都认为，重新开始举办这一运动会，无疑是件好事。于是，时隔两千多年后，人们首次在公元1896年重新举办了一届新的奥林匹克运动会；然而，这届运动会的举办地点并不是

however, but in Athens. The games used to be held only in Greece. Now they are held each time in a different country. Only Greeks used to be allowed to take part. Now, however, athletes from almost all the countries of the world are invited to compete. Only men used to take part. Now women from all over the world compete also. War used to be stopped when the time for the games arrived. Now the games are stopped when war is on.

From what we have learned of the Spartans' training, we might guess that they used to win most of the athletic prizes, and they did.

Do the Spartans still continue to win most of the prizes in the New Olympic Games?

No. Not even the Greeks now carry off the chief prizes, because Greece is just one small nation among many.

奥林匹亚，而是雅典。这一运动会，过去只是在希腊国内举行。而如今，每一届奥运会都是在不同的国家举行。在过去，只有希腊人才能参加比赛。而如今，世界各国的运动员几乎全都应邀参加比赛了。在过去，只有男子才能参加比赛。而如今，世界各地的女子也都来参加比赛了。过去举办奥运会的时候，战争常常会停止。而如今，要是正在打仗，奥运会就无法举行了。

从目前所知的斯巴达人的训练情况来看，我们可以猜出，他们通常获得大多数运动项目的冠军；事实上，他们也的确如此。

而在新的奥林匹克运动会上，斯巴达人是不是仍然会继续赢得大多数奖项呢？

不是的。即便是如今的希腊人，也无法夺得大多数主要的奖项了，因为希腊只是全世界众多国家中的一个小国啊。

16 A Bad Beginning

Have you ever heard of the Seven-League Boots, the boots in which one could take many miles at a single step?

Well, there is a still bigger boot; it is over five hundred miles long, and it is in the Mediterranean Sea.

No, it's not a real boot, but it would look like one if you were miles high in an airplane and looking down upon it.

It is called Italy.

Something very important happened in Italy, not long after the First Olympiad in Greece. It was so important that it was called the Year 1, and for a thousand years people counted from it as the Greeks did from the First Olympiad and as we do now from the birth of Christ. This thing that happened was not the birth of a man, however. It was the birth of a city, and this city was called Rome.

The history of Rome starts with stories that we know are fairy tales or myths in the same way that the history of Greece does. Homer told about the wanderings of the Greek, Odysseus. A great many years later a poet named Virgil told about the wanderings of a

16　邪恶的开端

你们听说过"千里鞋",就是一双一步就能跨出去好多英里的靴子吗?

哦,世界上还有一只比这更大的靴子呢;这只巨靴有500多英里长,位于地中海上。

不,这并不是一只真正的靴子;不过,假如你坐在离地面几英里高的飞机上向下看的话,它倒真像是一只靴子呢。

这只"靴子",就叫意大利。

在希腊的第一个奥林匹亚周期过后不久,意大利发生了一件极其重大的事情。这件事情如此重大,因此那里的人将这一年称为元年;而在接下来的一千年里,那里的人们一直都是从这一年开始纪年的,就像古希腊人是从第一个奥林匹亚周期,而我们则是从基督降生开始纪年那样。然而,这一事件并不是某个人物的出生。这一事件,是一座城市的诞生;而这座城市,就叫罗马。

罗马的历史,是从我们所知的童话故事或者神话传说开始的,与希腊历史一样。荷马曾经讲述过古希腊人奥德修斯的漫游经历。许多年后,一位叫作维吉尔的诗人则又讲述了一位名叫埃涅阿斯的特洛伊人的漫游经历。

在特洛伊城遭到焚毁的时候,埃涅阿斯逃出了该城,开始寻找新的家园。几年

Trojan named Æneas.

Æneas fled from Troy when that city was burning down and started off to find a new home. Finally after several years, he came to Italy and the mouth of a river called the Tiber. There Æneas met the daughter of the man who was ruling over that country, a girl by the name of Lavinia, and married her, and they lived happily ever after. The children of Æneas and Lavinia ruled over the land, and they had children, and their children had children, and their children had children, until at last boy twins were born. These twins were named Romulus and Remus. Here ends the first part of the story and the trouble begins, for they did not live happily ever after.

At the time the twins were born, a man had stolen the kingdom, and he feared that these two boys might grow up and take his stolen kingdom away from him. So he put the twins in a basket and set them afloat on the river Tiber, hoping that they might be carried out to sea or upset and be drowned. This, he thought, was nearly all right, so long as he didn't kill them with his own hands. But the basket drifted ashore instead of going out to sea or upsetting, and a mother wolf found the twins and nursed them as if they were her own babies. A woodpecker also helped and fed them berries. At last a shepherd found them and brought them up as if they were his own sons until they grew up and became men. This sounds a good deal like the story of Paris who was left out to die and was found and brought up by a shepherd also.

Each of the twins then wished to build a city. But they could not agree which one was

之后，他最终来到了意大利，来到了一条叫作台伯河的河口。在那里，埃涅阿斯碰到了当时意大利国王的女儿，一个叫作拉维妮娅的姑娘，并且娶她为妻，此后他们一直都生活得很幸福。后来，埃涅阿斯和拉维妮娅夫妇的孩子成了这个国度的统治者，并且子子孙孙、一代又一代地传承下去，直到最后诞生了一对孪生兄弟。这对孪生兄弟，一个叫作罗慕路斯，另一个叫作瑞摩斯。至此，罗马的第一段历史便结束了，而麻烦也就此开始，因为此后罗马人的生活便不再幸福了。

这对孪生兄弟出生的时候，王国的大权已经被一个人窃取了；那个人很担心，这对孪生兄弟长大后，会将他窃取的王国再从他的手中夺走。于是，他便把这对双胞胎放进一只篮子，并将篮子扔到台伯河上顺水漂流，希望这对双胞胎会漂到大海上去，或者篮子会翻到河里，从而将他们淹死。他以为，只要没有亲手杀死他们，这样做就没有什么不妥。可是，篮子却没有漂到大海上去或者翻倒，而是漂到了岸边；一头母狼发现了这对双胞胎，便把他们当成自己的幼崽一样喂养起来。一只啄木鸟也来帮忙，衔来浆果喂给他们吃。最后，一位牧羊人发现了这对双胞胎，便把他们带回家去，像自己的亲生儿子一样抚养，直到他们长大成人。这一过程，听上去与帕里斯的故事很相似；帕里斯也是被人扔到野外等死，后来也是被一位牧羊人发现并抚养长大的。

当时，两兄弟都希望建立一个城市。但是，对于该由谁来主导建立城市这一问题，两兄弟之间却产生了争执；而在因为这个问题而发生争吵的过程中，罗慕路斯杀死了自己的孪生兄弟瑞摩斯。然后，罗慕路斯便在台伯河畔、他和兄弟被母狼救

to do it, and in quarreling over the matter, Romulus killed his own twin brother Remus. Romulus then built the city by the Tiber River, on the spot where he and his brother had been saved and nursed by the mother wolf. Here there were seven hills. This was in 753 B.C., and he named the city Roma after his own name, and the people who lived there were called Romans. That is why, ever afterward, the Roman kings always said they were descended from the Trojan hero Æneas, the great-great-great-grandfather of Romulus.

Don't you believe this story? Neither do I. But it is such an old, old story everyone is supposed to have heard it even though it is only a legend.

In order to get people for the city which he had started, it is said that Romulus invited all the thieves and bad men who had escaped from jail to come and live in Rome, promising them that they would be safe there.

Then as none of the men had wives, and there were no women in his new city, Romulus thought up a scheme to get the men wives. He invited some people called Sabines, who lived nearby, both men and women, to come to Rome to a big party.

Romulus and Remus with the wolf
罗慕路斯、瑞摩斯以及喂养他们的那头母狼

They accepted, and a great feast was spread. In the middle of the feast, when everyone was eating and drinking, a signal was given, and each of the Romans seized a Sabine woman for his

起并抚养长大的地方建立了一座城市。如今，这个地方有七座小山。这件事情，发生在公元前753年；罗慕路斯用自己的名字，将这座城市命名为罗马；而生活在此处的人，也因此而被称为罗马人。自此以后，古罗马的历代帝王之所以总说自己是特洛伊英雄和埃涅阿斯的后裔，原因就在于此。

你们是不是不相信这个故事呢？我也不相信。不过，就算只是一种传说，它也是一个非常非常古老的故事，所以大家都应当听说过。

据说，为了让人们到他建立的这座城市里来，罗慕路斯曾经邀请所有的小偷和逃犯前来罗马定居，并且承诺说，他们在罗马会很安全。

然后，由于这些人都没有老婆，使得他新建的这座城市里没有女人，所以罗慕路斯便想出了一个让这些人都娶上老婆的计策。他邀请居住在附近地区的一些萨宾人，其中既有男人也有女人，到罗马来参加一场盛大的宴会。

萨宾人接受了邀请，于是一场盛宴便开始了。在宴会期间，正当大家都在大吃大喝的时候，有人发出了一个暗号，于是每个罗马人便都抓住一名萨宾女人当自己

wife and ran off with her.

The Sabine husbands immediately prepared themselves for war against the Romans, who had stolen their wives. When the battle had begun between the two armies, the Sabine women ran out in the midst of the fighting between their new and old husbands and begged them both to stop. They said they had come to love their new husbands and would not return to their old homes.

What do you think of that?

It sounds like a pretty bad beginning for a new city, doesn't it? and you may well wonder how Rome turned out — a city that started with Romulus killing his brother and that was settled by escaped prisoners who stole the wives of their neighbors. We'll see if the Romans continued to do such wicked things as their city grew older.

的妻子，然后带着她跑了。

那些萨宾女人的丈夫，马上准备跟那些抢走了他们妻子的罗马人开战。两军开始战斗后，那些萨宾女人都跑出来，插到正在作战的现任和前任丈夫之间，请求双方罢战。她们说，自己已经爱上了现在的丈夫，不会再回到原来的家里去了。

你们怎么看待那种情况呢？

一座新城市是这样开始建立起来的，听上去相当邪恶，不是吗？你们可能还想知道，罗马后来怎么样了；毕竟，这个城市一开始便是罗慕路斯杀死了自己的兄弟后建立的，然后定居其中的又是一些抢走他人妻子的逃犯。随着这座城市的历史渐久，我们便会看出，罗马人还会不会继续干这种伤天害理的事情了。

17 Kings with Corkscrew Curls

After Rome's bad start she had one king after another, and some of these kings were pretty good and some were pretty bad....

The most important city in the world at this time was far away from Rome on the Tigris River. This city was called Nineveh, and here lived the kings of the country called Assyria, which I told you about some time ago.

As usual, the chief thing we hear about Assyria and the Assyrians is that they were fighting with their neighbors. This, however, was not the fault of their neighbors.

The Assyrian kings who lived in Nineveh wanted more land and power, and so they fought their neighbors in order to take their land away from them. These kings had long corkscrew curls. They were such vicious fighters that they were feared far and near. They treated their prisoners terribly; they skinned them alive, cut off their ears, pulled out their tongues, bored sticks into their eyes, then bragged about it. They made the people whom they conquered pay them huge sums of money and promise to fight along with them whenever they went to war.

Assyria became so strong and powerful that it owned a lot of the world, the land between the rivers called Mesopotamia, and the land to the east, north, and south, and Phoenicia, and even Egypt.

17　一头卷发的国王

罗马城建立起来之后，便有了一任又一任的国王；而这些国王当中，有些人非常高尚，有些人却相当邪恶……

此时，在底格里斯河附近有一个城市叫尼尼微，它是世界上最有名的城市之一，离罗马很远，而住在那里的，就是我在前面已经跟你们说过的亚述古国的历代国王。

照例，我们所知的关于亚述和亚述人的主要情况，便是他们不断地与邻国打仗。然而，引发战争的过错，却不在于他们的邻国一方。

居住在尼尼微的亚述历代国王都想要获得更多的土地和权力，所以他们便发动战争，想要夺取邻国的土地。这些国王都有着长长的螺旋状卷发。他们都凶狠善战，令远近各族都闻风丧胆。他们对待俘虏的时候非常残忍；他们会活剥俘虏的皮、割掉俘虏的耳朵、割掉俘虏的舌头、用棍子捅进俘虏的眼睛里，之后还到处吹嘘。他们强迫那些被征服的民族向他们上缴大笔钱财，还迫使被征服者保证随时跟着他们出征。

于是，亚述古国的实力变得越来越强大，不但占领了世界上的许多地方，拥有了底格里斯、幼发拉底两河之间的美索不达米亚，和由此往东、往北、往南以及腓

This big, big country of Assyria was ruled by the kings at Nineveh, who lived in great magnificence. They built wonderful palaces for themselves, and on each side of the way that led to the palace, they placed rows of huge statues of bulls and lions with wings and men's heads. These winged animals are what are called *cherubs* in the Bible.

Perhaps you have heard a pretty little baby angel called a cherub. Isn't it strange that these Assyrian monsters should be called cherubs also?

When the Assyrian kings were not fighting men, they were fighting wild animals, for they were very fond of hunting with bow and arrow, and they had pictures and statues made of themselves on horseback or in chariots fighting lions. Often they would capture the animals they hunted alive and put them in cages so that the people could come and see them. This was something like a zoo such as we have nowadays.

The rulers of Assyria had very strange names. Sennacherib was one of the most famous. Sennacherib lived about 700 B.C. Once upon a time Sennacherib was fighting Jerusalem. His whole army was camped one night when as they lay asleep something happened, for when the morning came, none woke up; all were dead, both men and horses. An English poet named Byron has written a poem called *The Destruction of Sennacherib* describing this event. Perhaps they were poisoned; what do you think?

Ashurbanipal was another king who ruled later —

An Assyrian cherub
亚述古国的小天使

尼基的大片土地，甚至还包括埃及。

这个巨大广袤的亚述古国，由住在尼尼微的国王们统治着；而国王们所住的宫殿，则非常奢华富丽。他们为自己建造了许多令人惊叹的宫殿，而在每一条通往宫殿的道路两旁，都摆放着一排排巨大的、长有翅膀的人首牛身和人首狮身雕像。这些长有翅膀的动物，就是《圣经》中所称的"小天使"。

你们或许听说过，一个小小的、婴儿般的天使才叫小天使。可亚述古国的这些怪兽也叫小天使，是不是很奇怪呢？

当亚述古国的国王们不与其他国家打仗的时候，他们便会去跟动物作战；他们都很喜欢用弓箭狩猎，还叫人画了许多画、刻了许多雕像来描绘他们骑在马上或者驾着战车与狮子搏斗的场景。他们通常都会活捉猎物，然后用笼子关起来，这样人们便可以来观看这些猎物了。这可有点儿像是我们今天的动物园呢。

亚述古国的统治者，名字都稀奇古怪得很。其中最著名的一个，便是辛那赫瑞布。辛那赫瑞布生活在公元前700年左右。有一次，辛那赫瑞布正在跟耶路撒冷打仗。一天晚上，他手下的整支军队扎下营寨、睡熟了之后，发生了一件怪事，因为第二天天亮后，竟然没有一个人醒来；所有的人和马匹，全都死了。一位叫作拜伦的英国诗人曾经写过一首诗，叫作《辛那赫瑞布之死》，描述了这一事件。或许他们是被人下了毒；你们认为呢？

about 650 B.C. He was a great fighter too, but he was also very fond of books and reading; so Ashurbanipal started the first public library. The books in that first public library were, however, very peculiar. Of course they were not printed books, and they were not even made of paper. They were made of mud with the words pressed into the clay before it dried. This writing was cuneiform, which I have already told you about. The books were not arranged in bookcases either, but were placed in piles on the floor. They were, however, kept in careful order and numbered so that a person who wanted to see a book in the library could call for it by its number.

Assyria reached the height of her power during the reign of Sennacherib and Ashurbanipal, and everything in Nineveh was so lovely for the Ninevites that the time when Ashurbanipal reigned was called the Golden Age.

Although everything in Nineveh was so lovely for the Ninevites, everywhere else the Assyrians were hated and feared, for their armies brought death and destruction wherever they went.

It came to pass that not long after Ashurbanipal died, two of the neighbors of Nineveh could stand it no longer. These two neighbors were the king of Babylon, who lived south, and a people called the Medes, who lived to the east. The kings of Babylon and the Medes got together and attacked Nineveh, and together they wiped that city off the face of the earth. This was in 612 B.C. — Six-One-Two — and the power of Nineveh and Assyria was killed dead. This, therefore is called the Fall of Nineveh, the end of Nineveh. We might put up a tombstone.

亚述巴尼拔是后来统治过亚述古国的另一位国王，其时大约是公元前650年。他也是一位骁勇善战的国王，但他还很喜欢书籍和阅读；于是，亚述巴尼拔便创建了世界上的第一座公共图书馆。然而，这个公共图书馆里的藏书，却非常奇特。它们当然不是印刷出来的书籍，甚至也不是用纸张制成的。它们都是用泥巴制成，都是趁着泥巴还没有干的时候，就把文字压上去形成的。这种文字，就是我前面已经跟你们说过的楔形文字了。藏书也不是整整齐齐地码放在书架上，而是堆放在地板上的。然而，这些书籍都按照精心制定的顺序保存着，并且标上了编号；这样，一个人到图书馆去看某一本书时，按照编号就可以把书取来了。

在辛那赫瑞布和亚述巴尼拔两位国王统治的那个时期，亚述古国达到了实力的巅峰；当时尼尼微的一切对于尼尼微人来说都非常美好，因此，他们便将亚述巴尼拔统治的这一时期称为"黄金时代"。

尽管尼尼微的一切对于尼尼微人来说都非常美好，但其他地方的人对亚述人却是又恨又怕，因为亚述军队所到之处，带来的都是死亡和毁灭。

就在亚述巴尼拔死后不久，尼尼微的两个邻居再也无法忍受亚述古国的压迫了。这两个邻居，一个是南方古巴比伦王国的国王，另一个则是居住在东边的米堤亚人。古巴比伦和米堤亚两国的国王联合起来攻打尼尼微，并且一起将这座城市夷为了平地。这场战争，发生在公元前612年：6—1—2，尼尼微和亚述古国的政权就此覆灭了。因此，这一事件，史称"尼尼微衰亡"，即尼尼微的终结。我们可以为它立上一块这样的墓碑。

18 A City of Wonders and Wickedness

The king of Babylon had beaten Nineveh. But he didn't stop with that. He wanted his Babylon to be as great as Nineveh had been. He went on conquering other lands to the left and right until Babylon, in its turn, became the leader and ruler of other countries. Was Babylon, also, in its turn, to fall, as Nineveh had fallen?

When at last the king of Babylon died, he left his vast empire to his son. Now, the king's son was not called John or James or Charles or anything simple like that. It was — Nebuchadnezzar, and I wonder if his father called him by that long name or shortened it to a nickname like *Neb*, for instance, or *Chad*, or perhaps *Nezzar*. This is the way Nebuchadnezzar wrote his name, for he used cuneiform writing. How would you like to write your name in such an unusual way?

Nebuchadnezzar set to work and made the city of Babylon the largest, the most magnificent, and the most wonderful city in the world. He made the city in the shape of a square and surrounded it with a wall fifty times as high as a man — fifty times — whew! — and so broad that a chariot could be driven along the top, and in this wall he made one

18　奇迹和邪恶并存的城市

古巴比伦的国王已经打败了尼尼微。可他并没有就此止步。他希望让自己统治下的古巴比伦，变得像以前的尼尼微那样强大。于是，他并没有停止战争，而是继续征服其他土地，直到古巴比伦王国变成其他国家的领袖和统治者。那么，古巴比伦最终会不会也像尼尼微那样衰亡呢？

待巴比伦的这位国王去世之后，他便把这个广袤的帝国留给了自己的儿子。注意，这位国王的儿子，可不是叫约翰、詹姆士、查理或其他简单的名字。他叫尼布甲尼撒；我可不知道，他的父亲平常是叫他这个长长的全名呢，还是简短一点，只叫像"尼布""甲尼"或者"尼撒"这样的昵称。下面就是尼布甲尼撒将自己的名字写下来的样子，因为他用的是楔形文字。你们喜不喜欢用这种与众不同的方式来写你们的名字呢？

尼布甲尼撒继位后，便开始动手把巴比伦城建成世界上最庞大、最宏伟、最美

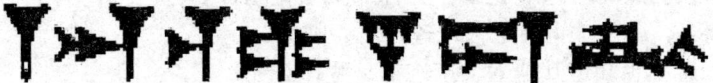

Name of Nebuchadnezzar in cuneiform writing
用楔形文字书写的"尼布甲尼撒"这个名字

hundred huge brass gates. The Euphrates River flowed under the wall, across the city, and out under the wall at the other side.

Nebuchadnezzar could not find anyone in Babylon who was beautiful to be his queen. The Babylonian women must have felt pretty bad — or mad — about that. He went to Media, the country that had helped his father conquer Nineveh. There he found a lovely princess, and so he married her and brought her home to Babylon.

Now, Media was a land of hills and mountains, whilst Babylon was on level ground and without even a hill in sight. Nebuchadnezzar's queen found Babylonia so flat and uninteresting that she became homesick, and she longed for her own country with its wild mountain scenery. Just to please her and keep her contented, Nebuchadnezzar set to work and built a hill for her, but the strange thing was he built it on top of the roof of his palace! On the sides of this hill he made beautiful gardens, and these gardens he planted not only with flowers but also with trees, so that his queen might sit in the shade and enjoy herself. These were called Hanging Gardens. The Hanging Gardens and the tremendous walls were known far and wide as one of the Seven Wonders of the World.

Would you like to know what the other Wonders were?

Well, the pyramids in Egypt were one; the magnificent statue of Zeus at Olympia, where the Olympic Games were held, was another — so those two plus the Hanging Gardens make three.

Nebuchadnezzar believed in many gods, like the ones the Phoenicians worshiped. The

妙的城市。他将该城建成正方形，四周都有城墙，并且城墙竟然有一个人的五十倍高：嗬，五十倍呀！城墙很宽阔，战车都能在上面走；而在这道城墙上，他还开了一百扇巨大的铜制城门。幼发拉底河在城墙之下流淌，穿过整座城市，再从另一面的城墙之下流出。

尼布甲尼撒发现，巴比伦王国里没有一个才貌足以当他王后的美女。对此，古巴比伦的女人们心中一定都很难过，或者很生气呢。于是，尼布甲尼撒便前往曾经帮助过他父亲征服尼尼微的米堤亚。他在该国发现了一位美丽的公主，因此娶她为妻，并带着她回到了巴比伦。

注意，米堤亚是一个山峦密布的地方，而巴比伦却坐落于平原上，连一座小山也看不到。尼布甲尼撒的王后发现巴比伦一坦平洋、毫无意思之后，便开始思念自己的家乡，向往起家乡那种山峦起伏的景色来。为了取悦妻子并满足她的愿望，尼布甲尼撒开始行动起来，为她人工建造出了一座小山；而奇怪的是，他竟然还将这座小山建在王宫的屋顶之上呢！在这座小山四面的山坡上，他布置了许多美丽的花园，并且这些花园里不仅种着花花草草，还栽上了树木，好让他的王后可以坐在树荫下玩得高兴一点儿。这些花园，史称"空中花园"。古巴比伦的空中花园和巨型城墙举世闻名，属于"世界七大奇迹"之一哩。

那你们想不想知道其他六大奇迹都是些什么呢?

好吧，埃及的金字塔是一大奇迹；举办奥林匹克运动会的奥林匹亚那尊宏伟的宙斯雕像则是另外一大奇迹；这样，它们再加上空中花园，便有三大奇迹了。

Jews away off in Jerusalem believed in one God. Nebuchadnezzar wanted the Jews to worship his gods, but they would not. He also wanted them to pay him taxes, and they would not. So he sent his armies to Jerusalem, destroyed the city, burnt the beautiful Temple that Solomon had built, and brought the Jews and all their belongings to Babylon. There in Babylon Nebuchadnezzar kept the Jews prisoners, and there in Babylon the Jews remained prisoners for seventy years.

Babylon had become not only the most magnificent city in the world; it had become also the most wicked. The people of Babylon gave themselves up to the wildest pleasures. Their only thought seemed to be, "Let's eat, drink, and be merry"; they thought nothing of the morrow; the more wicked the pleasure the more they liked it.

But although Nebuchadnezzar seemed able to do and able to have everything in the world he wanted, he finally went crazy. He thought he was a bull, and he used to get down on his hands and knees and eat grass, imagining he was a beast of the field.

And Babylon, in spite of its tremendous walls and brass gates, was doomed. Babylon was to be conquered. It didn't seem possible. How could it be conquered, and who was to do the conquering? You would probably never guess.

尼布甲尼撒崇拜众多神灵，它们与腓尼基人所崇拜的那些神灵没什么两样。可在相距遥远的耶路撒冷，犹太人却只信奉一个上帝。尼布甲尼撒希望犹太人也来信奉他所信奉的那些神灵，可犹太人不愿意。他还想要犹太人向他上交税赋，可犹太人也不愿意。于是，他便派大军去攻打耶路撒冷，摧毁了这座城市，焚毁了所罗门建造的那些美丽神庙，还将犹太人和犹太人所有的财物全都掳到了巴比伦。到了巴比伦后，尼布甲尼撒又把犹太人关进了监狱；因此，那些犹太人便在巴比伦的监狱里做了七十年的囚犯。

此时，巴比伦不仅成了当时世界上最宏伟壮观的城市之一，也变成了世界上最为邪恶的城市。巴比伦人全都纵情于声色犬马，尽情享乐。他们似乎一心只想着"我们吃吧，喝吧，快活吧"。他们只顾眼前享乐，根本就不考虑未来；而越是纵情享乐，他们就越喜欢那样的生活。

不过，尽管尼布甲尼撒似乎无所不能，似乎能够得到世界上他所想要的一切，可他最终却疯了。他以为自己是一头公牛，因此曾经四肢着地，趴下去啃青草吃，还幻想着自己就是原野上的一头野兽。

而巴比伦呢，尽管有着巨大的城墙和铜制城门，最终却难逃劫数。巴比伦终将会被敌人攻克。原来这种情况似乎是不可能出现的。它是怎样被攻破的，又是谁将它攻破的呢？结果你们很可能永远也猜不到。

19 A Surprise Party

When I was a boy I was always told, and you have probably been told the same thing: "You can have no dessert until you have eaten your dinner."

No matter whether I was hungry or not, "No dinner, no dessert." This was a rule that my father said was "like the laws of the Medes and Persians".

I didn't know then who the Medes and Persians were, but I know now that they were two Indo-European peoples living next to Babylon — you remember Nebuchadnezzar had married a Median woman — and that they were governed by laws, which were fixed so hard and fast and were so unchangeable, that we still speak of any such thing that does not change as like "the laws of the Medes and Persians".

The Medes and the Persians had a religion, which was neither like that of the Jews nor like that of the Babylonians. It had been started by a Persian named Zoroaster, who was a wise man like Solomon. Zoroaster went about among the people, teaching them wise sayings and hymns. These wise sayings have been gathered into a book. Zoroaster taught that there were two great spirits in the world, the Good Spirit and the Bad Spirit.

The Good Spirit, he said was Light, and the Bad Spirit Darkness. The Good or Light he

19　宴会奇袭

在我小时候，大人总是对我说：

"你不把饭吃完的话，就别想吃甜点。"

你们很可能也听大人这样说过。

不管我的肚子饿还是不饿，都是"不吃完饭，就没有甜点"。这是一条规矩；我的父亲曾说，它"就像是米堤亚人和波斯人的法律一样"。

那时我并不知道谁是米堤亚人，谁又是波斯人。可如今我却知道，他们是紧挨着巴比伦的两个印欧民族；你们应该都还记得，尼布甲尼撒娶了一个米堤亚姑娘为妻呢。这两个民族都是依法治国，而他们的法律也都制定得非常严格、不可更改，因此我们如今在谈到一些不可更改的东西时，仍然会说它们就像"米堤亚人和波斯人的法律"一样。

米堤亚人和波斯人信奉同一种宗教；可这种宗教，既不同于犹太人所信奉的宗教，也不同于古巴比伦人所信奉的宗教。这种宗教，是由一个叫作琐罗亚斯德的波斯人创立的，他是一个像所罗门那样的智者。琐罗亚斯德曾经深入各地的民众当中，向他们传播箴言和颂歌。这些箴言，已经被人汇编成书了。琐罗亚斯德说，世界上有两种主要的神灵，即善良之神和邪恶之神。

called Mazda. The Persians kept a fire constantly burning on their altar. They thought the Good Spirit burned in the fire, and they had men watch over the flame to see that it never went out. These men who watched the flame were called Magi, and they were supposed to be able to do all sorts of wonderful things, so that we call such wonderful things *magic*, and the people who are able to do them we call *magicians*. At the time of this story which I'm telling you, the ruler of the Medes and the Persians was a great king named Cyrus.

But before I go on with this story, I must tell you about a little country not far from Troy. This little country was called Lydia. Perhaps you may know a girl named Lydia. I do. Lydia was ruled over by a king named Croesus, who was the richest man in the world. When we want to describe a man as very wealthy, we still say he is "as rich as Croesus".

Croesus owned nearly all the gold mines, of which there were a great many in that country, and besides this he collected money in the form of taxes from all the cities near him.

Before the time of Croesus, people did not have money such as we have now. When they wished to buy anything, they simply traded something they had for something they wanted — so many eggs for a pound of meat or so much wine for a pair of sandals. To buy anything expensive, such as a horse, they paid with a lump of gold or silver, which was weighed in the scales to see just how heavy it was. It is hard for us to think how people could get along without cents and nickels, dimes, quarters and dollars — with no money at all — and yet they did.

Croesus, in order to make things simpler, cut up his gold into small bits. Now, it was not easy for everyone to weigh each piece each time it was traded, for he might not have

他说，善良之神就是光明，而邪恶之神则是黑暗。他将善良之神或者光明之神称为玛兹达。波斯人的祭坛上都点着长明灯。他们认为，善良之神在火中燃烧，所以他们会派专人守护，确保火苗永远不灭。守护圣火的这些人叫作魔法师；人们认为，他们能够做出各种各样的奇妙之事来，因此我们将这种奇妙之事称为"魔术"，而将能够做出这种奇妙之事的人称为"魔术师"。在我将要给你们讲述的这个故事所发生的那个年代，统治着米堤亚人和波斯人的，是一位名叫居鲁士的伟大国王。

不过，在继续讲述这个故事之前，我还得跟你们说一说一个离特洛伊不远的小国家。这个小国家叫作吕底亚（Lydia）。或许，你们可能认识一个叫作莉迪娅（Lydia）的小姑娘。我就认识一个。当时，吕底亚由一个叫作克罗伊斯的国王统治着，他是世界上非常富有的人。所以，如今倘若想要说一个人非常富有，我们仍然会说他"富比克罗伊斯"呢。

吕底亚国内有许多的金矿，这些金矿几乎全都是克罗伊斯的；除此之外，他还用税收的形式，向附近地区的所有城镇索要钱财。

在克罗伊斯当上国王之前，人们并没有如今我们所用的这种钱币。他们想要买什么东西的时候，只会用自己已有的东西去交换想要的东西，比如用多少鸡蛋换一磅肉，或者用多少葡萄酒换一双拖鞋。而要购买贵重物品的话，比如说一匹马，他们就会用一块金子或者银子，在秤上称一称重量之后去购买。我们很难想象，在没有五分钱、一角钱、两角五分或者一美元，在没有任何钱币的情况下，人们是怎样过的；不过，他们那时的确没有钱币。

为了让事情变得简单一点，克罗伊斯便把金子分成了小块。注意，要做到每次

any scales handy. So Croesus had each piece weighed and stamped with its weight and with his name or initials to show that he guaranteed the weight. These pieces of gold and silver were only lumps with Croesus's seal pressed into them, but they were probably the first real money even though they were not round and beautifully engraved like our coins.

Now, Cyrus, the great Persian king, thought he would like to own this rich country of Lydia with all its gold mines, so he set out to conquer it.

When Cyrus was on the way, Croesus sent in a hurry to the oracle in Greece to ask what was going to happen and who was going to win. You will remember what I said about the oracle at Delphi and how people used to ask the oracle questions — to have their fortunes told, as some people still do today.

The oracle replied to Croesus's question: "A great kingdom shall fall."

Croesus was delighted, for he thought the oracle meant that Cyrus's kingdom would fall. The oracle was right, but not in the way Croesus had thought.

A great kingdom did fall, but it was his own kingdom of Lydia and not Cyrus's that fell.

But Cyrus was still not satisfied with the

Delphic oracle
特尔斐神谕处

买卖东西时都把每块金子称一称，是件很不容易的事情，因为一个人可能手边根本就没有带秤。于是，克罗伊斯便将每块小金子都称上一遍，然后将重量、他的名字或者姓氏的首字母标在金子上，以示他保证每块金子的重量准确无误。这些金、银，不过是印有克罗伊斯印记的小金块和小银块罢了；然而，尽管它们不是圆形的，上面也不像我们如今的硬币那样刻着美丽的图案，但它们很可能就是世界上第一批真正的钱币呢。

此时，居鲁士这位伟大的波斯国王动起了心思，想要占领吕底亚这个富庶的国家，以及该国所有的金矿；于是，他便开始攻打吕底亚。

得知居鲁士正在率军前来进攻的消息后，克罗伊斯急忙派人前往希腊的神谕处，询问接下来的局势如何，以及哪一方将会获胜。你们可能还记得我在前面对特尔斐神谕处的介绍，以及当时的人为什么会向神提问。他们的目的，就是希望神指出他们的命运前程；而如今，有些人还在干这种事情呢。

对于克罗伊斯的问题，神是这样回答的：

"一个伟大的王国将被征服。"

克罗伊斯很高兴，因为他觉得，神谕的意思是指居鲁士的王国将被征服。虽然神谕说得没错，可结果却不是克罗伊斯所想的那样。

一个伟大的王国的确被征服了；但被征服的，却是克罗伊斯自己的吕底亚王

capture of Lydia, and so at last he attacked Babylon.

Now, the people in Babylon who thought of nothing but pleasure were busy feasting and drinking and having a good time. Why should they worry about Cyrus? Their city had walls that were so high and thick and was protected by such strong gates of brass that it seemed as if no one could possibly have captured it.

But you remember that the Euphrates River ran beneath the walls and crossed right through the city. Well, one night when the young prince of Babylon named Belshazzar was having a party and enjoying himself, feeling quite certain that no one could enter the city, Cyrus made a dam and turned the waters of the river to one side. Then Cyrus's army marched into the city through the dry riverbed and captured the surprised Babylonians without even a fight. It is supposed that some of the Babylonian priests helped him to do this and even opened the gates, for Babylon had become so wicked that they thought it time for it to be destroyed.

Old Lycurgus would have said, "I told you so. People who think of nothing but pleasure never come to a good end."

This surprise party was in 538 — 5 and 3 are 8.

Two years later Cyrus let the Jews, who had been carried away fifty years before from Jerusalem, return to the home of their fathers, thus ending the Babylonian Captivity.

Today the only thing left of this great city of Babylon — Babylon the Wicked, Babylon the Magnificent, Babylon with all its great walls and brass gates and Hanging Gardens — is a mound of earth

国，而不是居鲁士的王国。

可是，在攻下了吕底亚之后，居鲁士却仍不满足，所以最终他又去攻打巴比伦了。

此时，巴比伦那些除了享乐什么也不想的人，正在忙着大吃大喝、尽情享乐。他们为什么要担心居鲁士来进攻呢？他们的巴比伦，城墙又高又厚，还被极其坚固的铜制城门保护着，所以看上去似乎无人可以攻破。

不过，你们应当还记得，幼发拉底河是在巴比伦的城墙之下穿城而过的。于是，有天晚上，正当巴比伦那位叫作伯沙撒的年轻王子正在举行宴会、尽情享乐，并且自信满满地认为无人能够攻入城内的时候，居鲁士却派人筑起了一道水坝，将河水引到了另一侧。然后，居鲁士的大军便经由干涸了的河床进入了巴比伦城，不费一枪一弹，便俘虏了那些大惊失色的巴比伦人。据说，是巴比伦的一些祭司暗中协助了居鲁士，甚至打开了城门；因为他们觉得，巴比伦已经变得极其堕落，应该将它毁灭了。

莱克格斯如果还活着，他定然会说："我早说过会这样的。除了享乐什么也不想的人，必定不会有好下场。"

这场宴会奇袭，发生在公元前538年；这很好记，5加3等于8。

两年后，居鲁士便将五十年前从耶路撒冷俘虏过来的那些犹太人全都放回去与父母团聚，从而结束了"巴比伦囚房"时期。

如今，巴比伦这座伟大的城市，这个邪恶的巴比伦、辉煌的巴比伦、有着牢固城墙和铜制城门及"空中花园"的巴比伦，就只剩下一堆黄土啦。

20 The Other Side of the World: India

India is a country east of Persia. The people who live there are called *Indians*. The Indians, of course, are entirely different from Native Americans who were called Indians when early explorers believed they had reached India or the East Indies.

You may remember that India was one of the very early civilizations that grew up along a river valley. Do you remember the name of the river — Here's a hint. It sounds like India. Did you remember? It's the Indus River.

India is a very old country. Its modern neighbor, Pakistan, used to be part of India, too. Long, long ago — about 2500 B.C. — the people living along the Indus River, in what is now India and Pakistan, sailed up and down the river to trade with each other. They invented a system of writing to keep their records. They built large cities with wide, straight streets. Their houses even had bathrooms with drains that were connected to a city sewer system. Did you think that modern people were the only ones to have sewer systems? If you did, you were wrong. You can see that ancient Indians thought up this healthy system long before we did.

About a thousand years after the ancient Indians built their first cities along the Indus

20 世界的另一边：印度

印度是波斯以东的一个国家。生活在那里的人，被称为印度人。当然，印度人（Indian）和美洲的印第安人（Indian）是一个完全不同的民族，只是因为早期的探险家到达美洲时，以为自己到的是印度或者东印度群岛，才把美洲的土著称为印第安人。

你们可能还记得，印度是沿着河流流域发展起来的早期文明古国之一吧。你们还记得那条河流叫什么吗？给你们一点儿提示吧。它听起来与"印度"差不多。你们记起来了吗？这就是印度河。

印度是一个非常古老的国度。现代印度的邻国巴基斯坦，原来也属于印度。很久、很久以前，即公元前2500年左右，人们都在如今印度和巴基斯坦所在的地方沿着印度河而居，并且驾着船只往来于河上，相互进行贸易。他们发明了一套书写系统，来记录自己的历史。他们建立了一座座有着宽阔、笔直大道的城市。他们的房子里，甚至有带下水道的浴室呢；而那些下水道，则与整座城市的排水系统相连。你们是不是以为，只有现代人才懂得修建排水系统呢？如果是这样，那你们就错了。你们看看，古代印度人想出这种卫生系统，可比我们早了很久呢。

距古代印度人沿着印度河建立起第一批城市差不多一千年后，印度西边的一

River, people from the west invaded their land. These people were Indo-Europeans who came from somewhere near Persia. When they first arrived, these newcomers did not know how to write. They were strong warriors though and gradually conquered more and more of India. The original Indians and the newcomers learned from each other and adopted some of each others' customs.

In the course of time there came to be four chief *castes*, or classes, of people in India. No one in one caste would have anything to do with a person in another caste. A boy or girl in one caste would never play with a boy or girl in another caste. A man from one class would never marry a woman from another. No one from one class would eat with someone from another class.

The top caste was made up of the priests and scholars. In the next caste were people like rulers and warriors. Then, in the third caste, came farmers and merchants. Fourth, and last, were laborers, men who chopped wood, or dug the soil, or carried water.

But they weren't the lowest! There were other people so low that they didn't even belong to a caste, and so they were outcasts and *untouchables*. Even today, though India is trying to make changes and caste distinctions have been made illegal, these people are the ones who sweep the streets, clean the gutters, collect the garbage, and do the dirty work that no one else will do.

India today is terribly crowded with people. It is about one-third the size of the United States but has more than three times as many people. Think what that means!

些民族侵入了他们的土地。这些入侵者都属于印欧民族，来自波斯附近。初来乍到的时候，这些人还不知道写字。但他们都骁勇善战，因此逐渐征服了印度越来越多的地方。原来的印度人和这些新来者相互学习，并且相互接受了对方的一些风俗习惯。

随着时间的推移，印度人中出现了四大"种姓"，或者说四大等级。一个种姓里的人，不会与另一个种姓里的人相往来。一个种姓里的小朋友，绝对不会与属于另一个种姓的小朋友玩耍。一个种姓里的男子，决不会娶到属于另一个种姓的女子。而一个种姓里的人，也不会与属于另一个种姓里的人一起吃饭的。

最高一级的种姓，由僧侣和学者组成。第二级种姓是各级官吏和武士。接下来的第三大种姓，则是农民和商人。而最后的第四个种姓，就是体力劳动者，比如劈柴、翻地或者挑水的人。

不过，第四种姓的人的等级并不是最低的呢！还有一些人的地位极其低下，甚至不属于任何一个种姓，所以他们都属于无家可归者和贱民。即便是到了今天，尽管印度正在努力改变这一点，并且已将种姓歧视定为非法，但这些人仍然干着打扫大街、清理下水道、清扫垃圾以及没人会去干的一些脏活儿。

如今的印度，已经人满为患了。该国的面积只有美国国土的三分之一左右，可人口却有美国的三倍多。想象一下，这意味着什么吧！

虽说如今绝大多数印度人都信奉印度教，但从公元前300年到公元400年这七百年间，佛教却在印度逐渐盛行。佛教是这样产生和发展起来的：

Most Indians today follow the Hindu religion, but from about 300 B.C. to 400 A.D. — seven hundred years — Buddhism was very popular. It happened this way.

About 500 B.C. there was born a prince in India by the name of Gautama. Gautama saw so much suffering and trouble in the world that he felt it was not right that he himself, just because he by chance had been born rich, should be happy while others were miserable and unhappy. He gave up the life to which he had been born, a life of ease and luxury with all its good things, and spent his entire time trying to make things better for his people.

Gautama taught the people to be good; he taught them to be honest; and he taught them to help the poor and the unfortunate. After a while people began to call him Buddha, and he was considered so holy and pure that at last they came to think that he must be a god himself, and so they worshiped him as a god.

These people who believed in Buddha were called Buddhists, and many others quickly became Buddhists, too. Buddhism seemed so good that we do not wonder that great numbers of people became Buddhists.

Buddhists thought their religion was so good that they wanted everybody else to become Buddhists. They sent missionaries across land and sea all the way to the island of Japan, and this new religion spread far and wide. Today there are more Buddhists in the world than there are people in the United States.

You can see that India is a very important place. It is the home of one of the world's oldest civilizations and two of the world's important religions.

公元前500年左右，印度诞生了一位王子，名叫乔达摩[1]。乔达摩看到世界上有这么多的痛苦与灾难，所以他认为，自己只是因为碰巧生于富贵之家便生活幸福，而其他人却生活得悲惨而不幸，这种情况是不对的。于是，他放弃了生而拥有的幸福人生，抛下了那种安逸而奢华的生活，以及那种生活中的一切奢侈之物，用毕生的时间来让自己的子民生活得更好。

乔达摩教导人们向善；他教导人们要诚实；他还教导人们要帮助贫困者和不幸者。不久之后，人们便开始尊称他为佛陀。由于人们认为他极其圣洁，所以最后他们开始觉得，乔达摩本人一定是一位神灵，于是他们便把他当作神灵来崇拜了。

这些信奉佛陀的人被称为佛教徒；而不久之后，其他许多人也纷纷变成了佛教徒。佛教看上去非常不错，因此许多人变成佛教徒也就不足为怪了。

佛教徒认为他们的这种宗教非常好，所以希望其他所有的人全都变成佛教徒。他们派遣使徒，一路翻山越岭、漂洋过海，远达日本岛，于是这种新的宗教便到处传播开来了。如今，全世界的佛教徒人数比整个美国的人口还要多哩。

你们看得出，印度是一个非常重要的国度。它不但是世界上最古老文明之一的发祥地，也是世界两大宗教[2]的发源地。

---

[1] 乔达摩（Gautama），全名乔达摩·悉达多（Gautama Siddhārtha），古印度迦毗罗卫国的净饭王太子，是著名的思想家和佛教的创始人。因他本身为释迦族人，故被后人尊称为释迦牟尼。

[2] 此处当然是指前面已经提到了的印度教和佛教啦。

21 All the Way Around the World in China

About the same time that Gautama was starting Buddhism in India, a man in China, a great wise man named Confucius, was teaching the people of China what they ought to do and what they ought not to do. His teachings filled several books and formed what came to be a way of life for the Chinese and many other people in Asia.

Confucius taught that people should be loyal and obey their kings and also that rulers had a duty to take care of their people. He believed that this would bring peace and harmony in China. He taught people to obey their parents and teachers and to honor their ancestors. This sounds something like one of the Ten Commandments: "Honor thy father and thy mother."

Confucius also taught the Golden Rule, the same Golden Rule that you are taught today, only instead of saying, "Do unto others as you would have others do unto you" he said, "Do not do to others what you would not want others to do to you."

China had one of the earliest civilizations in the world. Maybe you remember the name of the river that was the cradle of Chinese civilization. It was the Huang River, or Yellow River, that overflowed with thick yellow mud. This mud fertilized the soil where people

21 概说中国

在乔达摩正在印度开创佛教的时候，中国有一个人，一个叫作孔子的伟大智者，也正在教导中国人该做什么、不该做什么。他的教导记录在好几本书里，并且后来变成了中国人和亚洲其他许多人的一种生存之道。

孔子教导人们应当忠诚，应当服从君主，还教导说统治者有义务照顾好手下的人民。他认为，这样就能给中国带来和平与和谐。他教导人们应当孝顺父母、师长，并且敬奉祖先。这一点，听上去与《十诫》中"应当孝敬父母"这一条倒是有点儿相似呢。

孔子还教给了人们一条"黄金法则"；它就是你们如今在《圣经》中学到的那条"黄金律"，只是表达方式不一样罢了。孔子说的并不是"你们愿意人怎样待你们，你们也要怎样待人"，而是"己所不欲，勿施于人。"

中国是世界上最早的文明古国之一。可能你们还记得那条孕育了中华文明的河流的名字吧。这条河流，就是河底全是黄色泥沙的"黄河"，或者说"黄色之河"。这种泥沙使土壤变得很肥沃，从而让人们可以种植庄稼。人们起初沿着黄河而居，后来又沿着扬子江而居；扬子江亦称"长江"。

中国距我们前面已经讲到过的那些地方都非常遥远。它与古代世界的其他国

grew their crops. People settled first along the Huang and then also along the Yangtze River, also called the Long River.

China is very far away from all the other places we have been talking about. It was isolated from the rest of the ancient world. The Himalaya Mountains lie to the west and the Gobi Desert to the north. On the south are more mountains and seas. On the east lies the great Pacific Ocean that stretches all the way to the west coast of the United States. In the days before large sailing ships and way before airplanes, the Chinese had very little contact with any other people. So Chinese culture developed all by itself.

We know the Chinese had a written language as early as 1500 B.C. at a time when the Shang dynasty ruled northern China. You can see that Chinese writing is still very different from the writing in any other country. The Chinese never switched to an alphabet but continue to use characters — a different character for each word. It must be very hard to learn to read and write Chinese.

We have to learn only twenty-six letters. Boys and girls in China have to memorize about six hundred characters before they can do even basic reading and writing.

Many inventions were made and used in China before the rest of the world ever heard of them. Around the time of Christ, the Chinese were making silk, porcelain, and paper. By this time, the Chinese did trade with some of the other people we have read about. Chinese silk was in great demand by Romans and their neighbors around the Mediterranean.

By 600 A.D. the Chinese had invented printing and used printing presses. A few

家都不相连。中国的西部矗立着喜马拉雅山脉，北部则是戈壁沙漠。该国的南边，还有更多的山脉和河域。而其东边，则是一望无际、一直延伸到美国西海岸的太平洋。在还没有大型帆船和航空线路的那个时代，中国人很少与其他民族进行接触。因此，中华文化是独立发展起来的。

我们知道，早在公元前1500年，中国就已经有了文字，当时正是商朝统治着中国的北方地区。你们可以看出，如今的汉字仍然与其他国家的文字大相径庭呢。中国人一直都没有转而采用字母文字，而是继续使用汉字；每个汉字的字形，都是不相同的。

我们只需学26个字母。可中国的小朋友却需要记住600个左右的汉字，才能进行基本的读写。

有许多的发明创造，在世界上其他国家都还没有听说过的时候，就已经在中国出现并加以应用了。几乎还是在基督降生的时候，中国人就已经生产出丝绸、瓷器和纸张了。到了此时，中国人开始与我们前面说过的其他一些民族有了贸易往来。古罗马人及地中海地区的一些国家，对中国丝绸的需求量都非常

Huang River
汉字"黄河"

Yangtze River
汉字"长江"

centuries later, they were making the magnetic compass, which was such a great help to the sailors. Do you know what a compass is? It's a little gadget with a needle that always points to the north. Knowing which way was north made it possible for sailors to know which way they were sailing — even when they were way out in the ocean, too far from land to be able to see the shore. Maybe someone in your class or neighborhood has a compass and can share it for everybody to see.

The Chinese also figured out how to immunize against the dread disease smallpox. They also were first to discover how to make explosive powder, the kind that we use both for gunpowder and for fireworks.

From all this, you can see that the Chinese may have been relatively isolated, but they were very busy making things that the rest of the world found really exciting when people learned about them.

巨大。

大约到公元600年的时候，中国人已经发明了印刷术，开始使用印刷机了。几百年后，他们又发明了磁性罗盘；这种罗盘，可是水手们的一大帮手呢。你们知道罗盘是什么吗？这是一种很小巧的装置，其中有一根指针，总是指向北方。只要知道哪边是北，即便是在驾船驶入茫茫的海洋深处，离陆地很远，根本看不到海岸的时候，水手们也知道自己正在朝着哪个方向航行。或许你们班上或者你们的邻居中，有的人家里就有罗盘，那么不妨拿出来让大家都瞧一瞧。

中国人还发明了预防天花这种可怕疾病的办法。他们也是第一个发现如何制造火药的民族；火药就是我们用来制造弹药和烟花的那种东西。

从这些情况，你们可以看出，虽说中国人可能相对与世隔绝，可他们却一直在不停地进行发明创造；而这些发明创造一旦传到世界各地，便让世人全都激动不已。

22 Rich Man, Poor Man

Whenever I pass a group of children playing ball, I almost always hear someone shout, "That's no fair!"

There always seem to be some players who think the others are not playing fair. Sides are always quarreling.

They need an umpire.

When Athens was young there were two sides among the people — the rich and the poor, the aristocrats and the common people — and they were always quarreling. Each side was trying to get *more* power, and each side said the other wasn't playing fair.

They needed an umpire.

Athens had had kings, but the kings took the side of the rich, and so finally the Athenians had kicked out the last king, and after that they would have no more kings.

About the year 600 B.C. things became so very bad that a man named Draco was chosen to make a set of rules for the Athenians to obey. These rules he made were called the Code of Draco.

Draco's Code made terrible punishments for anyone who broke the rules. If a man stole

22 富人、穷人

每当我经过一群正在打球的小朋友身边，几乎总是会听到有人嚷嚷着说："那样根本就不公平！"

似乎总是有人觉得其他人没有公平地进行比赛。因此，比赛双方总是争吵不休。

他们需要一个裁判。

而在雅典刚刚崛起的时候，雅典人便分成了两派：一派是富人，一派是穷人；一派是贵族，一派是平民。两派之间，总是争吵不休。每一派都想要获得更大的权势，并且每一派都说对方做得不公平。

他们需要一个裁判。

虽说雅典有国王，但国王站在富人一边；于是，后来雅典人便将最后一任国王扫地出门，此后雅典就再也没有国王了。

到了公元前七世纪的时候，由于雅典的形势变得极其糟糕，所以雅典人便选出了一个叫作德拉古的人，让他来制定出一套雅典人必须遵守的法律法规。他所制定的这套法规，被称为《德拉古法典》。

《德拉古法典》中制定了异常严酷的措施，来惩处那些违法犯罪的人。如果有

anything even as small a thing as a loaf of bread, he was not just fined or sent to jail; he was put to death! No matter how small the wrong a man had done, he was put to death for it. Draco explained the reason for such a severe law by saying that a thief deserved to be put to death and should be. A man who killed another deserved more than to be put to death, but unfortunately there was no worse punishment to give him.

You can understand how much trouble the laws of Draco caused. They were so hard that a little later another man was called upon to make a new set of laws. This man was named Solon, and his laws were very just and good. We now call senators and other people who make our laws *solons* after this man Solon who lived so long ago, even though their laws are not always just and good.

Still the people were not satisfied with Solons laws. The upper classes thought the laws gave too much to the lower classes, and the lower classes thought they gave too much to the upper. Both classes, however, obeyed the laws for a while, although both classes complained against them.

But about 560 B.C. a man named Pisistratus stepped in and took charge of things himself. He was not elected nor chosen by the people. He simply made himself ruler, and he was so powerful that no one could stop him. It was as if a boy made himself captain or umpire without being chosen by those on the team.

There were others from time to time in Greece who did the same thing, and they were called *tyrants*. So Pisistratus was a tyrant. Nowadays only a ruler who is cruel and unjust

人行窃，哪怕只是偷一个像面包这样小的东西，也会被判处死刑，而不是罚款或者蹲监狱！无论一个人所犯的过错是多么微小，他也会被处以死刑。德拉古曾经解释了采取此种严刑酷法的理由，他说小偷罪行当诛，所以理应处死。杀人者本来应当处以比死刑更重的刑罚，但可惜的是，除了死刑，便没有更加严厉的刑罚可以用于惩处杀人犯了。

你们完全可以想象，德拉古制定出来的这种法律必定引发了许许多多的问题。由于这套法典过于严苛，所以不久之后，雅典人便要求另一个人来制定出一部新的法律。这个人叫梭伦，而他制定出来的法律，在当时也非常公正、非常合理。我们如今之所以将我国负责制定法律的参议员和其他人士叫作立法议员（solons），就是根据梭伦（Solon）这个古代人物的名字来的，尽管这些立法议员所制定的法律，并非始终都很公正、很合理的。

但是，雅典人对梭伦制定的法律仍然感到不满意。上层贵族认为，法典给予了下层平民太多的权力，而下层平民则认为法律给予了上层贵族太多的权力。不过，尽管两个阶层都有所不满，他们还是暂时遵守了梭伦制定出来的这套法律。

但是，到了公元前560年左右，一个叫作庇西特拉图的人介入进来，一手控制了国家大权。他并不是经过推选或者由民众选举出来的。他完全是自封为王；由于他的势力非常强大，因此无人能够制止他这样做。这就好比是一个小朋友没有经过队员推选，便自任队长或者裁判一样。

古希腊历史上经常有其他的人这样干，人们将这些人都称为"暴君"。所以，

is called a tyrant. Pisistratus, however, settled the difficulties of both sides, and though a tyrant in the Greek sense, he was neither cruel nor unjust. In fact, Pisistratus ruled according to the laws of Solon, and he did a great deal to improve Athens and the life of the people. Among other things he did, he had Homer's poems written down, so that people could read them, for before this time people knew them only from hearing them recited. It is remarkable how histories can be passed down orally — just by telling the story. In cultures without writing, people had to have very good memories.

The people put up with Pisistratus and also with his son for a while. Finally the Athenians got tired of the son's rule and drove all the Pisistratus family out of Athens in 510 B.C.

The next man to try to settle the quarrels of the two sides was named Cleisthenes. It is hard, sometimes, to learn the name of a stranger to whom we have just been introduced unless we hear his name several times. I will say over his name so that you can get used to hearing it:

Cleisthenes;

    Cleisthenes;

        Cleisthenes.

Your parents may be poor or they may be rich.

If they are poor each has one vote when there is an election.

If they are rich each has one vote but only one vote and no more.

庇西特拉图就是一位暴君。如今，只有那种非常残暴、非常不公正的统治者，才会被称为暴君。然而，庇西特拉图却解决了贵族与平民之间的种种纷争；并且，尽管他被古希腊人称为暴君，可他却既不残暴，也很公正。事实上，庇西特拉图是遵照梭伦所制定的律法来统治希腊的，并且他还做出了巨大的努力，来促进雅典的发展和改善人民的生活。除了其他一些贡献，他还命人将《荷马史诗》书写下来供人们阅读，因为此前人们只是听人朗诵才能了解《荷马史诗》。历史怎么能够只通过讲述故事便口头传承下去？这可真是非比寻常啊。在那些没有文字的文化群落里，人们必须具有超常的记忆力才行呢。

古希腊人容忍庇西特拉图和他的儿子统治了一段时间。最后，他们厌倦了庇西特拉图儿子的统治，便在公元前510年将庇西特拉图家族全都赶出了雅典。

接下来，又出现了一个试图平息贵族和平民纷争的人物，叫作克里斯提尼。有的时候，除非多听几次，否则我们就很难记住刚刚结识的陌生人的名字。所以，这个人的名字我会多说几遍，好让你们熟悉起来：

克里斯提尼；

    克里斯提尼；

        克里斯提尼。

你们的父母既有可能是穷人，也可能很富有。

如果他们是穷人，那么在选举时，他们每人都可以投上一票。

如果他们是富翁，那么在选举时，他们每人也可以投上一票；但他们各自只有

If people break the laws, whether they are rich or whether they are poor, they must go to jail.

It was not always so; it is not always so even now. But long ago it was much worse.

Cleisthenes gave every man a vote — rich and poor alike — but he did not give women a vote. In ancient times, women often were kept out of politics. Still, the people of Athens believed that Cleisthenes ruled wisely and well. Cleisthenes started something called *ostracism.* If for any reason the people wanted to get rid of a man, all they had to do was to scratch his name on any piece of a broken pot or jar they might find and drop it in a voting-box on a certain day. If there were enough such votes, the man would have to leave the city and stay away for ten years. This was called ostracism, from the Greek name for such a broken piece of pottery, on which the name was written. Even today we use this same word to speak of a person whom no one will have anything to do with, whom no one wants around, saying he had been ostracized.

Have you ever been sent away from the table to the kitchen or to your room for misbehaving?

Then you, too, have been ostracized.

Ostracism
陶片放逐法

一票，没有多的。

如果人们违反了法律，那么无论是贫是富，他们都必须去坐牢。

但情况并非总是这样；即便是现在，也并非始终都是这样。但是，在很久以前的古代，这种情况还要糟糕得多。

克里斯提尼规定，在选举中每个男人都有一票，并且不论贫富，都一视同仁；但他没有赋予妇女以选举权。在古代，女性通常都是不准干预政治的。尽管如此，雅典人却都认为克里斯提尼的统治非常英明。克里斯提尼还开创了一种叫作"陶片放逐法"的制度。如果出于某种原因，雅典人想要除掉某个人的话，那么他们只需从破陶罐、破陶壶上随便找来一块碎片，将那个人的名字写在上面，并在某个固定的日子将碎片投进一个选票箱里就行了。假如这种选票达到了足够的数量，那个人就必须离开雅典，在外漂泊十年。根据古希腊人对这种写有名字的破陶片的叫法，人们便把这种制度叫作"陶片放逐法"。即便是到了今天，我们在谈到一个任何人都不愿再与之打交道、任何人都不希望看到的人时，还会用到这个词，说他已经被"流放"了呢。

你们有没有过因为调皮捣乱、因为没有礼貌而被父母从饭桌上赶到厨房或者卧室去的经历呢？

要是有的话，那你们也是被"流放"过啦。

23 Rome Kicks Out Her Kings

In 509 B.C. something happened in Rome. There were two classes of people in Rome, just as there were in Athens: the wealthy people who were called *patricians*, and the poor people who were called *plebeians*. We use the same words now and call people who are rich and aristocratic patricians, and the people who are poor and uneducated plebeians. The patricians were allowed to vote, but the plebeians were not allowed to vote.

At last, however, the plebeians had been given the right to vote. But in B.C. Rome had a king named Tarquin. He didn't think the plebeians; should be allowed to vote, and so he said they should not. The plebeians would not stand this, and therefore they got together and drove Tarquin out of the city, as the Athenians had driven out their king. This was in 509 B.C., and Tarquin was the last king Rome ever had.

After King Tarquin had been driven out, the Romans started what is called a republic, something like our own country, but they were afraid to have only one man as president for fear he might make himself king, and they had had enough of kings.

So the Romans elected *two men* each year to be rulers over them, and these two men they called consuls. Each consul had a bodyguard of twelve men. These men were given

23 罗马废除国王

公元前509年，古罗马发生了一件大事。像雅典社会一样，罗马社会也分成了两大阶层，即被称为贵族的富人和被称为平民百姓的穷人。如今我们仍然沿用了这两种称呼，将有钱人和名门世族称为贵族，而将那些贫困且未受过教育的人称为平民。古罗马的贵族拥有选举权，平民则没有选举权。

然而，平民最终还是获得了选举权。但在公元前，罗马有一个叫作塔克文的国王。他认为平民不应当拥有选举权，所以剥夺了平民的此种权利。平民无法容忍这种做法，便团结起来，将塔克文逐出了罗马城，就像雅典人将国王逐出雅典那样。这件事情发生在公元前509年，所以塔克文便成了古罗马的最后一任国王。

塔克文国王被驱逐之后，罗马建立了一个所谓的"共和国"，有点儿与我们美国相似；可罗马人很害怕只由一个人来担任总统，因为他们担心这个人会自立为王，而他们已经受够国王的统治了。

于是，罗马人便每年选举两个人出来统治国家，并将这两人称为"执政官"。每位执政官都配有一支由十二个人所组成的卫队。这些侍卫被称为"执束杆侍从"；每位执束杆侍从手中都持着一把捆插着斧头的木棒。这束木棍上，斧头从其

the name *lictors*, and each lictor carried an ax tied up in a bundle of sticks. This bundle of sticks with the ax-head sticking out in the middle or at the end was known as *fasces* and signified that the consuls had power to punish by whipping with the sticks or by chopping off one's head with the ax. Some modern coins and postage stamps have fasces pictured on them.

Perhaps you have seen fasces used as ornaments or decoration around monuments or public buildings.

One of the first two consuls was named Brutus the Elder, and he had two sons. The king, Tarquin, who had been driven out of the city, plotted to get back to Rome and become king once more. He was able to persuade some Romans to help him. Among those whom he persuaded were, strange to say, the two sons of Brutus — the new consul of Rome.

Brutus found out this plot and learned that his own children had helped Tarquin. Then Brutus had his sons tried. They were found guilty, and in spite of the fact that they were his own children, he had the lictors put both of them to death as well as the other traitors to Rome.

Tarquin did not succeed in getting back the rule of Rome in this way. The next year he tried again. This time he got

Lictor carrying fasces
手持束杆的执政官侍从

中部伸出或者插在棍束的一端；它被称为"束杆"[1]，表示执政官有权用木棍责打一个人，或者是用斧头砍下一个人的脑袋，以此来实施惩罚。如今有些国家的硬币和邮票上，仍然还印有"束杆"的图案呢。

你们或许在一些纪念碑或者公共建筑物上看到过用于装饰和点缀的束杆吧。

在古罗马的两位首任执政官中，有一位叫作老布鲁特斯，他有两个儿子。那个被逐出城去的国王塔克文密谋回到罗马，想再次登上王位。他很有本事，说服了一些罗马人来协助他。说来也怪，罗马新任执政官老布鲁特斯的两个儿子竟然也被他说服了。

老布鲁特斯发现了这个阴谋，并且得知了自己的两个儿子竟然也是塔克文同谋的消息。于是，老布鲁特斯便将两个儿子全都送上了审判台。他们被判有罪；尽管他们是自己的亲生儿子，但老布鲁特斯还是命令执束杆侍从将两人处死，就像对待其他背叛罗马的人一样。

塔克文用这种方法回到罗马的阴谋没有得逞。第二年，他又故伎重施。这一次，

---

[1] 束杆（fasces），原本是古罗马执政官出行时所带的权杖，后来在二十世纪上半叶被意大利的法西斯党用作标志，因此出现了音译的"法西斯"一词，所指的意思也变成了对内实行强权、暴力、恐怖统治，对外实施侵略扩张政策的极端独裁形式。

together an army of his neighbors, the Etruscans, and with this army he attacked Rome.

Now, there was a wooden bridge across the Tiber River, which separated the Etruscans from the city of Rome. In order to keep the Etruscans from crossing into the city, a Roman named Horatius, who had already lost one eye in fighting for Rome, gave orders to have this bridge broken down.

While the bridge was being chopped down, Horatius, with two of his friends, stood on the far side of the bridge and fought back the whole Etruscan army. When the bridge was cracking under the blows of the Roman soldiers, Horatius ordered his two friends to run quickly to the other side before the bridge fell.

Then Horatius, all by himself, kept the enemy back until at last the bridge crashed into the river. Horatius then jumped into the water with all his armor on and swam toward the Roman shore. Though arrows the Etruscans shot were falling all around him, and though his armor weighed him down, he reached the other side safely. Even the Etruscans were thrilled at his bravery, and, enemies though they were, they cheered him loudly.

There is a very famous poem called *Horatius at the Bridge*, which describes this brave deed.

A few years after Horatius, there lived another Roman named Cincinnatus. He was only a simple farmer with a little farm on the bank of the Tiber, but he was very wise and good, and the people of Rome honored and trusted him.

One day when an enemy was about to attack the city — for in those days there always

他从邻国伊特鲁里亚人那里招募了一支军队，并率领着这支军队开始攻打罗马。

当时，在隔开伊特鲁里亚人和罗马城的台伯河上，有一座木桥。为了不让伊特鲁里亚人过河攻进城来，一位叫作贺雷修斯、曾经在为罗马而战斗的过程中失去了一只眼睛的罗马人，便下令将这座桥毁掉。

就在罗马人砍倒木桥的过程中，贺雷修斯和他的两个朋友站在木桥的那一端，与整支伊特鲁里亚大军战斗。当木桥在罗马士兵的全力猛击下开始破裂后，贺雷修斯便命令他的那两位朋友赶紧趁着桥还没垮的时候跑过桥去。

然后，贺雷修斯便孤身一人阻挡敌军，直到木桥最终垮塌，掉进河里。接下来，贺雷修斯纵身一跃，带着全副铠甲跳进河里，游向罗马城那边的河岸。尽管伊特鲁里亚军队射出的乱箭如雨点般地落在他的四周，尽管身上沉重的铠甲让他的身子不住地往下沉，但他最终还是安全地游到了对岸。虽然彼此是敌人，但伊特鲁里亚人也叹服他的勇猛，都大声为他欢呼。

后来，有人还写了一首非常著名的诗歌，叫作《桥头的贺雷修斯》，描述了他的这一英勇事迹。

贺雷修斯去世几年之后，罗马又出了一个名叫辛辛纳图斯的人物。他原本只是一个农民，在台伯河岸边有一个小小的农庄；可他非常聪明、善良，罗马城里的人都尊重他、信任他。

有一天，当一支敌军正准备攻打罗马时，罗马人必须选出一位领袖和将军来；在那个时候，似乎到处都有敌人，而敌人也似乎总有各种各样的借口来攻打罗马。

seemed to be enemies everywhere ready to attack Rome on any excuse — the people had to have a leader and a general. They thought of Cincinnatus and went and asked him to be dictator.

Now, a dictator was the name they gave to a man who in a case of sudden danger was called upon to command the army and in fact all the people during the time of the danger. Cincinnatus left his plow, went with the people to the city, got together an army, went out and defeated the enemy, and returned to Rome, all in twenty-four hours!

The people were so much pleased with the quick and decisive way in which Cincinnatus had saved Rome that they wanted him to keep right on being their general in time of peace. Even though they hated kings so much, they would have made him king if he would have accepted.

But Cincinnatus did not want any such thing. His duty done, he wanted to return to his wife and humble home and his little farm. In spite of what many would have thought a wonderful chance, he did go back to his plow, choosing to be just a simple farmer instead of being king.

The city of Cincinnati in Ohio is named after a society which was founded in honor of this old Roman, who lived nearly five hundred years before Christ.

罗马人想到了辛辛纳图斯，便请他来担任独裁官。

注意，"独裁官"是罗马人在紧急情况下推举一个人出来，并且要求这个人指挥军队，实际上是在这一危险时期内指挥罗马全国民众时，给这个人所加的头衔。于是，辛辛纳图斯放下了自己的铧犁，跟着人们进入罗马城，召集起了一支军队，出城打败了敌人，然后又返回了罗马；这一切，全都是在24个小时里做到的呢！

对于辛辛纳图斯如此迅捷、如此果断地挽救了罗马，古罗马的民众都非常满意，于是他们希望辛辛纳图斯在和平时期能够继续担任他们的将军。尽管罗马人都非常憎恶国王，但要是辛辛纳图斯答应的话，他们也情愿拥立他为国王。

可辛辛纳图斯根本不想要这些东西。完成了自己的使命之后，他便想要回到妻子身边，回到他那个简陋的家和小小的农庄里去。尽管许多人会觉得这是一个千载难逢的机会，可他却决定做一位普通的农民，而不去做国王，因而解甲归田了。

美国俄亥俄州的辛辛纳提市，就是根据一个社团的名称而命名的；而那个社团，则为了纪念辛辛纳图斯这位生活在公元前500年左右的古罗马人而成立的。

24 Greece vs. Persia

Do you know what those two little letters vs. mean between Greece and Persia in the name of this story?

Perhaps you have seen them used on football tickets when there was to be a match between two teams as, for example, Harvard vs. Yale.

They stand for *versus*, which means *against*.

Well, there was to be a great match between Greece and Persia, but it wasn't a game; it was a fight for life and death, a fight between little Greece and great big Persia.

Cyrus, the great Persian king, had conquered Babylon and other countries, as well, and he had kept on conquering until Persia ruled most of the world, all except Greece and Italy.

About the year 500 B.C. the new ruler of this vast Persian Empire was a man named Darius. Darius looked at the map, as you might do, and saw that he owned and ruled over a large part of it. What a pity, thought he, that there should be a little country like Greece that did not belong to him!

Darius said to himself, "I must have this piece of land called Greece to complete my

24　希腊对波斯

这个故事的标题中，你们知道"希腊"与"波斯"之间的那个"对"字的意思吗？

也许你们曾经见到这个字用于两支橄榄球队进行比赛的门票上；比如说，"哈佛大学队对耶鲁大学队"。

它指的是"较量"，也就是"对抗"的意思。

好吧，希腊和波斯两国之间将会进行一场重大的比赛；但这并不是一场运动比赛，而是一场生死较量，是一场发生在小小的希腊与强大广袤的波斯之间的战争。

居鲁士这位伟大的波斯国王已经征服了巴比伦及其他一些国家，并且此后一直都在继续征伐，直到最后，波斯统治了世界上除希腊和意大利以外的大部分地区。

公元前500年左右，统治着这个广袤的波斯帝国的新一任君主，是一个叫作大流士的人。像你们可能会做的那样，大流士没准看了看地图，发现自己拥有和统治着地图上的大部分地区。他想：遗憾的是，竟然还有希腊这样一个小小国家没有归入我的治下！

大流士便对自己说："我必须占领这个叫作希腊的地方，让我的帝国版图变得完整起来。"除此之外，希腊人也给他带来了一些麻烦。他们曾经协助大流士的一

empire." Besides, the Greeks had given him some trouble. They had helped some of his subjects to rebel against him. Darius said, "I must punish these Greeks for what they have done and then just add their country to mine."

He called his son-in-law and told him to go over to Greece and conquer it.

His son-in-law did as he was told and started out with a fleet and an army to do the punishing. But before his fleet could reach Greece it was destroyed by a storm, and he had to go back home without having done anything.

Darius was very angry at this, mad with his son-in-law and mad with the gods who he thought had wrecked his ships, and he made up his mind that he himself would go and do the punishing and conquering the next time.

First, however, he sent his messengers to all the Greek cities and ordered each of them to send him some earth and some water as a sign that they would give him their land and become his subjects peaceably without a fight.

Many Greek cities were so frightened by the threat of Darius and by his mighty power that they gave in at once and sent earth and water as they were told to do.

But little Athens and little Sparta both hotly refused to do so, in spite of the fact that they were only two small cities against the vast empire of Darius.

Athens took Darius's messenger and threw him into a well, saying, "There is earth and water for you; help yourself"; and Sparta did likewise. Then these two cities joined their forces and called on all their neighbors to join with them to fight for their native land

些属国起兵造反。大流士说："我一定要惩罚这些希腊人，让他们为自己的行为付出代价，然后再将他们的国家并入我的帝国版图。"

于是，他招来自己的女婿，命令他率军前往希腊，去征服该国。

他的女婿便奉命行事，率领一支舰队和一支军队出发前去征服希腊。可是，还没等他到达希腊，一场暴风雨便将他的舰队打了个七零八落，所以他只能一事无成地返回了波斯。

对此，大流士极其震怒；他对自己的女婿大发雷霆，还痛斥众神，因为他觉得是这些神灵毁掉了他的战舰。然后，他决心下一次进行亲征，要亲自去惩罚和征服希腊。

然而，他先是派遣使者前往希腊的各个城邦，命令它们各自献出一点儿土和水，以此来表明它们愿意把土地献给他，和平地变成他的臣民而不用他大动干戈。

大流士的恐吓和强势，让希腊的许多城邦都感到害怕，因此它们纷纷遵命，马上派人向大流士献出了土和水。

可小小的雅典和小小的斯巴达这两个城邦，却坚决拒绝这样做，只有它们这两个小小的城邦与大流士那个广袤的帝国对着干。

雅典人抓住大流士的使者，将他扔进了一口水井里，并说："下面就有土和水，您自己取吧。"而斯巴达人的做法也差不多。然后，这两个城邦又将军队联合起来，并且呼吁它们的邻邦也与之联合起来，为保卫祖国而与大流士及波斯帝国战斗。

against Darius and Persia.

Darius made ready to conquer Athens and then Sparta.

In order to reach Athens his army had to be carried across the sea in boats. Of course, in those days there were no steamboats. Steamboats were invented nearly two thousand years later.

The only way to make a boat go was with sails or with oars. To make a large boat move with oars, it was necessary to have a great many rowers — three rows one above the other on each side of the boat.

Such a boat was called a trireme, which means three rows of oars. It took about 600 of these boats to carry Darius's army over to Greece. Each of these 600 boats carried, besides the rowers or crew, about 200 soldiers. You can see for yourself how many soldiers Darius had in this army, if there were 600 shiploads of them and 200 soldiers on each ship. Yes, that is an example in multiplication — 120,000 soldiers — that's right.

The Persians sailed across the sea; and this time there was no storm, and they reached the shore of Greece safely. They landed on a spot called the plain of Marathon, which was only about twenty-six miles away from Athens. You will see presently why I have told you just the number of miles — twenty-six.

When the Athenians heard that the Persians were

A trireme
三列桨座战船

大流士准备先征服雅典，然后再去攻取斯巴达。

要想到达雅典，他手下的大军必须先坐船过海。在那个时候，世界上当然还没有轮船。差不多要到两千年之后，轮船才发明出来哩。

唯一能够让一条船前进的办法，便是给船只装上船帆或者船桨。而要想用船桨划动一艘大型船只的话，则需要很多很多的桨手：船的上下三层，每层的每一边都各需三排桨手。

这种船只，便叫作"三列桨座战船"，意思就是指船的每一边都有三排船桨。大流士的军队需要六百艘左右这样的战船，才能渡海前往希腊。除了桨手或者说船员之外，这六百艘战船的每一艘上大约可坐二百名士兵。这样，你们自己就可以算一算，要是每艘战船上有二百名士兵、总共有六百艘战船的话，大流士这支军队究竟有多少兵力了。没错，这是一道乘法练习题：一共是十二万名士兵，那就对了。

于是，波斯人便渡海进击了；这一次，海上没起风暴，所以他们都安然无恙地到达了希腊海岸。他们在一个叫作马拉松平原的地方登陆，这里距雅典只有26英里左右。你们马上就会明白，我为什么会正儿八经地跟你们说起这段距离的准确数字，即26英里。

得知波斯大军正在前来的消息之后，雅典人希望斯巴达人能够信守承诺，马上

coming, they wanted to get Sparta to help in a hurry, as she had promised to do.

Now, there were no telegraphs or telephones or railroads, of course, in those days. There was no way in which they could send a message to Sparta except to have it carried by hand.

They called on a famous runner named Pheidippides to carry the message. Pheidippides started out and ran the whole way from Athens to Sparta, about one hundred and fifty miles, to carry the message. He ran night and day, hardly stopping at all to rest or to eat, and on the second day he was in Sparta.

The Spartans, however, sent back word that they couldn't start just then; the moon wasn't full, and it was bad luck to start when the moon wasn't full, as nowadays some superstitious people think it bad luck to start on a trip on Friday. They said they would come after a while, when the moon was full.

The Athenians couldn't wait for the moon. They knew the Persians would be in Athens before then, and they didn't want them to get as far as that.

So all the fighting men in Athens left their city and went forth to meet the Persians on the plain of Marathon — twenty-six miles away.

The Athenians were led by a man named Miltiades, and there were only ten thousand soldiers. Besides these, there were one thousand more from a little nearby town, which was friendly with Athens and wished to stand by her — eleven thousand in all. If you figure it out, you will see that there were perhaps ten times as many Persians as there were

赶来支援。

注意，那个时候世界上当然也还没有电报、电话或铁路之类的通讯、交通设施。除了派人前往，他们就没有办法把信息传达给斯巴达人。

于是，雅典人便让一个叫作斐力庇第斯的著名长跑运动员去送信。斐力庇第斯马上动身，带着情报从雅典一直跑到斯巴达，两地之间相距大约一百五十英里。他日夜兼程地跑着，途中既没有停下来休息，也没有吃东西，第二天便赶到了斯巴达。

然而，斯巴达人却回话说，他们那时还没法马上动身前去支援；因为当时月亮还没有盈满，而他们认为，在月亮不圆的时候出发，是会招来霉运的；这种观念，与如今一些迷信的人认为在星期五动身出行会招来霉运的观念是一样的。

雅典人可等不及月亮变圆了。他们知道，波斯大军在月圆之前就会兵临雅典城下，而雅典人则不希望波斯大军长驱直入。

于是，雅典的士兵便倾巢行动起来，出城而去，前往26英里之外的马拉松平原，去迎击波斯大军。

雅典军队的将领是一个叫作米太亚德的人，他们的兵力只有一万人。除此之外，还有附近一些小城邦拼凑起来的一千多兵力；这些小城邦都与雅典交好，希望与雅典并肩战斗。所以，雅典这一方的总兵力就是一万一千人。要是算一算的话，你们就会看出，波斯兵力差不多是希腊兵力的十倍；也就是说，有十名波斯士兵来对付一名希腊士兵呢。

Greeks, ten Persian soldiers to one Greek soldier.

The Greeks, however, were trained athletes, as we know, and their whole manner of life made them physically fit. The Persians were no match for them. In spite of the small number of Greeks, the large number of Persians were beaten, and beaten badly. Of course the Greeks were far better soldiers than the Persians, for all their training made them so, but more than all this, they were fighting for themselves to save their homes and their families.

Perhaps you have heard the fable of the hound who was chasing a hare. The hare escaped. The hound was made fun of for not catching the little hare. To which the hound replied, "I was only running for my supper; the hare was running for his life."

The Persian soldiers were not fighting for their homes or families, which were away back across the sea; and it made little difference to them who won, anyway, for most were merely hirelings or slaves; they were fighting for a king because he ordered them to.

Naturally the Greeks were overjoyed at this victory.

Pheidippides, the famous runner, who was now at Marathon, started off at once

The first marathon race
第一届马拉松长跑比赛

然而我们知道，希腊人都是训练有素的运动健将，而他们那种健康的生活方式，也使得他们的体格都非常强健。波斯人在这方面根本比不上他们。因此，尽管希腊人兵力少，但兵力众多的波斯大军却被打败了，而且是被打得一败涂地。希腊的军队当然要比波斯大军优秀得多，这是因为所受的训练使得他们一个个都成了优秀的战士；但除此之外，他们还是为自己而战，为挽救自己的家园和家人而战。

你们或许听说过一则寓言，说的是一头猎犬追逐一只野兔的故事。野兔最终逃脱了。猎犬则因为逮不住一只小小的野兔而受到了嘲笑。对此，猎犬回答道："我只是为了自己的晚饭而追击，可野兔却是为了性命而逃跑哩。"

波斯士兵并不是为了他们的家园和家人而战，因为他们的家人和家园都远在身后大海的那一边；而且，哪一方获胜对他们来说也没有太大的分别，因为波斯大军中的大多数人都只是雇佣兵或者奴隶。他们只是听从国王的命令，为那位国王而战罢了。

自然，希腊人都为这次胜利而感到欢欣鼓舞。

此时正在马拉松平原上的那位斐力庇第斯便马上动身，跑回26英里之外的雅典

to carry the joyful news back to Athens, twenty-six miles away. He ran the whole distance without stopping for breath. He had not had time to rest up from his long run to Sparta, which he had taken only a few days before, and so fast did he run this long distance that as soon as he had reached Athens and gasped the news to the Athenians in the marketplace he dropped down dead!

In honor of this famous run, they have nowadays in the new Olympic Games, what is called a Marathon race, in which the athletes run this same distance: twenty-six miles. This battle of Marathon took place in 490 B.C. and is one of the most famous battles in all history, for the great Persian army was beaten by one little city and its neighbor, and the Persians had to go back to their homes in disgrace.

A little handful of people, who governed themselves, had defeated a great king with a large army of only hired soldiers or slaves.

But this was not the last the Greeks were to see of the Persians.

城，去报告这一喜讯。他一口气跑完了全程，途中根本就没有停歇。几天之前，他刚刚长距离跑到斯巴达，之后也来不及充分休息；而这一次长跑时，他的速度又很快，所以他一回到雅典，在市场上气喘吁吁地将喜讯告诉了雅典人之后，马上便倒在地上死去了！

为了纪念马拉松战争的胜利和表彰斐力庇第斯的功绩，人们如今在新的奥林匹克运动会里加入了一个叫作马拉松赛跑的项目；参赛运动员所跑的距离，与斐力庇第斯所跑的距离相同，都是26英里。这场马拉松之战，发生在公元前490年；因为一个小小的城邦联合其邻国打败了强大的波斯军队，让波斯人不得不灰溜溜地滚回老家去，所以此战也成了世界历史上最有名的战事之一。

一群自行治国、数量不多的希腊人，打败了大流士这位率领着一支由雇佣兵或奴隶所组成的大军的伟大国王。

但是，这并不是希腊人与波斯人之间的最后一战。

25 Fighting Mad

Darius was now angrier than ever, and still more determined to whip those stubborn Greeks, who dared to defy him and his enormous power; and he began to get ready for one more attempt. This time, however, he made up his mind that he would get together such an army and navy that there would be no chance in the world against it, and he made a solemn oath to destroy the Greeks. So for several years he gathered troops and supplies, but something happened, and in spite of his oath he did not carry out his plan. Why? You guessed it. He died.

But Darius had a son named Xerxes — pronounced as if it began with a Z.

When I was a boy, there was an alphabet rhyme that began, "A is for Apple," and went on down to "X is for Xerxes, a great Persian king." I learned the rhyme, though I did not know at that time anything about either Xerxes or Persia.

Xerxes was just as determined as his father had been that the Greeks must be beaten, so he went on getting ready.

However, the Greeks also were just as determined that they must not be beaten, so they, too, went on getting ready, for they knew the Persians would sooner or later come back

25　战争狂人

此时，大流士比以前更加恼火，而彻底打败那些顽固不化的希腊人的想法也更加坚定了，因为那些希腊人竟然胆敢藐视他和他的巨大权威；于是，他便开始再次备战。然而，这一次他却下定决心，要组建一支世界上无人能敌的陆军和海军，还庄严地发下誓言，要彻底消灭希腊人。因此，在好几年里，他都一直在招募人马、筹集给养；可后来发生了一件事情，使得他尽管发过誓，却还是没有实现自己的计划。为什么呢？你们猜猜看吧。原来，他死掉啦。

不过，大流士有一个儿子，叫作薛西斯；这个名字，在英文里的发音就像是以字母Z开头似的。

我小的时候，曾经学过一首记忆字母表的儿歌，其中第一句是"A代表苹果（Apple）"，一直往下，直到"X指薛西斯（Xerxes），伟大的波斯王"。虽然记住了这首儿歌，但那时我对这个薛西斯或者波斯的情况，却一无所知。

薛西斯与他过世的父亲一样，决心打败希腊，所以他继续备战。

然而，希腊人也同样下定了决不能被波斯打败的决心，也在积极备战；因为他们都知道，波斯人早晚还会回来，再次攻打希腊的。

当时，雅典有两个重要的人物，并且两人都想要成为雅典的领袖。其中一人叫

and try again.

At this time there were two chief men in Athens, and each was trying to be leader. One was named Themistocles — pronounced *The MIS to kleez* — and the other Aristides — pronounced *Ar is Tl deez*. Notice how many Greek names seem to end in the letters es.

Themistocles urged the Athenians to get ready for what he knew was coming, the next war with Persia. Especially did he urge the Athenians to build a fleet of boats, for they had no boats and the Persians had a great many.

Aristides, on the other hand, didn't believe in Themistocles's scheme to build boats. He thought it a foolish expense and talked against it.

Aristides had always been so wise and fair that people called him Aristides the Just. Even so, some people wanted to get rid of him, because they thought he was wrong about building a fleet of boats and Themistocles was right. They waited till the time came to vote, when they could ostracize anyone they wanted to get rid of. Do you remember who started this custom? Cleisthenes — about 500 B.C.

When the day for voting came, a man who could not write and did not know Aristides by sight happened to ask his help in voting. Aristides inquired what name he should write, and the man replied, "Aristides."

Aristides did not tell who he was, but merely said:

"Why do you want to get rid of this man? Has he done anything wrong?"

"Oh, no," the voter replied. "He hasn't done anything wrong," but with a long sigh he

作地米斯托克利斯[1]，地—米斯—托—克利斯；另一个人叫亚里斯泰迪斯，亚—里斯—泰—迪斯。注意，希腊人名字中用"斯"字结尾的，可真不少呢。

地米斯托克利斯敦促雅典人做好准备，因为他明白，他们与波斯人的下一场战争即将到来。他尤其坚持让雅典人组建一支船队，因为当时他们没有战船，而波斯军队却拥有大量的船只。

而另一方面，亚里斯泰迪斯却并不赞同地米斯托克利斯建造船只的计划。他认为这是一种浪费钱财的愚蠢做法，因此反对这样做。

由于一向聪明、公允，因此人们都称亚里斯泰迪斯为"亚青天"。但即便如此，还是有一些人想要除掉他，因为那些人觉得，他在建造船队这一问题上的观念是错误的，而地米斯托克利斯的想法是对的。于是他们便等着投票日的到来；到了那时，他们就可以根据"陶片流放法"，来放逐任何一个他们想要除掉的人了。你们还记得是谁创立了这种方法吗？是公元前500年左右的克里斯提尼啊。

到了投票日，碰巧有一个不会写字、也不认识亚里斯泰迪斯的人，要亚里斯泰迪斯帮他投票。亚里斯泰迪斯问他要写谁的名字，那个人回答说："写亚里斯泰迪斯。"

亚里斯泰迪斯并没有向那人表明自己的身份，只是说：

---

[1] 地米斯托克利斯（Themistocles），多译成"地米斯托克利"，因为它词尾的"（e）s"的发音非常轻。本书之所以将其译成"地米斯托克利斯"，是为了配合下文中说的希腊人名多"斯"字的说法。同样，对于下文中的"亚里斯泰迪斯"，我们通常也都是音译为"亚里斯泰迪"。

said, "I'm so tired of hearing him always called *The Just*."

Aristides must have been surprised by this unreasonable answer, but nevertheless he wrote his own name for the voter, and when the votes were counted, there were so many that he was ostracized.

Though it did not seem quite fair that Aristides should be ostracized, it was fortunate, as it turned out, that Themistocles had his way, and it was fortunate the Athenians went on preparing for war.

They built a fleet of triremes. Then they got all the cities and towns in Greece to agree to join forces in case of war. Sparta, on account of its fame as a city of soldiers, was made the leader of all the others in case war should come.

And then, just ten years after the battle of Marathon in 490 B.C. the great Persian army was again ready to attack Greece. It had been brought together from all parts of the vast Persian Empire and was far bigger than the former army with its 120,000 men, although that was a large army for those days.

This time the army is supposed to have consisted of over two million soldiers — two million; just think of that! The question then was how to get so many soldiers over to Greece. Such a multitude could not be carried across to Greece in boats, for even the largest triremes only held a few hundred men, and it would have taken — well, can you tell how many boats, to carry over two million? Probably many more triremes than there were in the whole world at that time. Xerxes decided to have his army march to Greece,

　　"您为什么想要放逐这个人呢？是因为他干了什么坏事吗？"

　　"哦，不是的，"那人回答道，"他没有干任何坏事。"长叹了一声后，那人又说："我只是因为总是听人叫他'青天'，听得烦了。"

　　听到这样不可理喻的回答，亚里斯泰迪斯当时一定很惊讶；可尽管如此，他还是帮那人在陶片上写下了自己的名字。经过计票之后，要求放逐他的票数很多，于是他便被流放了。

　　虽然流放亚里斯泰迪斯显得不那么公平，但后来却表明，幸好地米斯托克利斯按照自己的计划行事，也幸亏雅典人积极进行了备战呢。

　　他们建造了一支由三列桨座战船组成的船队。然后，他们又说服了希腊的所有城邦和小市镇，让它们全都同意在爆发战争的时候将军队联合起来作战。由于拥有"战士之城"的美名，所以斯巴达被推选为战时所有城邦的领袖。

　　接下来，在公元前490年发生的马拉松之战恰好过去十年之后，强大的波斯军队再次准备攻打希腊了。这支军队，是由广袤的波斯帝国各地的军队集结而成的，规模远远超过了上一支兵力为十二万人的军队，尽管十二万兵力在当时也算是一支大军了。

　　这一次，波斯大军的兵力据说超过了两百万人；你们不妨想象一下，有两百万呢！当时的问题，就是怎样才能把这么多的士兵派往希腊。人数这么多，是不可能再乘坐船只渡海前往希腊的，因为就算是当时最大的三列桨座战船，也只能容纳几百人；而要把两百多万兵力送到海那边去的话，要用多少艘船只，你们能告诉我

the long way but the only way round. So they started.

Now, there is a strip of water called a strait, something like a wide river, right across the path the Persian army had to take. This strait was then called the Hellespont. It is, of course still there, but if you look on the map you will find it is now called the Dardanelles. There was no bridge across the Hellespont, for it was almost a mile wide, and they didn't have bridges as long as that in those days. Xerxes fastened boats together in a line that stretched from one shore to the other shore, and over these boats he built a floor to form a bridge so that his army could cross upon it.

Hardly had he finished building the bridge, however, when a storm arose and destroyed it. Xerxes, in anger at the waves, ordered that the water of the Hellespont be whipped as if it were an enemy or a slave he were punishing. Then he built another bridge, and this time the water behaved itself, and his soldiers were able to cross over safely.

So vast was Xerxes's army that it is said to have taken it seven days and seven nights marching continuously all the time in two long unbroken lines to get over to the opposite shore. Xerxes's fleet followed the army as closely as they could along the shore, and at last they reached the top of Greece. Down through the north of Greece the army came, overrunning everything before it, and it seemed as though nothing on earth could stop such numbers of men.

吗？很可能比当时整个世界上所有三列桨座战船加起来的总数还要多得多呢。因此，薛西斯决定让军队经由陆地，行军前往希腊；虽说路途遥远，但这是唯一可行的办法。于是，波斯大军便开拔了。

注意，在波斯军队前往希腊的必经之路上，有一片狭窄的水域，叫作"海峡"，它有点儿像是一条宽阔的河流。这个海峡，当时叫作赫勒斯滂。当然，这个海峡如今仍然位于那里；不过，如果看一看地图，你们就会发现，如今它叫作"达达尼尔海峡"了。赫勒斯滂海峡上面没有桥梁，因为这个海峡差不多有一英里宽，当时的人还建造不出这么长的桥梁来。于是，薛西斯下令将战船联结起来，排成一列，从这边的海岸一直延伸到对岸；然后，他又令人在船上铺上木板，从而形成一座浮桥，好让波斯军队能够从上面越过海峡。

然而，他刚刚建好这座浮桥，海上便风雨大作，海浪将浮桥打了个七零八落。薛西斯迁怒于海浪，便下令鞭笞赫勒斯滂海峡里的海水，就像是在惩罚一名敌人或者奴隶似的。然后，他又搭建起了一座浮桥；这一次，海水平静得很，所以他手下的大军便安全地渡过了赫勒斯滂海峡。

据说，薛西斯所率的这支军队兵力实在是太庞大了，所以分成两列、连续行军，也用了七天七夜才全部渡过海去，到达对岸。薛西斯的船队则沿着海岸，尽可能地紧靠大军前进，最后终于到达了希腊的北端。然后，波斯大军便从希腊北部挥师向南，并且所向披靡、势如破竹，似乎世界上再也没有什么可以阻挡住这支如此庞大的军队了。

26 One Against a Thousand

There is a little narrow passageway with the mountains on one side and the water on the other through which the Persians had to go to reach Athens. This pass is called Thermopylae, and you might guess what Thermopylae means if you notice that the first part is like Thermos bottle, which means *hot* bottle. As a matter of fact, Thermopylae meant Hot Gateway and was so named because this natural gateway to Greece had hot springs near by.

The Greeks decided that it was best to stop the Persians at this gate — to go to meet them there first before they reached Athens. In such a place a few Greek soldiers could fight better against a much larger number.

It also seemed wise to send picked Greek troops to meet the Persians, the very best soldiers in Greece with the very bravest general to lead them.

The Spartan king, who was named Leonidas — which in Greek means like a lion — was chosen to go to Thermopylae, and with him seven thousand soldiers — seven thousand soldiers to block the way of two million Persians! Three hundred of these were Spartans, and a Spartan was taught that he must never surrender, never give up. A Spartan

26 以一敌千

波斯大军要想抵达雅典，就必须经过一条狭窄的羊肠小道；这条小路，一边是山，另一边则是水。这个山隘，叫作"塞莫皮莱"（Thermopylae）；假如注意到这个英文单词的前半部分和"热水瓶"（Thermos bottle）的前半部分有点儿相似（Thermos 指"热的"）的话，那你们就可以猜出"塞莫皮莱"（Thermopylae）的意思了。事实上，"塞莫皮莱"（Thermopylae）指"温泉关"；之所以叫这个名字，是因为这个通往希腊的天然关隘附近，有许多眼温泉。

希腊人认为，最好的办法莫过于在这个关隘阻击波斯大军；也就是说，在敌人兵临雅典城下之前，首先到温泉关去迎击敌人。在这样一个地方，少量的希腊士兵就可以更好地抗击为数众多的敌人。

派遣经过精心挑选出来的希腊士兵前去迎击波斯大军，派遣最勇猛的将领统帅希腊最精良的战士，这似乎也是一种很明智的做法。

当时，斯巴达的国王叫作列奥尼达，这个名字在希腊语里是"勇如雄狮"的意思；他被推选出来前往温泉关，而随同他出征的，是七千士兵：要用七千士兵，阻住两百万波斯大军的去路！这些士兵中，有三百名是斯巴达人，而斯巴达人接受的教导就是决不投降、决不放弃。一位斯巴达的母亲，曾经对自己的儿子这样说道：

mother used to say to her son:

"Come back *with* your shield or *on* it."

When Xerxes found his way blocked by this ridiculously small band of soldiers, he sent his messengers ordering them to surrender, to give themselves up.

What do you suppose Leonidas replied?

It was what we should expect a Spartan to answer, brief and to the point; that is, *laconic*. He said simply:

"Come and take us."

As there was nothing left for Xerxes to do but fight, he started his army forward.

For two days the Persians fought the Greeks, but Leonidas still held the pass, and the Persians were unable to get through.

Then a Greek traitor and coward, who thought he might save his own life and be given a rich prize by Xerxes, told that king of a secret path over the mountains by which he and his army might slip through and get around Leonidas and his soldiers who blocked the way.

The next morning Leonidas learned that the Persians had found the secret path and were already on the way to pen him in from behind. There was still a chance, however, for his men to escape, and Leonidas told all those who wanted to do so to leave. Those who remained knew that the fight was absolutely hopeless and that it meant certain death for all of them. In spite of this, however, one thousand men, including all the three hundred

"要么手持盾牌回来，要么就躺在盾牌上回来。"

薛西斯发现自己的去路被一支人数少得不可思议的军队阻住之后，便派使者前去命令对方投降。

你们觉得，列奥尼达会怎样回答呢？

不出我们所料，斯巴达人的回答既简短，又一针见血；也就是说，是一种"拉科尼亚式"的回答。他只是说了一句：

"来打败我们吧。"

薛西斯除了战斗便别无选择了；于是，他便令大军向前推进。

波斯军队与希腊军队战斗了两天，但列奥尼达却仍然死死地守住了这个关隘，使得波斯大军无法通过。

接下来，希腊人里出现了一个叛徒、一个胆小鬼；他以为叛变可以保住自己的性命，并且认为薛西斯还会给他一大笔赏金，因此便告诉薛西斯国王，他知道有一条翻山而过的秘道；薛西斯和他的大军可以偷偷翻过去，将挡住去路的列奥尼达及其手下的士兵包围起来歼灭。

第二天上午，列奥尼达得知了波斯军队已经发现那条秘道、并且已经从背后向他包抄过来了的消息。不过，当时他手下的士兵仍然还有逃脱的机会，因此列奥尼达便让那些想要逃走的士兵赶紧走。而那些留下来的人呢，他们全都清楚这场战斗毫无取胜的可能，并且这就意味着他们全都会战死疆场。但尽管如此，还是有一千人马留下来，其中就包括那三百名斯巴达勇士，他们都坚守在统帅的身边；他们

Spartans stood by their leader, for, said they:

"We have been ordered to hold the pass, and a Spartan obeys orders, and never surrenders, no matter what happens."

There Leonidas and his thousand men fought to the bitter end until all except one of their number was killed.

The gateway to the city of Athens was now open, and things looked very bleak for the Greeks, for there was nothing to prevent the Persians from marching over the dead bodies of Leonidas and his men straight on to Athens.

The Athenians, wondering what was to happen to them, hurriedly went to the oracle at Delphi and asked what they should do.

The oracle replied that the city of Athens itself was doomed, that it would be destroyed, there was no hope for it, but that the Athenians themselves would be saved by wooden walls.

This answer, as was usually the case in whatever the oracle said, was a riddle, the meaning of which seemed hard to solve. Themistocles, however, said that he knew the answer. You remember that it was he who had been working so hard to have a fleet of ships built. Themistocles said that the oracle meant these ships when it spoke of the wooden walls.

The Athenians, following the supposed advice of the oracle, left their city as Themistocles told them and went on board the ships, which were not far away, in a bay

说，自己这样做的原因是：

"我们接到的命令就是守住关隘；无论出现什么样的情况，斯巴达士兵都会服从命令，决不投降。"

列奥尼达和他手下那一千名勇士浴血奋战到了最后一刻；除了一个人，其他士兵全都英勇战死了。

这样，通往雅典城的这个关隘便畅通无阻了，而希腊的局势似乎也变得严峻起来；因为再也没有什么东西可以阻止波斯大军踏着列奥尼达及其手下的遗体，向着雅典城长驱直入了。

雅典人不知道会有什么样的命运降临到他们身上，便急急忙忙地跑到特尔斐神谕处，问他们该怎么办。

神谕回答说：雅典城本身在劫难逃，注定会被摧毁，没有任何保存下来的希望；但雅典人却会被木墙所拯救。

这个回答，与神谕通常所说的东西一样，也是个难解的谜题，它的意思似乎微妙得很。然而，地米斯托克利斯却说，他知道神谕的意思。你们都还记得吧，正是他，曾经力主希腊组建起一支船队。地米斯托克利斯说，神谕里面所说的木墙，就是指这些船只。

于是，雅典人便遵照神谕给出的、他们信以为真的建议，按照地米斯托克利斯的吩咐，弃城登船了；那些船只都离城不远，停靠在一个叫作萨拉米斯的海湾里。

波斯大军来到雅典后，发现它竟然成了一座空城。于是，他们到处放火，毁

called Salamis.

The Persian army reached Athens and found it deserted. They burned and destroyed the city as the oracle said. Then they marched on to the Bay of Salamis, where the Athenians were on board the ships. There, on a hill overlooking the bay, Xerxes had a throne built for himself so that he could sit, as if in a box at the theater looking at a play, and watch his own large fleet destroy the much smaller one of the Greeks with all the Athenians on board.

The Greek fleet was commanded, of course, by Themistocles. His ships were in this narrow bay or strait of water, somewhat in the same way that the soldiers of Leonidas had been in the narrow valley at Thermopylae.

Themistocles, seeing that the Bay of Salamis looked somewhat like the Pass of Thermopylae, had an idea. He made believe he was a traitor like the traitor at Thermopylae and sent word to Xerxes that if the Persian fleet divided and one half stayed at one end of the strait and the other half closed off the other end of the strait, the Greeks would be penned in between and caught as in a trap.

Xerxes thought this a good idea, so he gave orders to have his ships do as Themistocles had suggested. But Xerxes, sitting smiling on his throne, had the surprise of his life. The result was just the

Xerxes on his throne watching Battle of Salamis
薛西斯坐在御座上注视着萨拉米斯湾之战

掉了整座城市，就跟神谕所说的情形一样。然后，他们又向萨拉米斯湾进军，因为雅典人都躲在这个海湾里的船只上。在一座俯瞰着海湾的小山上，薛西斯命人修建了一把御座；这样，他就可以像是坐在戏院的包厢里看戏似的，坐在那里看着手下的大型舰队去消灭那支规模小得多，并且躲藏着全部希腊人的希腊舰队。

希腊舰队当然是由地米斯托克利斯指挥着。他把船只全都部署在那片狭窄的海湾或者海峡里，方法与列奥尼达将手下的士兵部署在温泉关那条狭窄的山谷之中有点儿类似。

看到萨拉米斯湾的地形与温泉关有点儿相似之后，地米斯托克利斯想出了一个主意。他假装自己是一个叛徒，就像温泉关的那个叛徒一样，然后派人去跟薛西斯说，如果波斯舰队分开来，一半守在海峡的一端，另一半则扼住海峡另一端的话，希腊人就会被夹在中间，成为瓮中之鳖。

薛西斯觉得这个主意不错，便下令舰队按照地米斯托克利斯所建议的那样调动部署。可是，坐在御座上面带笑容的薛西斯，后来却大大地吃了一惊。结果与他所

opposite of what he had expected. With the Persian fleet separated in two parts, the Greeks in between could fight both halves of the divided fleet separately, and the space was so narrow that the Persians' ships got in the way of each other and rammed and sank their own boats.

The Persian fleet was completely beaten, and the proud and boastful Xerxes, with most of his army and all the navy that was left, made a hasty retreat back to Persia the way they had come.

This was the last time the Persians ever tried to conquer little Greece.

If Themistocles had not had his way and built such a strong fleet, what do you think would have become of Athens and Greece!

想的情况正好相反。由于波斯舰队分成了两部分,因此位于中间的希腊舰队便可以分别进击两头的波斯舰队;又因为海面非常狭窄,所以波斯人的战船相互拥挤、碰撞,从而弄沉了很多己方的战船。

波斯舰队被彻底打垮了,而得意扬扬、自吹自擂的薛西斯便赶紧率领大部分陆军和剩下来的海军,急急忙忙地从原路逃回了波斯。

这就是波斯人最后一次企图征服弱小的希腊的经过。

假如地米斯托克利斯没有坚持按照自己的想法去做,没有组建起一支舰队,那么你们觉得,雅典和希腊又会落得个什么样的下场呢!

27 The Golden Age

When we were talking about the Stone Age and the Bronze Age, I told you that later we should also hear of a Golden Age.

Well, we have come to the Golden Age now. This doesn't mean that people at this time used things made of gold, nor that they had a great deal of gold money. It means — well, let us see what sort of a time it was, and then you can tell what it means.

After the wars with Persia, Athens seemed to have been cheered up by her victory to do wonderful things, and the next fifty years after the Persians were driven out of Greece — that is, 480 to 430 B.C. — were the most wonderful years in the history of Greece, and perhaps the most wonderful years in the history of Europe.

Athens had been burned down by Xerxes. At the time it happened this seemed like a terrible misfortune. But it wasn't. The people set to work and built a much finer and much more beautiful city than the old one had been.

Now, the chief person in Athens at this time was a man named Pericles. He was not a king nor a ruler, but he was so very wise and such a wonderful speaker and such a popular leader that he was able to make the Athenians do as he thought best. He was like

27 黄金时代

前面说到"石器时代"和"青铜器时代"的时候，我曾经跟你们说过，日后我们还会听到一个黄金时代的。

那么，现在我们就来说一说这个黄金时代。所谓的"黄金时代"，并不是说生活在那个时代的人使用的都是用黄金制成的东西，也不是说他们拥有很多的金币。它的意思是——好吧，我们先来看一看这究竟是一个什么样的时代，然后你们就可以说出它的意思了。

与波斯的那几场战争结束之后，雅典人似乎一直都为自己获得的胜利所鼓舞，从而干出了种种了不起的大事；因此，从波斯人被赶出希腊之后起的那五十年，即从公元前480年至公元前430年，就是希腊历史上最精彩的五十年，或许也是欧洲历史上最辉煌的一个时期。

当时，雅典已经被薛西斯烧成了一片焦土。雅典刚被焚毁的时候，看上去真是一场可怕的灾难。但其实不是。因为随后雅典人便开始动手，兴建起了一座比原来更加精致，也要美丽得多的城市。

此时，雅典的主要人物是一个叫作伯里克利的人。虽说他既不是国王，也不是统治者，但他极其聪明睿智，极其擅长演说，也是一个深受爱戴的领导人，因此他

the popular captain of a football or soccer team who is a fine player himself and makes fine players of all the others on his team. Athens was his team, and he trained it so well that all the players were tops in their positions. Some people became great artists. Some people became great writers. Others still became great *philosophers*. Do you know what philosophers are? They are wise men and women who know a great deal and love knowledge.

The artists built many beautiful buildings, theaters, and temples. They made wonderful statues of the Greek gods and goddesses and placed them on the buildings and about the city.

The philosophers taught the people how to be wise and good.

The writers composed fine poems and plays. The plays were not like those we have nowadays but were all about the doings of the gods and goddesses.

The theaters were not like those we have nowadays, either. They were always out of doors, usually on the side of a hill, where a grandstand could be built facing the stage. There was little or no scenery, and instead of an orchestra of musicians, there was a chorus of singers to accompany the actors. The actors wore false faces or masks to show what their feelings were, a *comic* mask with a grinning face when they wanted to be funny and a *tragic* mask with a sorrowful face when they wanted to seem sad.

Perhaps you have seen pictures of these masks, for in the decorations of our own theaters these same comic and tragic masks are sometimes used.

能够让雅典人去做他认为最好的事情。他就像是一位广受欢迎的橄榄球队队长或足球队队长，自己既是一名优秀的球员，也让手下的其他队员成了优秀的球员。雅典就是他的球队，而他将球队训练得如此完美，因此所有球员都成了各个位置上的佼佼者。有些人变成了伟大的艺术家。有些人变成了伟大的作家。还有一些人，则变成了伟大的哲学家。你们知道什么是哲学家吗？哲学家都是一些有智慧、懂得很多知识并且热爱知识的人。

那些艺术家建造了许多美丽的楼房、剧院和庙宇。他们雕刻了希腊众神的美妙雕像，并将这些雕像放置在建筑上，或者布置在城市的四周。

那些哲学家教导人们如何变得聪明睿智和善良。

那些作家则创作出了许多精美的诗歌和戏剧。那时的戏剧并不像我们今天所看的戏剧，它们演的全都是一些与众神相关的故事。

而那时的剧院，也与我们如今的剧院不一样。那时的剧院总是露天的，通常设在山坡上，因为在山坡上可以修建一个朝着舞台的大看台。当时的戏剧很少或者说根本就没有什么舞台布景，并且没有乐队，而是由一帮歌手一起给演员伴唱。演员们都戴着表示喜怒哀乐等情感的假面具；想要表达滑稽可笑的时候，他们就戴咧嘴而笑的"喜剧"面具，而想要表现悲伤的时候，他们则戴上表情悲痛忧伤的"悲剧"面具。

Tragic and comic masks
悲剧面具和喜剧面具

Athens had been named after the goddess Athena, who was supposed to watch out for and look after the city. The Athenians thought she should have a special temple. Accordingly, they built one to her on the top of a hill called the Acropolis. This temple they called in her honor the Parthenon, meaning the *maiden*, one of the names by which she was known.

The Parthenon is considered by some people to be the most beautiful building in the world, although as you see by the picture, as it is today, it is now in ruins. In the center of this temple was a huge statue of Athena made of gold and ivory by a sculptor named Phidias. We are told that it was the most beautiful statue in the world as the Parthenon was the most beautiful building, but it has completely disappeared, and no one knows what became of it. One might guess, however, that the gold and ivory tempted thieves, who may have stolen it piece by piece.

Phidias made many other statues on the outside of the Parthenon, but most of these have been carried away and put in museums or have been lost or destroyed.

This statue of Athena and the other sculptures on the Parthenon made Phidias so famous that he

The Parthenon
巴台农神殿

没准你们都看到过这种面具的图片呢；因为在如今的剧院里，我们有时也会用到这种喜剧面具或者悲剧面具。

雅典是以雅典娜女神的名字命名的，因为人们认为，雅典娜是雅典城的守护神。雅典人觉得，雅典娜应当有一座特别的神庙才是。于是，他们便在一座叫作"阿克罗波利斯"[1]的小山丘上，为雅典娜修建了一座神庙。为了向雅典娜致敬，他们将这座神庙叫作"巴台农神殿"；"巴台农"的意思就是"少女"，而"少女"也是人们对雅典娜的称呼之一呢。

有些人认为，巴台农神殿是世界上最漂亮的一座建筑；但如今你们在这张照片上看到的，却是已经严重受损了的巴台农神殿。这座神庙的中央，矗立着一尊巨大的雅典娜雕像；这是由一个叫作菲狄亚斯的雕刻家，用黄金与象牙制作而成的。据说巴台农神庙是世界上最漂亮的建筑之一，而这尊雅典娜雕像，则是世界上最美丽的一座雕像呢；不过，这尊雕像已经彻底消失了，并且没人知道它是怎么消失的。不过，有人可能会猜想，没准是雕像上的黄金和象牙招来了窃贼，将它一点一点地偷走了。

菲狄亚斯还在巴台农神殿的外面雕刻出了许多雕像，但其中的绝大部分如今要

---

[1] 阿克罗波利斯（Acropolis），原是雅典的一个山丘城邦。如今，人们将这座山丘以及上面的神庙统称"雅典卫城"，即守卫雅典的雅典娜女神所居的地方。

was asked to make a statue of Zeus to be placed at Olympia, where the Olympic Games were held. The statue of Zeus was finer even than the one he had made of Athena and was so splendid that it was called one of the Seven Wonders of the World. You remember the pyramids of Egypt and the Hanging Gardens of Babylon were two others of the Seven Wonders. It is interesting that each of these three Wonders was located in a different continent. Can you tell which was in Africa, which in Asia, and which in Europe?

Phidias has been called the greatest sculptor who ever lived, but he did a thing which the Greeks considered a crime and would not forgive. We do not see anything so terribly wrong in what he did, but the Greeks' idea of right and wrong was different from ours. This is what he did. On the shield of the statue of Athena that he had made, Phidias carved a picture of himself and also one of his friend Pericles. It was merely a part of the decoration of the shield, and hardly anyone would have noticed it. But according to the Greek notion, it was a sacrilege to make a picture of a human being on a statue of a goddess. When the Athenians found out what Phidias had done, they threw him into prison, and there he died.

The Greeks used different kinds of columns on their buildings, and these columns are used in many public and in some private buildings today. I'll tell you what each kind is like; then see how many you can find.

The Parthenon was built in a style called *Doric*.

The top of the column is called the capital, and the capital of the Doric column is

么被挪进了博物馆，要么丢失了，要么便是毁坏了。

这尊雕像，以及巴台农神殿里的其他雕塑作品，使得菲狄亚斯名声大噪；于是，人们又请他制作了一尊宙斯的雕像，安放在举办奥林匹克运动会的奥林匹亚山上。这尊宙斯神像，比他雕刻的雅典娜神像还要精美，并且极其宏伟壮观，因此被人们称为世界七大奇迹之一。你们都还记得古埃及的金字塔和古巴比伦的"空中花园"也各是七大奇迹之一吧。有意思的是，这三大奇迹分别处于三个不同的大洲呢。你们能说出其中哪处奇迹位于非洲、哪处奇迹位于亚洲、而哪处奇迹又位于欧洲吗？

虽然菲狄亚斯被人们称为有史以来最伟大的雕塑家，可他却干了一件事情，并且被希腊人认为是一种不可饶恕的罪行。他做的那件事情究竟有什么严重的过错，我们并不明白，因为希腊人的是非观念与我们的并不相同。他干了什么呢？原来，在那尊雅典娜神像手持的盾牌上，菲狄亚斯刻上了自己的肖像，还把朋友伯里克利的像也刻了上去。那不过是盾牌上的一点儿装饰罢了，几乎没有人会注意到。可在希腊人看来，把凡人的形象刻在一尊女神的雕像上，是一种亵渎神灵的行为。于是，雅典人在发现了菲狄亚斯的所作所为之后，便把他关进了监狱；最后，菲狄亚斯便死在了监狱里。

古希腊人在建筑中，经常使用不同种类的圆柱；而这些圆柱，如今也经常用在许多的公共建筑和一些私人建筑上。我会跟你们说说每一种圆柱的样子，再来看一看你们能够找出多少种圆柱来。

巴台农神殿所用圆柱的风格，叫作"多利克式"。

圆柱的顶端，叫作"柱顶"；而多利克式圆柱的柱顶，样子就像是一个顶上罩

shaped like a saucer with a square cover on top of it. There was no base or block at the bottom of the column. It rested directly on the floor. As the Doric column is so plain and strong-looking, it was called the man's style.

The second style is called *Ionic*.

The capital of the Ionic column has a base, and the capital has ornaments like curls underneath the square top, and the column has a base.

As this column is more slender and more ornamental than the Doric, it was called the woman's style.

The third style is called *Corinthian*.

The capital of the Corinthian column is higher than either of the other two and still more ornamental. It is said that the architect who first made this column got his idea for its capital from seeing a basketful of toys that had been placed on a child's grave as was the custom instead of flowers. The basket had been covered with a slab, and the leaves of the thistle called the acanthus had grown up around the basket. It looked so pretty that the architect thought it would make a beautiful capital for a column, and so he copied it.

I asked some boys which one could find the most columns. The next day one boy said he had

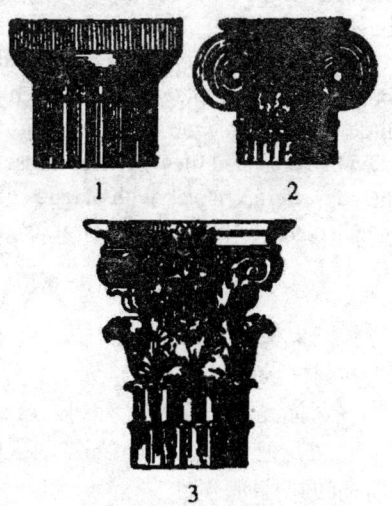

1. Doric 2. Ionic 3. Corinthian
1. 多利克式柱头 2. 爱奥尼亚式柱头
3. 科林斯式柱头

着正方体的盘子。这种圆柱的底部没有基座或者垫石，是直接立在地面上的。由于多利克式圆柱非常朴实，又很牢固，因此人们说它是一种具有男子汉气概的阳刚风格。

第二种圆柱的风格，叫作"爱奥尼亚式"。

爱奥尼亚式圆柱的柱顶有一个基座，而这个方形基座下的柱顶有像卷发那样的装饰，并且整个柱体之下还有基座。

由于这种圆柱比多利克式圆柱更加细长、装饰也更多，因此人们说它是一种具有女性之美的阴柔风格。

第三种圆柱的风格，叫作"科林斯式"。

科林斯式圆柱的柱顶，比其他两种风格的圆柱柱顶都要高，并且装饰也更加繁复。据说，首次建造这种圆柱的那位建筑师，是看到一名小朋友的坟上放着一篮子的玩具而不是鲜花（当时的风俗就是如此）之后，才想出了这种柱头的样式。当时，那只篮子的上面盖着板子，而四周则长着一种叫作莨苕的蓟类植物。篮子、板子、叶子一体，看上去非常漂亮；那位建筑师觉得，把圆柱的柱头设计成这个样子会很好看，于是他便依样画瓢，设计出了这种样式。

我曾经让一些小男孩去找一找，看谁找到的圆柱最多。第二天，第一个男孩说他看到自家门口有两根爱奥尼亚式的圆柱，一边一根。第二个男孩说他在银行边上

seen two Ionic columns, one on each side of the door of his house. The second had seen ten Doric columns on the savings bank. But the third said he had seen 138 Corinthian columns.

"Where on earth did you see so many?" I asked.

"I counted the lampposts from my house to the school," he said. "They were kind of Corinthian columns."

One of the friends of Pericles was a man named Herodotus. He wrote in Greek the first history of the world. For this reason Herodotus is called the Father of History, and someday if you study Greek you may read what he wrote in his own language. Of course, at that time there was very little history to write. What has happened since *hadn't* happened then. He wrote about Egypt and other parts of the ancient world. He wrote about places so far away that most Greeks had never visited them. One was Kush, in Africa way south of Egypt. Mostly Herodotus's history was a story of the wars with Persia, which I have just told you about.

In those days every once in a while a terrible contagious disease, called a *plague*, would break out, and people would be taken sick and die by the thousands, for the doctors knew very little about the plague or how to cure it. Such a plague came upon Athens, and the Athenians died like poisoned flies. Pericles himself nursed the sick and did all he could for them, but finally he, too, was taken sick with plague and died. This happened at the very end of the Golden Age, which has been called in honor of its greatest man, the Age of Pericles.

看到了十根多利克式的圆柱。可第三个小男孩却说，他看到了一百三十八根科林斯式的圆柱。

"你究竟是在哪里看到了这么多的科林斯式圆柱呢？"我问他。

"我把从家里到学校这一路上的路灯杆都数了一遍，"他说，"它们都是科林斯式的圆柱呀。"

伯里克利有一个名叫希罗多德的朋友。这个希罗多德，用希腊语写出了第一部世界历史。由于这个原因，希罗多德便被后人称为"历史之父"；将来你们如果学习希腊语的话，可能就会读到他用希腊语写成的这部世界历史。当然，那个时候还没有多少历史可以记载。自那时以后的历史，都还没有出现呢。他记载下来的，是古埃及和古时其他一些地区的历史。他还记述了绝大多数古希腊人没有到过的一些遥远之地的情况。其中之一便是"古实国"，那个地方位于埃及以南的非洲。希罗多德所记载的历史，主要叙述的就是古希腊与波斯之间的历次战争；这段历史，前面我刚刚给你们讲述过。

那个时候，每隔一段时间就会爆发一场可怕的、叫作"瘟疫"的传染病，让成千上万的人染病、死去。因为当时的医生对瘟疫了解甚少，也不知道如何治疗。雅典曾经爆发过这样的一场瘟疫；当时的雅典人，就像是中了毒的苍蝇一样，纷纷死去。伯里克利曾经亲自去护理病人，并且竭尽全力帮助他们，可最终他自己也染上疫病去世了。这场瘟疫，正是发生在"黄金时代"的末期；而为了纪念伯里克利这位极其伟大的人物，人们便将这个时代叫作"伯里克利时代"。

28 When Greek Meets Greek

The Golden Age, when Athens was so wonderful, lasted for only fifty years.

Why, do you suppose, did it stop at all?

It stopped chiefly because of a fight.

This time, however, the fight was not between Greece and someone outside, as in the Persian Wars. The fight was between two cities that had before this been more or less friendly — mostly less — between Sparta and Athens. It was a family quarrel between Greeks. The fight was all because one of these cities — Sparta — was jealous of the other — Athens.

The Spartans, as you know, were fine soldiers. The Athenians were fine soldiers, too. But ever since Themistocles had beaten the Persians at Salamis with the ships he had built, Athens had had a fine fleet as well, and Sparta had no fleet. Furthermore, Athens had become the most beautiful and most cultured city in the whole world.

Sparta did not care much about Athens's beautiful buildings and her education and culture and that sort of thing; that did not interest Sparta. What did make Sparta jealous was Athens' fleet. Sparta was inland, not on nor near the seashore as Athens was; so Sparta

28 当希腊人遇上希腊人

雅典这个如此美妙的"黄金时代"，仅仅持续了五十年。

你们觉得，这个"黄金时代"为什么会没有再继续下去了呢？

它主要是由于一场战争才结束的。

然而，这次战争却并不是像希波战争那样，并不是一场希腊人与外人之间的战争。这场战争，发生在大多数时间并不友好的两个城邦，即斯巴达和雅典之间。这是希腊人之间的一次内部纷争。战争的起因，则是因为两个城邦之一的斯巴达嫉妒另一城邦雅典。

大家都知道，斯巴达人很是骁勇善战，而雅典人也都是非常出色的战士。不过，自地米斯托克利斯在萨拉米斯湾率领他所组建起来的舰队大败波斯人之后，雅典又拥有了一支精良的舰队，可斯巴达却没有。而且，雅典还变成了世界上最美丽、文化最发达的一座城市。

对雅典那些漂亮的建筑、雅典的教育和文化等方面，斯巴达并不怎么在意；这些东西，对斯巴达可没有什么吸引力。让斯巴达嫉妒的，是雅典的舰队。斯巴达是个内陆城邦，不像雅典那样沿海；因此，斯巴达根本就不可能拥有一支舰队。然而，这个城邦并不想让雅典超过自己；因此，斯巴达便找了一个莫须有的借口，率

could not have a fleet at all. That city did not intend, however, to let Athens get ahead; therefore, on one excuse or another, Sparta with all of its neighbors started a war against Athens with all of *its* neighbors.

Sparta was in a part of Greece that was called by the hard name, the Peloponnesus. In those days, people did not think this a hard name, for they were as familiar with it as you are with such a name as Massachusetts, for instance, which would seem just as hard to a Greek as Peloponnesus does to you. This war between Athens and Sparta was, therefore, called the Peloponnesian War from the fact that it was not only Sparta but all of the Peloponnesus that fought against Athens.

We think a war lasts entirely too long if it lasts four or five years, but the Peloponnesian War lasted twenty-seven years! There is a saying, "When Greek meets Greek then comes a tug of war!" which means to say, "When two equal fighters such as Athens and Sparta, both Greek, meet each other in battle, who knows how it will end?"

I am not going to tell you about all the battles that took place during these twenty-seven years, but at the end of this long and bloody war, both cities were tired and worn out, and the glory of Athens was gone. Although Sparta was ahead, neither city ever amounted to much afterward. The Peloponnesian War mined them both. That's the way war does!

All during the Peloponnesian War there was a man in Athens by the name of Socrates who, many think, was one of the wisest and best men who ever lived. He was called a philosopher and went about the city teaching the people what was right and what they

领其所有邻邦，发动了一场针对雅典的战争。

斯巴达位于希腊一个名称很绕口、叫作"伯罗奔尼撒"的地区。在当时，人们可不觉得这是一个复杂的名称，因为他们都很熟悉这个地方，就像你们熟知诸如"马萨诸塞"这样的名称似的；而对于古希腊人来说，"马萨诸塞"这个名称，也会像"伯罗奔尼撒"对于你们来说那样绕口呢。因此，雅典和斯巴达之间的这场战争，便被叫作"伯罗奔尼撒战争"。事实上，整个伯罗奔尼撒地区的城邦也全都参与了对雅典的作战，而并非只有斯巴达参战。

倘若一场战争打上四五年，我们就会觉得这场战争实在是太过旷日持久了；可是，伯罗奔尼撒战争竟然持续了二十七年！有句谚语说得好："希腊人相遇，必有场恶斗！"意思就是说："倘若像雅典和斯巴达这两个同属希腊、同样骁勇善战的城邦在战场上相见的话，谁知道他们会缠斗到什么时候呢！"

这二十七年里，双方之间进行的那一场场战斗的具体情况，我并没有打算跟你们细说；不过，到了这场旷日持久而又血腥残酷的战争结束时，这两个城邦全都疲惫不堪、元气大伤，而雅典的辉煌也一去不复返了。尽管斯巴达占据了上风，但此后这两个城邦全都没有什么作为了。伯罗奔尼撒战争把双方都毁了。战争的后果，就是这样！

在整个"伯罗奔尼撒战争"期间，雅典有个人叫作苏格拉底；许多人都觉得，他是有史以来最睿智和最善良的人物之一呢。他被人们称为哲人，在城里到处讲学，教导人们分辨善恶对错和告诫他人应当干什么。不过，他在实践中并不是简单

ought to do. But instead of actually *telling* the people what he thought was right, he asked them questions which made them see what was right. In this way, chiefly by asking questions, he led people to find out for themselves what he wanted them to know. This kind of teaching, simply by asking questions, has ever since been called Socratic.

Socrates had a snub nose and was bald and quite ugly, and yet he was very popular with the Athenians, which may seem strange, for the Athenians loved beautiful faces and beautiful figures and beautiful things, and Socrates was anything but beautiful. It must have been the beauty of Socrates's character that made them forget his ugliness, as I know some boys and girls who think their teacher is perfectly beautiful and just because she is so good and kind they love her, although she is really not pretty at all.

Socrates had a wife named Xantippe. She had a bad temper and was the worst kind of a grouch. She thought Socrates was wasting his time, that he was a loafer, as he did no work that brought in any money. One day she scolded him so loudly that he left the house, whereupon she threw a bucket of water on him. Socrates, who never answered back, merely remarked to himself:

"After thunder, rain may be expected."

Socrates didn't believe in all the Greek gods, Zeus, Aphrodite, and the rest, but he was careful not to say so himself, for the Greeks were very particular that no one should say or do anything against their gods. Phidias, you remember, was thrown into prison for merely putting his picture on the shield of the goddess Athena, and one would have been put to

地将自己认为正确的东西说教给人们，而是向他们提出问题，在回答问题的过程中让他们明白孰对孰错。所以，他主要是用这种提问的方式，引导人们自己去发现他想要人们明白的道理。因此，这种纯属通过提问来进行引导的教育方式，此后便被称为"苏格拉底问答法"。

虽说苏格拉底长着一个蒜头鼻子，并且秃顶、长相丑陋，可他却备受雅典人的爱戴；这似乎奇怪得很，因为雅典人都喜欢漂亮的脸蛋、漂亮的人物和漂亮的东西，可苏格拉底却一点儿也不漂亮。一定是苏格拉底的性格之美让他们忘记了他面目的丑陋；我知道，有些小朋友觉得他们的女老师非常漂亮、非常公正，尽管这只是因为她对这些小朋友都非常温和、亲切，而其实她根本就算不上漂亮。

苏格拉底的妻子叫作赞西佩。她的脾气非常暴躁，是那种最爱发牢骚的人。她觉得苏格拉底是在虚度自己的光阴，认为他是个游手好闲的人，因为他不去干活，赚不回一分钱来养家。有一天，她又大声责骂苏格拉底，苏格拉底只好出门而去；可就在此时，她又泼了一盆水到他身上。吵架的时候，苏格拉底从不与她顶嘴，只是对自己说：

"响雷过后，马上就会下雨的。"

苏格拉底并不信奉诸如宙斯、阿弗洛狄忒以及其他的希腊诸神；可他很谨慎，自己从不说出来，因为希腊人在信仰这个问题上很是较真儿，不准任何人说出或者做出对诸神不利的事情。你们都还记得吧，菲狄亚斯仅仅是把自己的形象刻在雅典娜女神塑像的那面盾牌上，就被关进了监狱呢。因此，倘若有人去教唆年轻人不信

death for teaching young men not to believe in the gods.

At last, however, Socrates, as he had feared he would be, was charged with not believing in the Greek gods and with teaching others not to believe in them. For this he was condemned to death. He was ordered to drink a cup of hemlock, which was a deadly poison. Socrates's pupils, or disciples, as they were then called, tried to have him refuse to drink the cup, but he would not disobey the order; and so, when he was nearly seventy years old, with all his disciples around him, he drank the cup of hemlock and died.

Although Socrates lived many hundreds of years ago, he believed and taught some things that people today also believe.

One of these things he believed was that each of us has inside a *conscience*, which tells us what is right and what is wrong; we don't have to read from a book or be told by another what is right or what is wrong.

Another thing he taught was that there is a life after death and that when we die our souls live on.

No wonder he was not afraid himself to die!

奉神灵的话，这个人肯定就会被处死的。

然而，苏格拉底担心的事情最终还是发生了；他因为不信奉希腊众神并教唆其他人不信奉诸神而受到了指控。由于这个原因，他被判处了死刑。他被迫喝下一杯毒芥酒；那是一种致命的毒药。苏格拉底的学生们（当时称为门徒），试图让他不喝那杯毒酒，可他却不想违抗命令；所以，当时已经年近七十的苏格拉底，便在自己所有门徒都围在身边的情况下，喝下了那杯毒酒，与世长辞了。

尽管苏格拉底生活在几千年以前，但他所信奉和倡导的一些东西，如今的人却依然还在信奉着呢。

他所信奉的观点之一，便是我们每个人内心深处都有一种"良知"，让我们能够分辨对错；因此，我们不一定非得通过看书学习或者接受教导才能明辨是非。

他所倡导的另一观点，便是有来世；也就是说，我们死后，灵魂会继续存在。

所以，他根本不害怕自己死去，这也就不足为怪了！

29 Wise Men and Otherwise

Have you ever been playing in your yard when a strange boy who had been watching from the other side of the fence asked to be let into the game, saying he would show you how to play? You didn't want him around, and you didn't want him in, but somehow or other he got in and was soon bossing everybody else.

Well, there was a man named Philip who lived north of Greece, and he had been watching Sparta and Athens — not playing but fighting — and he wanted to get into the game. Philip was king of a little country called Macedonia, but he thought he would like to be king of Greece also, and it seemed to him a good time, when Sparta and Athens were down and out after the Peloponnesian War, to step in and make himself king of that country. Philip was a great fighter, but he didn't want to fight Greece unless he had to. He wanted to be made king peaceably, and he wanted Greece to do it willingly. He thought up a scheme to bring this about, and this was his scheme.

He knew, as you do, how the Greeks hated the Persians, whom they had driven out of their country over a hundred years before. Although the Persian Wars had taken place so long ago, the Greeks had never forgotten the bravery of their forefathers and the tales of

29　智者与庸人

你们正在自家院子里玩儿的时候，一个一直在栅栏外边看着、但你不认识的小男孩突然说他想进来告诉你们怎么玩；虽然你们不想跟他玩、不想让他进来，可他不知怎么的，却还是进来了，并且很快开始对每个小朋友发号施令。你们有没有过这样的经历呢？

好吧，古希腊北部有一个人叫作腓力，他一直关注着斯巴达和雅典这两个城邦，当然这两个城邦并不是在玩儿，而是在打仗；而且，腓力也想参与进去。腓力是一个叫作马其顿的小国的国王，但他也希望自己能够成为整个希腊的国王；而待伯罗奔尼撒战争结束，斯巴达和雅典全都千疮百孔、虚弱不堪之后，他便觉得介入此次战争、让自己当上希腊国王的大好机会来了。腓力骁勇善战，很了不起；但除非迫不得已，否则他并不想与希腊开战。他希望自己能够兵不血刃地当上希腊的国王，希望希腊人心甘情愿地请他去当国王。为了达到这一目的，他想出了一条计谋；下面我们就来说一说这条计谋。

他明白希腊人极其讨厌波斯人，你们也明白这一点，对不对？因为一百多年前，他们刚刚把波斯人赶出希腊呢。尽管希波战争是很久以前的事情了，希腊人却永远不会忘记自己先辈们的英勇无畏，不会忘记先辈们战胜波斯人的传奇经历。父

their victories over the Persians. These stories had been told them over and over by their parents and grandparents, and they loved to read and reread them in Herodotus's history of the world.

So Philip said to the Greeks, "Your ancestors drove the Persians out of Greece, to be sure, but the Persians went back to their country, and you didn't go after them and punish them as you should have done. You didn't try to get even with them. Why don't you go over to Persia and conquer it now, and make the Persians pay for what they did to you?"

Then he slyly added, "Let me help you. I'll lead you against them."

No one seemed to see through Philip's scheme — nobody except one man. This man was an Athenian named Demosthenes.

Demosthenes, when he was a boy, had decided that he would someday be a great speaker or orator, just as you might say you are going to be a doctor, or an aviator, or a teacher when you grow up.

Demosthenes had picked the one profession which by nature he was worst fitted for. In the first place, he had such a very soft, weak voice that one could hardly hear him. Besides, this, he stammered very badly and could not recite even a short poem without hesitating and stumbling so that people laughed at him. It seemed absurd, therefore, that he should aim to be a great speaker.

But Demosthenes *practiced and practiced* and practiced by himself. He went down on the seashore and put pebbles in his mouth to make it more difficult to speak clearly. Then

母和爷爷奶奶们一遍又一遍地给他们讲述这些故事,而他们也喜欢一遍又一遍地到希罗多德所写的《世界历史》一书中去阅读这些故事。

于是,腓力便对希腊人说:"你们的先辈确实把波斯人赶出了希腊,可波斯人回到了自己的祖国,你们并没有追击,没有给他们以应有的惩罚。你们现在为什么不前去征服波斯,让波斯人为曾经对你们做过的事情付出代价呢?"

接着,他又狡诈地补充说:"让我来帮助你们吧。我会领着你们去对付他们。"

似乎没有人看穿腓力的计谋,只有一个人除外。这个人,就是一个名叫狄摩西尼的雅典人。

狄摩西尼在小的时候就已经下定决心,将来要做一名伟大的演说家或者雄辩家,就像你们可能会说自己长大后要做一位医生、一名飞行员或者老师那样。

狄摩西尼选择的,是他天生就最不适合去干的一种职业。首先,他的声音又柔又弱,人们很难听清楚他说的是什么。除此之外,他还结巴得厉害,连朗诵一首短诗都断断续续、磕磕巴巴,弄得大家都嘲笑他。因此,他立志成为一名伟大的演说家的想法似乎荒唐得很呢。

但是,狄摩西尼却独自一遍又一遍地坚持练习、练习、再练习。他来到海边,将鹅卵石含在嘴里,使得自己更加难以清楚地讲话。然后,他又对着汹涌咆哮的海浪说话,假装自己正在对着群情激愤的民众演说;他们试图盖过他的声音,因此他演讲的声音必须非常响亮才行。

he spoke to the roaring waves, making believe that he was addressing an angry crowd, who were trying to drown the sound of his voice, so that he would have to speak very loud indeed.

At last, by keeping constantly at it, Demosthenes did become a very great speaker. He spoke so wonderfully that he could make his audience laugh or make them cry whenever he wanted to, and he could persuade them to do almost anything he wished.

Now, Demosthenes was the man who saw through Philip's scheme for conquering Persia. He knew that Philip's real aim was to become king of Greece. So he made twelve speeches against him. These speeches were known as *Philippics*, as they were against Philip. So famous were they that even today we call a speech that bitterly attacks anyone a Philippic.

The Greeks who heard Demosthenes were red-hot against Philip while they listened to him. But as soon as they got away from the sound of Demosthenes's words, the same Greeks became lukewarm and did nothing to stop Philip.

At last, in spite of everything that Demosthenes had said, Philip had his way and became king over all Greece.

Before, however, he could start out, as he had promised, to conquer Persia, he was killed by one of his own men, so that he was unable to carry out his plan.

Philip had a son named Alexander. Alexander was *only* twenty years old, but when his father died he became king of Macedonia and also of Greece.

通过坚持不懈的练习，狄摩西尼最后真的变成了一位伟大的演说家。他的演讲极其精彩。所以，只要他愿意，他随时都可以让听众哈哈大笑，或者让听众流泪痛哭；他也可以说服听众，去做他所希望的任何事情。

此时，只有狄摩西尼看穿了腓力要希腊人去征服波斯背后的计谋。他明白，腓力的真正目的是要当上希腊的国王。于是，他进行了十二场演说来反对腓力。人们将这些演说统称为"痛斥腓力的演说"，因为它们都是反对腓力的。这些演讲如此有名，以至于即便到了今天，我们还会将一场猛烈抨击他人的演说称作是一场"痛斥腓力的演说"呢。

听了狄摩西尼演讲的那些希腊人，在听他演说的时候全都群情激愤，坚决反对腓力。可一旦离开演讲现场，听不到狄摩西尼的声音后，这些希腊人便又变得漠然置之，不会采取任何行动去阻止腓力实施其计谋了。

最终，尽管狄摩西尼什么都说了，但腓力还是阴谋得逞，当上了整个希腊的国王。

然而，在遵守承诺、出发去征服波斯之前，他就被自己的一名手下刺杀了，因此他也没有办法再实现自己的计划了。

腓力有个儿子，叫作亚历山大。当时，亚历山大才二十岁；但父亲死后，他便继承大统，成了马其顿和希腊两国的国王。

亚历山大很小的时候，有一次看到一些人怎么也驯服不了一匹桀骜不驯的小马；那匹小马乱蹦乱跳，没人能够骑上去。亚历山大请求父亲让他去试一试，看他

When Alexander was a mere child, he saw some men trying without success to tame a young and very wild horse that shied and reared in the air so that no one was able to ride it. Alexander asked to be allowed to try to ride the animal. Alexander's father made fun of his son for wanting to attempt what those older than he had been unable to do, but at last gave his consent.

Now, Alexander had noticed what the others, although much older, had not noticed. The horse seemed to be afraid of its own shadow, for young colts are easily frightened by anything dark and moving, as some children are afraid of the dark at night.

Alexander turned the horse around facing the sun, so that its shadow would be behind, out of sight. He then mounted the animal and, to the amazement of all, rode off without any further trouble.

His father was delighted at his son's cleverness and gave him the horse as a reward. Alexander named the horse Bucephalus and became so fond of him that when the horse died Alexander built a monument to him and named several cities after him.

Now, Alexander was a wonderful boy, but he had such a wonderful teacher named Aristotle that some people think part, at least, of his greatness was due to the teacher.

Aristotle was probably the greatest teacher who ever lived. If there were more great teachers like Aristotle, it seems likely there would have been more great pupils like Alexander.

Aristotle wrote books about all sorts of things — books about the stars called

能不能驾驭这匹马儿。看到儿子想要尝试连大人都无法做到的事情，亚历山大的父亲觉得很好笑，但最终还是磨不过儿子，便同意他去试一试。

此时，亚历山大注意到了大人们并没有留意的一个细节：那匹马儿似乎很害怕自己的影子，因为小马驹很容易被黑乎乎的和移动着的东西惊着，就像一些小朋友在黑漆漆的夜里觉得很害怕似的。

亚历山大牵着小马，让它转过身来，对着太阳，这样它的影子就落到了身后，看不到了。然后，他跨上马背，毫无困难地骑着马儿扬长而去，让在场的人全都惊得目瞪口呆。

他的父亲对儿子的聪明机智大感高兴，便将那匹小马奖给了他。亚历山大给这匹马儿起了个名字，叫作布塞弗勒斯；他非常钟爱这匹马儿，因此在马儿死了之后，他不仅为它建了一座纪念碑，还将好几座城市都以它的名字来命名。

此时，亚历山大还只是一个很优秀的小男孩；可他有一位非常了不起的老师，名叫亚里士多德。有些人认为，亚历山大后来之所以伟大，至少部分功劳应当归功于他的这位老师呢。

亚里士多德很可能是有史以来最了不起的一位老师。假如世界上像亚里士多德这样的伟大导师更多一些，可能就会出现更多像亚历山大这样了不起的学生了。

亚里士多德写了很多的书，内容几乎涉及了方方面面：那些关于日月星辰的书，叫作天文学著作；那些关于动物的书，叫作动物学著作；还有很多其他学科的著作，比如心理学和政治，你们可能听都没听说过这些学科呢。

astronomy, books about animals called zoology, and books on other subjects that you probably have never even heard of, such as psychology and politics.

For hundreds of years these books that Aristotle wrote were the schoolbooks that boys and girls studied, and for many years they were the only schoolbooks. Nowadays, schoolbooks usually change every few years after they are written. See how remarkable it was that Aristotle's schoolbooks should have been used for so long a time.

Aristotle had been taught by a man named Plato, who was also a great teacher and philosopher. Plato had been a pupil of Socrates, so that Aristotle was a kind of *grand-pupil* of Socrates. You have heard of the Wise Men of the East. These were the three Wise Men of Greece.

Socrates,

Plato,

Aristotle.

Some day you may read what they wrote or said over two thousand years ago.

千百年来，亚里士多德所写的这些著作，都是孩子们学习的教材，并且在很长一段时间里，它们也是学校里唯一用到的教材。如今，一种教材在编写出来数年之后就会进行修订。亚里士多德所写的教材能够用上那么久的时间，所以你们完全可以看出，它们是多么的不同凡响了。

亚里士多德的老师叫作柏拉图，他也是一位了不起的导师，一位伟大的哲学家。柏拉图又是苏格拉底的门徒，所以亚里士多德可以说是苏格拉底的"徒孙"。你们已经听说过东方的一些智者了。下面则是古希腊的三位智者。

苏格拉底，

柏拉图，

亚里士多德。

将来，你们可能还会看到他们在两千多年前所写的著作或者论述呢。

30 A Boy King

When you are twenty years old, what do you think you will be doing?

Will you be attending college?

Will you be working, or what?

When Alexander was twenty, he was king of both Macedonia and Greece. But Macedonia and Greece were entirely too small for this wonderful young man. He wanted to rule a much bigger country; in fact, he thought he would like to rule the whole world; that was all — nothing more.

So Alexander went right ahead with his father's plan to conquer Persia. The time had come to pay back Persia for that last invasion one hundred and fifty years before.

He got together an army and crossed the Hellespont into Asia and won battle after battle against the first Persian armies that went out to stop him.

He kept moving on, for Persia was a vast empire.

Soon he came to a town where in a temple there was kept a rope tied into a very farfamed and puzzling knot. It was called the Gordian Knot, and it was very famous because the oracle had said that whoever should undo this knot would conquer Persia. No

30 少年国王

你们觉得，等长到二十岁的时候，你们会在干什么呢？

那时，你们是不是正在上大学呢？

那时，你们是不是已经参加工作，或者正在干别的什么事情呢？

亚历山大二十岁的时候，已经是马其顿和希腊两国的国王了。可对这个非凡的年轻人来说，马其顿和希腊两国都太小了。他想要统治一个更大的国家；事实上，他想要统治整个世界。除此之外，他就别无所求了。

于是，亚历山大便一往无前，开始实施他父亲要征服波斯的未竟之业了。向波斯复仇，洗雪一百五十年前波斯最后一次入侵之耻的时候，已经到来。

他召集了一支军队，跨过赫勒斯滂海峡，进入亚洲，并且接连打了几场胜仗，击溃了一拨拨前来迎击他的波斯先头部队。

然后他继续进击，因为当时的波斯帝国疆域广袤无垠。

不久之后，他便来到了一个城镇；那里有一座神庙，庙里保存着一根绳子，绳子上打着一个远近闻名、令人费解的结。这个绳结，叫作"戈尔迪之结"；它之所以有名，是因为神谕说，解开这个结的人将征服波斯。但是，以前一直都没有人能够解开这个绳结。

one had ever been able to untie it.

When Alexander heard the story, he went to the temple and took a look at the knot. He saw at once that it would be impossible to untie it, so, instead of even trying, as others had done, he drew his sword and with one stroke cut the knot in two.

Now when a person settles something difficult, not by fussing with it as one untangles a snarl, but at a single stroke, cutting through all difficulties, we say he "cuts the Gordian Knot".

From that time on, Alexander conquered one city after another and never lost any battle of importance until he had conquered the whole of Persia.

He then went into Egypt, which belonged to Persia at that time, and conquered that country, too. To celebrate this victory, he founded a town near the mouth of the Nile and named it after himself, Alexandria. He started there a great library that later grew to be so big that there were said to be five hundred thousand books in it — that is, half a million — and was the largest library of ancient times. The books were not like those in the library of Ashurbanipal nor the kind we have now, of course, because printing had not been invented. They were every one of them written by hand, and not on pages, but on long sheets which were rolled up on sticks to form a scroll.

In the harbor of Alexandria was a little island called Pharos, and on this island some years later was built a remarkable lighthouse named for the island, the Pharos. It was really a building more like a modern skyscraper with a tower. It was over thirty stories

亚历山大听到了这个传说之后，就前往神庙去看那个绳结。他一眼就看出，那个绳结是不可能解开的；所以，他根本就没有像其他人那样试着去解开绳结，而是拔出剑来，一下子就把那个绳结劈成了两半。

如今，倘若一个人解决了某个难题，并且不是像解死结似的大费周章，而是轻而易举地一下子完全解决掉，那么我们就说他是"劈开了戈尔迪之结"（即快刀斩乱麻）。

从那时起，亚历山大便征服了一座又一座城市，并且从未在重大战事中打过败仗，最终征服了整个波斯。

接下来，他又进军埃及，并将该国征服了；当时，埃及也是波斯的属国。为了庆祝这次大捷，他在尼罗河入海口的附近修建了一座城市，并且以自己的名字命名，称之为亚历山大。他在亚历山大还兴建了一座大型的图书馆；这座图书馆的规模后来变得极其宏大，据说藏书达五十万册，即一百万册的一半，从而成了古代最大的一座图书馆呢。当然，那里的藏书并不是像亚述巴尼拔的藏书那样，也不像如今我们所看的这种书，因为那时还没有发明印刷术。其中的每一本书都是手写的，并且不是一页一页，而是写在长长的纸张上，然后再用棍子将它们卷起来，形成一个卷轴。

亚历山大港内有一座小岛，叫作法罗斯；许多年以后，人们在这座小岛上修建了一座非比寻常的灯塔，并以该岛命名，称之为"法罗斯灯塔"。实际上，那座灯塔更像是一栋有塔顶的现代摩天大楼呢。它有三十多层楼高；由于当时的房屋都只有一两层楼高，所以这座灯塔就显得极其不寻常了，在数英里之外也能看到它的灯

high, which seemed most remarkable at that time when most buildings were only one or two stories high, and its light could be seen for many miles. The Pharos of Alexandria was called one of the Seven Wonders of the World. You have already heard of three others, so this makes the fourth.

Alexandria grew, in the course of time, to be the largest and most important seaport of the ancient world. Now, however, the Pharos and the library and all the old buildings have long since disappeared.

Alexander did not stay very long in any one place. He was restless. He wanted to keep on the move. He wanted to see new places and to conquer new people. He almost forgot his own little country of Macedonia and Greece. Instead of being homesick, however, as almost any one would have been, he kept going farther and farther away from home all the time. We should call such a man an adventurer or an explorer, as well as a great general. Alexander kept on conquering and didn't stop conquering until he had reached far-off India.

There in India his army, which had stayed on with him all the way, became homesick and wanted to go back. They had been away from home for more than ten years and were so far off that they were afraid they would never get back.

Alexander was now only thirty years old, but he was called Alexander *the Great*, for he was ruler of the whole world — at least, most of it that was then known to most Greeks,

光。因此，亚历山大港的法罗斯灯塔也被称为世界七大奇观之一。在前面，你们已经听说过三大奇观了，所以"法罗斯灯塔"便是其中的第四个。

随着时光流逝，亚历山大港慢慢变成了古代世界最大和最重要的一个海港。然而到了如今，法罗斯灯塔、亚历山大图书馆以及几乎所有的古代建筑，都早已不复存在了。

亚历山大在每一个地方都不会停留太久。他是个永不满足的人。他希望继续前进。他想要看到新的地方，想要征服新的民族。他几乎已经将马其顿和希腊这两个小小的国家抛到了脑后。然而，他并不像绝大多数人那样思念着自己的家乡，而是一直越走越远，一天天地远离了自己的故乡。我们应当称这样的人为"冒险家"或者"探险家"；同时，亚历山大也是一位伟大的将领。他不停地征战、征战，一直打到了遥远的印度。

到了印度之后，他手下那些一路跟随着他征战的士兵却开始想念家乡，希望回去了。他们已经离开家乡十多年了，如今又身处这样遥远的异乡，因此都担心自己再也回不去了。

此时，虽说亚历山大刚刚三十岁，他却被人们称为"亚历山大大帝"，因为他几乎统治了整个世界，起码也是统治着当时绝大多数希腊人所

A scroll, pens and ink
卷轴和笔、墨

except Italy, which was still only a collection of little, unimportant towns at that time. When Alexander found there were no more countries left for him to conquer, he was so disappointed that he wept!

At last, when there was nothing more to conquer, he agreed to do what his army begged him and started slowly back toward Greece.

He got as far as Babylon, the city once so large and so magnificent. There he celebrated with a feast, but while feasting and drinking he suddenly died. He never reached Greece.

This was in 323 B.C. when he was but 33 years old. You can remember these figures easily, for they are all 3's except the middle figure in the date, which is one less than 3.

Alexander the Great had conquered the largest country that had ever been under the rule of one man, and yet this was not the only reason we call him the Great.

He was not only a great ruler and a great general, but — this may surprise you — he was also a great teacher. Aristotle had taught him to be that.

Alexander taught the Greek language to the people he conquered so that they could read Greek books. He taught them about Greek sculpture and painting. He taught them the wise sayings of the Greek philosophers, Socrates and Plato and his own teacher, Aristotle. He trained the people in athletics as the Greeks did for their Olympic Games.

Alexander had married a beautiful Persian woman named Roxana, but their only child was still a baby, not born until after his father's death; so when the great king died there

知的这个世界的绝大部分,只有意大利除外;那个时候,意大利全境仍然还只是一些规模极小、微不足道的城镇罢了。亚历山大发现世界上已经没有更多国家可供自己征服之后,由于太过失落,他甚至哭了!

最后,到了他认为再也无地可以征服的时候,亚历山大便同意了士兵们的请求,开始踏上了返回希腊的漫漫归途。

后来,他抵达了巴比伦这个曾经非常强大、极其辉煌的城市。他在巴比伦举办了一场庆功宴会;可是,就在宴会上尽情享受、大吃大喝的时候,他却突然死了。因此,他再也没有活着回到希腊。

这一事件,发生在公元前323年,当时他年仅三十三岁。你们很容易就能记住这两个数字,因为它们全都由数字"3"组成,只是年份中间的那个数字不是"3",而是比"3"小"1"的数字"2"罢了。

亚历山大大帝掌控着有史以来由一位君主所统治过的最大国家,但这并不是我们称他为"大帝"的唯一原因。

他不但是一位伟大的君主、一位伟大的将领,还是一位了不起的老师呢;这一点,或许会让你们觉得很是惊奇。正是他的老师亚里士多德,教他成为一名伟大的老师。

亚历山大曾经教那些被他征服的民族说希腊语;这样一来,那些民族也可以阅读希腊书籍了。他将希腊雕塑、绘画方面的知识教给了这些民族。他将苏格拉底、柏拉图和他自己的老师亚里士多德等这些希腊哲人的至理名言教给了那些民族。他还按照希腊人为参加奥林匹克运动会而训练的方法,训练那些民族。

亚历山大娶了一个叫作罗克珊娜的波斯美女,但当时他们唯一的孩子还是个小

was no one to rule after him. He had told his generals before he died that the strongest one of them should be the next ruler; they must fight it out among themselves.

His generals did fight to see who should win, and finally four of them who were victorious decided to divide up this great empire and each have a share.

One of his generals was named Ptolemy I, and he took Egypt as his share and ruled well; but the others did not amount to much, and after a while their shares became unimportant and went to pieces. Like a toy balloon which stretches and stretches as you blow it up, Alexander's empire grew bigger and bigger until — all of a sudden — *pop* — nothing was left but the pieces.

宝宝，他是父亲死后才出生的；因此，这位伟大的君主去世后，便没人来继承他的王位了。去世之前，他曾对自己手下的将领说过，他想让其中最强大的一位将领继任王位；因此，他们必须通过比试，才能决定究竟由谁来继承王位。

他手下的那些将领们的确进行了比试，来确定获胜者。最后，有四位将领获胜了；于是，他们决定将这个伟大的帝国分裂开来，每人统治其中的一部分。

其中有位将领叫作托勒密一世，他得到了埃及，并且将埃及治理得很好；而其他三位将领却不成大器，所以不久之后，他们各自的地盘便变得无足轻重，接着又分崩离析了。就像你们在吹一个气球的时候，气球越来越大，然后突然"呼"的一声便破了，只剩下气球碎片那样，亚历山大的帝国疆域也变得越来越辽阔，然后突然之间，便土崩瓦解了。

31 Picking a Fight

Every dog has his day.

A tennis or track champion wins over the one who was champion before and then has a few years during which he or she is unbeaten. Sooner or later, however, some younger and better athlete wins and in turn takes the championship.

It seems almost the same way with countries as with people. One country wins the championship from another, holds it for a few years, and then, when older, finally loses it to some new-comer.

We have seen that

Nineveh was champion for a while; then

  Babylon had a turn; then

    Persia had a turn; then

      Greece; and, lastly,

        Macedonia.

You may wonder who was to be the next champion after Alexander's empire went to pieces — who was to have the next turn.

When Alexander was conquering the world, he went east toward the rising sun, and

31　挑起争端

风水轮流转。

一名网球选手或田径运动员打赢了前任冠军之后，他的冠军位置将会保持几年。然而，迟早会有某个更年轻、更优秀的运动员来将他打败，然后占领冠军的位置。

对于民族和国家来说，差不多也是这样。一个国家从另一个国家手中夺得霸主位置之后，会保持数年；接着，这个国家就会慢慢衰落，并且最终败给某个新崛起的国家。

我们已经看到，

尼尼微做过一段时间的霸主；接着

  轮到巴比伦；接着

    轮到波斯；接着

      轮到希腊；最后，

        则是马其顿。

你们或许很想知道，亚历山大大帝治下的波斯帝国四分五裂之后，谁会是下一任霸主；也就是说，接下来又会轮到哪一个国家？

亚历山大大帝在征服世界的时候，一直都是朝着旭日升起的东方以及南方进军

south. He paid little attention to the country to the west toward the setting sun. Rome, which we have not heard of for some time, was then only a small town with narrow streets and frame houses. It was not nearly important enough for Alexander to think much about. Rome itself was not thinking of anything then except keeping the neighboring soldiers out.

In the course of time, however, Rome began to grow up and was not only able to take care of itself but could put up a very stiff fight. Rome fought and won battles with most of the other towns in Italy, until at last Rome became champion of the whole of the boot. Then the Romans began to look around to see what other countries there were outside of Italy that they might conquer.

Perhaps you have noticed that Italy, the boot, seems about to kick a little island as if it were a football. This island is Sicily, and just opposite Sicily across the Mediterranean in North Africa was a city called Carthage.

Carthage had been founded by the Phoenicians many years before and had become a very rich and powerful city. Over the years, Phoenicians mixed with the local North Africans called Berbers and formed a unique culture.

They planted big farms with fruit trees and olive trees. They owned herds of cattle and sheep and horses. Wealthy families owned large country estates.

As Carthage was by the sea, it had built many ships and traded with all the other seaports along the Mediterranean, just as the old Phoenician cities of Tyre and Sidon had done. By now, Carthage controlled the whole western end of the Mediterranean Sea.

的。对于地处太阳落下的西边的那个国家，他却没怎么注意。我们有段时间没有谈到罗马了；当时，该国还只是一个街道狭窄、只有木屋的小城镇呢。所以这里没什么重要的，不值得亚历山大来考虑太多。而当时罗马本身也正在一心一意地抵御邻国的侵略；除此之外，该国什么也没有考虑。

然而，随着时光流逝，罗马开始慢慢发展起来，不仅能够保护好本国，还能承受一场非常激烈的大战了。罗马与意大利的其他绝大多数城邦都交过战，并且打了一场又一场胜仗，最后罗马终于变成了意大利这只"靴子"全境内的霸主。然后，罗马人便开始环顾四周，看意大利以外有哪些国家可以去征服。

也许你们已经注意到，意大利这只"靴子"，似乎是准备去踢一个小岛，好像这个小岛是一个足球似的。那个小岛，便是西西里；而隔着地中海与西西里岛相望的北非，则有一座叫作迦太基的城市。

迦太基是腓尼基人在多年以前建立起来的，此时已经变成了一座非常富庶、非常强大的城市。在那段时间里，腓尼基人与北非那个叫作"柏柏尔人"的当地人融合起来，形成了一种独特的文化。

他们耕作着大片大片的农田，农田里都是果树和橄榄树。他们饲养着成群的牛羊和马匹。一些富裕的家庭，还拥有广袤的田庄。

由于靠近海洋，因此迦太基建造了许多的船只，并且与地中海沿岸的其他所有海港都有贸易往来，就像古时的蒂尔和西顿那两个城市的做法一样。到了此时，迦太基已经控制了地中海地区的整个西部。

Carthage did not like to see Rome getting so strong and growing so big and becoming so powerful. In other words, Carthage felt challenged by Rome.

Rome, on her side, was jealous of the wealth and trade of Carthage. So Romans anxiously looked around for some excuse to get into a fight with their rival across the sea.

Now, you know how easy it is to pick a quarrel and start a fight when you are looking for trouble. One boy sticks out his tongue, the other gives him a kick, and the fight is on.

Well, two countries are at times just like little boys; they start a fight with just as little excuse, and though they call the fight war it is nothing but a *scrap*. Only there are no parents to come along and make them both go home.

It didn't take long for Rome and Carthage to find an excuse, and a war was started between them. The Romans called this fight a Punic War, for Punic was their name for Phoenician, and the Carthaginians originally were Phoenicians.

As Carthage was across the water, the Romans could not get there except in boats. But Rome had no boats. Rome was not on the seashore and knew nothing about making boats, nor about sailing them.

The Carthaginians, on the other hand, had many, many boats, and were old and experienced sailors.

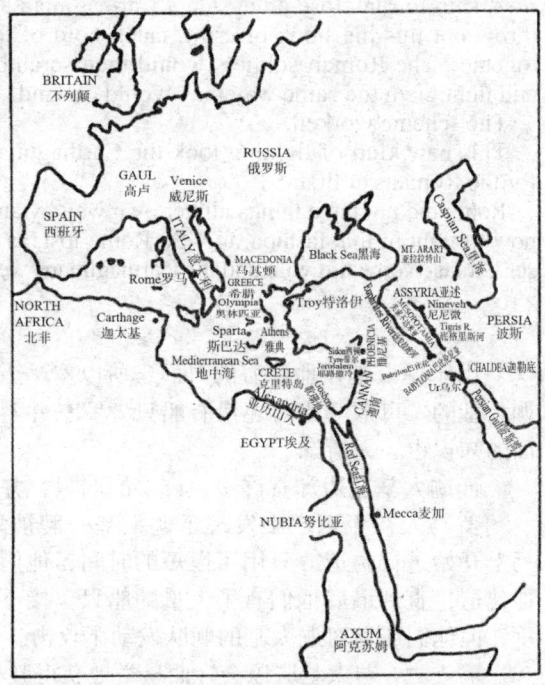

Map of Mediterranean showing Carthage, Spain, etc
地中海地区的迦太基、西班牙等国图

迦太基可不愿意看到罗马变得如此厉害，不愿看到罗马的疆域变得如此辽阔、势力变得如此庞大。换句话来说，就是迦太基觉得自己受到了罗马的威胁。

而另一方面，罗马也很嫉妒迦太基的富裕和发达的贸易。因此，罗马急不可耐地想要找一个借口，与这个隔海相望的对手打上一仗。

如今你们都明白，倘若成心找茬的话，挑起一场争吵、打上一架是很容易做到的一件事情。只需要一个小男孩伸出舌头做鬼脸，另一个小男孩再踢他一脚，两人便开始打架了。

注意，有的时候，两个国家就像是两个小男孩，它们之间只要有一点儿鸡毛蒜皮的小事，便可以掐上一架；尽管它们将这样的争吵叫作战争，但实际上这只是一种性质不同的打架罢了。不过，两国之间可不像两个小男孩那样，有父母前来让他们各自回家。

罗马和迦太基没过多久便找到了一个借口，于是双方之间便开始了一场战争。罗马人将这场战争叫作"布匿战争"，因为他们称腓尼基人为"布匿人"，而迦太基人又是腓尼基人的后裔。

Romans happened to find the wreck of a Carthaginian ship that had been cast ashore, and they at once set to work to make a copy of it. In a remarkably short time they had built one ship, then another and another, until they had a great many ships. Then, though the Romans were new at the game, they attacked the Carthaginian fleet.

It would seem that the Carthaginians could easily have won, for the Romans knew so little about boats. In sea battles, before this, the fighting had been done by running into the enemy and ramming and sinking their ships.

The Romans knew they were no match for the Carthaginians in this sort of fighting. So they thought up a way in which they could fight them as on land.

To do this they invented a kind of big hook which they called a *crow*. The idea was for a ship to run close alongside a Carthaginian ship and, instead of trying to sink her, to throw out this big hook or crow, catch hold of the other ship, and pull both boats close together. The Roman soldiers would then scramble over the sides into the enemy's boat and fight them the same way they would on land.

The scheme worked.

This new kind of fighting took the Carthaginians by surprise, and they were no match for the Romans at first.

Rome did not have things all her own way by any means. The Carthaginians soon learned how to fight in this fashion, too. So Rome lost, as well as won, battles both on land and on sea. At last Rome did win, and the Carthaginians were beaten. Thus ended the first Punic War.

由于迦太基在地中海的对面，所以罗马人除了坐船渡海，否则是没有办法到达迦太基的。可罗马当时还没有船只。罗马并不是个海滨城邦，对造船、驾船航海方面的知识也一无所知。

而迦太基这边却有许多、许多的船只，并且航海经验丰富。

罗马人在无意之中发现了迦太基一艘被海浪冲到岸上的失事船只，于是他们马上开始进行仿造。只用了极短的时间，他们便建造了一艘船，然后便一艘接一艘地建造，直到最后他们有了大量的船只。接下来，尽管罗马人在海战方面还是个新手，但他们还是对迦太基的舰队发动了攻击。

看上去，迦太基应该会轻而易举地获得胜利才是，因为罗马人很不了解舰船。在以前的海战中，作战双方所使用的战术，都是冲进敌军，用己方船只撞沉敌人的战船。

罗马人很清楚，在这种战斗中，他们不是迦太基人的对手。于是，他们便想出了一个办法，使得他们可以像在陆地上一样与迦太基人作战。

为此，他们发明了一种叫作"乌鸦"的大铁钩。发明这个的目的是，让一艘船只驶到迦太基战船的一侧后，不是试图去直接将敌舰撞沉，而是抛出那个大铁钩或者说"乌鸦"，让它勾住敌舰，然后将两艘战船拉得并排靠拢起来。这样，罗马士兵便可以从船舷爬上敌船，像在陆地上一样与敌人作战了。

这个计谋很有效。

这种新的战斗方法，打了迦太基人一个措手不及，因此一开始的时候迦太基人根本就不是罗马人的对手。

不过，罗马人也并不是一直都占据着上风。迦太基人很快也学会了这种作战方式。因此，罗马在陆战和海战方面都是有输有赢。最后，罗马的确胜利，而迦太基人也的确被打败了。这样，就结束了第一次布匿战争。

32 The Boot Kicks and Stamps

The Carthaginians were not beaten for good. They were only waiting for another chance to get even. As, however, they had been unsuccessful in attacking Italy from in front as they had been doing, they made up their minds to attack from the back. Their scheme was to go the long way round through Spain and down into Italy from the north.

In order to do this, first of all they had to conquer Spain so that they could get through. They did this, however, rather easily, for the Carthaginians had a very great general named Hannibal. Then came the great difficulty, to get into Italy by this back way.

Across the top of the *boot*, at the north of Italy, there are the great mountains called the Alps. They are miles high and covered even in summer with ice and snow. There are crags and steep cliffs along which anyone passing who made a single misstep would be dashed to death thousands of feet below.

It was the Alps, therefore, that formed a bigger and better wall than any city or country could possibly build. Of course the Romans thought it impossible for any army to climb over such a terribly high and dangerous wall.

Time and again there have been things that people call impossible to do, and then

32 "靴子"左右出击

迦太基人并没有被彻底打垮。他们只是在等待机会，准备向罗马人复仇。然而，由于他们从正面对意大利发动进攻一直没能取胜，所以他们决定从意大利的后方去发动进攻。他们的计划，就是经由西班牙绕上一个大圈子，然后再从北方南下，进入意大利。

为此，他们必须首先征服西班牙，这样才能取道该国去进攻罗马。他们攻下西班牙却没有费什么力气，因为迦太基人有一个非常了不起的将领，叫作汉尼拔。接下来，经由这条后方道路进入意大利就变成一个巨大的难题了。

在意大利这只"靴子"的顶端，即意大利的北部，横亘着一道叫作阿尔卑斯的巨大山脉。这条山脉的顶上连夏季也覆盖着皑皑的冰雪。在这里翻山越岭的时候，一路上全都是悬崖峭壁，脚下一不留神，便会跌下数千英尺深的悬崖，摔得粉身碎骨。

因此，阿尔卑斯山脉形成了一道巨大而坚固的屏障，比任何一座城市或者一个国家人工修筑的城墙或者边界都要牢靠。自然，罗马人也认为，任何一支军队都是不可能翻越这道高耸入云而又危险重重的屏障的。

可人们称之为不可能的事情，往往有人去做并且最终做到；这种情况，已经是

someone has come along and done them.

People said it was impossible to fly. Then someone did it.

People said it was impossible to cross the Alps with an army.

Then Hannibal came along, and before the Romans knew what had happened, he had done it. He had crossed the Alps with his army and was in at the back door! Hannibal brought with him elephants from Africa. These were the *tanks* of ancient warfare and were highly valued. Can you imagine the long columns of soldiers and elephants crossing those high mountains?

The Romans were unable to keep him from marching on toward their city, winning battle after battle as he came along. They were unable to prevent his marching up and down Italy, conquering other towns in Italy and doing pretty much as he pleased. It seemed as if Rome were beaten and would lose all of Italy.

Now, in some games, if you can't defend your own goal, it may be a good plan to try attacking your opponent's goal.

Romans thought they would try this plan. While Hannibal was attacking, Rome would attack Carthage while its general was away and there was no strong goalkeeper to defend that city.

The Romans sent a young man named Scipio with an army to do this.

First, however, Scipio went to Spain to cut Hannibal off from the way he had come.

Scipio then went over to Africa to attack Carthage itself.

屡见不鲜了。

人们曾经说，人类不可能飞上天去。

可接下来，有人却做到了这一点。

当时的人们说，一支军队是不可能越过阿尔卑斯山脉这道天险的。

可接下来，汉尼拔出现了，并且不待罗马人明白这是怎么回事，他就已经做到了这一点。他率军翻越了阿尔卑斯山脉，来到了意大利的后门！汉尼拔的大军中，装备着许多来自非洲的大象。大象就是古时战场上的"坦克"，得到了人们的极大重视。你们想象得出一队队由士兵和大象组成的队伍翻越阿尔卑斯这座高山时的壮观情景吗？

罗马人根本无法阻挡汉尼拔的大军向罗马城节节逼近，并且一路上汉尼拔所向披靡，打了一场又一场胜仗。罗马人无法阻止汉尼拔率军在整个意大利境内左奔右突，攻取意大利的其他城邦，并且为所欲为。似乎罗马已经被打垮，而整个意大利也将沦陷了。

注意，在有些比赛中，倘若你们无法守住自己的地盘，那么试着去进攻对手的地盘，可能不失为一个好办法呢。

罗马人决定试一试这个办法。当汉尼拔正在意大利四处进击的时候，罗马人则去攻打迦太基了；因为此时迦太基的那位将领不在城内，没有实力强大的守军来保卫迦太基城。

罗马派遣一位叫作西庇阿的年轻人，率军前去攻打迦太基。

不过，西庇阿首先攻入了西班牙，从而切断了汉尼拔的退路。

The Carthaginians, frightened at being attacked with their general and his army far off in Italy, sent as fast as they could for Hannibal to come home. When at last he arrived, it was too late. Scipio fought a famous battle at Zama near Carthage, and the Carthaginians were beaten, beaten a second time by the Romans. Thus ended the second Punic War in 202 B.C. This is another easy name and easy date:

Zama — 202 B.C.

The Romans had won two wars against Carthage; you would think that they would now have been satisfied. But they weren't. They thought they had not beaten Carthage badly enough. They were afraid Carthage was not quite dead or that it might come to life. They thought there might be a little spark left that might start a fire if it weren't trampled out.

Now, it is bad sport to pummel your opponent after he is beaten, and Carthage was beaten — beaten, black and blue. Yet a few years later the Romans attacked again for the third and last time.

Carthage was unable to defend itself, and the Romans destroyed the city. Later, though, the Roman general Julius Caesar rebuilt the city. Still later, the Romans built other cities nearby, with fine roads connecting them and with great aqueducts bringing them water. Today we can visit the Roman ruins in what is now Tunisia.

接下来，西庇阿便率军前往非洲，去进击迦太基本土。

迦太基人惊慌失措，因为他们的那位将领和大军，此时都在遥远的意大利；于是，他们便赶紧派人去通知汉尼拔回国。可当汉尼拔终于率军回到迦太基的时候，为时却已太晚了。西庇阿在迦太基附近的扎马打了一场著名的大仗，迦太基人再次被罗马人打败了。这样，第二次"布匿战争"就在公元前202年结束了。这个地名和年代也很容易记住：

扎马之战——公元前202年

罗马人已经打赢了两场与迦太基进行的战争；你们可能会想，如今他们应该心满意足了吧。可他们才没有满足呢。他们认为，罗马还没有将迦太基打得一败涂地。他们担心，迦太基还没有被彻底击溃，还有可能会卷土重来。他们认为，如果不斩草除根的话，那么星星之火可能就会形成燎原之势。

如今，假如在对手被打败之后继续进攻的话，就会被人认为是一种很没有风度的行为；而此时的迦太基，也确实已经被打败，并且被打得遍体鳞伤了。可是，几年过后，罗马人又第三次攻打了迦太基；这也是罗马的最后一次进攻。

此时的迦太基根本无法自卫，于是罗马人便摧毁了这座城市。不过，后来罗马将领恺撒又重建了迦太基城。再后来，罗马人又在迦太基城附近兴建了许多其他的城市，它们之间都有宽阔的道路相连，并且有巨大的沟渠给这些城市供水。今天，我们还可以在如今的突尼斯参观到古罗马人所建城市的遗迹呢。

33 The New Champion of the World

You can well imagine how proud all the Romans now *were* that they were Romans, for Rome was the champion fighter of the world. If a man could toss his head and say, "I am a Roman citizen," people were always ready to do something for him, afraid to do him any harm, afraid what might happen to them if they did. Rome was ruler not only of Italy but of Spain and North Africa. Like other earlier nations, once Rome had started conquering, it kept on conquering, until by 100 B.C. Rome was ruler of almost all the countries bordering the Mediterranean Sea — all except Egypt.

The New Champion of the World, who was to be champion for a great many years, was very businesslike and practical.

The Greeks loved beautiful things, beautiful buildings, beautiful sculpture, beautiful poems. The Romans copied the Greeks and learned from them how to make many beautiful things, but the Romans were most interested in practical and useful things. For example, now that the Romans ruled the world, they had to be able to send messengers and armies easily and quickly in every direction to the end of the empire and back again. It was necessary to have roads, for of course there were no railroads then. Now, an ordinary

33 新的世界霸主

你们完全可以想象，此时所有的古罗马人都对自己身为罗马人感到有多么的自豪，因为古罗马已经成了世界的霸主。如果一个人抬起头来，说"我是罗马公民"的话，人们往往就会很乐意为他服务，害怕做出令他不高兴的事情，担心要是这样做了的话，自己又会有什么下场。当时，古罗马不但统治着意大利，还统治着西班牙和北非地区。就像古代的其他民族一样，古罗马一旦开始征伐，之后就不断地攻城略地；直到公元前100年，古罗马统治了地中海沿岸几乎所有的国家，只有埃及除外。

这个新的世界霸主，在后来很长的一段时间里都一直保持着霸主地位；古罗马非但治理务实，也很讲求实际。

古希腊人热爱美丽的事物、漂亮的建筑、精美的雕塑和优雅的诗歌。虽说古罗马人效法古希腊人，并从古希腊人那里学到了制造各种美丽之物的技能，但古罗马人对实用之物却最感兴趣。例如，既然此时已经统治了整个世界，那么古罗马就必须能够向四面八方便利而迅速地派遣信使和军队，使之能够往来于帝国最边远的地区才行。因此，古罗马就必须修筑公路，因为那时当然还没有铁路。注意，倘若只是简简单单地清理了一下地面便修建出一条普通的公路的话，不久该公路就会变

road made by simply clearing away the ground gets full of deep ruts and in rainy weather becomes so muddy that it can hardly be used at all.

Rome set to work and built roads. These roads were like paved streets. Large rocks were placed at the bottom for a foundation, smaller stones placed on top, and large, flat paving-stones laid over all. Thousands of miles of such roads were built to all parts of the empire. One could go from almost anywhere all the way to Rome on paved roads. We still have an expression, "All roads lead to Rome." So well were these roads made that many of them still exist today, two thousand years after they were built.

The Romans also showed their practical minds by making two very important city improvements. If you live in a city, you turn on a spigot and you get plenty of pure water whenever you want it. The people in cities at that time, however, usually had to get their water both for drinking and for washing from wells or springs nearby. These springs and wells often became dirty and made the people very sick. Every once in a while because of such dirty water there were those terrible plagues, those terribly contagious diseases like the one I told you about in Athens when people died faster than they could be buried.

The Romans wanted pure water, so they set to work to find lakes from which they could get pure water. As oftentimes these lakes were many miles away from the city, they then built big pipes to carry the water all the way to the city. Such a pipe was not made of iron or terra-cotta as nowadays, but of stone and concrete, and was called an *aqueduct*, which in Latin means *water-carrier*. If this aqueduct had to cross a river or a valley, they built a

得坑坑洼洼、布满深深的车辙印，并且在下雨的时候还会变得泥泞不堪，几乎无法行走。

于是，古罗马便开始着手修筑公路。这些公路，就像一条条铺得平平整整的街道。路下有大石做路基，顶层是小石子，而最上面则铺有巨大而平整的石板。这种公路修筑了数千英里，通往帝国各地。一个人几乎可以从帝国的任何地方，一直沿着平整的公路前往罗马。我们如今仍然有这样一种说法呢："条条大路通罗马。"这些道路都修得极其牢固；到了两千多年后的今天，其中的许多道路还依然存在呢。

古罗马人还在城市发展方面做出了两个重大的改进，从而显示出了他们的实用思想。你们如果是城里人的话，那么不管什么时候，只要打开水龙头便有净水可用，并且想用多少就有多少。然而，当时那些居住在城市里的人，通常却必须到附近的水井或泉眼去打水，才会有水喝，才会有水洗东西。这种泉水或井水经常会受到污染，使得人们得上重病。由于喝了这种受到了污染的水，所以每隔一段时间，便会爆发一场可怕的瘟疫，出现种种可怕的传染病，就像我在前面跟你们说过的雅典那场瘟疫一样；当时死的人太多，埋都埋不过来呢。

古罗马人希望自己有干净的水可用，于是他们便开始找出一些水质干净的湖泊来获取净水。通常来说，这些湖泊距城市都有好几英里远；所以，古罗马人便铺设了一些巨大的管道，将湖水一路输送到城里去。这种管道，并不是如今那种用钢铁或者陶瓷制成的管道，而是用石头和混凝土制成的，因此被称为"水渠"；在拉丁

bridge to hold it up. Many of these Roman aqueducts are still standing and in use today.

Now, up to this time waste water, after it had been used, and also every other kind of dirt and refuse, was simply dumped into the street. This naturally made the city or town filthy and unhealthy and was another cause of plagues.

The Romans, however, built great underground sewers to carry off this dirt and waste water and empty it into the river or into some other place where they thought it would do no harm and cause no sickness. Now we know that it's not good to dump sewage into rivers because they can become polluted. Then if people drink that water, they'll get sick. The Romans knew that they had to get the sewage off the city streets, but they didn't know how to avoid polluting their rivers. Nowadays, every large city has aqueducts and sewers as a matter of course, but the Romans were the first Europeans to build them on a large scale.

One of the most important things that Rome did was to make rules that everyone had to obey; laws, we call them. Many of these laws were so fair and just that some of our own laws today are copied from them.

Roman aqueduct
古罗马的引水渠

All the cities and towns of the Roman Empire had to pay money or taxes to Rome. Rome therefore became a very wealthy city. Millions of this money, which was brought to

语里，"水渠"的意思就是指"引水的沟渠"。如果一条水渠必须跨越河流或者山谷的话，古罗马人还会架设一座桥梁来支撑水渠。古罗马的这些水渠中，有许多都保存至今，并且仍在使用呢。

注意，直到此时，人们用过的废水和其他各种各样的污物、垃圾，都是直接倾倒在大街上。这种做法，自然会让城市和乡镇都变得污秽不堪、毫不卫生，也是引起瘟疫的又一个原因。

然而，古罗马人却聪明得很。他们修建了一条条巨大的地下排水沟来收集这种污水和废水，并将它们排到河流中去，或者排到他们认为不会有害、不会引起疾病的其他地方去。如今我们已经明白，将污水排入河流是没有好处的，因为此种做法会让河水受到污染。这样一来，如果喝了河水，我们就会得病。古罗马人知道，他们必须把污水从大街上排走；可他们并不知道，如何才能不让河流也受到污染。事实上，虽说如今每座大城市里都建有引水渠和下水道，可古罗马人却是欧洲第一个大规模地铺设引水渠和排水沟的民族呢。

古罗马人的重大贡献之一，便是制定了人人都必须遵守的准则；这些准则，我们称之为法律。他们制定的法律当中，许多都制定得非常公正、合理，以至于如今美国的法律当中，有一些还是仿照它们制定出来的哩。

her, was spent in putting up beautiful buildings in the city, temples to the gods, splendid palaces for the rulers, public baths, and huge open-air places called *amphitheaters* where the people could be amused.

The amphitheaters were something like our football and baseball fields or stadiums. They did not have football or baseball, however. They had chariot races, and deadly fights between men, or between men and animals. Chariots were small carts with large wheels drawn by two or by four horses and driven by a man standing up. Perhaps you have seen chariot races in the circus.

The sport that the Romans enjoyed most of all was a fight of gladiators. Gladiators were very strong and powerful men who had been captured in battle by the Romans. They were made to fight with one another or with wild animals for the amusement of the crowds. These gladiatorial fights were very cruel, but the Romans enjoyed seeing blood shed. They liked to see one man kill another or a wild animal. It was so amusing. The movies would not have interested them half as much. Usually the gladiators fought until one or the other was killed, for the people were not, as a rule, satisfied until this was done.

Sometimes, however, if a gladiator, who had been knocked out, had shown himself particularly brave and a good fighter or a good sport, the people seated all around the amphitheater would turn their thumbs *up* as a sign that his life was to be spared by the other gladiator. The winning gladiator, before killing his opponent whom he had down, would wait to see what the people wished. If they turned their thumbs *down*, it meant he

罗马帝国的所有城邦和市镇，都必须向罗马缴纳钱财或者税赋。因此，罗马便变成了一个富甲天下的城市。缴纳上来的这些钱财，都被罗马人大把大把地用于在城中建造美丽的高楼大厦、祭祀神灵的庙宇、供君主居住的辉煌宫殿、公共浴室，以及被称为"竞技场"的供人们娱乐的大型露天场所。

露天竞技场有点儿像是我们如今的足球场、棒球场或者体育场。然而，露天竞技场并没有足球比赛，也不会举行棒球比赛。这里举行的是两轮战车竞赛，以及男人与男人之间或者是男人与动物之间的殊死搏斗。两轮战车的车斗很小，车轮却很大，由两匹或者四匹马儿拉着；赶车的人则站在车上。你们没准都在马戏团里看见过这种两轮战车赛跑呢。

古罗马人最喜欢的一项竞技运动，便是角斗士之间的格斗。角斗士都是古罗马人在战场之上俘虏过来的，他们一个个全都身强力壮、孔武有力。古罗马人让这些角斗士彼此格斗，或者是与野兽搏斗，以此来取悦观众。角斗士的这种搏斗极其残酷，可古罗马人却很喜欢看这种血腥的场面。他们喜欢看到两人相互残杀，或者杀死一头野兽。这太好玩了。如今的电影对他们来说，可能连一半的吸引力也达不到呢。角斗士一般会搏斗到其中有一人被杀死；因为通常来说，观众不看到这个，就不会觉得满意。

然而，有的时候，假如一名被打倒在地的角斗士表现出了非凡的勇猛，表明自己是一名优秀的格斗手或者很有气度的话，那么坐在露天竞技场周围的观众便会竖起他们的大拇指，表示另一名角斗士应当饶他一命。而获胜的角斗士在杀死已经被

was to finish the fight by killing his man.

Although Rome had become such a fine and beautiful and healthy city in which to live, the rich people were getting most of the money that came there from all over the empire. They were getting richer and richer all the time, while the poor people, who got nothing, were getting poorer and poorer all the time. The Romans brought the people they conquered in battle to Rome and made them work for them without pay. These were slaves and they did all the work. It is said that there were more than twice as many slaves as Romans — two slaves for every Roman citizen.

Now, Scipio, who had conquered Hannibal in the Punic War, had a daughter named Cornelia Gracchi, and she had two sons. They were very fine boys, and Cornelia was naturally very proud of them.

One day a very rich Roman woman was visiting Cornelia and showing off all her rings and necklaces and other ornaments, of which she had a great many and was very proud.

When she had shown off all she had, she asked to see Cornelia's jewels.

Cornelia called to her two boys, who were playing outside, and when they came in to their mother she put her arms around them and said:

"*These are my* jewels."

But boys who are jewels when they are young do not always turn out to be jewels when they grow up. You may wonder how Cornelia's jewels turned out.

When they grew up, the Gracchi, as they were called, saw such great extravagance

他打倒的对手之前，会等一会儿，看观众希望他怎么做。假如观众的拇指都朝下，那就意味着他应当杀死对手，结束搏斗。

尽管此时的罗马已经变成了一个非常完善、美丽、卫生且适于居住的城市，但从帝国各地进贡上来的钱财却大部分都归富人所有。他们变得越来越富有，而穷人什么也得不到，因此变得越来越贫困。古罗马人将战争中俘虏的人带往罗马，迫使这些人无偿地替他们工作。这些人全都是奴隶，各种各样的苦活儿都由他们来干。据说当时奴隶的数量甚至达到了古罗马人的两倍多，即平均起来，每位罗马市民都拥有两名奴隶呢。

此时，曾在"布匿战争"中打败了汉尼拔的那位西庇阿有个女儿，名叫科妮莉亚·格拉古，她生了两个儿子。他们都是非常优秀的孩子，所以科妮莉亚自然以他们为傲。

有一天，一位罗马的阔太太前来拜访科妮莉亚，并且向她炫耀自己的戒指啊、项链啊，以及其他的首饰；这位阔太太有很多这样的首饰，因此得意扬扬。

炫耀完所有的首饰之后，她便要求看一看科妮莉亚的珠宝首饰。

科妮莉亚将正在外面玩耍的两个儿子叫了进来；等他们进屋走到母亲身边后，她便伸手抱住两个儿子，说：

"他们就是我的宝贝。"

不过，凡是小时候属于父母掌上明珠的孩子，长大以后却不见得一定仍然是宝贝。你们或许很想知道，科妮莉亚的这两个宝贝，最后都变成了什么样的人。

among the rich and such great misery among the poor that they wanted to do something about it. They saw that the poor had hardly anything to eat and no place to live. This did not seem fair. They tried to lower the price of food, so that the poor might be able to buy enough to eat. They tried to find some way to give the poor at least a small piece of land where they might raise a few vegetables. They were partly successful in bringing this about. But the rich people didn't like giving up anything to the poor, and they killed one of the Gracchus brothers, and later they killed the other one, also. These were Cornelia's jewels.

　　长大成人后，这对格拉古兄弟，由于对富人的穷奢极欲、穷人的困苦不堪看得太多，所以便想做点什么来改变这种情况。他们看到，穷人既没有吃的，也没有房子居住，这似乎很不公平。于是，他们便尽力降低食品的价格，好让穷人买得起够吃的粮食。他们想方设法，觉得起码也要给穷人一小块土地来种植一点儿蔬菜才是。他们实现了这一目标的一部分。不过，罗马的富人却不愿意分给穷人一点点东西，因此他们便谋杀了格拉古兄弟中的一个，后来又杀害了另一个。这两兄弟，就是科妮莉亚真正的宝贝。

34 The Noblest Roman of Them All

Here's a puzzle for you:

A man once found a very old piece of money that had on it the date *100* B.C.

That couldn't be so. Why not? See if you can tell without looking at the answer at the bottom of the page.[1]

In the year 100 B.C. was born in Rome a boy who was named Julius Caesar.

If you had asked him when he was born, he would have said in the Year 653.

Why do you suppose?

Because Roman boys counted time from the founding of Rome in 753 B.C. and Caesar was born 653 years after the city was founded. That makes it 100 years before Christ, doesn't it?

Pirates seemed to be everywhere in the Mediterranean Sea at that time — *Pirates*. Now that Rome was ruler of the world, there were many ships carrying gold from different parts of the empire to Rome. The pirates sailed up and down, lying in wait to capture and rob

---

[1] People living 100 years before Christ was born could not have known when he was to be born and so could not put such a date on the coins they made.

34　最高贵的罗马人

下面给你们出一个智力问答题：

有一次，一个人发现了一枚非常古老的硬币，上面刻有"公元前100年"的日期。

这不可能是真的。为什么呢？你们能否不看这一页下端的答案，就说出原因来呢？[1]

公元前100年，罗马诞生了一个小男孩，名叫尤利乌斯·恺撒。

假如你问问他，看他是哪一年出生的，他就会回答你说是653年。

你们认为，这又是为什么呢？

这是因为，古罗马人是从公元前753年罗马建城的时候开始纪年的，而恺撒正是在罗马建城的653年之后出生的。这一年，正好是公元前100年，对不对呢？

那个时候，地中海上似乎到处都有海盗，那可是真正的海盗在出没呢。古罗马统治了大片领土之后，有许多的船只将帝国各地的金银财宝运送到罗马去。海盗们

---

[1] 生活在基督降生前100年的人，不可能知道基督将会降生，所以也不可能将这样一个日期刻在他们制造出来的硬币上啊。

these ships laden with gold.

When Caesar grew to be a young man, he was sent off to sea to fight these pirates, and he was captured by them. The pirates kept Caesar a prisoner and sent to Rome saying they would not let him go unless Rome sent them a great deal of money. Caesar knew that he would be killed if the money was *not* sent. He knew, too, that he might be killed anyway. He was not only not afraid, but he told the pirates that if he lived to get back home he would return with a fleet and punish every one of them. When at last the money came they let him go, nevertheless. They thought Caesar would not dare to do what he said. They thought he was just *talking big*. At any rate, they did not believe he would be able to catch them. Caesar, however, kept his word, came back after them as he said he would do, and took them prisoners. Then he had them all put to death on the cross, which was the Roman way of punishing thieves.

The far-off places of the Roman Empire were always fighting against Rome, trying to get rid of the foreign rule, and they had to be kept in order by a general with an army. As Caesar had shown such bravery in fighting the pirates he was given an army and sent to fight two of these far-off places — Spain and a country north of Spain then known as Gaul, which is now France.

Caesar conquered these countries, and then he wrote a history of his battles in Latin, which of course was his own language. Nowadays this book, called *Caesar's Commentaries*, is usually the first book read by those who study Latin.

便在地中海上四处游弋，守株待兔，想伺机夺取这些满载黄金的船只。

恺撒长大成年之后，曾被派到海上去与这些海盗作战，可他却被海盗俘虏了。海盗们将恺撒关了起来，并且派人到罗马去，说除非罗马送给他们一大笔钱，否则他们就不会放人。恺撒明白，如果罗马不送赎金来的话，他就会被海盗杀掉。他也明白，不管送不送赎金，自己都有可能被海盗杀掉。所以，他不但毫不畏惧，还对那些海盗说，如果活着回到罗马的话，他就会率领一支舰队回来报仇，每一名海盗都逃不掉。尽管如此，当罗马送来赎金后，海盗们最终还是释放了恺撒。他们觉得，恺撒根本就不敢再来报仇的。他们以为，恺撒当时不过是吹吹牛、说说大话罢了。反正，他们觉得恺撒根本就抓不住他们。然而，恺撒却说到做到，后来真的回去找海盗们报仇，并将他们全都关了起来。然后，他又按照罗马惩处盗贼的律法，将这些海盗判处死刑，全部钉死在十字架上。

古罗马帝国那些偏远的属国一直都在反抗罗马，试图摆脱外族的统治，因此必须有一名将领统帅一支军队，才能维持好这些地方的秩序。由于恺撒在与海盗作战的过程中表现出了非凡的勇气，因此罗马当局命令他率领一支军队，前去与两个偏远地区的叛军作战；这两个地方，一个是西班牙，另一个则是位于西班牙以北、当时叫作高卢的地方，也就是如今的法国。

恺撒征服了这两个国家，然后用拉丁语记录下了自己的作战经过；拉丁语自然也是他的母语。这本书，如今叫作《高卢战记》，通常都是学习拉丁语的人要阅读的第一部原著。

In 55 B.C. Caesar crossed over in ships to the island of Britain, conquered a large part of it, and went back again next year, in 54 B.C.

Caesar was becoming famous for the way he conquered and ruled over the western part of the Roman Empire. Besides this, he was very popular with his soldiers.

Now there was in Rome at this time another general named Pompey. Pompey had been successfully fighting in the eastern part of the Roman Empire while Caesar had been fighting in the west. Pompey had been a great friend of Caesar, but when he saw how much land Caesar had conquered and how popular he was with his soldiers, he became very jealous of him. Notice how many quarrels and wars are caused simply by jealousy. You have heard of at least two already.

While Caesar was away with his army, Pompey went to the Roman Senate and persuaded the senators to order Caesar to give up the command of his army and return to Rome.

When Caesar received the order from the Senate to give up his command and return to Rome, he thought over the matter for some time. Then at last he made up his mind that he would return to Rome, but he would not give up his command. Instead, he decided that he and his army would take command of Rome itself.

Now, there was a little stream called the *Rubicon* which separated the part of the country over which Caesar was given charge from that of Rome. The Roman law forbade any general to cross this stream with an army ready to fight — this was the line beyond which he must not pass, for the Romans were afraid that if a general with an army got too

公元前55年，恺撒乘船渡海前往不列颠岛，征服了岛上的大部分地区，并在第二年，即公元前54年，再次率军远征这个岛屿。

恺撒由于一路征伐、所向无敌，并统治着古罗马帝国西部而变得名声大噪了。除此之外，他也很受军中士兵的爱戴。

当时，罗马还有另一位将领，叫作庞培。当恺撒正在古罗马帝国西部征战的同时，庞培也在古罗马帝国东部地区取得了一场场大捷。庞培本是恺撒的知交密友，但当他看到恺撒攻取了那么多的地方，又深受军中士兵的爱戴之后，却开始对他极为嫉恨起来。请注意，仅仅是因为嫉妒，就引发了多少纷争和战争啊。你们起码已经听到了两次了，对不对呢？

就在恺撒率军出征之后，庞培便来到罗马的元老院，说服元老们下令，让恺撒交出军队的指挥权并返回罗马。

恺撒接到元老院要他交出军队指挥权并返回罗马的命令后，曾经仔细地考虑了一段时间。最后，他决定返回罗马，但他不愿交出指挥权。相反，他决定率军夺取并控制罗马的大权。

注意，在恺撒受命管理的国土与罗马管辖的疆域之间，隔着一条叫作卢比孔的小河。古罗马的律法规定，禁止任何一位将领率领一支准备作战的军队越过这条小河。所以，这是一条任何将领都不得逾越的界线，因为罗马人担心，如果一位将领统帅着军队离罗马太近的话，这位将领没准会自立为王呢。

close to Rome he might make himself king.

When Caesar decided not to obey the Senate, he crossed this stream — the Rubicon — with his army and marched on to Rome.

People now speak of any dividing line from danger as "the Rubicon" and say that a person "crosses the Rubicon" when he takes a step from which there is no turning back, when he starts something difficult or dangerous which he must finish.

When Pompey heard that Caesar was coming, he took to his heels and fled to Greece. In a few days Caesar had made himself head not only of Rome but of all Italy. Caesar then went after Pompey in Greece and in a battle with his army beat him badly.

Now that Pompey was out of the way, Caesar was the chief ruler of the whole of the Roman Empire.

Egypt did not yet belong to Rome. Caesar next went there and conquered that country. Now, in Egypt there was ruling a beautiful queen named Cleopatra. Cleopatra was so charming that she seemed able to make everyone fall in love with her. Cleopatra flirted with Caesar and so fascinated him that he almost forgot everything else. Although he had won Egypt, he allowed Cleopatra to remain queen over that country.

Just at this time some people in the far eastern part of the empire started a war to get rid of the rule of Rome. Caesar left Egypt, traveled rapidly to the place where the enemy were, made quick work of conquering them, then sent back the news of his victory to Rome in the most laconic (do you remember what that means?) description ever given of a battle. There were only three words in the message. Although the messenger could have

恺撒决定不服从元老院的命令之后，便率军越过了这条小河，并向罗马进军。

如今，人们还把所有与危险境地分隔开来的界线叫作"卢比孔河"；而当一个人采取果断措施且不留后路、开始去做某种不得不做的困难或危险之事时，人们还会说这个人是"跨过了卢比孔河"。

庞培得知恺撒率军向罗马逼近的消息后，便溜之大吉、逃往希腊了。没过几天，恺撒不仅成了罗马的首脑，而且成了整个意大利的领袖。然后，恺撒又率军挺进希腊、追击庞培，并在一场战役中大败庞培。

解决掉庞培之后，恺撒便成了整个古罗马帝国的元首。

当时，埃及仍然没有臣服于古罗马帝国。因此，恺撒接下来便挥师南下埃及，征服了这个国家。此时，统治着埃及的是一位美丽的女王，名叫克利奥帕特拉。克利奥帕特拉非常迷人，似乎能让每个见到她的人都爱上她。克利奥帕特拉对恺撒大送秋波，令他神魂颠倒，使得他几乎把其他的一切全都抛到了脑后。尽管已经战胜了埃及，但他答应让克里奥帕特拉继续以女王的身份统治该国。

就在此时，在古罗马帝国遥远的东部地区，一些人揭竿而起，发动了一场战争，准备摆脱罗马的统治。恺撒便离开了埃及，率军火速赶往敌人所在的地方，迅速镇压了叛乱，然后用历史上描述一场战斗时最拉科尼亚式的（你们还记得这个词的意思吗？）话语，将大捷的消息送回了罗马。这则消息，只用了三个词。尽管信使携带一份三千字的捷报信件与携带一份只有三个词的捷报信件同样轻而易举，但

carried three thousand as easily as three words, Caesar sent a message that would have been short even for a telegram. He wrote, "Veni, vidi, vici," which means, "I came, I saw, I conquered."

When Caesar at last got back to Rome, the people wanted to make him king, or said they did. Caesar was already more than king, for he was head of the whole Roman Empire. But he wasn't called king, for there had been no kings since 509 B.C., when Tarquin was driven out. The Romans had been afraid of kings and hated them, or were supposed to hate them.

A few of the people thought that Caesar was getting too much power and believed it would be a terrible thing to make him a king. They therefore decided on a plot to prevent such a thing happening. One of these plotters was a man named Brutus, who had been Caesar's very best friend.

One day when Caesar was expected to visit the Roman Senate, they lay in wait for him until he should appear — in the same way I have seen boys hide around the corner for some schoolmate, against whom they had a grudge, until he should come out of school.

Caesar came along, and just as he was about to enter the Senate the plotters crowded around him, and one after another they stabbed him.

Caesar, taken by surprise, tried to defend himself; but all he had was his stylus, which was a kind of pen he used for writing, and he could not do much with that, in spite of a famous saying, "The pen is mightier than the sword."

When at last Caesar saw Brutus — his best friend — strike at him, his heart seemed

恺撒所发的这则消息，即便是对于如今的电报而言，也是非常简短的了。他如此写道："Veni, vidi, vici。"意思就是："我来了，我看到了，我战胜了。"

恺撒最终回到罗马后，古罗马人都希望拥立他做国王，至少嘴上都说他们希望这样。当时，恺撒的权力其实已经大过国王的了，因为他是整个古罗马帝国的元首。只是他没有国王的名义，因为自公元前509年塔克文被赶下台之后，罗马就没有过国王了。古罗马人对历任国王一直都既害怕、又痛恨，而他们事实上也理应痛恨这些国王。

少数人觉得恺撒的权力过大，并且认为让他当国王会是一件可怕的事情。因此，他们便策划了一个阴谋，想要阻止恺撒称王。参与这一阴谋的人里，有个人叫作布鲁特斯，他一直都是恺撒最要好的朋友。

有一天，由于恺撒预订前往罗马元老院，所以他们便在暗中埋伏，等着他出现；这就像我曾经见到一些小朋友躲在角落里，等着与自己斗过气的同学走出校门，要吓他一跳似的。

恺撒按约前来，就在他正要进入元老院的时候，那些参与这一阴谋的人便一拥而上，你一剑我一刀地向他捅去。

恺撒大吃一惊，试图自卫；但他随身只携带着一支用来写字的铁笔。虽然有句名言说得好："笔能杀人。"但在此时，他的铁笔却没有多大用处。

最后，当恺撒看到他最好的朋友布鲁特斯也向他刺来之后，顿时痛心无比，便

broken and he gave up. Then, exclaiming in Latin, "Et tu, Brute!" which means, "And thou, O Brutus!" he fell down dead. This was in 44 B.C.

Antony, one of Caesar's true friends, made a speech over Caesar's dead body, and his words so stirred the crowd of people that gathered round that they would have torn the murderers to pieces if they could have caught them.

Shakespeare has written a play called *Julius Caesar*, and the month of July is named after him.

Now whom do you suppose Antony called "The Noblest Roman of Them All"?

"Julius Caesar"?

No, you're wrong. Brutus, the friend who stabbed Caesar, was called, "The Noblest Roman of Them All." Why, do you suppose?

You'll have to read Antony's speech at the end of the play to find out.

Caesar was pronounced in Latin *kaiser*; and in later years the rulers of Germany were called this, and those of Russia by the shortened form, *czar*.

不再抵抗了。接着，他用拉丁语喊道："Et tu, Brute！"意思就是："还有你啊，布鲁特斯！"然后便倒在地上死去了。这一事件，发生在公元前44年。

安东尼是恺撒真正的朋友之一，他在恺撒的遗体边发表了演讲。他的讲话激起了周围民众的极大愤慨：假如抓到了凶手，他们早就把凶手撕成碎片了。

莎士比亚曾经写过一部戏剧，叫作《裘力斯·恺撒》，而如今的七月（July），也是根据恺撒的名字来命名的。

那么，你们觉得，安东尼所说的"他们当中最高贵的罗马人"指的是谁呢？

"恺撒大帝吗？"

不是的，你们想错了。用刀刺向恺撒的那位"朋友"布鲁特斯，才是当时被称为"他们当中最高贵的罗马人"。

你们认为那是为什么呢？

你们必须到莎士比亚所写的那部戏剧末尾去读一读安东尼的话，才能明白其中的缘故。

恺撒（Caesar）这个名字在拉丁语中被写成"kaiser"，即"皇帝"的意思，故后来德国的历代君主都被称为"kaiser"，而俄罗斯的君主则是用其缩写形式czar，即"沙皇"。

35 An Emperor Who Was Made a God

A person is famous who has a town or a street named after him or her.

Will you ever do anything great enough to have even an alley named after you?

Just suppose a month, one of the twelve months of the year, was given your name!

Millions upon millions of people would then write and speak your name forever!

I'm going to tell you about a man who not only had a month named after him but who was made a god!

After Caesar had been killed, three men ruled the Roman Empire. One of these three men was Antony, the friend of Caesar, who made the famous speech over his dead body. The second was Caesar's adopted son, who was named Octavius. The name of the third you don't need to know, for Antony and Octavius soon got rid of him. Then no sooner had they forced him out than each of these two began to plot to get the share of the other.

Antony's share, over which he ruled, was the eastern part of the empire. The capital of this part was Alexandria in Egypt, hence Antony went there to live.

In Egypt Antony fell in love with Cleopatra, as Caesar before him had done, and he finally married her.

35 被奉为神灵的皇帝

假如有一座城市或者一条大街以一个人的名字来命名，那么这个人一定是位名人。

你们想不想去做一些了不起的事情，以便将来哪怕有一条小巷子能用你们的名字来命名呢?

想象一下，要是一年十二个月份当中，有一个月份用的是你们的名字，那你们该有多威风啊!

那样的话，就会有千百万的人不停地写下和说出你们的名字，直到永远了!

下面，我就打算跟你们来说说一个人;不但有一个月份是以他的名字来命名的，而且他还被人们尊奉为神灵!

恺撒遇刺身亡之后，古罗马帝国便由三个人统治着。这三个人当中，第一个就是恺撒的朋友安东尼，他曾在恺撒的遗体边发表过演讲。第二个人则是恺撒的养子，名字叫作屋大维。第三个人的名字你们没有必要知道，因为安东尼和屋大维很快就除掉了他。接着，刚刚将第三个人挤走，安东尼和屋大维两人便开始阴谋夺取对方的地盘了。

安东尼所统治的地盘，是古罗马帝国的东部地区。这一地区的都城是埃及境内

Octavius, in the west, which was his share, then made war on Antony and Cleopatra together, and in the end beat them both. Antony felt so bad at being beaten by Octavius that he committed suicide.

His widow, Cleopatra, thereupon, flirted with Octavius as she had with Julius Caesar and Antony, hoping to make him also fall in love with her and so win him in that way.

It was no use. Octavius was a different kind of man from both Julius Caesar and Antony. He was cold-blooded and businesslike. He had no heart for love-making. He would not let a woman charm him or turn him aside from his plan, which was to be the greatest man in the world!

Cleopatra saw that it was no use trying to fool him. Then she heard that she was going to be taken back to Rome and paraded through the streets, as was done with any other prisoners taken in battle. She could not stand such a shame as that, and so she made up her mind she would not be taken back to Rome.

Now, in Egypt there is a kind of snake called an asp, which is deadly poisonous. Taking one of these asps in her hand, she uncovered her breast and let it bite her, and so she died.

Octavius was now ruler over all the countries that belonged to Rome, and when he returned home to that city, the people hailed him Emperor. He then gave up the name Octavius and had himself called *Augustus Caesar*, which is like saying, *His Majesty, Caesar*. This was in 27 B.C. The Romans had got rid of their kings in 509. From now on Rome had emperors, who were more than kings, for they ruled over many countries.

的亚历山大港，所以安东尼住在那里。

在埃及，安东尼就像之前的恺撒那样，也爱上了克利奥帕特拉，并且最终娶了她为妻。

接下来，地盘在古罗马帝国西部的屋大维，便发动了一场讨伐安乐尼和克利奥帕特拉两人的战争，并且最终打败了他们。安东尼对自己被屋大维打败一事耿耿于怀，便自杀了。

他的遗孀克利奥帕特拉随即便像对付恺撒和安东尼两人那样，开始勾引屋大维，希望他也会爱上自己，从而用这种方式获得他的宠爱。

可这样做根本没有用处。屋大维这个人，与恺撒和安东尼两人都大不相同。他冷酷无情，讲求实际。他不喜欢谈情说爱。他既不会允许一个女人把自己迷住，也不会因为女人而放弃自己的计划；这个计划，就是变成世界上伟大的一位统治者！

克利奥帕特拉明白，想要骗取他的感情是没有用处的。后来她又听说，屋大维打算把她带回罗马去，像对待那些在战争中俘虏的囚犯一样，将她游街示众。她可受不了这种奇耻大辱，因此下定决心，绝对不能被屋大维带回罗马去。

当时，埃及有一种叫作角蝰的蛇类，剧毒无比。于是，克利奥帕特拉手中抓着一条这样的蝰蛇，然后解开胸前的衣襟，让蛇咬了自己一口，然后就中毒死去了。

此时，屋大维已经统治了古罗马帝国的所有属国；因此，待他回到故乡罗马城后，古罗马人便都三呼万岁，称他为"皇帝"。接下来，他便舍弃了"屋大维"这个原名，而让人叫自己"奥古斯都·恺撒"，就像称呼他为"皇帝陛下"一样。这

Octavius, now with his name changed to Augustus Caesar, was only thirty-six years old when he became sole master of the Roman world. Rome was the great capital of this vast empire.

Augustus set to work to make Rome a beautiful city. He tore down a great many of the old buildings made of brick and put up in their place a remarkable number of new and handsome buildings of marble. Augustus always bragged that he found Rome brick and left it marble.

One of the finest buildings in Rome, the Pantheon was built. Pantheon means the temple of all the gods. Do not mix this with the Parthenon in Athens, for the two buildings are quite different, and though the names look something alike and sound something alike, they mean quite different things. Parthenon is from the goddess Athena Parthenos; Pantheon is from the two words *Pan theon*, which means *all gods*.

The Pantheon has a great dome made of brick and mortar. This dome is shaped like a bowl turned upside down, and in the very center of the top of the dome is a round opening called an eye. This open eye is the only "window" in the building, but through it, even on a cloudy day, enough light comes so that you can clearly see the whole handsome interior.

So magnificent did the city become with all these wonderful buildings, and so permanently did it seem to be built, that it was known as The Eternal City and is still so spoken of.

是公元前27年的事情。古罗马人在公元前509年曾经废除了国王。而从此时起，古罗马帝国便有了皇帝；历任皇帝的权力比国王更大，因为他们统治着许多的国家。

此时已经改名的屋大维，在当上整个古罗马帝国的独裁者时，年纪刚刚三十六岁。罗马则成了这个广袤帝国的伟大首都。

接下来，奥古斯都便开始把罗马变成一个美丽的城市。他下令拆掉了许多用土砖建成的老房子，并在这些地方建起了一栋栋崭新而漂亮的大理石建筑。后来奥古斯都还经常夸口，说自己得到的是罗马的砖头，而留给罗马的却是大理石呢。

罗马城中修建的最精美的建筑之一，便是万神殿（Pantheon）。所谓的"万神殿"，就是祭祀所有神祇的庙宇。你们可不要把它与雅典的巴台农神庙（Parthenon）混淆起来，因为这两座神庙大相径庭；虽然两者的英语名称看上去差不多，发音也有点儿相似，但它们所指的东西却完全不同。巴台农（Parthenon）这个名称源于雅典娜·巴台农（Athena Parthenos）[1]这位女神的名字，而万神殿（Pantheon）这个名称则由Pan和theon这两个拉丁单词组成，它们合起来即指"所有的神"。

万神殿有一个巨大的、用砖和灰泥砌成的圆形屋顶。这种屋顶，就像是一只倒扣过来的碗，而在屋顶的正中央开有一个圆孔，叫作"天眼"。这个敞开的"天

---

[1] 雅典娜·巴台农（Athena Parthenos），是希腊神话中智慧女神雅典娜的全称。"巴台农"（Parthenos）本义指"处女、贞女"，古希腊神话中一些女神的名字后多附有这个词，亦有人将其音译为"帕耳忒诺斯"。

There was a public square in Rome called the Forum. Here markets were held and the people came together for all sorts of things. Around the Forum were erected temples to the gods, courthouses, and other public buildings. The courthouses were something like the temples that the Greeks built, only the columns were put on the inside of the building instead of on the outside.

Triumphal arches also were erected to celebrate great victories. When a conquering hero returned from the war, he and his army passed through such an arch in a triumphal parade.

There had been in Rome a great amphitheater that is supposed to have held more people than any structure that has ever been built — two hundred thousand, it is said, or more than all the people who live in some good-sized cities. This was called the Circus Maximus. It was at last torn down to make room for other buildings.

Another amphitheater was the Colosseum, but this was not built until some time after Augustus had died. It held about the same number as the

Roman Pantheon
罗马的万神殿

眼",是万神殿里唯一的一扇"窗户";但即便是在阴天,从中透进来的光线也足以让人看清殿内气派美观的景物。

有了这些奇妙的建筑,罗马城便变得富丽堂皇起来;加上这些建筑似乎都牢固无比,因此罗马声名赫赫,被人们称为"不朽之城",而如今也依然还有人这么称呼它呢。

罗马还有一个被称为"市集"的公共广场。这里是个市场,古罗马人都到这里来买各种各样的东西。"市集"四周建有神庙、法院以及其他的公共建筑。古罗马的法院与希腊人修建的神庙有点儿相似,只不过法院的圆柱是在建筑内部,而不是立在建筑外部。

罗马还修建了许多的凯旋门,来纪念历次重大的胜利。当一位攻城略地的英雄从战场之上归来的时候,他和手下的军队都会从这种凯旋门下经过。

罗马城中曾经有过一座巨大的露天竞技场,据说其中可以容纳的人数超过了有史以来人类建造的其他任何建筑;据说它能够容纳下二十万人,这比如今一些中等规模的城市中所居住的人口还要多哩。这个地方,就叫"大竞技场"。最终,为了给其他建筑腾出地方,这个大竞技场被拆掉了。

罗马还有一个露天竞技场,叫作"圆形斗兽场",但它是奥古斯都去世一段时间之后才修建起来的。罗马斗兽场所能容纳的人数,与如今美国最大的体育场可以容纳的人数差不多。这里举行的竞技项目,就是角斗士之间的格斗以及角斗士与野

largest stadium in this country does today. Here were held those fights between men, called gladiators, and wild animals that I have already told you about. It is still standing, and, though it is in ruins, you can sit in the same seats where the old Roman emperors did, see the dens where the wild animals were kept, the doors where they were let into the arena, and even bloody marks that are said to be the stains made by the slain men and beasts.

So many famous writers lived at the time of Augustus that this has been called the Augustan Age. Two of the best known Latin poets lived at this time. These poets were Virgil and Horace. Virgil wrote the *Æneid*, which told of the wanderings of Æneas, the Trojan, who settled in Italy, and was the great-great-great-grandfather of Romulus and Remus. Horace wrote many short poems called odes. They were long songs of shepherds and shepherdesses and songs of the farm and country life. People liked his songs, and many still name their sons after him.

When Augustus Caesar died, he was made a god because he had done so much for Rome; temples were built in which he was worshiped, and the month of August was named after him.

兽之间的搏击，我在前面已经跟你们介绍过这种搏击的情况了。如今这个斗兽场依然存在；尽管它已经成为一片废墟，但你们还是可以到古罗马那些皇帝曾经坐过的位置上去坐一坐，看一看原来关着野兽的小房子、将野兽放到竞技场上去的那一道道门，甚至还能看到一些血迹，据说这些血迹都是一些被杀死的角斗士和野兽留下来的呢。

奥古斯都在位的时候，古罗马涌现出了许多著名的作家，因此人们一直将这个时期称为"奥古斯都时代"。有两位著名的拉丁诗人，都生活在这一时期。这两位诗人，一位是维吉尔，一位是贺拉斯。维吉尔著有史诗《埃涅阿斯纪》，讲述了特洛伊人埃涅阿斯漂泊漫游的经历；埃涅阿斯最后在意大利定居下来，成了罗慕路斯和瑞摩斯的曾曾曾祖父。贺拉斯则写了许多叫作"颂歌"的短诗。它们都歌颂了男女牧羊人之间的爱情，以及乡村和田园生活的美好。人们都很喜欢他的这些颂歌，因此如今还有很多人给自己的儿子起名为"贺拉斯"呢。

奥古斯都死后，由于他生前为罗马做出了那么多的贡献，所以人们便将他尊奉为神灵，古罗马人还建了许多神庙来敬奉他；而八月（August）也是根据他的名字"奥古斯都"（Augustus）来命名的。

36 "Thine Is the Kingdom, the Power, and the Glory"

Augustus Caesar had been Ruler of the World.

He had found Rome brick and left it marble.

He had had a month named after him, and He had been made a god!

Surely no one could ever be greater than he! Yet a greater man than he was living at the very same time — although Augustus himself knew nothing about Him and lived and died without ever having heard of Him. This man was born in the eastern part of Augustus's empire in a tiny little village called Bethlehem, and His name was Jesus.

For many, many years after Jesus was born no one except His family and friends knew or cared anything about His birth or paid the slightest attention to it.

Jesus was a Jew, the son of a carpenter. As a boy and young man He led a very simple and quiet life working in His father's shop. He did not begin to preach until He was more than thirty years old. Then He went about teaching the people what we learn today as the Christian religion.

He taught that there was one God over all.

He taught brotherly love, that one should love one's neighbor as oneself.

36 "国度、权柄和荣耀，全是你的"

奥古斯都曾经是整个世界的主宰。

他得到的罗马是一座用砖头砌成的城市，而留下的却是用大理石打造的罗马城。

他的名字被用于命名一个月份，而且他还被人们尊奉成了神灵！

世界上肯定再也没有比他更伟大的人了！不过，就在同一时期，还生活着一个比他更加伟大的人，尽管奥古斯都本人对这个人一无所知，并且生前、死时甚至都没有听说过这个人的名字。这个人名叫耶稣，他出生于奥古斯都治下的古罗马帝国东部一个叫作伯利恒的小村庄。

耶稣降生之后的许多、许多年里，除了他的家人和朋友以外，根本就没有人知道或者在意他的降生，也没有人注意到他的降生。

耶稣是个犹太人，他的父亲是一位木匠。青少年时期，他都在父亲的作坊里干活，过着一种非常简朴、宁静的生活。直到三十多岁后，他才开始传道。然后，他便开始四处游历，将我们如今所学的基督教教义，教导给当时的人们。

他教导说，世间只有一个上帝。

他教导说，人们要像兄弟般地相互友爱，一个人应当像爱自己一样地去爱

He taught the Golden Rule; that is, "Do unto others as you would have them do unto you."

He taught that there was a life after death for which this short life on earth was only a preparation; that therefore you should "lay up your treasures in heaven" by doing good works here.

Some of the Jews listened to Jesus and believed what He taught them. They thought He was going to set them free from the rule of the Romans, which they hated. Some of the temple priests, however, were afraid of what Jesus taught. Because so many people listened to Him and believed in Him, the priests were afraid they would lose their influence to a man whose ideas they believed were wrong. So they plotted to have Him put to death.

Now the men who were plotting Jesus's death could not have Him put to death without the permission of the Roman ruler of that part of the empire where Jesus lived. This ruler was named Pilate. So they went to Pilate and told him that Jesus was trying to make Himself king. Jesus of course meant and always said that He was a heavenly ruler and not an earthly king. These men knew that Pilate would not care at all what religion Jesus taught. There were all sorts of religions in the Roman Empire — those that believed in idols and those that believed in the sun, moon, and so on. One more new religion made little difference to the Romans, and Jesus would not be put to death simply for teaching another. But the priests knew if they could make Pilate believe that Jesus was trying to

邻居。

他将"黄金律"教导给人们，即"你们愿意人怎样待你们，你们也要怎样待人"。

他教导说，人死后会去到另一个世界，而尘世的短暂生活，只是为去到另一个世界所做的一种准备；因此，人们应当通过在尘世积德行善，从而"将财富积聚在天堂里"。

一些犹太人聆听着耶稣的布道，并且相信他所教导的东西。他们认为，耶稣会把他们从古罗马人的统治之下解救出来，因为他们都痛恨古罗马人的统治。然而，一些神庙里的祭司却害怕耶稣所传的教义。由于聆听耶稣教义并信仰耶稣的人实在太多，所以祭司们都很害怕，害怕他们会失去对那些信奉错误宗教的人的影响力。于是，他们便要阴谋诡计，准备处死耶稣。

当时，那些阴谋杀死耶稣的人，只有得到统治此地的罗马总督的允许，才能将他处死。那个总督名叫彼拉多。于是，他们便到彼拉多那里去，对他说耶稣正在准备自立为王。耶稣当然说过，并且一向都说他是一位天国之王，而不是一位尘世之王。这些人都明白，彼拉多总督根本就不在乎耶稣宣传的是一种什么样的宗教。当时古罗马帝国各地有着各种各样的宗教，有信奉多神教的，有信奉日月星辰等天体的。多一种新的宗教对古罗马人来说并无大碍，耶稣也不会只是因为宣传了一种新的宗教就被处死。但是，那些祭司们却明白，要是他们能够让彼拉多总督相信耶稣正在准备自立为王的话，那就是一项可以把耶稣钉死在十字架上的大罪了。彼拉多

make Himself a king, that was a thing for which He could be crucified. Pilate did not believe much in what they said against Jesus. It was a small matter to him. But he wanted to please them and keep his government in order, so he told them he would have Jesus put to death because they wanted it. So He was crucified.

Jesus had chosen twelve of his fellow Jews to teach what he told them. These twelve men were called apostles. After Jesus was crucified, the apostles went through the land teaching the people what He had taught them. Those who believed in and followed His teachings were called disciples of Christ (the Greek word for "messiah") or Christians. The apostles were teachers; the disciples were pupils.

One tiling that no Christian, or Jew either, could do was worship the Roman emperor. Most people in the empire found it easy to add one new god, but Christians, of course, could not do that. The Romans thought that these disciples of Christ were trying to start a new world empire and that they were against Rome and the emperor and should be arrested and put in prison. The Christians, therefore, held their meetings in secret places, sometimes even underground, so that they would not be found and arrested.

After a while the leaders of the Christians became bolder. They came out of their secret places and taught and preached openly, although they knew they might sooner or later be thrown into prison and perhaps killed. Indeed, so strongly did they believe in the teachings of Christ that they seemed even glad to die for His sake, as He had died on the cross for them.

In the first hundred years after Christ, there were a great many Christians put to death

总督却不怎么相信他们给耶稣编排出来的那些坏话。对他来说，这都是不值一提的小事。不过，彼拉多总督想让这些祭司们高兴，从而稳定他对犹太地区的统治，便对他们说，因为他们希望那样，所以他会把耶稣处死。于是，耶稣便被钉死在了十字架上。

耶稣生前已经选定了十二个信徒，来继续宣传他教导给人们的那些教义。这十二个人被称为"使徒"。耶稣被钉死在十字架上之后，这些使徒便四处行走，向人们宣传耶稣对他们的教导。那些信仰并追随耶稣教义的人，称为基督的门徒（"基督"一词是希腊语，代表"弥赛亚"），或者基督徒。因此，使徒就是老师，门徒则是学生。

基督徒或者犹太人无法忍受的一件事情，就是崇拜罗马皇帝。古罗马帝国中的大多数人都觉得，增加一个新的神灵是一件并不难办的事情，可基督徒当然做不到这一点。所以，古罗马人都以为这些基督门徒正在准备创立一个新的世界帝国，以为他们都在反抗古罗马帝国以及古罗马帝国的皇帝，因此应当全都抓起来关进监狱里才行。于是，基督徒便只能在秘密的地点碰头，有时甚至是在地下集会，以免被人发现并抓起来。

过了一段时间之后，基督徒中的一些领袖变得大胆一些了。他们不再藏身于隐秘之处，开始公开地进行教义宣传和布道，尽管他们明白，自己迟早会被关进监狱，或许还会被当局处死。事实上，由于他们都坚定不移地信奉基督的教义，因此他们甚至很乐意为了基督而赴死，就像基督为了他们而在十字架上受难那样。

because they were thought traitors. Christians who died for Christ's sake were called *martyrs*. The first martyr was named Stephen. He was stoned to death about 33 A.D.

One of the men who helped in putting Stephen to death was a man named Saul. Saul was a Roman citizen and, like other Roman citizens, was proud of that fact. He thought the Christians were enemies of his country, and he did everything he could to have the Christians punished. Then, all of a sudden, Saul had a change of heart and came to believe in the religion of the very people whom he had been fighting. Whatever Saul did or whatever he believed, he did or believed with his whole soul. Though he had never seen Christ, he became one of the chief Christians and then was made an apostle and was called by bis Roman name, Paul.

Paul preached the new religion far and wide just as earnestly as he had fought against it at first. Then he, too, was condemned to death. Paul, however, was, as I have said, a Roman citizen, and a Roman citizen could not be put to death by the ordinary judges who were not Roman citizens nor in the ordinary way by crucifying. So Paul appealed to the emperor, but he was put in prison in Rome and afterward beheaded. He is now known as St. Paul.

Peter was another of the chief apostles. Christ had said to him, "I will give unto thee the keys of the kingdom of heaven." Peter, too, was thrown into prison, and was sentenced to be crucified. He asked to be crucified with his head downward. He thought it too great an honor to die in just the same way as his Lord. On this spot in Rome where Peter was put to death was built long afterward the largest church in the world, the Cathedral of St. Peter.

在基督受难后起初的那一百年中，有许多的基督徒都因为被冤枉成奸人而处死了。那些为基督舍生就死的基督徒，被人们称为"殉道者"。第一位殉道者名叫司提反，他是公元33年左右被人们用乱石砸死的。

在协助处死司提反的人当中，有一个人叫作扫罗。扫罗是罗马人，并且像其他罗马人一样，都以自己是罗马人为荣。他认为基督徒都是古罗马帝国的敌人，因此千方百计地想让基督徒受到惩罚。接下来，扫罗的内心却突如其来地发生了变化，他开始信奉起原来一直与之做斗争的那些人的宗教来。无论扫罗做什么或者信奉什么，他都是全心全意地去做、去信奉。尽管他从未见过耶稣本人，可他却成了最重要的基督徒之一，然后又被选为使徒，而人们也用他的罗马名字"保罗"来称呼他。

保罗到处不遗余力地宣传这种新的宗教，跟起初他与这种新的宗教做斗争时一样诚心诚意。这样，后来他也被当局判处了死刑。然而，我在前面已经说过，保罗是罗马人，而那些不是罗马人的普通法官，是不能判处一个罗马人死刑，或者随随便便地将他钉死在十字架上的。因此，保罗便向罗马皇帝上诉；可他最终还是被关进了罗马的监狱，后来又被砍了头。如今，人们都称他为"圣保罗"。

彼得也是一名重要的使徒。基督曾经对他说过："我要把天国的钥匙给你。"后来，彼得也被关进了监狱，并且被当局判处了被钉死在十字架上的刑罚。他提了一个要求，希望低着头被钉死。他觉得，能够用一种与耶稣基督受难时完全相同的方式死去，是一种莫大的荣耀。很久、很久以后，在罗马城中彼得受难殉道的那个地方，人们还修建了一座世界上最大的教堂，即圣彼得大教堂。

As everything before Christ's birth is called B.C. and everything since his birth is called A.D., you would naturally suppose that 0 would be the date of His birth.

It was not until some five hundred years later that people began to date from Christ's birth. And then, when they did begin to date from this event, they made a mistake. It was found out that Christ was really born four years before He was supposed to have been born — that is, in 4 B.C. — but when the mistake was found out, it was then too late to change.

由于耶稣基督降生以前的一切都被称为"公元前",而基督降生之后的一切都叫作"公元",因此你们自然就会认为,公元0年就是基督降生的年份。

实际上,直到大约五百年后,人们才从基督降生开始纪年。可是,就在人们真的要从这一事件开始纪年的时候,他们却犯下了一个错误。后来发现,耶稣基督真正的降生时间,比人们以为他降生的那一年早了四年,也就是公元前4年;不过,等到人们发现这个错误时,却已经太迟,来不及对我们的纪年方式加以改正了。

37 Blood and Thunder

I once had a big Newfoundland dog, and he was one of the best friends a boy ever had. I don't know who it was that named him; he was named before I got him; but whoever it was must either have been ignorant of history or a bad chooser of names. He was called Nero, and even a dog would have hated such a name, had he known whose it once was.

Every good story usually has a villain to make it interesting. The story of Rome has plenty of villains, but one of the worst was Nero. He was a Roman emperor who lived not long after Christ, and he is considered one of the crudest and wickedest rulers that ever lived.

He killed his mother. He killed his wife. He killed his teacher, who was named Seneca. Seneca was a very good teacher, too.

We think that Nero ordered both Peter and Paul put to death, for they were executed at the time of Nero's rule.

Nero seemed to take great pleasure in making others suffer. He loved to see men torn to pieces by wild beasts; it amused him greatly. I have seen boys who liked to throw stones at dogs just to hear them yelp, or tear the wings off butterflies. Such boys must have some

37　鲜血与雷霆

我曾经养了一条体型很大的纽芬兰犬，它是作为男孩的我最好的朋友之一。我不知道是谁给这条狗起的名字，因为到我家来之前，它就已经有名字了；但不管是谁起的，这个人要么是不懂历史，要么就是个特别不会起名字的家伙。这条狗名叫尼禄；要是小狗知道历史上是谁曾经叫过这个名字的话，它一定不会喜欢这样一个名字。

每一个好故事中，通常都有一个坏蛋，以便让故事变得有意思。在关于罗马的故事中，有很多的坏蛋，但其中最坏的坏蛋之一，便是尼禄。他是罗马皇帝，生活的年代是在耶稣基督死后不久；人们都认为，他是有史以来最残暴、最邪恶的统治者之一呢。

他杀死了自己的母亲。他杀死了自己的妻子。他杀死了自己的老师塞内卡。塞内卡也是一位很优秀的老师。

我们认为，是尼禄下令将彼得和保罗两人判处了死刑，因为这两个人正是尼禄在位的那个时期被处死的。

尼禄似乎以折磨别人为乐。他喜欢看到别人被野兽撕成碎片；这让他觉得非常有意思。我曾经看到过这样一些小男孩，他们喜欢拿石头去砸小狗，目的只是为了

Nero in them; don't you think?

If a man was a Christian, that gave Nero an excuse to torture him horribly. Nero had some of the Christians wrapped in tar and pitch, then placed around the garden of his palace and set fire to, as if they were torches. It is even said that Nero set Rome on fire just for the fun of seeing the city burn. Then he sat in a tower and, while he watched the blaze spreading played on a stringed instrument. The saying is that "*Nero fiddled while Rome burned.*" The fire burned day and night for a whole week and destroyed more than half the city. Nero then laid the blame on the Christians, who, he said, started the fire. Did you ever blame someone else for something you had done?

Some think Nero really was crazy, and we hope he was, for it is hard to think any human being who was not crazy could act as he did.

Nero built himself an immense palace and overlaid it extravagantly with gold and mother-of-pearl. It was known as Nero's House of Gold. At its front door he put up a colossal statue of himself in bronze fifty feet high. Both the House of Gold and the statue were later destroyed, but the Colosseum, which was built a few years afterward, was named Colosseum from this *coloss-al* statue of Nero that was once there.

Nero was very conceited. He thought he could write poetry and sing beautifully. Although he did both very badly, he liked to show off, and no one dared to laugh at him. Had anyone been so bold as to make fun of him or even to smile, he would have had that person put to death instantly.

听到小狗痛得大叫，或者喜欢撕下蝴蝶的翅膀。这样的小男孩，心肠必定有点儿像尼禄，你们觉得是不是这样呢？

如果有人是基督徒，那么尼禄就有借口来狠狠地折磨这个人了。尼禄曾经将一些基督徒全身浇上焦油和沥青，然后再将他们放在皇宫四周的花园里，点上火，把他们当成火把烧。据说尼禄甚至还曾经在罗马城内纵火，只是因为他觉得看到城中着火会很有趣。纵火之后，他便坐在一座高塔上面，一边看着火势蔓延，一边弹琴。有句谚语，说"罗马失火，尼禄奏乐"，就是这么来的。这场大火，没日没夜地整整烧了一个星期，将罗马城毁掉了大半。然后尼禄又将责任归咎于基督徒，说这场火是基督徒放的。你们以前有没有把自己做的错事，归咎到别人身上过呢？

有些人认为，当时的尼禄实际上已经疯了，而我们也但愿如此，因为没有疯而干出他那样的疯狂之举，实在是令人难以想象的。

尼禄为自己修建了一座巨大无比的宫殿，并且一掷千金，在殿中到处铺满了金银珠宝。这座宫殿，人称"尼禄的金殿"。在宫殿的前门，他为自己建造了一尊硕大的青铜雕像，高达五十英尺。"金殿"和这座雕像后来都毁掉了，但数年之后修建的圆形斗兽场，就是根据此处曾经矗立着的、尼禄的那尊"硕大的"雕像而命名为"圆形斗兽场"的。

尼禄其人，极其自负。他认为自己诗写得好，歌唱得也很美妙。尽管在这两方面的本领实际上都糟糕得很，但他却喜欢炫耀，因为没有人胆敢嘲笑他。倘若有人如此大胆敢去取笑他，甚至只是微微一笑，他也会马上将这个人处死。

Even Roman people who were not Christians feared and hated Nero. The military rebelled against him. Before they had a chance to do anything, Nero heard what they were planning, and in order to save himself the disgrace of being put to death by his own people he decided to kill himself. He was such a coward, however, that he couldn't quite bring himself to plunge the sword into his breast. Finally, his slave, impatient to finish the job, shoved the blade in. Thus was Rome rid of one of its worst rulers.

So much for the first part of this *blood and thunder* story. Here is the second part:

The Jews in Jerusalem didn't like to have Rome rule over them. They never had. Like the Christians, the Jews could not worship the emperor as a god. But they were afraid to do much about it. In the Year 70 A.D. they rebelled; that is, they said they would no longer obey Rome or pay money to the government. The emperor sent his son, who was named Titus, with an army to put an end to the rebellion, to punish them as if they were disobedient children.

The Jews crowded into their city of Jerusalem to make a last stand against the Romans. But Titus destroyed that city completely and the Jews in it, a million of them, it is supposed. Then he robbed the great temple of all its valuable ornaments and brought them back to Rome. The great temple was then destroyed.

To celebrate this victory over Jerusalem an arch was built in the Forum at Rome, and through this arch Titus and his army marched in triumph. On this arch was carved a procession, showing Titus leaving the city of Jerusalem with the temple ornaments. Chief

连那些不是基督徒的罗马人，也对尼禄又怕又恨。罗马军队开始起来造反了。但是，还没等到他们有机会动手，尼禄便得知了他们的计划；为了保住自己的面子，不遭到被手下臣民处死的羞辱，他决定自杀。然而，他又是一个胆小鬼，根本就没有勇气把剑刺进自己的胸膛。最后，他手下的一名奴隶等得不耐烦了，便一把将剑捅进了他的胸膛。于是，古罗马便除掉了该国最坏的一位君主。

这就是"鲜血与雷霆"这个故事的前半部分。下面则是后半部分：

生活在耶路撒冷的犹太人，不想要罗马来统治他们。他们从来都不愿接受罗马的统治。与基督徒一样，犹太人也坚决反对将罗马皇帝当作神灵来崇拜。不过，他们一直都害怕在这方面表现得太明显。公元70年，他们终于起来反抗了；也就是说，他们宣布不再服从罗马的统治，也不再向罗马政府缴纳钱财税赋了。罗马皇帝便派皇子提图斯率军前去镇压，准备像惩罚不听话的孩子一样，好好地惩罚惩罚犹太人。

犹太人纷纷涌入耶路撒冷城，准备与罗马军队决一死战。不过，最终提图斯还是彻底摧毁了这座城市，彻底消灭了城中的犹太人；据说，当时城中的犹太人多达一百万呢。然后，他又洗劫了所罗门建造的那座伟大的神庙，将其中所有的珍宝全都带回了罗马。于是，那座伟大的神庙就此毁掉了。

为了庆祝此次耶路撒冷大捷，罗马的"市集"上还修建了一座拱形的凯旋门，让提图斯及其大军穿过这道凯旋门，得胜还朝。这座拱门上雕有一队人马，表现的是提图斯带着所罗门神庙里的珍宝离开耶路撒冷城时的情景。在这些珍宝中，最主

among these ornaments was a golden seven-branched candlestick he had taken from the temple. Today we see many copies in brass of this famous seven-branched candlestick. It is called a *menorah*, which is the Hebrew word for candlestick.

The city was rebuilt later, but most of the Jews who survived have ever since been living in many other countries of the world. When people leave their homeland and spread, it is called a *diaspora*.

The third part of this story is the *thunder*.

In Italy there is a volcano named Vesuvius. You remember that *volcano* came from the name Vulcan, the blacksmith god, and people imagined that his forge in the heart of a volcano made the smoke and flame and ashes. From time to time this volcano, Vesuvius, thunders and quakes and spouts forth fire and throws up stones and gas and boils over with red-hot melted rock called lava. It is the hot inside of the earth exploding. Yet people build houses and towns nearby and live even on the sides of the volcano. Every once in a while their homes are destroyed when the volcano quakes or pours forth fire. Yet the same people go right back and build again in the same place!

There was at the time of Titus a little town named Pompeii near the base of Vesuvius. Wealthy Romans used to go there to spend the summer. Suddenly, one day in the year 79 A.D., just after Titus had become emperor, Vesuvius began to spout forth fire. The people living in Pompeii rushed for their lives, but they didn't have time to get away. They were smothered with the gases from the volcano before they had time to move and, falling

要的是一件他从神庙里掠夺而来的金制七支烛台。如今，我们还可以看到人们根据这件著名的七支烛台仿造而成的许多铜烛台呢。这种烛台，在希伯来语里叫作"米洛拿"（menorah），也就是"扦枝烛台"的意思。

后来，虽说人们重建了耶路撒冷城，但幸存下来的犹太人自此以后便流落到了世界各国。倘若人们纷纷离开故乡，散布到各地，那就叫作"大迁徙"。

这个故事的第三个部分，便是"雷霆"。

意大利有一座火山，叫作维苏威火山。你们应该还记得，"火山"（volcano）一词来源于火神伏尔甘（Vulcan），即那个本是铁匠的神灵的名字。因为人们以为，是他那个位于火山深处的铁匠铺子，才让火山喷吐出烟雾、火苗和灰烬。维苏威火山会时不时地发出雷鸣般的巨响，然后地动山摇，源源不断地向空中喷出火焰、岩石和气体，并且流出沸腾翻滚、炽热的熔岩；这种熔岩，叫作"火山岩浆"。这是地球炽热的内部发生了爆炸。可尽管如此，人们还是在附近地区建起了房屋和市镇，甚至还居住在火山的山坡之上。每隔一段时间，当火山剧烈震动、喷出火焰的时候，他们的家园都会被火山摧毁。可喷发过后，这些人又会回来，

Vesuvius erupting, Pompeii in foreground
维苏威火山正在喷发，山前就是庞贝古城

down dead, were buried deep in a boiling rain of fire and ashes, just where they happened to be when the eruption, as it is called, took place.

The people and their houses lay buried beneath the ashes for nearly two thousand years, and in the course of time everyone had forgotten there ever had been such a place. People came back as they had before and built houses over the spot where everyone had forgotten there once was a city. Then one day a man was digging a well over the spot where Pompeii had once been. He dug up a man's hand — no, not a real hand, but the hand of a statue. He told others, and they set to work and dug and dug to see what else they could find until the whole town was dug out. And now one can go to Pompeii and see it very much as it was in 79 A.D. before it was destroyed.

There are houses of the Romans who went there to spend their vacations. There are shops and temples and palaces and public baths and the theater and the market place or forum. The streets were paved with blocks of lava, once melted stone. They still show ruts which were worn into them by the wheels of the chariots that the Romans used to drive. Stepping stones were placed at some crossings, so that in case of heavy rains, when the streets were full of water, one could cross on them from curb to curb. These stepping stones are still there. The floors of the houses were made of bits of colored stone to form pictures. These are called mosaics. They are still there. In the vestibule of one house, there is in the floor a mosaic picture of a dog. Under it are the Latin words, Cave canem. What does that mean? Can you guess? It means, *Look out for the dog*!

在同一个地方重新修建房子哩!

在提图斯那个时代,维苏威火山的山脚下有一座叫作庞贝的小城。古罗马的富人常常到这里来避暑。公元79年,那时提图斯刚刚当上罗马皇帝不久,有一天维苏威火山突然开始喷出火焰。居住在庞贝的人赶紧逃命,可已经来不及了。因为不等他们逃走,火山喷出的气体便让他们窒息了;而倒在地上死去之后,他们的尸体又被深深地埋到了滚烫炽热的岩浆和火山灰下,留在我们所称的"火山喷发"时他们恰好所处的位置上。

这些人和他们的房屋,在火山灰下埋藏了差不多两千年;而随着时光流逝,人们也都不记得还有这样一个地方了。后来,人们又像以前那样回到了这里,再次建起了房屋;再也没人记得,这里曾经有过一座城市。接下来,有一天,一个人正在庞贝古城曾经所在的那个地方打一口水井。他挖出了一个人的一只手;不,不是真的人手,而是一尊雕像的手。他把这事告诉了其他的人,于是他们便开始起劲挖掘,看能不能找到别的东西,最终把整个庞贝古城都发掘了出来。如今,我们还可以到庞贝古城去参观,看一看公元79年它被火山摧毁之前的样子呢。

城中有古罗马人为了前往庞贝避暑而修建的许多房屋。城里有商店、庙宇、宫殿、公共浴室、剧院,还有集市或者说广场。街道上铺有一块块的熔岩,就是熔化过的石块。这些石块上,如今仍然看得出古罗马人经常驾驶的两轮马车留下的车辙印呢。有些十字路口还安有垫脚石,以便在下大雨、街上全都是水的时候,人们能够踩着它们过街。这些垫脚石如今也保存下来了。城中房屋的地板上铺有彩色石

The bones of the people who were caught and buried alive in the ashes were also found. There were also found bronze ornaments worn by the women, vases that decorated the home, pots and pans and dishes, and lamps which they used to light the houses. Beds and chairs were found just as they had been buried. Still more remarkable, cakes were found on the table, a loaf of bread half eaten, meat ready to be cooked, a kettle on the fire with the ashes still underneath it — beans and peas and *one egg* unbroken — probably the oldest egg in the world!

子，并且拼出了各种图案。这些彩色图案被称为"马赛克"，它们也保存下来了。在一栋房子的前厅，地板上竟然拼有一只小狗的马赛克图案。图案下方还拼有一句拉丁语：Cave canem。你们能猜出它是什么意思吗？这句话的意思就是：小心恶犬！

那些猝不及防就被活活地埋在火山灰下的人的遗骨，也被发掘出来了。人们还发掘出了女性佩戴的青铜饰品、装点家里所用的花瓶、锅碗瓢盆以及家中照明所用的灯具。一些床和椅子被发掘出来的时候，仍然保持着被掩埋之前的样子呢。而更令人称奇的是，发掘出来的桌子上还有蛋糕、已经被人咬过的半块面包、准备下锅的肉，以及炉火上烧着的一只水壶，而水壶下仍有炉灰，炉灰中还有蚕豆、豌豆和一只没有打破的鸡蛋：它很可能是世界上最古老的一个鸡蛋了！

38 A Good Emperor and a Bad Son

Rome's wicked emperor, Nero, had been dead a hundred years when there came to the throne a new emperor named Marcus Aurelius. He was just as good as Nero was bad. Many people think he was one of the noblest and greatest men who ever lived.

At this time most of the Romans had very little religion of any sort. They were not Christians, but neither did they put much faith in their own gods — Jupiter and Juno and the rest. They honored them because they had been brought up to honor them and because they thought that if they didn't honor them, they might have bad luck. So they took no chances.

But instead of believing in such gods, many other Romans followed the teachings of some wise man, or philosopher, and tried to obey the rules that he had made.

About 300 B.C. a Greek philosopher named Zeno had taught a philosophy called Stoicism. His ideas became popular, and a century later they spread to Rome. Many Romans liked Stoicism because it taught good behavior, wisdom, and strength to suffer hardship and pain. Seneca, the teacher whom Nero killed, became a Stoic and wrote about Stoicism.

38　好皇帝，坏儿子

古罗马那位邪恶的皇帝尼禄死了一百年后，一位叫作马可·奥勒留的新皇登上了罗马帝国的皇位。可以说，尼禄有多邪恶，马可·奥勒留便有多善良。许多人都认为，他是有史以来最高尚、最伟大的人物之一。

此时，绝大多数古罗马人对任何一种宗教都没有什么信仰。虽说他们不是基督徒，但他们对自己的神灵，即朱庇特、朱诺以及其他诸神，也不怎么虔敬。他们之所以敬奉这些神灵，是因为从小到大家人一直教导他们要敬奉这些神灵，是因为他们觉得，如果不敬奉这些神灵，就会给自己招来噩运。所以，他们敬奉这些神灵，不过是谨慎从事、力求万全罢了。

但是，尽管并不信仰这些神灵，许多罗马人却还是遵从着某位智者或者说哲人的教导，并且尽量按照这位智者或哲人制定的准则去行事。

公元前300年左右，有位名叫芝诺的古希腊哲学家曾经宣扬过一种叫作"斯多亚主义"的哲学。他的思想渐渐广为流传开来，一个世纪之后便传播到了罗马。许多古罗马人都喜欢斯多亚派哲学，因为这种哲学教导的是良好的品行、智慧以及承受磨难和痛苦的力量。尼禄杀死的那位老师，即塞内卡，也变成了斯多亚派哲学的一名信徒，并且写了一些关于斯多亚派哲学的著作。

A hundred years later, along came the emperor Marcus Aurelius. He was a Stoic, too, and he needed to be, for he had a hard and difficult life. He wrote down his thoughts, now called his *Meditations*. He didn't intend to have his thoughts published; he just wrote them down to remind himself how he ought to think and behave.

Here are some of the ideas that Marcus Aurelius believed in:

★ *I must calmly endure pain and suffering.*

★ *I must put up with everything that happens, no matter how bad it may seem. Whatever happens has been caused by God, and God is good. Therefore everything that happens is good.*

★ *I must always do my duty.*

★ *I must not seek pleasure.*

★ *Good behavior is the best thing in life.*

★ *I must obey the laws of God.*

★ *All men are brothers, and I must treat everyone as well as if he were my brother.*

Marcus Aurelius was a good Stoic. He followed his own rules, and he always did what he thought was his duty. He was kind to people, was good to the poor, and managed to get rid of much of the cruelty and brutality in the gladiators' shows.

Even today, people — thousands of them — read Marcus Aurelius's *Meditations*. Some

又过了一百年，马可·奥勒留这位皇帝登台了。他也是一名斯多亚主义者，因为他曾经有过一段非常艰难困苦的生活。他把自己的思想记录下来，汇集成了如今人们所称的《沉思录》一书。他并没有想过要把自己的思想发表出来，公之于众；将它们记录下来，只是为了提醒他自己，应当怎样去思考和行动。

下面就是马可·奥勒留坚信的一些观点：

★我必须平心静气地忍受痛苦与磨难。

★我必须忍受世间的一切，无论情况看起来有多么糟糕。世间所发生的一切，全都是上帝安排的。上帝是善良的，因此世间的一切也都是善良的。

★我必须始终尽职尽责。

★我决不能追求享乐。

★行为端正是人生中最好的东西。

★我必须服从上帝的律法。

★人人皆为兄弟，我必须像对待自己的兄弟一样对待所有的人。

马可·奥勒留是一位优秀的斯多亚主义者。他遵循着自己的准则，并且始终履行着自认为属于他的那些义务。他待人和善，对穷人也很仁慈，并且曾经想方设法让角斗士的搏击表演不再残忍、野蛮。

即便是到了如今，仍有成千上万的人去阅读马可·奥勒留的《沉思录》。他的

of his sayings sound almost as though they come from the Bible. Even today, too, people who bear pain and hardship without a murmur are described as stoic.

One of Marcus Aurelius's rules was "Forgive your enemies." Though Marcus Aurelius was not a Christian, nevertheless he was more moral in the way he acted than some of the later emperors who *were* Christians!

Like many people who are very good themselves, Marcus Aurelius was unable to bring up his son to be good. Commodus, his son, was just as bad as his father was good. When the son grew up and was able to choose for himself and do as he pleased, he forgot all about doing his duty and behaving well and obeying the laws of God. Instead, Commodus's one thought was pleasure, and the worst kind of pleasure at that. Commodus forgot his father's ideas about being kind to others and treating them like brothers. He thought only of giving himself a good time.

Commodus was an athlete and had beautiful muscles and a handsome figure, of which he was so proud that he had a statue made of himself. The statue showed him as the strong and muscular god Hercules. Commodus made the people worship him as if he were this god. Just to show off his muscles and his muscular ability, he himself took part in prizefights. He poisoned or killed anyone who found fault with or criticized him. He led a wild and dissipated life, but at last he met the end that he deserved. Many attempts to kill him failed, but finally he was strangled to death by a wrestler.

Pleasure! For Commodus, pleasure meant feasting too much and drinking too much

一些说法，看上去差不多就像是出自《圣经》。而即便是到了如今，那些毫无怨言地忍受痛苦和磨难的人，也还是被人们称为斯多亚主义者呢。

马可·奥勒留的准则之一，就是"宽恕敌人"。尽管马可·奥勒留不是一名基督徒，但他的行为与后来一些身为基督徒的皇帝的做法比起来，却更高尚啊！

与许多自身非常善良的人一样，马可·奥勒留也无法将自己的儿子培养成一个善良之人。他的儿子叫康茂德，坏得透顶；父亲马可·奥勒留有多善良，他的儿子康茂德便有多邪恶。康茂德长大成人，能够自己做主、随心所欲之后，便将履行自己的职责、品行端正和服从上帝的律法这些方面全都抛到了脑后，忘得一干二净了。相反，康茂德一心想的就是享乐，并且还是最堕落的一种享乐。康茂德忘记了父亲关于善待他人、待人如兄弟的思想。他心中所想的，只是让自己尽情享乐这一件事情。

康茂德是个运动健将，肌肉发达，身材很好；他对这一点感到非常骄傲，因此还为自己建了一座雕像。这尊雕像，让他显得好像是强壮有力、肌肉发达的大力神赫拉克勒斯一样。康茂德还让人们把他当成大力神一样来敬奉。身为皇帝的他还亲自参加过拳击比赛，可目的却只是为了炫耀自己的肌肉和力大无穷。只要有人指责或者批评他，他就会把那人毒死或者杀死。他过着放荡不羁、荒淫无耻的生活，所以最终落了个罪有应得的下场。许多人都想要刺杀他，可无人成功；而最终，他却被一名摔跤手勒住脖子勒死了。

快乐！对于康茂德来说，就是尽情地吃喝玩乐，以及通宵达旦地举行放荡无度的宴会。但是，尽管还有其他的种种快乐，有着种种善良高尚的快乐，可康茂德对

and going to wild all-night parties. But there are other kinds of pleasure, good kinds, and Commodus had nothing to do with them.

About the same time as Zeno, there lived another Greek wise man, or philosopher, named Epicurus. His ideas, too, became popular in Rome, and thousands followed his teachings. The Epicureans — the followers of Epicurus — thought that the highest good was pleasure, but the pleasure must be of *the right kind*.

Here are a few of the pleasures that the Epicureans considered good:

★ *Being honest and truthful*
★ *Being just to others*
★ *Friendship with good people*
★ *Simple, clean living*
★ *Freedom from superstition*
★ *Freedom from fear*
★ *Quiet study*
★ *Calmness*

Any pleasure that causes pain, thought the Epicureans, is not really a pleasure — not at all. How much happier Commodus would have been if he had followed the ideas of Epicurus instead of his own wild, selfish ideas!

它们却毫无兴趣。

与芝诺差不多同一时代，古希腊还有另一名智者，或者说哲人，叫作伊壁鸠鲁。他的思想也在罗马帝国传播开来，有成千上万的古罗马人遵循着他的教导。伊壁鸠鲁学派的信徒，即伊壁鸠鲁的追随者，认为快乐就是最高的善，但此种快乐，当然应是高尚正确的快乐。

下面就是伊壁鸠鲁学派认为属于善的几种快乐：

★为人正直、诚实
★待人公允
★与善良之人为友
★过简朴而正派的生活
★不崇尚迷信
★无所畏惧
★安静地学习
★心静如水

伊壁鸠鲁学派的人认为，任何会引起痛苦的快乐都不是真正的快乐，或者说根本就不是快乐。假如康茂德遵从了伊壁鸠鲁的思想，而不是遵从自己那种放荡堕落、自私无比的思想，那他可能就会幸福得多呢！

39 I_H_ _S_ _ _ _ V_ _ _ _

The name of this story I'm going to put at the end, for you wouldn't know what it means, anyway, until you have heard the story, and so it's no use looking ahead.

All through the years since Christ was crucified, some people who said they believed in Christ had been terribly treated — *persecuted*, we call it — because they were Christians. They had been flogged; they had been stoned; they had been torn with iron hooks. They had been roasted and burned to death. Yet, strange as it may seem, in spite of this terrible treatment, more and more people were becoming Christians every day. They believed so strongly in life after death, and they believed that they would be so much happier after death if they died for Christ's sake, that they seemed even glad to suffer and to be killed. At last the emperor himself put a stop to all these persecutions. This is how it happened.

About the year 300 A.D. Rome had an emperor by the name of Constantine. Constantine was not a Christian. His gods were the old Roman gods. He probably did not put much faith in them, however.

Well, once upon a time Constantine was fighting with an enemy when he dreamed one night that he saw in the sky a flaming cross. Beneath this cross were written the

39   I_H_ _S_ _ _V_ _ _ _

这个故事的标题，我要到最后才会说明；因为在没有听完整个故事之前，你们是不会明白这个标题的意思的。所以，提早解释它的意思没有什么用。

自耶稣基督在十字架上受难以来的多年里，那些说他们信奉基督的人，都因为身为基督徒而受到了残酷的对待；这种残酷对待，我们称之为"宗教迫害"。他们有的遭到鞭笞，有的被人用石头砸死，有的被人用铁钩撕死。有的人还被架到火上烤，然后被活活烧死了。然而，令人觉得奇怪的是，尽管有着如此残酷的迫害，但每天还是有越来越多的人皈依基督教。他们都坚信死后有另一个世界，认为自己如果为基督而献身的话，他们在死后的来世便会幸福得多，因此他们似乎都很乐意承受苦难，很乐意被人杀死。最后，古罗马皇帝亲自制止了所有这些针对基督徒的迫害行为。下面就来说一说这件事情的经过。

公元300年左右，罗马有一位皇帝，叫作君士坦丁。君士坦丁皇帝并不是基督徒。他信奉的，还是罗马原来的那些神灵。然而，他对这些神灵很可能也不怎么信得过。

有一次，君士坦丁正在率军与敌人作战；一天晚上，他做了一个梦，梦见天空中有一个熊熊燃烧着的十字架。十字架的下方，写着这样一行拉丁文字：In hoc

Latin words, *In hoc signo vinces*. In English this is, "In this sign thou shalt conquer." Constantine thought this meant that if he carried the Christian cross into battle, he would conquer. He thought it would at least be worthwhile to give the Christian god a trial. So he marked the sign of the cross on the shields carried by his soldiers, and he did win the battle. To celebrate his victory, the Roman Senate built the Arch of Constantine, a triumphal arch with three openings, in the Forum of Rome. After this, Constantine made Christianity a legal religion in the Roman Empire. It is believed that he was baptized just before he died. From that time on, all the Roman emperors who came after Constantine — all except one — were Christians.

Constantine's mother was named Helena. She became a Christian. Then she gave up her life to Christian works and built churches at Bethlehem and on the Mount of Olives. It is said that she went to Palestine and found the actual cross on which Christ had been crucified three hundred years before and sent part of it to Rome. When she died she was made a saint. She is now called St. Helena.

Constantine built a church over the spot where St. Peter was supposed to have been crucified. Many years later, this church was torn down so that a much larger and grander church in honor of St. Peter might be built there.

Constantine did not care for Rome. He preferred to live in another city in the Eastern part of the Roman Empire. This city was called Byzantium.3 So he moved from Rome to Byzantium and made that city his capital. Byzantium was called New Rome, and then the

signo vinces。翻译成英语，这句话的意思就是："见此标志，汝当取胜。"君士坦丁皇帝认为，这是说，如果带着基督教的十字架去作战的话，他就会获胜。他心想，去试一试基督教的上帝是否灵验，起码也是值得的。于是，他便下令把军中所有的盾牌都画上十字架，然后真的就打赢了这场战斗。为了庆祝这次胜利，罗马元老院还修建了一座"君士坦丁凯旋门"呢；那是一座开有三个门洞的胜利之门，建在罗马广场上。此后，君士坦丁便宣布基督教在整个罗马帝国的统治范围内是一种合法的宗教了。据说，他在去世之前还接受了洗礼，成为一名基督徒。从那时起，除了一个人，君士坦丁之后的历任罗马皇帝便都信奉基督教了。

君士坦丁的母亲叫作海伦娜。她也皈依了基督教。然后，她便毕生从事基督教事业，在伯利恒和橄榄山上修建了教堂。据说她还前往巴勒斯坦，找到了三百年前基督被钉在上面的那个真正的十字架，并将这个十字架的一部分送往了罗马。她去世之后，被追授为圣徒。因此，如今人们都称她为圣海伦娜。

君士坦丁还在据说是圣彼得在十字架上受难的那个地方，修建了一座教堂。许多年后，人们又将这座教堂拆了，打算修建一座更加巨大、更加宏伟的教堂来纪念圣彼得。

君士坦丁不喜欢罗马。他宁愿住在罗马帝国东部的另一座城市里。那座城市，叫作拜占庭。所以，他便从罗马搬到了拜占庭，并把后者当成古罗马帝国的首都。拜占庭又被称为新罗马，后来又改名为"君士坦丁之城"。在希腊语中，"城市"

name was changed to Constantine's city. In Greek, the word for *city* is *polis*. We see the word used in Anna*polis* and Indiana*polis*. Constantine's City became Constantinepolis, and then shortened to Constantinople.

Hardly had the Roman Empire become Christian before a quarrel arose between those Christians who believed one thing and those who believed another. The chief thing they quarreled about was whether Christ was equal to God the Father or not equal to Him. Constantine called the two disagreeing sides together at a place called Nicaea to settle the question. There the leaders of each side argued the matter hotly. Finally, it was decided that the Christian Church should believe that God the Son and God the Father were equal. Then they agreed to put what they believed in words. This was called a creed, which means *believe*, and because it was made at Nicaea it was known as the Nicene Creed, which many Christians still say every Sunday.

Before the time of Constantine, there were no weekly holidays in the Roman Empire. Sunday was no different from any other day. People worked or did just the same things on Sunday as they did on other days. Constantine thought Christians should have one day a week for the worship of God — a *holy* day, or holiday, as we call it — so he made Sunday the Christian day of rest, a *holy* day such as Saturday is for Jews and Friday is for Muslims.

Although Constantine was head of the Roman Empire, there was another man whom all Christians throughout the world looked to as their spiritual head. This man was the Bishop

---

一词是"波利斯"（polis）。我们可以看到，"安那波利斯"（Annapolis）[1]、"印第安纳波利斯"（Indianapolis）[2]等地名中，都用到了这个词。所以，"君士坦丁之城"便变成了"君士坦丁波利斯"，后来又被缩写成了"君士坦丁堡"（Constantinople）[3]。

罗马帝国刚刚皈依基督教不久，基督教内部观点不同的两派之间便发生了一场纷争。两派争执的主要问题，就是耶稣基督究竟是不是等同于天主圣父。君士坦丁将各执一词的两派召集到一个叫作尼西亚的地方，来解决这一问题。双方的主要人物在那里就这一问题进行了激烈的论争。最后，双方决定，基督教会应当认定圣子等同于圣父。然后，他们又一致同意，将此次论争所达成的共识用文字记录下来。这一记录，被称为《信经》，也就是"信条"的意思；又由于它是在尼西亚记录下来的，因此人们称之为《尼西亚信经》。如今，许多的基督徒在礼拜日里还会诵读这部《信经》呢。

在君士坦丁继位以前，罗马帝国并没有周末假期。星期天与其他日子没什么区别。在星期天，人们仍然要干活，或者像其他日子一样，该干什么就干什么。君士坦丁认为，基督徒每周都应当有一天来礼拜上帝才是；这一天是个宗教节日（holyday），后来人们将其缩写为holiday，即如今我们所称的"假日"。于是，他便将

---

[1] 安那波利斯（Annapolis），美国马里兰州的首府。

[2] 印第安纳波利斯（Indianapolis），美国印第安纳州的首府。

[3] 君士坦丁堡（Constantinople），土耳其西北部港口城市伊斯坦布尔（Istanbul）的旧称。

of Rome. In Latin he was called *Papa*, which means the same thing in Latin that it does in English, *father*. So the bishop of Rome was called *Papa*, and this became *pope*. St. Peter was supposed to have been the first bishop of Rome. For many centuries the pope was the spiritual ruler of all Christians everywhere, no matter in what country they lived.

As now you know what the name of this story means, I'm putting it here:

In Hoc Signo Vinces

星期日定为基督徒的休息日，定为宗教节日，就像星期六是犹太人的宗教节日、星期五是穆斯林的宗教节日一样。

尽管君士坦丁是罗马帝国的元首，但还有一个人却被全世界的基督徒视为精神领袖。这个人，就是罗马主教。在拉丁语中，他被称为"爸爸"（Papa），它的意思和英语中这个词的意思是一样的，都是指"父亲"。于是，罗马主教便被人们称为Papa，后来这一称呼则演变成了"教皇"（Pope）。据传，圣彼得是第一任罗马主教。在数个世纪里，无论基督徒生活在哪个国家，教皇都是各地所有基督教徒的精神统治者。

听到这里，你们就会明白这个故事标题的意思了。我把它写下来吧：

In Hoc Signo Vices（见此标志，汝当取胜）

40 Barbarian Invaders

But Rome with the Roman Empire had had its day. The empire had risen as high as it could. It was Rome's turn to fall. It was Rome's turn to be conquered. But you cannot guess what people were to do the conquering and to be next in power.

For centuries there had been Germanic tribes living on the northern borders of the Roman Empire. Every now and then they tried to cross over the border into Roman lands, and the Romans had to be constantly fighting them to keep them back where they belonged. Julius Caesar had fought with them. So had Marcus Aurelius and so had Constantine. The Romans called these people *barbarians*, which is what they called all people who were not Romans. The Romans believed that all barbarians were fierce and warlike.

Many of these Germanic people had light hair and blue eyes; that is, they were what we call blonds. The Greeks and Romans and other people who lived around the Mediterranean Sea had dark hair and dark eyes. They were what we call brunettes.

Although some of the Germanic peoples had moved into the Roman Empire, many lived in sparsely populated areas, not in cities. They lived in huts made of wood,

40 野蛮的侵略者

但是，罗马以及罗马帝国的全盛时期已经过去了。这个帝国，已经达到了其势力的顶峰，该轮到罗马衰落了，该轮到罗马被人征服了。不过，你们不可能猜得出，哪个民族会来征服罗马，然后掌握罗马大权呢。

几个世纪以来，罗马帝国北部边境一直生活着一些日耳曼部落。他们时不时地试图越过边境，进入罗马帝国的领土；因此，古罗马人不得不经常与之打仗，以便把他们赶回原来的地方去。恺撒与他们交过战。马可·奥勒留、君士坦丁这两位皇帝也与他们打过仗。古罗马人将这些日耳曼人称为"野蛮人"；当然，他们将所有不是罗马人的民族全都叫作野蛮人。古罗马人认为，所有的野蛮人全都是凶悍而好战的。

这些日耳曼人当中，许多人都长着浅色的头发和蓝色的眼睛；也就是说，他们就是我们如今所称的"金发碧眼者"。而生活在地中海沿岸的古希腊人、古罗马人以及其他民族，却都是黑头发、黑眼睛。他们则是我们如今所称的"黑发黑眼者"。

尽管这些日耳曼人中有一些已经迁徙到了罗马帝国里，但许多人都生活在人烟稀少的地区，而不是生活在城市里。他们住着用木头搭建而成的小房子，房子有的

sometimes of branches woven together — like a large basket. The women raised vegetables and took care of the cows and horses. The men did the hunting and fighting and blacksmithing. Blacksmithing was very important, for the blacksmith made the swords and spears with which they fought and the tools with which they worked. That is why the name *Smith* was so honored among them.

When the men went to battle they wore the heads of animals they had killed, an ox's

时候还是用树枝缠织在一起搭建起来的，就像一个巨大的篮子。妇女种植菜蔬、照料牛马。男子则负责打猎、作战和铁器加工。打铁这种工作非常重要，因为他们打仗所用的刀剑、长矛，以及干活所用的工具，都是铁匠打造出来的。这就是"史密斯"（Smith，即"铁匠"的音译）这个名字在他们当中大受敬重的原因。

当男人们去打仗时，他们都会戴上自己曾经猎杀过的兽头，比如一个双角保存完整的公牛头，或者一个狼头、熊头或者狐头。这样做，是为了让他们看起来显得

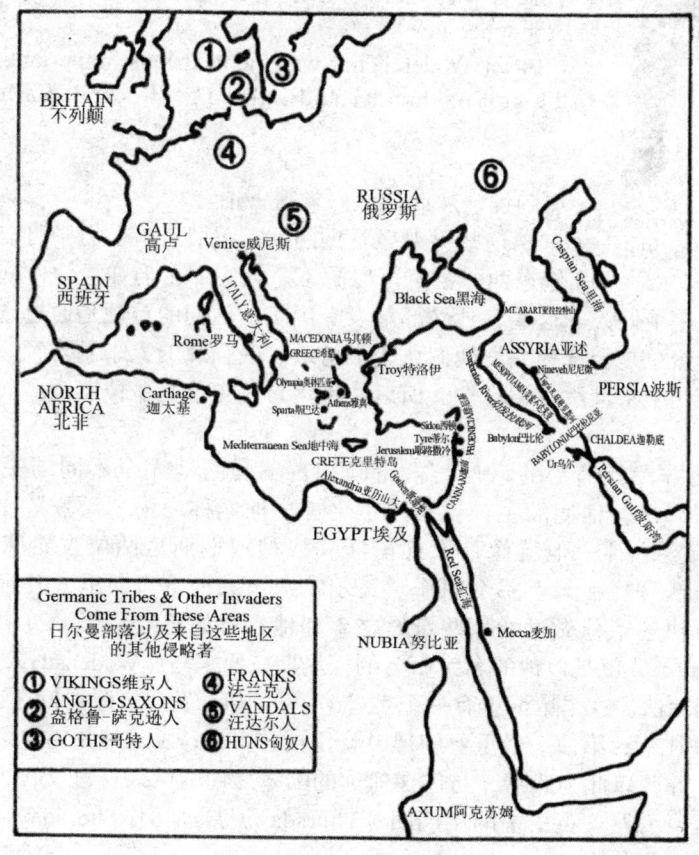

Invasions from the north
北方民族入侵图

head, horns and all, or the head of a wolf or bear or fox. This was to make themselves look fierce and to frighten the enemy.

Bravery was the chief thing the men thought good. A man might lie, he might steal, he might even commit murder, but if he was a brave warrior, he was called a good man. The Germanic tribes did not have a king. They elected their chiefs, and of course they always chose the man who was the bravest and strongest. But he could not make his son ruler after him. He was more like a president than a king.

These northern people had an entirely different set of gods from those of Greece and Rome. Their chief god, as you might guess, was the god of war, and they called him Woden. Woden was also the god of the sky. He was like the two Greek gods, Zeus and Ares, put together. Woden was supposed to live in a wonderful palace in the sky called Valhalla, and many tales are told of the wonderful things he did and of the adventures he had. Wednesday, which was once Wodensday, is named after him. That is why there is a letter *d* in this word, although we don't pronounce it.

After Woden, Thor was the next most important god. He was the god of thunder and lightning. He carried a hammer with

Germanic warrior
日耳曼部落的勇士

更凶悍，从而让敌人觉得害怕。

这些男人最看重的就是勇敢。一名男子可以撒谎，可以偷东西，甚至可以犯下杀人大罪，但如果他作战勇猛，人们就会说他是一个好人。这些日耳曼部落没有国王。他们的首领是通过选举产生的，因此他们自然总是会选择一位他们认为最勇敢、最强壮的人来做首领。不过，一位首领不能让儿子来继承首领之位。所以，部落首领更像是一位总统，而不像是一位国王。

这些北方民族信奉的，是与古希腊和古罗马两地完全不同的一系列神灵。你们没准猜得出，他们的主神就是战争之神，他们称之为"沃登"（Woden）。沃登也是天空之神。他就像是天神宙斯和战神阿瑞斯这两位古希腊神灵的结合体。据说，沃登住在天上一个叫作"瓦尔哈拉"的神奇宫殿里，并且有许多的神话传说，都讲述了他做过的那些奇妙之事和他有过的冒险经历。英语中的星期三（Wednesday），就是以他的名字命名的；星期三原来写作Wodensday，后来才演变成了如今的写法。这个单词里有一个字母d，可它却不发音，原因就在这里。

从沃登往下，第二个最重要的神灵就是托尔（Thor）。他是雷电之神。他手持一把铁锤，并曾以此为武器，与住在遥远的酷寒之地的巨人打过仗，人们将那些巨人叫作"冰巨人"。英语中的星期四（Thursday）曾经写作Thorsday，就是用这个托尔的名字来命名的。

还有一位神灵叫作蒂乌（Tiu），我们用他的名字命名了星期二（Tuesday），

which he fought great giants who lived in the far-off cold lands and were called *ice-giants*. Thursday, which was once Thorsday, is named after him.

Another god was named Tiu, and from his name we get Tuesday, and another Freya, from whom we get Friday, so that four out of seven of our days are named after Germanic gods, in spite of the fact that none of us believe in these gods.

Of the other three days of the week, Sunday and Monday of course are named after the sun and moon, and Saturday is named after a Roman god, Saturn.

About the year 400 A.D. these northern neighbors were becoming particularly troublesome to the Romans. They began to push their way down into the northern part of the Roman Empire, and after a few years the Romans could hold them back no longer. Two of these Germanic tribes went over into Britain, and the Romans who were living there found it wisest to get out, go back to Rome, and leave the country and its native people to the invaders.

These tribes who settled in Britain were known as Angles and Saxons. So the country came to be called the land of the Angles, or, for short, *Angle-land*. After the words *Angle-land* were said over for many years, they became *England*, which is what we call the country today. The people of England are still known by the full name *Anglo-Saxons*, and this is the name by which we call anyone descended from these tribes of Angles and Saxons who settled in Britain about 400 A.D.

Another tribe called the Vandals went into Gaul. Gaul is where France is now. Then

而星期五（Friday）则源于另一位叫作弗雷娅（Freya）的女神。因此，虽然我们都不信奉这些日耳曼神灵，但我们一周的七天中，却有四天都是以这些神灵的名字来命名的呢。

至于一周当中的其他三天，星期日（Sunday）和星期一（Monday）当然分别是用太阳（sun）和月亮（moon）来命名的，而星期六（Saturday）用的则是古罗马的农神萨杜恩（Saturn）的名字。

到了公元400年左右，这些与罗马帝国相邻的北方民族，开始变成古罗马人最为头疼的一种麻烦了。他们开始南下，向罗马帝国的北部地区推进；几年之后，古罗马人便再也无法将他们赶走了。这些日耳曼部落中，有两个部落漂洋过海，登上了不列颠岛；而当时住在那里的古罗马人发现，他们最明智的做法就是撤出不列颠岛，回到罗马去，并将那片国土和当地的居民留给入侵者。

在不列颠岛上定居下来的这两个部落，就是盎格鲁人和撒克逊人。于是，该国后来便被叫作"盎格鲁人之地"，简称"盎格鲁之地"（Angle-land）。在"盎格鲁之地"这个名称用了多年之后，慢慢就演变成了今天我们称呼该国时所用的"英格兰"（England）了。如今，英国人的全称依然是"盎格鲁–撒克逊人"；而对于所有属于这些于公元400年左右在不列颠定居下来的盎格鲁和撒克逊部落后裔，我们也是这样称呼他们的。

还有一个叫作汪达尔人的部落则进入了高卢。高卢就是如今法国所在的地方。然后，他们继续南下，进入西班牙，并且巧取豪夺、烧杀掳掠，无恶不作。他们还

they kept on down into Spain, stealing, smashing, burning, and destroying. They crossed over by boats into North Africa. They damaged or destroyed everything they came upon. So today when anyone damages or destroys property wickedly, we call him a *vandal*. If you cut up your desk, tear your books, or scratch names on walls or fences, you, too, are a vandal.

A tribe called the Franks followed the Vandals into Gaul, and there they stayed, giving the name *France* to that country.

The people north of Italy were the Goths. They had a leader by the name of Alaric. Alaric and his Goths crossed over the mountains into Italy and robbed or destroyed everything of value they could lay their hands on. They then entered Rome and carried away whatever they wanted, and the Romans could not stop them. But the worst was yet to come.

坐船渡海，进入了北非。一路之上，他们大肆烧杀，所到之处尽被损毁。因此，如今倘若有人恶意破坏或损毁他人财物，我们就会说这人是个汪达尔人（即蓄意破坏分子）。如果你们在课桌上乱刻乱画、撕坏书本，或者在墙上、篱笆上乱写名字，那么你们也是汪达尔人哩。

一个叫作"法兰克人"的部落，在汪达尔人之后进入了高卢，并在这里定居下来，因此该国便叫作法兰西。

意大利北部的那个民族，叫作哥特人。他们有个头领，名叫阿拉里克。阿拉里克率领手下的哥特人翻山越岭，进入了意大利，并且将一路上见到的值钱之物全都洗劫一空、损毁殆尽。然后，他们又攻入罗马，将喜欢的东西尽数掳走，可古罗马人却无力阻止他们。不过，最糟糕的情况还在后头呢。

41 Barbarians Meet the Champions of the World

Farther north and to the east was a tribe of people who were considered by both the Romans and the Germanic tribes to be very fierce. They were called Huns. They lived far off in the eastern forests, in a part of the world that no one then knew much about.

Even the Germans themselves, fierce fighters though they were, feared the Huns, and it was chiefly because they were afraid of them and wanted to get away from them as far as they could that the Germans went over the borders into the Roman Empire. It was much easier to fight the Romans than it was to fight the Huns.

The leader of the Huns, named Attila, boasted that nothing ever grew again where his horse had trod. He and his Huns had conquered and laid waste the country all the way from the East almost to Paris. At last a Roman-Germanic army made a stand against them and fought a great battle at a place not so very far from Paris, a place called Châlons.

The Germans fought desperately; they fought madly; and the Huns were beaten. It was lucky they were beaten, for if they had won, these wild barbarians might have conquered and ruled the world. So the battle of Châlons, 451 A.D., is written in history in capital letters and large figures — CHÂLONS, 451.

41 野蛮人碰上了世界霸主

在遥远的北方和东方，有一个部落；古罗马人和日耳曼部族都认为，那是一个非常凶悍的民族。他们被称为匈奴人。匈奴人居住在与罗马相距极其遥远的东方森林地带，当时人们还不是很了解那个地区。

即便是本身非常骁勇善战的日耳曼人，也对匈奴人心存畏惧；正是由于他们害怕匈奴人，觉得离匈奴人越远越好，所以他们才越过边境，侵入罗马帝国。因为他们觉得与罗马人打仗，要比与匈奴人打仗轻松得多呢。

匈奴人的首领叫作阿提拉；他曾经夸口说，自己手下大军的铁蹄所到之处，寸草不生。他率领手下的匈奴人从东方一路征伐过来，几乎打到了巴黎，把所到之处全都夷为了平地。最终，一支由古罗马人和日耳曼人组成的联军背水一战，与匈奴人在距巴黎不远一个叫作沙隆的地方打了一场大仗。

在这场大仗中，日耳曼人殊死奋战，杀红了眼；于是，匈奴人被打败了。幸亏他们被打败了；因为匈奴人若是打赢此次大战的话，这些野蛮人可能便会征服并统治整个世界了。所以，公元451年发生的这场沙隆之战，在史书上提到时都是用粗体，以便表明此战非常重要：沙隆之战，公元451年。

阿提拉及其手下的匈奴大军在沙隆之战中被打败后，便去追击古罗马人。他们

After Attila and his Huns had been beaten at Châlons, they then went after the Romans. Turning back they went down into Italy, where there was no one able to stop them. They destroyed everything as they moved on. The people of the country didn't even attempt to fight. They thought the Huns were monsters and simply fled before them. On to Rome the Huns went.

Now, there was in Rome at this time a pope named Leo I which means Lion. Leo, of course, was neither a soldier nor a fighting man, but he and his cardinals and bishops went out from Rome to meet Attila. They were not clad in armor, and none of them carried any weapons with which to fight. The pope and those with him were dressed in gorgeous robes and richly colored garments. It seemed as if they must be slaughtered by Attila and his Huns like lambs before wolves.

Something strange happened when Attila and the pope met; exactly what no one knows. Perhaps Attila was awed by the pomp and splendor of those Christians. Perhaps he feared what heaven might do to him if he destroyed those holy beings who had come out to meet him as if from heaven. At any rate, he did not destroy them, nor did he enter Rome, but turned about and left Italy, left it for good and all, and he and his Huns returned to the unknown land to the north from which they had come.

Now that the dreaded Attila was out of the way, the Vandals in Africa saw their chance to attack Rome. Attila had barely left Italy before the Vandals crossed over from Africa and sailed up the Tiber to Rome. They captured the city without any difficulty, helped

掉转头来，南下攻进了意大利，并且无人能敌，所向披靡。进军途中，他们将一切全都夷为了平地。意大利民众甚至都没有想过要进行抵抗。他们觉得匈奴人都是怪物，所以完全是闻风而逃。于是，匈奴人便朝罗马挺进。

注意，此时的罗马教皇叫作利奥一世，"利奥"（Leo）的意思就是"雄狮"。当然，利奥一世既不是士兵，也不是军队里的作战人员；可他还是带领手下的主教们出了罗马城，前去会见阿提拉。他们既没有身着盔甲，也没有人手持战斗武器。教皇及其随从人员，全都穿着华丽的长袍和色彩艳丽的衣服。看起来，他们好像是"羊入虎口"，一定会被阿提拉及其率领的匈奴大军残忍地杀害的。

可阿提拉与教皇会面之后，怪事却发生了；没有人清楚这是怎么回事。或许，是那些基督徒的气势让阿提拉产生了敬畏之心吧。或许，是因为他害怕，如果杀了这些仿佛是从天堂下来会见他的神圣之人，那么上天可能会惩罚他吧。不管是出于什么原因，反正他没有杀死这些人，也没有进入罗马城，而是掉转马头离开了意大利，并且是永远地离开了意大利；而他手下的匈奴大军，也都撤回了他们那个不为人知的北方老家。

可怕的阿提拉走了，身处非洲的汪达尔人便觉得攻打罗马的机会已经到来。阿提拉刚刚率军撤出意大利，汪达尔人便从非洲驾船渡海，并沿着台伯河而上，前去攻打罗马了。他们几乎不费吹灰之力便攻下了罗马城，然后在城里毫不客气地大肆劫掠，并将罗马所有的金银财宝全都洗劫一空。

多么可怜的古罗马城啊！这座不朽之城，最终还是被敌人踩在脚下，并且永

themselves to everything they wanted, and carried away all Rome's treasures.

Poor old Rome! The *Eternal* City was at last beaten, beaten for good! It had been the champion for a great many years. But now all Rome's strength was gone. The city was no longer able to defend itself. Rome's last emperor had the high-sounding name *Romulus Augustulus*, the same name as the first king, Romulus, with the addition of Augustulus, which means the little Augustus. But in spite of his high-sounding name, Romulus Augustulus could do nothing.

It was in the year 476 that Rome was beaten. The western half of the empire, of which Rome had been the capital, broke up into pieces, and the pieces were ruled over by various Germanic rulers. Like Humpty Dumpty, Rome had had a great fall, and all the king's horses and all the king's men couldn't put it together again. Only the eastern part, of which Constantinople was the capital, still went on. This eastern half was not conquered by the barbarians, and it still kept going for nearly a thousand years longer until — but wait till we come to that time in history.

People speak of this date, 476, as the end of Ancient History. A date like 476 is very convenient and definite, and people like definite dates, but of course Ancient History didn't come to a sudden end the way one year comes to an end on December 31 and another year begins at once. You might say that Ancient History began to fade away long before 476 and that a new era began to fade in over a long period of time both before and after 476. Still, 476 is a good date to remember.

远地踩在脚下！许多年来，它一直都是世界霸主。可如今，古罗马的所有实力全都荡然无存了。这座城市，甚至无法再保护自己。罗马帝国的最后一任皇帝有个非常夸张的名字，叫作罗慕路斯·奥古斯都鲁斯；其中，非但"罗慕路斯"与罗马帝国第一任皇帝的名字相同，而且还加上了指"小奥古斯都"的"奥古斯都鲁斯"。不过，尽管拥有这样一个冠冕堂皇的名字，但对于罗马的衰落，罗慕路斯·奥古斯都鲁斯皇帝却无能为力。

罗马是在公元476年被打败的。此后，曾以罗马为首都的帝国西部地区便分崩离析，由许多的日耳曼统治者分而治之了。罗马就像是蛋壳先生[1]一样，摔了一大跤，就算国王召集所有人马，也无法再将它拼凑复原了。只有以君士坦丁堡为首都的东部地区，还继续存在着。东部地区并没有被野蛮民族征服，此后又继续存在了差不多一千年之久，直到——我们还是等上一等，到了那个历史时期再说吧。

因此，人们便把这个时间，即公元476年，当成是世界古代历史结束的时间。像公元476年这样的日期，既方便易记，又准确明了，而人们也很喜欢准确明了的日期；不过，古代历史当然不会突如其来地结束，不会像一年在十二月三十一号终

---

[1] 蛋壳先生（Humpty Dumpty），同名英文童谣中的人物，译名不统一，有"矮胖子""鸡蛋男孩""蛋头先生"及音译"汉普蒂·邓普蒂"等。这首童谣的原文是：Humpty Dumpty sat on a wall, Humpty Dumpty had a great fall; All the king's horses and all the king's men, Couldn't put Humpty together again（矮胖子，坐墙头，栽了一个大跟斗；国王呀，齐兵马，破蛋难圆没办法）。如今这个词多用于指身材矮胖的人，或者指一经损坏便无法再修复的东西。

This new era, called the Middle Ages or the medieval period, began, then, in 476 and lasted until 1453. What happened in 1453? You will learn that later.

During the early part of the Middle Ages, till, about the year 1000, the Germanic peoples were the chief people in Europe. They were quick to learn many things from the Romans whom they had conquered. Even before they had conquered Rome, most of them had already become Christians. They also learned Latin.

Without the unity of the Roman Empire, people no longer traveled very much or very far. This meant that people from places like Spain and Italy and Gaul didn't talk to each other very often. Over the years they began to use different expressions and to pronounce words differently. As centuries passed, the common people no longer spoke the old classical Latin but spoke what were really the new languages of Spanish, Italian, and French. These were different from Latin and different from each other, too. However, because they all grew out of Latin, they have a lot of words that are very much alike.

In Britain, the Anglo-Saxons would have nothing to do with the Romans and would not use the Roman language but kept their own language. After a while this language of the Anglo-Saxons was called English. The Anglo-Saxons also kept their own religion until about one hundred years later, or about 600 A.D.

At that time some English slaves were being sold in the slave-market in Rome. They were very handsome. The pope saw them and asked who they were.

止、随即马上开始第二年那样。你们不妨说，古代历史是在公元476年之前很久就已经开始慢慢地终结，而一个新的时代则是在这一年之前及之后的很长一段时间里慢慢地出现的。尽管如此，公元476年仍然是一个很好记忆的年份。

因此，这个称为中古时期或者中世纪的新时代，便是从公元476年开始，一直持续到了公元1453年。那么，1453年又出现了什么情况呢？你们日后自然就会知道的。

从中世纪早期到公元1000年左右，日耳曼各族都是欧洲的主要民族。他们非常聪明，很快就从征服的古罗马人那里学到了许多的东西。甚至在古罗马还没有被征服的时候，他们中的大多数人就已经皈依了基督教呢。他们还学会了拉丁语。

由于罗马帝国不再统一，所以人们便不像以前那样经常旅行或者远走了。这就意味着，像西班牙、意大利和高卢这些地方的人，彼此之间便不会经常交流了。因此，许多年后，他们开始使用不同的语言表达，对单词的发音也不同了。几个世纪之后，普通民众便不再说原来那种古典的拉丁语，而是开始说西班牙语、意大利语、法语这些真正的新语言了。这些语言既与拉丁语不同，彼此之间也有差异。然而，由于它们全都起源于拉丁语，因此这些语言中有许多的单词都很相似。

在不列颠，盎格鲁-撒克逊人与古罗马人并无往来，也不使用拉丁语，而是保持着自己的语言。不久后，盎格鲁-撒克逊人所说的这种语言，便被人们称为英语了。除此之外，盎格鲁-撒克逊人还保留着自己的宗教，直到差不多一百年后，即到了公元600年左右，他们才皈依了基督教。

当时，罗马的奴隶市场上还可以买到一些英国奴隶。他们的长相都很英俊。教皇看到了之后，就问他们都是些什么人。

"They are Angles," he was told.

"Angles!" exclaimed he. "They are handsome enough to be 'angels,' and they should certainly be Christians."

Rome sent some missionaries to England to convert the English: to change Angles to angels. So at last the English, too, became Christians.

"他们都是盎格鲁人（Angles）。"教皇手下的人回答说。

"盎格鲁人！"教皇大声说，"他们这么英俊，完全可以做'天使'（angels）啊，他们当然应该成为基督徒才是。"

于是，罗马教皇便派了一些传教士前往英格兰，去让英国人信奉基督教，让盎格鲁人变成天使。因此，英国人最终也变成了基督徒。

42 New Places — New Heroes

Germanic kings were ruling over pieces of the Western Empire, but in Constantinople a Roman was still ruling over the Eastern Empire. This Roman was named Justinian. Now, up to this time there had been a great many rules or laws by which the people were governed. There were so many of these rules and they were so mixed up that one law would tell you you could do one thing and another would tell you you couldn't. It was as if your mother said you could stay up till nine o'clock tonight and your father said you must go to bed at eight. It was hard for people to tell, therefore, what one must do and what one must not do.

In order to untangle this snarl, Justinian had a set of laws made for the government of his people, and many of these were so good and so just that they are still the law today. If you notice that Justinian begins with *Just*, this will help you to remember that he was the one who made *just* laws.

Another thing Justinian did that has lasted to the present time was to build in Constantinople a very beautiful church called Santa Sophia. Though it is no longer a church, it is still standing after all these years and is a beautiful sight to see. Still another thing he did that you could never guess. It had nothing to do with war or law or buildings.

42 新的地方，新的英雄

虽说此时西罗马帝国各地为日耳曼族的国王们所割据，但在君士坦丁堡，却仍然是罗马皇帝在统治着东罗马帝国。这位罗马皇帝名叫查士丁尼。注意，到此时为止，罗马人民要遵守一大堆的法律法规。由于法律法规太多，因此弄得混淆不清，比如这条法律规定你可以做某件事情，可另一条法律却又规定你不能做。这就好比是你们的妈妈说你们可以待到晚上九点才睡，可你们的爸爸却说你们八点就必须上床那样。因此，人们很难搞清楚自己究竟必须做什么、不能做什么。

为了解决这个问题，查士丁尼便另行制定了一套律法来管理罗马人民；这套律法非常完善、公正，所以如今仍在使用。如果你们注意到"查士丁尼"（Justinian）这个名字的前面部分就是"公正"（Just）一词，那就不难记住，正是这位皇帝，制定出了公正的法律。

查士丁尼还有一项成就，一直影响到了今天；这项成就，就是他在君士坦丁堡修建了一座非常漂亮的教堂，叫作圣索菲亚大教堂。尽管这儿如今不再是教堂了，但经历了如此漫长的岁月后，它却仍然屹立着，变成了一道美丽的风景。他还干了一件大事，你们肯定猜不到。这件大事，与战争、律法或者建筑都毫无关系。

Travelers from the Far East, where China now is, had brought back tales of a wonderful caterpillar that wound itself up with a fine, thin thread over a mile long, and they told stories of how the Chinese unwound this thread and wove it into cloth of the finest and smoothest kind. This thread, as you might guess, was called silk, and the caterpillar that made it was called the silkworm. People in Europe had seen this beautiful silk cloth, but how it was made had been a mystery — a secret. They thought it so wonderfully beautiful that it was supposed to have been made by fairies or elves or even sent down from heaven. Justinian found out about these caterpillars and had men bring these silkworms into Europe so that his people also might make silk cloth and have silk ribbons and fine silk garments, and therefore we give him the honor of starting the manufacturing of silk in Europe.

About the same time that Justinian lived, there was a king in *France* named Clovis. Clovis belonged to the Germanic tribe called the Franks, which gave the name France to that country. Clovis believed in Thor and Woden as all of his people did. Clovis had a wife named Clotilda, whom he loved very dearly. Clotilda thought all the fighting and cruelty, which her people seemed to like, was wrong. She had heard about the religion of Christ, which did not believe in quarreling and fighting, and she thought she would like to be a Christian. So she was baptized. She then tried to persuade her husband, Clovis, to become a Christian, also.

Clovis was just then going to war — the very thing the Christians preached against. However, just to please his wife, he promised her, if he won the battle, he would become a

当时，一些到过遥远的、如今中国所在的东方去旅行的人，带回了许多的传说，说那里有一种神奇的小毛虫，能够用一根长达一英里的精细丝线将自己缠绕起来，并且描述了中国人如何将这根丝线解开，然后再用它织成最精美、最光滑的布料的过程。你们可能猜得出，这种丝线就是蚕丝，而吐出蚕丝的那种小毛虫，就是蚕。虽说欧洲人曾经见到过这种漂亮的真丝布料，可生产这种布料的方法却一直是一个谜，一个秘密。由于觉得这种布料实在是精美绝伦，他们曾经还以为这种布料是仙女或精灵编织出来的，甚至是从天上掉下来的呢。查士丁尼发现了这些小毛虫的秘密，便命人带了一些回欧洲，从而让古罗马人也可以织出真丝布料，也可以拥有丝绸缎带和精美的丝绸服装；因此，我们便把开创欧洲丝绸生产业的荣耀，归于查士丁尼。

差不多与查士丁尼同一时期，法国有位国王，叫作克洛维。克洛维属于一个叫作法兰克的部落，法兰西这个国名也是由此而来的。克洛维及其手下的臣民敬奉的都是雷神托尔和主神沃登。克洛维的王后名叫克洛蒂尔达，他非常宠爱她。克洛蒂尔达认为，法国人的热衷战争和残暴行为都是不对的。她曾经听说过基督教，听说这种宗教不提倡争斗和战争，因此她希望自己也能成为一名基督徒。于是，她接受了洗礼。然后，她又尽力说服了自己的丈夫克洛维，想让他也变成一名基督徒。

当时，克洛维正在准备发动一场战争，而这正是基督徒坚决反对的。但是，为了让妻子高兴，他便答应她说，假如打赢了这场战争，他就会皈依基督教。后来他

Christian. He did win, and he kept his word and was baptized and had his soldiers baptized also. Clovis made Paris his capital, and Paris is still the capital of France.

It was about this same time, also, that a king named Arthur was ruling in England. Many stories and poems have been written about him, most of which are mythical. Although we know these stories are not historically true, they are, nevertheless, important and interesting — like those tales that are told about the heroes of the Trojan War.

It was said that there was a sword called Excalibur stuck so fast in a stone that no one could draw it out except the man who should be king of England. All the nobles had tried without success to draw the sword, when one day a young boy named Arthur pulled it out with the greatest ease, and he was accordingly proclaimed king.

King Arthur chose a company of the nobles to rule with him, and as they sat with him at a round table they were known as the Knights of the Round Table. Tennyson, a great English poet, has written in verse an account of the doings of King Arthur and his knights in a long poem called *The Idylls of the King*, which you will have to read yourself, for we must go on to the next story.

确实打赢了，并且信守诺言，不但自己受洗成了基督徒，还让手下的士兵也都接受了洗礼。克洛维定都巴黎，而如今巴黎仍然是法国的首都呢。

也是差不多与此同时，统治英国的是一个叫作亚瑟的国王。人们写了许多描述亚瑟王事迹的故事和诗歌，但其中绝大多数都是神话传说。尽管我们知道这些故事都不是真实的历史，但它们还是非常重要，也很有意思，就像描述特洛伊战争中那些英雄人物的传说一样。

据说，当时有一把"王者之剑"牢牢地插在一块石头当中；除了注定要当英格兰国王的那个人之外，是没有人能够将它拔出来的。所有的贵族都去尝试过，但无人能把它拔出来；后来有一天，一个叫作亚瑟的小男孩却轻而易举地将这把剑拔了出来；于是，他便被人们尊奉为英格兰国王了。

亚瑟王选择了一些贵族来与他一起统治英国。由于他们与亚瑟王一起议事的时候，都是围坐在一张大圆桌旁，因此人们便将他们称为"圆桌骑士"。丁尼生这位伟大的英国诗人曾经写过一首长篇韵律诗《国王之歌》，描述了亚瑟王及其手下骑士们的事迹；这首诗你们得自己去读，因为我们接下来必须讲下一个故事了。

43 Being Good

What do you mean by *being good*?

The Germans thought being good was being brave.

The Athenians thought that whatever was beautiful was good.

The Stoics thought that doing one's duty and suffering hardship calmly was being good.

The Epicureans thought the right kinds of pleasure were good.

The martyrs thought being good meant suffering and dying for Christ's sake.

Ever since the time of the martyrs, some Christians who wanted to be very, very good indeed, went off into the wilderness and lived by themselves. They wished to be far away from other people, so that they could spend all their time praying and thinking holy thoughts. This, they believed was being good.

One of the strangest of these men who wanted to get away from others was named St. Simeon Stylites. He built for himself a pillar or column fifty feet high, and on the top of it he lived with room only to sit but not to he down. There on the top he lived for many years, day and night, winter and summer, while the sun shone on him and the rain rained on him, and he never came down at all. He could be reached only by a ladder, which his

43　为善

你们觉得，"为善"是什么意思呢？

日耳曼人认为，为善就是勇敢。

雅典人认为，凡属美的东西就是善。

斯多亚派信徒认为，尽自己的义务、毫无怨言地忍受苦难就是为善。

伊壁鸠鲁学派则认为，正确的快乐才是善。

而殉道者却认为，为善指的就是为基督而承受苦难、为基督而牺牲。

自从有了殉道者之后，一些希望自己品行变得实实在在、非常非常高尚的基督徒，便开始来到荒野之中，离群隐居起来。他们希望远离别人，这样他们就能够一心一意地进行祷告，一心一意地去思考神的旨意了。他们认为，这样做就是为善。

这些希望远离别人的人当中，最奇怪的一位要算圣西蒙·斯泰莱特了。他给自己修建了一根高达五十英尺的圆柱，然后住在圆柱顶上的一间房子里；那间房子很小，只够他坐着，没法躺下来。他在柱子顶上生活了许多年，不论白天黑夜、寒来暑往，日晒也好、雨淋也罢，他都从来没有下来过。只有搭上梯子才能爬到他那里去，而他的朋友们也都是搭梯子给他送吃的。他觉得，只有远离尘世、高高在上，才是过一种圣洁生活的最佳办法。虽然我们觉得这个人完全疯了，但他所认为的为

friends used to take him food. High up out of the world, he thought he could best lead a holy life. That was his idea of being good although we should think such a person simply crazy.

In the course of time, however, men and women who wanted to lead holy lives, instead of living alone as they had done at first, gathered in groups and built themselves homes. The men were called monks, the women nuns or virgins, and the houses where they lived were known as monasteries or abbeys. The head monk of an abbey was called an abbot, from the Aramaic word *abba*, which means *father* in the language that Jesus spoke. The abbot ruled over the other monks like a father over his children, giving them orders and punishing them when he thought they needed it. Abbesses were in charge of their nuns in the same way.

In the five hundreds there lived an Italian monk named Benedict. He believed very strongly that one must work if he was to be holy, that work was a necessary part of being holy. He thought, also, that monks should have no money of their own, for Christ had said in the Bible, "If thou wilt be perfect, go and sell that which thou hast, and give to the poor." (Matthew 19:21) Benedict started an order for those people who would agree to three things:

The first thing they were to agree to was to have no money.

The second thing was not to marry.

The third thing was to obey the abbot or abbess.

善，就是这样的。

然而，随着岁月的流逝，那些希望过圣洁生活的人却不再像起初那样离群索居，而是开始聚集在一起，为自己建造共同的家园了。这些人中，男的称为修道士，女的叫作修女或者圣女；而他们居住的地方，则叫修道院或者隐修院。修道院里领头的修道士，叫作"院长"（abbot），这个词源自阿拉米语[1]中的abba一词，在犹太语中是"父亲"的意思。修道院院长就像父亲管教孩子那样，管理着其他的修道士，吩咐他们做这做那，并在他认为需要的时候对犯有过错的修道士进行惩罚。女修道院院长管理手下修女的方式，也是如此。

公元500年的时候，意大利有一位名叫本尼迪克特的修道士。他坚信，一个人如果想要变得圣洁起来，就必须工作，因为他认为工作是让人变得圣洁起来的一个不可或缺的组成部分。他还认为，修道士不应当拥有钱财，因为基督在《圣经》中说过："你若愿意作完全人，可去变卖你所有的，分给穷人。（参见《马太福音》19：21）"本尼迪克特创立了一个修道会，规定认可下述三个方面的人才能加入这个修道会。

他们必须认可的第一件事情，就是个人不能拥有钱财。

第二件事情，就是不得结婚。

---

[1] 阿拉米语（Aramic），公元前 9 世纪通用于古叙利亚的一种语言，属于闪米特语族，后来一度成为西南亚地区（包括以色列）的通用语。直到公元 70 年左右，它都是以色列犹太人的日常用语。

Men and women who joined this order were called Benedictines.

Now, you might think there would have been hardly anyone who would promise for life three such things as to have no money, to obey the abbot — no matter what he told them to do — and never to marry. Nevertheless, there were a great many in every country of Europe who did become Benedictines.

Usually monks or nuns lived in little bare rooms like prison cells, and ate their very simple meals together at a single table in a room called the refectory. They sang praise at sunrise and sunset, and four times during the day besides; they even woke up at midnight to sing prayers. Singing praise was their main job, but not all they had to do. Work of every kind they were obliged to do, and they did it joyfully, whether the work was scrubbing floors or digging in the garden. People who had been rich and people who had been poor all followed the same rules.

Sometimes a monastery was situated in a barren or swampy spot on land that had been given the monks because it was not good or, even worse than no good, dangerously unhealthy. But the monks set to work and drained off the water, tilled the soil, and made the waste places bloom like the rose. They then raised vegetables for their table, fodder for their horses and cattle and sheep. Everything they ate or used or needed, they raised or made.

They did not only the rougher handwork; they did fine handwork, too. Movable type had not been invented, and printing was not known in Europe at this time. Books had to be

第三件事情，就是服从修道院院长的指令。

加入这个修道会的人，就叫本笃会修士（或修女）。

如今，你们或许会认为，几乎没有人会去承诺终生奉行这三件事情，即不拥有钱财、不论对错都要服从修道院院长的指令以及终生不结婚。但尽管如此，欧洲各国中的确还是有很多人都加入了本笃会呢。

通常来说，修士或修女都住在一间间小得就像是牢笼的小房间里，并且在一间叫作饭堂的房间里，坐在一张桌子旁集体就餐，吃的也非常简单。日出和日落时分，他们都会唱赞美诗；除此之外，白天当中他们还会唱上四次。他们甚至还会在半夜起来唱祷文。他们的主要工作就是唱赞美诗，但这并不是他们的全部工作。他们必须干各种各样的活儿，可无论是擦洗地板还是在花园里松土，他们都会满怀喜悦之心地去干的。不管以前是富是贫，他们都遵守着同样的规定。

有的时候，修道院会坐落在一处贫瘠而多沼泽的地方；这种地方正是因为不好，甚至可能会危及人们的身体健康，才让给修道士们去用的。可修道士们会马上行动起来，排干积水、耕种土地，让这片荒地像玫瑰般地绽放出生命的光彩来。然后，他们又会种植菜蔬供自己食用，种植饲料来喂养马、牛、羊。他们吃的、用的和所需的一切，全都是自己生产或者制造出来的。

他们不但从事着较为粗重的体力劳动，还会从事一些优雅精细的手头工作。当时，活字印刷术还没有发明，而欧洲人对印刷术也还是一无所知。书籍只能用人工来抄写，所以，能读会写的修士和修女，便成了抄写书籍的不二人选。他们会将那

written by hand, and the monks and nuns who had reading and writing skills were the ones to do this job. They copied the old books in Latin and Greek. Sometimes one monk would slowly read the book to be copied, and several other monks at one time would copy what he dictated. In this way a number of copies would be made.

The pages of the books were not made of paper but of calfskin or sheepskin, called vellum, and this vellum was much stronger and lasted much longer than paper.

These old books which the monks wrote were called *manuscripts*, which means *handwritten*. Many of these may now be seen in museums and libraries. Some of these manuscripts have been beautifully hand painted with loving care and the initial letters and borders ornamented with designs of flowers and vines and birds and pictures in red and gold and other colors. If monks and nuns hadn't done this copying, many of the old books would have been lost and unknown to us.

The monks also kept diaries, writing down from day to day and year to year an account of the important things that happened. These old diaries, or chronicles, as they were called, tell us the history of the times. As there were then no newspapers, if these chronicles had not been written we should not know what went on at that time.

The monks were the best educated people of those days, and they taught others — both

Monk copying a manuscript
修道士正在抄写手稿

些用拉丁语和希腊语写成的古籍抄写下来。有的时候，是由一名修道士慢慢地朗读需要抄写的书籍，而其他几名修道士则根据他朗读的内容同时进行抄写。这样，一次就可以抄写出好多份副本了。

这些书籍的书页并不是纸张，而是用小牛皮或者羊皮制成的"皮纸"；这种皮纸比纸张结实得多，保存时间也要长久得多。

由修士抄写出来的这些古籍，叫作"手稿"，也就是"手抄本"的意思。如今，在各大博物馆和图书馆里，我们还能看到很多这样的古籍。这些手稿当中，有一些还经过了精心手绘，美丽异常，单词的首字母和边框都饰有花草、藤蔓、小鸟、以及红色、金色和其他颜色的图案呢。倘若不是修士、修女们这样抄写下来，那么许多古籍就会佚失，而我们今天也就看不到它们了。

修士和修女们还会记日记，日复一日、年复一年地把发生的重大事件记录下来。这些古老的日记又称为"编年史"，向我们描绘了当时的历史。由于那个时候还没有报纸，因此，如果没有这些编年史，我们就不知道当时的情况。

那个时候，修道士的教育程度最高，因此他们还会把自己懂得的知识教给别

young and old — the things they themselves knew. The monasteries were also inns for travelers, for anyone who came and asked for lodging was received and given food and a place to sleep whether he had any money to pay or not.

Monks and nuns helped the poor and needy. The sick, too, came to monasteries to be treated and taken care of, so that a monastery was often something like a hospital, too. Many people who had received such help or attention made rich gifts to the monasteries, so they became very wealthy, although neither monks nor nuns could own so much as a spoon for themselves.

So you see monks and nuns were not merely holy; they were lights in an age when the world had grown dull and dangerous. Yes, they were lights, and there were other lights too shining in those years. You will read about them a little later in this book.

人；而他们的学生，则有老有少。修道院也是旅行者停留的客栈，因为无论是谁来借宿，都不会遭到拒绝；修道院既会提供吃的，也会提供睡觉的地方，有没有钱来付账都不打紧。

修士和修女们都会接济穷人和困难人群。病人也会来到修道院里接受治疗和照料，所以修道院常常也有点儿像是医院。许多接受过这种帮助或者照料的人，都会送给修道院丰厚的礼物作为报答；因此，尽管修士和修女个人连一把汤匙都没有，但整个修道院却非常富裕。

所以，你们便可以看出，修士和修女都不只是圣洁而已；在整个世界都变得阴暗沉闷而危险重重的那个时代，他们就是一盏盏明灯。是的，他们就是明灯；不过，在那个年代，也还有其他的明灯在黑暗中发出光芒。在本书稍后的章节中，你们就会看出这一点。

44 A Christian Kingdom in Africa

By the time of the Roman Emperor Constantine, Christianity had been taught all around the Roman Empire; in countries like Italy and Greece in southern Europe; in the countries like Syria and Turkey in the Middle East; and in countries like Egypt and Libya in North Africa. One of the most important early Christians, St. Augustine, was bishop of the North African city of Hippo. He was a famous teacher and writer. The very first monks lived in Egypt, usually out in the desert. The Egyptian city of Alexandria, which Alexander the Great had built so long ago, became important in the Christian world. The bishops of Alexandria were leaders in the early church.

Missionaries traveled beyond the Roman Empire, not only north into Europe but also south into Africa. Some of these missionaries went south of Egypt into Nubia and Axum. Nubia lay directly south of Egypt and today is called Sudan. Axum is southeast and is part of the modem nation of Ethiopia. You already know that Nubia has a history going back as far as Egypt's history. Axum also has a long history that I will tell you now.

Axum was located on the shore of the Red Sea. It is just a short distance across the water from Arabia. A thousand years before Christ, some people from Saba on the tip of

44　非洲的基督教王国

到了罗马皇帝君士坦丁在位的时候，基督教已经在整个罗马帝国境内传播开来了，并且传播到了意大利和希腊这样的南欧国家，传到了叙利亚和土耳其这样的中东国家，以及埃及和利比亚这样的北非国家当中。圣奥古斯丁是早期最重要的基督教信徒之一，他曾是北非城市希波的主教。他还是一位著名的导师和作家。非洲最初那批修道士都集中在埃及，他们通常都住在沙漠之中。亚历山大这座埃及港市，是亚历山大大帝很久以前建立的；如今，它在基督教世界里已经变得非常重要。亚历山大的历任主教，都是早期基督教会里的领袖人物。

传教士们的足迹，踏到了罗马帝国以外的地方；他们不但向北进入了欧洲，也向南进入了非洲。其中有些传教士还前往埃及以南的地方，进入了努比亚和阿克苏姆。努比亚位于埃及的正南方，如今叫作苏丹。阿克苏姆在埃及的东南面，是如今埃塞俄比亚这个国家的一部分。你们已经知道，努比亚的历史和埃及的历史一样漫长。阿克苏姆也有着悠久的历史，下面我就来跟你们说一说。

阿克苏姆位于红海之滨。它距红海对岸的阿拉伯半岛不远。公元前1000年的时候，一些原本生活在阿拉伯半岛最南端的沙巴地区的人迁徙到了阿克苏姆，在这里定居下来，并与当地人混居在一起。后来，阿克苏姆的国王征服并统治了沙巴。因

Arabia migrated to Axum, settled, and mixed with the people there. Later, the kings of Axum conquered and ruled Saba. You can see these two peoples had a lot to do with each other over the years.

One Queen of Sheba (a place also known as Saba) is said to have gone to Jerusalem at the invitation of the Hebrew King Solomon. Perhaps she was one of his wives. In any case, there is a legend that has been told for many years in Ethiopia that the kings there are descended from King Solomon and the Queen of Sheba. Even the last king of Ethiopia, Haile Selassie, who ruled until 1974, claimed that the famous Biblical king and queen were his great great great, great ... grandparents.

Because of its long seacoast, Axum became a trading center. Ships from Axum sailed north along the Red Sea to Egypt, south in the Indian Ocean along the east coast of Africa, and across that ocean all the way to India. The ships carried valuable goods like gold and ivory and spices. Axum also sent caravans across the desert to trade with places that could not be reached by water. Axumite merchants traded with the Roman Empire. Merchants from Rome and Greece came to live in Axum to conduct business there. Axum became a very rich kingdom. The kings wore luxurious robes and rode in chariots pulled by elephants. One king of Axum is particularly famous. This is King Ezana, who came to the throne around 330 A.D., just around the time of the Roman Emperor Constantine.

Like most ancient rulers, King Ezana was a military leader. He extended his empire by conquering his neighbors. But he is best known because he converted to Christianity. He

此你们都可以看出，这两个民族之间，在这一时期的彼此交往一定是非常频繁的。

据说，一位示巴（这个地方也被称作沙巴）女王曾经受到希伯来国王所罗门的邀请，到过耶路撒冷。或许，这位女王还是所罗门的妻子之一呢。不管是不是，反正埃塞俄比亚有一个古老的传说，称当地的国王都是所罗门王和示巴女王的后裔。即便是在埃塞俄比亚王位上掌权到了1974年的最后一任国王海尔·塞拉西一世，也说《圣经》中这两位著名的国王和女王是他的曾曾曾曾……祖父母呢。

由于有着漫长的海岸线，因此阿克苏姆就成了一个贸易中心。来自阿克苏姆的船只沿着红海一直向北，航行到了埃及，向南则在印度洋里沿着非洲东海岸航行，还穿过整个印度洋，到达了印度。这些船只上装载的，都是贵重商品，比如黄金、象牙和香料。阿克苏姆还派遣商队穿过沙漠，去跟那些无法经由水路抵达的地方的人们做生意。阿克苏姆王国的商人与罗马帝国有贸易往来。而罗马和希腊的商人也远道而来，住在阿克苏姆打理生意。于是，阿克苏姆便成了一个非常富裕的王国。阿克苏姆的国王们都穿着华丽的长袍，坐着用大象拉着的两轮马车。有位阿克苏姆国王尤其出名。他就是公元330年左右登上王位的埃扎那国王，此时与罗马皇帝君士坦丁在位差不多属于同一时期呢。

跟绝大多数古代统治者一样，埃扎那国王也是一位军事领袖。他通过征服邻国，让阿克苏姆帝国的疆域不断扩大。但他之所以有名，则是因为他皈依了基督教。在两位来自叙利亚的年轻基督徒的引领下，他皈依了基督教。传说这两位年轻人要么是因为在红海中所坐的船只失了事，要么是因为被海盗俘虏，才来到阿克

was converted by two young Christians from Syria who were brought as slaves to Axum. Legend has it that these young men either were shipwrecked or were captured by pirates in the Red Sea. Since they knew how to write, they were brought to the king's court to work as scribes. One worked particularly hard to convert King Ezana. When he succeeded, Ezana made Christianity the official religion of his nation. The Christians of Axum were in close contact with the Christians of Alexandria, Egypt. At first, Christians in both Egypt and Axum held their services in Greek. Later they began to worship in their own languages, Coptic in Egypt and Ge'ez in Axum. The king of Axum had the Bible translated into Ge'ez.

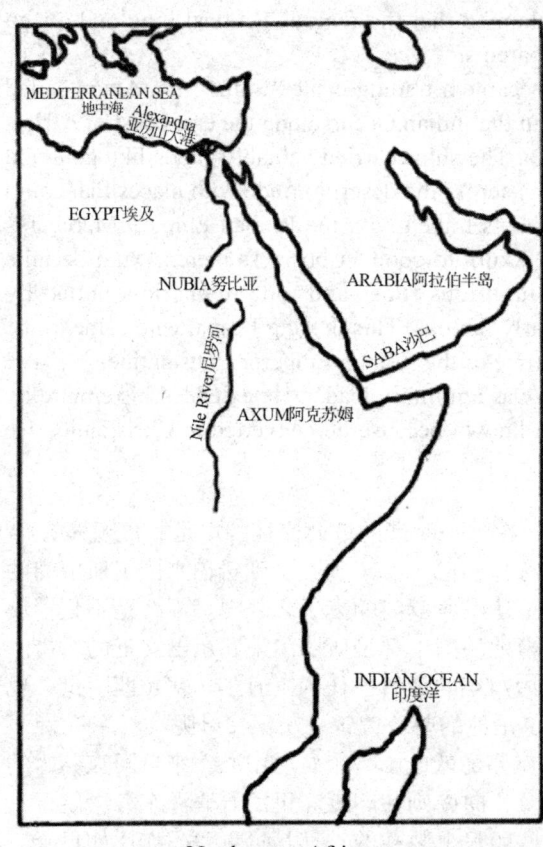

Northeasten Africa
非洲东北部

Axum remained a Christian kingdom through the centuries. In the Middle Ages, when the Christian countries in Europe were building the great cathedrals that you will read about in later chapters, the kings of Axum were also building great churches. Some of these

苏姆王国的。由于他们会写字，因此被带到国王的王宫中去当书记。其中一人尤其卖力，希望埃扎那国王能够皈依基督教。成功之后，埃扎那国王便将基督教定为本国的官方宗教。阿克苏姆王国里的基督徒，与埃及亚历山大港的基督徒之间，联系非常密切。起初，埃及和阿克苏姆两地的基督徒，是用希腊语进行祷告的。后来，他们都开始用本国的语言来礼拜上帝：在埃及的基督徒用的是科普特语，而在阿克苏姆的基督徒则用吉兹语[1]。阿克苏姆国王还让人把《圣经》翻译成了吉兹语。

阿克苏姆一直都是一个基督教国家，持续了几百年。到了中世纪，当欧洲各个基督教国家都开始大兴土木，修建起一座座宏伟壮观的大教堂时，阿克苏姆的国王也正在修建许多宏大的教堂；欧洲国家的情况，你们在后面的章节中将会看到。阿

---

[1] 科普特语（Coptic）和吉兹语（Ge'ez），即古埃及语和古埃塞俄比亚语，如今都已经很少有人使用了。

are unlike any other churches that you will ever see. One king, a man named Lalibela, sent stone carvers into a remote mountain area. First the carvers cut deep down into underground rock and made trenches. Then the workers were lowered into the trenches to carve the actual churches out of the solid rock. One has the shape of a cross. The largest is more than one hundred feet long. Inside, beautiful paintings with bright colors and gold leaf decorate the walls and altars. If you travel to Ethiopia, you can still visit these churches today.

Several centuries after the time of King Ezana, Axum was cut off from most of the Christian world. Arabs, whom you will read about in the next chapter, conquered all of North Africa and established a new religion called Islam. Some people in Egypt continued to be Christians, but most Egyptians and also many Nubians were converted to Islam. Axum was cut off from many of its old trade routes, so Axum's wealth declined. The country did manage to preserve its independence and its religion. Because they were so far away, Europeans lost track of the Ethiopian Christians. But they were still there. And now we have rediscovered their history.

克苏姆兴建的那些教堂当中，有一些与你们看到过的教堂都全然不同。有一位名叫拉利贝拉的国王，曾经派了一些石雕匠到一个遥远的山区里去。首先，那些石雕匠会一直向下开凿，在地下岩石中凿出一条条大沟来。然后，石匠们便被放到这些沟壕里，在坚硬的岩体上雕出真正的教堂来。其中有一座石雕教堂，外形竟然还是一个十字架哩。而其中最大的一座，则有一百多英尺长。在教堂内部，墙壁和祭坛上还装饰着许多颜色亮丽的精美壁画和黄金树叶。如今要是你们去埃塞俄比亚旅行的话，还能参观到这些教堂呢。

埃扎那国王去世几个世纪后，阿克苏姆便同其他大多数基督教国家都断绝了往来。这是因为，阿拉伯人征服了整个北非，并且建立了一种叫作伊斯兰教的新宗教；在下一章，你们就会看到阿拉伯人的相关情况。虽说埃及有一些人仍然信仰基督教，但绝大多数古埃及人和许多的古努比亚人却皈依了伊斯兰教。阿克苏姆过去的许多贸易线路也都中断了，因此阿克苏姆的财富也日渐减少。这个古国曾经的确试图保持独立，并且保护着本国的宗教。但由于相距极其遥远，所以欧洲人便与埃塞俄比亚的基督徒失去了联系。不过，这些基督徒仍然留在埃塞俄比亚。而如今，我们又重新发现了他们的历史。

45 Muhammad and the Early Years of Islam

We have already heard about two religions that began in the part of the world we now call the Middle East. These are Judaism and Christianity. In this story, I'll tell you about a third religion that began in the same area. This religion is called Islam.

Every hundred years is called a century, but a thing that seems a little strange is this — the hundred years from 500 to 600 is called the sixth century, not the fifth; the hundred years from 600 to 700 is called the seventh century, not the sixth, and so on. Well, we have now reached the seventh century, the six hundreds, and we are to learn of a man who was to make a change in the whole world.

There lived in Arabia a man named Muhammad. He was born into humble circumstances. Because his parents died when he was young, he was raised by an uncle. His uncle operated camel caravans, which transported passengers and goods much as trains or trucks do today. The Arabian city of Mecca, where Muhammad lived, was the center of the caravan trade. These camel caravans traveled across the Arabian Desert to North Africa and to the lands along the eastern end of the Mediterranean Sea. Although Muhammad had little formal education, he traveled to many wonderful places with the

45 穆罕默德和早期的伊斯兰教

我们已经知道，有两种宗教都发源于如今我们称之为中东的这一地区。这两种宗教，就是犹太教和基督教。在这一章中，我将跟你们说一说发源于同一地区的第三种宗教。这种宗教，叫作伊斯兰教。

虽然我们都知道，每一百年叫作一个世纪，但有个方面却似乎有点儿奇怪，那就是：从公元500年至公元600年这一百年，我们称之为六世纪，而不是五世纪；从公元600年至公元700年的这一百年，我们称之为七世纪，而不是六世纪；其余的则依此类推。好吧，我们现在正是说到了七世纪，也就是从基督降生时算起的第六个一百年。在此，我们将介绍一位即将改变整个世界的人物。

阿拉伯半岛上有一个人，叫作穆罕默德。他出生在一个贫贱的家庭里。由于父母在他还小的时候就去世了，所以他是由伯父养大的。他的伯父经营着一支骆驼队，用于运送旅客和货物，就像今天的火车和汽车似的。穆罕默德生活的麦加城，当时正是阿拉伯半岛的商队贸易中心。这些骆驼商队穿越阿拉伯沙漠，前往北非以及地中海东部的沿海地区。尽管穆罕默德没有接受过多少正规教育，但他跟随着商队到过许多奇妙的地方，见识过各种各样的人物。他在替伯父打工的过程中，遇到了一个很富有的阿拉伯女性。两人不久后就结了婚，幸福地生活在一起。穆罕默德

caravans and met many different kinds of people. While working for his uncle, he met a wealthy Arabian woman named Khadija. They were soon married and lived happily together. Muhammad and Khadija had four daughters.

A remarkable thing happened to Muhammad when he was around forty years old. According to Muslim tradition, the story is told that he was visiting a mountain in the desert, where he often went to study and think. One day the angel Gabriel appeared and delivered a message from God. Muhammad listened to this message and set out to teach it to others. But Muhammad did not intend to start a whole new religion.

He believed in the same God that the Jews and Christians worshiped. In Arabia there were Jews and Christians, as well as others who still worshiped idols. These groups often fought over their religious differences. Muhammad hoped that his teachings would make them more understanding of one another.

Muhammad saw a lot of unjust and bad behavior around him. He taught that people should change their selfish ways of living and be more concerned for those less fortunate.

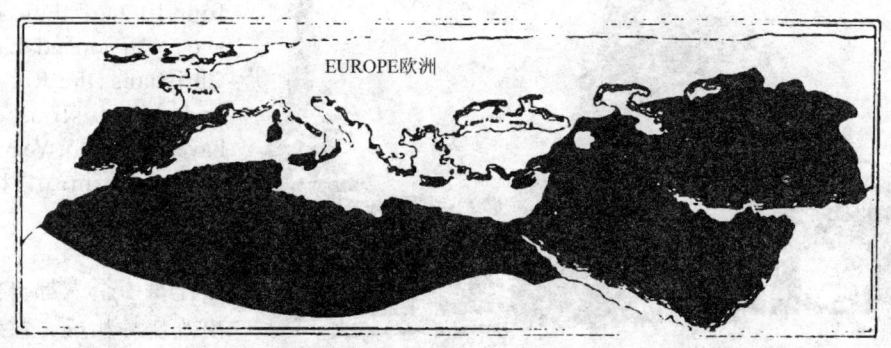

World of Islam
伊斯兰教的范围

夫妇一共生了四个女儿。

在穆罕默德年近四十的时候，发生了一件不同寻常的事情。据穆斯林的传说，此事发生的时候，他在沙漠当中一座自己常去那儿学习和思考的山上游玩。有一天，天使加百列[1]在他面前现身，给他带来了神的旨意。穆罕默德聆听了这一旨意，然后开始将旨意传达给其他的人。不过，穆罕默德当时并没有想过要创立一种全新的宗教。

他与犹太人和基督徒一样，信奉同一个神。在阿拉伯半岛上，既有犹太人、基督徒，也有其他一些仍然信仰多神教的人。这些群体之间，经常会因为宗教信仰不同而争斗不休。穆罕默德希望，自己的教义能够让他们更多地理解彼此。

穆罕默德看到，自己的身边存在着许多既不公正、又不道德的做法。他教导人们应当改变种种自私的生活方式，应当更加关注那些不幸的人。不过，他当然无

---

[1]　加百列（Gabriel），基督教《圣经》中替上帝把好消息报告给世人的天使，是七大天使中的报喜天使。参见《但以理书》8：16和《路加福音》1：26等处。

But, of course, it is impossible to get everyone to agree to change. A new religion began, instead, among those people who believed in Muhammad's teachings. His followers became known as Muslims, and their religion is called Islam. Islam means "submission" to God.

Khadija was the first to follow her husband's teachings. Soon others in Mecca followed, but there were some who wanted to stop Muhammad's teachings. In 622 A.D. Muhammad and his followers moved from Mecca to the city of Medina. This first migration is called the Hegira. Some years later, they returned to Mecca, but Muslims today still teach the story of the angel Gabriel appearing before Muhammad and of the Hegira.

The Muslims began their calendar with the year of the Hegira, calling 622 A.D. the Year 1, just as Christians began their calendar from the year of Jesus's birth and the Romans from the year of the founding of their city. Have you noticed that the Christians, the Romans, and the Muslims each have a different Year 1?

Muhammad lived

In 622 A.D. Muhammad and his followers moved from Mecca to the city of Medina
公元622年，穆罕默德及其信徒从麦加迁徙到了麦地那城

法让每一个人都自愿做出改变。相反，在那些信奉穆罕默德教义的人当中，却兴起了一种新的宗教。他的信徒被称为穆斯林，而他们所信奉的这种宗教则称为伊斯兰教。所谓的"伊斯兰"，就是指"顺从"神。

穆罕默德的夫人是第一个信奉他的教义的人。很快，麦加的其他人也纷纷变成了穆罕默德的信徒；但是，还有一些人却想要阻止穆罕默德教义的扩散。公元622年，穆罕默德及其信徒从麦加迁徙到了麦地那。这第一次迁徙，被称为"圣迁"[1]。几年后，他们又回到了麦加；不过，人们直到如今还在讲述着天使加百列在穆罕默德面前显灵和圣迁的故事呢。

穆斯林就是从"圣迁"这一年开始纪年的，他们把公元622年称为元年，就像基督徒从耶稣基督降生那一年开始纪年、罗马人从罗马建城那一年开始纪年一样。你们有没有注意到，基督徒、罗马人和穆斯林各自的元年都不相同呢？

---

[1] 圣迁（Hegira），专指公元622年穆罕默德率信徒从麦加逃亡到麦地那的过程，亦用于指伊斯兰教纪元。Hegira 本身指"逃亡，迁徙"。

only ten years after the Hegira; that is, until 632 A.D. The new Muslim leaders were called caliphs. The caliphs continued to spread Muhammad's teachings. The first caliph was Abu Bakr; the second was named Omar. These teachings from God were written down and became the Qur'an (sometimes spelled as Koran), the Muslim holy book. "Qur'an" comes from a word that means "to recite" because Muslims learn to recite the Qur'an when they are young.

"Allah" is the Arabic word for God. Muslims believe that Muhammad was the last of God's prophets. They also believe that Abraham, Moses, and Jesus were also God's prophets.

Muslims worship in a building called a mosque, just as Christians worship in a church, and Jews worship in a synagogue or temple. They also pray five times each day, if possible, wherever they may be. A man called a muezzin goes out on the balcony of a minaret, or tower, of a mosque and calls aloud, "Come to prayer. Come to prayer. There is but one God, and He is Allah."

When Muslims pray, they face toward the city of Mecca because the holiest shrine of Muslims, called the Ka'ba, is located there. At least once in their lifetime, Muslims try to make the pilgrimage to the

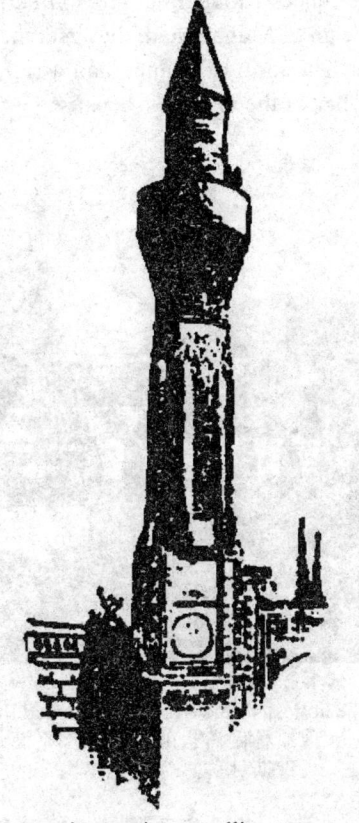

"圣迁"之后,穆罕默德只活了十年就去世了;也就是说,穆罕默德只活到了公元632年。后来,新的穆斯林领袖被称为哈里发。历任哈里发继续传播着穆罕默德的教义。第一任哈里发叫阿卜·巴克尔,第二任哈里发则是奥马尔。穆斯林将这些源自神的教义记录下来,形成了穆斯林的圣书《古兰经》(Qur'an,有时也被拼成Koran,译为《可兰经》)。"古兰"(Qur'an)一词本义指的是"诵读",因为穆斯林在幼年时期就得学会诵读《古兰经》。

Muezzin on minaret calling to prayer
宣礼员在清真寺的尖塔上召唤穆斯林去做祷告

"安拉"(Allah)一词,是阿拉伯语里对伊斯兰教所信仰的唯一神的称呼。穆斯林认为,穆罕默德是神派来的最后一位先知。

穆斯林都在清真寺里做礼拜,就像基督徒在教堂、犹太人在犹太教堂或神庙里礼拜神一样。无论身处何地,只要做得到,穆斯林每天都要做五次祷告。一到时间,就会有一个叫作"宣礼员"的穆斯林走到清真寺尖塔的阳台上,大声喊道:"都来祷告吧。都来祷告吧。世间只有一个神,那就是真主安拉。"

穆斯林在祷告的时候,都是面朝麦加城,因为穆斯林最神圣的圣殿"克尔白"就位于麦加。所有的穆斯林在一生当中,起码都会尽量去圣城麦加朝圣一次。

holy city of Mecca.

During the early years of Islam, its leaders were building an empire, much of it in the lands that had once been a part of the Roman Empire. Muslim armies traveled around the Mediterranean, through the Middle East, all the way to Constantinople.

At Constantinople, the gateway from Asia to Europe, they were turned back by Christians, who poured hot tar and burning oil from the walls of the city. The Muslims tried many times to capture Constantinople but without success. Muslim armies also went westward through North Africa, across the Strait of Gibraltar into Spain and across the Pyrenees Mountains into southern France. In 732 A.D., just one hundred years after the death of Muhammad, they met their match near the town of Tours' in France.

The king of France had a right-hand man named Charles, who had been nicknamed Charles the Hammer because he could strike such terrific blows. Charles was also called Mayor of the Palace, which meant that he was the chief servant of the king. Charles the Hammer and his French soldiers defeated the Muslims and kept them from moving farther into Europe.

In just a century, Islam had spread far and wide.

When Muslims pray, they face toward the city of Mecca ... the holiest shrine of Muslims called the Ka'ba is located there.
穆斯林做祷告的时候，都是面朝麦加城的方向……
穆斯林称之为"克尔白"的圣殿，就位于麦加

在伊斯兰教兴起的初期，穆斯林的领袖们便建立起了一个帝国，其中的大部分疆域都曾经是罗马帝国的领土。穆斯林的大军横扫地中海周围，穿过中东地区，一路挺进君士坦丁堡。

而在君士坦丁堡这个从亚洲前往欧洲的门户，他们却被基督徒挡住了；基督徒从城墙上面泼下滚烫的沥青和燃烧着的油料，阻住了他们的去路。穆斯林多次强攻，想要攻下君士坦丁堡，却都没有成功。穆斯林的大军还向西挺进到北非，越过直布罗陀海峡，攻入了西班牙，然后又越过比利牛斯山脉，进入了法国南部。就在距穆罕默德去世正好一百年的公元732年，穆斯林军队在法国的图尔城附近遇上了劲敌。

当时，法国的国王手下有一个名叫查理的得力干将；因为他打起仗来就像铁锤那样强大有力，因而得了个"铁锤查理"的绰号。查理还被人们称为"大内总管"，也就是说，他是国王最主要的亲信。"铁锤查理"率领手下的法军打败了穆斯林，从而没有让穆斯林大军继续向欧洲深入扩张。

People in countries bordering the Mediterranean, from Constantinople, all the way around North Africa on the southern edge, and north through Spain into France, lived under Muslim rulers. Many ordinary people had become Muslim. Even today, Islam is the main religion in the Middle East and North Africa.

　　仅仅用了一个世纪，伊斯兰教便名扬天下，大范围地传播开来了。地中海周围各国，从君士坦丁堡起，沿着北非南端一路向西，再向北经由西班牙到法国，这一大片地区全都落入了穆斯林君主的统治之下。即便是到了如今，伊斯兰教也仍然是中东和北非地区的一种主要宗教。

46 Arabian Days

Perhaps you have read the *Arabian Nights*.

This is the story of

In the one hundred years after Muhammad died, the Muslims conquered the Middle East and North Africa. Soon after that, they conquered Persia and lands farther east. Before long, their empire was larger than the Roman Empire had been. For the Middle East and North Africa, the centuries that followed were indeed Arabian Days. Although they failed to conquer most of Europe, over the years people there learned many things from the Muslims.

The Phoenicians invented our alphabet, but the Arabs invented the figures which we use today in arithmetic. 1, 2, 3,4, and so on are called Arabic figures. The Romans used letters instead of figures: V stood for 5, X for 10, C for 100, M for 1000, and so on. Think how difficult it must have been for a Roman boy to add such numbers as

IV
XII
+ MC
XCII
VII

They could not be added up in columns as we do. When you think of multiplying and dividing with Roman numbers, it seems almost impossible, for example:

MCVII
× XIX

46 阿拉伯时代

你们可能都看过《一千零一夜》了吧。这个故事，却叫"阿拉伯时代"[1]。

在穆罕默德去世后的那一百年里，阿拉伯人征服了中东和北非地区。不久之后，他们又征服了波斯，以及更远的一些东方地区。很快，他们建立的这个帝国的疆域，便超过了以前的罗马帝国。对于中东和北非地区来说，接下来的那几个世纪，实际上就是阿拉伯人的时代。尽管阿拉伯人没能征服欧洲的绝大部分地区，但这些年间欧洲人也从阿拉伯人那里学到了不少的东西。

腓尼基人发明了我们如今所用的字母表，而阿拉伯人则发明了如今我们在算术中所用的数字。1、2、3、4等数字，就叫阿拉伯数字。罗马人用的是字母，而不是数字：比如V代表5，X代表10，C代表100，M代表1000，等等。想象一下，要是让古罗马的一个小男孩来算一算下面这道加法题，该有多困难啊：

IV
XII
+ MC
XCII
VII

这种数字，是没法像我们这样用竖式来计算的。如果想用罗马数字来进行乘法和除法运算的话，那就似乎更加做不到了，例如：

MCVII
× XIX

---

[1] 《一千零一夜》（Arabian Nights）和"阿拉伯时代"（Arabian Days），这里用的是对比的手法。《一千零一夜》（Arabian Nights）直译就是"阿拉伯之夜"，而"阿拉伯时代"（Arabian Days）直译则是"阿拉伯的白天"。注意，《一千零一夜》也译为《天方夜谭》（其中的"谭"，就是"谈"），是一部古代阿拉伯、波斯、印度等地的民间故事集。

Occasionally you may see Roman figures still used — on clock faces, for instance — but all the figures that you use every day in your arithmetic are Arabic figures.

Another thing:

The Arabs built many beautiful buildings; these buildings look quite different from those that the Greeks and Romans and Christians built. The doors and window openings, instead of being square or round, were usually horseshoe-shaped. On the top of their mosques they liked to put domes shaped something like an onion, and at the corners they put tall spires or minarets from which the muezzin could call aloud the hour for prayer. They covered the walls of their buildings with beautiful mosaics and designs. The Muslims, however, were very careful that these designs were not copies of anything in nature, for they had a commandment in the Qur'an something like the Christian commandment, "Thou shalt not make . . . any likeness of anything that is in heaven above, or that is in the earth beneath, or that is in the water under the earth." Because of this commandment, most Muslims never made drawings or pictures of any living thing, neither of plants nor animals. They thought they would be breaking the commandment if they did. So they made designs out of lines and curves without copying anything from nature. These designs were called *arabesques*, and although they were not like anything in nature, they were often very beautiful.

Still another thing:

In Arabia there grew a little bush on which were small berries with seeds inside. The

如今，你们偶尔也会看到，还有人在使用罗马数字，比如用在时钟的钟面上；不过，你们每天在算术课上使用的数字，却全都是阿拉伯数字。

阿拉伯人的贡献，还有一个方面。

阿拉伯人修建了许多漂亮的建筑；那些建筑，样子都与古希腊人、古罗马人和基督徒所建的大不相同。阿拉伯人修建的这些建筑上，门啊、窗啊既不是方形的，也不是圆形的，而通常是马蹄形的。他们所建的清真寺，屋顶都喜欢盖成圆形的穹顶，样子有点儿像是洋葱头，而在寺的四角则喜欢建有尖顶或尖塔；到了祷告的时候，宣礼员就是在这种尖塔上大声进行召唤的。他们还会将建筑物的墙壁贴满美丽的马赛克和图案。然而，在这样干的时候，阿拉伯人却非常细心，不会让那些图案与自然界里的任何东西相似；因为他们的《古兰经》里也有一条戒律，它与基督教的下述戒律是一样的："你们不应制造出……与天上、地下或者水中之物有任何相似之处的东西。"由于有这条戒律，所以绝大多数阿拉伯人从来都不会画下任何生物；他们既不会画植物，也不会画动物。他们认为，如果画了，就是违反了这条戒律。于是，他们便用不是仿照自然界中任何东西的线条、弧形来构造图案。这些图案，被称为阿拉伯式花饰；尽管它们与自然万物都不相似，但它们通常都非常漂亮。

阿拉伯人的贡献，还有一个方面。

阿拉伯半岛上生长着一种矮小的灌木，上面结有浆果，浆果里面有籽儿。绵羊似乎很喜欢吃这种浆果，并且在吃完后，它们还会变得非常活泼。于是，阿拉伯人

sheep seemed to like these berries and, when they ate them, became very lively. The Arabs themselves tried eating the seeds of these berries with the same effect. Then they made a drink out of these seeds by roasting and grinding them and boiling them in water. This was coffee — which the Arabs had discovered and which is now drunk all over the world.

Another drink made from berries, often from grapes, is alcohol. The Muslims did not like what alcohol does to people who drink it, and so they forbade every Muslim from drinking anything containing alcohol, such as wine, beer, or whiskey.

Still another thing:

Woolen cloth which people used for clothing was made from the hair of sheep or goats. As it took the hair of a great many such animals to make a very little cloth, woolen cloth was expensive. The Arabs found out a way of making cloth from a plant, the cotton plant, which of course was much cheaper. Then in order to decorate the cloth and make it pretty and attractive, they stamped the plain cloth with wooden blocks shaped in different forms and dipped in color. This printed cloth that the Arabs invented was called *calico*.

Still another thing:

The Arabs made swords and knives of such wonderful steel that the blades could be bent double without breaking. The blades were said to be so keen they could cut through the finest hair if floated on water, a thing that only the sharpest razor will do, and yet at the same time so strong that they could cut through a bar of steel. Such swords were made in the East at a place called Damascus, which is in Syria, and in the West at a place called

试着亲口吃了一点点这种浆果里面的籽儿，之后也变得精力充沛起来。后来，他们便将这种籽儿烘干、磨碎并用水煮，制作出了一种饮料。这种饮料就是咖啡，它是由阿拉伯人发现的；而如今，全世界的人都在喝它呢。

还有一种用浆果，通常是用葡萄制成的饮料，那就是酒。阿拉伯人不喜欢看到人们喝了酒之后的样子，因此禁止所有的穆斯林饮用任何含有酒精的饮料，比如葡萄酒、啤酒或者威士忌。

阿拉伯人的贡献，还有一个方面。

人们用于制造服装的羊毛布料，是用绵羊或山羊的毛织成的。由于编织出一件小小的衣服就要剪下许多许多只羊儿的羊毛，因此毛料非常昂贵。阿拉伯人发现了用棉花这种植物来织布的办法，而棉花自然会便宜得多。然后，为了装点布料，让布料看上去漂亮而讨人喜欢，他们又用木块蘸上颜料，在白布上印出不同的图案来。阿拉伯人发明的这种印有图案的布料，就叫作印花布。

阿拉伯人的贡献，还有一个方面。

阿拉伯人的刀剑，都是用非常神奇的钢铁制作而成的，刀刃或剑刃哪怕对折起来也不会断裂。据说这种刀剑的刃口非常锋利，能够切断漂在水面上的一根细发；这种事情，只有最为锋利的剃须刀才能做到呢。而与此同时，刀刃又非常坚固，能够砍断铁棍；因此，完全可以说它是吹毛断发、削铁如泥。这种刀剑，是在东方一个叫作大马士革的地方（如今在叙利亚境内）和西方一个叫作托莱多的地方（今属西班牙）制造出来的；因此，这些刀剑便被人们称为大马士革刀剑或托莱多刀剑。

Toledo, which is in Spain; and so these swords and knives were known as Damascus or Toledo blades. Unfortunately, no one now knows the Arabs' secret for making such marvelous blades. It is what is called a lost art.

Near where Babylon once was, the Arabs built a city named Baghdad. You have heard of it if you have ever read any of the *Arabian Nights*, for most of these stories were told about Baghdad. It was the eastern capital of the Muslims. There in Baghdad the Arabs built a great school that was famous for many, many years. At Cordova in Spain was the western capital of the Muslims, and there they built another great school. Later, after Islam spread south of the Sahara Desert to West Africa, Muslims there built another wonderful school in a city called Timbuktu.

I might tell you many other things these people did — how they made clocks with pendulums to keep time — people had no real clocks before; how they started wonderful libraries of books; and so on — but this is enough for the present to show you what intelligent people they were.

The Arabs belong to the Semite family, the same family to which the Phoenicians and Jews belong. The Arabs were as clever as their cousins the Phoenicians, who, you remember, were very clever, but they were also as religious as their other cousins the Jews, who, you remember, were very religious.

The Muslims had ideas about women that are different from ours. Most thought it was immodest for a woman to show her face to men, and so every woman had to wear a thick

可惜的是，如今阿拉伯人制造这种神奇刀剑的秘诀已经失传了。这就是人们所谓的失传工艺。

阿拉伯人还在古巴比伦城所在之处的附近，兴建了一座叫作巴格达的城市。如果看过《一千零一夜》，那么你们肯定已经听说过这座城市，因为书中的很多故事都曾提到过巴格达。这里是阿拉伯人的东方之都。阿拉伯人在巴格达开设了一所了不起的学校；许多年里，这所学校都赫赫有名呢。西班牙的哥多华，则是西方都城；在那里，阿拉伯人也开设了一所伟大的学校。后来，当伊斯兰教传播到撒哈拉沙漠以南的西非地区后，穆斯林又在当地一个叫作廷巴克图的城市里兴建了一所令人称奇的学校。

我还可以跟你们说出阿拉伯人做过的其他许多贡献；比如，他们用钟摆做成时钟来计时，而在此以前人们还没有真正的时钟；他们建立了许多不可思议的图书馆等。不过，目前你们只需知道这么多，明白这些阿拉伯人有多聪明就行了。

阿拉伯人与腓尼基人和犹太人一样，也属于闪米特族。阿拉伯人也跟同族的腓尼基人一样聪明；你们应该都还记得，腓尼基人是极其聪明的。同时，阿拉伯人在宗教上又与犹太人一样虔诚；你们应该也还记得，犹太人在宗教上是极其虔敬的。

绝大多数穆斯林认为，女性让男人看到自己的脸是一种很不端庄的做法，因此不管是外出还是在有男性的场合，每位女性都必须戴上厚厚的面纱，将自己的脸遮挡起来，只能将眼睛露在外面。戴着这样的面纱，女性就能够看到别人，可别人却看不到她的脸。穆斯林认为，戴上面纱可以保护女性。穆斯林的教义中还规定，一

veil which hid her face — all except her eyes — whenever she went out where there were men. With such a veil she could see but not be seen. Muslims believed their women would be protected by wearing the veil. Muslims also taught that one man might have up to four wives, if he could protect them all and care for them equally.

One other thing that the Muslims did was to copy and save the writings of the Greek poets and philosophers like Aristotle. Many of these were lost in Western Europe after the fall of Rome. You will see later that Muslim scholars saved these writings and gave them back to Europeans to study centuries later.

个男人最多可以娶上四位妻子，条件则是他能够保护她们，并且一视同仁地照料好她们。

穆斯林还有一项贡献，那就是：他们将古希腊的诗人们以及像亚里士多德那样的哲学家的著作抄写并保存下来了。古罗马衰落之后，这些著作中的许多都在西欧失传了。你们在后面的章节中将会看到，正是穆斯林的学者们将这些著作保存下来，并在几百年后又将它们送回欧洲，让欧洲学者们去进行研究。

Muslim veiled woman standing by
Saracenic ornamental arch
一位戴着面纱的穆斯林女性站在
装饰风格为萨拉逊式的拱门边

47 Two Empires, Two Emperors

Europe had been *in the dark* for three hundred years. You know what I mean. There were not enough educated people to make it bright.

The Arabs were bright, but they were not in Europe.

In 800 there was a man — a king — who by his might and power was able to join the pieces of Europe together once again to form a new Roman Empire. He was not a Roman, however, but a Frank. Franks, you remember, were one of the Germanic tribes that ruled Europe after the end of the Roman Empire. This king of the Franks was named Charles. He was a grandson of the Charles the Hammer who had stopped the Muslims at Tours, and he was called by the French name Charlemagne, which means Charles the Great.

Charlemagne at first was king of France alone, but he was not satisfied to be king of that country only. He soon conquered the countries on each side of him, parts of Spain and Germany. He built his capital in a place in Germany called Aachen, or Aix-la-Chapelle in French. At Aix-la-Chapelle there were warm springs which made fine baths, and Charlemagne was very fond of bathing and was a fine swimmer.

A large part of Italy was then ruled over by the pope. But the pope was having a good

47 两个帝国，两位皇帝

欧洲曾经在黑暗之中过了三百年的时间。你们都明白我的意思吧？因为当时受过良好教育的人不多，没法给欧洲带来光明。

阿拉伯人虽说辉煌灿烂，可他们不是欧洲人啊。

公元800年，欧洲出了一个人物，一位皇帝；凭借自己的能力和权势，他本来是可以将欧洲四分五裂的各个地区重新统一起来，建立一个新的罗马帝国的。不过，他可不是罗马人，而是法兰克人。你们都还记得吧，法兰克人是罗马帝国终结之后，曾经统治过欧洲的日耳曼部族当中的一个。这位法兰克国王，名叫查理。他就是曾经抵抗过穆斯林大军的那位"铁锤查理"的孙子；他的法语名字叫作"查理曼"，意思就是"查理大帝"。

查理曼起初只是法国国王，可他并不满足于只做这一个国家的国王。不久之后，他便征服了法国两侧的一些邻国，征服了西班牙和德国的部分地区。他把首都建在德国境内一个叫作亚琛的地方；在法语里，亚琛（Aachen）叫作Aix-la-Chapelle。亚琛的春季非常暖和，很适合游泳；而查理曼正好非常喜欢游泳，并且技术也很不错。

当时，意大利的大部分地区都由教皇统治着。不过，教皇却与意大利北部的一

deal of trouble with some tribes in the north of Italy, and he asked Charlemagne if he wouldn't come down and conquer them. Charlemagne was quite ready and willing to help the pope, so he went over into Italy and easily settled those troublesome tribes. The pope was grateful to Charlemagne for this and wished to reward him.

Now, Christians everywhere used to make trips to Rome in order to pray at the great Church of St. Peter, which had been built over the spot where St. Peter had been crucified. Well, at Christmas time in the Year 800 Charlemagne paid such a visit to Rome. On Christmas day he went to the Church of St. Peter and was praying at the altar when the pope came forward and put a crown on his head. The pope then hailed him *Emperor*, and as the pope at that time could make kings and emperors, Charlemagne became emperor of Italy added to the other countries over which he already ruled. Charlemagne's empire was now like a new but smaller Roman Empire, but with this big difference: it was ruled over not by a Roman, but by a Frank.

In those days, few people had any education, and hardly anyone could read or write. Charlemagne wanted an education. He was so anxious to know everything there was to be known. He wanted to be able to do everything anyone could do, but there was no one in his own country who knew enough or was able to teach him. In England, however, there was a very learned monk named Alcuin. He knew more than anyone else in Northern Europe, so Charlemagne invited Alcuin to come over from England and teach him and his people. Alcuin taught both Christian literature and also some Latin and Greek writings that had survived the years of warfare in Europe.

些部族矛盾重重，摩擦不断；因此，教皇便问查理曼能不能南下征服这些部族。查理曼早已做好准备，也很乐意帮教皇这个忙；因此，他便率军挺进意大利，轻而易举地解决了那些令人讨厌的部族。教皇非常感激查理曼，便想要报答他。

当时，各地的基督徒经常前往罗马，以便能到圣彼得大教堂里去祷告；这座教堂，就建于圣彼得在十字架上受难的那个地方。公元800年的圣诞节，也正是出于这个原因，查理曼来到了罗马。圣诞节那天，查理曼便前往圣彼得大教堂；当他正在祭坛前祷告的时候，教皇走上前去，将一顶皇冠戴到了他的头上。然后，教皇又高呼他为"皇帝"。由于当时教皇能够册封国王和皇帝，所以查理曼便成了意大利当时他已经实际统治的那些国家的皇帝。此时，虽说查理曼的帝国就像一个新的、只是面积稍小了一点儿的罗马帝国，但二者之间却存在一个重大的差别：统治这个帝国的不是罗马人，而是一位法兰克人。

在那个时候，极少有人接受过教育，也几乎没有人能读会写。查理曼希望自己能够接受教育。他渴望了解一切未知的东西。他希望自己能够去做任何人都可以做到的事情；可在他自己的国家里，却没人如此博学多识，能够去教导他。不过，当时的英格兰却有一位知识非常渊博的修道士，名叫阿尔昆。他的学识，比北欧地区的任何人都要渊博；因此，查理曼便邀请阿尔昆离开英格兰，到他这里来教导他和他的臣民。来了之后，阿尔昆不但向他们传授了基督教文学，还将经历了欧洲连年战火之后幸存下来的一些拉丁语和希腊语著作，传授给了他们。

Charlemagne learned all these things very easily, but when it came to the simple matter of learning to write he found this very hard. He did learn to read, but he seemed unable to learn to write. It is said that he slept with his writing pad under his pillow and practiced whenever he awoke. Yet he never learned to write much more than his name. He did not begin to study until he was a grown man, but he kept on studying all the rest of his life. To make sure that others would have the opportunity he missed, Charlemagne ordered every monastery in his kingdom to open a school. He also opened a school right in his own palace. Why do you suppose he did that?

In spite of the fact that Charlemagne's daughters were princesses, he had them taught how to weave and sew and make clothes and cook just as if they had to earn their own living. Although Charlemagne was such a rich and powerful monarch and could have everything he wanted, he preferred to eat plain food and dress in plain clothes. He did not like all the finery that those about him loved. One day, just to make his nobles see how ridiculously dressed they were in silks and satins, he took them out hunting in the woods while a storm was going on, so that he could laugh at them. You can imagine how their silk and satin robes looked after being soaked with rain, covered with mud, and torn by briers.

Although his tastes were simple in matters of dress, he made his home a magnificent palace. He furnished it with gold and silver tables and chairs and other gorgeous furniture. He built in it swimming pools and a wonderful library and a theater and surrounded it with beautiful gardens.

At this time and all through the Dark Ages people had a strange way of finding out

查理曼非常轻松地学会了这些知识；可他发现，学习写字这件简单的事情，对他来说却非常困难。他的确学会了阅读，但他似乎怎么也学不会写字。据说他连睡觉的时候也把写字板放在枕头下，一醒来就开始练习。尽管如此，除了自己的名字，他始终都没有学会写字。虽然他是在成年之后才开始学习的，但在余下的一生中，他一直坚持学习。为了确保其他人不像他那样失去学习的机会，查理曼还下令在国内的每座修道院里都开设一所学校。他甚至还在自己的皇宫里面设立了一所学校。你们认为，他为什么要那样做呢？

尽管查理曼的女儿们都贵为公主，但他还是请了人，来教她们织布、缝纫、做衣服、烧饭，好像她们日后必须自己出去谋生似的。尽管查理曼是一位富甲天下、有权有势的君主，想要什么就有什么，但他宁愿粗茶淡饭，衣着朴素。他与身边的人完全不同，一点儿也不喜欢华丽的服装。有一天，为了让手下的王公贵族明白他们穿着绫罗绸缎的时候有多可笑，他便带着这些人在风雨大作之时到森林里去打猎，以便好好地嘲弄他们一番。你们可以想见，那些王公贵族身上的绫罗绸缎被雨淋湿、被污泥沾满、被荆棘撕破后的样子，该有多么的可笑啊。

虽然在穿着方面喜欢简朴，但查理曼的皇宫却建得富丽堂皇。皇宫中用的都是金银桌椅，而其他的家具也非常豪华。他还在皇宫中修建了好几个游泳池、一座图书馆和一个戏院，并在皇宫周围修建了一座座美丽的花园。

在这一时期以及整个"黑暗时代"，人们都是用一种非常古怪的方法来判定一

whether a person had stolen or committed a murder or any other crime. The person suspected was not taken into court and tried before a judge and a jury to see whether he was telling the truth and had done the thing or not. Instead he was made to carry a redhot iron for ten steps, or to dip his arm into boiling water, or to walk over red-hot coals. If he were not guilty, it was thought no harm would come to him, or if he was burned, it was thought that the burn would heal right away. This was called *trial by ordeal*. It probably started from the story told in the Bible of Shadrach, Meshech, and Abednego, who, you remember, in the time of Nebuchadnezzar, had walked through the fiery furnace unharmed because they had done no wrong. Though Charlemagne was so intelligent, he believed in the trial by ordeal. Today we have no such cruel and unfair way of finding out whether one is guilty or not. Yet we say of a person who has a lot of trouble that seems to be a test of his character, "He is going through an ordeal."

While Charlemagne was living, there was a caliph in far-off Baghdad named Harun, which is the Arabic spelling of Aaron. You may have heard of him if you have read any of the *Arabian Nights*, for the stories of the *Arabian Nights* were written at this time, and Harun is described in them. Although Harun was a Muslim, not a Christian, and though he was ruler of an empire that fought the Christians, nevertheless he admired Charlemagne very much. To show how much he thought of him, he sent him valuable presents — among other things, a clock which struck the hours, which you remember, was an invention of the Arabs. This was a great curiosity, for there were then no clocks in Europe. People had to tell time by the shadow the sun cast on a sundial, or else by the amount of water or sand

个人是否犯了偷盗、杀人或者其他罪行的。嫌疑人不是被带到法庭上，由法官和陪审团来审理，看他说的是不是真话、是不是犯下了罪行，而是必须手持一根烧红的铁条走上十步，或者将胳膊伸进沸水，或者在烧得通红的炭火上行走。人们认为，如果这个人无罪，那他就会毫发无伤；即便是被烧伤、烫伤了，伤口也会马上愈合。这种方法，叫作神断法。它很可能起源于《圣经》中关于沙德拉、米煞和亚伯尼歌等人的故事；你们应该都还记得，在尼布甲尼撒时期，这几个人都曾经因为没有过错而安然无恙地走过了炽热的火炉。尽管查理曼非常聪明，但他也相信神断法。如今，我们已经不用这样残忍而不公正的方式去判定一个人有罪无罪了。可我们在说到一个人面临着诸多考验其品德的麻烦时，还是会说"他正在经受神断"呢。

查理曼在世之时，遥远的巴格达有一位叫作亚伦（Harun）的哈里发，他的名字在阿拉伯语里拼作Aaron。如果看过《一千零一夜》，你们就一定听说过这个人物；因为《一千零一夜》正是在这个时期写成的，其中提到亚伦的一些故事。虽然亚伦是一位穆斯林而不是基督徒，尽管他身为一个正在与基督徒打仗的帝国的皇帝，但他还是非常仰慕查理曼。为了表明自己极其敬重查理曼，他还送了很多贵重的礼物给查理曼，其中包括一个报时的时钟；你们都还记得吧，时钟可是阿拉伯人发明的。这真是一件稀奇之物，因为当时的欧洲还没有时钟呢。人们只能根据太阳在日晷仪上投下的影子来判断时间，否则便只能根据从一个壶中注入另一把壶中的水或沙子的量来判断时间。他还送了一头大象给查理曼；这头大象，即便是在这位

that dripped or ran out from one jar to another. He also sent Charlemagne an elephant, which was a great curiosity at the court of the Frankish king.

Harun was a very wise and good ruler over the Muslims, and that is why he came to be called *al-Rashid*, which means *the Just*. Do you remember what Greek was also called *the Just*? Harun used to disguise himself as a workman and go about among his people. He would talk with those he met along the street and in the market place, trying to find out how they felt about his government and about things in general. He found they would talk freely to him when he was dressed in old clothes, for then they did not know who he was but thought him a fellow workman. In this way, Harun learned a great deal about his people's troubles and what they liked or didn't like about his rule. He then would go back to his palace and give orders to have rules and laws made to correct anything that seemed wrong or unjust.

After Charlemagne died there was no one great enough or strong enough to hold the new Roman Empire together, and once again it broke up into small pieces; and, "All the king's horses and all the king's men could not put it together again."

法兰克国王的宫廷里，也是一件极其稀罕的东西呢。

亚伦是一位非常睿智、非常优秀的君主；正因为如此，他才被人们称为"阿-拉希德"（al-Rashid），它的意思就是"青天"。你们还记不记得，哪个古希腊人也曾被人们称为"青天"[1]呢？亚伦经常化装成工匠，去臣民当中微服私访。他会跟自己在街道上或市场上碰到的人交谈，尽量了解民众对他的统治和一些大政方针方面的看法。他发现，自己穿着破旧衣服的时候，百姓往往会对他畅所欲言；因为他们不知道他是什么人，以为他也是一位同行的工匠。这样，亚伦就了解到了百姓的许多困苦，了解到百姓喜不喜欢他的统治。接下来，待回到皇宫后，他就会下令制定一些法律法规，来纠正那些似乎不对或不公正的做法。

查理曼死后，再也没有一个能力非凡、势力强大的人来维持这个新的帝国的统一，因此帝国便再一次四分五裂了；这可真是应了那句童谣呢："国王呀，齐兵马，破蛋难圆没办法。"

---

[1] 作者注：是亚里斯泰迪斯（Aristides）。

48 Getting a Start

England is just a little island.

It was quite an unimportant little island in 900 A.D. Much later, England grew rich and strong and, for a while, had an empire spread all over the world.

England is still just a little island.

But it is now an important island in the world!

About one hundred years after Charlemagne — that is, 900 — there was a king of England named Alfred. When Alfred was a boy he had a hard time learning to read, for he did not like to study. In those days many of the hand-written books made by the monks had pretty drawings and letters made in bright colors and even in gold. One day Alfred's mother showed such a book to her children and promised to give it to the one who could read it first. That was a game. Alfred wanted to win the book, so, for the first time in his life, he really tried. He studied so hard that in a very short time he had learned to read before his brothers. Alfred won the book.

When Alfred grew up, England was being troubled by pirates. These pirates were cousins of the English — a Germanic tribe called Danes. The English had long ago

48 刚刚起步

英格兰是一个小小的岛屿。

公元900年的时候，它还是一个非常不起眼的小岛。但过了很久以后，英格兰却开始变得越来越富裕、越来越强大，并且曾经有过一段时间，还变成了一个势力遍布整个世界的大帝国。

英格兰仍然只是一个小小的岛屿。

可如今，它却是世界上非常重要的一个岛屿了！

查理曼去世大约一百年之后，即公元900年左右，英格兰有位国王叫作阿尔弗雷德。阿尔弗雷德小的时候，曾经费尽了九牛二虎之力才学会看书，因为他很不喜欢学习。那个时候，修道士们所抄写的许多书籍中都有精美的图画和文字，它们的色彩都很亮丽，甚至还有金色的。有一天，阿尔弗雷德的母亲给孩子们拿了一本这样的书，并且答应把这本书送给第一个能够阅读它的孩子。那实际上就是一场比赛。阿尔弗雷德想要得到这本书，于是他生平头一回开始实实在在地用功。他学习非常刻苦，因此只用了很短的时间，便学会了阅读，学得比自己的兄弟都要快。因此，阿尔弗雷德便得到了这本书。

阿尔弗雷德长大后，英格兰经常受到海盗（丹麦的日耳曼人）的侵扰。这些海

become Christians and civilized, but the Danes were still rough and wild. They came over from their own country across the water, landed on the coast of England, robbed the towns and villages, and then sailed back to their homes, carrying off everything valuable they could lay their hands on — like bad boys who climb a farmer's fence and steal apples from his orchard. At last the Danes became so bold that they didn't even run away after robbing the country; they were like the bad boys who stick out their tongues and throw stones at the farmer who comes after them. The king's armies went out to punish these pirates, but, instead of beating, they were beaten. It began to look as if these Danes, who were able to do pretty much as they pleased, might conquer England and rule over the English.

Once when things looked pretty bad for England, King Alfred was without an army. Alone, ragged, tired out, and hungry, he came to the hut of a shepherd and asked for something to eat. The shepherd's wife was baking some cakes by the fire, and she told Alfred he should have one if he watched them while she went out to milk the cow. Alfred sat down by the fire, but in thinking about what he could do to beat the Danes he forgot all about the cakes, and when the shepherd's wife returned they were all burned. Thereupon she scolded him roundly and drove him off, not knowing that it was her king that she was treating in this way, for he never told her who he was.

Alfred decided that the best way to fight the Danes was not on land but on the water, so he set to work to build boats bigger and better than those the Danes had. After a while he had something of a fleet, and the boats he built were bigger than those of the Danes, but

盗与英国人同族，属于日耳曼部族。英国人很久以前就皈依了基督教，并且进入了文明社会，可此时的丹麦人却依然很粗鲁、很野蛮。他们从本国渡海而来，在英格兰沿海登陆，劫掠市镇和村庄，然后再坐船回去，带着所有能够到手的贵重之物，就像调皮的男孩子爬过农民的篱笆，到果园里偷苹果似的。最后，丹麦人变得胆大包天，劫掠之后也不逃走了；他们就像那些偷了苹果之后，还向追赶他们的农民吐舌头、扔石子的坏孩子一样。可国王手下的军队前去惩罚这些海盗时，却不是打败了海盗，而是被海盗打败了。看上去，这些为所欲为、无恶不作的丹麦人，似乎可以征服英格兰，可以统治英国人了。

有一次，形势似乎变得对英格兰极为不利，阿尔弗雷德国王手下的军队全军覆灭了。他独自一人，衣衫褴褛、疲惫不堪、饥肠辘辘地来到一位牧羊人的小屋前，要牧羊人给他点儿吃的。那位牧羊人的妻子正在火上烤蛋糕；她对阿尔弗雷德说，如果她出去给奶牛挤奶的时候他能帮着照看火上的蛋糕，就给他一块蛋糕吃。阿尔弗雷德在火边坐下来，可由于他心里一直在想着用什么办法才能打败丹麦人，因此把蛋糕的事情忘了个一干二净；当牧羊人的妻子挤完牛奶回屋时，蛋糕都已经烤煳了。于是，她把他痛骂了一顿，之后就赶走了他；她并不知道，自己如此对待的这个人，就是本国的国王，因为他始终都没有透露自己的身份。

阿尔弗雷德判断，打败丹麦人的最好办法不是陆战，而是水战，因此他便下令，开始建造比丹麦人所乘船只更大、性能更好的船只。不久之后，他便组建起了一支小舰队，而他所造的船只也比丹麦人的船只大；可是，由于体型太大，这些船

they were so big that they could not go into the shallow water without running aground. The Danes' boats, on account of their small size, could go safely close in to shore. In deep water, however, Alfred's fleet was very strong and powerful. This was the first navy that England ever had. England's navy became the largest in the world for a while, and Alfred the Great was the one who started it more than a thousand years ago.

After fighting with the Danes for many years, Alfred finally thought it best to make an agreement with them and give them a part of England to live in if they would promise to stop stealing and live peaceably. The Danes did agree to this, and they settled down peaceably on the land that Alfred gave them — and then became Christians. Over the years, the Danes and the English married each other and raised families. Eventually they became one nationality and no one knew any more whose ancestors were Danes and whose were English.

Alfred made very strict laws and severely punished those who did wrong. Indeed, it is said that the people of England were so careful to obey the law in his reign that one might leave gold by the roadside, and no one would steal it.

Alfred not only built a navy and made wise laws, but he, like Charlemagne, started a school at court for both children and grownups, many of whom were as ignorant as the children. He did many other useful things besides.

He invented, for instance, a way of telling time by a burning candle. You have heard how wonderful the clock, that which Harun al-Rashid sent to Charlemagne one hundred

只无法在浅水区航行，否则便会搁浅。而丹麦人的船只由于体型小，却可以安全地靠近岸边。然而，在深水区，阿尔弗雷德的舰队却威力巨大。这是英国有史以来组建的第一支海军。不久之后，英国海军便变成了世界上规模最大的一支海军；而这支海军，正是阿尔弗雷德大帝在一千多年前创建起来的。

与丹麦人打了多年仗之后，阿尔弗雷德大帝觉得，最好还是与丹麦人议和；如果丹麦人答应不再盗掠，老老实实过日子的话，还可以在英格兰划出一块地方来让他们居住。丹麦人同意了这个条件，并在阿尔弗雷德划给他们的那个地区老老实实地定居下来，后来也变成了基督徒。在此后的许多年里，丹麦人与英国人之间开始相互通婚，共同组建家庭。最终，他们变成了一个民族，再也没人知道谁的祖先是丹麦人、谁的祖先又是英国人了。

阿尔弗雷德大帝制定了严格的法律，毫不留情地惩处那些作奸犯科的人。实际上，据说在阿尔弗雷德统治期间，英国人都非常小心，可以说是他们非常遵纪守法，路不拾遗；就算不小心将金子掉在路边，也不会被人偷偷捡走呢。

阿尔弗雷德大帝不仅创建了一支海军、制定了一些英明的法律，还像查理曼大帝一样，在宫廷里为儿童和成年人开设了一所学校，因为成年人中还有很多的人都像儿童那样没有文化。除此之外，他还干了许多有利的事情呢。

例如，他发明了一种用燃烧的蜡烛来计时的方法。你们已经知道，在当时的人看来，一百年前亚伦·阿-拉希德送给查理曼大帝的那座时钟是多么的神奇。虽然自鸣钟如今已是极其常见之物，但在英格兰根本没有任何钟表的那个时代，阿尔弗

years before, was thought to be. Although striking clocks are, of course, very common nowadays, it was an extraordinary thing then when there were no clocks nor watches at all in England. Alfred found out how fast candles burned down and marked lines around them at different heights — just the distance apart that they burned in one hour. These were called *time-candles*.

Candles were also used for lighting but when they were carried outdoors, they were very likely to be blown out by the wind. So Alfred put the candle inside of a little box, and in order that the light might shine through the box, he made sides of very thin pieces of cow's-horn, as glass then was very scarce.

Such inventions may seem very small and unimportant, and they are when you think of the marvelous inventions and wonderful machines that are made by the thousands nowadays. These inventions of Alfred were no more than the household ideas for which some magazines now offer only a few dollars apiece. But I have told you about them just to show you how ignorant the English, as well as other Germanic tribes of Europe, were in those days. How much superior were the Arab thinkers with their striking clocks. The English were just getting a start.

雷德大帝发明的这种方法也是非比寻常的。阿尔弗雷德算出了蜡烛燃烧的速度，然后在蜡烛上刻下高度不同的刻线；两根刻线之间的距离，就是蜡烛在一个小时内燃烧的长度。这种蜡烛，就叫"计时蜡烛"。

虽说蜡烛可用于照明，但若是在室外点着的话，它们却很容易被风吹灭。于是，阿尔弗雷德大帝便把蜡烛装进一个小盒子里；为了让光线能够从盒中透出来，他又用很薄的牛角片做盒子的四边，因为这些牛角片就像当时还极其罕见的玻璃一样透明。

这些发明可能看上去都很微小，很不足称道；要是你们想到如今成千上万种奇妙的发明和人们制造出来的种种神奇机器的话，也确实如此。阿尔弗雷德大帝的这些发明，与如今一些只值几美元的杂志上刊登的"家用妙招"相比，确实也强不到哪儿去。但我之所以告诉你们这些，是为了说明那时的英国人和欧洲其他的日耳曼部族究竟有多愚昧。而当时的那些阿拉伯思想家和他们发明的时钟，又是多么的先进啊。与他们相比，英国人不过是刚刚起步罢了。

49 The End of the World

What would you do if you knew the world was coming to an end next week, or even next year?

The people who lived in the tenth century thought the Bible[1] said something that meant that the world was coming to an end in the Year 1000 — which was called the millennium from the Latin word meaning a thousand years.

Some people were glad that the world was coming to an end. They were so poor and miserable and unhappy here that they were anxious to go to heaven, where everything would be fine and lovely — if they had been good here. They were particularly good and did everything they could to earn a place for themselves in heaven when this old world should end.

Others were not so anxious to have the world come to an end. But, they thought, if it were coming to an end so soon, they might as well hurry up and enjoy themselves here while they still had a chance.

Well, the Year 1000 came, and nothing happened. At first people simply thought that a mistake had been made in counting the years — that there had not really been one

---

[1] Book of Revelations, chapter 20.

49   世界末日

假如你们知道，下个星期或者明年就是世界末日的话，你们会怎么办呢？

生活在十世纪的人都认为，《圣经》[1]中有些内容的意思就是，世界末日将在公元1000年到来。公元1000年被称为"千禧年"；这个词源于希腊语，指的就是一千年。

有些人对世界即将迎来末日感到很高兴。在这个世界上，他们都穷困潦倒、苦不堪言、毫不幸福，因此他们的心中都在渴望着，只要此生善良、没有作恶，死后他们就会升入天堂；而天堂里的一切，全都是纯粹、美好的。他们都是些特别善良的人，并且竭尽全力，以便在这个旧世界走向末日之后，他们能够升入天堂。

还有一些人则并不那么急于让世界走向末日。不过，他们觉得，如果世界末日真的很快就会到来的话，那他们就不妨趁着还有机会，在此生抓紧时间，及时行乐呢。

---

[1] 《圣经》启示录第 20 章。

thousand years since Christ's birth. The years went by, and still people waited for the end. They reread their Bibles and thought perhaps it meant a thousand years after Christ's *death*, instead of his birth. As time went on, without any change, they began to think the end was delayed for some reason they could not explain. It was not for many years after the millennium that most people came at last to realize that the world was not going to stop after all.

Every once in a while someone who thinks he knows more than others says the end of the world is not far off, but we may be quite sure that the world will keep on going long after we have all grown up and died and our children have done the same.

At this time, when people were looking for the end of the world, there was in the north of Europe a people who did not become Christians until around the year 1000 and cared nothing about what the Bible said as to the end of the world. They belonged to the same family as the Danes who had come to England in the time of Alfred. They were called Norsemen or Vikings. They were bold seafaring men, as hardy and unafraid as the Phoenician sailors of old. Their boats were painted black and had prows carved with figures of sea monsters or dragons. They sailed the northern seas and went farther westward toward the setting sun than any other sailors that we know about had ever gone. They had discovered Iceland and Greenland, and at last under their chief who was named Leif Ericson they reached the shores of America. About the same year that the Christians in Europe were expecting the end of the world — the Year 1000 — the Vikings had gone to what some people thought was the end of the world.

The Vikings called this new place Vineland or Wineland because they found grapes,

好吧，公元1000年到了，可什么事情也没有发生。起初，人们只是以为自己的纪年出现了错误，因为此时距基督降生实际上还不到一千年。随着一年一年过去，人们还在等着世界末日的到来。他们一遍又一遍地反复阅读了《圣经》之后，又认为《圣经》可能是指，世界末日的降临时间是在基督死后一千年，而不是基督降生后的一千年。由于岁月流逝，一切却都没有改变，他们又开始认为，世界末日是由于某种他们无法解释的原因而被推迟了。直到千禧年过去很久，绝大多数人才终于认识到，世界根本就没有什么末日。

每隔一段时间，就会有一些自以为比别人高明得多的人说，世界末日不远了；但我们完全可以肯定的是，待我们这一代人全都长大成人、直到死去，待我们的孩子那一代也全都长大成人、直到死去之后很久，世界仍然不会走向末日哩。

此时，正当人们都在琢磨着世界末日这个问题的时候，北欧有个民族却一直对《圣经》中所说的世界末日问题毫不在意。他们与阿尔弗雷德大帝时期迁徙到英格兰的那些丹麦人同族。他们被称为维京人，或者维京人。他们都是些胆大妄为的水手，与腓尼基水手一样吃苦耐劳、无所畏惧。他们将船只都漆成黑色，船头还刻有海怪或者巨龙的形象。他们在北部海域游弋，并且朝着日落的方向往西航行，所到之处比我们所知的其他任何一个海上民族到达的都要远。他们发现了冰岛和格陵兰岛，最终又在莱夫·埃里克森这位首领的带领下，来到了美洲沿海。差不多就在欧

from which wine is made, growing there. They told stories called sagas about their voyages to Vineland, and we can still read these stories. In the sagas, Vineland is described as a beautiful country, rich with grass and timber and wild wheat, with abundant animals and fish, and mild in winter. The Vikings met people living there whom we now call Native Americans.

We're not sure exactly where these adventurous people went. We know that they reached Newfoundland, Canada and they may have gone as far south as Cape Cod in Massachusetts. The Vikings did not stay for very long in America, although they continued to sail the North Atlantic. We can only wonder if Columbus knew about the Vineland sagas and their stories about the land across the Atlantic, west of Europe.

洲的基督徒正期待着世界末日的同一年，即公元1000年，维京人却来到了有些人以为的世界尽头。

维京人将这个新发现的地方命名为"葡萄地"或"葡萄酒之地"，因为他们在这里发现，当地人种植着用于酿造葡萄酒的葡萄。他们有一些讲述自己如何航海抵达"葡萄地"的传奇故事，叫作"英雄传说"，如今我们依然可以读到这些故事呢。在这些英雄传说里，"葡萄地"被描述为一个美丽的国度，那里草木茂密，到处都是野生的小麦，并且飞禽走兽和鱼类相当丰富，冬季也不寒冷。维京人还遇到了生活在当地的民族，即如今我们所称的美洲印第安人。

这些喜欢冒险的人曾经都到过哪些地方，我们并不完全了解。我们只知道，他们到达过纽芬兰、加拿大，甚至可能南下，远至马萨诸塞州的科德角。尽管一直都在北大西洋海域航行，但维京人在美洲并没有停留很长的时间。如今我们只能怀疑，哥伦布是不是知道关于"葡萄地"的这些英雄传说，是不是知道维京人讲述的关于欧洲西部大西洋对岸这片土地的故事呢？

50 Real Castles

You may think that castles belong only in fairy tales of princes and princesses.

But about the Year 1000 there were castles almost everywhere over Europe, and they were not fairy castles but real ones with real people in them.

After the downfall of Rome in 476, the Roman Empire was broken to pieces like a cut-up puzzle-map, and people built castles on the pieces, and they kept on building castles up to the 1400's. This is why and how people built them and why they at last stopped building them.

Whenever any ruler, whether he was a king or only a prince, conquered another ruler, he gave to his generals, who had fought with him and helped him to win, pieces of the conquered land as a reward instead of paying them in money. The generals in turn gave pieces of their land to the chief men who had been under them and helped them in battle. These men who were given land were called lords or nobles, and each lord was called a vassal of him who gave the land. Each vassal had to promise to fight with his lord whenever he was needed. He could not make this promise lightly in an offhand way, however. He had to do it formally so that it would seem more binding. The vassal had to

50   真正的城堡

你们有可能觉得，城堡只是神话传说里才有，只有王子和公主才会住在城堡里。

但在公元1000年左右，欧洲各地几乎都有城堡哩。而且，它们都不是神话故事中的那种城堡，而是真正的城堡，里面住着的也是真正的人。

古罗马在公元476年灭亡之后，整个罗马帝国便四分五裂，变得像是一幅拆散开来了的拼图，而人们就是在这些四分五裂的土地上修建起了一座座城堡，并且直到十五世纪还在修建呢。下面就来说一说人们为什么要修建城堡、如何修建城堡，以及他们最终为什么不再修建城堡等问题。

不管是国王还是王子，每当一位统治者征服了另一位统治者后，都会把被征服土地的一部分当作奖赏，分封给那些随之征战、助其取胜的将领，而不用给他们金钱作为奖赏。那些将领们又把自己所获封地的一部分，分封给手下那些头领和建有战功的人。这些获得了封地的人，被称为领主或者贵族；而每位领主，就是封给他们土地的那位统治者手下的诸侯或者封臣。每位封臣都必须承诺，一旦需要，必须随时跟随主人去打仗。然而，封臣的这种承诺并不是随随便便、轻而易举地做出的。他们必须正式宣誓，从而让这种承诺看上去更具约束力。封臣必须跪在主人的面前庄严宣誓，一旦主人召唤，他便会随同主人去打仗。这一过程，称为"效

kneel in front of his lord, and make the solemn promise to fight when called upon. This was called *doing homage*. Then once a year, at least, thereafter, he had to make the same promise over again. This method of giving away land was known as the Feudal' System.

Each of these lords or nobles then built himself a castle on the land that was given him, and there he lived like a little king with all his workpeople about him. The castle was not only his home, but it had to be a fort as well to protect him from other lords who might try to take his castle away from him. He usually placed it on the top of a hill or a cliff, so that the enemy could not reach it easily, if at all. It had great stone walls often ten feet or more thick. Surrounding the walls there was usually a ditch called a *moat* filled with water to make it more difficult for an enemy to get into the castle.

In times of peace, when there was no fighting, the men farmed the land outside the castle; but when there was war between lords, all the people went inside the castle walls, carrying all the food and cattle and everything else they had, so that they could live there for months or even years while the fighting was going on. A castle, therefore, had to be very large to hold so many people and animals for so long a time, and often it was really like a walled town.

Medieval women managed many of the things that went on inside the castle — cooking, spinning thread, weaving cloth, overseeing the servants, and

城堡、吊桥、护城河与骑士
Castle, drawbridge, moat, and knights

忠"。此后，封臣每年至少都必须宣一次同样的誓言。这种分封土地的方式，就是我们所称的"封建制度"。

然后，这些领主或贵族便会在获封的土地上为自己修建一座座城堡，并且像小皇帝一样，同自己的手下生活在城堡里。城堡不但是他的家，还必须是一座堡垒，能够保护领主不受到可能想要夺取城堡的其他领主的进犯才行。领主通常都会把城堡建在山顶，或者建在悬崖上；这样，就算有敌来犯，也可以使得敌人无法轻易到达。城堡都修有巨大的石墙，且通常都厚达十多英尺。城墙四周，通常都有一道叫作"护城河"的壕沟，沟中有水，从而使得敌人更加难以攻入城堡。

在平时，即不打仗的时候，领主手下的人会耕种城堡外面的土地。一旦领主之间爆发战争，所有的人就会带着全部的粮食、牲畜以及其他家当进入城堡；这样，在战争持续期间，他们在城堡里面过上数月甚至数年都没有问题。因此，一座城堡必须建得极其庞大，才能容纳下这么多的人和牲畜，让他们在里面住上这么久的时间；所以，城堡实际上往往就像是一座修有城墙的市镇。

在中世纪，城堡里的许多事情都是由女性来负责的，比如做饭、纺线、织布、监管仆役、照料牲畜，等等。有的时候，男人们外出打仗动不动就是好几个月，甚

taking care of the animals. When the men were away at war, sometimes for months or even years at a time, the women were in charge of all the farming activities and the family's money as well. Because there were so many wars, many women became widows. In that case, they took total charge of the family estates.

Inside the walls of the castle were many smaller buildings to house the people and animals and for cooking and storing the food. There might even be a church or chapel. The chief building was, of course, the house of the lord himself and this was called the *keep*.

The main room of the keep was the Great Hall, which was like a very large living room and dining room combined. Here meals were served at tables which were simply long and wide boards placed on something to hold them up. These boards were taken down and put away after the meal was over. That is where we get the names *boarding and boarding house*. There were no forks nor spoons nor plates nor saucers nor napkins. Everyone ate with his fingers and licked them or wiped them on his clothes. Table manners were more like *stable* manners. The bones and scraps they threw on the floor or to the dogs, who were allowed in the room. Itchy scratchy! What a mess! At the end of the meal towels and a large bowl of water were brought in so that those who wished might wash their hands. Do you suppose anybody washed the floor?

After dinner the household was entertained during the long evenings with songs and stories by men called minstrels, who played and sang and amused the company.

Shut up within the castle walls, it seemed as if the lord and his people would be

至是好几年，所以女性还得干所有的农活，负责家庭开支。由于那时经常打仗，因此许多女性都成了寡妇。在那种情况下，所有家业就全得由女性来照管了。

城堡里面建有许多较小的房子，用来住人、关牲口、做饭和储存粮食等。其中甚至还可能建有一座教堂或者小礼拜堂呢。当然，城堡中最主要的建筑还是领主自己所住的房子，被称为城堡的"主楼"。

主楼中的主要房间，便是大堂；它就像是一间非常巨大的客厅，同时也是餐厅。这里吃饭时所用的饭桌，其实只是用一块块又长又宽的木板搭在支架上做成的。吃完饭后，这些板子便会拆下去收起来。英语中所说的"膳宿"（boarding）和"膳宿公寓"（boarding house）两个词，便是由此处所用的木板（board）一词而来的。当时人们在吃饭的时候，既不用刀叉、汤匙、盘子、碟子，也不用餐巾。大家都是直接用手，吃完后把手舔上一舔，或者在衣服上蹭上一蹭就算完事。当时的人几乎没有什么餐桌礼仪。他们会将骨头和剩饭随手扔在地上，或者扔给狗吃，因为他们那时允许小狗进屋。那种场面，可真是一地狼藉、乱成一团呢！吃完饭后，仆人会拿来毛巾和一大盆水，想洗手的人便可以洗洗。你们觉得，那时会有人去擦地板吗？

晚饭过后，一家子便会聚在一起，聆听那些所谓的"吟游诗人"唱歌、讲故事，来度过漫漫长夜；这些"吟游诗人"，吹、拉、弹、唱样样在行，都是以取乐周围的人为生。

既然城墙围得严严实实，那么领主及其手下的人似乎就是绝对安全的，城堡完

absolutely safe against any attacks of his enemies. In the first place, any enemy would have had to cross the moat or ditch filled with water, which surrounded the castle. Across this moat there was a drawbridge to the entrance or gate of the castle. In the entrance itself was an iron gate called a portcullis, which was usually raised like a window to allow people to pass. In time of war the drawbridge was raised. But in case an enemy was seen approaching and there was not time to raise the drawbridge, this portcullis could be dropped at a moment's notice. When the drawbridge was raised there was no way of getting into the castle except by crossing the moat. Anyone trying to do this would have had stones or melted tar thrown down on him. Instead of windows in the wall of the castle there were only long slits through which the fighters could shoot arrows at the enemy. At the same time, it was very difficult for anyone on the outside to hit the small crack-like openings with an arrow.

Yet attacks *were* made on castles. Sometimes the enemy built a tall wooden tower on wheels. This they would roll up as close as they could get to the walls, and from its top shoot directly over into the castle.

Sometimes they built tunnels from the outside right under the ground, under the moat, and under the castle walls into the castle itself.

Sometimes they built huge machines called battering-rams, and with these they battered down the walls.

Sometimes they used machines like great sling-shots to throw stones over the walls. Of

全可以抵挡住敌人的任何进攻了。首先，敌人必须越过那道注满了水且环绕在城堡四周的护城河或者壕沟。护城河上有一座吊桥，通往城堡的入口或者大门。而城堡入口本身又是一道大铁门，称为"吊闸"，平时一般都是像一扇窗户那样升起来，好让人们进出。而到了打仗的时候，吊桥就会升起来。不过，万一看到敌人逼近的时候来不及升起吊桥，那么城堡里的人就会立即放下城堡入口处的那道吊闸。倘若吊桥升起来了，那么敌人除了游过护城河，就没有别的办法进入城堡了。而敌人在横渡护城河的时候，城堡里的人就会居高临下地用石块砸他们，用烧熔了的沥青浇他们。城堡的城墙上没有窗户，只开了一些长长的缝隙，士兵们可以从这些缝隙里向敌人射箭。与此同时，对于城堡外面的敌人来说，他们的箭矢却很难射进这些缝隙中去。

然而，人们还是会去攻打城堡。有的时候，敌人会建造一个底下装有轮子的、高高的木架。这样，他们就可以推着这个木架尽可能地靠近城墙，并从木架顶上将箭矢直接射入城堡里面。

有的时候，敌人还会从城堡外面挖掘地道，从底下穿过护城河，然后再从城墙底下挖进城堡内部。

有的时候，敌人会建造一种叫作"攻城槌"的巨型机械，并用它来将城堡的城墙撞塌。

有的时候，敌人还会用一种像是巨型弹弓的机械，将石块投掷到城堡里去。当然，那个时候既没有大炮，也没有炮弹；既没有枪支，也没有火药，所以也只能投

course there were no cannons nor cannonballs nor guns nor gunpowder then.

The lord and his family were the rich people; all the others were little better than slaves. In times of peace most of the common people lived outside the castle walls on the land called the *manor*. The lord gave them just as little as he could and took from them just as much as he could. He had to feed and take some care of them, so that they could fight for him and serve him, just as he had to feed and take care of his horses that carried him to battle, and the cattle that provided him with milk and meat. But he didn't treat the people who served him as well as he did his domestic animals. The common people had to give their time and labor and a large part of the crops they raised to the lord. They themselves lived in miserable huts more like cowsheds, with only one room that had a dirt floor. Above this was perhaps a loft reached by a ladder where they went to bed. Bed was usually only a bundle of straw, and they slept in the clothes they wore during the day.

These workpeople were called *serfs*. Sometimes serfs could stand this kind of life no longer, and they would run away. If a serf was not caught within a year and a day, he was a free man. But if he was caught before the year and a day were up, the lord might whip him, brand him with hot irons, or even cut off his hands. Indeed, a lord could do almost anything he wished with his serfs except kill them — or sell them.

What do you think of the Feudal System?

掷石块啰。

　　城堡里的领主及其家人都是富人，而其他的人则比奴隶好不了多少。平时，绝大多数平民百姓都生活在城堡外面那片叫作"领地"的土地上。领主对平民都很苛刻，所给甚少，索取却甚多。领主之所以必须养活并适当照料好手下的那些平民，是为了让平民能够替他去打仗并服侍他，就像他必须养活并照料好自己的马匹才能骑着马匹去打仗，必须养活并照料好自己的牛羊才能有奶可喝、有肉可吃那样。但是，领主对待服侍他的平民，却还没有他对待家畜那样好呢。平民必须花时间和劳力去服侍领主，还得把自己所种收成中的大部分交给领主。平民自己住的，都是看上去更像牛棚的肮脏小屋；这种小屋只有一间房子，地板则邋遢无比。而这间房子的上方，或许还有一间阁楼，必须搭一架梯子才能爬上去，那就是他们睡觉的地方。床铺呢，通常都只是一捆稻草罢了；他们睡觉的时候，身上也仍然会穿着白天干活时所穿的衣服。

　　这些替领主干活的人，就叫"农奴"。有的时候，农奴们无法再忍受这样的生活，便会逃跑。如果在一年零一天的时间里，一名逃跑的农奴没有被领主抓回来的话，那他就成了一个自由民。不过，倘若在一年零一天之内抓住了逃奴的话，领主就可以鞭打逃奴，用烧红的烙铁在逃奴身上烙下标记，甚至可以砍掉逃奴的双手。事实上，除了杀掉或者卖掉农奴，领主几乎想怎样处置，就可以怎样处置农奴呢。

　　那你们觉得，封建制度好还是不好呢？

51 Knights and Days of Chivalry

Those years in history which I have been telling you about are known as the days of chivalry — which means the times of ladies and gentlemen. The lord and his family were the gentlemen and the ladies. All the other people, by far the greater number, were just common people.

There were no schools for these common people. Little was done for them. They were taught to work and nothing else. The sons of a lord of a castle, however, were very carefully taught. Even they were taught only two things, how to be gentlemen and how to fight. Reading and writing were thought of no importance; in fact, it was usually considered a waste of time to learn such things.

This is the way the son of a lord was brought up. He stayed with his mother until he was seven years old. When he reached the age of seven he was called a page; and for the next seven years — that is, until he was fourteen, he remained a page. During the time he was a page, his chief business was to wait on the ladies of the castle. He ran their errands, carried their messages, waited on tables, etc. He also learned to ride a horse and to be brave and courteous.

51　骑士和骑士时代

我正在向你们介绍的这个历史时代，被称为"骑士时代"，也就是贵妇和绅士盛行的那个时代。领主及其家人，便是绅士和贵妇。至于其他的人，尽管数量比贵妇和绅士要庞大得多，却都只是平民。

当时这些平民百姓并没有学校可上。他们享受的权利很少。他们一生下来被教要去干活，除此之外就没有别的了。可是，城堡领主的儿子们却会受到细心的教导。不过，即便是他们，接受的教育也只有两个方面，就是如何做一名绅士和如何打仗。当时的人认为，阅读和写字根本就不重要；事实上，学习这些东西，往往还会被人们认为是浪费光阴哩。

领主的儿子都是这样培养长大的：他会由母亲照料到七岁。过了七岁之后，他就被称为"小听差"了；而在接下来的七年中，也就是说，直到十四岁，他都一直会是一个"小听差"。在当"小听差"的这段时间里，他的主要任务就是服侍城堡里的贵妇。他要替贵妇们跑腿，替贵妇们送信，侍候贵妇们就餐，等等。他还要学会骑马，学会变得勇敢和谦恭有礼。

长到十四岁后，他就成了一名"侍从"，并且在接下来的七年里一直担任"侍从"；这也就是说，一直要当到他满二十一岁。在担任"侍从"的这段时间里，他

When he was fourteen years old, he became a squire and remained a squire for the next seven years; that is, until he was twenty-one. During the time he was a squire he waited on the men, as he had waited on the ladies when he was a page. He attended to the men's horses, went to battle with them, led an extra horse, and carried another spear or lance, in case these should be needed.

When he was twenty-one years old, if he had been a good squire and had learned the lessons that he was taught, he then became a knight. Becoming a knight was an important ceremony like graduating exercises, for the grown boy was now to take up the business of a man.

To get ready for this ceremony, first, he bathed. This may not seem worth mentioning, but in those days one very rarely took a bath, sometimes not for years. He was then dressed in new clothes. Thus washed and dressed, he prayed all night long in the church. When day came, he appeared before all the people and solemnly swore always to do and to be certain things:

To be brave and good
To fight for the Christian religion
To protect the weak
To honor women

These were his vows. A white leather belt was then put on him and gold spurs fastened

服侍的是男人，内容与他当"小听差"时服侍那些贵妇的没什么两样。他要照料男人们的马匹，随同他们出去打仗，并且另外多牵一匹马、多带一支长矛，以备急时所需。

长到二十一岁之后，如果他是一名优秀的"侍从"，并且已经学会了别人教给他的那些知识，那么他就会升为一名"骑士"。升任骑士与毕业典礼一样，是一项重大的仪式；因为它意味着，这个已经长大成人的小伙子如今应当承担起成年男人的义务了。

准备好参加这场典礼之前，他首先需要沐浴。这一点似乎没有什么必要提及；可在那个时候，人们难得洗一次澡，有时甚至几年才洗上一次呢。接下来，他会穿上崭新的衣服。沐浴完、穿戴好新衣之后，他会一整夜都在教堂里祈祷。第二天天亮之后，他便会来到众人之前庄严宣誓，承诺始终都会做到下述几个方面：

勇敢，善良
捍卫基督教
保护弱者
尊重女性

这些就是他的誓言。接下来，有人会给他系上白色的牛皮腰带，帮他的靴子装上金色的马刺。这一切都完成之后，他便跪下来，而领主则会用剑身轻击他的双

on his boots. After this had been done, he knelt, and his lord struck him over the shoulders with the flat side of a sword, saying as he did so, "I dub thee knight."

A knight went into battle covered with a suit of armor made of iron rings or steel plates like fish scales, and with a helmet or hood of iron. This suit protected him from the arrows and lances of the enemy. Of course if they had had any shot or shell, armor would have been no use at all, but they had no such things then.

Knights were so completely covered by their armor that when sides became mixed up in fighting, they could not tell one another apart. It was impossible to know who were friends and who were enemies.

So the knights wore, on the outside of the coat that went over their armor, a design of an animal, such as a lion, or of a plant or a rose or a cross or some ornament, and this design was known as a coat of arms.

A knight, as I told you, was first of all taught to be a gentleman, and so we sometimes speak of one who has good manners and is courteous, especially to ladies, as knightly or chivalrous. When a knight came into the presence of a lady he took off his helmet. It meant, "You are my friend, and so I do not need my helmet." That is why gentlemen raise their hats nowadays when they meet ladies.

But the most important thing the knights had to learn was to fight. Even their games were play fights.

Each country and each age has had its own games or sports in which it has taken special

肩，并且一边做一边说："我授予你骑士称号。"

骑士去打仗的时候，都会披着一身用圆形铁片或者像鱼鳞般的钢片制成的铠甲，戴着一顶钢盔或者铁制的兜帽。这身铠甲会保护他，使他不会被敌人的弓箭或长矛所伤。当然，假如那时的人有子弹或者炮弹的话，那么铠甲就毫无用处了；不过，当时他们可没有这种东西呢。

由于骑士全身都裹在铠甲里面，因此双方混战起来的时候，他们完全分辨不出对方来。在这种情况下，是不可能分清谁是朋友、谁是敌人的。

于是，骑士们便在铠甲的外层标上一种动物的图案，比如一头狮子，或者标上像玫瑰这样的植物图案，或者标上十字架和其他的装饰性图案，以便区分敌我。这种图案，就叫作"盾形纹章"。

我在前面已经跟你们说过，骑士接受的最重要的教育，便是学会做一名绅士；因此，如今我们在谈到一个彬彬有礼、谦恭客气的人，尤其是一个对女士们很有礼貌的人时，还会说这个人很有"骑士风度"呢。骑士来到有女士在场的地方时，都会取下头盔。这样做的意思是："您是我的朋友，所以我用不着戴头盔。"如今的绅士在碰到女士时，之所以会摘下帽子，原因就在于此。

不过，骑士要学会的最重要的一件事情，就是打仗。即便是他们进行的比赛，也都是格斗比赛。

每个国家、每个时代，都分别有令人觉得特别愉快的比赛或者运动项目。古希腊人有自己的奥林匹克运动会。古罗马人有自己的战车比赛和角斗竞赛。我们美

delight. The Greeks had their Olympic Games. The Romans had their chariot races and gladiatorial contests. We have football and baseball. But the chief sport of the knights was a kind of sham battle called the tournament.

The tournament was held in a field known as the lists. Large crowds with banners flying and trumpets blowing would gather around the lists to watch the sham fight, as crowds nowadays flock to a big football game waving pennants and tooting horns. The knights on horseback took their places at opposite ends of the lists. They carried lances, the points of which were covered so that they would not make a wound. At a given signal, they rushed toward the center of the field and tried with their lances to throw each other off their horses. The winner who succeeded in throwing the other knights was presented with a ribbon or a keepsake by one of the ladies, and a knight thought as much of this trophy of victory as the winner of a cup in a tennis tournament nowadays.

Knights were very fond of hunting with dogs. But they also hunted with a trained bird called a falcon, and both lords and ladies delighted in this sport. The falcon was trained like a hunting dog to catch other birds, such as wild ducks and pigeons, and also small animals. The falcon was chained to the wrist of the lord or lady, and its head was covered with a hood as

Man with falcon
带着猎鹰的男子

国人如今有橄榄球和棒球比赛。而中世纪骑士的主要运动项目，则是一种称为"比武大会"的模拟格斗竞赛。

比武大会是在一个叫作"比武场"的场地上进行的。许多挥舞着旗帜、吹着喇叭的观众会将比武场围得水泄不通，来观看模拟格斗比赛；就像如今的观众挥舞着三角小旗、嘟嘟地吹着喇叭，涌去观看一场重大的橄榄球比赛一样。骑士们骑着马儿，在比武场的两端各就各位。他们都手持长矛，只是矛尖都用东西包上了，使得他们在比赛中不会受伤。信号发出之后，他们便冲向场地中央，竭力用自己的长矛将其他骑士一个个都挑下马来。成功地将其他骑士全都挑下马来的获胜者，将会获得由一位女士来颁发的缎带或者纪念品；骑士们都十分重视这种战利品，就像如今人们非常看重网球锦标赛中的优胜奖杯一样。

骑士们都非常喜欢带着猎犬去狩猎。不过，他们也会带着一种经过训练的、叫作"猎鹰"的鸟儿去狩猎，而领主、贵妇们也都很乐意进行这种狩猎活动。猎鹰被训练得像猎犬一样，能够捕到其他的鸟儿，比如野鸽子，以及一些小动物。领主或贵妇会把猎鹰拴在手上；在带着猎鹰出去打猎的时候，则会用头套把猎鹰的头蒙

it was carried out to hunt. When a bird was seen, the hood was removed, and the falcon, which was very swift, would swoop down upon its prey and capture it. Thereupon the hunter would come up, take the captured animal, and put the hood on the falcon again. The men, however, usually preferred hunting the wild boar, which was a kind of pig with sharp tusks, for this was more dangerous and therefore supposed to be more of a man's sport.

上。他们看到鸟儿之后，就会把猎鹰的头套取下，而敏捷迅速的猎鹰便会向猎物猛扑过去，将其逮住。随即，狩猎者便会跟上来，取下猎鹰逮住的猎物，然后再次把猎鹰的头用头套蒙上。然而，男人们通常都更喜欢去猎杀野猪，那是一种长着锋利獠牙的猪；由于猎杀野猪更加危险，因此被认为是更适合于男人的一种狩猎活动。

52 A Pirate's Great Grandson

When Alfred was king, the Danes had raided England. At the same time their cousins the Norsemen had raided the coast of France.

King Alfred at last had to give the Danes a part of the English coast, and they then settled down and became Christians.

The French king likewise did the same thing. In order to save himself from further raids, he gave the Norsemen a part of the French coast. The Norsemen then, as the Danes had done, settled down and became Christians.

These Norsemen who raided France were led by a very bold and brave pirate named Rollo. In return for this gift of land Rollo was supposed to do homage by kissing the king's foot. But Rollo thought it beneath him to kneel and kiss the king's foot, so he told one of his men to do it for him. His man did as he was told, but he didn't like to do it, either. As he kissed the king's foot he raised it so high that he tipped his Majesty over backward.

The part of France that was given the Norsemen came to be called Normandy, and it is so called today, and the people were known thereafter as Normans.

In 1066 there was a very powerful duke ruling over Normandy. His name was William,

52　了不起的海盗后裔

阿尔弗雷德大帝在位的时候，丹麦人曾经劫掠过英格兰。

与此同时，跟丹麦人同族的维京人，也曾经劫掠过法国的沿海地区。

阿尔弗雷德大帝最后不得不将英国沿海的一部分地区分给丹麦人，而这些丹麦人定居下来后，都皈依了基督教。

当时的法国国王也是这样做的。为了不再受到侵扰，他将法国沿海的一部分地区让给了维京人。后来，这些维京人便像丹麦人一样，在这里定居下来并变成了基督徒。

这些劫掠法国的维京人的头领，是一名非常胆大、非常勇敢的海盗，名叫罗洛。据说，为了回报法国国王将这片土地赐予他们，罗洛应当亲吻国王的脚来向法国国王效忠。可罗洛觉得，跪下来亲吻国王的脚有损自己的尊严，因此便叫手下的一个人去代他效忠。虽说手下遵照他的命令去做了，可这位手下其实也不喜欢干这种事情。因此，他在亲吻法国国王的脚时，竟然把国王的脚抬得老高，让那位陛下仰天摔了一跤哩。

法国国王赐给维京人的这个地方，后来便被叫作"诺曼底"；这一名称一直延续到今天，而那里的人此后也被称作"诺曼底人"了。

and he was descended from Rollo the pirate. Perhaps your name may be William. If you have any English or French ancestors, you may even be descended from this William.

William was strong in body, strong in will, and strong in rule over his people. He could shoot an arrow farther, straighter, and with more deadly effect than any of his knights. No one else was strong enough even to bend the bow he used.

William and his people had become Christians, but according to their idea, the Christian God was more like their old god, Woden, under a new name. William believed that, "might made right", for he was descended from a pirate, and he still acted like a pirate. Whatever he wanted he went after and took, even though he was supposed to be a Christian.

Norman raising king's foot
诺曼底人抬起国王的脚

Now, William was only a duke, not a king, and he wanted to be a king. In fact, he thought he would like to be king of England, which was just across the channel from his own dukedom. Besides, the English king Edward was William's cousin, so he thought that gave him a good claim to the throne.

It so happened that a young English prince named Harold was shipwrecked on the coast of Normandy and was found and brought before William. Now, it seemed

1066年的时候，统治诺曼底的是一位非常有权势的公爵。他名叫威廉，是罗洛的后裔。你们当中，或许也有人名叫威廉呢。要是你们的祖先是英国人或者法国人的话，那你们有可能就是这位威廉大公的子孙。

威廉身高力壮，意志坚定，统治臣民的手段也强大有力。他开弓射箭的时候，他射的箭比手下的所有骑士都要射得远、射得准，杀伤力也更大。甚至连他所用的那把强弓，也无人有那么大的力气去拉开哩。

虽说威廉及其手下的臣民都已经皈依了基督教，但在他们看来，基督教的上帝更像是他们原来的那个上帝，即主神沃登，只不过换了个名字罢了。威廉认为，"强权就是公理"。由于他是一名海盗的后裔，因此行事风格仍然与海盗没什么不同。虽说他是一名基督徒，但无论自己想要什么，他都会竭尽全力去弄到手的。

此时，威廉还只是一位公爵，而不是国王，可他却想要做国王。事实上，他希望做英国的国王，而英国则正好隔着英吉利海峡，与他的公爵领地隔海相望。此外，当时英国的国王爱德华是威廉的表亲，因此，他觉得这就是他登上英国王位的一个很好的理由。

likely that some day Harold would be king of England, and William thought this a good chance to get England for himself. Before he would let Harold leave, he made the young man promise that when his turn came to be king, he would give England to William just as if that country were a horse or a suit of armor that could be given away. In order that this promise should be solemnly binding, William made Harold place his hand on the altar and swear, just as people place a hand on the Bible nowadays, when they take an oath. After Harold had sworn on the altar, William had the top lifted and showed Harold that below it were the bones of some of the Christian saints. Swearing on the bones of a saint was the most solemn kind of an oath one could possibly take. It was thought one would not dare to break such an oath for fear of the wrath of God.

Harold then returned to England. But when the time came that he should be king, the people naturally would not let him give England to William. Besides that, Harold said that such an oath, which he had taken against his will, an oath which had been forced on him by a trick, was not binding. So Harold became king.

When William heard that Harold had been made king, he was very angry. He said that he had been cheated and that Harold had broken his oath. At once he got ready an army and sailed over to take the country away from Harold.

As William landed from his boat, he stumbled and fell headlong on the shore. All his soldiers were shocked and greatly worried by this, for they thought it very bad luck — a

说来也巧，那时有位叫作哈罗德的年青王子刚好在诺曼底海岸遭遇了海难事故，被人发现后，被带到了威廉面前。当时，哈罗德王子似乎将来定会继承王位，成为英国国王的；因此，威廉觉得这是一个大好的、可以将英国据为己有的机会。在送哈罗德王子回英国去之前，他让这位年轻人答应，一旦这位年轻人继承大统，成了英国国王，就会将英国拱手奉送给自己。好像该国是一匹马儿或者一副铠甲，可以随便送人似的。为了让这一承诺具有神圣的约束力，威廉还让哈罗德把手放在祭坛上发誓，就像如今的人在发誓时把手放在《圣经》上那样。待哈罗德在祭坛前发过誓之后，威廉又将祭坛的坛顶掀起来，让哈罗德看了看祭坛下一些基督教圣徒的骸骨。在基督圣徒的骸骨之上发的誓，是最神圣的一种誓言。据说，由于害怕遭到天谴，因此人们是不敢不遵守自己发下的这种誓言的。

然后，哈罗德便返回了英国。不过，到了他继承王位之时，英国人民自然不允许他将英国拱手送给威廉。非但如此，哈罗德还称，那个誓言是自己违心所发，是在阴谋所迫的情况下无奈地发下的，因此没有约束力。于是，哈罗德便当上了英国国王。

威廉得知哈罗德被拥立为英国国王的消息之后，顿时狂怒不已。他说自己被人欺骗了，说哈罗德没有恪守自己发下的誓言。他马上召集了一支军队，渡海前去，准备从哈罗德手中将英国抢过来。

就在威廉下船登岸的时候，他的脚下一个踉跄，一头摔倒在海滩上。他手下的将士们非常震惊，同时也对此感到忧心忡忡，因为他们认为这是一个不好的兆头，

bad omen, the Greeks would have called it. But William was quick-witted, and as he fell he grabbed up some of the earth in both hands. Then, rising, he made believe he had fallen on purpose and, lifting his hands in the air, exclaimed that he had taken up the ground as a sign that he was going to have all the land of England. This changed the bad omen into good luck.

The battle started, and the English fought furiously to defend themselves against these foreigners who were trying to take their country away from them. Indeed, they had almost won the battle when William gave an order to his men to pretend they were running away.

The English then followed, wildly rejoicing, and running pell-mell after the Normans. Just as soon, however, as the English were scattered and in disorder, William gave another signal, and his men faced about quickly. The English were taken by surprise, and before they could get into fighting order again, they were defeated, and Harold, their king, was shot through the eye and killed. This was the Battle of Hastings, one of the most famous battles in English history.

Harold had put up a brave fight. But luck was against him. Only a few days before this, he had had to fight a battle with his own brother, who in a traitorous way had got together an army against him. We are sorry for Harold, and yet it was probably better for England that things turned out as they did — yet who can tell?

William marched on to London and had himself crowned king on Christmas day, 1066. Ever since then he has been known as William the Conqueror, and the event is called the

即古希腊人所称的"凶兆"。可威廉却非常机灵，在摔倒的时候双手就势分别抓了一把泥土。爬起来之后，他便假称自己是故意摔倒的，并且举起双手，声称他已经得到了土地，这就是他必将占领英国全部国土的预兆。这样，他就把凶兆变成了吉兆。

战斗打响了；英军作战时极其勇猛，誓死捍卫国土，抗击这些想要将英国从他们手中夺走的外国人。实际上，英军差不多已经要打赢了；可就在此时，威廉却下令手下的军队假装打不过，假装准备逃跑。

见此，英军便兴高采烈、乱哄哄地跟在诺曼底人的后面，开始追击。然而，就在英军四处分散、乱成一团的时候，威廉发出了另一个信号；于是，他手下的军队马上掉头开始反击。英军被打了个措手不及，还不待他们再次形成战斗队形，便被打垮了；而英王哈罗德的眼睛也被箭矢射中，死于乱军之中。这就是黑斯廷斯之战，也是英国历史上最著名的战役之一。

哈罗德进行了英勇的战斗。可他的运气太不好了。就在此战的前几天，他还不得不与自己的兄弟打了一仗；那位兄弟背叛了他，召集了一支军队来攻打他。虽然我们都替哈罗德感到难过，但形势如此发展，很可能对英国更加有利；不过，这种事情谁又说得清楚呢？

威廉率军进入了伦敦，并在1066年加冕，成了英国国王。此后，他就被世人称为"征服者威廉"。从此以后，统治英国的便是一条新的王室血脉，即一个诺曼底家族、一个海盗家族了。

Norman Conquest. After this England had a new line of kings — a Norman family and a pirate family — to rule over her.

William divided England up among his nobles as if it were a pie, and gave each a share in the feudal way. They had to do homage to him as his vassals and promise to fight for him and to do as he said. Each of William's nobles built a castle on the property he was given. William himself built a castle in London by the Thames River. On the same spot Julius Caesar had built a fort, but it had disappeared; and Alfred the Great had built a castle there, but it, too, had disappeared. But the castle William built is still standing today. It is known as the Tower of London.

William was a splendid boss and very business-like. He set to work and had a list made of all the land in England, a list of all the people and of all the property they had. This record was called the Domesday Book and was something like the *census* now taken in this country every ten years. This list gave the name of everyone in England and everything each owned, even down to the last cow and pig. If your ancestors were living in England then you can look in the Domesday Book and find their names, how much land they owned, and how many cows and pigs they had.

In order that no mischief might take place at night, William started what was called the *curfew*. Every evening at a certain hour a bell was rung. Then all lights had to be put out, and everyone had to go indoors — supposedly to bed.

One thing, however, that William did made the English very angry. He was extremely

威廉把英格兰当成是一块大大的馅饼，分给了自己手下的贵族；按照分封制度，每位贵族都分到了一块领地。这些贵族必须向他宣誓效忠，成为他的封臣，并且承诺替他去打仗，遵奉他的号令行事。威廉手下的每一名贵族，都在自己所获得的封地内修建了城堡。威廉自己也在伦敦城内的泰晤士河边修建了一座城堡。恺撒曾经在这个地方修筑了一处要塞，可此时要塞已经化为尘土了；阿尔弗雷德大帝也曾经在这里建过一座城堡，可此时城堡也已无影无踪。但是，威廉所建的那座城堡，至今却仍然屹立在那里。如今，人们称它为"伦敦塔"。

威廉是一位杰出的领袖，行事风格非常务实。他着手制定了一份列出英格兰所有土地明细的清单，以及一份列出了英国所有人口和财产明细的清单。这份文件，叫作《末日审判书》，有点儿像是如今美国每十年进行一次的"人口普查"。这份清单中，包括了英国每一个人的姓名、每个人拥有的财产，甚至细到每一头牛和每一头猪。假如你们的祖辈是英国人，那么你们完全可以到这份《末日审判书》中去找一找他们的名字，看他们当时拥有多少亩土地、养了多少头牛和猪呢。

为了不让人们在夜间作奸犯科，威廉还创立了一种叫作"宵禁"的制度。每天晚上，到了某个时刻，就会敲响一口大钟。然后，所有的灯火都必须熄灭，每个人也都得待在家里，他们全都只能上床睡觉了。

然而，威廉却做了一件事情，让英国人极为愤怒。威廉特别热衷于狩猎，但伦敦附近却没有适合他打猎的地方。为了有一个打猎的场所，他毁掉了许多的村舍和

fond of hunting, but there was no good place where he could hunt near London. In order to have a place for hunting, he destroyed a large number of village houses and farms and turned that part of the country into a forest. This was called the New Forest, and though it is now about nine hundred years *old* it is still called *New* to this day.

On the whole, William, although descended from a pirate, gave England a good government and made it a safe place to live. Since that time, no foreign country has ever conquered England. So 1066 was almost like the Year 1 for the English.

农田，然后将那片乡村改成了森林。这个地方，就叫"新森林"；尽管迄今已经过了几百年，但如今这里还是叫作"新森林"[1]呢。

总的来说，尽管威廉身为海盗后裔，但他还是把英国治理得井井有条，使得英国成了一个适宜生活的国家。从那时起，就几乎没有外族敢去征服英国了。因此，对于英国人来说，1066年几乎就是他们历史上的元年呢。

---

[1] 新森林（New Forest），伦敦郊区的一个国家森林公园，亦音译为"新福瑞斯特"。

53 A Great Adventure

Have you ever played the game called "Going to Jerusalem" in which everyone scrambles to get a seat when the music stops playing?

Well, all during the Middle Ages, that is, the period between ancient times and modern times, "Going to Jerusalem" was not a game but a real journey which Christians everywhere in Europe wanted to take and did take if they could. They wanted to see the actual spot where Christ had been crucified, to pray at the Holy Sepulcher, and to bring back a palm leaf as a souvenir, which they could show their friends, hang on the wall, and talk about all the rest of their lives.

There were always some good Christians — and also some bad ones — going to Jerusalem. Sometimes they went all by themselves, but more often they went with others. As of course there were no such things as trains in those days, poor people had to walk nearly the whole way from France and from England, from Spain and from Germany, and so it took them many months and sometimes years to reach Jerusalem. These travelers were called *pilgrims*, and their trip was called a *pilgrimage*.

Jerusalem at that time had been conquered by the Turks, who were Muslims. The Turks did

53 一场伟大的探险

你们有没有玩过一种叫作"到耶路撒冷去"[1]的游戏呢？在这种游戏里，音乐一停，每个人都必须赶紧抢到一把椅子坐下。

好吧，在整个中世纪，也就是介于古代和现代之间的那个时期，"到耶路撒冷去"可不是一种游戏，而是一场真正的旅行；欧洲各地的基督徒都想进行这样的旅行，并且只要条件允许，他们也的确会前往耶路撒冷。他们都想实地看一看基督受难的那个地方，想要在基督的墓前做一做祷告，并且带回来一片棕榈叶做纪念；然后，他们会向亲戚朋友炫耀这片棕榈叶，把它挂在墙上，并且一生中都会不断地提到它。

前往耶路撒冷的，往往都是一些善良的基督徒，当然也会有一些心地不好的基督徒。有的时候，他们会孤身前往，但更多的时候还是与其他基督徒一起前往耶路撒冷。由于那个时候当然还没有火车这样的交通工具，穷人差不多一路都得步行，从法国、英国、西班牙、德国等地千里迢迢而来，因此往往会花上几个月，有时甚至要花上几年的时间，才能到达耶路撒冷。这些旅行者，被称为"朝圣客"，而他们的这种旅行，就叫作"朝圣"。

当时，耶路撒冷已经被土耳其人占领了。土耳其人很不喜欢这些前来瞻仰耶稣

---

[1] 到耶路撒冷去（Going to Jerusalem），亦称 musical chairs（音乐座椅），也就是我们所说的抢座椅游戏。

not like these Christian pilgrims who came to see Christ's tomb, and they didn't treat them very well. Indeed, some of the pilgrims on their return told frightful stories of the way they had been treated by the Turks and the way the holy places in Jerusalem were also treated.

Just before the Year 1100, there was a pope at Rome named Urban. Urban heard these tales that the pilgrims told, and he was shocked. He thought it was a terrible thing, anyway, for the Holy City, as Jerusalem was called, and the Holy Land, where Jerusalem was located, to be ruled over by Muslims instead of by Christians. So Urban made a speech and urged all good Christians everywhere to get together and go on a pilgrimage to the Holy Land, with the idea of fighting the Turks and taking the city of Jerusalem away from them. Jerusalem was a holy city for the Muslims, too, as it was for the Jews. No wonder there have been so many wars to control that city.

Now, there lived at that same time a monk whom people called Peter the Hermit. A hermit is a man who goes off and lives entirely by himself, usually in a cave or hut where no one can find him or go to see him, where he can spend all day in prayer. Peter the Hermit thought such a life was good for his soul, that it made him a better man to be hungry and cold and uncomfortable.

Peter the Hermit had made a pilgrimage to Jerusalem and was very angry at what he saw there. He, too, began to tell people everywhere he went how disgraceful it was for them to allow Christ's tomb to belong to Muslim rulers and called on everyone to start on a pilgrimage with him to save Jerusalem. He talked to people in the churches, on the street corners, in the marketplaces, on the roadside. He was such a wonderful orator that

墓的基督教朝圣客，因此在对待他们时，态度都非常粗暴。事实上，有些朝圣者回去后，还说起过他们被土耳其人虐待的可怕经历，说耶路撒冷城内各个圣地的境遇也很糟糕。

就在公元1100年之前，罗马有位教皇，名叫乌尔班。乌尔班听到了朝圣者述说的这些情况之后，极为震惊。他认为，无论从哪个方面来看，当时称为"圣城"的耶路撒冷以及耶路撒冷所在的"圣地"被非基督徒统治着，是一件不幸的事情。于是，乌尔班发表了一次演讲，号召世界各地善良的基督徒全都团结起来，前往圣地朝圣；当然，他的目的其实是要这些基督徒与土耳其人作战，并从后者手中将耶路撒冷城夺过来。不过，耶路撒冷同时也是穆斯林和犹太人的圣城。因此，人们为了控制这座城市而爆发过多场战争，就不足为奇了。

注意，当时还有一位修道士，人称"隐修士彼得"。所谓的隐修士，就是那种脱离社会、完全独居的人；这种人通常都住在山洞或者小屋里，没有人能够找到或者去看望他，因此他可以一心一意地整天祈祷。隐修士彼得认为，这样的生活对他的灵魂有好处，因为经受饥饿、寒冷和不适，会让他成为一个更好的人。

隐修士彼得曾到耶路撒冷朝过圣，而在耶路撒冷的所见所闻，也让他觉得非常生气。于是，他也开始向所到之处的人们宣传，说让耶稣基督的圣墓落在非基督徒统治者的手里有多么屈辱，并且号召大家都同他一起，发动一场旨在拯救耶路撒冷的朝圣运动。在教堂中、街角上、市场里、马路边，他不停地对碰到的人们进行宣

those who heard him wept at his descriptions and begged to go with him.

Before long, thousands upon thousands of people, old and young, men and women, and even some children had pledged themselves to join a band to go to Jerusalem and take it away from the Muslims. As Christ had died on the cross, they cut pieces of red cloth in the form of a cross and sewed them on the fronts of their coats as a sign that they were soldiers of the cross. These pilgrims were called *Crusaders*, which is the Latin word for a crossbearer. As they knew they would be gone a long time and perhaps never return, some sold all they had and left their homes. Some men left their wives in charge. Not only poor people, but lords and nobles and even princes, joined the army of the Crusaders, and there were, besides the crowds on foot, large companies of those who rode on horseback.

The plan was to start in the summer of 1096, four years before 1100, but a great many were so anxious to get started that they didn't wait for the time that had been set. With Peter the Hermit and another pious man named Walter the Penniless as their leaders, they started off before things were really ready.

They had no idea how very far off Jerusalem was. They hadn't studied geography nor maps. They had no idea how long it would take, no idea how they would get food to eat on their journey, no idea where they would sleep. They simply trusted in Peter the Hermit and believed that the Lord would provide everything and show them the way.

Onward they marched, "Onward, Christian Soldiers," thousands upon thousands, toward the east and far-off Jerusalem. Thousands upon thousands of them died from disease and from hunger on the way. Every time they came within sight of another city,

讲。他的演讲技艺高超得很；凡是听他演讲的人，无不因为他的描述而涕泪交流，因此纷纷请求跟他一起去。

不久，便有成千上万的人，包括男女老少，甚至还有一些小朋友，都发誓加入前往耶路撒冷的人马，去把这座城市从穆斯林的手中夺取过来。由于耶稣基督是在十字架上受难的，因此这些人便用一些红布剪成十字架的样子，然后缝在自己所穿衣服的前襟上，以此来表明他们都是捍卫十字架的战士。于是，这些朝圣者便被称为"十字军"，十字军在拉丁语中就是"背负十字架的人"的意思。由于他们知道自己这一去长路漫漫，可能永远都回不来了，因此有些人还变卖掉了自己的全部家产。有些人则留下妻子守家。加入十字军的，不但有穷苦百姓，也有领主和贵族，甚至还有王公大臣；因此，除了步行的人，十字军里也有大队的骑兵。

十字军原本计划在1096年的夏季，也就是公元1100年的四年之前动身，但由于许多人都急不可耐，因此他们还没等到预定的时间便开始动身了。在隐修士彼得和另一位叫作"穷汉瓦尔特"的虔诚信徒的率领下，他们在没有真正做好准备的情况下，便仓促启程了。

他们当时并不清楚耶路撒冷究竟有多远。他们没有学过地理，也没有研究过地图。他们不知道这一路行来究竟要多久，既不知道一路上如何获得食品给养，也不知道到哪里去睡觉休息。他们只是非常信任隐修士彼得，认为上帝会给他们准备好一切，并且会给他们指路。

they would ask, "Is this Jerusalem?" so little did they know of the long distance that still lay between them and that city.

When the Muslim army in Jerusalem heard that the Crusaders were coming, they went forth to meet the Christians in order to defend their city against the European invaders. The Muslims killed almost all of the Crusaders who had started out with Peter ahead of the rest. Those Crusaders, who had started out later, marched on, as had been planned at the beginning.

Finally, after nearly four years, only a small band of that vast throng that had set out so long before reached the walls of the Holy City. When at last they saw Jerusalem before them, they were wild with joy. They fell on their knees and wept and prayed and sang hymns and thanked God that He had brought them to the end of their journey. Then they furiously attacked the city. The Christians fought so hard that at last they captured Jerusalem. Then they entered the gates and killed thousands, so that it is said the streets of the Holy City ran with blood. This seems strange behavior for the followers of Christ, who preached against fighting and commanded, "Put up thy sword, for he that taketh the sword shall perish by the sword."

The Crusaders then made one of their leaders named Godfrey ruler of the city. Most of the other Crusaders who were left then went back home. Some stayed, though, because they saw that they could have more land and greater riches than they had at home in Europe.

他们不断前进；在"前进，捍卫基督教的战士"这样的口号声中，成千上万的人一路向东，往遥远的耶路撒冷进发。他们当中，有成千上万的人因为疾病和饥饿而死在路上。每当一座新的城市映入眼帘后，他们都会问："是耶路撒冷吗？"因为他们根本就不知道，自己与耶路撒冷之间，仍然隔着千山万水呢。

耶路撒冷的穆斯林军队得知十字军正在前来的消息后，为了捍卫这座城市，不让耶路撒冷遭到欧洲侵略者的进攻，他们便主动出击，去迎战基督徒。隐修士彼得率领的、先于其他人出发的那支十字军，几乎被穆斯林军队斩杀殆尽了。而那些动身较迟的十字军，则按照起初制定的计划，继续前进。

最终，差不多四年之后，这支几年以前就开始动身前来的庞大十字军中，只有一小支队伍终于抵达了圣城耶路撒冷的城墙之下。终于看到耶路撒冷就在眼前之后，这些人全都欢呼雀跃起来。他们纷纷跪下，泪流满面，一边祈祷，一边唱着赞美诗，感谢上帝引领他们抵达了旅程的终点。然后，他们便开始向耶路撒冷发起猛攻。这些基督徒奋力鏖战，最终攻下了耶路撒冷。接下来，他们便进入城中并大肆屠杀，据说当时这座圣城的街道上简直是血流成河呢。追随耶稣基督的信徒干出这种残暴的事情，似乎奇怪得很；因为耶稣基督宣传的教义就是反对战争，他还要求世人："收起你们的刀剑吧，因为凡动刀剑的人，必死在刀剑之下。"

接下来，十字军便推举一位叫作戈弗雷的头领来统治耶路撒冷。然后，其他幸存下来的大多数十字军战士便都返回家乡去了。不过，有些人却留了下来，因为他们明白，与欧洲的家乡相比，他们在这里可以获得更多的土地和更多的财富。

54 Tick-Tack-Toe; Three Kings in a Row

Here are three kings:
Richard of England,
Philip of France, and
Frederick Barbarossa of Germany.
If you say their names over several times, they keep ringing through your mind and you can't seem to stop thinking them whether you want to or not.

Jerusalem was captured. But it didn't stay captured very long. Muslims attacked and won it back again.

The Christians started a Second Crusade. Thereafter about once in a lifetime during the next two hundred years there was one Crusade after another — eight or nine in all. Sometimes these later Crusades won back Jerusalem for a while, but for a while only. Sometimes they did not succeed at all.

The Third Crusade took place about a hundred years after the first; that is, nearly 1200 A.D. These three kings — Richard of England, Philip of France, and Frederick Barbarossa — started on the Third Crusade. But they didn't all finish. I'll tell you about them in three-

54　井字过三关[1]；连续三王

当时，欧洲有三位国王：
英国的理查德，
法国的腓力，
德国的腓特烈·巴巴罗萨。
如果你们把这三个名字说上几次的话，它们就会不停地在你们的脑海中回响；这样一来，不管愿不愿意，你们似乎都会情不自禁地想起这三位国王了。

此时，耶路撒冷已经被征服。不过，基督徒并没有占领这座城市很久。穆斯林发起进攻，再一次把耶路撒冷夺回去了。

于是，基督徒又发动了第二次十字军东征。此后的两百年间，差不多每一代人都发动过一次十字军东征，接连不断，总共达到了八次之多哩。有的时候，这些后来的十字军会夺回耶路撒冷，守上一段时间，但据守的时间都很短暂。有的时候，他们根本就打不过穆斯林。

第三次十字军东征，是在第一次十字军东征差不多一百年之后进行的；也就是

---

[1]　井字过三关（Tick-Tack-Toe），一种游戏，亦称"画井字"或者"画三棋"。游戏中，两人轮流在井字棋盘的方格内画"×"或"○"，谁先将自己画过的三个方格连成一行，谁就获胜。

two-one-order.

Frederick's name, Barbarossa, meant Red Beard, for in those days it was the custom to give kings nicknames that described them. Frederick's capital was in Aix-la-Chapelle, as Charlemagne's had been, but Frederick was king only of Germany. When a young man, he had tried to make his country as large and powerful as the new Roman Empire that Charlemagne had made. But he was not a great enough man, and so was unable to do what Charlemagne had done. Frederick was quite old when he started out on the Third Crusade with the other two kings. But he never reached Jerusalem, for in crossing a stream on the way, he was drowned. So much for Frederick, the third king.

The second king, Philip of France, was jealous of the first king, Richard, because Richard was so very popular and well liked by the Crusaders. Philip finally gave up the Crusade and went back to France.

Richard of England was then the only king left on the Crusade. It would have been

英国的理查德、法国的腓力和德国的腓特烈·巴巴罗萨
Richard of England, Philip of France, and Frederick Barbarossa

说，是在公元1200年左右进行的。第三次十字军东征，就是由这三位国王，即英国的理查德、法国的腓力和德国的腓特烈·巴巴罗萨发起的。不过，他们并没有全都完成此次东征。我会按照从第三位国王到第二位国王、再到第一位国王的顺序，来跟你们说一说他们的情况。

腓特烈的名字"巴巴罗萨"是"红胡子"的意思；这是因为，在那个时候，给国王们取个外号来描述他们，这种做法可是蔚然成风呢。腓特烈的都城就是查理曼大帝曾经待过的亚琛，不过腓特烈只是德意志的国王。年轻的时候，腓特烈曾经想让自己的国家变得像查理曼大帝的新罗马帝国那样疆域宽广、势力强大。可他的才能不足，因此无法像查理曼大帝那样称雄天下。与其他两位国王发起第三次十字军东征的时候，腓特烈已经年迈体衰了。他最终并没有抵达耶路撒冷，因为在途中过一条小河的时候，他掉到河里淹死了。第三位国王腓特烈的情况，就是这些。

第二位国王，即法国的腓力，他很嫉妒第一位国王理查德，因为理查德国王很受十字军士兵们的欢迎和爱戴。后来，腓力便不再随着十字军东征，返回法国去了。

于是，英国的理查德便成了率领十字军进行东征的唯一一位国王。其实，如果

better if he, too, had gone back to his country instead of gallivanting off on a Crusade. But he thought going on a Crusade was much better sport than staying at home and working over the difficult business of governing his people.

Richard was kind and gentle, yet strong and brave. Richard the Lion-Hearted they called him. He was hard on wrongdoers but fair and square. People loved him, but they feared him, too, for he punished the wicked and those who misbehaved.

Even Richard's enemies admired him. The Muslim king of Jerusalem at the time of this Third Crusade was named Saladin. Saladin, though being attacked by Richard, admired him very much and even became his friend. So Saladin, instead of fighting Richard, finally made a friendly agreement with him to treat the Holy Sepulcher and the pilgrims properly. As this arrangement was satisfactory to everyone, Richard left Jerusalem to Saladin and started back home.

On his way home Richard was captured and put in prison by the son of Frederick Barbarossa and held for a large ransom from England. Richard's friends did not know where he was and did not know how to find him.

Now, it so happened that Richard had a favorite minstrel named Blondel. Blondel had composed a song of which Richard was very fond. When Richard was taken prisoner, Blondel wandered over the country singing everywhere this favorite song in the hope that Richard might hear it and reveal where he was. One day he happened to sing beneath the very tower where Richard was imprisoned. Richard heard him and answered by singing

他也返回英国，而不是轻率地领着十字军去东征的话，结局可能会更好的。可他却觉得，率领十字军去东征，要比待在国内解决那些治国安民方面的难题更有意思。

虽说理查德国王性情温和，但他同时也很坚强、勇敢。人们都称他为"狮心王理查德"。他对违法犯罪的人非常严厉，同时也很光明磊落。人民都爱戴他，但同时也很畏惧他，因为他不会放过一个坏蛋，会严厉地惩处那些作奸犯科的人。

即便是敌人，也很尊重理查德国王。第三次十字军东征期间，耶路撒冷的穆斯林国王叫萨拉丁。尽管遭到了理查德的进攻，但萨拉丁还是非常敬重理查德，甚至与他成了朋友。因此，萨拉丁并没有与理查德交战，而是与他签订了一份友好协定，同意恰当地对待圣墓教堂和朝圣者。由于这一协定让各方都觉得很满意，所以理查德便同意耶路撒冷仍由萨拉丁统治，自己则动身回国去了。

可在回国的路上，理查德国王却被腓特烈·巴巴罗萨的儿子俘虏，成了他的阶下囚，并被后者当成人质，准备向英国勒索一大笔赎金。理查德的朋友们都不知道他身处何处，也不知道如何才能找到他。

当时，理查德国王恰好有一个很宠信的"吟游诗人"，叫作布隆德尔。布隆德尔曾经谱写过一首歌曲，深得理查德喜爱。理查德国王被腓特烈·巴巴罗萨的儿子囚禁起来后，布隆德尔便到处流浪，并且一边走，一边吟唱着理查德国王最喜欢的这首歌曲，希望理查德国王能够听到他的歌声，从而透露出他被关押的地点。有一天，他恰巧来到了理查德国王被囚禁的那座高塔底下吟唱。理查德听到了他的歌声，便唱着那首歌曲的副歌作为回应。这样，他的朋友们便知晓了他被囚的地点；

the refrain of the song. His friends then knew where he was, the ransom was paid, and Richard was allowed to go free.

When, at last, Richard did reach England, he still had adventures. This was the time when Robin Hood was robbing travelers. Richard planned to have himself taken prisoner by Robin Hood, so that he might capture him and bring him to justice. Richard disguised himself as a monk and was captured as he had planned. But he found Robin Hood such a good fellow after all that he forgave him and his men.

Richard's coat of arms was a design of three lions, one above the other; and this same design of three lions now forms part of the shield of England.

After Richard's Crusade, there was a Fourth Crusade, and then in the year 1212 — which is an easy date to remember, because it is simply the number 12 repeated — one, two, one, two — there was a crusade of children only. This was known therefore as the Children's Crusade. It was led by a French boy about twelve years old named Stephen, who was named after the first Christian martyr.

Children from all over France left their homes and their mothers and fathers — it seems strange to us that their mothers and fathers let them start off on such a trip — and marched south to the Mediterranean Sea. Here they expected the waters of the sea would part and allow them to march on dry land to Jerusalem, as they had read in the Bible the waters of the Red Sea had done to allow the Israelites to leave Egypt. But the waters did not part.

Some sailors, however, offered to take the children to Jerusalem in their ships. They

而在支付了赎金之后，理查德便获得了自由。

理查德国王回到英国之后，他又经历了一次次的冒险。当时，正是罗宾汉四下劫掠旅行者财物的那个时代。理查德计划让自己被罗宾汉抓住，通过这种办法来逮住罗宾汉，从而将罗宾汉送交法办。理查德把自己伪装成一个修道士，并且像他所计划的那样被罗宾汉抓住了。可他发现罗宾汉完全是一个善良的人，因此他便赦免了罗宾汉及其手下的人。

理查德的盾形纹章，是一个有着三头狮子的图案，并且其中的狮子都是一头叠于一头之上；如今，这个三头狮子的图案，就成了英国盾形徽章上的一部分。

理查德的这次十字军东征之后，欧洲人又发动了第四次十字军东征；而接下来，在1212年，还出现了一场全部由小朋友组成的十字军东征；这个年份很好记忆，因为其中有两个12：1，2，1，2。因此，这场东征也叫作"童子十字军东征"。此次东征，由一个年纪才十二岁左右、名叫司提反的法国小男孩率领；他的名字，就是根据基督教第一位殉道者的名字来起的。

法国各地的儿童全都离家而去，离开了他们的母亲和父亲，开始向着南边的地中海进军；在我们看来，那些孩子的父母竟然允许他们去进行这样的旅行，这种做法是很奇怪的。孩子们都希望，地中海的海水会分开，从而让他们沿着干燥的海床进军到耶路撒冷，就像他们在《圣经》中都看到过的那样；《圣经》里称，红海的海水曾经分开来，让以色列人离开了埃及。可等他们到达之后，地中海的海水却并没有分开。

said they would do it for nothing, just for the love of the Lord. But it turned out that these sailors were really pirates, and as soon as they got the children on board their ships they steered them straight into the very land of their enemies, the Muslims. Here, it is said, the pirates sold the children as slaves. This is not a Grimm's fairy tale, and the pirates were not trapped by the children, so I cannot make a happy ending, for it was not.

The last or Eighth Crusade was led by a king of France called Louis. He was so pious and so devoted to the Lord that he was made a saint and ever after has been called St. Louis. Yet this Crusade failed, and ever since that time Jerusalem was ruled by Muslims until, in 1917, it was captured by the English, who kept it until 1948 when the state of Israel was established. Now, both Israeli Jews and Palestinians — Muslim and Christian — want control of the Holy City. It's very sad that this city that is so sacred to Jews, Christians, and Muslims is always at the center of a war.

Not all the Crusaders were good Christians. Like some people nowadays, a great many were Christian only in name. In fact, though strange to say, quite a number of the Crusaders were nothing but scalawags, looking for excitement and adventure, and they went on a Crusade merely as an excuse to rob and plunder.

The Crusades did not succeed in their object, which was to keep Jerusalem for the Christians. In spite of that, the Crusades did a great deal of good. When the Crusades first started, the Crusaders were not nearly as civilized as the people they went to conquer. But travel sometimes teaches people more than books, and it taught the Crusaders. They

　　然而，有一些水手却提出，可以用他们的船只把这些童子军带到耶路撒冷去。他们说，自己这样做并无所求，完全是因为他们热爱上帝。可结果却表明，这些水手实际上都是海盗；把孩子们全都骗上船后，他们便转过船头，径直朝敌国，即穆斯林控制的国家驶去。据说，海盗们后来把孩子们都卖给别人当了奴隶。这可不是《格林童话》里的故事，不是孩子们设计困住了海盗，所以我没法编出一个皆大欢喜的结局来，因为结局的确是不幸的。

　　最后一次，也就是第八次十字军东征，是在一个叫作路易的法国国王领导下进行的。他非常虔诚，非常忠于上帝，所以他死后被追封为圣徒，并且此后就被称为"圣路易"。不过，这次十字军东征却失败了；而自那时起，耶路撒冷便一直由穆斯林统治着，直到1917年英军攻陷此城。之后，耶路撒冷便由英国管辖，直到1948年以色列建国。如今，以色列的犹太人和巴勒斯坦人（其中既有穆斯林，也有基督徒）都想控制这座圣城呢。这座对犹太人、基督徒和穆斯林都非常神圣的城市，却总是处于战争的核心，这一点可真是令人觉得无比遗憾啊。

　　并非所有的十字军士兵都是善良的基督徒。跟如今有些人一样，其中的许多人不过都是名义上的基督徒罢了。说来也怪，十字军里的许多人，实际上都是一些只想寻求刺激和冒险的流氓无赖；而他们加入十字军进行东征，也只是为自己去打家劫舍、四处掳掠找个借口罢了。

　　历次十字军东征并没有实现它们的目标，也就是没有为基督徒守住耶路撒冷。虽说如此，十字军东征还是有着巨大贡献的。首次发动东征的时候，十字军士兵的

learned the customs of the other lands through which they went. They learned languages and literature. They learned history and art.

There were then no public schools. Only a very, very few people had any education at all. The Crusades then did what schools might have done. They taught the people of Europe and opened up to them a whole new world of culture and knowledge.

文明程度还不如他们前去征服的那个民族呢。可是，旅行有时能够教给人们一些书本以外的知识，而十字军则正是这样。他们了解了自己经过的其他国家的风俗习惯。他们学到了这些国家的语言和文学。他们学到了历史和艺术。

当时，欧洲还没有公立学校。只有极少数、极少数的人接受过教育。所以，历次十字军东征实际上是完成了学校的教育使命。它们不但教育了欧洲人，还在欧洲人面前打开了一个文化和知识的新世界。

55 Three Kingdoms in West Africa

At the same time that medieval kingdoms like England and France were becoming important in Europe, three kingdoms in West Africa also grew strong and wealthy. They were called Ghana, Mali, and Songhay. These kingdoms were south of the Sahara Desert, along the Niger River. On your map each kingdom is outlined with a different kind of line.

This part of Africa was very wealthy because gold was mined there. For many centuries, the peoples of West Africa traded their gold with close neighbors and also with the Berber people north of the Sahara Desert. Some of the gold from West Africa was sold in the Roman Empire.

There are lots of good stories about the gold miners and traders. When the miners had gold to trade, they would carry their nuggets far away from the mines. They didn't want strangers to find out exactly where the gold came from. The miners would wait in a place that both sides agreed upon. The traders would come and leave what they had to trade. After the traders were out of sight, the miners would leave some gold. Then they would hide. They didn't want to meet the traders, who might force them to tell the location of the mines. The traders would then return and see how much gold had been left. If they thought it was a fair trade, they would take the gold and go home. If they thought that not

55 西非三王国

就在英国、法国这种中世纪王国在欧洲变得日益重要起来的同时，西非有三个王国也变得越来越强大、越来越富庶了。这三个王国，分别叫作加纳、马里和桑海。它们都位于撒哈拉沙漠以南的尼日尔河流域。在下页的地图上，每个王国的边界都用不同的线条标出来了。

非洲这一地区非常富庶，因为这里开采出了金矿。几百年来，西非各个民族都用自己开采出来的黄金同邻近民族进行贸易，也与撒哈拉沙漠以北的柏柏尔人进行贸易。来自西非地区的一些黄金，在罗马帝国境内也有出售呢。

关于西非地区的淘金者和商人，有着许多很有意思的传说。倘若淘金者有黄金出售，他们就会带着金块到距金矿很远的地方去。他们可不想让陌生人知道自己的黄金是从哪里开采出来的。淘金者会在买卖双方商定的一个地方等候买家到来。买家来了之后，便会将用于交易的东西放下，然后转身就走。等买家走得看不见了，淘金者便会现身，留下一些黄金。然后他们就会躲起来。他们不想与买家碰面，因为买家可能会强迫他们说出金矿的位置。接下来，买家又会返回来，看淘金者留下了多少黄金。假如买家觉得交易公平，他们就会拿上黄金回家去。而倘若觉得淘金者留下的黄金不够，他们就会再回来一次，等着淘金者留下更多的黄金。双方都对

enough was offered, they would back off once more and wait for the miners to leave more gold. When both sides were satisfied with the trade, they would all go home. It was like swapping baseball cards. Both sides had to be happy or there was no trade.

One thing that the West Africans needed to get in trade was salt. Can you guess why? West Africa is very hot. In those days with no refrigerators, salt was used to preserve food. Perhaps you've tasted beef jerky, which is meat that has been dried and preserved by salting. You can think of many other ways we keep our food from spoiling now, but in those days, salt was scarce and valuable. Even today we still use salt as a preservative, and we still say someone is "worth his salt" when he does a job well.

交易觉得满意后，便会各自回家。这倒有点儿像是交换棒球卡呢。双方都必须觉得满意才行，否则交易就不会成功。

西非人需要通过交易获得的物品之一，便是食盐。你们能够猜到那是什么原因吗？这是因为，西非地区的天气非常炎热。在那个时候，由于没有冰箱，因此人们都是用盐来腌存食物的。你们可能都吃过牛肉干吧，它就是风干了的、用盐腌制过的牛肉。你们如今可以想出其他许多不让食物变坏的方法来；可在那个时候，食盐却极其稀少，也相当贵重呢。即便是到了今天，我们也还在用食盐来保存食物，并且倘若有人干得很不错，我们也还会说他"配得上他所吃的盐（即很能干）"呢。

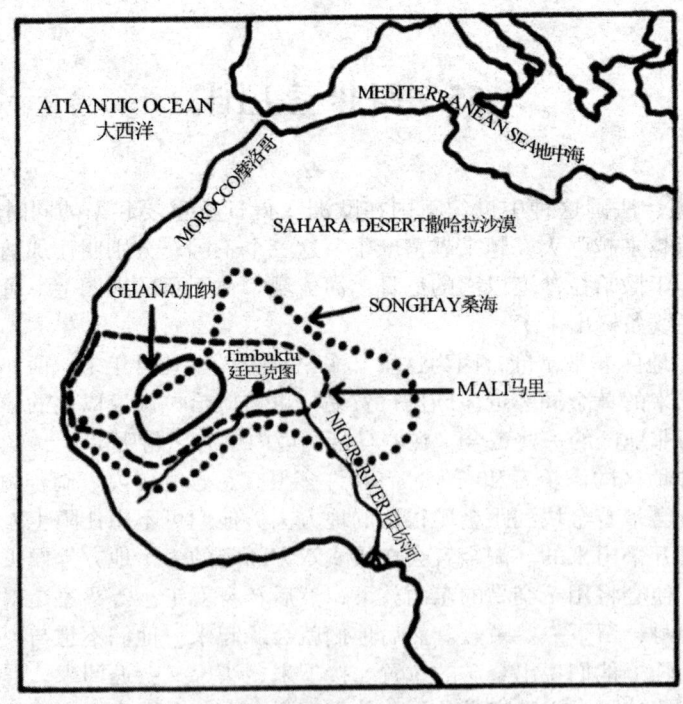

Medieval kingdoms of West Africa
中世纪西非地区的王国

It just so happened that there was a lot of salt on the north side of the Sahara Desert. So, the people of the Niger River area traded with the Berbers of North Africa — gold for salt. Salt was so valuable that West Africans and Berbers traded an even weight of gold for salt — one pound of gold for one pound of salt. That's how valuable salt was. How would you like to be able to make that trade today?

All that gold made a number of the kingdoms in West Africa very wealthy. First a kingdom called Ghana grew large by conquering many of its neighbors. The king's power came from his well-trained army, a skillful cavalry, and gold. When the king of Ghana held an audience, he was surrounded by signs of his power and wealth: pages holding shields, swords with gold handles, horses covered with gold cloths, and the king's own horse tied to a sixty-pound gold nugget! Despite all this wealth, Ghana eventually declined in power, as all empires do sooner or later.

Mali was the next rich, important empire in West Africa. One king, Sundiata,5 conquered the cities important in the trade crossing the Sahara. He also conquered rich gold fields. This king was not only rich, but he was also smart. Whenever his army conquered ncw land, he put the soldiers to work converting it to farm land — until it was time for the next battle. Soon Mali was one of the richest farming areas in West Africa, so this kingdom had plenty to eat as well as having gold and a powerful army.

The most famous king of Mali was Mansa Musa, who ruled during the 14th century.

恰巧，撒哈拉沙漠以北的地区食盐产量巨大。因此，尼日尔河地区的人便与北非的柏柏尔人进行贸易，即用黄金换取食盐。当时，由于食盐非常贵重，所以西非地区的人都是以等重的黄金来换取食盐，即用一磅[1]黄金换取一磅食盐呢。当时的食盐就有那么贵重呀。如果如今还能有这样的生意，你们觉得怎么样呢？

正是黄金，使得西非的许多王国都富庶得很。起初，是一个叫作加纳的王国征服了许多邻国，疆域变得辽阔起来。该国国王的权势全都来自于他手下那支训练有素的军队，即一支精良的骑兵，以及黄金。加纳国王接受臣民觐见的时候，会把他的权威和财富展现得淋漓尽致：侍从们都手持盾牌，他们所佩的刀剑都配有金制手柄，马匹都披着黄金布料，而国王的坐骑竟然拴在一块重达六十磅的金块之上！不过，尽管富甲一方，但加纳最终还是衰落下去了。

马里则是西非地区第二个富庶而重要的帝国。该国有一位叫作松迪亚塔的国王，他征服了穿越撒哈拉沙漠那条贸易线路上的所有重要城市。他还占领了许多储量丰富的金矿区。这位国王不但富有，而且非常聪明。只要攻取了新的国土，他就会让手下的士兵动手，将占领过来的土地变成农田，然后再去发动下一场征战。所以，马里很快就变成了西非地区最富庶的农耕区之一，使得该国在拥有黄金和一支强大军队的同时，还有充足的粮食。

马里王国最出名的一位国王是曼萨·穆萨，他在位的时候是十四世纪。他将帝国疆域向西扩张到了大西洋沿岸，当时可能统治着八百万人口哩。穆斯林商人纷

---

[1] 磅（pound），英制重量单位，有常衡磅（即普通磅）和金衡磅（即用于衡量黄金重量）之分。常衡磅的 1 磅相当于 0.454 千克，而金衡磅的 1 磅相当于 0.373 千克。

He extended his empire westward to the Atlantic Ocean and ruled perhaps eight million people. Muslim traders, both Arabs and North Africans, came to Mali, and Mansa Musa converted to Islam. Like all devout Muslims, he made a pilgrimage to Mecca. Mansa Musa's pilgrimage made *him* famous! His route took him through Cairo, Egypt. He traveled with 500 slaves, each carrying a six-pound gold staff. There were also one hundred elephants, each said to be carrying one hundred pounds of gold. Several hundred camels carried food, weapons, and other things that the pilgrims needed. In Egypt and in Arabia, Mansa Musa gave away a lot of gold. Muslims are expected to be generous, and Mansa Musa was. He also used his gold to buy presents for the people he met along the way. While he was traveling, someone asked Mansa Musa how big his kingdom was. He replied, "A year." What do you think he meant by this? Did you guess? He meant that it took him a year to travel from one end of his kingdom to the other.

When Mansa Musa came home, he brought with him artists and architects to build mosques in the city of Timbuktu and other cities in Mali. He also brought scholars and many books to start a library. Most of the books were written in Arabic, the language used by many Muslims. Timbuktu became a center of learning, and a large book market opened there. Astronomers, mathematicians, philosophers, and poets flocked to the city with its large library and many mosques. Doctors and lawyers worked and taught there. The king supported them all. A lot of foreigners came to visit Timbuktu. Some of these visitors

纷来到马里，其中既有阿拉伯人，也有北非人，因此后来曼萨·穆萨也皈依了伊斯兰教。跟所有虔诚的穆斯林一样，他也曾经前往麦加朝圣。可曼萨·穆萨的这次朝圣却非比寻常，让他自己变得名扬天下了！他是取道埃及的开罗前往麦加的。去朝圣的时候，他带着五百名奴隶，而每名奴隶都带着一根重达六磅的旗杆。他还带了一百头大象，据说每头大象都驮着一百磅黄金呢。此外，还有几百匹骆驼，驮着朝圣人马的食物、武器以及朝圣所需的其他物品。到了埃及和阿拉伯半岛后，曼萨·穆萨将许多黄金都分赠出去了。穆斯林应当乐善好施，而曼萨·穆萨正是如此。他还用黄金换取礼物，分送给一路上遇到的那些人。途中曾经有人问曼萨·穆萨说，他的王国究竟有多大。他回答说："一年。"你们认为，他说的这句话是什么意思呢？你们猜得出吗？他的意思就是：从王国的这一头出发，他得用一年的时间才能走到那一头哩。

　　曼萨·穆萨回国的时候，带回了许多能工巧匠和建筑师，来帮他在廷巴克图和马里的其他城市兴建清真寺。他还带回了一些有学问的人和许多书籍，用来开设一座图书馆。大多数书籍都是用阿拉伯语写的，这是许多穆斯林所用的语言。于是，廷巴克图便变成了一个学问中心，并且市内还开设了一个规模很大的图书市场。由于藏书丰富，又有许多清真寺，因此天文学家、数学家、哲学家和诗人等全都蜂拥而至。许多医生和律师也来到这里工作、教学。国王为所有这些人都提供了支持。许多外国人都来廷巴克图参观、游览。这些游客当中，有些人将自己的旅行经历记录下来了，使得我们如今还能看到他们的描述。一位从北非来的穆斯林旅行者还发现了一件令人震惊的事情：这里的女性竟然可以上学，并且竟然像男性一样受到人

wrote about their trips, so we can read what they said. One Muslim traveler who came from North Africa discovered an astonishing thing: Women were allowed to study and were treated with as much respect as the men!

After Mansa Musa died, the empire of Mali began to split apart. Soon a third important empire, Songhay, arose in the Niger River area. In Songhay, the king's wealth again was based on gold, and he commanded strong armies. The king, Sunni Ali Ber, expanded Songhay until its empire was larger than Mali had ever been. He died in 1492, the year that Columbus set sail for the Americas. After this time, Songhay was weakened by foreigners, first by Moroccans from North Africa and then by the Portuguese who began sailing and trading along the African coast. The king of Songhay no longer had the power or wealth to hold his territory together. After a thousand years of wealthy empires, the lands along the Niger River split into small kingdoms.

们的尊重！

　　曼萨·穆萨死后，马里帝国就开始分裂。不久，第三个重要的帝国，即桑海帝国，便在尼日尔河地区崛起了。在桑海，国王的财富根基也是黄金，并且国王手中也掌握着一支支强大的军队。国王桑尼·阿里·贝尔不断扩张，直到桑海帝国的疆域超过了马里帝国曾经的疆域。他死于1492年，也就是哥伦布航海前往美洲探险的那一年。此后，桑海帝国的势力便不断地遭到外族的侵蚀而削弱了；在这些外族中，先有北非的摩洛哥人，然后又是刚刚开始沿着非洲海岸航行和贸易的葡萄牙人。桑海国王的实力或财富，都不足以再维持帝国领土的统一了。在历经了一千年，其间有三个富甲一方的帝国相继崛起并衰落之后，尼日尔河流域地区便分裂成了许许多多的小王国。

56 Bibles Made of Stone and Glass

In Europe during the Middle Ages, people often went to church every day and often several times a day. They did not go only when there was a church service. They went to say their prayers by themselves; they went to tell their troubles to the priest, to get advice from him, to bum a candle to the Virgin Mary, or simply to chat with their friends.

All during the Crusades and immediately after the Crusades, the chief thing that many people thought about was their church.

Almost everyone in Europe was a Christian although many towns had Jewish residents as well. You may remember that Jews had been forced to leave the Holy Land way back in 70 A.D. by the Romans. Some had made their way to Europe.

For Christians, there was only one church in a neighborhood, and everyone went to the same church, for there were no Baptists, nor Episcopalians, nor Methodists; all were just Christians.

The church was everyone's meetinghouse, so people naturally gave as much money and time and labor as they could to make their church the best that could be built. That is why there were built in France and other parts of Europe at this time many of the finest

56 石头与玻璃制成的《圣经》

在中世纪的欧洲，人们往往每天都要去教堂做祷告，并且经常是一天要去好几次。他们并非只是在教堂做礼拜的时候才去。他们去教堂，是为了独自做祷告；他们去教堂，是为了向牧师诉说自己碰到的问题，是为了听取牧师提出的建议，是为了向圣母马利亚焚烛叩拜，或者只是为了与朋友们在那里聊聊天。

在整个十字军东征期间，以及随后的那段时间里，许多人心中所想的头等大事，便是他们的教堂。

在欧洲，几乎人人都是基督徒；不过，许多城镇里也有犹太教居民。你们可能都还记得，早在公元70年，犹太人便被罗马人逼着离开了圣地耶路撒冷。后来，有些犹太人便迁徙到了欧洲。

对于基督徒来说，一个社区只会设立一座教堂，并且大家去的都是同一座教堂，因为当时还没有浸礼会、圣公会、卫理公会等教派；大家全都是一样的基督徒。

由于教堂是大家的会堂，所以人们自然会竭尽所能，花钱、花时间和劳动力来把教堂修建得最好。那个时候，法国与欧洲的其他地区之所以都修建了许多全世界最精美的教堂和大教堂，原因即在于此。这些教堂和大教堂如今依然存在；由于它

churches and cathedrals in the world. These churches and cathedrals are still standing, and because they are so beautiful, people go long distances to see them.

Do you know what a cathedral is? A cathedral is not just a large church. It is the church of a bishop. In the chancel of this church, there is a special chair for the bishop. This bishop's chair is called in Latin a *cathedra*, and so his church is named a cathedral after this chair.

These churches and cathedrals were nothing like the old Greek and Roman temples; they were not like anything that had ever been built before.

If you have ever built a house out of blocks, you probably did it this way: first you stood two blocks upright, and then you laid another block across the top of these for a roof. This is the way the Greeks and Romans built.

But the Christians throughout Europe at that time did not build in this way at all.

When you were building toy houses, instead of laying a single block across the two standing ones, you may perhaps have tried leaning two blocks together like the sides of a letter A for a roof. If you did, you know what happened: the two leaning blocks pushed over the sides, and *crash*! everything tumbled. Well, these churches were built somewhat in this way, with stones arched across the standing stone columns. But to keep the stone arches from pushing over the standing stone columns, the builders put up props or braces. These props or braces were made of stone, too, and these props of stone were called *flying buttresses*.

们都非常漂亮，所以人们都不远万里地前来参观呢。

你们知道大教堂是什么吗？大教堂可并非只是一座规模很大的教堂。它还是主教所住的教堂。在这种大教堂的圣坛之上，有一把专供主教坐的椅子。主教的座椅在拉丁语中被称为cathedra，因此主教所住的教堂也就根据这把椅子的名字，被称为大教堂（cathedral）了。

这些教堂和大教堂，与古希腊和古罗马的那些神殿完全不同；它们也不同于人们以前修建的任何建筑。

假如你们以前用积木搭过房子，那你们很可能是这样做的：首先是垂直地放上两块积木，然后再用一块积木横着搭在这两块垂立的积木上面，当作屋顶。古希腊人和古罗马人也是这样修建房屋的。

可在当时，全欧洲的基督徒却完全不是这样来修建房屋的。

你们在搭建玩具房子的时候，也有可能不会用一块积木横着搭在两块直立的积木上，而是可能试着将两块积木斜搭在一起，形成一个就像是字母A的两边那样的形状，以此来做屋顶。假如试过这种方法的话，那你们肯定明白，结果会是什么样子：那两块斜搭在一起的积木会相互挤推，从而咔嚓一声，整堆积木都倒了。可是，那些教堂正是用与这有点儿类似的方法修建起来的；它们都是用石头搭成拱形，横跨在直立的石柱之上。不过，为了不让石拱挤压直立的石柱，建筑人员还会建造一些支柱或者支架。支柱或者支架也是石制的，而这些石制的支柱，就叫"飞拱"。

意大利人觉得，这简直就是一种疯狂的建筑方法。他们以为，这种建筑必定会

The people in Italy thought this a crazy way of building. They thought such buildings must be shaky and might easily topple over — like a house of cards. The Goths who had conquered Italy in 476 were considered wild and ignorant and after that people called anything wild and ignorant *Gothic*. People called all buildings such as I have just described *Gothic*, although the Goths had nothing to do with the buildings.

Indeed, from my description you, too, may think such buildings propped up by flying buttresses must have been tottering and ugly, but they were neither. They were not rickety, for though occasionally one that was not carefully built did collapse, the largest and best are still standing today. Although there were old-fashioned people who thought no building was beautiful that was not built in the Roman or Greek style, we have come to admire the great beauty of these so-called Gothic buildings.

There were other ways in which the Gothic churches were different from the Greek and Roman temples. Before a Gothic church was started, a very large cross was first drawn on the ground with its head towards the east, because that is the direction of Jerusalem. On this cross-

Flying buttresses — apse of Notre Dame
飞拱——巴黎圣母院的后殿

摇摇晃晃，一不小心就会倒塌下来，就像一座用纸牌搭成的房屋似的。人们曾经认为，征服意大利的哥特人都很野蛮、很无知；所以，此后人们便将所有野蛮无知的东西，全都称为"哥特式"的。因此，人们把我刚才所描述的所有建筑也都称为"哥特式"，尽管哥特人与这些建筑毫无关系呢。

的确，从我的描述来看，你们可能也会以为，这些用飞拱支撑起来的建筑一定都是摇摇欲坠、丑陋不堪的，可事实上它们既稳固，又美观。它们不会摇摇晃晃，因为尽管偶尔确实会有一两座建得不怎么细致的房子倒塌，但那些规模大、完美的房屋，直到今天却仍然屹立在那里。虽然有些老派的人认为，除了用古罗马和古希腊的风格来修建，世界上就没有建得漂亮的建筑了，可对于这些所谓的哥特式建筑，我们如今却开始越来越欣赏了。

哥特式教堂还有其他一些方面，也与古罗马或古希腊的神殿不一样。人们在动工修建一座哥特式教堂之前，都会先在地上画出一个巨大的十字架，并让十字架头朝东方，因为那是耶路撒冷所在的方向。按照这种十字形的设计图把教堂建成后，倘若从上往下看，整个教堂的布局也会呈十字架形，并且祭坛始终都会朝着东方。

哥特式教堂都建有漂亮的尖顶或者说箭楼；它们就像手指一样，直指苍穹。其中的门窗顶上都既不是方的，也不是圆的，而是尖的，就像祈祷时合拢的双掌

shaped plan, the church was built so that if you looked down from above on the finished building, it was shaped like a cross with the altar always toward the east.

Gothic churches had beautiful spires or *arrows*, which have been likened to fingers pointing to heaven. The doorways and windows were not square or round at the top, but pointed, like hands placed together in prayer.

Nearly the whole side of a Gothic church was made of glass. These large windows were not, however, plain white glass, but beautiful pictures made of colored glass. Small pieces of different colors were joined together at their edges with lead to make what looked like wonderful paintings. These pictures were much finer than ordinary paintings, for the light shone through the stained glass and made the colors brilliant as jewels — blue like the clear sky, yellow like sunlight, red like a ruby. These pictures in glass told stories from the Bible. They were like colored illustrations in a book. The people who could not read, and very few could read, were able to know the Bible stories just by looking at these beautiful illustrations.

Statues of saints and angels and characters in the Bible were carved in the stonework of the church. The churches were like Bibles of stone and glass.

Besides these holy things, strange, grotesque beasts were also made in stone — monsters like no animal that has ever been seen in nature. These creatures were usually put on the outside edge or corner of the roof or they were used for waterspouts and called *gargoyles*. They were supposed to scare away evil spirits from the holy place.

那样。

　　一座哥特式教堂，几乎都有一整面玻璃侧墙。不过，侧墙上那一扇扇巨大的窗户上，并非只是普通的透明玻璃，而是用彩色玻璃构成了许多美丽的图案。人们用铅将无数小片彩色玻璃的边缘黏合在一起，使得它们看上去就像是一幅幅奇妙的图画。这些图案比普通的油画要精致得多，因为光线会透过彩色玻璃照射进来，使得这些彩色玻璃就像珠宝一样熠熠生辉：蓝的就像是明净的天空，黄的就像是金色的阳光，红的就像鲜艳的红宝石。这些玻璃图画描述的都是《圣经》中的故事。它们就像是一本书中的彩色插图。那些不识字的人，只需观看这些美丽的插图，便能明白《圣经》中的故事；而在当时，识字的人还极少呢。

　　教堂的石墙之上，都刻有《圣经》中提及的圣徒、天使和人物的雕像。因此，一座座教堂就像是一部部用石头和玻璃制成的《圣经》啊。

　　除了这些神圣之物，教堂里还有一些奇妙而古怪的野兽雕像它们都是一些在自然界里见不到的怪物。这些怪物雕像，通常都雕在屋顶的外侧或角落里，或者用于做排水口，被称为"雨漏"。人们认为，它们可以吓走恶魔，不让恶魔进入圣地。

　　如今，没人知道设计并建造这些哥特式教堂的都是些

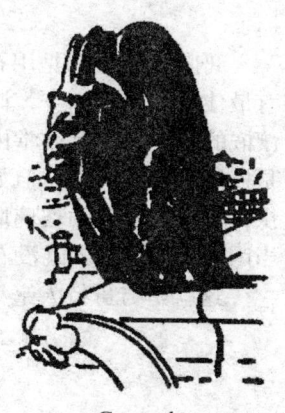

Gargoyle
雨漏

No one now knows who were the architects or the builders of these Gothic churches or who were the sculptors or artists. Almost everyone did some work on the church. Instead of giving money, men and women gave time and labor. Men carved stone or made stained glass. Women sewed and embroidered vestments and altar cloths.

Some of these Gothic churches took hundreds of years to build, so that the workmen who started them never lived to see them finished. Some of the most famous cathedrals are Canterbury Cathedral in England, the Cathedral of Notre Dame in Paris, Cologne Cathedral in Germany, and Chartres Cathedral in France.

Cologne Cathedral took the longest of all to build, as it was not entirely finished until about seven hundred years after it was begun! Some of the cathedrals were destroyed during the many wars fought since the Middle Ages.

Gothic churches were built, with loving care, of stone and jeweled glass. Nothing but the best was thought good enough. Today many churches are still built with spires, pointed doors, and some stained-glass windows, and often the altar is toward the east. But although they imitate the Gothic style in these things, they seldom have stone ceilings, as Gothic churches had, nor flying buttresses, nor walls of stained glass. Real Gothic was enormously expensive and difficult, and nowadays people haven't the time, the money, nor the interest to build in such a way.

That is the story of Gothic churches that the Goths had nothing to do with.

什么人，也没人知道是谁雕刻或设计出这些雕像了。几乎每个人都为教堂的修建出了力。男男女女，就算没有出钱，也是出了时间和劳力。男人们雕刻石头或者制作彩色玻璃。女人们则缝缝补补，绣出法衣和祭坛上所用的布料。

这些哥特式教堂当中，有一些花了几百年的时间才建成，因此动工修建这些教堂的工人，到死都没有看到它们完工呢。其中最著名的一些大教堂，有英国的坎特伯雷大教堂、巴黎的圣母院、德国的科隆大教堂，以及法国的沙特尔大教堂，等等。

其中，科隆大教堂修建的时间最久；因为自动工之后，前后花了约七百年的时间，这座教堂才全部完工！从中世纪以来，一些大教堂都在连绵不断的战火中被毁掉了。

哥特式教堂都是用石头和饰有宝石的玻璃精心修建而成的。因为人们觉得，只有最佳才够好。如今，许多教堂仍然建有尖塔、尖形拱门，以及一部分用彩色玻璃镶嵌的窗户，并且教堂内的祭坛通常也是朝向东方。不过，尽管它们在这些方面都是模仿哥特式风格，但如今的教堂很少有哥特式教堂的那种石制天花板了，没有飞拱，也没有彩色的玻璃墙壁了。真正的哥特式教堂造价极其昂贵，并且修建起来相当困难；如今的人既没有时间、资金，也没有兴趣再用这种方法来修建教堂了。

这就是与哥特人毫无关系的哥特式教堂的历史。

57 John, Whom Nobody Loved

Richard the Lion-Hearted, whom every-body loved, had a brother named John, whom nobody loved.

This brother John became king, but he turned out to be a very wicked king.

He is another one of the villains in history, whom we do not like, but like to hear about, and like to clap when he gets what he deserves.

John was afraid that his young nephew named Arthur might be made king in his place, so he had him murdered. Some say he hired others to do the killing; some say he murdered him with his own hands. This was a very bad beginning for his reign, but things got worse and worse as time went on.

John got into a quarrel with the pope in Rome. The pope at that time said what should be done and what should not be done in churches everywhere. The pope ordered John to make a certain man bishop in England, and John said he wouldn't do it. He wanted another man, a friend of his, to be bishop. The pope then said he would close up all the churches in England if John didn't do as he was told. John said he didn't care. Let the pope go ahead and close up all the churches if he wanted to. So the pope ordered all churches in

57　没人喜欢的约翰

人见人爱的"狮心王"理查德有个没人喜欢的弟弟，名叫约翰。

这位约翰弟弟后来登上了王位；可最终表明，他却是一个非常邪恶的国王。

他是历史上的又一名恶棍；虽说我们都不喜欢这样的恶棍，大家却喜欢听这种恶棍的故事，并且在听到恶棍得到应有的下场之后都会拍掌称快呢。

约翰很担心自己的小侄子亚瑟可能取代他登上王位，于是便谋杀了亚瑟。有的人说，他是雇人将亚瑟杀死的；还有的人则说，他是亲手谋杀了亚瑟。他的统治以这种方式开始，本来就是一件很糟糕的事情；可随着时光流逝，情况还变得越来越糟糕了呢。

约翰与罗马的教皇之间产生了矛盾。人们在世界各地的教会中应当怎样做、不应当怎样做，这一切本来都是当时的教皇说了算。教皇命令约翰让某个人当英国的主教，可约翰却不答应。他想要另一个人当主教，因为那个人是他的朋友。教皇便说，如果约翰不按照教皇所说的去做，教皇便要关闭英国的所有教堂。约翰回答说他不在乎，教皇想这样干的话，就让他去关掉所有的教堂好了。于是，教皇便下令关闭英国的所有教堂，并且一直要关到约翰让步为止。现在来看，这样做并没有太大的影响；可我曾经跟你们说过，在那个时候，去教堂祷告就是大家生活里唯一重

England to be closed until John should give in. Nowadays this might not have made much difference, but then, as I have told you, the church was the one most important thing in everyone's life; in fact, nothing else mattered so much. The closing of the churches meant that no services could be held in any church. It meant that children could not be baptized, and so, if they died, it was believed they could not go to heaven. It meant that couples could not be married. It meant that the dead could not be given a Christian burial.

The people of England were shocked. It was as if heaven had put a curse on them. They were afraid that terrible things would happen to them. Of course the people blamed John, for he was the cause of the churches being closed. They were so angry at him that he became scared — afraid what his people might do to him. When at last the pope threatened to make another man king of England in John's place — yes, the pope had as much power as that — John, in fear and trembling, gave in and agreed to do everything that at first he had said he would not do and more besides. But John was pig-headed. He was always doing the wrong thing and sticking to it.

John had an idea that the world was made for the king and that people were put upon the earth simply so that the king might have servants to work for him, to earn money for him, to do what he wished them to do. Many of the kings of olden days felt the same way, though they did not go as far as John did. John would order people who were rich to give him whatever money he wanted. If they refused to give him all he asked, he would put them in prison, have their hands squeezed in an iron press until the bones cracked and the blood ran, or he would even put them to death.

要的事情呢，事实上其他任何东西都没有教堂那样重要。关闭教堂，就意味着所有教堂都没法举行礼拜仪式了。它意味着孩子没法接受洗礼；人们认为，这样这些孩子长大、死后就没法上天堂了。它意味着男女没有办法结婚。它也意味着没法给逝者举行符合基督教教义的葬礼了。

英国人民都很震惊。这就好比是他们受到了天堂的诅咒似的。他们都担心，噩运会降临到自己身上。人们当然都是异口同声地指责约翰，因为他才是导致教堂被关闭的始作俑者。他们都很愤怒，弄得约翰很害怕，害怕民众会对他做出什么出格的事情来。最后，当罗马教皇威胁说要推举另一个人来取代约翰当英国国王后，约翰便提心吊胆、战战兢兢地屈服了，除了答应起初断然拒绝的所有事情外，还做出了其他的让步；是的，当时的罗马教皇有权力废立各国的国王呢。不过，约翰是个极其顽固的家伙。他总是在做错误的事情，并且还固执己见，一错到底。

约翰有一种想法，以为整个世界就是为国王而存在的；世界上之所以会有普通民众，不过是为了让国王有仆役来替他干活、替他挣钱并供他随心所欲地来驱使罢了。古时候的许多国王都有这种想法，不过他们可不像约翰那样极端。约翰命令富人给他缴纳钱财，无论他要多少，就得给多少。如果胆敢拒绝他的要求，约翰就会把他们关进监狱，将他们的双手放进一个铁夹子里猛夹，直到骨头断裂、鲜血淋漓才罢手，或者将他们判处死刑。

约翰的行径变得越来越恶劣，他手下的贵族终于忍无可忍了。于是，他们抓

John got worse and worse until at last his barons could not stand his actions any longer. So they made him prisoner and took him to a little island in the Thames River called Runnymede. Here they forced John to agree to certain things that they had written down in Latin. This was in the Year 1215; and 1215 was a bad date for John, but a good date for the English people. This list of things which the barons made John agree to was called by the Latin name for a great agreement or charter, which is *Magna Carta*.

John did not agree to the Magna Carta willingly, however. He was as angry and furious as a spoiled child, who kicks and screams when forced to do something he does not want to do. He had to agree, nevertheless.

John was unable to write his name, and thus he could not sign the agreement as people sign contracts nowadays. But he wore a seal ring that was used by people who could not sign their names, and this seal he pressed into a piece of hot wax which was dropped on the agreement where one would have signed.

John agreed in the Magna Carta to give the barons some of the rights that we think every human being should have anyway, without an agreement. For instance, a person certainly has the right to keep the money he earns, and he has the right not to have it taken away from him unlawfully. A person also has the right not to be put in prison or be punished by the king or anyone else unless he has done something wrong and unless he has had a fair trial. These are two of the rights that John agreed to in the Magna Carta. There were quite a number of others.

John didn't keep his agreement, however. He broke it the very first time he had a good

住了约翰，把他送到泰晤士河中一个叫作兰尼米德的小岛上囚禁起来。在这里，他们逼迫约翰答应了他们用拉丁语写下来的一些条件。这一事件，发生在1215年；因此，虽说1215年对于约翰来说是个糟糕的年份，可对于英国人民来说，1215年却是一个大吉大利的好年份哩。贵族们迫使约翰答应的这些条件，在拉丁语里称为《大宪章》，就是一份"重大条约"或者"章程"的意思。

然而，约翰并不是心甘情愿地认可《大宪章》。他暴跳如雷、怒火中烧，就像一个被宠坏了的孩子在被迫去做自己不愿意做的事情时那样拳打脚踢、尖声高叫。但尽管如此，他还是不得不同意这些条件。

约翰不会写自己的名字，所以他当然无法像如今的人签署合同时那样来签署《大宪章》这份协议。可他随身携带着一枚印章戒指，过去那些不会写字的人都是用这种印章戒指来代替签名的；于是，他便在滴在协议签名处的一团热蜡上按下了那枚印章，算是签名了。

在这份《大宪章》中，约翰同意给予贵族一些政治上的独立与经济权益；可在我们看来，哪怕是没有签署什么协议，那些权利也都是每个人应当拥有的。例如，一个人有权保护自己的劳动所得，并且有权保护此种所得不会被人非法剥夺。一个人除非违反了法律规定并经过公正的审判，否则也拥有不被国王或其他人关进监狱、施加惩处的权利。可这正是约翰国王在《大宪章》里同意的两种权利呢。《大宪章》里还有其他许多的条款。

chance, as a person usually does when he is forced to agree to something against his will. But John died pretty soon; and so, as far as he was concerned, the Magna Carta didn't matter much. However, kings who came after him were made to agree to the same things. So after 1215 the king in England was supposed to be the servant of the people, and not the people servants of the king as they had been before that time.

然而，约翰并没有遵守自己所签的这份协定。一找到机会，他就像一个人在被迫违心地答应了某件事情之后通常所做的那样，撕毁了这份协议。不过，约翰国王不久后就驾崩归天了；因此，对他来说，《大宪章》其实是没有什么关系的。然而，继他之后的历任国王，却都不得不认可《大宪章》里的所有条款。因此，1215年之后，人们便认为英国国王是民众的公仆，而不再像以前那样，认为民众是国王的仆役了。

58 A Great Story Teller

Far away from England,
      Far off in the direction of the rising sun,
           Far beyond Italy and Jerusalem and the Tigris and Euphrates and Persia was a country called Cathay — C-A-T-H-A-Y.

If you looked down at your feet, and the world were glass, you would see Cathay on the other side.

Cathay is the same place we now call China. There had been people living in Cathay, of course, all through the centuries that had passed, but Europeans knew little of this land or of its people.

In the thirteenth century or twelve hundreds, Mongols, who came from the north, were ruling China. Soon, it seemed that they might conquer all the other countries whose histories we have been hearing about. The ruler of the Mongols was a fierce fighter named Genghis Khan. Genghis Khan had an army of Tartar horsemen who were terrific fighters.

Genghis usually found some excuse for making war on others, but if he couldn't find a good excuse, he made up one, for he was bent on building an enormous empire.

58   了不起的故事先生

在离英国非常非常遥远、朝着日出的东方而去，距意大利、耶路撒冷、底格里斯河、幼发拉底河和波斯依然非常非常遥远的地方，有个叫作"中国"的国家。

假如地球是透明的，那么你们看一看自己的脚底下，就会看得见位于地球那一边的中国呢。

在过去的千百年里，中国当然一直有人生活着，只是欧洲人对这片土地以及生活在这个国度里的人知之甚少罢了。

在十三世纪，或者说公元1200年到公元1300年之间，中国一直是由来自北方的蒙古人统治着。很快，这些蒙古人似乎完全可以去征服其他的各个国家了；那些国家的历史，我们在前面都已经说过了。蒙古人的首领，是一位非常凶悍善战的人，叫作成吉思汗。成吉思汗手下有一支由蒙古骑兵所组成的大军；那些骑兵，则个个都是令人生畏的勇士。

成吉思汗在向别的国家发动战争的时候，通常都会找个借口出来；可如果找不到什么好借口的话，他就会编造出一个理由来，因为他一心所想的，就是建立一个广袤庞大的帝国。

成吉思汗率领手下的铁骑，横扫了从契丹直到欧洲的大片土地。他们一路上烧杀

Genghis and his horsemen swept over the land from Cathay toward Europe. They burned and destroyed thousands upon thousands of towns and cities and everything in their way. No one was able to stop them.

Genghis Khan had conquered the whole land from the Pacific Ocean to the eastern part of Europe. At last he stopped. With this kingdom he seemed to be satisfied. He might well have been satisfied, for it was larger the Roman Empire or that of Alexander the Great.

Even when Genghis died, things were no better, for his son was just as fierce a fighter as his father and conquered still more territory.

But the grandson of Genghis Khan was much less warlike than his grandfather had been. He was named Kublai Khan, and he was quite different from his father and grandfather. He made his capital at a city in China called Peiping, now called Beijing, and ruled over this vast empire that he had inherited from his father. Kublai built magnificent palaces and surrounded himself with beautiful gardens, and he made such a wonderful capital for himself that Solomon in all his glory did not live in such splendor as did Kublai Khan.

Now, far, far off from Beijing and the palace of Kublai Khan, in the north of Italy was a city built on the water. Its streets were of water, and boats were used instead of carriages. This city was called Venice. About the Year 1260 there were living in Venice two brothers named Nicolo and Maffeo Polo. The Polos got an idea in their heads that they would like to see something of the world. So these two Venetian merchants started off toward the

拂掠，毁掉了成千上万座城镇，以及所到之处的一切。无人能够挡住他们的去路。

成吉思汗曾经征服了从太平洋沿岸往西、直到欧洲东部的大部分土地。最后，他不再征战了。拥有如此广袤的一个王国，他似乎已经心满意足了。他也应当心满意足才是，因为这个王国的疆域已经超过了罗马帝国，超过了亚历山大大帝的帝国呢。

即便是成吉思汗死后，帝国的形势也没有什么变化，因为他的儿子像父亲一样骁勇善战，仍然在不断地攻城略地。

不过，成吉思汗的孙子却没有他的祖父那样好战了。成吉思汗的孙子叫作忽必烈可汗，他与自己的父亲、祖父都大不相同。他把都城建在中国境内一个当时叫作"大都"、如今叫作"北京"的城市，并且统治着从父亲手里继承下来的这个大帝国。忽必烈修建了许多辉煌灿烂的宫殿，所居之地到处都是美丽的花园；他为自己建立了如此奇妙的一座都城，就连荣耀无比的所罗门王过得也没有忽必烈那样奢华呢。

此时，在距北京和忽必烈可汗的皇宫很远、很远的意大利北部，有一座建在水上的城市。那座城市里的街道全都是水路，人们来去所用的都是小船而不是马车。那座城市叫作威尼斯。公元1260年左右，威尼斯有两兄弟，分别叫作尼科洛·波罗和马费奥·波罗。波罗兄弟脑海中出现了一个想法，那就是他们应当去看一看世界。于是，这两位威尼斯商人便像故事书中那些出发去寻找出路的男孩子一样，朝着日出的方向而去，准备动身去探险。他们一直朝着东方行进，经历了几年的旅程之后，终于来到了忽必烈可汗那个花园般的首都，来到了忽必烈可汗那座金碧辉煌

rising sun looking for adventure, just like boys in storybooks who go off to seek their fortunes. After several years of travel, always toward the east, they at last came to the gardens and to the magnificent palace of Kublai Khan.

When Kublai Khan heard that strange white men from a far-off place and an unknown country were outside the palace, he wanted to see them. They were brought into his presence. They told Kublai Khan all about their own land. They were good story-tellers, and they made it interesting. They told him also about the Christian religion and many other things that he had never heard of. After several years, the Polos went home to Venice.

The emperor was so much interested in the Polos and in the stories they told about their country that he wanted to hear more. In 1271 the Polos returned to China with Nicolo's teenage son, Marco. The emperor persuaded them to stay with him and tell him more. He gave them rich presents. Then he made them his advisers and assistants in ruling his empire. The Polos stayed on for years and years and years and learned the language and came to be very important people in Cathay.

At last after they had spent about twenty years in Cathay, the Polos thought it was about time to go home and see their own people again. They begged leave to return. Kublai Khan did not want them to go. In the end though he did let them go, and they started back to what once had been their home.

When they at last arrived in Venice, they had been away so long and had been traveling

的皇宫。

忽必烈可汗听说皇宫外面来了两个陌生的白人，并且得知这两个白人来自远方一个无人所知的国度之后，便想要见一见他们。于是，两人被带到了忽必烈可汗的面前。他们把本国的情况全都一五一十地告诉了忽必烈可汗。他们很会讲故事，因此叙述得非常有意思。他们还给忽必烈可汗介绍了基督教的情况，将许多他闻所未闻的事情都告诉了他。几年后，波罗兄弟便返回威尼斯去了。

忽必烈可汗对波罗兄弟以及他们讲述的、关于意大利的故事产生了浓厚的兴趣，因此希望多听他们说一说。1271年，波罗兄弟带着尼科洛那个十多岁的儿子马可再次来到了中国。忽必烈可汗说服他们留下来，给他多说一些事情。他赐给了他们很多很多的礼物。然后，他又聘请这两兄弟当自己的顾问和助手，帮助他来治理整个帝国。波罗兄弟在中国待了一年又一年，既学会了中文，也成了元朝非常重要的两个人物。

最后，他们在元朝待了近二十年后，波罗兄弟觉得他们应该回家去看一看本国人了。他们恳求皇帝允许他们离去后再回来。忽必烈可汗并不想让他们走。不过，最终他还是答应了他们的请求；于是，他们便启程，回到曾经是自己家乡的意大利去了。

回到意大利后，由于他们离家的时间太久，游历的地方又太远，因此已经没人认识他们了。他们几乎已经忘掉家乡话该怎么说了，因此说起话来就像外国人一样洋腔怪调。他们身上所穿的衣服，由于长途跋涉而变得破旧不堪、衣衫褴褛。他们

so far that no one knew them. They had almost forgotten how to speak their own language, and they talked like foreigners. Their clothes had become worn out and ragged by their long trip. They looked like tramps, and not even their old friends recognized them. No one would believe that these ragged, dirty strangers were the same fine Venetian gentlemen who had disappeared almost twenty years before.

The Polos told their townspeople all about their adventures and the wonderfully rich lands and cities that they had visited. The townspeople only laughed at them, for they thought them story tellers.

The Polos then ripped open their ragged garments, and out fell piles of magnificent and costly jewels, diamonds and rubies and sapphires and pearls — enough to buy a kingdom. The people looked in wonder and amazement and began to believe.

Marco Polo told his stories to a man who wrote them down and made a book of them called *The Travels of Marco Polo*. This is an interesting book for you to read even today, although we cannot believe all the tales he told. We know that he exaggerated a great many things, for he liked to amaze people.

Marco Polo described the magnificence of Kublai Khan's palace. He told of its enormous dining hall, where thousands of guests could sit down at the table at one time. He told of a bird so huge that it could fly away with an elephant. He said that Noah's Ark was still on Mount Ararat, only the mountain was so high and so dangerous to climb on account of the ice and snow with which it was covered that no one could go to see if the ark really was there.

的样子就像是流浪者，甚至连老朋友们也认不出来了。没人相信这两个衣衫褴褛、肮脏不堪的陌生人，就是差不多二十年前离家的那两位威尼斯绅士呢。

波罗兄弟将自己的冒险经历，以及他们到过的那些极其富庶的国家和城市的情况，全都告诉了威尼斯的同乡。可听了之后，威尼斯市民却只是嘲笑他们，因为他们以为波罗兄弟只是两个故事先生呢。

于是，波罗兄弟撕开破破烂烂的外衣；一堆堆金光闪闪、贵重无比的珠宝、钻石、红宝石、蓝宝石和珍珠一下子掉了出来，多得可以买下一个王国。人们都惊得目瞪口呆，这才开始相信他们的话了。

马可·波罗把他的经历告诉了一个人；那个人将这些经历记录下来，写成了一本书，叫作《马可·波罗游记》。即便是对于今天的你们来说，这也是一本很有意思的书；尽管我们无法相信他所述说的那些传奇故事全部都是真实的，但这本书还是值得一读。我们知道，他夸大了许多的事情，因为他喜欢让人们感到惊讶。

马可·波罗描述了忽必烈可汗那座皇宫的辉煌壮观。他描述了宫中巨大的餐厅，那里一次可以容纳数千位宾客坐下来吃饭。他还提到了一种鸟儿，大得可以抓住大象飞行。他还说挪亚方舟仍然停在亚拉拉特山上；只是那山又高又危险，加上冰雪覆盖，爬不上去，因此无人能够去看一看。挪亚方舟是否真的还泊在那里呢？

59 "Thing-a-ma-jigger" and "What-cher-may-call-it" or a Magic Needle and a Magic Powder

About this same time that Marco Polo returned from his travels, people in Europe began to hear and talk about a magic needle and a magic powder that did remarkable things, and some said that Marco brought them back from Cathay, but now we know that it was Arab sailors who carried many of the wondrous things from China to the Mediterranean, where Europeans learned of them.

One of these wonderful things was a little magic needle. The little magic needle, when floated on a straw or held up only at its middle, would always turn towards the north no matter how much you twisted it. Such a needle put in a case was called a compass.

Now, you may not see why such a little thing was so remarkable. But strange as it may seem, this little thing really made it possible to discover a new world.

Perhaps you have played the game in which a child is blindfolded, twisted around several times in the center of the room, and then told to go toward the door or the window or some other point in the room. You know how impossible it is for one who has been so turned round to tell which way to go, and you know how absurd one looks who goes in

59 "小小装置"和"无名之物"，或者魔针和魔粉

差不多与马可·波罗游历回来的同一时期，欧洲人开始听说世界上有一种非常神奇的魔针和一种魔粉了。有些人说它们是马可·波罗从元朝带回欧洲的；不过，我们如今已经知道，是那些把很多神奇之物从中国带到地中海地区的阿拉伯水手让欧洲人得知了它们的存在。

那些神奇之物中，有一样便是一根小小的魔针。这根小小的魔针，无论把它扭成什么样子，如果把它放到一根稻草上在水面漂浮着，或者只是撑起它的中点，那么它始终都会转过来朝向北方。将这样的魔针装在盒子里，就成了"指南针"。

注意，你们可能不明白，这件小东西为什么会如此的不同寻常。但看上去奇怪的是，这件小东西确实让人们发现一个新世界成为可能呢。

或许你们都玩过这样一种游戏：把一个小朋友的眼睛蒙上，让他在房子中间转几个圈，然后再走向门、窗或者房间里其他指定的方向。要是玩过的话，你们就会知道，转了几圈之后，那个小朋友就没法知道自己要朝哪个方向走了；当他朝着自己以为正确的方向，其实却是正好相反的方向走去时，看上去有多么可笑啊。

其实，在大海上航行的水手，正是有点儿像这样一个被蒙住了眼睛的小朋友。

quite the opposite direction when he thinks he is going straight.

Well, the sailor at sea was something like such a blind-folded child. Of course, if the weather were fine, he could tell by the sun or the stars which way he should go. But when the weather was cloudy and bad, there was nothing for him to go by. He was then like the blindfolded child. He might easily become confused and sail in just the opposite direction from the way he wanted to go without knowing the difference.

This was perhaps one of the chief reasons why most sailors, before the compass was used, had not gone far out of sight of land. They were afraid they might not be able to find their way back. So most sailors traveled only to that part of the world that could be reached without going far out of sight of land.

But, with the compass, sailors could sail on and on through storms and cloudy weather and keep always in the direction they wanted to go. They simply had to follow the little magnetic needle suspended in its box. No matter how much the boat turned or twisted or tossed, the little needle always pointed to the north. Of course sailors did not always want to go north, but it was very easy to tell any other direction if they knew which was north. South was exactly opposite, east was to the right, and west was to the left. All they had to do was to steer the boat on the course in whatever direction they wished.

It was a long while, however, before sailors would use a compass. They thought it was bewitched by some magic, and they were afraid to have anything to do with such a thing. Sailors are likely to be superstitious, and they were afraid that if they took the compass on

当然，如果天气晴朗的话，水手可以根据太阳或者星星来判断自己的航行方向。不过，假如是阴天，即天气不好的话，他就没有可以参照的东西了。这样一来，水手就跟蒙上了眼睛的小朋友没有什么分别。他很容易迷路，很容易与自己所希望去到的方向背道而驰，并且还浑然不觉呢。

在使用指南针以前，绝大多数水手之所以都不会让船只驶到离陆地太远的海域，一个主要的原因或许就在于此。他们都害怕自己找不到回来的路。因此，绝大部分水手都只到过世界上离陆地不太远的地方。

不过，有了指南针之后，水手们便可以驾船一直航行，并且不管海上是风雨肆虐还是阴云密布，始终都能朝着正确的方向航行了。他们只需按照那枚悬在盒子里的小小磁针所指出的方向来行驶就行了。无论船只转几个圈、拐几次弯，无论船只如何颠簸，这枚小小的磁针始终都会指向北方。当然，水手们并非总是想要向北航行的；但只要知道哪个方向是北，要判断其他方向就很容易了。南方正对着北方，而右手边是东方，左手边则是西方。他们只需掌好舵，让船只始终朝着他们想要前去的方向航行就是了。

然而，过了很久之后，水手们才用上指南针。他们都以为，指南针上被施了某种魔法，所以都不敢去用这种带有魔法的东西。水手们通常都比较迷信；那时的水手都担心，要是把指南针带到船上的话，它可能也会给船只施上魔法，从而给他们带来噩运。

另一种神奇之物，便是火药。

board it might bewitch their ship and bring them bad luck.

The other magic thing was gunpowder.

Never before 1300 had there been such things in Europe as guns or cannons or pistols. All fighting had been done with bows and arrows or swords or spears or with some such weapons. A sword can only be used on a man a few feet away, but with guns an enemy may be killed and walls battered down miles away. After gunpowder was invented, the armor that the old knights wore was of course no longer of any use, for it could not protect them from shot and shell. Gunpowder has changed fighting completely and made war the terrible thing it has become.

Although Marco Polo was supposed to have told about gunpowder and its use in cannons as he had seen it in the East, most people think it was the Arabs who brought the knowledge to Europe. However it happened, we're sure it was in Asia that people first discovered how to put certain ingredients together that resulted in an explosive. It was quite a while, however, before gunpowder was made strong enough to do much damage. In fact, it was over a hundred years before fighting with guns entirely took the place of fighting with bows and arrows in Europe.

在公元1300年之前，欧洲一直都没有步枪、大炮或手枪这样的武器。所有的战争，一直都是用弓箭、刀剑、长矛之类的武器来进行的。刀剑只能杀伤几英尺开外的敌人；而有了枪支，就可以在数英里之外射杀敌人或者轰塌城墙了。发明了火药之后，古时骑士们所披的铠甲自然没有什么用处了，因为它们根本无法保护身穿铠甲的人不受子弹和炮弹的杀伤。火药彻底改变了战争，使得战争变成了一件可怕的事情。

尽管有人认为，马可·波罗提到他在东方国家看到了火药，看到了火药用于大炮的情况，但大多数人都觉得，是阿拉伯人把火药的知识带到了欧洲。不管真相如何，我们都可以肯定，是亚洲人民首先发现了把某些成分混合起来制造成炸药的方法。然而，又过了很久，人们制造的火药才拥有了巨大的破坏力。事实上，又过了一百多年，欧洲各国才不再用弓箭打仗，而是彻底用枪支作战了。

60 Thelon Gest Wart Hate Verwas

Is this another Latin heading?

No, it's English.

Don't you understand English?

It was 1337, and Edward III was king of England. He also owned some land in France, which the French king wanted to take away from him. Edward III decided he wanted to rule France as well as England. He said he was related to the former king of France and had a better right to the country than the one who was ruling. So he started a war to take France, and the war he started lasted more than a hundred years. This is known as the Hundred Years' War and it is:

The Longest War that Ever Was!

The English army sailed over from England and landed in France. The first great battle was fought in 1346 at a little place called Crécy. The English army was on foot and was made up chiefly of the common people. The French army were mostly knights clad in armor on horseback.

60 史上最久的战争

这一章的标题（Thelon Gest Wart Hate Verwas），难道又是拉丁语吗？

不是，这是英语。

你们难道还看不懂英语吗？

这个故事发生在1337年，当时的英国国王是爱德华三世。法国有一部分土地也是他的，可法国国王却想要从他手中夺取这些土地。爱德华三世则决定，他要当英国和法国两国的国王。他说自己是法国前任国王的亲戚，所以比此时的那位法国国王更有权力来当法国的国王。于是，他便发动了一场攻取法国的战争；而这场战争，竟然持续打了一百多年。这场战争，史称"百年战争"，它也是

人类历史上持续时间最久的一场战争！

英军从英格兰乘船渡海，登上了法国的国土。1346年，双方之间爆发了第一场大战，地点则是在一个叫作克雷西的小地方。英军都是徒步进军，并且士兵主要都是由平民组成的。而法军呢，大部分却是骑着战马、身披铠甲的骑士。

The French knights on horseback thought themselves much finer than the common English soldiers who were on foot. The English soldiers, however, used a weapon called the longbow, which shot arrows with terrific force, and they completely whipped the French knights in spite of the fact that the knights were nobles, were trained to be fighters, rode on horses, and were protected by armor.

Cannons were used by the English in this battle for the first time. The cannons, however, did not amount to much nor do very much harm. They were so weak that they simply tossed the cannonballs at the enemy as one might throw a basketball or football. They scared the horses of the French but did little other damage. But this was the beginning of what was before long to be the end of knights and armor and feudalism.

After the battle of Crécy, a horribly contagious disease called *bubonic plague* attacked the people of Europe. It was like the plague in Athens in the Age of Pericles, but this plague did not attack just one city or country. It was supposed to have started in Cathay, and it spread westward until it reached Europe. There was no running away from it. It spread far and wide over the whole land and killed more human beings than any war that has ever been. The bubonic plague was called Black Death, because black spots came out all over the body of anyone who caught it, and he was certain to die within a few hours or a day or two. There was no hope. No medicine had any effect. Many people committed suicide just as soon as they found they had the disease. Many died just from fright, actually "scared to death".

法国那些骑着战马的骑士们都觉得，他们比那些徒步行军的普通英军士兵要优秀得多。然而，英军却有一种叫作"长弓"的武器，能够用强大的力量发射弓箭；因此，尽管法军里的那些骑士都是贵族，都是训练有素的战士，并且骑着战马，又有铠甲护身，可英军还是把法军打了个落花流水。

英军在这场战役中还首次使用了大炮。然而，在此战中大炮却没有发挥出什么作用，也没有给敌人造成很大的伤害。这种大炮发射时的力量都很小，因此向敌人发射炮弹时，情形完全就像是一个人投篮球或者橄榄球那样。虽说炮弹让法军的战马受到了惊吓，但除此之外，却没有什么杀伤力。但这是一个开端；不久之后，火炮便终结了骑士、铠甲的那个时代和封建制度。

克雷西战役之后，欧洲各国人民当中突然爆发了一种可怕的、叫作"腺鼠疫"的传染病。这场瘟疫，就像伯里克利时期雅典爆发的那场瘟疫一样；而这一次，瘟疫袭击的也不只是一个城市或者一个国家。据说此种瘟疫始于元朝，然后向西蔓延，直到欧洲。人们逃无可逃。它席卷了整个欧洲；丧生于这场瘟疫中的人数，比历史上任何一场战争中杀死的人都要多。腺鼠疫又叫"黑死病"，因为感染了这种病的人，全身都会出现黑色的斑点，并且在得病几小时或者一两天之后就一定会死去，没有任何治愈的希望。所有药物都不起作用。许多人在发现自己染上这种疾病之后，马上就自杀了。还有许多人则完全是吓死的，那可是真正的"吓得要命"呢。

这场瘟疫持续了两年的时间，有数百万人受到了感染。欧洲三分之一的人口，都死于这场瘟疫。整座整座城镇的人全都病死了，许多地方甚至没有剩下活人来掩

It lasted two years, and millions upon millions caught the disease. One third of the people of Europe died of it. Whole towns were wiped out, and in many places no one was left to bury the dead. Dead bodies lay where they had fallen — on the street, in the doorway, in the marketplace.

The crops in the fields went to waste, for there was no one to gather them. Horses and cows roamed over the country at will, for there was no one to care for them. The plague attacked even sailors at sea, and ships were found drifting about on the water with not a soul alive left on board, with not even one left to steer the ship.

What if it had killed every last man, woman, and child in the world! What then would have been the future history of the world?

As if there were not enough people dead already, the Hundred Years' War still went on year after year. The soldiers who had fought at Crécy had been dead for years. Their children had grown up, fought, and died; their grandchildren had grown up, fought, and died; and their great grandchildren had done the same; and the English army was still fighting in France. The French prince at that time was very young and weak, and the French were almost in despair — hopeless — because they had no strong leader to help them drive out the English after all these many years.

Now, in a little French village there was living a poor peasant girl, a shepherdess, called Joan of Arc. As she watched her flocks of sheep, she had wonderful visions. She heard voices calling to her, telling her she was the one who must lead the French armies and

埋尸体。大街上、家门口、市场上，到处都是死尸。

　　田野里的庄稼因为无人收割，所以全都白白浪费了。马匹、牛羊在乡间随意流浪，因为没有人来照料它们。这场瘟疫甚至蔓延到了海上的水手当中；一些船只被发现在海上随波逐流，船上没有剩下一个活人，甚至连个掌舵的人都没有了。

　　要是世界上剩下的所有男人、女人和孩子全都染上这种瘟疫而死去的话，那将是多么可怕的情景啊！要是那样的话，世界未来的历史又会是个什么样子呢？

　　但英法两国间的这场"百年战争"却仍然年复一年地进行着，仿佛是死的人还不够多似的。那些在克雷西战役中英勇作战的士兵，都已经死了好多年了。他们的孩子长大后也去打仗，然后也死了；他们的孙子长大后又去打仗，然后也死了；他们的曾孙也一样，可英军仍然还在法国打仗。那时法国的王子还很小，性格也很懦弱，所以法军几乎陷入了绝望的境地，毫无取胜的希望；因为经过这么多年之后，他们再也没有一位强有力的领导人来帮助他们赶走英军了。

　　此时，法国的一座小山村里有一个贫苦的农家小女孩；她是牧羊女，名叫贞德。她在放牧羊群的时候，产生了许多神奇的幻觉。她听到有声音在召唤她，说她是注定要领导法国军队并将法国从英国手中挽救出来的那个人。于是，她便去见王子手下的贵族，将自己看到的幻象告诉他们。可他们一点儿也信不过她，既信不过她的幻觉，也不相信她能够做到自己以为能够做到的那些事情。

　　不过，为了考验她，他们让另一个人假扮法国王子坐到金銮宝座上，而真正的王子则与贵族们站在一旁。然后，他们便宣贞德进殿。贞德进入宫殿后，看了一

save France from England. She went to the prince's nobles and told them her visions. But they did not put any faith in her or her visions, and they did not believe she was able to do the things she thought she could.

To test her, however, they dressed up another man as the prince and put him on the throne while the prince stood at one side with the nobles. Then they let Joan into the room. When Joan entered the royal hall, she gave one look at the man who was seated on the throne and dressed up as the prince. Then without hesitating she walked directly past him and went straight to the real prince. Before him she knelt and said, "I have come to lead your armies to victory." The prince at once gave her his flag and a suit of armor, and she rode out at the head of all the army and had the prince crowned king.

The French soldiers took heart again. It seemed as if the Lord had sent an angel to lead them, and they fought so hard and so bravely that they won many battles.

The English soldiers, however, thought that it was not the Lord but the devil who had sent Joan and that she was not an angel but a witch, and they were very much afraid of her. At last, the English made her prisoner. The French king, whom she had saved, didn't even try to save her, in spite of all she had done for him. Now that things were going his way, he didn't like to have a woman running things, and the soldiers didn't like to have a woman ordering them around, and they were glad to be rid of her.

The English tried her as a witch, judged

眼坐在金銮宝座上、化装成王子的那个人。接着，她便毫不犹豫地径直从那位假王子身边过去，走向真正的王子。她在真王子面前跪下，说："我是来率领您手下的军队走向胜利的。"王子马上便将自己的令旗和一副铠甲交给她，然后贞德便骑马站在法军前面，让王子顺利加冕成了国王。

法国士兵重新鼓起了勇气。似乎是上帝派了一位天使前来领导他们，因此他们都奋勇作战，并且节节取胜。

然而，英军却认为贞德不是上帝派来的，而是魔鬼派来的，认为她不是天使而是巫婆，因此都非常害怕她。最终，英军俘虏了贞德。可她拯救下来的

Joan of Arc at the stake
被处以火刑的圣女贞德

那位法国国王，连想都没想过要去营救她，尽管她为他做了那么多的贡献。由于此时形势对他有利了，法国国王又不喜欢由一位女性来管理国家大事，而法军也不喜欢听一位女性领袖的号令，因此他们都很高兴敌人把贞德除掉呢。

英军把贞德当成女巫进行了审判，判决她犯了施弄巫术之罪，然后就把她绑在

her guilty of being a witch, and then they burned her alive at the stake.

But Joan seemed to have brought the French good luck, to have put new life into their armies, for from that time on, France increased in strength, and, after more than a hundred years of fighting, at last drove the English out of the country. In more than one hundred years of fighting, hundreds of thousands of people had been wounded and crippled and blinded and killed, and after it all England was no better off, just the same as when it started — all the fighting all for nothing.

柱子上活活烧死了。

可贞德似乎给法国带来了好运，似乎已经给法军注入了新的活力；因为从那时起，法国的实力便日益增强，并在经历了长达一百多年的战斗之后，最终将英军赶出了法国。在这场长达一百多年的战争中，有千百万人受伤、致残、致盲或者丧生；而此战之后，英国的情况却没有什么好转，而是与发动这场战争之初的形势没什么两样。可以说，在这场旷日持久的战争中，英国完全是一无所获哩。

61 Print and Powder or Off with the Old, On with the New

Up to this time there was not a printed book anywhere in Europe. There was not a newspaper. There was not a magazine. All books had to be written by hand. This, of course, was extremely slow and expensive, so there were very few of even these handwritten books. Only kings and very wealthy people had any books at all. Such a book as the Bible, for instance, cost almost as much as a house, and so no poor people could own such a thing. Even when there was a Bible in a church, it was so valuable that it had to be chained to keep it from being stolen. Think of stealing a Bible!

Actually, if you remember, the Chinese invented printing. Later, people began to print books in a new way. First the printer put together wooden letters called type, and then smeared them with ink. Then he pressed paper against this inky type and made a copy. After the type was once set up, thousands of copies could be made quickly and easily. Then he could take the letters apart and use them to make the next page. This, as you of course know, was printing. It was printing with movable type. It all seems so simple, the wonder is that no one had thought of this type of printing thousands of years before.

61 印刷术和火药——弃旧迎新

直到此时为止，整个欧洲都还没有一本印刷出来的书籍。这里既没有报纸，也没有杂志。所有书籍都只能用人工进行抄写。自然，人工抄写的速度很慢，而且费用巨大，因此，连这种人工抄写的书籍也很少呢。只有国王或者非常富有的人，才会拥有几本书籍。例如，买一本像《圣经》这样的书，费用几乎跟买一栋房子差不多，因此没有哪个穷人买得起这样的东西。就算是教堂里有一本《圣经》吧，可由于书籍太过贵重，所以也得用链子把书拴住，以免被人偷走才行。想一想吧，竟然有人去偷一本《圣经》！

实际上，如果你们都还记得的话，此时中国人已经发明了印刷术。后来，人们又开始用一种新的办法来印刷书籍了。首先，印刷工将一种叫作"活字"的木质字母集中排列起来，然后将它们全都涂上墨汁。接下来，印刷工又把纸张压在这种沾满了墨汁的活字上面，便制作出了一张影印件。活字一旦排列好顺序，那么复制出成千上万份影印件就很快捷、很轻松了。然后，印刷工又把活字拆散，再用它们去印刷第二页。你们当然都知道，这一过程就是印刷。这一技术，就是活字印刷术。看起来简单得很吧，可奇怪的是，几千年之前却没有人想到过这种印刷方法呢。

人们普遍认为，是一位叫作古登堡的德国人制作出了欧洲的第一本印刷书籍。

It is generally believed that a German named Gutenberg made the first printed book in Europe. And what book do you suppose it was that he printed? Why, the book that people thought to be the most important book in the world — the Bible. It took Gutenberg five years to make such a big book, and he finished it in 1456.

The first dated book printed in England was made by an Englishman named Caxton. It was called *Sayings of the Philosophers*, and was printed in 1477.

Before this time few people, even though they were kings or princes, knew how to read. There were no books to teach them how to read and few books for them to read if they had learned. So what was the use of learning?

You can see how difficult it must have been for people throughout the Middle Ages, without books or newspapers or anything printed, to learn what was going on in the world, or to learn about anything that one wanted to know.

Now that printing had been invented, all that was changed. Storybooks, schoolbooks, and other books could be made in large numbers and more cheaply. People who never before were able to have any books could now own them. People could now read all the famous stories of the world and learn about geography, about history, about anything they wanted to know. The invention of movable type was soon to change everything.

The Hundred Years' War had at last come to an end soon after the invention of printing.

Gutenberg at his press, comparing a printed sheet with a manuscript
古登堡在印刷机旁比对印刷页面与手稿

你们觉得，他印刷出来的，是一本什么样的图书呢？哦，就是人们觉得属于世界上最重要的那本书——《圣经》。古登堡花了五年，才把这本大书印出来；他印完《圣经》的时间，是在1456年。

英国第一本有史可查、印刷出来的图书，是一个叫作卡克斯顿的英国人印制的。那本书叫作《哲人箴言录》，印刷于1477年。

在此以前，就算是国王或王子，也很少有人识字。因为当时根本没有书籍去教他们如何阅读，而就算他们识字，也几乎无书可看啊。因此，他们学会识字又有什么用呢？

你们完全可以看出，由于没有图书、报纸或其他印刷品，因此在整个中世纪，人们要得知世界上发生的事情或者得知一个人想要知道的东西，究竟有多困难。

发明印刷术之后，这一切便都发生了变化。故事书、学校教材和其他书籍都可以大批量地印刷出来，并且成本也要低廉得多了。那些以前买不起书的人，如今买得起了。人们如今也可以阅读到世界上其他国家的著名故事，并且学习到地理、历史以及其他任何想学的知识了。活字印刷术的发明，必将很快地改变一切。

印刷术发明之后不久，"百年战争"也终于结束了。

At the same time something else that was a thousand years old came to an end.

The Muslims, whom we haven't heard of for a long time, had tried to capture Constantinople in the seventh century but had been stopped, as I told you, by tar and pitch that the Christians poured down on them.

Now in 1453 the Muslims once again attacked Constantinople. This time, however, the Muslims were Turks, and they didn't try to batter down the walls of the city with arrows. They used gunpowder and cannon. Against the power of this new invention the walls of Constantinople could not stand, and finally the city fell. Constantinople became Turkish and the magnificent Church of Santa Sophia, which Justinian had built a thousand years before, was turned into a mosque for Muslim worship. This was the end of all that was left of the old Roman Empire — the other half of which had fallen in 476.

Ever after the downfall of Constantinople in 1453, wars were fought with gunpowder. No longer were castles of any use. No longer were knights in armor of any use. No longer were bows and arrows of any use — against this new kind of fighting. There was a new sound in the world, the sound of cannon — firing: "Boom! boom! boom!" Before this, battles had not been very noisy except for shouts of the victors and the moans of the dying. So some people call 1453 the end of the Middle Ages and the beginning of Modern History.

Gunpowder had put an end to the Middle Ages. The invention of printing and that little magic needle, the compass, did a great deal to start what we call Modern History.

与此同时，还有一种历史已达千年之久的东西，也宣告结束了。

我们已经很久没有说起的那些穆斯林，在七世纪的时候曾经想要攻陷君士坦丁堡；但是，我在前面已经跟你们说过，基督徒从城墙之上倒下滚烫的沥青，挡住了这些穆斯林。

到了1453年的时候，穆斯林再一次对君士坦丁堡发动了攻击。然而，这一次进攻的穆斯林是土耳其人，他们并没有想过要用弓箭去把君士坦丁堡的城墙射塌。他们用的是火药和大炮。君士坦丁堡的城墙，根本就承受不起这种新发明的武器的威力，所以该城最终还是陷落了。于是，君士坦丁堡便落到了土耳其人手里，而查士丁尼在一千年前修建的那座辉煌无比的圣索菲亚教堂，也变成了穆斯林做礼拜的清真寺。这就结束了古罗马帝国留下来的一切；而古罗马帝国的另一半，早在公元476年就灭亡了。

自1453年君士坦丁堡陷落后，战争便一直是用火药来进行的了。城堡再也没有用处，身披铠甲的骑士再也没有用处，而弓箭在这种新型的战争中再也没有任何用处了。世界上出现了一种新的声音，那就是大炮开火时的轰鸣："轰隆！轰隆！轰隆！"此前，交战时的声音并不大，只有胜利者的欢呼声和垂死者的呻吟声。因此，有些人认为1453年就是中世纪结束、现代历史发端的一年。

火药终结了中世纪。而印刷术的发明，以及那根小小的、称为"指南针"的魔针，则极大地促进了我们所称的现代历史的发展。

62 A Sailor Who Found a New World

What book do you like best?

Alice in Wonderland?

Gulliver's Travels?

One of the first books to be printed and one that children at that time liked best was

The Travels of Marco Polo.

One of the boys who loved to read these stories of those far-away countries of Asia with their gold and precious jewels was an Italian named Christopher Columbus. Christopher Columbus was born in the city of Genoa, which is in the top of the *boot*. Like a great many other boys who were born in seaport towns, he had heard the sailors on the wharves tell yarns of their travels, and his greatest ambition in life was to go off to sea and visit all the wonderful lands of which he had read and been told. At last the chance came, and, though only fourteen years old, he made his first voyage. After that, Columbus made many other voyages and grew to be a middle-aged man, but he never got to the countries he had

62　发现新大陆的水手

你们最喜欢看的是什么书呢？

是《爱丽丝梦游仙境》？

还是《格列佛游记》呢？

在人类印刷出来的第一批图书中，当时的小朋友最喜欢看的就是：

《马可·波罗游记》。

游记当中那些故事所讲述的，都是遥远的亚洲各国黄金遍地、奇珍异宝无数的情况；而在喜欢看这些故事的男孩子当中，有一位意大利的小朋友，名叫克里斯托弗·哥伦布。克里斯托弗·哥伦布出生于热那亚，该地位于意大利这只"靴子"的顶上。与许多出生于海港城市的小朋友一样，他曾听码头上的水手们讲述过许多的游历奇闻，因此他人生最大的梦想便是乘船出海，去看一看自己读到过、听到过的所有神奇国度。后来，机会来了；尽管当时还只有十四岁，可他却开始了自己的首次航海。那一次之后，哥伦布又进行过多次航海，年纪也慢慢进入了中年；不过，他却一直没有去过自己在《马可·波罗游记》中读到过的那些国度。

read about in *The Travels of Marco Polo*.

Many sea captains of that time were trying to find a shorter way to India than the long and tiresome one that Marco Polo had taken. They felt sure there was a shorter way by sea, and now that they had the compass to guide them, they dared to go far off searching for such a waterway.

By this time many books had already been printed. Some of these books on travel were written by the old Greeks and Romans. Some had been written by Arabs. The navigators knew that the world was round, even though some uneducated medieval folk believed it to be flat. Columbus had read these books and he said to himself that if the world is really round, one should be able to reach India by sailing toward the west. It should be much easier and shorter that way than if one took a boat to the end of the Mediterranean Sea and then went over land for thousands of miles the way Marco Polo had gone.

The more Columbus thought of the idea, the surer he was that this could be done and the more eager he was to get a ship to try out his idea. Of course, being only a sailor, he had no money to buy or hire a ship in which to make the trials and he could find no one to help him.

First Columbus went to the little country called Portugal. Portugal was right on the ocean's edge. It was to be expected then that the people of Portugal would be famous sailors, and they were — as famous as the Phoenicians had been of old. Columbus thought they might be interested and help. Besides, the king of Portugal was extremely interested

那个时候，许多船长都在试图寻找一条通往印度，比马可·波罗曾经走的那条又漫长又烦人的线路更短的航线。他们确定有一条较短的海上航线；而有了指南针来导航之后，他们便敢于走得更远，去找出这样的一条水路了。

到了这个时候，人们已经印刷出了很多的书籍。那些关于游历的书籍中，有一些是古希腊人和古罗马人写的。有一些则是阿拉伯人写的。尽管一些没有受过教育的中世纪人以为地球是平的，但当时的那些航海家却都明白地球是圆的。哥伦布阅读了这些书籍后，便在心里想：如果地球的确是圆的，那么人们向西航行的话，应当也能到达印度。与乘船到达地中海的一端，然后再像马可·波罗那样从陆路千里迢迢地前往印度相比，向西的那条航线航行起来将会更加容易，航程也会更短的。

哥伦布对这个问题考虑得越多，就越确信这种想法可行，也越发渴望获得一条船只去验证这个想法。当然，由于他只是一名水手，因此他既没有钱去买下或租用一条船来尝试，也找不到人来帮助他。

哥伦布首先来到了葡萄牙这个小国。葡萄牙正好临近大西洋。可以预见，那时的葡萄牙人应该都是大大有名的水手，而他们也的确如此，就像古时的腓尼基人那样有名。因此，哥伦布认为葡萄牙人可能会有兴趣，从而为他提供帮助。除此之外，当时的葡萄牙国王也对发现新的土地极感兴趣哩。

然而，葡萄牙国王却像其他人那样，认为哥伦布是个傻瓜，因而不愿和他打交道。不过，那位国王还想要完全确认，哥伦布的那种想法毫无意义。此外，就算世界上存在新的大陆，国王也希望由自己去发现呢。因此，他便偷偷地派了手下的一

in discovering new lands.

But the king of Portugal thought, as the others did, that Columbus was foolish and would have nothing to do with him. The king wanted to make quite sure, however, that there was nothing in Columbus's idea. Furthermore, if there were any new land, he wanted to be the first to discover it himself. So he secretly sent some of his sea captains off to explore. After a while they one and all returned and stated that they had been as far as it was safe to go, and that positively there was nothing at all to the west but water, water, water.

Columbus in disgust then went to the next country — Spain — which at that time was ruled by King Ferdinand and his Queen Isabella. King Ferdinand and Queen Isabella were just then too busy to listen to Columbus. They were fighting with the Muslims, who had been in Spain ever since 732, when, you remember, they got as far north as France. At last Ferdinand and Isabella succeeded in driving the Muslims out of their country, and then Queen Isabella became very much interested in Columbus's ideas and plans and finally promised to help him. She even said she would sell her jewels, if necessary, to give him the money to buy ships. So Columbus, with her help, was able to buy three little ships named the *Niña*, *Pinta*, and Santa Maria. So small were these three boats that nowadays we would be afraid to go even out of sight of shore in them.

At last everything was ready, and Columbus set sail from the Spanish seaport of Palos with about a hundred sailors. Directly toward the setting sun into the broad Atlantic,

些船长去探险。不久之后，船长们便一个接一个地返回来，说他们已经在安全许可的程度内尽可能地远航了；并且，他们都极其肯定地报告说，西方什么也没有，只有海水、海水、还是海水。

哥伦布非常厌恶葡萄牙国王的做法，便来到了下一个国家，即西班牙；当时，统治西班牙的是斐迪南国王和伊莎贝拉王后。斐迪南国王和伊莎贝拉王后那时都太忙，根本就没有时间来听取哥伦布的想法。他们当时正在与穆斯林交战，那些穆斯林自公元732年以来就一直留在西班牙；你们应该都还记得吧，他们曾经向北远征到了法国呢。最后，斐迪南国王和伊莎贝拉王后成功地将这些穆斯林赶出了自己的国家；而接下来，伊莎贝拉王后便对哥伦布的想法和计划产生了很大的兴趣，并且最终答应帮助他。她甚至还说，如果有必要的话，她可以卖掉自己的珠宝首饰，然后把钱交给哥伦布去购买船只呢。因此，哥伦布在她的帮助之下，购买了三艘小船，分别叫作"尼娜号""平塔号"和"圣玛利亚号"。这三艘船都非常小；要是如今我们去乘坐的话，可能都不敢驶到岸上看不见的地方去呢。

一切终于就绪之后，哥伦布便率领大约一百名水手，从西班牙的帕洛斯港起航了。哥伦布亲自掌舵，径直朝着日落的方向，驶入了茫茫的大西洋。他驾船驶过了加纳利群岛，然后一直往前，夜以继日，始终朝着同一个方向航行。

看你们能不能理解这样一种观点吧，那就是：整个世界上，只存在到此时为止我们一直都在研究的那些地方。那个时候，除了极少数人，几乎每个人都是这样想的哩。请试着忘记你们已经听说过的那些关于南北美洲的知识吧。那时的人，当然还

Columbus steered. Past the Canary Islands he sailed, on and on, day and night, always in the same direction.

See if you can get this idea — the idea that almost everyone had at that time except a few Scandinavians — that all there was of the world was what we have so far been studying about. Try to forget that you ever heard of North and South America. They, of course, knew of no such lands. Try to think of Columbus on deck scanning the waves in the daytime or peering off in the darkness at night, hoping sooner or later to sight, not a new land — he wasn't looking for a new land — but for China or India.

Columbus had been out for over a month, and his sailors began to get worried. It seemed impossible that any sea could be so vast, so endless, with nothing in sight before, behind, or on either side. They began to think about returning. They began to be afraid they would never reach home. They begged Columbus to turn back. They said it was crazy to go any farther; there was nothing but water ahead of them, and they could go on forever and ever, and there would never be anything else.

Columbus argued with them, but it was no use. Finally he promised to turn back if they did not reach something very soon. As the days went on still with nothing new, the sailors plotted to throw Columbus overboard at night and so get rid of him. They would then sail home and tell those back in Spain that Columbus had fallen overboard by accident.

At last, when all had given up hope except Columbus, a sailor saw a branch with berries on it floating in the water. Where could it have come from? Then birds were seen flying —

不知道有这两处大陆存在。请试着想象一下哥伦布白天站在甲板上观察洋流，或者夜里在黑暗中瞪大眼睛眺望，希望自己看到的并不是一处新大陆时的情形吧；因为他一心寻找的，并不是一处新大陆，而是中国或者印度啊。

哥伦布率船出海一个多月后，他手下的水手们都开始担心起来。世界上似乎不可能有一个海洋会如此辽阔广袤，会如此无边无际，会前后左右全都望不到头哩。他们开始打退堂鼓，想掉头回去。他们开始害怕，担心自己再也回不了家。他们请求哥伦布掉头回去。他们说，再往前走就是疯了；前面除了茫茫的海水，什么也没有，因此他们可能会永远向前航行下去，却永远什么也找不到呢。

哥伦布与他们据理力争，但毫无用处。最后他只得答应说，如果他们不能很快到达什么地方，那就掉头回去。随着日子一天天过去，情况却毫无变化，于是那些水手们便密谋，准备哪天晚上把哥伦布丢下船去，从而除掉他。然后，他们便可以起航回家，并告诉西班牙国内的人，说哥伦布是意外掉下了船。

最后，到了所有的人都不再抱有希望、只有哥伦布除外的时候，一名水手却看到海面上漂着一根枝条，上面还结着浆果。这根枝条是从哪儿来的呢？接下来，他们又看到空中有小鸟在飞；小鸟一向都是不会飞得离岸边太远的。然后，在一个漆黑的夜晚，在起航两个多月后，他们终于看到前边远远地有微弱的灯光在闪烁。很可能，世间再也没有哪种微弱的灯光，能像此时这样令他们欣喜若狂了。灯光只意味着一件事情，那就是有人类，以及陆地。陆地，终于看到陆地了！1492年10月12日清晨，他们那三条船终于靠岸了。哥伦布跳下船，双膝跪地，喃喃祈祷，感谢上

birds that never get very far away from shore. Then one dark night, more than two months after they had set sail, they saw far off ahead a twinkling light. Probably no little light ever gave so much joy in the world. A light meant only one thing — human beings — and land, land — land at last! On the morning of October 12, 1492, the three boats ran ashore. Columbus leaped out, and falling on his knees, offered up a prayer of thanks to God. He then raised the Spanish flag, took possession of the land in the name of Spain, and called it *San Salvador*, which means in Spanish, Holy *Saviour*.

Now, Columbus thought this land was India or nearby islands called the Indies that he had at last reached, though of course we know now that two great continents, North and South America, blocked his way to India. In fact, he had only landed on a little island in the Bahamas off the coast of America.

Columbus and his sailors soon saw that people lived on this island. Columbus claimed the land for Spain. You may wonder how he thought he could do this when the land obviously already belonged to the people living there. One reason was that in those days, Europeans thought that if people were not Christians, then they had no rights. And so Columbus believed that he could simply take over their country and call it his own. Besides that, he hoped that someday the new land might make him rich.

Since Columbus thought that he had reached India, he called the people he found on the island Indians. *We*, of course, know that they were really Native Americans and not Indians. And *we* know that Native Americans had been living there for many centuries

帝。然后，他升起西班牙国旗，以西班牙的名义占领了这片土地，称之为"圣萨尔瓦多"，它在西班牙语里就是"圣救世主"的意思。

当时，哥伦布以为自己最终到达的这片大陆就是印度，或者是距印度不远的所谓"东印度群岛"；但如今我们当然清楚，有两个大陆，即北美洲和南美洲，挡住了他前往印度的去路。实际上，他到达的，不过是位于美洲沿海的巴哈马群岛中的一个小岛罢了。

哥伦布和他率领的水手，很快便看到了生活在这个岛屿上的人。哥伦布宣布，这片土地归西班牙所有。你们可能会觉得奇怪，他怎么会觉得自己有权这样做，因为那片土地显然早就属于那些生活在当地的人了。其中的一个原因，就是在那个时候，欧洲人认为凡是不属基督徒的人都没有任何权利。因此，哥伦布觉得，他完全可以占领这些人的国家，将其据为己有。除此之外，他还指望着这片新的土地将来会让他变成富翁呢。

由于哥伦布以为自己已经到达印度，所以他把自己在这座小岛上看到的人称为印第安人。我们如今当然知道，这些人其实是真正的美洲土著，而不是印度人。我们也知道，这些真正的美洲土著，在哥伦布还没有想起要向大西洋起航之前，早就在这里生活数百年的时间了。

哥伦布接着前往附近的其他岛屿；可他并没有如愿以偿，几乎没有找到黄金和宝石，也没有看到马可·波罗所描述的那种种奇观。由于出海远航已经很久了，因此他便开始沿着来时的航线，动身返回西班牙。他带了几名美洲土著回去给国内的

before Columbus even thought of sailing out into the Atlantic.

Columbus went on to other islands nearby; but he found very little gold and few precious stones such as he had expected, or the wonders that Marco Polo had described; and as he had been away so long, he started back again to Spain the way he had come. With him he took several Native Americans to show the people at home, and also some tobacco, which he found them smoking and which no one in Europe had even seen or heard of before.

When he at last reached home safely again, people were overjoyed at seeing him and hearing of his discoveries. Everyone was wildly excited — but only for a while. People soon began to say it was nothing for Columbus to have sailed westward until land was found, that anyone could do that.

One day when Columbus was dining with the king's nobles, who were trying to belittle what he had done, he took an egg and, passing it around the table, asked each one if he could stand it on end. No one could. When it came back to Columbus, he set it down just hard enough to crack the end slightly and flatten it. Of course, *then* it stood up. "You see," said Columbus, "it's very easy if you only know how. So it's easy enough to sail west until you find land after I have done it once and shown you how."

人看，还带了一些烟草；他发现美洲土著都吸烟，而欧洲人以前既没看到过，也没听说过烟草这种东西呢。

待他最终安然无恙地回到西班牙后，人们见到他、听到他说起自己的发现时都非常高兴。大家都欣喜若狂；可这种狂热，却只持续了一阵子。人们很快就开始说，向西航行、发现新大陆的功劳其实与哥伦布毫不相干，任何人都做得到。

有一天，哥伦布正在陪国王手下的贵族们吃饭，那些贵族都试图贬低哥伦布的功劳；这时，他拿起一个鸡蛋，让在座的每个人都看一看，问他们当中有哪一个能够把鸡蛋立起来。没有人做得到。而当鸡蛋传回哥伦布那里后，他拿起鸡蛋在桌子上轻轻一敲，把一头敲平。

Columbus arguing with his crew
哥伦布与他手下的船员据理力争

自然，他随后就把鸡蛋立起来了。"你们看，"哥伦布说，"如果掌握诀窍，做起来就非常容易。所以，只有在我做过一次，告诉你们怎样做之后，你们向西航行并发现新的土地才变得容易得很。"

哥伦布后来又向美洲大陆航行了三次，也就是说，他总共进行了四次航海；不

Columbus made three other voyages to America, four in all, but he never knew he had reached the Americas. Once he landed in South America, but he never reached the mainland of North America.

As Columbus did not bring back any of the precious jewels or wonderful things that those in Spain expected him to, people lost interest in him. Some were so spiteful and jealous of his success that they even charged him with wrongdoing, and King Ferdinand sent out a man to take his place. Columbus was put in chains and shipped home. Although he was promptly set free, Columbus kept the chains as a reminder of men's ingratitude and asked to have them buried with him. After this, Columbus made one other voyage, but when at last he died in Spain, he was alone and almost forgotten even by his friends. What an end for the man who had once been such a hero!

Of all the people of whom we have heard, whether kings or queens, princes or emperors, none can compare with Columbus. Alexander the Great, Julius Caesar, Charlemagne, were all killers. They took away. But Columbus *gave*. He gave us a new world. Without money or friends or luck, he stuck to his ideas through long years of discouragement. Although made fun of and called a crank and even treated as a criminal he never

> gave up,
>> gave out, nor
>>> gave in!

过，他始终都不知道自己到达的是美洲。有一次他曾经登上了南美洲，可他一直都没有到达过北美大陆。

由于哥伦布没有带回西班牙人所期待的宝石和神奇之物，所以人们对他便没有了兴趣。有些人因为非常嫉妒他的成就，甚至还指控他有不法行为，于是斐迪南国王便派人取代了他的职位。哥伦布被五花大绑地送回了国内。尽管随后就被释放了，但哥伦布却把捆绑自己的锁链留了下来，时时提醒自己注意人们的忘恩负义，并且要求死后将这条锁链与自己葬在一起。这件事情过后，哥伦布还进行过一次航海；可最后他在西班牙去世时，却孑然一身，连朋友们都差不多忘记了他。这位曾经的英雄人物，结局又是多么的悲凉啊！

我们前面提到的那些人里面，无论是国王、王后，还是王子或者皇帝，都没有人能够与哥伦布相提并论。亚历山大大帝、恺撒大帝、查理曼大帝，都是些嗜杀成性的人。他们都四处掠夺。可哥伦布所做的，却是给予。他给了我们一个新的世界。尽管没有钱、没有朋友，运气也不好，但他在漫长的岁月中却毫不气馁，一直坚持着自己的理想。尽管被人嘲笑、被人称为怪物，甚至被人当成罪犯对待，可他却从不

> 放弃、
>> 泄气，也从不
>>> 屈服！

63 Fortune Hunters

The New World had no name. It was simply called *the New World*, as one might speak of *the new baby*.

It had to have a name, but what should it be? Of course if we could have chosen the name, we should have called it *Columbia* after Columbus. But another name was selected, and this is how it happened.

An Italian named Americus Vespucci made a voyage to the southern part of the New World. Then he wrote a book about his travels. People read his book and began to speak of the new land that Americus described as Americus's country. The New World came to be called America after Americus, although in all fairness it should have been named after Columbus; don't you think so? Children sometimes have names given them which they would like to change when they grow up. But then it is too late. We sometimes speak and sing of our country as Columbia, although that is not the name on the map. We call a great many cities and towns and districts and streets Columbus or Columbia in memory of Christopher Columbus.

After Columbus had shown that there was no danger of falling off the world and that

63　淘金的人

哥伦布发现的那个新世界，当时并没有命名。人们只是称它为"新大陆"，就像一个人提到"新生儿"那样。

这处新大陆必须有一个名称才是，可应当给它起一个什么样的名称呢？如果可以选择的话，我们当然会用哥伦布的名字，将它称为"哥伦比亚"。但事实上，人们选择的却是另一个名称；下面，我们就来说说这是怎么回事。

有一位名叫阿美利哥·维斯普奇的意大利人，曾经航海到达过这个新大陆的南部。后来，他将自己的游历写成了一本书。人们看了他的这本书后，在谈到阿美利哥描述的这处大陆时，便开始将它称为"阿美利哥之国"了。于是，人们便用阿美利哥的名字，给这个新大陆命了名；可凭良心说，其实应当用哥伦布的名字来命名才对。你们觉得，是不是这样呢？有的时候，小朋友们会不喜欢家长给自己起的名字，想长大以后再改名。可长大后，却已经太迟了。虽说我国（编者注，作者为美国人，故称我国）在地图上的名称是"美国"，但我们有时也会将美国说成或者唱成"哥伦比亚"啊。为了纪念哥伦布，我们还将许许多多的城市、小镇、地区和街道，全都命名为"哥伦布"或者"哥伦比亚"呢。

哥伦布的航海行为表明，人们不会有从世界的边缘掉下去的危险，并且遥远的

there really was land off to the west, almost everyone who had been hunting for India now rushed off in the direction Columbus had taken. "Copy cats!" A genius starts something; then thousands follow — imitate. Every sea captain who could do so now hurried off to the west to look for new countries, and so many discoveries were made that this time is known as the Age of Discovery. Most of these men were trying to get to India. They were after gold and jewels and spices, which they thought they would find in India in great quantities.

西方确实存在大陆；故自此以后，几乎每一个一直在寻找印度的人，便都急忙沿着哥伦布所航行的方向而去了。"真是东施效颦啊！"天才开创出某种东西来，然后成千上万的人便会去仿效，即模仿。因此，每一位有这本领的船长，此时便都一拥而上，赶紧往西航行，去寻找新的国度了；由于人们有了诸多发现，所以这一时期便被称为"大发现时代"。这些人当中的绝大多数，原本都是想要前往印度的。他们寻找的，是黄金、珠宝和香料；他们还以为，这些东西在印度遍地都是哩。

Map shows limited European knowledge of the continent. Compare with map in story 65.
这张地图表明，欧洲人对非洲大陆的了解非常有限。将它与第65章中的地图比较一下。

（图中文字：hispania：伊比利亚半岛；Gades：加的斯；Granat：格拉纳达；Sardinia：撒丁岛；Mare mediterrancum：地中海；Malta：马耳他；Sicilia：西西里岛；Syros：锡罗斯岛；Magna：麦格纳；Candia：干地亚；Cyprus：塞浦路斯；Mauri：毛里；M. Vimea：比梅斯山；Cyrene：昔兰尼；Marmaried：马尔马里；Alexandria：亚历山大；ÆGYPTUS：埃及；Syene：色耶尼；Niles R.：尼罗河；Syria：叙利亚；ARABIA deserea：阿拉伯沙漠；Medina：麦地那；ARABIA Pelrea：阿拉伯半岛；ARABIA Felix：阿拉伯福地；Mare Rubru：红海；Insole Canariae：内加那利群岛；Capul Viride：佛得角群岛；Nigritæ：尼日尔部落；Oara M.：奥拉山；Garamantes：加拉曼特人；LIBYA Interior：利比亚内陆；Regnum MELLI：梅里王国；LIBYA desertum：利比亚沙漠；REGNUM Orguene：奥奎尼王国；NVBIAE Regnum：努比亚王国；Monoculi：摩罗古里；REGNVM Habesin：哈比辛王国；REGNVM de Seylam：塞兰姆王国；QVIOLA Regnum：奎奥拉王国；AFRICÆ extremitas：非洲之角；Zapanala aurisodina：赞普纳拉奥里索迪那；Vasco da gama：瓦斯科·达·伽马；15th century map of Africa：15 世纪的非洲地图）

Now we can understand why people might go long distances in search of gold and precious stones, but they also went after spices — such as cloves and pepper — and you may wonder why they were so eager to get spices. You yourself may not like pepper very much, and you may dislike cloves. But in those days they didn't have refrigerators, and meats and other foods were often spoiled. We would have thought such food unfit to eat. However, they covered it with spices to kill the bad flavor, and then food could be eaten that otherwise one could not have swallowed. Spices didn't grow in Europe — only in warmer countries. People paid big prices to get them, and that is why men made long journeys after them.

A Portuguese sailor named Vasco da Gama was one of those who were trying to get to India all the way by water. He did not, however sail west as Columbus had done, but *south* down around Africa. Others had tried before to get to India by going south and around Africa but none had gone more than part way. Many frightful stories were told by those who had tried but had at last turned back. These stories were like the tales of Sinbad the Sailor. They said that the sea became boiling hot; they said that there was a magnetic mountain which would pull out the iron bolts in the ship, and the ship would then fall to pieces; they said there was a whirlpool into which a ship would be irresistibly drawn — down, down, down to the bottom; they said there were sea serpents, monsters so large that they could swallow a ship at one gulp. The southern point of Africa was called the Cape of Storms, and the very name seemed to be bad luck, so that it was changed to the Cape of Good Hope.

　　如今，对于当时的人不远千里地去寻找黄金和宝石这一点，我们是能够理解的；可他们同时也在寻找香料，比如丁香和胡椒。你们可能会觉得奇怪，他们为什么会那么渴望得到香料呢？你们自己可能很喜欢胡椒，却不喜欢丁香呢。但在那个时候，人们没有冰箱，所以肉类和其他食物经常会变质、坏掉。我们会觉得，这种变了质的东西是吃不得的。然而，当时的人却会用香料将异味去除，这样一来，变了质的食物也可以吃了；否则的话，它们就会让人难以下咽。欧洲种不了香料，香料只能生长在气候较为温暖的国家。当时的人都是花大价钱去购买香料；而他们之所以不远万里地去寻找香料，原因也正在于此。

　　一位名叫达·伽马的葡萄牙水手，正是那些试图通过水路到达印度的人当中的一个。然而，他并没有像哥伦布那样向西航行，而是向南，绕过非洲航行。别的航海家以前也曾经尝试过向南航行，想要绕过非洲前往印度，可他们全都是半途而废。那些尝试过这条航线，可最终还是掉头回来了的人，讲述了许多可怕的故事。这些故事，就像《辛巴达历险记》中的传说一样。他们说，大海会变得像开了锅一样滚烫；他们说，海上有一座巨大的磁山，会把船上的铁制螺钉全都吸走，这样一来，船只就会解体；他们说，海上有一个巨大的旋涡，一艘船会毫无抵抗之力地被它吸沉，一直吸到旋涡的底下去；他们还说，海上有海蛇，那是一种巨大的怪兽，一口就能吞掉一艘船呢。非洲最南端的那个海角，原本叫作"风暴角"；可由于这个名字听上去不吉利，于是人们便将它改成了"好望角"。

　　尽管有那么多骇人听闻的故事，达·伽马还是继续向南航行。在经历了千辛

In spite of all such scary stories, Vasco da Gama kept on his way south. Finally, after many hardships and many adventures, he passed around the Cape of Good Hope. He sailed on to India, got the spices that were so highly prized, and returned safely home. This was in 1497, five years after Columbus's first voyage, and Vasco da Gama was the first modern European to go to India by water.

There's one thing you always have to remember about these *discoveries*. That is this — that there were *some* people who did know about these places all along! The Native Americans knew about America. The Scandinavians or Vikings did, too. The Indians knew about India and so, you will soon see, did a lot of other people.

England did not want to be left out of the search for new wealth across the ocean. In the same year that Vasco da Gama reached India, a man named John Cabot set sail from England on a voyage of discovery. His first trip was a failure,

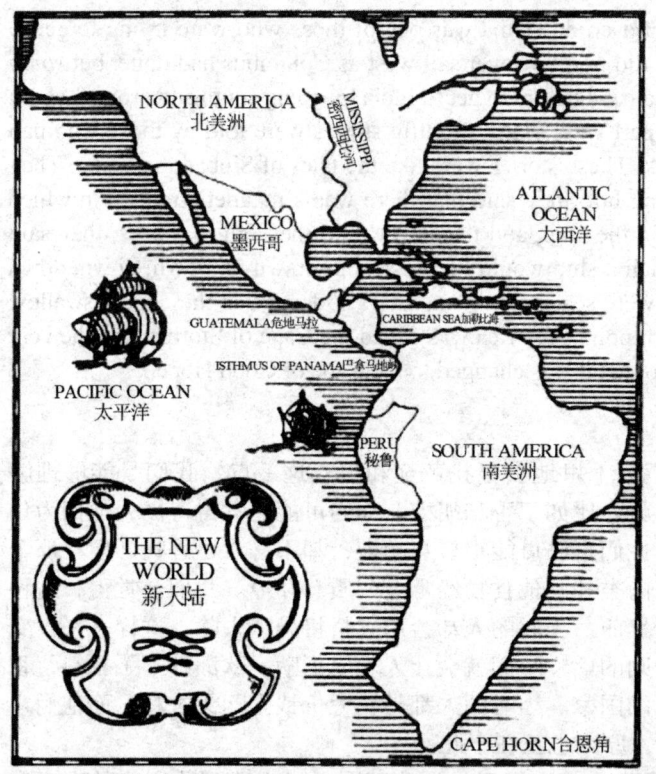

Americas drawn from a map in 1570.
Compare with two maps in story 78.
1570年绘制的一幅地图上的南、北美洲。
将它们与第78章中的两幅地图比较一下。

万苦和许多次动人心魄的冒险之后，他最终绕过了好望角。然后，他继续航行，抵达了印度，得到了当时价格极为昂贵的香料，并且安全地返回了国内。这次航海，是在1497年进行的，也就是在哥伦布首次航海的五年之后；而达·伽马也成了经由水路前往印度的第一位现代欧洲人。

在这些发现当中，有一个方面你们必须始终牢记才行。那就是：当时有一些人，自始至终都很了解这些地方！美洲的土著自始至终都很了解美洲。印度人自始至终都很了解印度；而你们很快也会看到，其他许多民族对自己的故土也都是了如指掌呢。

英国可不想任由别的国家跨越大西洋去寻找新财富，而自己却置身事外。就在达·伽马抵达印度的同一年，一位名叫约翰·卡伯特的人从英国起航，开始了自己的航海发现。虽说他的第一次航海以失败而告终，但他又试了一次，最后抵达了

but he tried again and finally came to Canada and sailed along the coast of what is now the United States. These countries he claimed for England, but he returned home, and England did nothing more about his discoveries until about a hundred years later.

Another Spaniard, named Balboa, explored the central part of America. He was on the little strip of land that joined Central and South America which we now call the Isthmus of Panama. Suddenly he came to another great ocean. This strange new ocean he named the South Sea, for although the Isthmus of Panama connects Central and South America, it bends so that one looks *south* over the ocean.

Then came the longest trip of all. A Portuguese named Magellan wanted to find a way to India *through* the New World, for he thought there must be some opening through which he might pass this new land that blocked the way. He tried to get his own country to help him. Again Portugal made the same mistake it had made in the case of Columbus. The Portuguese government would not listen to Magellan. So Magellan went to Spain, and Spain gave him five ships.

With these five ships, Magellan sailed off across the sea. When he reached South America, he sailed south along the shore, trying to find a passage through the land. One place after another seemed to be the passage for which he was looking, but each one turned out to be nothing but a river's mouth. Then one of his ships was wrecked, and only four were left.

With these four ships, he still kept on down the coast until he finally reached what is

加拿大，并且沿着如今美国所在的海岸航行过。虽说他宣布这些土地全都归英国所有，但他后来回了国；而英国也直到大约一百年之后，才对他的这些发现有所行动。

还有一位叫作巴尔沃亚的西班牙人，则到中美洲地区进行了探险。当时，他来到了连接中美洲和南美洲的那片窄窄的大陆上，如今我们将那里叫作巴拿马地峡。突然之间，他又进入了另一个浩瀚的大洋之中。他将这个新发现的奇怪海洋命名为"南海"，因为尽管巴拿马地峡将中美洲和南美洲连了起来，但这条地峡却是弯的，因此从地峡上看去，这个大洋就是在南面。

接下来，就出现了当时距离最远的一次航海。一位名叫麦哲伦的葡萄牙人想找出一条穿过新大陆到达印度的航线来；因为他觉得，必定存在着某个出口，他也可以经由这个出口，越过阻住他去路的那个新大陆。他千方百计地要得到祖国的协助。可葡萄牙君主却又像对待哥伦布那样，犯了同样的错误。葡萄牙政府不愿听取麦哲伦的意见。于是，麦哲伦便去了西班牙，而西班牙给了他五艘船。

有了这五艘船，麦哲伦便开始起航去横渡大西洋了。到达南美洲之后，他又沿着美洲海岸向南航行，试图找出一条穿过这片大陆的水道。他们来到了一个又一个地方，起初这些地方似乎都是他正在寻找的那种水道，可最终却表明，每一处都不是，每一处都是河流的入海口。后来，他手下有一艘船失了事，因此他就只剩四艘船了。

率领着这四艘船，他继续沿着海岸向南航行，最终抵达了如今的合恩角。他率

now Cape Horn. Through the dangerous opening there, since called after him the Straits of Magellan, he worked his way. One ship deserted and went back home the way it had come. Only three were then left.

With these three ships, he at last came into the great ocean on the other side, the same ocean that Balboa had called the South Sea. This Magellan named the *Pacific*, which means *calm*, because after all the storms they had had, it seemed so calm and quiet. However, food and water became scarce and finally gave out. Magellan's men suffered terribly from thirst and hunger and even ate the rats that are always to be found on shipboard. Many of his men were taken sick and died. Still he kept on, though he had lost most of the crew with whom he had set out. At last he reached what are now the Philippine Islands. Here he and his men got into a battle with the local people, and Magellan was killed. There were now not enough men left to sail three ships, and so one of these was burned, and only two were then left.

Two of the ships, however, of the five with which Magellan had started, still kept on. Then one of these was lost, disappeared and was never heard of again, and only a single ship, named the *Victoria*, remained. It seemed as if not one

From an old print of Magellan's Victoria
麦哲伦所率"维多利亚号"的一幅古老版画

领船队,奋力通过了这个危险重重的地方;此后,这个地方便根据他的名字,被命名为麦哲伦海峡。其中有一艘船开了小差,沿着来时的航线返回了西班牙。这样一来,他就只剩下三艘船了。

率领着这三艘船,他最终驶入了美洲西侧那个广袤的海洋,也就是巴尔沃亚称之为"南海"的那个大洋之中。麦哲伦将这个大洋命名为"太平洋";"太平"的意思就是"平静",因为他们经历了麦哲伦海峡的狂风暴雨之后,这个大洋看上去风平浪静,显得非常的平和温驯。然而,他们的食物和淡水越来越少,最后全部用完了。麦哲伦手下的人饥渴难耐,连甲板上经常出没的老鼠都被他们抓来吃掉了。他手下的许多水手都染上了疾病,一个个地死去。尽管起航时那些船员中的大部分人都不在了,但他还是继续坚持航行。最后,他们到达了如今的菲律宾群岛。在这里,他和手下的人与当地人打了一仗,麦哲伦也在战斗中被敌人杀了。此时,剩下的人手不够再驾驶三艘船只,他们便烧掉了其中的一艘,所以只剩下两艘了。

然而,麦哲伦出发时所率的五艘船只中幸存下来的这两艘船,却依然继续着自己的航程。接下来,其中的一艘迷了路,消失在茫茫的大海中,且此后再也没有任何音讯了;因此,他们就只剩下了一艘船,只有那艘名叫"维多利亚号"的船了。当时,似乎不会有一艘船、一个人幸存下来,也不会有幸存者去给人们讲述这段传

ship, not one man, would be left to tell the tale.

Around Africa the *Victoria* struggled. Magellan's men, worn out with hunger and cold and hardships, still battled against wind and storm. At last a leaky and broken ship with only eighteen men sailed into the harbor from which it had set out more than three years before. Thus the *Victoria* — *Victory*! — Magellan's ship, but without Magellan — was the first ship to sail completely around the world. This voyage settled forever the argument that had been going on for ages, whether the earth was round or flat for a ship had actually sailed around the world! In spite of this proof, for many more years thereafter, there were people who still would not believe the world was round.

奇故事了。

　　"维多利亚号"奋力绕过了非洲。虽然麦哲伦手下的人都被饥饿、寒冷和艰难险阻折磨得筋疲力尽，但他们还是英勇地同狂风暴雨、滔天巨浪进行着斗争。最后，这艘千疮百孔、又破又漏的船，带着仅存的十八人，终于驶入了三年多前起航的那个港口。这样，"维多利亚号"就成了世界上第一艘进行环球航行的船只；麦哲伦手下的这艘船，虽然没有了麦哲伦的领导，却还是取得了胜利！这次航海，解决了人们长久以来一直争论不休的一个问题，那就是地球究竟是圆的还是平的；因为，有一艘船实实在在围着地球航行了一圈！不过，尽管有了这一证据，但在此后更长的一段时间里，却还是有人认为地球不是圆的呢。

64 The Land of Enchantment or the Search for Gold and Adventure

All sorts of marvelous tales were told about the wealth and wonders of the New World.

It was said that somewhere in the New World there was a *Fountain of Youth*, and that if you bathed in it or drank of its water, you would become young again.

It was said that somewhere in the New World there was a city called El Dorado built of solid gold.

So everyone who liked adventure and could get enough money together went off in search of these things that might make him famous or healthy, wealthy or wise, or forever young.

One of these men was Ponce de Leon, a Spaniard. Ponce de Leon was looking for the *Fountain of Youth*. While searching for this lifegiving water, he found Florida. But instead of finding the Fountain of Youth, he lost his life in fighting with the people who already lived in Florida.

Another one of these men was Hernando de Soto. He was searching for El Dorado, the city of gold. While doing so, he discovered the longest river in the New World — the Mississippi. Instead of finding El Dorado, de Soto was taken sick with fever and died.

64 魅力之地：寻宝与冒险

关于新大陆，人们有着各种神奇的传说，说那里遍地是财富，到处是奇观。

据说新大陆的某个地方有一口"不老泉"，只要在里面泡一泡，或者喝一点儿泉水，一个人就可以返老还童。

据说新大陆上有一座城市，叫作埃尔多拉多，那里全都是用一块一块的黄金建成的。

因此，凡是喜欢冒险、筹得起足够旅费的人，便都纷纷前去寻找这些东西；因为，这些东西或是可以让他们名扬天下、身体健康，或是可以让他们富甲一方、聪明睿智，或是可以让他们永葆青春。

这些人当中，有一位便是西班牙人庞塞·德莱昂。当时，庞塞·德莱昂正在寻找不老泉。就在寻找这口生命之泉的过程中，他发现了佛罗里达。不过，他非但没有找到不老泉，相反却在跟那些已经在佛罗里达生活的人打仗时送了命。

这些人当中，还有一位就是埃尔南多·德·索托。当时，他寻找的是埃尔多拉多这座黄金城。就在寻找的过程中，他发现了新大陆上最长的河流，即密西西比河。德·索托也没有找到埃尔多拉多这座黄金城，反而染上了热病，死掉了。当

Now, the Spaniards, to make the Native Americans fear them, had said that de Soto was a god and could not die. In order to cover up the fact that de Soto had actually died, his men buried him at night in the river he had discovered. They then said that he had gone on a trip to heaven and would presently return.

The first country you come to south of the United States is called Mexico. Here lived at that time a nation of Indians known as Aztecs. These Aztecs had a very advanced civilization. They did not live in tents but in houses. They built fine temples and palaces. They made roads and aqueducts, something like those of the Romans. They had enormous treasures of silver and gold. Yet the Aztecs worshiped idols and sacrificed human beings to them. Their king was a famous chief named Montezuma.

A Spaniard named Cortés was sent to conquer these Aztecs. He landed on the shore of Mexico and burned his ships so that his sailors and soldiers could not turn back. The Aztecs had never seen horses, some of which the Spaniards had brought over across the water, and they were astonished at what seemed to them terrible beasts that the Spaniards rode. When the Spaniards fired their cannon, the Aztecs were terrified. They thought it was thunder and lightning that the Spaniards had let loose.

Cortés moved on toward the Aztec capital, the city of Mexico, which was built on an island in the middle of a lake. The people he met on the way fought desperately, but as they had only such weapons as men used in the Stone and Bronze Ages, they were no match against the guns and cannon of the Spaniards.

Montezuma, their chief, wishing to make friends, sent Cortés rich gifts, cartloads of

时，西班牙人为了让美洲的土著畏惧他们，便说德·索托是一位不死的神仙。为了掩盖德·索托事实上已经送命的真相，他手下的人在晚上偷偷地把他的尸体进行水葬，扔到了他所发现的密西西比河里。然后，他们便说德·索托到天堂去了，并且很快就会回来。

美国南边的第一个国家是墨西哥。当时，这里生活着一个叫作阿兹特克的印第安部族。这些阿兹特克人拥有很发达的文明。他们住的不是茅棚，而是房屋。他们修建了许多精美的神庙和宫殿。他们修筑了许多道路和沟渠，与古罗马人修筑的道路和沟渠有点儿相似。他们拥有大量的金银财宝。不过，阿兹特克人崇拜多神教，并且还用活人来献祭。他们的国王是一位大名鼎鼎的头领，叫作蒙特祖玛。

西班牙派了一个叫作科尔特斯的人，率军前去征服这些阿兹特克人。科尔特斯在墨西哥沿岸登陆后，便烧掉了自己的船只，目的是让手下的水手和士兵能够背水一战。西班牙人带了一些战马漂洋过海而来；由于阿兹特克人从来没有见过马儿，因此看到西班牙人竟然骑着这种似乎非常可怕的野兽，他们都很惊讶。而待西班牙人的大炮开了几炮之后，阿兹特克人更是惊恐不已。他们以为，西班牙人放出的是雷鸣和闪电呢。

科尔特斯率军朝着阿兹特克人的首都墨西哥城挺进；这座都城建在一个湖心岛上。一路上，阿兹特克人进行了殊死抵抗；可由于他们的武器都是些石器时代和青铜器时代的冷兵器，因此他们根本就不是拥有枪支大炮的西班牙人的对手。

gold, and when Cortés reached the capital city Montezuma treated him as a guest instead of an enemy and entertained him and could not do enough for him. Cortés told Montezuma all about the Christian religion and tried to make him a Christian also, but Montezuma thought his own gods just as good as the Christian God, and he would not change. Then suddenly Cortés took Montezuma prisoner, and terrible fighting began. At last Montezuma was killed, and Cortés succeeded in conquering Mexico, for though the Aztecs fought desperately and bravely, shot and shell were too much for them.

In Peru in South America was still another nation of civilized Indians even more wealthy than the Aztecs. They were called Incas, and it was said that their cities were paved with gold.

A Spaniard named Pizarro went to Peru to conquer it as Cortés had conquered Mexico. Pizarro told the ruler, who was called the Inca, that the pope had given the country to Spain. The Inca had never heard of the pope and must have wondered what the pope had to do with Peru and how he could give it away. Naturally the Inca would not give up his country to Spain. Then Pizarro *took* it away. He had but a few hundred men, but he had cannons, and of course the Incas could not stand up against cannon.

Another people found by the Spanish were the Mayas. The Mayas lived on land that today is in Mexico and also Guatemala. The Mayas had a written language that we are only beginning to figure out how to read. They also invented a calendar and had built observatories from which to watch the stars. They built tall pyramids that remind us of the

阿兹特克人的头领蒙特祖玛希望与西班牙人和平相处，便给科尔特斯送了很多的礼物，送了一车又一车的黄金；而等科尔特斯抵达墨西哥城后，蒙特祖玛又像对待上宾一样款待他，尽可能地满足他的要求，根本就没有把他当成敌人。科尔特斯给蒙特祖玛介绍了基督教的全部情况，试图让蒙特祖玛也皈依基督教；可蒙特祖玛认为，他们本族敬奉的那些神灵与基督教的上帝一样善良，不愿改变信仰。科尔特斯便发动突袭，囚禁了蒙特祖玛；于是，双方开始了惊心动魄的战斗。最终，蒙特祖玛被杀，科尔特斯成功地占领了墨西哥城；尽管阿兹特克人进行了殊死搏斗，作战英勇，但他们的血肉之躯毕竟挡不住炮弹和子弹啊。

而在南美洲的秘鲁，还有一个文明发达的印第安民族，甚至比阿兹特克人还要富裕呢。他们被称为印加人；据说，在他们的城市里，连道路上铺的都是黄金。

一位名叫皮萨罗的西班牙人率军前往秘鲁，想要像科尔特斯征服墨西哥那样去征服秘鲁。皮萨罗对秘鲁那位被称为印加国王的统治者说，教皇已经将这个国家赐给了西班牙。印加国王从来没有听说过什么教皇；当时他一定很不理解，不知道教皇与秘鲁有什么关系，自己又怎么能把国家交给别人。因此，印加国王自然不肯把自己的国家拱手送给西班牙。于是，皮萨罗便攻陷了这个国家。虽说手下只有几百兵力，但他有大炮；印加人自然也抵御不了大炮的猛攻。

西班牙人发现的另一个民族，就是玛雅人。玛雅人所处的地方，就在如今的墨西哥和危地马拉两国境内。玛雅人拥有书面文字，但如今我们才刚刚开始弄明白如何去阅读那些玛雅文呢。他们发明了一种日历，并且修建了用于观察天体的观象

ancient Egyptian pyramids. Like the Incas, the Mayas were conquered by Spanish guns.

The Aztecs, the Incas, and the Mayas — these are only three of many native peoples that were living in America when the Spanish came. And do you know — Incas, Aztecs, and Mayas are still alive today, and you can visit Central and South America and see some of the wonderful things they built.

France and other countries of Europe also sent out explorers to conquer parts of America, and then missionaries to teach Native Americans the Christian religion, but these you will hear more about when you study American history.

Many of the explorers were really pirates, even worse pirates than the Norsemen who raided England and France, because they murdered people who were without equal weapons to fight back. The excuse they often gave for doing so was that they wanted to make the natives Christians. No wonder that the natives did not think much of the Christian religion if it taught murder of people who could not defend themselves. The Muslims made converts with the sword, but the Christians made converts with shot and shell.

台。他们还修筑了许多高高耸立的金字塔；看到它们，就会让我们想起古埃及的那些金字塔来。玛雅人也像印加人一样，被西班牙人的枪炮征服了。

阿兹特克人、印加人和玛雅人，只是在西班牙人来到美洲之时，生活于美洲的众多土著民族中的三个罢了。你们知道吗，如今依然有印加人、阿兹特克人和玛雅人呢。倘若你们到中美洲和南美洲去走一走的话，还能看到他们修建的一些奇妙建筑。

法国以及欧洲的其他一些国家，也都纷纷派遣探险队，前去征服美洲的部分地区，然后又派传教士去向美洲的本地民族宣传基督教；不过，待你们学习美国历史时，就会了解到这些方面的更多内容。

许多探险者实际上都是海盗，甚至是比曾经劫掠过英国和法国的人更加可恶的海盗，因为他们屠杀的，都是没有武器来进行反击的人。他们为自己这样干而找出的借口，便是他们想让美洲的土著都皈依基督教。美洲的本地土著很不喜欢基督教，因为他们认为它教导的是屠杀手无寸铁的人，这一点从外来殖民者对他们的迫害来看便不足为奇了。

65 Along the Coast of East Africa

America was not the only place where adventurers sailed in search of excitement and wealth. While the Spanish were conquering the Aztecs, Incas, and Mayas in America, the Portuguese went to Africa. Just as Christopher Columbus was looking for a route to India by sailing west, the Portuguese were also looking for a way to sail to India and China. They decided to try sailing around Africa. They didn't know for sure that they could ever find an end to that continent — a way around — but they wanted to try.

Before Columbus got to America, several Portuguese explorers sailed south along the coast of West Africa. They passed the mouth of the Senegal River that had been in Mansa Musa's empire. Then they rounded the corner of the great continent and soon came to Benin, an empire in a part of Africa that is now Nigeria. Benin was ruled by a king called an *oba* and was known for its beautiful artwork. If you visit a large art museum, you can see carvings and statues and ceremonial masks made in Benin. Farther south still, the ships passed an empire called Kongo. One explorer even got as far as the very southern tip of Africa, but then he turned around and headed for home.

Five years after Columbus left Spain, Vasco da Gama left Portugal. He finally

65   东非沿海

美洲并不是探险者们起航前去寻找刺激和财富的唯一去处。就在西班牙人征服美洲阿兹特克人、印加人和玛雅人的同时，葡萄牙人则去了非洲。正如哥伦布想要寻找一条向西航行到印度的航线一样，葡萄牙人也正在寻找一条通往印度和中国的海上航线。他们决定试一试绕道非洲的那条航线。虽说没有十足的把握，也没法说自己一定能够绕道到达这个大陆的尽头，但他们还是想要试一试。

在哥伦布到达美洲之前，有一些葡萄牙探险者就已经沿着西非海岸向南航行过了。他们曾经驶过了位于曼萨·穆萨手下那个帝国境内的塞内加尔河河口。然后，他们又绕过了非洲的那个大陆角，很快抵达了贝宁；贝宁曾经是一个帝国，位置就在如今非洲的尼日利亚。当时统治贝宁的，是一个被称为"奥巴"的国王，而贝宁也因为其漂亮的艺术品而闻名于世。假如去一座大型的艺术博物馆参观的话，你们有可能会看到产自贝宁的雕刻品、雕塑和仪式上所戴的面具呢。再往南去，船队又经过了一个叫作刚果的帝国。有一位探险者甚至还来到了非洲的最南端；可后来他却没有继续航行，而是掉转船头回国了。

哥伦布从西班牙动身的五年之后，达·伽马从葡萄牙起航了。他最终成功地率领船队绕过了非洲的最南端，进入了印度洋。之后，他便沿着非洲东部海岸向北航

succeeded in sailing around that southern tip of Africa and into the Indian Ocean. He sailed up the east side of Africa. Then he traveled on toward India. While he was still in East Africa, he found wonderful cities that he thought nobody knew about.

Way back, in fact, some Europeans *had* known that these cities were there. Greeks and Romans as well as Egyptians all knew their way to East Africa. Soon after the time of Christ, a Greek guidebook for sailors told how to get to the different ports and said that ivory, tortoise shell, and coconut oil were traded there. During these early years, the towns were small, with perhaps one thousand people living in them.

Around 900 A.D. or about one hundred years after Charlemagne, at a time when very few Europeans were doing much traveling and all had forgotten about East Africa, an Arab geographer visited there. He was on his way home from a trip to India and China. He wrote that in East Africa the climate was warm and the land fertile and that gold and many other wonderful things were found there. We know

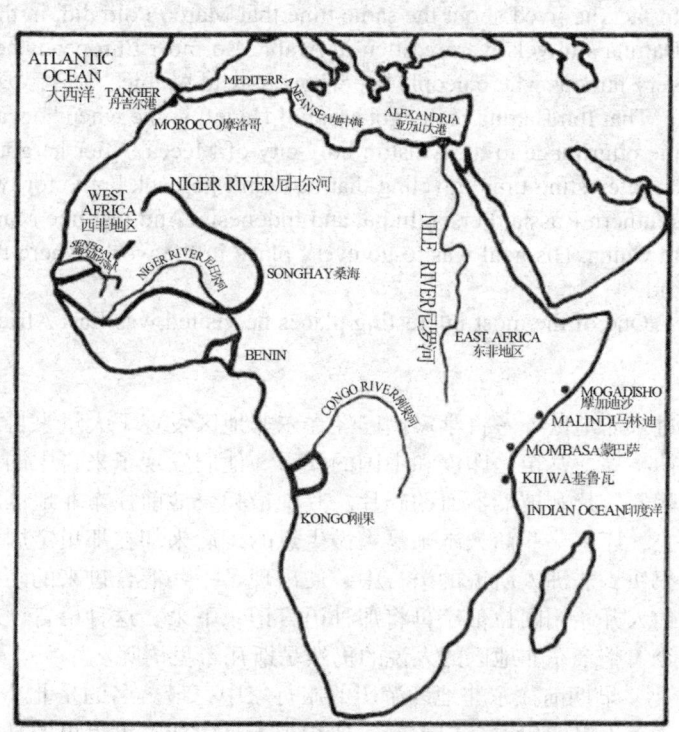

City states of East Africa
东非地区的城邦

行。接下来，他又率领船队朝印度驶去。在沿着东非海岸航行的过程中，他发现了许多奇妙的城市；而当时他以为，此前还没有人听说过这些城市呢。

实际上，很早以前，一些欧洲人就已经知道有这些城市存在了。古希腊人、古罗马人以及古埃及人全都知道怎么去东非地区。基督降生后不久的一本古希腊水手指南书上，就说明了前往不同海港的方法，还说在这些港口里可以买到象牙、玳瑁和椰子油呢。早期的时候，这些城镇的规模都很小，每座城镇里可能只有一千来口人。

公元900年左右，或者说查理曼大帝去世之后大约一百年左右，由于当时欧洲很少有人去旅行，所以大家都不记得东非地区的这些情况了；可是，一位阿拉伯的地理学家，却在此时来到了东非地区。当时，他是在印度和中国游历完后，正要回国的路上。他写道：东非地区气候温暖、土地肥沃，那里有着黄金和其他许许多多的奇妙之物。如今我们知道，在基督降生后最初的那一千年里，有很多的商人都到

now that a lot of traders visited East Africa during those first thousand years after Christ. Archeologists have found large numbers of coins from Persia, Greece, Rome, Arabia, and even India and China there. They have found pieces of pottery and glassware from China, India, and Arabia too. The Arabs visited East Africa most. In fact, some of the Arabs who went there to trade settled down and made their homes there. Soon the language spoken by the Africans had some Arab words mixed into it. Then Arabs began writing that language in Arabic letters. That language is called Swahili. Swahili is still spoken all through East Africa.

The most famous early traveler to visit East Africa was a Muslim from Tangier, a city in North Africa. His name was Ibn Battuta. He was the Marco Polo of the Muslim world. In fact, he lived about the same time that Marco Polo did, in the 1300s. The stories of Ibn Battuta's travels were written in Arabic, so most Europeans never read them, but he was very famous where people knew how to read Arabic.

That Ibn Battuta really got around! He left home when he was twenty years old to go on the pilgrimage to the Muslim holy city of Mecca. After he got there, he was having such an interesting time traveling that he didn't go back home for twenty five years. He visited southern Russia, Persia, India, and Indonesia. And just like Marco Polo, he got all the way to China. His goal was to go every place in the world where there were Muslims, and he did.

One of the most interesting places he visited was East Africa. A lot of the people there

过东非地区。考古学家们已经在东非地区发现了大量来自波斯、希腊、罗马、阿拉伯半岛、甚至是印度和中国的钱币。他们发现了来自中国、印度还有阿拉伯半岛的陶器碎片和玻璃器皿的碎片。其中最频繁地前往东非地区的，就是阿拉伯人。事实上，还有一些商人本来是去做生意的，后来却在那里定居下来，把家安在那里了。很快，非洲人所说的语言中，便出现了一些混合进来的阿拉伯语词汇。接着，阿拉伯人开始用阿拉伯字母将那种语言记录下来。这种语言，就叫"斯瓦希里语"。如今，整个东非地区的人说的仍然是斯瓦希里语呢。

早期前往东非地区游历的旅行家中，最著名的是北非丹吉尔港的一位穆斯林。这个人名叫伊本·白图泰。他相当于是伊斯兰世界里的马可·波罗。事实上，他与马可·波罗差不多生活在同一时期，即公元十四世纪。伊本·白图泰的游历故事是用阿拉伯语记录下来的，因此绝大多数欧洲人从来都没有看过；但在人们能够阅读阿拉伯语的那些地区，伊本·白图泰却是非常有名。

那个伊本·白图泰的确是个喜欢到处旅行的人！他在24岁的时候离家，去穆斯林的圣城麦加朝圣。抵达麦加之后，由于旅途太有意思了，所以他竟然有25年没有回过家。他到访过俄罗斯的南部、波斯、印度和印度尼西亚。与马可·波罗一样，他也历尽艰险，一路来到了中国。他的目标是到全世界有穆斯林的地方去转一转，而他也的确做到了这一点。

他游历过的最有意思的地方之一，便是东部非洲。那里的很多人都是穆斯林。你们都知道，虽然那里有一些人是阿拉伯人，但绝大多数还是非洲人。有的时候，非

were Muslims. As you know, some were Arabs. Most were Africans. Sometimes Africans had married Arabs, and their children were a mixture of the two.

By Ibn Battuta's time, the trading towns had grown into cities. They were city states, independent like the earlier Greek city states. Each city had its own ruler, and each was surrounded by countryside where men and women farmed. You can still visit many of these cities in East Africa. The cities had names like Mogadishu, Malindi, Mombasa, and Kilwa. Try saying those names. They may seem strange at first, but soon they will seem easy to you.

Ibn Battuta described Kilwa as the most beautiful town in the whole world. There were fountains and public squares, he said. The main palace was on a high cliff above the Indian Ocean, had one hundred rooms, and an eight-sided swimming pool. How would you like to have been a guest of the ruler in Kilwa?

The cities all had ports where large vessels tied up. Arab ships were sixty to seventy feet long. Even larger ships came from Persia and India. Occasionally Chinese fleets of hundreds of huge ships visited the East African ports. Africans sold gold, iron, and ivory in exchange for silks, glassware, and tools. Once, the city of Malindi sent a wonderful gift to the emperor of China. Can you imagine something — that was not gold — that the ruler of Malindi might think would be a good surprise for the wealthy and powerful Chinese emperor? Something that did not exist in China? It must have made a big impression on the Chinese, because they wrote all about it — and that's how we still know about this

洲人与阿拉伯人会相互通婚，因此他们的后代便成了非洲人和阿拉伯人的混血儿。

到了伊本·白图泰那个时候，以前进行贸易的小城镇都已经发展成了一座座城市。它们都是独立自主的城邦，就像早期古希腊的那些城邦一样。每个城邦都有各自的统治者，而城邦周围则是乡村，男男女女都在那里耕作。如今，你们仍然可以在东非地区看到许多这种的城邦呢。这些城邦都有自己的名称，比如摩加迪沙、马林迪、蒙巴萨和基尔瓦。试着说一说这些名称吧。它们一开始看上去会很陌生，可不久后，你们就会觉得很容易记住它们了。

在伊本·白图泰的描述中，基尔瓦是世界上最美丽的城市之一。他说，那里有喷泉和公共广场。该市的正殿位于高耸的悬崖之上，俯瞰着印度洋；其中有一百间房子，还有一座八边形的游泳池哩。那么，你们愿不愿意到基尔瓦城邦的统治者那里去做客呢？

那些城邦都有自己的海港，并且港口里都停满了大型船舶。阿拉伯人的船只一般是六十至七十英尺长。还有一些更大的船只，则是来自波斯和印度。偶尔也会有由数百艘大型船舶组成的中国船队来到东非的这些海港。非洲人用黄金、铁器和象牙，交换丝绸、玻璃制品和工具。马林迪城邦曾经派人送了一件奇妙的礼物给中国的皇帝。你们能够猜出，马林迪国王当时觉得，有哪种不是黄金制成的东西，会给那个富甲天下、实力强大的中国皇帝带去惊喜吗？是中国没有的什么东西吗？这件东西一定给所有的中国人都留下了极其深刻的印象，因为他们都记录下了这件东西；而我们如今仍然知道有这样一件礼物，也正是得益于他们的记载呢。好啦，你

gift. Well, have you guessed? It was a

That's certainly something they didn't have in China!

The rulers of those city states must have been pretty smart because one thing that they *didn't* have much of was war. There were some minor squabbles, but most of the cities didn't even have large fortifications except around the ports. They didn't think they needed them because they weren't fighting each other all the time. This meant that they could spend all their energy on trade and farming. I'm sure it's one reason why these cities were so prosperous.

Eventually, though, they were attacked. Then they had a real problem. Can you guess what country decided to take over these cities? I'll give you a hint. There was a country that wanted to take control of the trade routes — that wanted to move in on the trade with India and China. Well, you may have guessed it by now. That country was Portugal. When the Portuguese discovered that not only was there gold in Africa, but that the East Africans already had the trade with the East that both Portugal and Spain wanted, they were ready to move in.

The Portuguese came with big guns on their ships. When a city didn't just give in to them, they attacked. Mombasa was completely destroyed. All

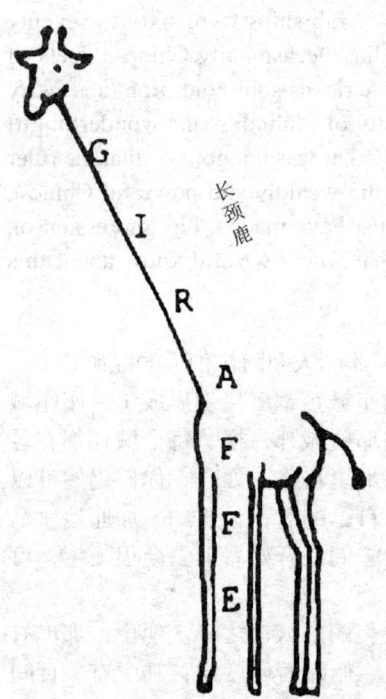

们猜到了没有？这件礼物，就是一头长颈鹿！

长颈鹿，当然是中国没有的一种东西！

这些城邦的统治者一定都是相当聪明，因为他们之间不经常干的一件事情，就是战争。鸡毛蒜皮的争执当然有，但除了海港四周，绝大多数城邦连大型的防御工事也没有修建。这些城邦显然是认为，自己不需要修建防御工事，因为它们之间并非动不动就打仗。这就意味着，它们可以把所有的精力都放在贸易和农耕上。我敢肯定，这就是那些城邦如此繁荣发达的一个原因呢。

不过，它们最终还是受到了攻击。这样一来，它们就面临着一个真正的问题了。你们能够猜出，是一个什么样的国家决定接管所有这些城邦吗？我给你们一点儿提示吧。当时有一个国家，想要控制所有的贸易线路，希望控制与印度和中国的贸易往来。好吧，现在你们可能已经猜到了吧。这个国家，便是葡萄牙。葡萄牙人发现非洲不但有黄金，而且东非人也已经与东方有了贸易往来（这可是葡萄牙和西班牙两国都觊觎已久的）之后，他们就准备好去插上一手了。

葡萄牙人驾驶着装有大炮的战船来了。倘若哪个城邦不肯屈服，他们就来硬的，直接攻打。蒙巴萨被彻底摧毁了。这个城邦里的人，也全都被葡萄牙人杀害了。

the people there were killed.

The East Africans knew they couldn't defeat the big ships and their cannon. So they used another strategy to get rid of the Portuguese. They stopped the gold trade. The miners stopped mining gold. The merchants stopped shipping gold. Gradually the ports closed down. The people from the cities moved into the countryside and became farmers. Now, the Portuguese weren't interested in farms so — except for keeping a few places where their ships could stop to get fuel and supplies on the long voyage to the Indies — they lost interest in East Africa. The people had lost their cities, but they had won their peace.

东非人知道自己无法战胜葡萄牙人的坚船利炮。于是，他们采取了另外一种策略，试图把葡萄牙人赶走。他们停止了黄金贸易。金矿不再开采黄金，商人们也不再运输黄金。于是，各个海港便逐渐凋敝下去了。人们从城镇搬到了乡下，变成了农民。当时，除了在前往印度的航线上保留了一些地方，以便让船只能够获得燃料和补给之外，葡萄牙人对农业可不感兴趣，因此他们对东非地区也就失去了兴趣。东非人民虽然失去了自己的城市，却赢得了和平安宁的生活。

66 Rebirth

Here is a long word for you; it is Renaissance.

It means *rebirth*.

Of course, nothing can be born again. But people call this time we have now reached the Renaissance, the time of rebirth. Here is the reason why they call it that.

You remember the Age of Pericles, don't you, when such beautiful sculptures and buildings were made in Athens? Well, in the fifteen hundreds not everyone was rushing off to the New World in search of adventure. While the voyages that I have told you about were taking place, there were living and working in Italy some of the greatest artists the world has ever known.

Architects built beautiful buildings something like the old Greek and Roman temples. Sculptors made statues that were almost as beautiful as those of Phidias. People began to take an interest once more in the old Greek writers, whose books were now printed for everyone to read. It seemed almost as if Athens in the Age of Pericles had been born again. That is why people speak of this time as the Renaissance.

One of the greatest of these artists of the Renaissance was a man named Michelangelo.

66 重生

在这里，你们将会看到一个较长的词语：文艺复兴。

所谓"复兴"，指的就是"重生"。

当然，没有什么东西可以再次出生。不过，人们还是将我们如今所要讲述的这个时代，称为"文艺复兴时期"，即一个重生的时代。下面，我就来说一说他们之所以这样做的原因。

你们都还记得伯里克利时代吧？当时，雅典修建了许多非常美丽的雕像和建筑，对不对呢？好吧，十六世纪的时候，也并不是所有的人全都急急忙忙地赶往新大陆探险去了。就在我前面已经提及的那一次次航海正在进行的时候，世界历史上非常伟大的一些艺术家，却正在意大利生活和工作着呢。

这一时期的建筑师，修建了许多美丽的、有点儿像是古希腊和古罗马时期的神庙。雕刻师们则雕刻出了几乎可与菲狄亚斯的作品相媲美的雕塑。这一时期的人们，开始再一次对古希腊时期的作家产生了兴趣；这是因为，当时那些作家的著作都被印刷出来，每个人都可以去阅读了。看上去，就像是伯里克利时代的古希腊如今又重生了。这就是人们之所以称这一时期为"文艺复兴时期"的原因。

文艺复兴时期最伟大的艺术家之一，是一个叫作米开朗琪罗的人。不过，米开

But Michelangelo was not just a painter; he was a sculptor, an architect, and a poet as well. Michelangelo thought nothing of spending years working on any statue or painting that he was doing. When he had finished, he had done something that people even now go from all over the world to see.

Nowadays, sculptors first model a statue in clay and then copy it in stone or cast it in bronze, but Michelangelo did not do this. He cut his figures directly out of the stone, without making a model first. It was as if he saw the figure imprisoned in the stone and then cut away the part that closed the figure in.

A large block of marble had been spoiled by another sculptor. Michelangelo saw a figure of David *in* it, and, setting to work, he cut this young athlete *out*.

He made also a statue of Moses sitting down. It is now in a church in Rome, and when you walk up to it, it is so lifelike that it seems as if you were in the presence of the prophet Moses himself. The guide tells you that when Michelangelo had finished this statue of Moses he was so thrilled by the figure he had created that, feeling it must come to life, he struck it on the knee with his hammer and commanded as he did so, "Stand up!" And then the guide shows you a crack in the marble to prove that the story is true!

The pope wanted Michelangelo to paint the ceiling of the Sistine Chapel. This is the pope's private chapel in Rome. At first Michelangelo didn't want to do the painting. He told the pope he was a sculptor and not a painter. But the pope insisted, and Michelangelo at last gave in. Once having agreed to do the work, however, Michelangelo gave himself

朗琪罗并非只是一位画家；他还是一位雕塑家、一位建筑师和一名诗人。米开朗琪罗在年复一年地雕塑、绘画的时候，什么也不曾想过。可一旦完工，那就是一件伟大的作品；即便到了如今，世界各地的人也还是会纷纷前去瞻仰他的杰作呢。

如今，雕刻师一般都是先用黏土做出雕塑的模型，然后再将它复制到石头上或者用青铜浇铸出来；可米开朗琪罗的做法却不是这样的。他是直接在石头上雕刻出手指来，而不用先做模型。这就好像是他看到石头里面本来就有手指，然后只是将包围着手指的那部分石头雕掉罢了一样。

有一次，另一位雕刻师雕坏了一大块大理石。可是，米开朗琪罗却在这块石头里面看出了大卫的形象，于是便动手雕出了那位年轻的运动员。

他还雕刻出了一尊摩西的坐像。这尊坐像如今保存在罗马的一座教堂里；倘若走上前去细看，雕像显得栩栩如生，让人觉得完全就像是面对着先知摩西本人似的。导游会告诉你们说，米开朗琪罗完成这尊雕像后，因为对自己雕出了这样一个人物感到非常激动，觉得它会活过来，所以用锤子在雕像的膝盖上敲了一敲，并且一边敲一边说："站起来！"接着，导游还会让你们去看看那尊雕像上的一条裂缝，以此来证明这个故事是真的呢！

当时的教皇想要米开朗琪罗去给西斯廷教堂的屋顶绘上油画。那座教堂，就是教皇在罗马的私人教堂。起初，米开朗琪罗不想去画。他对教皇说，自己是一位雕刻师，可不是画家。但教皇一直坚持，因此米开朗琪罗最终答应了。然而，一旦应承下来，米开朗琪罗便全心全意地扑到了这件工作上。

to it heart and soul.

For four years he lived in this room — the Sistine Chapel — and hardly ever left it day or night. Beneath the ceiling, he built himself a platform, and lying on this scaffold, he would read poetry and the Bible and work as the spirit moved him. Locking himself in, he would let no one enter, not even the pope himself. He wanted to be alone and to be left alone.

One day the pope, finding a door left open went into the chapel to see how things were getting along. Michelangelo, thereupon, accidentally dropped some of his tools, and they just barely missed hitting the pope on the head. The pope was very angry, but he never returned uninvited again.

People now go from all over the world to see this ceiling, which only can be viewed comfortably by lying on the floor or by looking at it in a mirror.

Michelangelo lived to be nearly ninety years old, yet he had very little to do with people. He could not stand being bored by them. He lived apart, in the company of the gods and angels that he painted.

Raphael was another famous Italian artist. He lived at the same time as Michelangelo. Raphael, however, was just the opposite of Michelangelo in most ways. Michelangelo liked to be by himself. Raphael loved

Michelangelo at work
工作时的米开朗琪罗

在四年的时间里，他一直都住在西斯廷教堂里，不分昼夜地工作，几乎从不出去。他在屋顶下方搭建了一座平台；他会躺在这个平台上阅读诗歌和《圣经》，而当心灵受到触动之后，他便又开始工作。他把自己锁在教堂里，任何人也不准进去，连教皇本人也不例外。他希望自己独自创作，希望别人不去打扰他。

有一天，教皇发现教堂的一扇门开着，便走了进去，想看看绘画工作进行得怎样了。躺在平台上的米开朗琪罗一不小心，掉了几把工具下去，差点儿砸中了教皇的脑袋。教皇非常生气，不过此后他再也没有不请自来了。

如今，世界各地的人都前来观看这座教堂的天花板；可游客只有躺在地上，或者用一面镜子反射，才能舒适地欣赏呢。

米开朗琪罗活到了近九十岁的高龄，不过他不太与人们打交道。让他们来烦自己，他可忍受不了。他孤身一人生活着，与自己所绘的上帝和天使为伴。

拉斐尔是另一位著名的意大利艺术家。他与米开朗琪罗属于同一时期的人。然而，在绝大多数方面，拉斐尔却与米开朗琪罗截然相反。米开朗琪罗喜欢独处，拉斐尔却喜欢有人做伴。他很受人们爱戴，身边经常围满了朋友和崇拜者；由于他既

company. He was very popular and constantly surrounded by his friends and admirers, for everybody loved him on account of his genius and kindly nature. Young men swarmed about him, drinking in his words and humbly copying everything he did. He had fifty or more pupils studying and painting under him, and they went along with him whenever he went out even for a walk. They almost worshiped the ground he walked on.

Raphael painted many beautiful pictures. One of the best known is *School of Athens*. He painted many pictures of the Virgin Mary with the infant Jesus. These are called *Madonnas*. One of the best known of these pictures of Mary and the Christ child is called *Sistine Madonna*. It was painted for a little church, but it is now in a great picture-gallery.

Raphael died when he was still a young man, but he worked so hard and so continuously that he has left a large number of pictures. He painted only the very important parts of his pictures himself — perhaps only the faces. The bodies and hands and clothing he usually left to be painted by his pupils. They were glad to be allowed to do even a finger of a painting on which their master had worked.

Leonardo da Vinci is another great artist who lived at this time. He could do any number of things exceptionally well. He would be called a jack-of-all-trades, but unlike most jacks-of-all-trades, he was good at everything. He was an artist, an engineer, a poet, and a scientist. He made, however, very few paintings, because he did so many things besides, but these few pictures are beautiful and famous. One of these is *The Last Supper*. It is considered, as is the *Sistine Madonna*, one of the greatest paintings in the world.

才华横溢，性格又很和善，所以大家都很喜欢他。年轻人都云集到他身边，用心聆听着他的话语，并且谦卑无比地模仿着他的一举一动。他带了五十多位学生，教他们绘画；无论他去哪里，即便是出去散散步，那些学生也都亦步亦趋地跟着他。连他走过的地面，学生们几乎都膜拜得很哩。

拉斐尔创作出了许多美丽的绘画。其中最有名气的画作之一，便是《雅典学派》。他还创作出了多幅关于圣母马利亚带着襁褓中的耶稣的画作。这些画作，被称为"圣母像"。这些关于圣母马利亚和儿时基督的画作中，最著名的作品之一被称为《西斯廷圣母》。这幅油画是为一座小小的教堂创作的，可如今它却保存在一座大大的画廊里了。

拉斐尔英年早逝，死的时候还很年轻；但他非常勤奋，笔耕不辍，因此留下了许多的画作。不过，这些画作上，他亲手所画的只是其中最重要的部位，没准他只画了脸部。至于其中人物的身体、四肢以及所穿的衣物，他通常都会留给学生们去画。能够获准在老师的作品上画一画，哪怕只是画上一根手指，那些学生也都高兴得很哪。

这一时期，还有一位伟大的艺术家，那就是达·芬奇。他对很多领域里都极其精通。他完全可以说是一个"万事通"；但与绝大多数"万事通"不同的是，他每件事情都很擅长。他既是艺术家、工程师、诗人，也是科学家。然而，他创作的绘画很少，因为除了绘画，他还有许多别的事情要做；不过，这些为数不多的画作却都很漂亮，也很有名。其中之一便是《最后的晚餐》。人们认为，这幅画作与《西

Unfortunately, it was painted directly on a plastered wall, and in the course of time much of the plaster with the paint has peeled off, so that there was little left of the original painting. Recently this painting was restored. The colors were brightened up so, once again, we can see its full beauty.

Leonardo usually painted his women smiling. One of his most famous paintings is the picture of a woman called *Mona Lisa*. She has a smile that is called *quizzical*. You can hardly tell whether she is smiling *at* you or *with* you.

斯廷圣母》一样，是世界上最伟大的绘画作品之一。可惜的是，这幅画是直接绘在一面灰墙上；而随着时间的流逝，墙上的许多灰泥都带着油彩剥落下来，因此原作几乎没有留下多少了。近来，人们又修复了这幅画作。画中的油彩变得明亮起来，从而让我们可以再次一睹整幅画作的美丽。

达·芬奇通常会让笔下的女性在画作中微笑。他最著名的画作之一，就是一幅女性的画像，叫作《蒙娜·丽莎》。这位女性的微笑，简直可以称之为"古怪"哩。欣赏这幅画作的时候，你几乎分不清她是在对着你微笑呢，还是在与你一起微笑。

67 Christians Quarrel

Some people say young boys and girls can't understand this chapter. They say it is too difficult. But I want to see if it is.

Up to this time, as I have told you before, in Western Europe had been one Christian religion — the Catholic. There was no Episcopalian, nor Methodist, nor Baptist, nor Presbyterian, nor any other denomination. All were just Christians.

In the sixteenth century, however, some people began to think that changes should be made in the Catholic religion.

Others thought changes should not be made.

Some said it was all right as it was.

Others said it wasn't all right as it was. So a quarrel started.

This is the way the trouble began. The pope was building a great church called St. Peter's in Rome. It took the place of the old church that Constantine had built on the spot where St. Peter was supposed to have been crucified head down. The pope wanted it to be the largest and finest church in the world, for Christ had said, "Thou art Peter, and upon this rock [Peter means rock in Latin] I will build my church . . . ." So the Church of St.

67　基督徒反目

有些人说，小朋友们可能无法理解这一章。他们说这一章太难了。但我还是想看一看，这一章对小朋友来说是不是真的很难。

我在前面已经跟你们说过，到此时为止，西欧各国一直都只信奉一种基督教，即天主教。当时既没有什么主教派，也没有什么卫理公会、浸礼会、长老会，以及其他的教派。大家都是基督徒。

然而，到了十六世纪，有些人却开始觉得，天主教必须有所改变才行了。

可其他一些人却觉得，基督教不应当有所改变。

有些人说，天主教现在这个样子挺好。

可其他一些人却说，天主教这个样子一点都不好。于是，双方便开始争吵起来。

问题就这样产生了。当时，教皇正在罗马修建圣彼得大教堂。这座教堂的位置，就在君士坦丁所建的那座老教堂之上；而那座老教堂，则正是建在传说中圣彼得被钉死在十字架上的那个地方。教皇希望这座圣彼得大教堂是世界上最大、最精美的一座，因为基督曾经说过：　"你是彼得，我要把我的教会建造在这磐石上［在拉丁语中，'彼得'就是指'岩石'］……"[1]因此，他打算让圣彼得大教堂成为基

---

[1]　你是彼得，我要把我的教会……(Thou art Peter, and upon this rock ...)，原文见于《圣经·马太福音》16：18。方括号中的内容是作者的注释。

Peter's was to be the Capitol of the Christian religion. Both Michelangelo and Raphael had worked on the plans for the new church. In order to get marble and stone and other materials for this Church of St. Peter, the pope did as others before him had done; he tore down other buildings in Rome and used their stone for the new church.

Besides all this the pope needed an enormous amount of money to build such a magnificent church as he had planned. So he started to collect from the people. Now, there was a man in Germany named Martin Luther who was a monk and a teacher of religion in a college. Martin Luther thought that not only this but also other things in the Catholic Church were not right. He made a list of ninety-five things that he thought were not right and nailed them up on the church door in the town where he lived, and he preached against doing these things. The pope sent Luther an order to stop, but Luther made a bonfire and burned it publicly. Many took sides with Luther, and before long there was a great body of people who had left the Catholic Church and no longer obeyed the pope.

The pope called on the king of Spain to help in this quarrel with Luther. The reason he called on him was this: the king of Spain was Charles V, the grandson of the Ferdinand and Isabella who had helped Columbus. He was not only a good Catholic but the most powerful ruler in Europe. The Spanish explorers had claimed large parts of America and so Charles was owner of a large part of the New World. But he was emperor not only of these Spanish settlements in America but of Austria and of Germany as well. It was quite natural that the pope should go to Charles for help.

督教的中枢。米开朗琪罗和拉斐尔那两位艺术大师，都曾经为这座新教堂的设计出过力。为了获得兴建这座圣彼得大教堂所需的石料和其他建材，教皇的做法与前人的做法没什么两样，就是将罗马城里的其他一些建筑拆掉，然后再用拆下来的石料去修建这座新教堂。

除此之外，教皇还需要一大笔资金，才能按照他的计划来修建起这样一座宏伟的教堂。于是，他开始向民众征税，以便募集资金。此时，德国有一个叫作马丁·路德的人；他是一名修道士，也是一所大学里的宗教导师。马丁·路德觉得，非但这件事情教皇做得不对，天主教会里的其他许多事情也是不对的。于是，他把自己认为不合理的95件事情一一列举出来，张贴在所住城市里的那座教堂的大门上，并且向民众宣传，要他们反对做这些事情。教皇下了一道命令，要路德别再那样干；可路德却点了一堆火，当众烧毁了这份命令。许多人都支持路德；所以不久之后，就有一大批民众退出了天主教会，不再听命于教皇了。

教皇便要西班牙国王帮助他，来解决他与路德之间的这场纷争。教皇之所以要求西班牙国王出面，原因在于：当时的西班牙国王是查理五世，是曾经帮助过哥伦布的斐迪南国王和伊莎贝拉王后的后代。他不但是一位虔诚的天主教徒，也是欧洲实力最强大的君主之一。西班牙的探险者已经把美洲的大部分地区攫为西班牙所有，因此查理五世还统治着新大陆上的大部分地区。不过，他实际上是一位皇帝，既统治着位于美洲的那些西班牙殖民地，同时还管辖着奥地利和德国。因此，教皇向查理五世求助，就是顺理成章的事情了。

Charles commanded Luther to come to a city named Worms to be tried. He promised Luther that no harm would be done him, and so Luther went. When Luther arrived at Worms, Charles ordered him to take back all he had said. Luther refused to do so. Some of Charles's nobles said Luther should be burned at the stake. But Charles, as he had promised, let him go and did not punish him for his belief. Luther's friends were afraid, though, that other Catholics might do him harm. They knew Luther would take no care of himself, and so they themselves took him prisoner and kept him shut up for over a year, so that no one could harm him. While Luther was in prison, he translated the Bible into German; it was the first time that the Bible had been written in that language.

The people who protested against what the pope did were called Protestants, and the new churches that grew from this protest are still called Protestant today. The time when these changes were made in the Catholic form of worship was called Re-form-ation, as the old religion was *reformed*.

Now, you may be a Catholic and your best friend may not be a Catholic, but that makes no difference in your friendship. But at that time those who were Catholics were deadly enemies of those who were not, and vice versa. Each side was sure it alone was right and the other side was wrong. Each side fought for the things it thought were right, fought the other side as furiously and madly and bitterly as if the other side were scoundrels and devils. Friends and relatives murdered each other because they thought differently about religion, and yet all were supposed to be Christians.

查理五世下令，要路德前往一个叫作沃尔姆斯的城市受审。他向路德承诺，说不会加害于他，于是路德便去了。路德抵达沃尔姆斯之后，查理五世便下令要他回收自己说过的所有话语。可路德拒绝这样做。查理五世手下的一些贵族说，应当把路德绑在火刑柱上烧死。可查理五世由于有言在先，所以还是释放了路德，并没有因为信仰问题而惩处路德。不过，路德的朋友们却害怕其他的天主教徒可能会加害于他。他们知道路德不会在意自己的安危，因此他们便亲自把路德囚禁起来，让他一年多没能出去宣传；这样一来，也就没有人能够加害于他了。在被囚禁起来的那一段时间里，路德将《圣经》翻译成了德语；这可是《圣经》第一次被翻译成了德语呢。

那些抗议教皇所作所为者，就被称为"抗议宗信徒"[1]；而此次抗议活动中形成的种种新的教派，如今也仍然被称为"抗议宗"。天主教礼拜形式上发生这些变化的这一时期，史称"宗教改革运动"；之所以如此，是因为旧的宗教得到了改革。

如今，你们可能是天主教徒，你们最好的朋友却可能不是天主教徒，但这一点并不会影响到你们之间的友谊。可是，当时的天主教徒却视那些非天主教徒为不共戴天的敌人，反过来也是如此。每一方都认为只有自己才是正确的，而对方是错误的。每一方都誓死捍卫自己认为正确的教义，都猛烈、狂热而怨气十足地攻击对方，好像对方是恶棍和魔鬼似的。朋友和亲戚会因为在宗教信仰方面的想法不同而

[1] 抗议宗信徒（Protestant），由英文单词 protest（抗议）而来，如今一般译为"新教徒"。此处译为"抗议宗信徒"，只是为了让小朋友们明白这一专称是怎么来的，所以下文会沿用通译。

Charles was greatly worried and troubled by the religious quarrels and other difficulties in his vast empire. He became sick and tired of being emperor and of having to settle all the many problems he had to solve. He wanted to be free to do other things that he was more interested in. Being king did not mean being able to do whatever you wanted, as some people think. Charles then did what few rulers have ever done voluntarily: He resigned — *abdicated*, as it is called — and gave up his throne to his son, who was named Philip II.

Charles, glad to be rid of all the cares of state, went to live in a monastery. There he spent his time doing what he liked — what do you suppose? — making mechanical toys and watches — until he died!

Now, the king of England at this time, when Charles was king of Spain, was Henry VIII. His last name was Tudor. So many kings had first names which were alike that such names were numbered to tell which Charles or Henry was meant and how many of the same name there had been before. Henry VIII was, at first, also a strong Catholic, and the pope had called him Defender of the Faith. But Henry had a wife whom he wanted to divorce because she had no son. Henry wanted a son to succeed him as king and keep England united. In order to divorce her so that he might marry again, he had to have the agreement of the pope because the pope was the only one who could give Henry a divorce. Now, the pope at Rome was head of the Christian Church in all of Europe and the Americas and said what Christians could do or could not do, no matter whether they were in Italy or Spain or England. Henry asked the pope to grant him this divorce. The pope, however, told

相互残杀，可实际上大家都应当是基督徒呢。

查理五世对自己手下那个广袤帝国里出现的宗教纷争和其他问题感到忧心忡忡，烦恼不已。他厌烦了当皇帝，厌倦了不得不去解决那些必须解决的问题。他希望自由自在地去干自己更感兴趣的其他事情。当一位国王，并不像一些人所认为的那样可以随心所欲。于是，查理五世便干出了历史上极少有君主自愿去做的一件事情：他辞职了，将王位传给了自己的儿子腓力二世；我们将他的这种做法，称为退位。

查理五世很高兴摆脱了所有的国家大事，便住进了一座修道院。在修道院里，他把时间全都放到了自己喜欢的事情上，直到去世；你们觉得，他喜欢干什么呢？告诉你们吧，竟然是制作机械玩具和钟表！

此时，也就是查理五世担任西班牙国王的时候，英国的国王正是亨利八世。亨利八世姓都铎。由于许多国王的名字都相似，因此人们会在他们的名字后面加上数字，以此来表明指的究竟是哪个查理、哪个亨利，并且说明之前已经有过多少个相同的名字了。起初，亨利八世也是一位坚定不移的天主教徒，教皇还曾称他为"护教者"[1]呢。可亨利八世由于妻子没有给他生个儿子，所以想和妻子离婚。亨利八世想要一个儿子来继承自己的王位，并让英国保持统一。要想休掉现任的妻子，以便可以再娶一位妻子，亨利八世就必须获得教皇的批准，因为教皇是唯一能够让亨利

---

[1] 护教者（Defender of the Faith），1512年教皇利奥十世赐给英王亨利八世的封号，也译为"卫护信仰者""护教功臣"等。

him he would not give him a divorce.

Now, Henry thought it was neither right nor proper that a man in another country — even if he *were* pope — should say what could be done in England. He himself was ruler, and he didn't intend to let any foreigner meddle in his affairs or give him orders.

Then Henry said that he himself would be head of all the Christians in England; then he could do as he wished without the pope's permission. So he made himself head, and then he divorced his wife. All the churches in England were now told by the king what they should do; the pope no longer had anything to say in the matter; the English churches obeyed the king, not the pope. This made the second big break in the Catholic Church.

After this, Henry VIII had five other wives, six in all; not of course all at one time, for Christians could only have one wife at a time. His first wife he divorced, the second he beheaded, the third died. The same thing happened to his last three wives: the first he divorced, the second he beheaded, and the third survived. Henry died before she did.

Is this too difficult for you to understand?

Henry VIII and his second wife Anne Boleyn
亨利八世和他的第二任妻子安妮·博林

八世离婚的人。此时，罗马教皇是整个欧洲及南北美洲基督教会的领袖；无论教徒是在意大利、西班牙还是在英国，能做什么、不能做什么，都是罗马教皇说了算。亨利八世请求教皇批准他离婚。然而教皇却说，他是不会批准亨利八世离婚的。

于是，亨利八世便觉得，由别国的一个人来决定英国人可以做什么，这种做法既不正确，也不合适，哪怕这个人身为教皇也不行。他自己就是一位君主，因此不希望让任何外国人来干涉他的事情，不希望任何人来对他发号施令。

接着，亨利八世便说自己要当英国基督徒的领袖；这样一来，他就可以为所欲为，不需要教皇批准了。因此，他便自封基督徒领袖，然后与妻子离了婚。至此，英国所有教堂的事务，便全由英国国王说了算，教皇在这方面不再有任何发言权，而英国各教堂服从的也是英王，而不是教皇了。这就形成了天主教会的第二次重大分裂。

此后，亨利八世又娶了五位妻子，也就是说，他总共娶了六位妻子；当然，他并不是一次就娶那么多，因为基督徒一次只能娶一位妻子。他将第一任妻子休了，将第二任妻子砍了脑袋，第三任妻子则死了。而他后来那三位妻子的遭遇也是一样：第一位被他休了，第二位被他砍了头，第三位则幸存下来了。因为第三任妻子去世之前，亨利八世就死了。

你们还觉得这一章很难理解吗？

68 Queen Elizabeth

King Henry VIII had two daughters.

One was named Mary, and one was named Elizabeth.

Their last name was of course Tudor, the same as their father's although we do not usually think of kings and queens as having last names.

King Henry had a son, also, and he was first to become king after his father died, for though he was younger than his sisters, a boy was supposed to be more fit to rule than a girl. But he didn't live long, and then Mary was the first of the two sisters to become queen.

Mary did not approve what her father had done when he turned against the pope and the Catholic Church. Mary herself was a strong Catholic and ready to fight for the pope and the Catholic Church. She thought that all those who did not believe as she did should be persecuted for heresy, or expressing beliefs opposed to the traditional Catholic Church. Like the queen in *Alice in Wonderland*, she was always saying, "Off with his head!" This seems to us very unchristian, but in those days their ideas about such things were different. Mary had so many people killed that she was called Bloody Mary.

68 伊丽莎白女王

英王亨利八世有两个女儿。

其中一个叫作玛丽，一个叫作伊丽莎白。

她们当然也都跟着父亲姓都铎，尽管我们通常都想不到国王和女王也会有姓。

亨利国王还有一个儿子；父亲死后，这个儿子是王位的第一继承人；虽然他比两个姐姐都小，但人们觉得一个男孩子肯定比女孩子更适合统治国家。可他的寿命不长，因此在这两姐妹中，玛丽后来便成了王位第一继承人，当上了英国女王。

玛丽并不赞同父亲反对教皇和天主教会的做法。玛丽本身是一个坚定的天主教徒，很愿意为捍卫教皇和天主教会而斗争。她认为，所有不像她那样坚定地信仰天主教的人，全都应该当成异教徒，并认为表达了与正统天主教相对的观点的人应被处死。就像《爱丽丝梦游仙境》中的那位女王一样，玛丽也总是在说："砍了他的头！"在我们看来，这种做法很不符合基督教的教义；可在那个时候，人们对这些事情的看法可大不一样呢。由于玛丽处死了很多的人，因此她被人们称为"血腥玛丽"。

玛丽的丈夫和她一样，也是一位坚定不移的天主教徒，并且比玛丽还要残忍嗜

Mary married a man who was just as strong a Catholic as she and even bloodier. He was not an Englishman, but a Spaniard, Philip II of Spain, son of Charles V, who had abdicated.

Philip II was much sterner than his father had been. Philip tried to make those who were Protestants, or who were supposed to be Protestants, confess and give up Protestantism. If they did not do so, they were tortured as the old Christian martyrs had been tortured. This was called the Inquisition. Those suspected of being Protestants were tormented in all sorts of horrible ways. Some were tied up in the air by their hands, like a picture hung on a wall, until they fainted from the pain or else confessed what they were told to confess. Some were stretched on a rack, their heads pulled one way and their legs the opposite way, until their bodies were nearly torn apart. Those who were found guilty of being Protestants were killed outright, burned to death, or put slowly to death, so that they would suffer longer. You should know that Protestants were not the only people who suffered under the Spanish Inquisition. A century earlier, Jews were tortured in the same way. Most left Spain to find new homes in North Africa or Europe.

The people whom Philip chiefly persecuted were the Dutch people in Holland. Holland then belonged to his empire, and a great many of the Dutch people had become Protestants.

Now, there was a Dutchman called William the Silent because he talked little but did a great deal. William was furious at the way his people were treated. He fought against

杀。他不是英国人，而是西班牙人；他是西班牙的腓力二世，即那个退了位的查理五世的儿子。

腓力二世的做法，要比他的父亲严酷得多。腓力想方设法地要让那些新教徒或者据说是新教徒的人忏悔，并且让他们不再信仰新教教义。假如这些人不照命行事，那他们就会像古时的基督教殉道者一样，受到残酷的拷问。这种拷问的过程，叫作"宗教审判"。在宗教裁判所，那些被怀疑是新教徒的人受到了各种各样的可怕折磨。一些人被绑着双手吊在空中，就像墙上挂的画那样，直到他们疼得晕过去，或者屈打成招后，这才会罢手。有些人被放到拉肢刑架上，头和脚分别被人向相反的方向拉伸，直到他们的身体几乎快被拉断时才停下。那些因为是新教徒而被判有罪的人，则要么被当场杀死，要么用火烧死，或者凌迟处死，从而让他们受苦的时间更久一点儿。你们应该明白，在西班牙宗教裁判所里受苦受难的，可并不只有新教徒。一个世纪以前，犹太人也受到了同样的折磨。因此，绝大多数犹太人才会离开西班牙，到北非或欧洲的其他地区去寻找新的家园。

腓力二世处决的人，主要还有荷兰的荷兰人。当时，荷兰是腓力二世所统治的那个帝国的属国，而很多的荷兰人都皈依了新教。

此时，荷兰有一个人，因为寡言少语、多干实事而被称为"沉默者威廉"。对于国民的遭遇，威廉觉得义愤填膺。他揭竿而起，与腓力二世做斗争，并且最终成功地让自己的祖国获得了自由，从而建立了荷兰共和国。不过，后来腓力二世却下令暗杀了"沉默者威廉"。

Philip and at last succeeded in making his country free and setting up the Dutch Republic. But William the Silent was murdered by order of Philip.

And that's the kind of man Bloody Mary had for a husband.

After Mary Tudor died, her sister, Elizabeth Tudor, became queen. Elizabeth was the strongest of Henry's three children. Elizabeth had red hair and was very vain and loved to be flattered. Many men loved her but she never married, and, as a woman who never marries was called a virgin, she was known as the Virgin Queen.

Elizabeth was a Protestant and was just as bitter against the Catholics as her sister and sister's husband had been against the Protestants.

A relative of Elizabeth was queen of Scotland. Scotland is a country north of England, but at that time it did not have the same ruler as England, and its queen was named Mary Stuart. Mary Stuart, Queen of Scots, was young, beautiful, and fascinating; but she was a Catholic, and so Elizabeth and she were enemies.

Elizabeth heard that Mary Stuart was trying to become queen of England as well as Scotland, so she had her, although a relative, put in prison. In prison Mary Stuart stayed for nearly twenty years and was then at last put to death by Elizabeth's orders. It is hard for us to understand how anyone could have her own relative killed in this coldblooded way, especially anyone who pretended to be a Christian, but in those times it was a very common custom, as we see when we hear of so many murders committed by the rulers of the people.

　　"血腥玛丽"正是选了这样一个男人当丈夫。

　　玛丽·都铎死后，她的妹妹伊丽莎白·都铎继任，成了英国女王。在亨利八世的三个孩子当中，伊丽莎白其实是最强硬的一个。伊丽莎白一头红发，非常自负，而且喜欢听别人的奉承话。许多男人都爱她，可她却终身未嫁；由于那些终身未嫁的女子都被称为"贞女"，因此她也被世人称为"童贞女王"。

　　伊丽莎白是一名新教徒；她在对付天主教徒的时候，完全就像自己的姐姐、姐夫对付新教徒那样残酷。

　　伊丽莎白的一位亲戚是苏格兰女王。苏格兰是英格兰北边的一个国家，可当时该国与英格兰并不是由同一位君主统治着；该国的这位女王，叫作玛丽·斯图亚特。苏格兰的玛丽·斯图亚特女王既年轻、漂亮，又很迷人；可她是一位天主教徒，因此伊丽莎白便与她成了仇敌。

　　伊丽莎白听说玛丽·斯图亚特正在图谋成为英格兰和苏格兰两国的女王，因此尽管两人是亲戚，伊丽莎白还是将她关进了监狱。玛丽·斯图亚特在监狱里关了差不多20年，最后又被伊丽莎白下令处死了。我们很难理解，一个人，尤其是一个假惺惺地认为自己是基督徒的人，怎么能够用如此冷酷无情的方式杀掉自己的亲戚？可在那个时代，这却是一种常见的做法呢；而我们在听说那些统治民众的君主全都干过许许多多的阴谋杀戮行径之后，就会明白这一点了。

　　腓力二世这个十足的天主教捍卫者，下定决心要惩罚自己的小姨子伊丽莎白，因为她把玛丽·斯图亚特这样一个虔诚的天主教徒杀害了。于是，他组建了一支庞

Philip II the great champion of the Catholics, made up his mind to punish Elizabeth, his sister-in-law, for killing such a good Catholic as Mary Stuart. So he got together a large navy of very fine ships called the Spanish Armada. All Spain was very proud of this fleet. It was boastfully called the Invincible Armada; *invincible means unconquerable*.

The Invincible Armada set forth in 1588 to conquer the English navy. Lined up in the shape of a half-moon, the ships sailed grandly toward England.

The English fleet was composed only of little boats. Instead of going out to meet the Armada in regular sea battle as the Spaniards expected, the English ships sailed out and attacked the Spanish ships from behind and fought one ship at a time. The English were better fighters, and their small boats were quicker and more easily managed. They could strike a blow and get away before a Spanish ship could rum around into position to fire. Gradually the English fleet sank or destroyed the big Spanish boats one by one.

Then the English set some old boats afire and started them drifting toward the Spanish fleet. As all boats at that time were of course made of wood, the Spaniards became frightened at these burning piles drifting down upon them, and part of the fleet sailed away. The rest tried to get back to Spain by sailing the long way round, north of Scotland. However, a terrible storm struck them, and almost all the boats were shipwrecked, and thousands of dead bodies were washed up on shore. The great Spanish Armada was destroyed, and with it ended the power of Spain at sea. Spain was no longer the great nation it had been.

大的海军，海军由许多精良的战船组成，号称是西班牙的"无敌舰队"。西班牙上下都为这支舰队而感到自豪。他们自负地称这支舰队为"所向披靡的无敌舰队"；而所谓的"所向披靡"，就是指"不可战胜"。

这支所向披靡的无敌舰队于1588年起航，前去征服英国海军。于是，舰队里的所有战船排成一个半月形，浩浩荡荡地朝英国驶去。

英国舰队里，全都是小型的战船。可英军的战船并没有像西班牙人所预计的那样出海迎敌，来与无敌舰队展开常规的海战；它们而是驶出了港口，从后部去袭击西班牙舰队，并且每次只与一艘敌船作战。英军比较善战，而他们的战船虽说较小，速度却更快，也更容易操纵。他们可以在发动一次袭击之后，不待西班牙的战船转过身来进入开火战位，就马上撤退。因此，英国舰队慢慢地将西班牙的那些大型战舰一艘接一艘地击沉或者消灭了。

接着，英军又将一些旧船点上火之后发动起来，让它们漂向西班牙舰队。由于当时的船只全都是木制的，因此看到这些顺水向他们漂来、燃着熊熊大火的船只后，西班牙人都大惊失色，有一部分战船便逃离了舰队。剩下的那些战船则想绕过苏格兰的北部，取远路返回西班牙。然而，路上它们又碰上了可怕的暴风雨，几乎所有船只都沉没了；后来，还有数千具士兵的尸体被海浪吹到了岸边呢。这支庞大的西班牙无敌舰队被彻底消灭，从而结束了西班牙称霸海上的历史。于是，西班牙不再是以前那个强大的国家了。

伊丽莎白女王登基之初，世界上疆域最广、实力最强大的国家就是西班牙；而

At the beginning of Elizabeth's reign, the largest and most powerful country in the world was Spain; at the end of her reign it was England that was the most powerful. Her fleet, which King Alfred had started far back, became one of the largest.

People at that time thought it impossible for a woman to rule as well as a man, but under Elizabeth's rule England in turn became the leading country of Europe. Elizabeth proved that a woman could rule England better than most kings had.

到她在位末期的时候，英国则成了世界上最强大的国家之一。她手下那支由阿尔弗雷德大帝在很久以前创立的舰队，也成了世界上规模最大的舰队之一。

那个时候，人们觉得一位女性是不可能像男性一样统治好一个国家的；可在伊丽莎白女王的统治下，英国却反而变成了欧洲首屈一指的国家。伊丽莎白的成就证明，女性也可以把英国治理得比历史上绝大多数王国都要更好。

69 The Age of Elizabeth

This story is about the Age of Elizabeth. I'm not going to tell you how old Elizabeth was, though she did live and reign a great many years.

I'm going to tell you some of the things that happened during her long life, for the time when she lived is called the Age of Elizabeth.

There was a young man named Raleigh' living when Elizabeth became queen. One day when it was raining and the streets were muddy, Elizabeth was about to cross the street. Raleigh saw her and, to keep her from soiling her shoes, ran forward, took off his beautiful velvet cape, and threw it in the puddle where she was about to step, so that she might cross upon it as upon a carpet. The queen was greatly pleased with this thoughtful and gentlemanly act and she made him a knight, so that he was then called Sir Walter Raleigh, and ever after that he was one of her special friends.

Sir Walter Raleigh was much interested in America. Cabot had claimed a great part of it for England almost a hundred years before, but England had done nothing about it. Raleigh thought something should be done about it; he thought English people should settle there, so that other countries like Spain, which had made so many settlements in America, would not get ahead of

69　伊丽莎白时代

这一章，讲的是"伊丽莎白时代"。我不是要告诉你们伊丽莎白女王有多大年纪[1]；不过她的确很高寿，也当了很多年的英国女王。

我要跟你们说的是，在她漫长的一生中所发生的一些事情；因为她所在的那个时期，就是所谓的"伊丽莎白时代"。

伊丽莎白登基当上女王的时候，英国有一个男子，名叫罗利。有一天，天上下着雨，街上泥泞不堪，当时伊丽莎白正想过街。罗利看到了她；为了不让她弄脏鞋子，罗利便跑上前去，脱下自己那身漂亮的天鹅绒斗篷，铺在她就要踏入的那处水坑上，使得她就像是踩在地毯上那样走过去。对这种非常体贴、非常具有绅士风度的行为，女王大感欣慰，便封他为骑士；从此以后，他就被称为沃尔特·雷利勋爵，并且成了女王的挚友之一。

沃尔特·雷利勋爵对美洲非常感兴趣。差不多一百年前，卡伯特早已将美洲的大部分地区宣布为英国所有，可英国对这些国土却一直不理不睬。雷利觉得，必须采取点儿什么措施才行了；他认为，英国人应当到那里去殖民，这样的话，其他一

---

[1]　在英语中，"时代"和"年纪"是同一个词，都是age。作者担心小朋友会将这两个意思混淆起来，所以才这样说。

England. Raleigh got together several companies of English people and sent them over to an island called Roanoke, which was just off the coast of the present state of North Carolina. At that time, however, almost the whole coast of the United States as far north as Canada was called Virginia. It had been named Virginia in honor of the Virgin Queen Elizabeth.

Some of these Roanoke colonists became discouraged with the hardships they had to suffer and so gave up and sailed back home again. Those who remained all disappeared. Where? No one knows. We think they must either have been killed or have died of starvation. At any rate, not one was left to tell the tale. Among these Roanoke colonists was the first English child born in America — a girl, who had been named Virginia Dare, for the queen was very popular and a great many girls were named Virginia after her.

Some tobacco was brought back from Virginia, and Sir Walter Raleigh learned to smoke. This was such a strange and unknown thing at that time that one day while he was smoking a pipe, a servant who saw smoke coming out of his mouth thought he was on fire and, running for a bucket of water, emptied it over his head.

Virginia is still famous for its tobacco. At first tobacco was supposed to be very healthful, for the Native Americans seemed to have very good health, and they smoked a great deal. Afterward, however, in the next reign, King James so hated tobacco that he wrote a book against it and forbade its use. Now we know that James was right and that tobacco can make people sick with deadly diseases.

After Queen Elizabeth died, Raleigh was put in prison, for it was said he was plotting

些已经在美洲拥有了许多殖民地的国家，比如西班牙，才不会胜过英国。于是，雷利召集了好几拨英国人，派他们漂洋过海，来到了一个叫作罗阿诺克的岛屿上；这个岛屿，就在如今美国北卡罗来纳州的近海地区。然而，那个时候，几乎美国的整个沿海地区，并且向北远至加拿大的沿海地区，都叫弗吉尼亚。人们之所以把这里叫作"弗吉尼亚"，正是为了向"童贞女王"伊丽莎白致敬呢。

来到罗阿诺克岛的那些殖民者当中，有些人由于不得不忍受那里的艰苦条件而变得灰心丧气，便放弃了殖民，回到了国内。而那些留下来的殖民者，却全都不见了。他们去哪里了呢？没人知道。我们认为，那些人要么是被人杀了，要么就是饿死了。不管怎么样，反正没人活下来给我们讲述那段悲惨的往事了。在罗阿诺克岛的那些殖民者当中，还包括了第一名在美洲出生的英国儿童呢；那是一个女孩，父母给她起名为维吉妮亚·戴尔。这是由于"童贞女王"伊丽莎白很受人爱戴，所以有许多女孩都随她而起名叫维吉妮亚[1]。

殖民者从弗吉尼亚带回了一些烟草，所以沃尔特·雷利勋爵学会了吸烟。当时，吸烟还是一件很古怪、人们还很不习惯的事情，因此有一天，正当罗利勋爵吞云吐雾的时候，一名仆人看到他的嘴里冒出烟来，还以为他身上起了火，便赶紧跑

---

[1] 维吉妮亚（Virginia），是由"处女，童贞"（virgin）一词加上词尾 -ia 构成，为欧美常见的女性名字。注意，我们在翻译外文的时候有音译和意译之分，Virgin Queen 译为"童贞女王"是意译，而 Virginia 译成"维吉妮亚"则是音译。另外，Virginia 作地名的时候，我们将其译成"弗吉尼亚"，以便与人名区分开来。

against the new king, James, who came after Elizabeth. The prison where he was placed was the Tower of London, the old castle that William the Conqueror had built. Here Raleigh was kept for thirteen long years, and to pass the time away he wrote a *History of the World*. But at last he was put to death as many other great men were also.

During the reign of Queen Elizabeth, there lived the great writer of plays, the greatest writer the world has ever known. This man was William Shakespeare.

Shakespeare's father could not write his name. Shakespeare himself spent only six years at school. As a boy he was rather wild, and he was arrested for hunting deer in the forest of Sir Thomas Lucy at Stratford.

When still a boy, Shakespeare married a girl older than himself named Anne Hathaway. After he had been married a few years he left her and their three children, left the little town of Stratford, and went up to the great city of London to seek his fortune. There, Shakespeare got a job working around a theater, holding the horses of those who came to see the plays. Then he got a chance to act in the theater, and he became an actor, but he did not become a very good one.

In those days the theaters had no scenery. A sign was put up to tell what the scene was supposed to be. For instance, instead of forest scenery, they would put up a sign saying, "This is a forest," or instead of a room scene a sign saying "This is a room in an inn." There were no actresses. Men and boys took the parts of both men and women.

Shakespeare was asked to change some of the plays that had already been written, so

出去提了一桶水，从他的头上淋了下去呢。

如今，弗吉尼亚仍然以盛产烟草而著称。起初，人们认为烟草对身体健康很有好处，因为美洲的土著似乎个个都身体很好，而他们也经常吸烟。然而到了后来，到了下一任国王在位的时候，英王詹姆斯由于极其讨厌烟草，便写了一本反对吸烟的书，并且禁止人们吸烟。如今我们知道，詹姆斯国王的看法是对的，因为烟草能够让人们得上致命的疾病。

伊丽莎白女王去世后，雷利勋爵被关进了监狱；原因则是，据说他打算阴谋反对继承伊丽莎白女王王位的新任国王詹姆斯。他被囚禁的地方就是伦敦塔，即"征服者威廉"所建的那座古老城堡。雷利勋爵在这里关了13年；为了打发时间，他便撰写了《世界历史》一书。不过，最终他还是像其他许多伟人一样，也被处死了。

在伊丽莎白女王治下，英国涌现出了一位伟大的剧作家，也是世界上有史以来最伟大的作家之一。这位作家，便是威廉·莎士比亚。

莎士比亚的父亲，连自己的名字也写不出来。莎士比亚本身则只在学校里上到了六年级。小的时候，莎士比亚非常桀骜不驯，还因为在斯特拉福德那片属于托马斯·卢西勋爵的森林里猎鹿，而被当局逮捕过呢。

莎士比亚很小就与一个年纪比他大、名叫安妮·海瑟薇的姑娘成了亲。结婚数年后，他便离开了她和他们所生的三个孩子，离开了斯特拉福德小镇，前往伦敦这座大城市寻找出路去了。到了伦敦后，莎士比亚先是在一家戏院边上工作，替那些前来看戏的人拴马。接下来，他得到了一个进戏院演戏的机会，于是便变成了一名

that they could be better acted. He did this very well; then he started in to write plays himself. Usually he took old stories and made them into plays, but he did it so wonderfully well that they are better than any plays that have ever been written before or since.

Though Shakespeare left school when only thirteen years old, he seems to have had a remarkable knowledge of almost everything under the sun. He shows in his plays that he knew about history and law and medicine. Some of the best known of Shakespeare's plays are *Hamlet, The Merchant of Venice, Romeo and Juliet*, and *Julius Caesar*.

Shakespeare made a good deal of money for those times — almost a fortune. Then he left London and went back to live in the little town of Stratford where he was born. Here at last he died and was buried in the village church. People wanted to move his body to a greater and handsomer place, to a famous church in London. But someone, perhaps Shakespeare himself, had written a verse which was carved on his tombstone. The last line of this verse said, "And curst be he who moves my bones"; so they never were moved, for no one dared to move them.

Shakespeare reading to Elizabeth
莎士比亚正在为伊丽莎白女王朗诵

演员；不过，他的演技并不是很出色。

那个时候，戏院里还没有什么舞台布景。演员会举起一块牌子，向观众说明舞台上应该是一种什么样的场景。比如说，演员们会举起一块上面写着"这是一座森林"的牌子，而不会将舞台布置成森林的样子；或者举起一块上面写着"这是客栈里的一个房间"的牌子，而不会将舞台布置成房间的样子。当时也没有女演员。男演员和男孩子们既演男人，也演女人的角色。

后来，有人请莎士比亚将一些已经写好的剧本进行修改，以便这些剧本能够更好地在舞台上演出。他在这方面很擅长；于是，接下来他便开始自己创作剧本。他通常是采用古时的一些故事传说作为素材，并将它们改编成剧本；不过，他改编得非常精彩，因此他写出的那些剧本都很优秀，简直可以说是空前绝后呢。

尽管莎士比亚13岁就辍学了，可他似乎对世界上差不多所有的领域都了如指掌，真是令人称奇。在他创作出来的剧本中，他表现出了历史、法律和医学等各方面的知识。莎士比亚最著名的一些戏剧作品，有《哈姆雷特》《威尼斯商人》《罗密欧与朱丽叶》等。

那个时候，莎士比亚赚了很多很多的钱，几乎成了富豪。然后，他便离开了伦敦，回到了自己出生的斯特拉福德小镇。他最终也是在这里去世的，并且被安葬在一座乡村教堂里。人们曾经想要把他的遗体挪到一个更大、更气派的地方，挪到伦敦一座著名的教堂里去。不过，有人曾经在他的墓碑上刻下了一首诗，没准还是莎士比亚自己刻上去的呢。诗的最后一句是："挪动吾之尸骨者，必受诅咒。"所以，他的遗骸一直都没有挪动，因为没有人敢去挪动啊。

70 James the Servant or What's in a Name?

What does your name mean? If it is
Baker or
　　Miller or
　　　　Taylor or
　　　　　　Carpenter or
　　　　　　　　Fisher or
　　　　　　　　　　Cook,
it probably means that at some time one of your ancestors was a
baker, or
　　miller, or
　　　　tailor, or
　　　　　　carpenter, or
　　　　　　　　fisher, or
　　　　　　　　　　cook.
If your name is Stuart or Steuart or Stewart or Steward, it may mean that at some time

70　公仆詹姆斯

你们的名字都有什么含意呢？假如你们叫
贝克尔，或者
　　米勒，或者
　　　　泰勒，或者
　　　　　　卡朋特，或者
　　　　　　　　费希尔，或者
　　　　　　　　　　库克的话，
那么很有可能，你们的祖先在某个时期曾经是一位
面包师，或者
　　磨坊主，或者
　　　　裁缝，或者
　　　　　　木匠，或者
　　　　　　　　渔夫，或者
　　　　　　　　　　厨师。
如果你的名字是斯图亚特、斯图尔特、斯图华特或者斯图尔德，那可能就意味

one of your ancestors was a steward, for in olden days people knew very little about spelling, and they spelled the same name in different ways. A steward was a chief servant.

There was a family named Stuart in Scotland, and from chief servants or stewards they had become rulers of the Scots. Mary Stuart, whom Elizabeth had beheaded, was one of them.

As Queen Elizabeth never married, she had no children to rule after her. She was the last of the Tudor family. The English had to look around for a new king, and they looked to Scotland.

Now, Scotland, as I have told you, was then a separate country and not a part of Britain as now. The son of Mary Stuart was then king of Scotland. His name was James Stuart. As he was related to the Tudors, the English invited him to come and rule over them. He accepted the invitation and was called James I. So we speak of his reign and that of his children as the reign of the Stuarts.

The Stuart family reigned for about a hundred years, that is, from 1600 to 1700, all except about eleven years when England had no king at all.

Many times the English must have been very sorry that they had ever invited James to be their king, for he and the whole Stuart family lorded it over the English people. They acted as if they were lords of creation, and the English people had to fight for their rights.

A body of men called Parliament was supposed to make the laws for the English people. But James said that Parliament could do nothing that he didn't like, and if they weren't

着你的祖先曾经是位管家；因为古时候人们对拼写不甚了解，所以他们会用不同的方式拼写同一个名字。所谓的"管家"，就是仆人的头儿。

苏格兰就有一个姓斯图亚特的家族；可他们却从仆人头子或者说管家，变成了苏格兰的君主。那个曾经被伊丽莎白砍掉了脑袋的玛丽·斯图亚特，就是这个家族中的一员。

由于伊丽莎白女王一直没有结婚，因此她没有孩子可以来继承王位。她是都铎家族中的最后一人。英国人不得不到处去寻找一位新的国王，于是他们便把目光转向了苏格兰。

注意，我在前面已经跟你们说过，那时的苏格兰还是一个独立的国家，并不是像现在这样，成了英国的一部分。当时，玛丽·斯图亚特的儿子是苏格兰国王。他的名字是詹姆斯·斯图亚特。由于他与都铎家族有亲戚关系，因此英国人便请他前来统治英格兰。他接受了邀请，被称为詹姆斯一世。这样，我们便将他在位以及他的孩子们在位的那个时期，叫作斯图亚特王朝。

斯图亚特王室统治了英国一百年左右，也就是说，从公元1600年至公元1700年；其中有十一年左右的时间，英国并没有国王。

英国人必定对他们邀请詹姆斯来当国王后悔不迭，因为他和整个斯图亚特王室，后来都是骑在英国人民的头上作威作福。他们的行为，就好像自己是万物之主一样；因此，英国人民不得不为了自己的权利而与之斗争。

为英国人民制定法律，本来应当由一个叫作议会的机构来负责。可詹姆斯却

very careful, he wouldn't let them do any governing at all. James said that whatever the king did was right, that the king could do no wrong, that God gave kings the right to do as they pleased with their subjects. This was called the Divine Right of Kings. Naturally the English people would not put up with this sort of thing. Ever since the time of King John, they had insisted on their own rights. The Tudors had often done things that the people didn't like, but the Tudors were English. The Stuarts, however, were Scottish, and the people looked on them as foreigners; what they permitted in one of their own family they wouldn't stand in these strangers whom they had invited into their family. So, of course, a quarrel was bound to start. But the real fight came with the next king and not with James.

During King James's reign, the Bible was translated into English. This is the Bible that is called the *King James Bible*.

Nothing much happened in England during James's reign, but in some other countries a great deal did happen although the king had little to do with it. English people made settlements in India, that far-away country that Columbus had tried to reach by going west; and these settlements there grew until India at last belonged to England. England had conquered a large empire and become a wealthy and powerful nation.

Settlements also were made in America; one was made in the South and one, in the North. Raleigh's settlement at Roanoke had disappeared, as I told you; but in 1607 a boatload of English men sailed over to America looking for adventure and hoping to make their fortunes by finding gold. They landed in Virginia and named the place where they

说，议会不能做他不喜欢的任何事情；并且威胁说，如果议员们不小心一点儿的话，他就会彻底剥夺他们的行政权力。詹姆斯说，国王所做的一切都是正确的，国王不可能犯错，上帝赋予了国王随心所欲地处置手下臣民的权力。这就是所谓的"君权神授"。英国人民自然不会容忍这种事情。自英王约翰统治时期以来，他们一直都在坚持捍卫自己的权利。虽说都铎王朝以前也经常做出民众不喜欢的事情来，可都铎王室毕竟都是英国人。然而，斯图亚特王室却是苏格兰人，而英国民众也都将他们视作外族；因此，有些事情他们虽说允许本国的一个王室去做，可倘若他们邀请到本国来的这些异族也做同样的事情，他们就不会容忍了。因此，双方之间必定会爆发纷争。不过，真正的斗争却出现在下一位国王的任期，而不是詹姆斯一世在位的时候。

在詹姆斯国王统治期间，《圣经》被翻译成了英语。这部翻译过来的《圣经》，便被称为《英王詹姆斯钦定版圣经》。

在詹姆斯一世统治期间，英格兰并没有发生过什么重大事件；但在其他一些国家，却发生了许多与这位英王无关的事件。英国人开始在印度建立殖民地，就是哥伦布曾经想要通过向西航行前往的那个遥远国度；而那些殖民地逐渐地发展壮大起来，最后整个印度都成了英格兰的属国。英格兰已经控制了一个庞大的帝国，变成一个富有而强大的国家了。

英国人也开始在北美洲建立殖民地；其中一个在南部，另一个则在北部。前面我跟你们说过，雷利勋爵在罗阿诺克岛上所建的那个殖民地已经没有了；但在1607

settled Jamestown after their king, James. But they found no gold, and as they were not used to work, they didn't want to do any. Their leader, Captain John Smith, took matters in hand and said that those that didn't work shouldn't eat. So then the colonists had to go to work.

Back in England people had learned to smoke, and so the colonists began to raise tobacco for the English people. The tobacco brought the colonists so much money that it proved to be a gold mine — of a different kind — after all. But the colonial gentlemen wanted someone to do the rough work for them. A few years later black people were brought over from Africa and sold to the colonists to do the rough work. This was the beginning of slavery in America, which grew and grew until, on big plantations in the South, almost all the work was done by slaves.

This system of slavery was of course very wrong and cruel, but it lasted for several hundred years. Greed lay at the root of this as well as many other evils.

A little later another company of people left England for America. These people were not looking for fortunes, however, as the Jamestown settlers had been. They were looking for a place where they might worship God as they pleased, for in England they were interfered with, and they wanted to find a place where no one would interfere with them. So this company of people left Plymouth, England in 1620 in a ship called the *Mayflower*, sailed across the ocean, and landed in a place they named Plymouth, in Massachusetts, and there they settled. More than half of them died the first winter from hardship and exposure

年，却有一船英国人漂洋过海，前往美洲去探险，希望通过在美洲找到黄金而发上大财。他们在弗吉尼亚登陆，并根据英王詹姆斯的名字，把他们拓殖的那个地方叫作詹姆斯敦。不过，他们并没有找到黄金；可由于这些人过去都没怎么干过活儿，因此大家都不愿意工作。他们的头领约翰·史密斯船长承担起了责任，说谁不干活，谁就没饭吃。这样一来，那些殖民者便不得不动手去干活了。

由于英国国内有许多人都学会了吸烟，因此那些殖民者便开始为英国人种植烟草。烟草让殖民者赚了很多很多的钱，因此最终表明，烟草实际上完全就是一座金矿；当然，这可是一座不同类型的金矿。但是，那些殖民地的上流人士，却希望有人来替他们干那些粗活儿。几年后，便有人将黑人从非洲掳掠过来，卖给殖民者去干粗重的活儿。美洲的奴隶制度便由此开始了；这种制度不断发展，最终使得北美洲南部的大种植园里，几乎所有的工作都是由奴隶去干了。

这种奴隶制度当然既不道德，又很残酷；不过，它却持续了实行了好几百年。这种制度以及其他诸多恶行的根源，就在于人性的贪婪。

不久之后，又有一批人离开了英国，前往美洲。然而，这些人却与詹姆斯敦那些殖民者不一样，他们并不是想到美洲来寻找发财的机会。他们寻找的，是一个能够让他们按照自己的意愿来敬奉上帝的地方；因为在英格兰，他们经常受到他人的干涉，所以他们希望找到一个无人能够干涉他们的地方。于是，这帮人在1620年乘坐一艘名叫"五月花号"的船只，从英格兰的普利茅斯出发，横渡大西洋，在某个地方登上了美洲；他们将这个地方命名为普利茅斯——就在如今的马萨诸塞州，

in the bitter weather that they have in the North; nevertheless, none of those who were left would go back to England. This settlement was the beginning of that part of the United States called New England. You will hear more about both settlements later when you study American history. At present we must see what was going on in England, for there were great goings on following the reign of James Stuart.

并且在此定居下来。抵达后的第一个冬天，有一多半人都因为环境恶劣、北方天气严寒而死掉了；但尽管如此，这些人却没有一个愿意再回到英格兰去。这次殖民，便开辟出了美国如今叫作"新英格兰"的那个地区。你们日后在学习美国历史的时候，还会了解到南、北两个殖民地的更多情况。而现在，我们必须去看一看英格兰的形势了，因为在詹姆斯·斯图亚特统治期过后，英国又发生了许多的重大事件。

71 A King Who Lost His Head

The next king was King Charles I. He was the son of King James, whom you have just read about, and he was "a chip off the old block". Like his father he believed in the Divine Right of Kings, that he alone had the right to say what should be done or what should not be done, and he treated the English people as King John had; that is, as if they were made simply to serve his pleasure and to do as he said.

But this time the people didn't carry him off, as they had King John, to agree to a paper. They started to fight. The king made ready to fight for what he thought his rights. He got together an army of lords and nobles and those who agreed with him. Those who took his side even dressed differently from those who were against him. They grew their hair in long curls and wore a broad-brimmed hat with a large feather and lace collars and cuffs of lace even on their breeches.

Parliament also got together an army of the people who wanted their rights. They had their hair cut short and wore a hat with a tall crown and very simple clothes. A country gentleman named Oliver Cromwell trained a regiment of soldiers to be such good fighters that they were called Ironsides.

71　掉了脑袋的国王

接下来的英国国王，便是查理一世。他是上一章刚刚讲到过的那个英王詹姆斯的儿子。他与父亲一样，相信"君权神授"，即只有他才有权决定民众应当干什么、不应当干什么；而在对付英国人民这个方面，他则与英王约翰一样，也就是说，似乎英国人民之所以存在，完全是为了服侍他一个人去享乐，完全是为了听他使唤似的。

但这一次，英国人民却没有将查理一世带走，然后逼他签署一份文件，不像曾经对付英王约翰那样了。他们开始揭竿而起，进行斗争。国王已经做好了准备，要为他自以为的那些权力而战。他召集了一支由领主和贵族组成的军队；这些领主和贵族，全都赞同他的观点。那些支持查理一世的人，甚至在穿着上也与反对查理一世的人不同。他们都留着长长的卷发，戴着宽边且插有一根大羽毛的帽子，衣领是花边的，连马裤的裤脚上也饰有花边呢。

英国议会也召集了一支军队，由那些想要捍卫自身权利的民众组成。他们都把头发剪得短短的，戴着高高耸起的帽子，衣着非常朴素。一位名叫奥利弗·克伦威尔的乡绅还训练了一个团的士兵；这些士兵全都骁勇善战，因此被称为"铁甲军"。

The king's army was made up of men who prepared for battle by drinking and feasting. The parliamentary army prayed before going into battle and sang hymns and psalms as they marched.

At last after many battles the king's army was beaten and King Charles was taken prisoner. A small part of Parliament then took things into their own hands, and though they had no right to do so, they tried King Charles and condemned him to death. They found him guilty of being a traitor and a murderer and other terrible things. He was taken out in front of his palace in London in the year 1649, and his head was cut off. People now feel that this was a shameful thing for the parliamentary army to do to the king, and even at that time only a part of the English people were in favor of it. He might have been sent away instead of being killed, or he might have had his office of king taken away from him.

Oliver Cromwell, the commander of the parliamentary army, then ruled over England for a few years. He was a coarse-looking person with very rough manners, but honest and religious, and he ruled England as a stern and strict father might rule his family. He would stand no nonsense. Once when he was having his picture painted — for there were no photographs then — the artist left out a big wart he had on his face. Cromwell angrily told him,

King Charles I and Oliver Cromwell
英王詹姆斯一世和奥利弗·克伦威尔

英王手下的军队，全都是由一些在备战的时候饮酒作乐、大摆宴席的人组成的。而议会所率的军队，在战前却是做祷告，而进军的时候还会高唱赞美诗和圣歌呢。

经过多次大战之后，最终英王的军队被打败，查理一世也沦为了阶下囚。接下来，议会里的一小部分人掌握了权力；尽管无权那样干，但他们还是对查理一世进行了审判，并且判处他死刑。他们判决查理一世犯有叛国罪、谋杀罪，还有其他诸多可怕的罪行。1649年，他被押到自己在伦敦城里的皇宫前面，被刽子手砍下了脑袋。如今的人认为，议会统率的军队如此处置国王查理一世是一件并不光彩的事情；并且，即便是在当时，也只有一部分英国民众赞同这样干。他们本来可以将他流放，而无须将他杀害的；或者，他们也可以废除他的王位。

接下来，议会军司令奥利弗·克伦威尔便统治了英国若干年。他是个长相粗鄙的人，行事风格粗鲁，但很诚实、严谨，因此在治理英国的时候，他就像是一位不苟言笑的严父管理家人那样。他不会容忍有人胡闹。有一次，他正在让人给自己画像，因为当时还没有照相机；画师没有把他脸上一个大大的瘤子给画出来。克伦威尔非常生气地对他说："照我的本来面目画，不管是瑕疵还是优点。"尽管自封为

"Paint me as I am, wart and all." Cromwell was really a king although he called himself Protector.

When Cromwell died, his son became ruler after him, just as if he were the son of a king, but the son was unable to fill his father's shoes. He meant well, but he hadn't the brains or the ability that his father had, and so in a few months he resigned. Oliver Cromwell had been so strict that the English people had forgotten about their troubles under the Stuarts. So in 1660 when the English found themselves without a ruler, they invited the son of the monarch they had beheaded, and once more a Stuart became king. This was Charles II.

Charles was called the Merry Monarch because all he seemed to think about was eating and drinking, amusing himself, and having a good time. He made fun of things that were holy and sacred. To revenge himself on those who had put his father to death he had those of them who were still living killed in the most horrible way one could think of. Those that were dead already, Oliver Cromwell among them, were taken from their tombs; then their dead bodies were hanged and afterward beheaded.

In his reign that old and terrible disease, the plague, broke loose again in London. Some people thought that God had caused it, that He was shocked by the behavior of the king and his people especially toward holy things, that He was punishing them. The next year, 1666, a great fire started and burned up thousands of houses and hundreds of churches. But the Great Fire, as it was called, cleaned up the disease and dirt and was therefore really a

"护国公"，克伦威尔实际上就是一位国王。

克伦威尔死后，他的儿子继位成了英国的统治者，就像他是王子，继任的是王位一样；不过，这位儿子却没有他父亲那样的才干。他的本意很好，可他没有父亲那样的头脑和能力，因此几个月之后就下台了。克伦威尔的统治使得英国人民全都忘记了他们在斯图亚特王室统治下的种种遭遇。因此，当英国人发现本国又没有君主之后，他们便在1660年向那位曾被他们砍掉了脑袋的君主的儿子发出了邀请，而斯图亚特王室的一位成员便再次成了英国国王。这位国王，就是查理二世。

查理二世被称为"快乐的国王"，因为他心中所想的，似乎全然是吃、喝、玩、乐和尽情享受。他曾经对一些神圣而庄严的东西大加嘲弄。为了报复那些曾经处死了他父亲的人，他用我们想象不到的、最可怕的方式，将其中仍然在世的人一个个全都杀了。而对于那些已经过世了的，其中包括克伦威尔，他还叫人将他们的坟墓掘开，然后将他们的遗体吊起来，最后再砍下遗体的脑袋。

查理二世在位期间，瘟疫这种古老而可怕的疾病在伦敦再一次爆发了。有些人认为，这是上帝造成的，因为上帝被英王及其臣民的所作所为，尤其是对他们亵渎神圣之事的做法震惊了，因此上帝才来惩罚他们。第二年，即1666年，伦敦又发生了一场大火灾，焚毁了数千座房屋和数百座教堂。不过，人们后来所称的这场"伦敦大火"，也赶走了城里的瘟疫，清除了城里的污物，因此实际上这还是一件好事哩。伦敦这座城市里，原来修建的一直都是木制房屋。大火之后，人们在重建房屋的时候，用的就是砖头和石块了。

blessing. London had been a city of wooden houses. It was rebuilt of brick and stone.

Only one more Stuart ruler shall I tell you about — or rather a royal pair, William and Mary — because in their reign the fight between the people and their kings was once for all finally settled. In 1689 Parliament drew up an agreement called the Bill of Rights, which William and Mary signed. This agreement made Parliament ruler over the nation, and ever since, Parliament — not the king — has been the real ruler of England. This was called the *Glorious Revolution*. It was glorious because there was no war. I think we have heard enough of the Stuarts for a while.

我还要跟你们再说一个属于斯图亚特王室的君主，或者说是一对王室夫妇，即威廉和玛丽；因为他们在位期间，最终彻底地解决了英国人民和国王之间的争斗问题。1689年，议会起草了一份叫作《权利法案》的协议，后来威廉和玛丽都签字同意了这份法案。这份协议规定，由议会来治理整个国家；所以，自此以后，英国的真正统治者便是议会，而不是国王了。这一过程，被称为"光荣革命"。之所以光荣，就是因为双方之间没有爆发战争。我认为，到此为止，我们对斯图亚特王朝的情况，了解得暂时足够了。

72 Red Cap and Red Heels

The last Louis I told you about was a saint — the Louis who went on the last Crusade.

I'm going to tell you now about two kings named Louis who were not saints — not by any means.

They were Louis XIII and Louis XIV and they ruled France while the Stuarts were reigning in the seventeenth century in England.

Louis XIII was king in name only. Another man told him what to do, and he did it. Strange to say, this other man was a great ruler of the church called a cardinal, who wore a red cap and a red gown. The cardinal's name was Richelieu.

Now, you are probably sick and tired of hearing about wars, but during the reign of Louis XIII, another long war started, and I must tell you something about it, for it lasted thirty years. It was therefore called the Thirty Years' War. It was different from most wars. It was not a war of one country against another. It was a war between the Protestants and Catholics.

Cardinal Richelieu was of course a Catholic and the real ruler of France, which was a Catholic country. Nevertheless, he took sides with the Protestants, for they were fighting

72 红帽子、红鞋跟

前面我跟你们说过的最后一位"路易"，是一位圣徒，就是发动最后一次十字军东征的那位法国国王路易。

而现在，我准备再跟你们说一说两个不是圣徒、但也名叫"路易"的人；这两个人，跟圣徒可一点儿也挨不上边哩。

他们就是路易十三和路易十四；两人统治着法国的时候，正是斯图亚特王朝统治着英国的时候。

路易十三只是名义上的国王。当时，另外有一个人告诉他该干些什么，而他不过是奉命行事罢了。说来也怪，这个人也是教会里一位了不起的领导人物，被称为"枢机"；他戴着红帽子，身穿红法袍。这位枢机，名叫黎塞留。

注意，虽说你们可能已经厌烦了听我再来说战争的事情，可路易十三在位期间，又爆发了一场旷日持久的战争；而我也必须跟你们说一说它的情况才行，因为这场战争持续打了30年呢。因此，它就被称为"三十年战争"。这场战争，与绝大多数战争都不一样。它不是一场由一个国家对另一个国家的战争，而是一场新教徒对天主教徒的战争。

枢机黎塞留当然是一名天主教徒，并且是法国的实际统治者，因为法国是一个

a Catholic country called Austria, and he wanted to beat Austria. Most of the countries in Europe took part in this war, but Germany was the battleground where most of the fighting was done. Even Sweden, a northern country of Europe which we have not mentioned before, took part. The king of Sweden at this time was named Gustavus Adolphus, and he was called the Snow King because he was king of such a cold country, and also the Lion of the North, for he was such a brave fighter. I am mentioning him particularly because of all kings and rulers in Europe at this time he was the finest character. Indeed, most of the other rulers thought only of themselves, and they would lie and cheat and steal and even murder to get what they wanted, but Gustavus Adolphus was fighting for what he thought was right. Gustavus Adolphus was a Protestant, and so he came down into Germany and fought on the side of the Protestants. He was a great general, and his army won. Unfortunately he himself was killed in battle. The Protestants came out ahead in the Thirty Years' War, and at last a famous treaty of peace was made called the Treaty of Westphalia. By this treaty it was agreed that each country should have whatever religion its ruler had; it could be Protestant or Catholic, as the ruler wished.

During the Thirty Years' War, the plague, that old deadly contagious disease we have heard of before, broke out in Germany. A little town named Oberammergau prayed that it might be spared. The townspeople vowed that if they were spared they would give a play of Christ's life once every ten years. They were spared, and so every ten years, ever since then, with only a few exceptions, they have been giving what is called the Passion Play.

天主教国家。尽管如此，黎塞留却支持新教徒这一边，因为新教徒正在与一个叫作奥地利的天主教国家作战，而黎塞留则希望打败奥地利。欧洲的绝大多数国家都参与了这场战争，但战场却是在德国，绝大多数战役也都发生在德国。连地处欧洲北部、我们前面已经提到过的瑞典，也参与了这场战争呢。此时的瑞典国王名叫古斯塔夫·阿道夫，由于他统治的瑞典气候非常寒冷，因此人们称他为"冰雪国王"；又因为他非常骁勇善战，所以人们还称他为"北方雄狮"。我之所以专门提到他，是因为在这一时期欧洲各国的国王当中，他是最杰出的人物之一。事实上，其他的君主当中，绝大多数人都只考虑自己的利益；为了达到自己的目标，他们可以干出撒谎、骗人、偷窃，甚至谋杀等行径来。可古斯塔夫·阿道夫呢，却是为了捍卫自己觉得正确的东西而战。古斯塔夫·阿道夫是一名新教徒，因此他率军南下进入德国，站在新教徒一边作战。他是一名了不起的将领，因此他的军队打赢了。可惜的是，他本人却在战斗中阵亡了。新教徒在"三十年战争"中占据了上风，于是双方最终签订了一份有名的和平条约，叫作《威斯特伐里亚条约》。在这份条约中，双方同意，每个国家都应当信奉该国君主所信奉的宗教；只要君主愿意，该国既可以信奉新教，也可以信奉天主教。

就在"三十年战争"期间，我们之前已经了解过的瘟疫这种古老而致命的传染病又在德国爆发了。奥伯阿默高这座小镇里的人纷纷向上帝祈祷，希望小镇可以幸免于难。小镇上的居民都发下誓言说，如果他们幸免于难的话，以后每十年就会演出一场关于基督生平的戏剧，以此来作为献给上帝的祭礼。他们后来的确逃过了一

Tens of thousands of tourists from all over the world travel to this little out-of-the-way town to see the townspeople act the story of Christ's life. The play is given on Sundays during the summer of the tenth year and lasts all day long. About seven hundred people take part. It is a great honor to be chosen to play the part of a saint, and it is the highest honor to be selected to play the part of Christ.

The next French king to rule after Louis XIII and Richelieu was Louis XIV.

The people in England had at last succeeded in getting the power to rule themselves through their Parliament. But in France, Louis would let no one rule but himself. He said, "I am the state," and he would let no one have a say in the government. This was the same as the Stuarts' Divine Right of Kings that the English people had put an end to. Louis ruled for more than seventy years. This is the longest time that anyone in history has ever ruled.

Louis XIV was called the Grand Monarch, and everything he did was to show off. He was always parading and strutting about as if he were the leading character in a play and not just an ordinary human being. He wore corsets and a huge powdered wig and shoes with very high red heels, to make himself appear taller. He carried a long cane, stuck out his elbows, turned out

Louis XIV
路易十四

劫；所以从那时起，他们每十年就会举办一届所谓的"耶稣受难剧"演出，其间只有少数几次没有举办。如今，每年都有成千上万的游客从世界各地来到这个偏僻的小镇，一睹小镇居民演出关于耶稣基督生平的故事。这出戏剧，通常都是在第十个年头的夏季演出，并且会演出一整天。每次都差不多有七百人参加演出。如果被选中扮演剧中的一位圣徒，那就是一种莫大的荣耀；而要是被选中扮演耶稣基督的话，那就是最高的荣耀了。

继路易十三和黎塞留之后，统治法国的下一任国王就是路易十四了。

英国人民通过议会，最终成功地获得了自治的权力。可在法国，路易十四除了自己，决不允许任何人来治理国家。他曾说过："我就是国家。"因此他不允许任何人在政府里拥有发言权。这种做法，与英国人民已经终结掉的、斯图亚特王朝的那种"君权神授"思想没什么两样。路易十四统治法国的时间长达七十多年。他也是世界历史上在位时间最长的一位君主。

路易十四被称为"伟大的君主"；他所做的每一件事情，都会拿出来炫耀。他经常举行阅兵活动，并且昂首阔步，仿佛自己就是一出戏剧中的主角，而不是普通人似的。他身穿紧身外套，头戴抹了粉的假发，脚上的靴子则有高高的红鞋跟，好让自己显得高一点儿。他喜欢随身携带着一根长长的手杖，胳膊向外突出，迈着八

his toes, and strutted up and down, for he thought these things made him seem grand, important, imposing.

All this may sound as if Louis were a strange person with no sense, but you must not get that idea. In spite of his absurd manners, he made France the chief power in Europe. He was almost constantly fighting other countries, trying to increase the size of France and to add to his kingdom, but I have already told you so much about so many fights, that I'm not going to tell you any more about his just now, for you would probably not read it if I did. So France had her turn as leader of all the other countries, as Spain and England had had theirs as well.

Louis built a magnificent palace at Versailles in which were marble halls, beautiful paintings, and many huge mirrors in which he could see himself as he strutted along. The palace was surrounded by a park with wonderful fountains. The water for the fountains had to be brought a long distance, and it cost thousands of dollars to have the fountains play just for a few minutes. Even today sightseers visit Versailles to see the magnificent palace rooms and to watch the fountains play.

路易十四准备就寝
Louis XIV getting ready for bed

字步，大摇大摆地走来走去；因为他觉得这样会让他显得高贵、显得重要，显得威风八面哩。

这一切，听起来会让人觉得路易十四似乎就是一个没有头脑的怪人；可你们千万不要这么想。虽说他的举止荒唐，可他却让法国变成了欧洲首屈一指的强国。他几乎一直都在跟别的国家打仗，千方百计地想要扩大法国的疆域，增加王国的领土；不过，由于我已经跟你们介绍过了那么多场战争的情况，因此我眼下不打算再跟你们介绍路易十四那些战争的情况。如果我介绍的话，你们很可能就不会自己去看了。这样，风水轮流转，法国便像以前的西班牙和英国那样，成了欧洲各国的领头羊。

路易十四在凡尔赛修建了一座辉煌壮观的皇宫；其中既有大理石的厅堂、美丽的油画，还有许多巨大的镜子，这样他就能看到自己趾高气扬地走来走去的样子了。王宫周围是一个公园，里面修建了许多奇妙的喷泉。这些喷泉所用的水，必须从很远的地方引来；哪怕只让喷泉喷上几分钟的时间，也要花费好几千美元呢。即便是到了今天，仍然有观光的人到凡尔赛来看这座辉煌宫殿里的房间，来观看这些喷泉喷水呢。

可是，路易十四并不是仅仅让自己置身于美妙的东西之间。他还把当时最有意

But Louis surrounded himself not only with beautiful things. He also surrounded himself with all the most interesting men and women of his time. All those who could do anything exceptionally well, all those who could paint well or write well or talk well or play well or look well, he brought together to live with him or near by him. This was called his court. They were the chosen few who looked down on all the others.

This was all very fine for the people who were lucky enough to be in Louis's court. But the poor people of France, ordinary farmers and the men and women who worked in the towns, were the ones who had to pay Louis's expenses and those of his court. They were the ones who had to pay for his parties and balls and feasts and for all sorts of presents that he gave his friends. We shall soon see what happened. The poor people would not stand that sort of thing forever. "The worm will turn," we say.

思的人全都招揽到了自己的身边。凡是极其精通某一方面事物的人物，凡是擅长绘画、写作、交谈、演戏或者长相俊美的人，他都招来与自己同住，或者将他们招到自己的身边。这些人，便组成了他那个所谓的"宫廷"。他们都是经过精心挑选的精英，根本就瞧不上其他的人。

对于那些运气够好，能够进入路易十四宫廷的人来说，这是一件非常美妙的事情。但是，法国的穷人、普通农民以及在城镇里工作的人，却是负担路易十四及其宫廷宠臣们各种花费的人。他们得负担路易十四举办种种晚会、舞会、宴会，以及给朋友们送各种礼物的花费。我们不久就会看到，后来导致了国家形成什么样的形势。穷人不会永远忍受这种事情的。这正是我们所说的："狗急了也会跳墙。"

73 A Self-Made Man

Who was the Father of his Country?

I know what you will say:

"George Washington."

But there was another man called *The Father of His Country* before Washington was born, and he was not an American.

In the northeast of Europe and in northern Asia, there is a great country twice as large as our own. Its name is Russia. Very little had been heard of Russia before the Year 1700, for although it was the largest country in Europe, its people were relatively isolated — that is living apart from the rest of Europe. The Russians were a branch of the large Indo-European family called Slavs. Genghis Khan and the Mongols had conquered Russia in the thirteenth century and ruled over the land. So, although the Russians were Christians, they were in some ways more like the people of the East than like Europeans. The men had long beards and wore long coats. The people counted on an abacus as the Chinese did. Long after serfdom had ended in Western Europe, a great many Russians still were serfs.

Well, just before 1700 there was born a Russian prince named Peter. When a small boy,

73 白手起家的人

谁是"国父"呢?

我知道你们都会回答说:

"乔治·华盛顿啊。"

不过,在华盛顿出生之前,还有一个人也被称为"国父",而且他也不是美国人。

在欧洲东北部和亚洲北部有一个伟大的国家,它的面积有美国的两倍。这个国家就是俄罗斯。在公元1700年以前,人们对俄罗斯的情况知之甚少,因为尽管它是欧洲面积最大的国家,可俄罗斯人却相对比较闭塞;也就是说,他们与欧洲其他各国都不怎么往来。俄罗斯人是斯拉夫人这个庞大的印欧语系民族中的一个分支。成吉思汗和蒙古人曾在十三世纪的时候征服过俄罗斯,并统治过这个国家。因此,尽管俄罗斯人都是基督徒,可他们在某些方面却更像是东方民族,而不像是欧洲人。俄罗斯男子都留着长长的胡须,并且身着长袍。他们像中国人一样,在算盘上进行计算。在西欧各国结束农奴制度很久以后,许多俄罗斯人却仍然还是农奴。

好了,就在公元1700年的前夕,俄罗斯诞生了一位王子,名叫彼得。小的时候,彼得很害怕戏水。可他觉得,自己作为一位王子竟然会害怕,这是件很丢人的

Peter was very much afraid of the water. But he felt so ashamed that he, a prince, should fear anything that he forced himself to get used to the water. He would go to it and play in it and sail boats on it, although all the time he was almost scared to death. At last he not only got over this great fear but he came to like the water and boats more than any other playthings.

When Peter grew up, the thing he wanted more than anything else in the world was to make his country important in Europe, for before this time it had not been. It was big but not great. He wanted his people to share the culture and wealth that other Europeans enjoyed. But before he could teach his own people, most of whom were very poor and ignorant, he had to learn himself. As there was no one in Russia who could teach him what he wanted to know, he disguised himself as a common laborer and went to the little country of Holland. Here he got a job in a shipbuilding yard and worked for several months, cooking his own food and mending his own clothes. While he was doing this, however, he learned all about building ships and studied many other things besides, such as blacksmithing, cobbling shoes, and even pulling teeth.

Then he went to England, and everywhere he went he learned all he could. At last he returned to his own country with the knowledge he had gained and set to work to make Russia over. First of all, Peter wanted Russia to have a fleet of ships as other nations had. But in order to have a fleet, he had to have water for his ships, and Russia had almost no land bordering on the water. So Peter planned to take a seashore away from the

事情，因此他强迫自己去戏水。他来到水边，在水里玩耍，在水上划船，尽管他其实一直都怕得要命。最后，他不但克服了这种巨大的恐惧，还喜欢上了水，喜欢上了在水中划船，并且戏水胜过了其他所有的玩具。

彼得长大后，他在这个世界上最大的心愿，就是让他统治下的俄罗斯变成欧洲的重要国家，因为此前俄罗斯在欧洲一直都无足轻重。俄罗斯的国土面积虽广，却并不伟大。他希望自己的人民能够分享其他欧洲人所享有的文化和财富。不过，在他能够教导本国民众之前，他自己首先必须学会这些东西才行；当时，他手下的子民绝大多数都非常贫穷，目不识丁。由于俄罗斯国内没有人能够将他想要了解的知识教给他，所以他将自己打扮成一名普通的劳力，前往荷兰这个小国家。他在荷兰的一家造船厂里找到了一份工作，干了好几个月的活儿，不但要自己做饭，还得缝补自己的衣服呢。然而，在打工的过程中，他不但掌握了所有的造船知识，还学到了其他许多的东西，比如铁器加工、修鞋，甚至拔牙。

接下来，他又去了英国，并且每到一处，都尽力了解当地的所有情况。最后，他带着自己学到的全部知识回到了祖国，开始改变俄罗斯。首先，彼得希望俄罗斯像别的国家一样，拥有一支本国的舰队。但是，要想拥有一支舰队，他必须拥有能够停放舰队的水域才行，而当时俄罗斯却几乎没有临海的领土。于是，彼得便制定计划，打算从邻国瑞典手中夺取一片沿海地区。

此时，瑞典的国王是查理。他是瑞典历史上第十二位名叫查理的国王。查理十二当时几乎还是个毛孩子，因此彼得觉得打败这个毛孩子、任意夺取瑞典的沿海

neighboring country of Sweden.

Now the king of Sweden at this time was Charles. He was the twelfth king named Charles that Sweden had had. Charles XII was hardly more than a boy, and Peter thought it would be an easy matter to beat this boy and help himself to whatever land he wanted on the water. But Charles was not an ordinary boy. He was an extraordinary boy, extraordinarily bright and gifted, and he had been unusually well educated besides. He knew several languages; he had learned to ride a horse when he was four years old and how to hunt and to fight. Besides all this, he feared neither hardship nor danger. Indeed, he was such a dare-devil that people called him the Madman of the North. At first Peter's army was beaten by Charles.

But Peter took his beating calmly, simply remarking that Charles would soon teach the Russian army how to win. Indeed, so successful was Charles at first in fighting Peter and all others who threatened him that the countries of Europe began to think of him as Alexander the Great come to life again, and they feared he might conquer them all. But at last the Russians did win against Charles, and Peter got his seashore. Peter then built the fleet for which he had been working and planning for so many years.

The capital of Russia was Moscow. It was a beautiful city but near the center of that country and far from the water. This didn't suit Peter at all. Peter wanted a fine city for his capital, but he wanted it right on the water's edge, so that he could have his beloved ships close to him. He picked out a spot not only on the water but mostly water, for it was

地区是件轻而易举的事情。但是，查理十二可不是个普普通通的孩子。他是个非同寻常的孩子，他聪明过人，天赋禀异；除此之外，他还接受了异常全面的教育。他懂好几种语言；四岁的时候，他就学会了骑马、打猎和作战。除了这些，他还毫不畏惧困难和危险。事实上，他极其勇猛无畏，人们都曾称他为"北方狂人"呢。因此，起初彼得所率的军队败在了查理十二的手下。

但是，面对失利，彼得却很冷静，他只是说查理十二很快就将教会俄罗斯军队如何去取胜。事实上，查理十二起初把彼得以及那些威胁过他的国家全都打了个落花流水，因此欧洲各国都以为他是亚历山大大帝再生，并且担心他可能将这些国家全都征服呢。不过，最终俄罗斯军队还是打败了查理十二；于是，彼得便获得了自己想要的沿海地区。接下来，彼得便开始组建舰队；而他为组建这支舰队，已经工作和计划多年了。

俄罗斯的都城是莫斯科。这是一座美丽的城市，但它位于该国的中心地带，距沿海地区非常遥远。这种情况，根本就不符合彼得的雄心壮志。彼得希望有一座漂亮的都城，但他希望这座都城位于海边，这样他就可以把自己所钟爱的舰队部署在身边了。于是，他选择了一个地方，那里不但临近海洋，而且绝大部分地区都是水，因为那里本来就是一片沼泽。接下来，他派出33万多人去将那片沼泽填平，然后就在这片沼泽之上修建了一座美丽的城市。这座城市被命名为圣彼得堡，以此来纪念守护神兼使徒彼得；而他自己的名字，也正是根据使徒彼得的名字来起的。圣彼得堡后来被更名为彼得格勒，后来又被改成列宁格勒；如今，这里恢复了原名，

chiefly a marsh. Then he put a third of a million people to work filling in the marsh, and on this he built a beautiful city. This city he called St. Petersburg in honor of his patron saint, the apostle Peter, after whom he himself had been named. The name of St. Petersburg was later changed to Petrograd and still later to Leningrad; and now it is again called St. Petersburg. After a revolution, which you will read about later, the capital was moved back to Moscow.

Peter improved the laws, started schools, and built factories and hospitals and taught his people arithmetic. He made his people dress like other Europeans. He made the men cut off their long beards, which he thought looked countrified. The men thought it indecent to have no beards so some saved them to be placed in their coffins in order that at the day of resurrection they could appear before God unashamed. He introduced all sorts of things that he found in Europe but which were unknown in his own country, and he really made Russia over into a great European nation. That is why he is called Peter the Great, the Father of his Country.

Peter fell in love with a poor peasant girl, an orphan named Catherine, and married her. She had no education, but she was very sweet and lovely and bright and quick-witted, so the marriage turned out happily. The Russians were shocked at the idea of having a queen who was not a princess and was so low-born. But Peter had her crowned, and after he died she ruled over Russia.

再次叫作圣彼得堡了。一场革命之后,俄罗斯的首都又迁回了莫斯科;日后,你们就会看到这次革命的情况。

彼得改善了律法,开设了学校,建造了工厂和医院,还教给他的臣民们算术知识。他让手下的臣民都像其他欧洲人一样穿衣服。他让男人都剪掉长须,因为他觉得长胡须看上去粗俗不堪。当时,男人们都觉得没有胡须很不体面,因此有些人还把剪下的胡须留了下来,准备死后放进棺材里;这样,到了复活日的时候,他们就可以毫无顾虑地来到上帝的面前了。彼得将自己在欧洲发现的、但俄罗斯还不了解的东西全都引入进来,真正将俄罗斯改造成了一个欧洲强国。人们之所以称他为"彼得大帝"或"国父",原因就在于此。

彼得爱上了一位贫穷的农家女孩、一个叫作凯瑟琳的孤儿,并且娶了她为妻。凯瑟琳没有上过学,但她非常温柔、可爱,既聪明又伶俐,因此他们婚后过得很幸福。娶一个不是公主、并且出身极其低贱的女子当王后,俄罗斯人曾经都大感震惊。可是,彼得却给她戴上了皇冠;彼得大帝驾崩之后,凯瑟琳还成了俄罗斯的君主呢。

74 A Prince Who Ran Away

If you put a P in front of Russia it makes — Prussia. This was the name of a little country in Europe that was later a part of Germany. Russia was big, and Peter made it great. Prussia was small, but another king made it also great. This king was named Frederick. He, too, lived in the eighteenth century, but a little later than Peter, and he, too, was called "the Great" — Frederick the Great.

Frederick's father, who was the second king of Prussia, had a hobby for collecting giants as you might collect postage stamps. Wherever he heard of a very tall man, no matter in what country and no matter what it cost to get him, he bought or hired him. This collection of giants he made into a remarkable company of soldiers, which was his special pride.

He was a very cranky, cross, and bad-tempered old king. He treated his children terribly, especially his son Frederick, whom he called Fritz. Fritz had curls and liked music and poetry and fancy clothes. His father didn't like this, for he wanted a son who would be a soldier and fighter. His father, when angry, used to throw dishes at him, lock him up for days at a time, and feed him on bread and water and whip him with a cane. Finally Fritz

74 离家出走的王子

如果你们在俄罗斯（Russia）这个单词的前面加上一个字母P，它就变成了普鲁士（Prussia）。这是欧洲的一个小国，后来变成了德国的一部分。俄罗斯国土广袤，而彼得大帝又让该国变得很强大了。普鲁士疆域虽小，但也有一位国王，曾经让它变得非常强大呢。这位国王，名叫腓特烈。他也生活在十八世纪，但比彼得大帝稍晚一点儿，并且他也被称为"大帝"，即腓特烈大帝。

腓特烈的父亲是普鲁士的第二任国王；他有一种搜罗巨人的业余爱好，就像你们有集邮的业余爱好那样。只要听说有身材非常高大的人，那么无论这个人住在哪个国家，无论要花多少钱才能将这个人搜罗过来，他都会将其买下来或者雇过来。他把搜罗来的这些巨人编成了一支无与伦比的军队，并且对此尤感自豪。

他是一位非常古怪、乖戾、脾气暴躁而又年老体衰的国王。他对自己的孩子很不好，尤其是对儿子腓特烈，他叫腓特烈"弗里茨"。弗里茨长着一头卷发，喜欢音乐、诗歌和奇装异服。可他的父亲却不喜欢这些东西，因为父亲希望儿子成为一名英勇无畏的战士和斗士。父亲发脾气的时候，常常用碗呀盘子什么的砸他，一次把他关上好几天，只给他吃面包、喝水，并且还用藤条抽打他。最后，弗里茨无法再忍受下去，便离家出走了。但是，后来他又被父亲手下的人抓住并送了回来。父

could stand it no longer, and he ran away. He was caught and brought back. His father was so angry with his son for disobeying and acting as he had done that he was actually going to have him killed — yes, put to death — but at the last minute was persuaded not to do it.

But here is a strange thing: When Fritz grew up to be Frederick, he turned out to be just what his father wanted him to be — a great soldier and fighter. He still loved poetry and even tried to write poems himself, and he was very fond of music and he played the flute very well indeed. But Frederick wanted above everything else to make his country important in Europe; for before his time it was of little account, and no one paid much attention to it.

Now, the neighboring country to Prussia was Austria. Austria was ruled over by a woman named Maria Theresa. Maria Theresa had become ruler of Austria at the same time that Frederick had become king of Prussia. Some people said that a woman should not rule a country and they wanted to use this as an excuse to start a war. Frederick's father had promised to let Maria Theresa alone — he had promised not to fight just because she was a woman — but when Frederick became king, he wanted to add a part of Austria to his own country, so he simply helped himself to the piece of Maria Theresa's country that he wanted. He didn't care if she was a woman or what his father had promised. Of course this started a war. Before long almost every country in Europe was fighting either with Frederick or against him. But Frederick not only succeeded in getting what he was after; he succeeded in holding on to it.

亲对儿子的叛逆不驯感到极其恼火，几乎打算杀了他；是的，他就是打算处死自己的儿子。但在最后一刻，终于有人说服了父亲，因此父亲才没有处死儿子。

不过很奇怪的是，弗里茨长大成人之后，最终却完全变成了一个符合父亲期望的人，变成了一名了不起的战士和斗士。他仍然热爱诗歌，甚至还亲自试着写过诗；他仍然非常喜爱音乐，事实上他的长笛吹得很不错。但是，腓特烈最希望的，还是让自己统治下的普鲁士变成欧洲一个重要的国家；因为在他继位以前，普鲁士一直都无足轻重，也没有什么人关注这个国家呢。

此时，普鲁士的邻国是奥地利。统治奥地利的是一位女性，名叫玛丽亚·特蕾萨。玛丽亚·特蕾萨登上奥地利君主之位，与腓特烈继任普鲁士国王属于同一时期。有些人说一个国家不该由女性来统治，他们都希望以此为借口，来发动一场战争。腓特烈的父王曾经答应过，不会去干涉玛丽亚·特蕾萨的事情；他之所以承诺不与奥地利打仗，仅仅是因为玛丽亚·特蕾萨是一个女人。可腓特烈继承王位之后，却希望将奥地利的一部分领土并入普鲁士的版图；于是，他便毫不客气地动手去夺取玛丽亚·特蕾萨治下的奥地利境内那处他想要吞并的领土了。他根本就不在乎玛丽亚·特蕾萨是不是一个女人，也不在乎自己的父王做出了什么样的承诺。这种做法，自然就引发了一场战争。不久之后，欧洲几乎所有的国家全都卷入了这场战争，要么是支持腓特烈，要么就是对抗他。可最终，腓特烈不但成功地攫取到了自己想要的领土，还牢牢地控制住了这处领土。

然而，玛丽亚·特蕾萨也不会轻易认输。她希望将腓特烈从她手中非法夺走

Maria Theresa, however, would not give up. She wanted to get back what had been wrongfully taken away from her. She began quietly and secretly to get ready for another war against Frederick. Quietly and secretly she got other countries to promise to help her. But Frederick heard of what she was doing, and suddenly he attacked her again, and for seven long years this next war went on. This was called the Seven Years' War. Frederick kept on fighting until he had beaten Austria for good and until he had gained his purpose, which was to make his little country of Prussia the most powerful country in Europe. He still held on to the part of Austria that he had at first taken away. Maria Theresa was a great queen, and she would have won against Frederick had he been an ordinary king. But she had too strong a ruler against her. Frederick was one of the world's smartest generals and too much for her.

The Seven Years' War, strange to say, was fought out not only in Europe but in far-off America, also. England had taken Frederick's side. France and other countries had taken sides against him. The English settlers in America, who were on Frederick's side, fought the French settlers, who were against him. When Frederick won in Europe, the English in America also won against the French in America. I am telling you all this because that is why we in America speak English instead of French today. If Frederick had lost in Europe and the English had lost in America, France would have won, and we here in America would probably now speak French instead of English.

Frederick, like some other kings we have heard of before, thought nothing of lying or

的领土再夺回来。她开始不声不响地暗暗筹谋，准备对腓特烈发动另一场战争。她不声不响，暗中让其他一些国家都答应给她提供帮助。不过，她的所作所为还是传到了腓特烈的耳中，因此腓特烈便再次对她发动了突然袭击；这第二场战争，整整打了七年之久。因此，这场战争便被称为"七年战争"。腓特烈征战不已，直到将奥地利彻底打败，直到实现了自己的目标，让普鲁士这个小国变成了欧洲实力最强大的国家之一，他才罢手。一开始便从奥地利攫取的那处领土，他仍然牢牢地掌控着。玛丽亚·特蕾萨本来也是一位了不起的女王；假如腓特烈只是一位普普通通的国王，她可能早就打败了他。可事实上，与她打仗的却是一位强有力的君主。腓特烈是世界历史上最厉害的统帅之一，因此她哪能对付得了啊。

说来也怪，"七年战争"不但在欧洲进行，而且还波及了遥远的美洲。英国站在腓特烈大帝这一边。法国和其他一些国家，则站在对抗腓特烈大帝的一方。美洲的英国殖民者都支持腓特烈大帝，因此他们与反对腓特烈大帝的法国殖民者之间也打起了仗。腓特烈大帝在欧洲打赢了之后，美洲的英国殖民者也打赢了法国殖民者。我之所以把这些情况都告诉你们，只是为了说明，这就是我们美国如今说英语而不说法语的原因。假如腓特烈大帝在欧洲战败，而美洲的英国殖民者也战败了、法国殖民者取胜了的话，那么如今我们在美国说的很可能就是法语而不是英语了。

与我们之前已经了解到的其他一些君主一样，腓特烈大帝觉得，如果为了打败其他国家而不得去撒谎、欺骗或偷窃的话，那也没什么大不了的。对他来说，正当手段也好，不正当的手段也罢，都没什么分别。不过，他对待本国的臣民时，却

cheating or stealing if he had to in order to get the better of other countries. Fair means or foul means made no difference to him. But his own people he treated as if they were his children and did everything he could for them. Like a lioness with her cubs, he fought for his family, even with the world against him.

There was a mill close by Frederick's palace that belonged to a poor miller. As it was not a pretty thing to be so near, the king wanted to buy it in order to tear it down and get rid of it. But the miller would not sell. Although Frederick the Great offered a large sum of money, the miller refused. A great many kings would simply have taken the mill and perhaps put the miller in jail or put him to death. Frederick did neither, for he thought his lowliest subject had his rights and that if he didn't want to sell he shouldn't be made to. He left the miller undisturbed, and the mill stands today as it did then, close to the palace.

Though Frederick was a German, strange to say, he hated the German language. He thought it the language of the uneducated. He himself spoke French and wrote in French and only spoke German when he had to talk to his servants or those who did not understand French.

像对待自己的孩子那样，为他们竭尽所能。他就像是一头带着幼崽的母狮，为自己的家人而战，哪怕因此要与整个世界为敌也在所不惜呢。

腓特烈大帝的王宫附近有座磨坊，它是一位贫穷的磨坊主的。由于磨坊离王宫太近了不好，因此腓特烈大帝想把磨坊买下来拆掉，然后再把那个地方清理干净。可磨坊主却不肯卖掉磨坊。尽管腓特烈大帝提出给他一大笔钱，可磨坊主还是不同意。许多国王都会径直抢走磨坊，没准还会将那位磨坊主关进监狱，甚至处死呢。可腓特烈大帝却没有这样做，因为他觉得哪怕是最低贱的臣民，也有自己的权利；要是磨坊主不想卖掉磨坊，那就不应当强迫他去卖掉。所以，他并没有惩处那位磨坊主；而那座磨坊呢，如今仍然像当时一样保留着，仍然保留在腓特烈大帝的皇宫附近。

奇怪的是，虽然腓特烈大帝是德国人，可他却不喜欢德语。他觉得，德语是一种没有教养的粗俗语言。他本人说的是法语，写东西时用的也是法语；只有在吩咐仆人或者跟那些不懂法语的人交谈时，他才会说德语呢。

75 America Gets Rid of Her King

Did you know that we once had a king?

His name was George.

No, George Washington wasn't a king.

This was another George.

You remember the Stuarts in England — James, Charles, and the rest of the family who ruled England for a hundred years from 1600 to 1700. Well, about 1700 England ran out of Stuarts — there were no more Stuart children.

As England had to have another king, they asked a distant relative of the royal family over from one of the German states to rule England. Yes, from Germany to rule England. His name was George, and the English called him George I. George couldn't even speak English. He was German and loved his own country much better than England. You can imagine what sort of king he was. His son, George II ruled after him, although he, too, was more German than English. But when the grandson, George III, came to the throne he was a born and bred Englishman. It was in this grandson's reign, in the reign of George III, that our country, the United States, was born.

75 美国摆脱了国王

你们知不知道，我们美国人曾经也有一位国王呢？

这位国王叫作乔治。

他可不是乔治·华盛顿。乔治·华盛顿不是国王。

这是另一个乔治。

你们应该都还记得英国的斯图亚特王朝，记得詹姆斯、查理，以及斯图亚特王朝的其他君主吧？他们在公元1600年到公元1700年间，统治了英国一百年。后来，到了公元1700年左右，英国便结束了斯图亚特王朝的统治，因为当时斯图亚特王室没有继承人了。

由于英国必须另立国王，所以英国人便要皇室的一位远亲从德意志的一个小国过来统治英国。是的，这位远亲是从德国过来当英国国王的。他叫乔治，英国人称之为乔治一世。当时，乔治一世甚至还不会说英语哩。他是德国人，对自己的祖国要比对英国热爱得多。你们可以想象一下，看他是一个什么样的国王。他死后，由他的儿子乔治二世继位；可乔治二世也与父亲一样，与其说他是英国人，还不如说他是德国人呢。不过，到了乔治一世的孙子乔治三世登上王位的时候，他就已经是一个土生土长的英国人了。正是在这位孙子的统治之下，即乔治三世在位期间，我

When a wheel turns over, we call it a *revolution*, which is a big name for a little thing.

When a *country* turns around, we also call it a revolution, which is a big name for a big thing.

Our country had started with the two little settlements, or *colonies*, as they were called, of Jamestown and Plymouth. It had grown and grown until there were a number of settlements along the coast of the Atlantic Ocean. Most of the people who had settled here first were English, and the king of England ruled over them. Soon people from other countries like Germany, Holland, Scotland, and Ireland came here. Africans were brought against their will to work as slaves. The king of England ruled over all these people, too. The king asked these people to send him money, which was called taxes. Now, the money collected from taxes was not, of course, for the king to put in his pocketbook to use as he liked. It was supposed to be spent on the people who were taxed, to be used for roads, schools, police, and such things that are for the good of all.

These people along the coast, who were paying money or taxes to the king far off across the water, thought they ought to have a vote to say how this money should be spent and on what it should be spent. But they did not have a vote, and they thought they ought not to have to pay taxes to the king away off in England.

One of the leading citizens of America at this time was a man named Benjamin Franklin. He was the son of a candlemaker, but from a poor boy, who had once walked the streets of Philadelphia with a loaf of bread under each arm, he had risen to a very honored position in the country. He had learned to be a printer and had started one of the first and

们的美国诞生了。

车轮滚动的时候，我们称之为"revolution"（转动）；这个词还指"革命"，所以，这可是大词小用呢。

一个国家发生变革的时候，我们也称之为"revolution"（革命），这才是大词大用啊。

我们美国起源于两个小小的定居点，也就是当时人们所称的"殖民地"：詹姆斯敦和普利茅斯。后来，殖民的范围日益扩大，直到大西洋沿岸出现了许多的殖民地。在这里拓居的殖民者，起初绝大多数都是英国人，因此都由英国国王管辖。不久之后，其他一些国家的人，比如德国人、荷兰人、苏格兰人和爱尔兰人，也纷纷来到了这里。其中还有非洲人，他们都是被强行掳掠过来当奴隶的。当时，这些人也全都接受英国国王的管辖。英王要求这些人给他交纳钱财，这种钱财被称为"赋税"。注意，通过赋税征收上来的钱财，当然并不是完全装进了英王的荷包里，任他可以随心所欲地去花。这笔钱应当花在交纳赋税的人民身上，用于修路、办学、设立警察，以及诸如此类的公共事业。

大西洋沿岸的这些殖民者都认为，既然要给远隔重洋、相距遥远的英国国王交纳钱财或赋税，那他们就理应拥有选举权，来决定这笔赋税应当怎样花、应当花在哪些事情上。可当时他们却没有选举权；因此大家都认为，他们不应当向远在英国国内的英王交纳赋税。

此时，美国的市民领袖当中，有一个叫作本杰明·富兰克林的人。他的父亲

best newspapers in the United States. He was a great thinker and had invented a stove and a lamp and had succeeded in getting electricity from the lightning in the clouds by flying a kite with a wire during a storm. He was one of the Wise Men of the West.

Franklin was sent over to England to try to get the king to change his mind about taxing the colonies or to bring about some sort of agreement with him. But King George was hardheaded, and Franklin was unable to stop the king from doing what he had made up his mind to do.

The people in America, finding that talking did no good, started in to fight. They raised an army. Then they tried to find a good man to command the army. Such a leader must be honest and brave; he must have a good mind; he must love his country; and he must be a good fighter. They looked around for a man who had all these qualities, and they found

Map of the thirteen original states
美国最初十三州地图

是一名蜡烛制造商；虽然小的时候家里很穷，但他还有过两只胳膊下各夹着一条面包在费城的大街上到处跑的经历，他后来在美国获得了极其高的地位。他当了印刷工，还创办了美国最早和最好的一份报纸。他是一位伟大的思想家，曾经发明了一种炉子和一种油灯，还曾在暴风雨中放飞一只带有电线的风筝，成功地从乌云中的闪电里引下了电流。因此，他是西方的智者之一。

富兰克林被派往英国，去想办法让英王改变向各殖民地征税的想法，或者与英王之间达成某种协议。可英王乔治却顽固得很：他下定了决心要做的事情，富兰克林是没有办法阻止的。

美洲的殖民者发现谈判没有任何用处之后，便开始起来战斗。他们组建了一支军队。然后，他们便想找一个优秀的人来统领这支军队。这位统帅必须正直诚实、勇敢无畏；他必须有优秀的头脑；他必须热爱自己的国家；他还必须是一名杰出的

one. The man they picked was honest and brave. A legend grew up that when this man was a boy, he had cut down a favorite cherry tree of his father's just to try a new hatchet he had been given. When this boy was asked by his angry father if he had done it, he answered honestly and bravely, "I cannot tell a lie; I did." Of course, now you know who it was — George Washington. We know now that this story was made up by a man who wrote a book about George Washington. It's not true, but it makes a good story, doesn't it?

George learned to be a surveyor — that is, a man who measures land — and when only sixteen years old he was employed to survey the large farm of Lord Fairfax in Virginia; that showed he had a good mind. He then had been a soldier and had fought bravely and well in the French and Indian War, as the Seven Years' War was called here. That showed that he loved his country and was a good fighter. George Washington was chosen to lead the American army against the English.

The Americans did not at first think of starting a new country. They simply wanted the same rights that Englishmen in England had. They soon found out that there was only one way to get those rights, and that was to start a new country, independent of England. So a man named Thomas Jefferson wrote a paper which was called a Declaration of Independence — can you say it? — because it declared that the colonies were going to be independent of England. There were fifty-six Americans chosen by the people to sign it. Each one of the signers would have been put to death as a traitor to England if the United States had not won, and each signer knew it, yet he signed it nevertheless. But just signing

战士。他们到处寻找具有这些品质的人，最后终于找到了一位。他们千挑万选地找到的这个人，既正直诚实，又英勇无畏。传说这个人小的时候，曾经为了试一试大人给他的一把新斧子，而砍掉了父亲最喜欢的一棵樱桃树。当暴跳如雷的父亲问这个小男孩，是不是他砍掉了樱桃树时，小男孩诚实而勇敢地回答说："我不能撒谎，是我干的。"自然，此时你们都知道这个人是谁了：他就是乔治·华盛顿。如今大家都知道，这个故事是一个曾经写了一本关于乔治·华盛顿的书的人编造出来的。虽然不是真的，可这个故事还是很不错，对不对呢？

乔治·华盛顿曾经通过当学徒而成了一名土地勘测员，即测量土地的人；他还只有十六岁的时候，就被雇去给弗吉尼亚的费尔法克斯勋爵测量大农庄呢，这说明他很有头脑。然后，他又当过兵，在法印战争中作战英勇、表现优异；这里所称的"法印战争"，就是前面提到的"七年战争"。这表明他热爱自己的祖国，也是一位优秀的战士。于是，乔治·华盛顿便被选去率领美国军队与英军作战。

起初，美洲殖民者并没有想过要开创一个新的国家。他们只是想要获得与英国国内人民同等的权利罢了。可他们不久之后就发现，要获得这些权利，只有一条路可走，那就是成立一个新的国家，摆脱英国的统治。于是，一位叫作托马斯·杰斐逊的人便写了一篇文章，题目就叫《独立宣言》；这篇文章宣布，大西洋沿岸那些殖民地都打算脱离英国而独立。美国民众选出了56名代表，在这篇文章上签了字。倘若美国打不赢这场战争，那么每个签字的人过后都会被英国当作叛国者判处死刑的；尽管每个签字的人都明白这一点，可他们还是义无反顾地在上面签上了自己的

this paper didn't make England give up the colonies. Oh, no! King George's armies tried to stop the colonies from getting away from the rule of England.

Washington had a very small army with which to fight the English army, and very little money with which to pay the soldiers or to supply them with food or clothes or powder and shot. One winter the soldiers nearly froze and starved to death, for they had little clothing and hardly any food but carrots, and it seemed as if the war could not go on unless they got help. Yet Washington kept up their spirits.

Benjamin Franklin was sent across the ocean, not to England this time of course, but to France to see if he couldn't get some help from that country. France hated England, because France had lost part of America, Canada, in the Seven Years' War, but at first France would not help. France took little interest in the fight, for Washington's army had lost a number of battles against the English, and people don't like to back a loser. The year after the Declaration of Independence, the American army beat the English badly at a place called Saratoga in New York State. The king of France then became more interested, and then he sent help to the colonies to carry on the war. A young French nobleman named Lafayette hurried over from France and fought under General Washington and did so well that he made a great name for himself.

England, seeing that things were going against her, now wanted to make peace with the Americans and give them the same rights that English citizens had, but it was then too late. At the beginning of the war, the Americans would have agreed to this and been

大名。不过，仅凭这份签了字的文章，可不会让英国拱手放弃这些殖民地。噢，绝对不行！英王乔治三世手下的军队，想方设法地要阻止这些殖民地摆脱英国的统治。

华盛顿手下与英军作战的兵力非常少，而用于支付士兵军饷，或者供应军队食品、衣物、火药、子弹的资金也不多。有一年冬天，士兵们差不多都要冻僵了，还饿得要命，因为他们没有什么衣服可穿，并且除了胡萝卜之外，几乎没有什么吃的东西；当时的形势，似乎只有在他们得到援助之后，这场战争才能继续打下去。不过，华盛顿却不停地给士兵们打气。

本杰明·富兰克林又被派到大西洋的那一边去；不过，这一次他当然不是去英国，而是去法国，看能不能从法国获得一些援助。法国不喜欢英国，因为法国在"七年战争"期间已经丢失了美洲殖民地的一部分地区，即加拿大；可就算这样，法国起初也并不愿意为美洲殖民者提供帮助。法国对这场战争没有什么兴趣，因为在与英军作战的过程中，华盛顿所率的军队已经打了多场败仗。但在《独立宣言》发表后的那一年，美国军队却在纽约州一个叫作萨拉托加的地方大败了英军。这样一来，法国国王对此的兴趣便大了一点，因此随后便向美洲殖民地派出了援军，帮助他们继续打下去。一位名叫拉斐特的法国贵族率军从法国匆匆赶去，编入了华盛顿将军的麾下作战；由于在作战中的表现极其优秀，因此他名声大噪。

此时，由于看到形势变得越来越不利于自己，所以英国便想要与美国人讲和，赋予他们与英国公民以同等的权利；可如今为时已晚。战争初期，美国人很可能会

glad to agree, but now they would agree to nothing less than complete independence from England; and so the war went on, for England would not let the colonies go.

The English had been beaten by the Yankees, as they called them, in the North, at Saratoga. Then they sent their general, Lord Cornwallis, to the south of our country to see if he could beat the people there. General Greene was put in command of the southern American soldiers. Lord Cornwallis tried to fight Greene, but Greene led Cornwallis a merry chase around the country until he was all tired out and finally went into a little place called Yorktown on the coast of Virginia. Here, Cornwallis and his army were caught fast so that they could not get out. On the side of the land was the American army, and on the ocean side were the French warships that had been sent over to help. Cornwallis had to surrender.

King George then said, "Let us have peace"; and in 1783 the war was ended by a treaty of peace, eight years after it had started, and the colonies were independent of England. This was called the Revolutionary War, and after it was over our country was called the United States.

There were just thirteen of these original colonies that joined as partners in this Union. That is why there are just thirteen stripes in our flag. Some people think thirteen is an unlucky number; but our flag with its thirteen stripes still waves over the land, and it has brought us good luck; don't you think so?

Washington was made the first President, and so he is called the Father of his Country; the First in War, the First in Peace, and the First in the Hearts of his Countrymen.

同意讲和，可能还会很乐意讲和呢；可到了如今，除了彻底摆脱英国而获得独立，他们是不会同意任何条件的了。于是，战争便继续进行下去，因为英国不允许这些殖民地摆脱自己的统治。

在北方的萨拉托加，英军已经被他们所称的"美国佬"打败了。接下来，他们便派英军统帅康华里勋爵率军前往美国南部，看能不能打败南方的美军。南方的美军由格林将军指挥。康华里勋爵想与格林将军决一死战，可格林将军却轻轻松松地牵着康华里勋爵的鼻子，在乡间绕着圈子到处追击，直到康华里勋爵所率英军全都疲惫不堪，最终进入了弗吉尼亚沿海一个叫作约克镇的小地方。在这里，康华里勋爵及其手下的英军陷入了重重包围之中，无法脱身了。陆上那一边是美国军队，海洋那一边则有被派来支援美军的法国军舰。困在中间的康华里便不得不缴械投降了。

于是，英王乔治说："我们讲和吧。"因此，1783年，这场战争在打了八年之后，便以双方签订了一份和约而宣告结束，而美洲这些殖民地也摆脱英国而获得了独立。这场战争，史称"革命战争"；而战争结束之后，我国便称为"美利坚合众国"了。

最初一起加入这个联邦的殖民地，一共有十三个。美国国旗上之所以刚好有十三道条纹，原因就在于此。有些人觉得十三是个不吉祥的数字，可美国那面带有十三道条纹的国旗，如今却仍然飘扬在这片土地上，并且给我们带来了好运；你们觉得是不是这样呢？

后来，华盛顿被推选为美国的第一任总统，也被人们称为"国父"了；因此，他既是战争中的第一人、和平时期的第一人，也是美国同胞心中的第一人。

76　Upside Down

Measles and Mumps are very catching.

So are Revolutions.

Just a little later than the Revolution of the thirteen colonies, the people in France had a Revolution, too. They saw how successful the Americans had been in their fight against the king of England, and so they rebelled against their own king and queen in France. This was called the French Revolution.

The reason the French people rebelled against their king was that they had very little, and the king and his royal family and nobles seemed to have everything. Both the Americans and the French rebelled against paying taxes. Although the English taxes were not very high, the Americans thought them unjust. The French taxes, however, not only were unjust but they took almost everything away from the people.

I have already told you how bad things were under Louis XIV, and they got worse until the people could stand it no longer.

At this time the king of France was Louis XVI, and his queen was named Marie Antoinette. The people were so poor that they had hardly anything to eat except a very

76　天翻地覆

麻疹和腮腺炎这两种疾病，都具有很强的传染性。

革命也是如此。

就在美国爆发革命后不久，法国人民也发动了一场革命。他们看到，美国人在对抗英国国王的斗争中取得了伟大的胜利，因此他们便在法国国内反抗本国的国王和王后了。这次革命，就叫"法国大革命"。

法国人民起来反抗国王的原因是，他们几乎一无所有，可国王、王室以及贵族阶层却似乎拥有一切。美国人民和法国人民都反对交税。尽管英国征收的税款不是很高，可美国人还是觉得这种做法不公平。然而，法国征收的赋税却非但不公平，而且几乎将人民的财产全都掠夺走了。

我已经跟你们说过，路易十四在位的时候，法国的社会形势极其糟糕；之后，这种形势还每况愈下，一直发展到了人们无法再容忍下去的程度。

此时法国的国王是路易十六，王后则叫玛丽·安托瓦内特。法国人民都非常穷苦，除了一种粗糙得很、味道很不好的黑面包之外，几乎没有什么吃的。他们被强制向国王和贵族交纳钱财，以便让国王和贵族们可以过得很优越，可以举办各种宴会；他们还不得不替国王和贵族们干各种各样的工作，并且完全是无偿或者接近无

coarse and bad-tasting kind of bread called black bread. They were compelled to pay the king and the nobles money so the king and nobles could live in fine style and have parties; and they had to do all sorts of work for nothing or next to nothing. If anyone complained, he was put in a great prison in Paris called the *Bastille* and left there to die. In spite of the fact that all the people were so terribly poor, the king and the queen and their friends lived in luxury and extravagance with everything in the world they wanted, all paid for by the poor people.

Neither the king nor his wife was really wicked. They were simply young and thoughtless. They meant well, but like a great many well-meaning people they lacked common sense and did not know how others lived. They didn't seem to understand that people *could* be poor, for they had so much themselves. Marie Antoinette was told that her subjects had no bread to eat. "Let them eat cake," she said.

To right the wrongs of the people, a body of many of the best men from all France gathered together and, calling themselves the National Assembly, tried to work out some plan to do away with all the injustice the people had been suffering. They wanted to make everyone free and equal and give everybody a say in the government. Their slogan was, *Liberté, égalité, fraternité*. In English this means, *Liberty, equality, brotherhood*.

The poor had become so furiously angry at the way they had been treated by the rich that they would stand things no longer, and a wild and angry mob of them attacked the old prison of the Bastille. They battered down the walls and freed the prisoners and killed the

偿的。有人如果胆敢发牢骚，就会被关进巴黎一座叫作"巴士底狱"的大型监狱里去，并且一直关到死。尽管所有民众都极其贫困，但法国国王、王后和他们的朋友们却生活奢靡，拥有他们所希望的一切，花的也全都是贫苦民众交纳上来的钱财。

法国国王和王后其实都并不恶毒。他们当时只是太年轻、太自私罢了。他们的本意是好的，可与许多怀有善意的人一样，他们却缺乏常识，不知道别人的生活状况。他们似乎并不理解，人民怎么可能会贫穷，因为他们自己很富有啊。有人曾经对玛丽·安托瓦内特说，她的臣民没有面包吃。"那就让他们吃蛋糕呀。"她竟然如此回答说。

为了纠正人民遭受的种种不公正，法国各地的许多杰出人士聚集在一起，组成了一个叫作"国民会议"的组织，试图制定出某种计划，来消除人民一直承受的所有不公平现象。他们想要做到人人自由、人人平等，让每个人在国家治理方面都有发言权。他们的口号，就是"自由、平等、博爱"。

一直以来，穷人都受到富人的欺压盘剥，对此他们已经极其愤怒，无法再容忍这种情况了；所以，其中一群狂热且怒不可遏的民众，便去攻打巴士底这座老监狱。他们捣毁了监狱的墙壁，释放了其中被关押着的囚犯，并且杀掉了巴士底狱的看守，原因仅仅在于这些看守都是国王手下的仆役。然后，他们又将监狱看守的头颅割下来放在杆子上，高高地举着它们在巴黎的大街小巷游行。当时，这座老监狱里只关押了七名囚犯，因此把他们释放出来并无大碍；可这次攻打监狱的行动却表明，人民不会再容忍国王任意监禁他们了。

guards of the Bastille simply because they were servants of the king. Then they cut off the heads of the guards and stuck them on poles and, carrying them aloft, paraded through the streets of Paris. There were only seven prisoners in the old jail, so that freeing them didn't matter much, but this attack was to show that the people would no longer allow the king to imprison them.

The Bastille was stormed on July 14, 1789. This was the beginning of what is called the French Revolution, and this day is celebrated in France in almost the same way that our Fourth of July is, for it was the French Declaration of Independence against their kings.

Lafayette, who was now back in France, the same Lafayette who had helped the Americans fight their king, sent the key of the Bastille over to George Washington as a souvenir that his own country had now overthrown its king and declared its independence.

The king and queen were living in the beautiful palace at Versailles, the palace that Louis XIV had built. Many of the king's nobles, when they heard what was taking place in Paris, became frightened and, deserting their king and queen, took to their heels and left the country. They knew pretty well what was going to happen, and they didn't wait to see.

Meanwhile the National Assembly drew up what was called a Declaration of the Rights of Man, which was something like our Declaration of Independence. It said that all men were born free and equal, that the people should make the laws, and that the laws should be the same for all.

Soon after the Declaration of Rights had been made, the angry mob from Paris, ragged

巴士底狱是在1789年7月14日遭到猛攻的。这就是所谓的法国大革命的开端，因此这一天被定为法国的国庆日。在这一天，人民会像美国庆祝7月4日国庆节那样进行庆祝，因为这一天就是法国人民对国王发出《独立宣言》的时间啊。

拉斐特此时已经回到了法国，这个拉斐特就是曾经帮助美洲殖民者对抗英国国王的那个人。他曾派人将巴士底狱的钥匙送给了乔治·华盛顿，以纪念自己的祖国如今已经推翻了国王，宣布独立了。

当时，法国国王和王后都住在凡尔赛那座漂亮的王宫里，也就是路易十四修建的那座宫殿。得知巴黎发生的情况之后，国王手下的许多贵族全都惊恐不已，便抛下了国王和王后，一个个都逃离了法国。他们根本无须等着去看，就很清楚接下来会出现什么样的状况。

与此同时，国民议会起草了一份称为《人权宣言》的文件，它与美国的《独立宣言》有点儿类似。这份宣言称：人类生而自由、生而平等，法律应当由人民来制定，并且应当做到法律面前人人平等。

《人权宣言》发表后不久，来自巴黎的那些狂怒不已、衣衫褴褛、样子古怪的暴民们，便都手持棍棒、石块，口里高喊着："面包，面包！"他们向十三英里外的凡尔赛进发，因为当时路易十六和玛丽·安托瓦内特仍然住在那里。暴民们纷纷冲上王宫外那道样子美丽、宏伟壮观的台阶。国王身边仅剩的几名护卫，根本无法挡住他们。暴民们抓住国王和王后，把他们当成囚犯带往巴黎。到了巴黎后，他们便将路易十六和玛丽·安托瓦内特两人囚禁起来。有一次，国王和王后试图乔装打

and wildlooking, carrying sticks and stones, and crying, "Bread, bread!" marched the thirteen miles to Versailles, where Louis and Marie Antoinette were still living. Up the beautiful grand staircase of the palace they rushed. The few guards remaining round the king were unable to hold them back. They captured the king and queen and took them prisoners to Paris. There they kept Louis and Marie Antoinette prisoners. Once the king and queen tried to escape in disguise but were caught before they could get out of the country, and they were brought back.

Then it was that the National Assembly drew up a *constitution* — a set of rules by which the country should be justly governed. This the king agreed to and signed.

That still wasn't enough. The people wanted no king at all to rule over them. So about a year later they started a real republic like our own, and the king was sentenced to death. A Frenchman had invented a kind of machine with a big knife for chopping off heads. This was called the *guillotine*, and it was used instead of an ax, for it was quicker and surer. The king was taken to the guillotine, and his head was cut off.

But the people did not settle down quiet and contented when they had got rid of their king. They were afraid that those who were in favor of kings might start another kingdom. The people chose red, white, and blue as their colors and the *Marseillaise* as their national song; and everywhere they marched they carried the tricolor, as they called the three-colored flag, and as they marched they sang the *Marseillaise*.

法国的革命群众和断头台
French revolution crowd and guillotine

扮后逃跑；可还没有跑出国去，便又被人抓住，带了回来。

接下来，国民议会制定了一部《宪法》，也就是用于公正地管理国家的一系列法律法规。国王认可了这部《宪法》，并在上面签了字。

可这样还是不够。人民根本就不想要什么国王来统治他们。因此，大约一年之后，他们便建立了一个与美国类似的、真正的共和国，国王也被判处了死刑。当时，一位法国人已经发明了一种用很大的刀片将人的脑袋砍下来的机械。这种机械叫作"断头台"，用于代替刽子手和斧头，因为这种机械砍起头来更快，也更可靠。于是，国王路易十六就被押到这种断头台上，砍掉了脑袋。

不过，废除国王之后，民众并没有平心静气、心满意足地安定下来。他们担心，那些支持君主制的人会再立一个王国。法国人民决定用红、白、蓝三色的国旗，用《马赛曲》作国歌；无论进军到哪里，他们都高举着三色国旗，并且一边行进，一边高唱着《马赛曲》。

Then began what is called the Reign of Terror, and that is a tale of blood. A man named Robespierre and two of his friends were leaders in the Reign of Terror. Anyone whom the people suspected of being in favor of kings they caught and beheaded. The queen was one of the first to have her head cut off. If anyone even whispered that there was a man, or a woman, or even a child who was in favor of kings, that man, woman, or child would be rushed to the guillotine. If anyone hated another and wished to get rid of him, all he had to do was to point him out as in favor of kings, and off he would be taken to the guillotine. No one was sure of his life for a day. He never knew what moment some personal enemy might accuse him. Hundreds, then thousands, of suspected people were beheaded, and a special sewer had to be built to carry off the blood. The guillotine, fast as it was, was too slow for the terrorists. It could cut off but one head at a time, and so prisoners were lined up and shot down with cannon.

People seemed to have gone wild, crazy, mad! They insulted Christ and the Christian religion. They put a pretty woman called the Goddess of Reason on the altar of the beautiful Church of Notre Dame and worshiped her instead of the Lord. They pulled down statues and pictures of Christ and the Virgin Mary. In their places they put statues and pictures of their own leaders. The guillotine was put up in place of the cross. They did away with Sundays. They made a week ten days long, and every tenth day they made a holiday instead of Sunday. They stopped counting time from Christ's birth, because they didn't want anything that had to do with Christ, and they began to call the year when the

接下来，法国便开始了所谓的"恐怖统治"；这可是一段血腥无比的时期。在"恐怖统治"时期，法国的领导人是一个叫作罗伯斯庇尔的人和他的两位朋友。任何人，只要有支持君主制的嫌疑，人们就会把他抓起来，砍掉他的脑袋。玛丽·安托瓦内特就是第一个因此而被砍掉了脑袋的人。只要有人谣传，说哪个男人、女人甚至小孩是保皇党，那么这个男人、女人或者小孩就会马上被抓起来送上断头台。假如有人憎恨另一个人、想要除掉这个人，那么只要告发说这人是个保皇党就行了，因为后者马上就会被押上断头台。没有人有把握说，自己能够活过今天。人们根本不清楚，什么时候就会有一个仇人出来指控自己是保皇党。成百上千、然后又是成千上万有嫌疑的人，全都被砍了头；人们甚至还修了一条专门的下水道，才能及时清理掉血污呢。然而，断头台砍头的速度虽说快得很，对于实施恐怖统治的那些人来说，砍头的速度却还是太慢了。断头台一次只能砍一个人的脑袋；可他们关押的犯人太多，因此只好让犯人排成一队，然后用大炮轰死呢。

此时的法国人民，似乎完全变得狂热、愚蠢而疯狂了！他们辱骂基督和基督教。他们将一尊叫作"理性女神"的美女雕像放到了漂亮的巴黎圣母院的祭坛上，把她当成上帝来礼拜。他们把基督和圣母马利亚的雕像和绘画全都拆毁了。而在原本放置这些雕塑和绘画的地方，他们则摆放上领袖们的雕塑和画像。断头台取代了十字架。他们取消了礼拜日。他们规定一周为十天，并且将第十天定为假日，以取代原来的礼拜天。他们不再从基督降生时开始纪年，因为他们不想要任何与基督相关的东西；所以，他们开始将共和国成立的那一年，即1792年，称为元年。

republic was started in 1792 the *Year 1*.

But Robespierre wished to rule alone, and he plotted against his two friends. One of these he had beheaded, and the other was killed in his bathtub by a girl named Charlotte Corday, who was in a rage at what he had done. So Robespierre was left alone. At last the people, in fear of this man who was such a monstrous and inhuman tyrant, rose up against him. When he found that he too, was to be put to death, he tried to commit suicide, but before he could do so, he was caught and taken to the guillotine, where he went to the same death to which he had sent countless others, and the Reign of Terror was ended.

但是，罗伯斯庇尔想独掌大权，于是他设下了阴谋来对付自己的那两位朋友。其中一人被他砍掉了脑袋，而另一位则被一个女孩杀死在家中的浴缸里；那个女孩名叫夏绿蒂·科黛，她是因为对他的所作所为感到极其愤怒，才刺杀了他。于是，此时就剩下罗伯斯庇尔一人大权独揽了。最后，法国人民由于很害怕这个令人恐惧且毫无人性的独裁者，便起来反对他。发现自己也会被别人处死后，罗伯斯庇尔曾经想过要自杀；可还没来得及这样做，他就被人抓住，押上了断头台，他就像被他处死的无数人那样被砍下了脑袋，而法国的"恐怖统治"时期也宣告结束了。

77 A Little Giant

At last the Revolution was stopped.

It was stopped by a young soldier only about twenty years old and sixty inches tall.

The Government was holding a meeting in the palace while an angry mob in the streets outside were trying to attack the palace. A young soldier had been given a few men and told to keep the mob away. The young soldier pointed cannons down each street that led to the palace, and no one dared to show himself. The young soldier was named Napoleon Bonaparte. He made such a fine record that people wanted to know who he was and where he came from.

Napoleon had been born on a little island called Corsica in the Mediterranean Sea. He was born just in time to be a Frenchman, for the island of Corsica had belonged to Italy and had only just been given to France a few weeks before he was born. As soon as he was old enough, he was sent off to a military school in France. There, his French schoolmates looked upon him as a foreigner and didn't have much to do with him. But Napoleon made high marks in arithmetic, and he loved hard problems. Once he shut himself up in his room to work over a hard problem, and there he stayed for three days and nights until he

77 小个子巨人

法国大革命终于结束了。

而结束法国大革命的，却是一位当时还只有20岁、身高60英寸[1]的年轻士兵。

当时，法国政府正在凡尔赛宫里开会，而外面的大街上，一群愤怒的民众正试图攻打凡尔赛宫。政府给一位年轻的士兵派了为数不多的兵力，让他去赶走那些民众。这位年轻的士兵下令，将大炮对准通往凡尔赛宫的每一条街道，因此那些民众都不敢露面了。这位年轻的士兵，名叫拿破仑·波拿巴。由于他在职业生涯中屡立奇功，因此人们都想知道他是谁、来自哪里。

拿破仑出生于地中海上一个叫作科西嘉的小岛上。他的出生时间很巧，使得他成了法国人；因为科西嘉岛以前一直属于意大利，只是在他出生前几个星期才刚刚割让给法国。他成长到刚够年龄后，就被送到法国的一所军校去上学。在军校里，同学们把他当成外国人，都不愿意跟他交往。不过，拿破仑在算术方面成绩优异，并且喜欢解决疑难问题。有一次，他把自己关在房间里解决一个疑难问题，三天三

---

[1] 英寸（inch），英制长度单位。1 英寸 =2.54 厘米。换算之后，拿破仑的身高约为 1.52 米。

had found the answer.

Napoleon showed early in his career that he was going to be a fine soldier, and when he was only twenty-six years old he was made a general.

Now, at this time all the other countries of Europe had kings. France had caught the fever of revolution from the Americans all the way across the ocean and had got rid of her kings. The kings of these other countries were afraid their people might catch the fever of revolution, too. All of these other countries became enemies of France because France had put an end to her kings. Besides that, the French army was invading France's neighbors to help them get rid of their kings. So, once again, war was on.

Napoleon was sent off to fight Italy. He had to cross the Alps, which Hannibal in the Punic Wars had crossed long before. But Hannibal had no heavy cannons when he crossed; it seemed impossible for Napoleon's army to cross with cannons. Napoleon asked his engineers, the men who were supposed to know about such things, if it could be done. They said they thought it was impossible.

"Impossible," Napoleon angrily replied, "is a word found only in the dictionary of fools." Then he shouted:

"There shall be no Alps!" and went ahead and crossed them. His army won in Italy, and when he returned to France he was greeted by the people as a conquering hero. But the men who were then governing France were afraid of him. They feared he might try to make himself king because he was so popular with the people. Napoleon, however, asked

夜没有出门，最终找到了答案。

拿破仑很早就表明，自己打算成为一名优秀的战士；而在26岁的时候，他就已当上了将军。

注意，此时欧洲的其他各国都有国王。法国却因为大洋彼岸的美国人而感染上了革命狂热症，所以废除了君主制度。其他各国的君主都很担心，本国民众可能也会感染上这种革命狂热症。由于法国废除了君主制度，因此欧洲其他各国都成了法国的敌人。除此之外，法国军队当时正在侵略邻国，以帮助邻国废除君主制度。于是，战争再一次爆发了。拿破仑被派去与意大利作战。他必须率军翻越阿尔卑斯山脉；在很久以前的"布匿战争"中，汉尼拔曾经率军翻越过这条山脉。可汉尼拔翻越阿尔卑斯山的时候，并没有携带重型火炮；因此，拿破仑所率的那支带着大炮的军队，似乎是不可能翻越这条山脉的。拿破仑曾经问过手下的工程技术人员，部队带着大炮能不能翻过去，因为工程技术人员应当很了解这些事情。工程师们都回答说，他们觉得是不可能翻越过去的。

"不可能，"拿破仑很生气地回答说，"这个词只有在傻瓜的词典中才看得到。"接着他大呼一声：

"没有什么阿尔卑斯山！"然后，他便一马当先，率领大军翻越了这条山脉。他的大军在意大利打了胜仗，因此回到法国后，法国民众都夹道相迎，把他当成是一位远征的英雄。不过，当时法国政府里那些掌权的人却很害怕他。他们担心，由于深受百姓爱戴，拿破仑可能会千方百计地要自立为王。然而，拿破仑却又主动请

to be sent to conquer Egypt because he had an idea he could get the better of the English there. He thought he might then cut England off from India, the colony that they had won in the reign of James I. England had lost America and didn't want to lose India, too.

The French Government was very glad to get rid of Napoleon, and so they sent him off to Egypt as he asked. He quickly conquered Egypt as Julius Caesar had done, but there was no Cleopatra to upset his plans. While he was conquering Egypt, his fleet, which was waiting for him at the mouth of the Nile, was caught and destroyed by the English fleet under a great admiral, if not the greatest that ever lived. His name was Lord Nelson.

Napoleon had no way to take his army back to France. He left his army in Egypt under command of another. He himself, however, managed to find a ship to take him back home. When he reached France, he found that the men who were supposed to be governing were quarreling among themselves, and, seeing his chance, he had himself made one of three men chosen to rule France. He was called first consul; and there were supposed to be two assistant consuls but the assistants were little more than clerks to do Napoleon's bidding. It was only a very short time before he was next made first consul for life. Then, not long after that, he became emperor of France and also king of Italy.

The other countries of Europe began to fear that Napoleon would conquer them, too, and make them also a part of France. All the other countries joined together to beat him. Napoleon planned to conquer England first, and he got ready a fleet to cross over to England. But his fleet was caught off Spain near a point called Trafalgar by the same

缨去攻打埃及，因为他觉得自己可以在埃及打败英国人。他认为，那样一来，就可以切断英国同印度的联络；印度这个殖民地，是英国在詹姆斯一世在位的时候从法国手中夺取过去的。英国已经失去了美洲，因此不想再失去印度。

法国政府很乐意摆脱拿破仑，因此批准了他的请求，将他派往埃及。他一举攻克了埃及，就像恺撒那样，不过此时却没有一位克利奥佩特拉来打乱他的计划了。就在他攻克埃及的过程中，他手下那支停泊在尼罗河河口等着他的舰队，却被一支英国舰队赶上并消灭掉了；当时指挥这支英国舰队的，就算不是有史以来最伟大的，也是很伟大的一位海军将领。他的名字叫纳尔逊勋爵。

这样一来，拿破仑就没法率军返回法国了。他将埃及的法军留下来，由另一位将领指挥。而他自己则设法弄到了一艘船，回到了国内。他回到法国后，发现本应治理国家的那帮人正在内讧；因此，在看到有机可乘之后，他便设法让自己成了被选中来统治法国的那三个人之一。他被称为"第一执政"；本来还有两位"助理执政"，可那两名"助理执政"比文书强不了多少，只是遵照拿破仑的命令行事罢了。只过了很短的一段时间，他又被确定终身担任"第一执政"。此后不久，他便成了法国皇帝，同时也是意大利的国王。

欧洲其他各国开始担心拿破仑会来把它们一个个全都征服，然后再把这些国家并入法国领土了。于是，其他各国便团结起来，一致想要打败他。拿破仑计划先征服英国，并且他还准备好了一支能够渡海前去进击英国的舰队。可他的这支舰队，却被同一位英国海军将领困在了西班牙沿海一个叫作特拉法尔加的地方附近；

English admiral, Lord Nelson, who had beaten him in Egypt. Before this battle, Nelson said to his sailors, "England expects every man to do his duty," and they did it. Napoleon's fleet was utterly destroyed, though Nelson himself was killed.

Napoleon then gave up the idea of conquering England, and he turned his attention in the opposite direction. He had beaten Spain and Prussia and Austria. Almost all Europe either belonged to him or had to do what he said. He then attacked Russia. It was a great mistake he made, for Russia was far off and very large, and it was wintertime and very cold. Still, he managed to reach Moscow way off in the center of Russia with his army. But the Russians burned the city and destroyed all the food, so that Napoleon had nothing with which to feed his army. It was terribly cold; there were deep snows; and, in retreating, his army suffered enormous losses. Napoleon himself soon made a beeline to Paris, leaving his soldiers to get back the best way they could. Men and horses died of cold and hunger by the thousands. Napoleon reached Paris, but his fortune had turned. All of Europe was getting ready to put an end to the tyrant, and it was not long after this that he was hemmed in and beaten by his enemies.

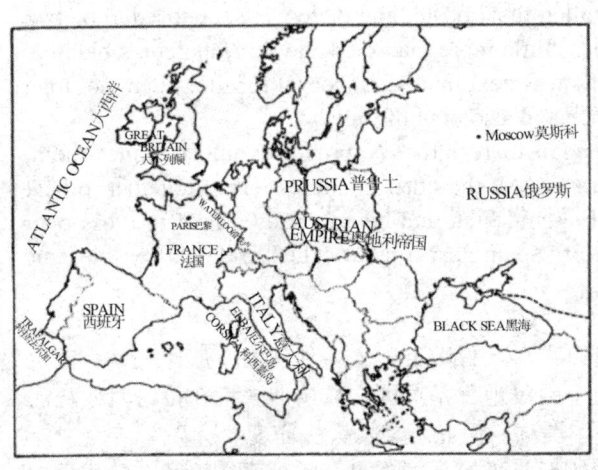

Europe in 1815
1815年的欧洲

那位海军将领，就是曾经在埃及打败了他的纳尔逊勋爵。特拉法尔加海战之前，纳尔逊勋爵曾对手下的海员们说："英国期待着我们每一个人都尽自己的义务。"而英军将士也做到了这一点。拿破仑的这支舰队被彻底消灭，但纳尔逊勋爵本人也在战斗中阵亡了。

于是，拿破仑便打消了征服英国的念头，将注意力转向了法国的东方。他打败了西班牙、普鲁士和奥地利。欧洲各国几乎要么成了他的属国，要么必须遵照他的命令去行事。然后，他又去攻打俄罗斯。这是他犯下的一个严重的错误，因为俄罗斯非但与法国相距遥远，而且国土非常广袤，而拿破仑进击的时候又是冬天，天气非常寒冷。尽管如此，他还是率军挺进到了位于俄罗斯中部的莫斯科。可俄军却在城中放起大火，烧掉了所有的粮食，使得拿破仑根本找不到什么东西来做军粮。当时天气极其寒冷，到处都是厚厚的积雪，因此在撤退的过程中法军损失惨重。拿破仑本人迅速回到了巴黎，而让手下的士兵们尽可能找容易的道路回国。成千上万的士兵、马匹，要么被冻死，要么被饿死了。虽说拿破仑回到了巴黎，可他的好运却走到了头。欧洲各国都已经做好准备，要结果掉这个暴君；此后不久，他就被敌人包围起来，打得一败涂地。

When Napoleon saw that he was beaten, he signed a paper saying that he would give up and leave France. This he did, sailing away to a little island called Elba, just off the coast of Italy, not far from the island where he was born.

But Napoleon, on the island of Elba, got an idea that all was not lost and that he might return to France and get back his power again. All of a sudden, to the surprise of France and the rest of the world, he landed on the coast of France. The French government at Paris sent an army of his old soldiers against him with orders to meet him and bring him to Paris in an iron cage. But when his old soldiers met their old general, they went over to his side, and so with them he marched on to Paris. The English and German armies were north of France and preparing to fight. Napoleon quickly got together an army and went forth to meet them. At a little town called *Waterloo*, Napoleon fought his last battle, for there he was utterly beaten by an English general named Wellington. This was the year 1815. We still speak and probably always will speak of any great defeat as a Waterloo.

There is a peculiar sentence which reads backward the same as forward. It is what Napoleon might have said after all was over. It is

Able was I Ere I Saw Elba.

After Napoleon was beaten at Waterloo, the English took him away and put him on a little island far off in the ocean where he could not possibly escape. It was a lonely spot

拿破仑看到自己被打败后，便签署了一份文件，说自己愿意放弃皇位，离开法国。后来他的确这样，坐船去了一个叫作厄尔巴的小岛上；那个小岛就在意大利沿海，离他出生的科西嘉岛不远。

但待在厄尔巴岛上的时候，拿破仑心想，他并没有失去一切，因此仍然可以回到法国，夺回自己的权力。于是，他突如其来地在法国沿海登陆，让法国和世界各国都大吃了一惊。巴黎的法国政府派遣一支由拿破仑的老部下所组成的军队，命令这支军队去迎击拿破仑，并把拿破仑关在一只铁笼子里，带回巴黎。可当那些老部下见到了自己的老将领之后，便全都临阵倒戈，投向了拿破仑那一边；于是，拿破仑便率领旧部向巴黎挺进。当时，英国和德国都有军队驻扎在法国北部，并且正在备战。拿破仑很快召集了一支军队，前去迎击英、德两军。在一个叫作滑铁卢的小镇，拿破仑打了自己一生当中的最后一仗；因为在这里，他被一个叫作威灵顿的英军将领彻底打败了。这一仗，发生在1815年。如今，我们仍然将一个人的重大失败称为"滑铁卢"，并且将来很可能还会一直这样说呢。

下面有一个很古怪的英语句子，从前面往后读跟从后面往前读是一样的。一切都结束之后，拿破仑可能会这样说的。这个句子就是：

ABLE WAS I ERE I SAW ELBA（见到厄尔巴岛之前，我本领通天）。

拿破仑在滑铁卢大败之后，英军把他押到了大西洋深处的一个小岛上，这样他

named St. Helena after the mother of Constantine. Here he lived for six years before he died.

Napoleon was probably the greatest general that ever lived, but that does not mean that he was the greatest man. Some say he was the worst, for just to make himself great, he killed hundreds of thousands of people and brought destruction and ruin to the whole of Europe wherever he fought his battles.

This brings us up into the nineteenth century, for Napoleon died in 1821. How long ago is that?

就不可能再逃脱了。那是一座孤零零的小岛，叫作圣赫勒拿，是以君士坦丁母亲的名字命名的。他在这个小岛上过了六年才死。

拿破仑很可能是有史以来最伟大的一名军事将领，可这并不意味着他是有史以来最伟大的人。有些人还说他是最坏的坏蛋呢，为了让自己名垂青史，他杀害了数十万人，并且因为四处打仗，而让整个欧洲变得千疮百孔、一片废墟。

由此我们便进入了19世纪，因为拿破仑死于1821年。那一年距现在又有多久了呢？

Napoleon at St. Helena
囚禁在圣赫勒拿岛上的拿破仑

78 Latin America and the Caribbean Islands

When you think about places like Mexico and South America and the Caribbean islands, you may think about wonderful beaches or the celebration of Carnival that is like Mardi Gras in New Orleans. But did you know that the first university in North America opened in Mexico before Jamestown was even thought of? Or do you know the name of Simon Bolivar, a hero in South America, who is known there as well as George Washington is known in the United States?

Mexico, which is part of North America, along with Central and South America and the island nations of the Caribbean all have long histories just as we do. Most people from the United States don't know those stories and usually don't know very much at all about the other countries in this hemisphere. So I'm going to tell you a little about these neighbors of ours, especially about several of their heroes. When you know these stories, you will know more about our neighbors to the south than most adults do! Try it out on your family. See if I'm right.

You remember that the Spanish conquered most of the islands of the Caribbean and then Central and South America and Mexico in the years after Columbus first crossed the Atlantic. The Spanish took over lands where many different groups of Native Americans

78 拉丁美洲和加勒比群岛

在想到像墨西哥、南美洲和加勒比群岛这样的地方时，你们想起的可能都是美丽的海滩，或者像新奥尔良狂欢节那样的嘉年华庆典活动吧。可是，你们知不知道，北美洲的第一所大学竟然是在墨西哥开设的，并且是在人们甚至还没有想到要建立詹姆斯敦的时候开设的呢？你们又知不知道，南美洲有位英雄人物，叫作西蒙·玻利瓦尔呢？他在南美非常有名，就像乔治·华盛顿在我们美国这样有名呢。

墨西哥是北美洲的一部分，它连同中美地区和南美洲以及加勒比海上的各个岛国，全都与我们一样，有着悠久的历史。绝大多数美国人都不知道这些地区的历史，对同处于这个半球的其他国家也不甚了解。因此，我打算给你们说一说这些邻国的情况，尤其要说一说这些国家中的几位英雄人物。听一听这些故事之后，你们对美国南方这些邻国的了解，就会比绝大多数大人都多了！到时，你们完全可以去考一考自己的家人，看我说得对不对。

你们都还记得吧，哥伦布首次横渡大西洋之后的那些年里，西班牙征服了加勒比海上的绝大多数岛屿，然后又征服了中美地区、南美洲和墨西哥等地。西班牙人占领了大片土地；许多不同的美洲土著民族，比如玛雅人、印加人和阿兹特克

like the Mayas, the Incas, and the Aztecs had been living. They found lots of gold and silver. They made the native people work in the gold and silver mines so that the precious metals could be shipped to Spain to make that nation richer. When other European countries saw the fabulous wealth, they wanted some too. Soon the Spanish had to share the "New World" with other people. Portugal occupied the land that we call Brazil today. England and France claimed the eastern part of North America. England, France, Holland, and even Denmark snatched up some of the islands and a little land along the coast of Central and South America, but Spain continued to control most of the land that we call Latin America today. The Spanish language spoken by the colonists is still the most common language in Latin America, which includes all the lands in the Americas south of the United States. And the Roman Catholic religion, followed by most of the Spanish settlers, is still the largest religion there.

Most of the early Spanish settlers were men. Many of them married Native American women. Soon there were a lot of people whose parents and grandparents were both European and Native American. These people are called *Mestizos*. People whose ancestors were only Europeans were called *Creoles*. In some places land owners brought slaves from Africa to do their work for them. Some people with African ancestors married Creoles or Mestizos. Soon people in Latin America came not only in all sizes and shapes but in all colors as well. The king and queen in Spain sent out officials to rule over all these people. The officials collected taxes, but they didn't let any of the people have much say in how

人，都曾经生活在这些土地上。西班牙人在这里发现了大量的黄金和白银。他们强迫当地的土著到金矿和银矿里去干活，并将这些贵重金属运回西班牙，从而让该国变得越来越富庶起来。欧洲其他国家看到了这种巨大的财富后，也都想要分上一杯羹。不久之后，西班牙就只能与其他国家共享这个"新大陆"了。葡萄牙占领了如今我们所称的巴西。英国和法国占领了北美洲的东部地区。英国、法国、荷兰，甚至连丹麦这样的小国，也分别蚕食了一些岛屿，以及中美地区和南美洲沿海的小部分土地；可西班牙却继续控制着如今我们所称的"拉丁美洲"的绝大部分地区。当时殖民者所说的西班牙语，至今仍是拉丁美洲最通用的语言；所谓的拉丁美洲，包括南、北美洲位于美国以南的所有区域。绝大多数西班牙殖民者所信奉的罗马天主教，至今仍是拉丁美洲传播范围最广的一种宗教呢。

早期的西班牙殖民者，绝大多数都是男人。他们当中的许多人都娶了美洲的土著女子为妻。不久之后，就有了很多父母或者祖父母一方是欧洲人、另一方是美洲土著的混血儿。这些混血儿被称为"梅斯蒂索人"。而那些祖辈都是欧洲人的人，则被称为"克里奥耳人"。在有些地方，地主们还会从非洲掳来奴隶，让奴隶来替他们干活。一些带有非洲血统的人，后来又与克里奥耳人或梅斯蒂索人通婚。不久之后，拉丁美洲的人非但个子、长相各种各样，连肤色也是五花八门了。西班牙国王和王后派出官员，到美洲来统治这些人。那些官员征收赋税，但不允许任何人在行政方式上有多少发言权。

你们完全可以想见，拉丁美洲和加勒比地区的这些殖民地中，一定有许多不幸

they would be ruled.

You can imagine that there were a lot of unhappy people in the colonies in Latin America and the Caribbean! The Creoles thought that they should run the government and keep all the gold and silver and other wealth found in America. The Native Americans and the Mestizos both believed that they should have as much power as the Creoles or the officials sent from Europe. And, of course, the slaves didn't like being slaves, and they wanted very much to be free. This was true not only in the Spanish colonies but everywhere throughout Central and South America and the Caribbean.

Can you guess what happened next?

If you guessed revolution, you are right. In fact, a lot of revolutions broke out all over the place. These came not too long after the American Revolution and the French Revolution that you already know about. Each revolution had its own battles and its own heroes. Here are just a few of the stories.

The first big revolution took place in Haiti. Haiti is

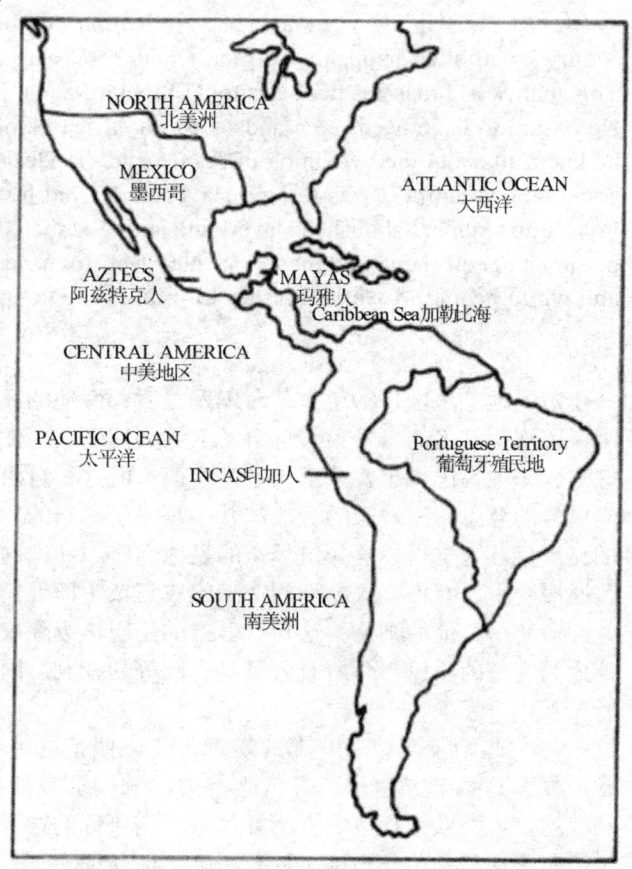

Colonial Latin America showing Native American civilizations
殖民时期的拉丁美洲，表明了美洲的土著文明

的人！ 克里奥耳人认为，他们应当由自己来管理政府，并且留住美洲发现的所有金银财宝。美洲土著和梅斯蒂索人则认为，他们应当拥有与克里奥耳人或欧洲派来的官员同等的权力。此外，那些奴隶当然也并不喜欢当奴隶，他们都渴望着获得自由。不但西班牙的殖民地情况如此，中美地区、南美洲和加勒比地区所有殖民地的情况，也是如此呢。

你们能够猜到，接下来发生了什么事情吗？

如果你们猜的是革命，那就对了。事实上，各地都爆发了一次又一次的革命。这些革命，都是在你们已经了解过的美国革命和法国大革命之后不久爆发的。每次革命，都进行了战斗，也都涌现出了各自的英雄人物。下面就是其中发生的一些故事。

第一次重大的革命发生在海地。海地是加勒比地区的一个岛国，当时是法国的

an island nation in the Caribbean and was a French colony. When the revolution began in France in 1789, people in Haiti heard all about it. They heard the famous slogan, *Liberté, égalité, fraternité*. Do you remember what that means? Well, the people in Haiti wanted their share of that liberty, equality, and brotherhood that everyone was talking about. But the Haitians didn't exactly agree on what that meant! The wealthy Creoles who owned most of the land thought it meant that they should be equal to French people in France. Ordinary people in Haiti, some of whom had a mixed racial background (whose ancestors were part French and part African) thought it meant that they should be equal to the wealthy Creoles. Slaves believed that it meant slavery should be abolished and all the former slaves should be full citizens with the same rights as all citizens. Before long, everybody was fighting everybody else.

One part of this fighting was a slave rebellion that began on the northern part of the island. As so often happens, a strong leader took charge and led his people to victory. This man was Toussaint L'Ouverture. Toussaint, as he is called, had been born a slave. He is said to have been the grandson of an African king. He could read and write, and he knew all about the revolution in France and the ideals of liberty and equality. He also knew how dreadful it was to be a slave. So he and his followers fought hard until the French government abolished slavery in Haiti, and then he continued to fight until he was put in charge of the government. He ruled well for several years. He asked black people and white people to work together to rebuild the country that had been torn apart by

一个殖民地。法国1789年大革命爆发之后，海地的民众都得知了这一消息。他们也听说了那个有名的口号："自由、平等、博爱"。你们还记得这个口号的意思吗？好吧，海地人民也想要分享大家都在谈论的这种自由、平等和博爱。可是，对于这句口号的意思，海地人的看法却并不是完全一致的！拥有绝大部分土地、非常富有的克里奥耳人觉得，这句口号指的是他们应当和国内的法国人一样平等。而海地的普通民众中，有一些人的种族背景比较复杂（即他们的祖先有部分法国血统和部分非洲血统），他们则认为这句口号指的是应该废除奴隶制度，以前的所有奴隶都应该成为完整的公民，与所有公民具有同等的权利。因此不久之后，这些人之间便开始相互斗争起来。

一场起始于海地岛北部的奴隶起义，便是这种斗争中的一个组成部分。跟往常一样，这场起义也是由一位强有力的领袖负责，他带领着手下的人民走向了胜利。这个人，就是杜桑·卢维杜尔。人们所称的这个杜桑，一出生就是个奴隶。据说他本来还是一位非洲国王的孙子呢。他能读会写，并且对法国爆发的这次大革命的情况了如指掌，也很了解自由、平等之类的理想。他也深知，身为奴隶是一件多么可怕的事情。因此，他和他的追随者们苦苦奋战，直到法国政府废除了海地的奴隶制度；然后他又继续斗争，最终被法国政府任命为海地政府的总督。他在任上井井有条地治理了好几年。他要求黑人和白人一起工作，重建那个被战争撕得四分五裂的国家，因此海地开始慢慢地恢复元气。接下来，拿破仑在法国掌握了大权，可拿破仑并不喜欢海地这个叫作杜桑的强势领导人。你们也可以说，拿破仑是在嫉妒

war, and Haiti began to recover. Then Napoleon came to power in France, and Napoleon didn't like this strong ruler named Toussaint. You might say that Napoleon was jealous of Toussaint. Or maybe Napoleon just decided that he wanted to control the island. In any case, Napoleon sent soldiers to Haiti. The general in charge of the French army played a mean trick on Toussaint. He invited Toussaint to be his guest for dinner. Then, when Toussaint came, the French general took him prisoner. Toussaint was sent to a prison all the way across the Atlantic in France. He died there a year later. But all was not lost. Soon a new leader named Jean-Jacques Dessalines took over the fight, and Haiti became an independent country. This is not a story with a completely happy ending though. After independence, a civil war broke out and Haiti had no real peace for many years.

In Spain's American colonies, there were a lot of unhappy people, too. Like the Haitians, they knew about the revolutions in the United States and in France. And they also had a lot of complaints about the conditions of their own lives. The Creoles were angry because people sent by the king from Spain had all the power, and they had none. All the people living in the Spanish colonies resented paying high taxes to the king of Spain. The Mestizos were angry with Spain just as the Creoles were. Native Americans knew that the Spanish had taken away their land, made them perform forced labor like slaves and killed many of their people. Most of all, these native peoples wanted their land back. Slaves in Latin America, like slaves everywhere, wanted to be free.

The first revolt against Spanish rule took place in South America, in what is now the

杜桑。或者说，拿破仑没准只是想要控制海地岛。不管怎么说，事实是拿破仑向海地派出了军队。负责指挥法军的那位将领，对杜桑玩了一种卑劣的花招。他邀请杜桑去做客，和他共进晚餐。接下来，待杜桑抵达之后，他便把杜桑囚禁了起来。后来，杜桑被漂洋过海地押到了大西洋对岸，关进了法国的一座监狱。一年后，他便在监狱里去世了。不过，海地并没有因此而失去一切。很快，一位名叫让-雅克·德萨林的新领导人接过了斗争的重任，最终使得海地变成了一个独立自主的国家。但是，这并不是一个结局非常完美的故事。独立后，海地又爆发了一场内战，因此许多年里都没有获得过真正的和平。

在西班牙的美洲殖民地中，也有许许多多不幸的人。像海地人一样，他们都得知了美国和法国爆发革命的消息。并且，他们对自己的生存状况也有着诸多的不满。克里奥耳人很恼火，因为西班牙国王从国内派来的人掌握着全部权力，而克里奥耳人自己却什么权力也没有。生活在西属殖民地的所有民众，对于必须向西班牙国王交纳高额赋税这一点，也都愤恨不已。梅斯蒂索人与克里奥耳人一样，也对西班牙人感到愤怒。美洲的土著民族都清楚，西班牙人夺走了他们的土地，强迫他们像奴隶一样劳动，还杀害了他们许多的同胞。最重要的是，这些本地民族都希望夺回自己的土地。而拉丁美洲的奴隶与世界各地的奴隶一样，都希望获得自由。

反对西班牙统治的第一场起义发生在南美洲，爆发于如今秘鲁这个国家所在的地方。这场起义由一个叫作图帕克·阿玛鲁的人领导；他是一名梅斯蒂索人，是印加王室的后裔。西班牙派来军队，杀害了图帕克·阿玛鲁及其追随者，这次起义就

nation of Peru. It was led by a man named Tupac Amaru, a Mestizo who was descended from Inca kings. The Spanish troops came and killed him and his followers, and that was the end of that. Latin America would have to wait a while for things to change.

A little after 1800, things really began to happen. First, in Europe, Napoleon conquered Spain, threw out the king, and made his own brother the new king of Spain. What do you think of that? Well, the people in Latin America saw it as a good excuse to declare independence. After all, their old king was no longer on the throne and clearly, they figured, Napoleon had no right to rule them. So the fighting began.

First, in Argentina, an army organized and won independence. The leading general, José de San Martin then decided on a dangerous plan. He led his armies across the high Andes mountains into Chile and later on to Peru to fight for independence in those places, too. Look at the map and see where those countries are. About one third of San Martin's soldiers were slaves to whom he had promised freedom for joining his army.

The best known hero in all Latin American history is Simon

Countries of Latin America and the Caribbean
拉丁美洲和加勒比地区各国

此结束。拉丁美洲还得等上一段时间，形势才会有所改变。

公元1800年刚刚过去，形势真的发生了变化。首先，在欧洲，拿破仑征服了西班牙，赶走了西班牙国王，并将他的兄弟扶植成了西班牙的新王。你们怎么看待这种情况呢？拉丁美洲的人民觉得，这是一个宣布独立的好理由。毕竟来说，原来的国王已经不再在位了，因此他们认为，拿破仑显然并没有权力来统治他们。于是，战争又开始了。

首先，阿根廷组建了一支军队并且赢得了独立。接着，领军的将领何塞·德·圣马丁制定了一个极其危险的计划。他率领手下的军队翻越高耸的安第斯山脉，进入智利，后来又进军秘鲁，去为那些地方也获得独立而战斗。看一看地图，找出这些国家都在哪里。圣马丁手下的士兵中，约有三分之一的人以前都是奴隶；他承诺说，只要他们加入他的军队，他就会让他们获得自由。

拉丁美洲历史上最有名的英雄人物，要算西蒙·玻利瓦尔了。正如我在本章

Bolivar. Just as I told you at the beginning, he is as famous in South America as George Washington is in the United States. Simon Bolivar was born in Caracas, Venezuela. He was the youngest of four children. His parents were wealthy Creoles who owned several houses, silver and copper mines, large herds of cattle, and large farms where sugar and cocoa were grown. You probably think that Simon must have been a very lucky little boy but, in fact, he was not. Simon's father died before he was three, and his mother died two weeks before his ninth birthday. The children all went to live in different places. Simon went to live with an uncle. This man was cold to Simon, and Simon missed the rest of his family very much.

When Simon was eleven, his uncle hired a young man to come tutor him. In those days, wealthy boys did not go to school. They had private tutors who came to their homes. Simon's new tutor was also named Simon — Simon Rodriguez. This young teacher taught Simon Bolivar all the new ideas that educated people were talking about. He taught him about the revolutions in the United States and France. He told him to look around him at the sad lives of the Native Americans and the slaves in Venezuela and to see how the Spanish wouldn't let people in their colonies rule themselves. With all this, it's not surprising that Simon Bolivar grew up to be a revolutionary.

In 1811, Creoles in Venezuela declared their independence from Spain. Just as we had to fight the British after we declared independence, the people of South America had to fight the Spanish to make their independence real. Simon Bolivar became one of the

开头告诉你们的那样，他在南美洲，就跟乔治·华盛顿在美国那样赫赫有名呢。西蒙·玻利瓦尔出生于委内瑞拉的加拉加斯。在兄弟姐妹四个当中，他的年纪最小。他的父母都是有钱的克里奥耳人，拥有房屋、银矿和铜矿、大群牲畜，以及种植糖料作物和可可的大型农庄。你们很可能会觉得，西蒙·玻利瓦尔一定是个很幸运的小男孩；可实际上，他并不幸运。他还不到三岁的时候，父亲就去世了；而母亲在他九岁生日的前两个星期也与世长辞了。兄弟姐妹们不得不分别到不同的地方去生活。西蒙·玻利瓦尔跟他的一个舅舅一起生活。这个舅舅很不喜欢西蒙·玻利瓦尔，因此西蒙·玻利瓦尔非常思念自己的家人。

西蒙·玻利瓦尔十一岁后，他的舅舅请了一位年轻人来当他的家庭教师。在那个时候，富人家的孩子都不去学校上学。他们都有私人的家庭教师，到家里来给他们上课。西蒙·玻利瓦尔的这位新老师也叫西蒙，叫西蒙·罗德里格斯。这位年轻的老师，把当时受过教育的人们正在纷纷谈论的所有新思想，全都灌输给了西蒙·玻利瓦尔。他给西蒙·玻利瓦尔介绍了美国革命和法国大革命的情况。他让西蒙·玻利瓦尔看一看周围那些美洲土著和委内瑞拉国内奴隶们的悲惨生活，看一看西班牙不让各个殖民地的人民当家做主的原因。这样一来，西蒙·玻利瓦尔成长为一个革命者，便不足为奇了。

1811年，委内瑞拉的克里奥耳人宣布该国脱离西班牙而独立。正如美国宣布独立之后不得不抗击英军一样，南美人民也不得不与西班牙人开战，才能让自己的独立变成现实。西蒙·玻利瓦尔成了起义军队里级别最高的领导人之一。第二年，

highest ranking officers in the rebel army. The next year, there was a terrible earthquake in Caracas that killed ten thousand of the rebel soldiers. A lot of people would have given up, but Simon Bolivar did not. He formed a new army and fought on. Finally he liberated Venezuela and then Colombia, Bolivia, and Ecuador. Bolivar was chosen president of the newly independent lands. He called this new country Gran Colombia in honor of Christopher Columbus.

Bolivar hoped to unite all the states of Latin America. But his plans never worked out. The places that broke away from Spanish rule split into the many separate countries of modern Central and South America. One country is named for the famous leader Bolivar. Can you pick it out on the map?

In most of the new countries, the wealthy people would not share the power with ordinary people, and they also refused to return any land to the Native Americans. Nor would they end slavery as Simon Bolivar wanted them to do. So all of Latin America's problems were not solved after independence. Still, Simon Bolivar is a hero in all the countries of South and Central America. He is known throughout the region as *El Libertador* — the Liberator.

Our nearest southern neighbor is Mexico. Take a minute and find Mexico on the map. Mexico used to be called New Spain, and it included such places as Texas, Arizona, New Mexico, and California. Mexicans rebelled against Spain just as the people in South America did. The first uprising was led by a Creole priest named Father Miguel Hidalgo.

加拉加斯发生了一次可怕的地震，有一万名起义军士兵在地震中丧生。许多人可能会因此而放弃斗争，可西蒙·玻利瓦尔并没有气馁。他组建了一支新军，继续与西班牙人战斗。最后，他不但解放了委内瑞拉，接下来还解放了哥伦比亚、玻利维亚和厄瓜多尔。将这几个刚刚独立的国家合并起来之后，玻利瓦尔便当选为该国总统。为了纪念克里斯托弗·哥伦布，他还将这个新的国家定名为"大哥伦比亚共和国"。

玻利瓦尔希望将拉丁美洲的所有国家全都统一起来。不过，他的计划一直都没有实现。摆脱了西班牙统治的那些地方，如今又分裂成了现代中美洲和南美洲的多个独立国家。其中有一个国家，就是用玻利瓦尔的名字命名的。你们能在地图上将这个国家找出来吗？

在绝大多数新成立的国家里，富人都不愿意与普通百姓共享权力，并且他们还拒绝将土地归还给美洲的原住民。他们也不愿意像玻利瓦尔所希望的那样，废除奴隶制度。因此，独立之后，拉丁美洲的所有问题依然没有得到解决。尽管如此，在南美洲和中美地区的所有国家，西蒙·玻利瓦尔仍然是一个英雄人物。这一地区的人，全都尊称他为"解放者"呢。

美国南方最近的一个邻国，就是墨西哥。请你们花上一分钟，在地图上将墨西哥这个国家找出来。墨西哥以前被称为"新西班牙"，其中还包括了像得克萨斯州、亚利桑那州、新墨西哥州以及加利福尼亚州等现在属于美国的地方。后来，像南美人民一样，墨西哥人也开始起义，开始反抗西班牙人的统治了。他们的第一次

He led a small group of Native Americans and others who joined him. They wanted to take some of the land from the few very wealthy people who owned it all and give some of it back to the native people from whom it had been taken, and to other poor people as well. The Spanish and the wealthy Creoles all went after him and, of course, they defeated his rebels. After Hidalgo was captured and executed, a Mestizo priest named Father José Maria Morelos led the fight. He, too, was captured and executed. In the end, the Creoles led the fight for independence from Spain, but they kept all the power in the hands of rich people. A general named Augustin de Iturbide actually declared Mexican independence in 1821. Soon after that, he was declared emperor, and the history of modem, independent Mexico had begun.

You can see from all this that there is a lot of history in the Americas south of the United States. All these new names may seem hard at first but, if you just think of them as people like George Washington, Benjamin Franklin, and Thomas Jefferson, you will understand what important people they are.

Now, you go try out some of those names on an adult you know and see how little most people from the United States know about our southern neighbors.

起义，是由一个叫作米格尔·伊达尔戈神父的克里奥耳牧师领导的。他手下只有一小支人马，由美洲土著以及其他一些加入进来的人所组成。他们希望从极少数非常富有、控制着所有土地的人手中夺取一部分土地，然后将其中的一部分土地返还给它们原来的所有者，另一部分则分配给其他的穷人。于是，西班牙人和当地富裕的克里奥耳人全都四处追捕他，最终当然是联合镇压了他所领导的这次起义。伊达尔戈被抓住并处死之后，一位名叫乔斯·玛利亚·莫雷洛斯的梅斯蒂索神父，领导人民继续战斗。后来，他也被抓住并处死了。最终，克里奥耳人又率领人民进行了摆脱西班牙统治的独立斗争，可他们却让所有的权力都掌握在富人手中。一位名叫阿古斯汀一世的将领，在1821年事实上宣布"伊瓜拉计划"，提出建立独立统一的墨西哥主张。此后不久，他就公开就任墨西哥皇帝；于是，现代独立的墨西哥的历史，便由此开始了。

由此，你们可以看出，美国以南的中美洲、南美洲地区的历史故事也丰富得很。一开始的时候，这些新的人名可能看上去很难记忆；但只要把他们看成是像乔治·华盛顿、本杰明·富兰克森和托马斯·杰斐逊那样的人，你们就会明白，他们都是些多么重要的人物了。

现在，你们就可以用这些名字，去考一考你们认识的某个成年人，看看绝大多数美国人对南方这些邻国的了解，少得有多么的可怜了。

79 From Pan and His Pipes to the Phonograph

Frogs croak.
Cats meow.
Dogs bark.
Sheep bleat.
Cows moo.
Lions roar.
Hyenas laugh.
But only birds and people sing.
And people can do what birds cannot.
They can also make music out of things.

Have you ever made a cigar-box fiddle or a pin piano or musical glasses?
In the long-ago story-book times, Apollo took a pair of cow horns and fastened between them seven strings made from the cow's skin. This was called a lyre. These strings he picked with his finger or with a quill, making a little tinkling sound that could hardly have

79 从潘及其排笛到留声机

青蛙呱呱。
小猫喵喵。
小狗汪汪。
绵羊咩咩。
母牛哞哞。
雄狮咆哮。
鬣狗大笑。
唯有鸟和人，可以来歌唱。
鸟儿的本领，没有人们大。
人可用万物，编成妙乐唱。

你们有没有做过烟盒小提琴、别针钢琴或者音乐酒杯之类的东西呢？
在传说中，很久、很久以前，太阳神阿波罗拿了一对牛角，然后用牛皮做成七根弦，拴在这对牛角之间。这件东西，叫作竖琴。他用手指或者用一根鸟翎拨动那些弦，就会发出一种细微的叮当之声；当然，那种声音是说不上非常美妙的。不

been very beautiful. Yet Apollo's son, Orpheus, is said to have learned from his father to play so beautifully on the lyre that the birds and wild beasts and even trees and rocks gathered around to hear him.

Pan, the god of the woods, who had goat's horns, and ears and legs and feet, tied together several whistles of different lengths and played on these as you might on a mouth organ. This instrument was called *Pan's pipes*.

The lyre and Pan's pipes were two of the earliest musical instruments. The first was a stringed instrument, the second a wind instrument. The long strings and long pipes made low notes; the short strings and short pipes made high tones.

From Apollo's lyre we get the piano with its many, many strings. Did you ever look at the inside of a piano and see the many strings of different lengths? They are, however, not picked as the strings of a lyre or harp are picked, but hammered by little felt-covered blocks as you touch the keys.

From Pan's pipes we get the great church organ with its pipes like giant whistles. You don't, of course, blow the pipes with your mouth as you do a whistle. The pipes are so big you must blow them with a machine.

We know what the instruments in olden times were like, but we don't know what the music that people made was really like; there were no phonographs or tapes to bottle up the sounds and, when uncorked a thousand years later, to pour forth the old notes once again. The music went off into thin air and was lost.

过，据说阿波罗的儿子俄耳甫斯却从父亲那里学会了用竖琴弹奏出美妙的音乐，使得百鸟、走兽甚至是树木、岩石都纷纷来到他身边，聆听他所奏的音乐呢。

潘是山林之神，长着山羊的角、耳朵、双腿和双脚；他曾将几个长短不一的哨子绑在一起，然后像如今你们吹口琴那样吹奏这些哨子。这件乐器，就叫作排笛。

竖琴和排笛是人类两种最早的乐器。竖琴是一种弦乐器，而排笛则是一种管乐器。长弦、长管发出来的，是低音；短弦、短管发出来的，则是高音。

根据阿波罗的竖琴，人们后来又发明了有许多根弦的钢琴。你们有没有看过一架钢琴的内部，看看里面有多少根长短不一的弦呢？但是，钢琴里的那些弦，并不是像竖琴的琴弦那样用来拨动的，而是在你们按下琴键的时候，通过包有棉布的小硬块的敲击来发出声音的。

从潘的排笛，我们得到了大型的教堂管风琴；这种大型管风琴的发音管，就像是一个个巨大的哨子。当然，人们并不是像吹哨子那样用嘴去吹那些发音管。因为发音管非常巨大，所以得用机器才能进行吹奏。

虽说我们知道古时的乐器是个什么样子，但我们并不了解古时人们吹奏出来的音乐究竟是个什么样子；因为那时并没有留声机、磁带来将这些音乐封存起来，无法让我们在一千年后打开它们时，再次流淌出古老的音乐来。音乐会飘向无形的空气中，消失得无影无踪。

直到公元1000年左右，音乐才能被人们用文字的形式记录下来。在此之前，所有的音乐都是通过用耳朵记住，然后再演奏出来的，因为那时还没有乐谱。一位名

It was not until about the Year 1000 A.D. that music could even be written down. Before then all music was played by ear, for there was no written music. A Benedictine monk named Guy, or, in Italian, Guido, thought of a way to write down musical notes, and he named the notes do, re, mi, fa, and so on. These were the first letters of the words of a hymn to St. John which the monks sang like the scale.

Another Italian is sometimes called the Father of Modern Music. His name is Palestrina, and he died in 1594. He set the church service to music, and the pope ordered all churches to follow it, but the people didn't like his music very much; that is, it was not what we call *popular*.

It was not until a hundred years later — that is, about 1700 — that the first great European musician lived who wrote music that was really popular, that the people in Europe and America loved, and that we still love today.

He was a German named Handel. His father was a barber, a dentist, and doctor, and he wanted his boy to become a great lawyer. But the only thing the boy liked was music.

In those days there were no pianos. There was a little instrument with strings which was played by touching keys. This was called a clavichord. Sometimes it had legs like a table. Sometimes it had no legs and was just laid on a table.

Handel, though only six years old, got hold of one of these instruments, and, without anyone finding out about it, he had it put up in his room in the attic of his house. After everyone had gone to bed at night, he would practice on this clavichord until late, when he was supposed to be in bed. One night his family heard sounds up under the roof.

叫盖伊（Guy）、在意大利语中写作圭多（Guido）的本笃会修道士，发明了一种将音乐符号记录下来的方法，并且将这些乐符命名为"朵、雷、咪、发"等等。它们就是修道士们吟唱给圣约翰的一首赞美诗中，每句第一个音节所用的阶名唱法。

还有一位意大利人，有时会被人们尊称为"现代音乐之父"。他名叫帕莱斯特纳，死于1594年。他曾给教堂的礼拜仪式配上音乐，后来教皇便下令所有的教堂全都这样做；可是，当时人们并不是很喜欢他的音乐，也就是说，他的音乐并不是我们如今所谓的流行音乐。

直到一百年后，即到了公元1700年左右，欧洲才出现了第一位伟大的音乐家；他所写的音乐确实非常流行，非但欧洲人和美国人都很喜欢，如今我们也依然很喜欢呢。

他是德国人，名叫汉德尔。他的父亲既是理发师、牙医，也是一名大夫；他曾希望，自己的儿子能够成为一名了不起的律师。可他的这位儿子，却只喜欢音乐。

那个时候，世界上还没有钢琴。当时只有一种通过触动琴键来弹奏琴弦的小型乐器。那种乐器叫作翼琴。有的时候，人们会给翼琴底下装上四根支架，使它就像一张桌子那样。有的时候，翼琴则没有安装支架，只是平放在桌子上。

汉德尔只有六岁的时候，就得到了一架这样的乐器；在大家都不知道的情况下，他把这架翼琴藏到了阁楼上他自己的房间里。晚上等全家人都上床睡觉之后，他就会在这架翼琴上练习，直到深夜；这个时候，他本来应当早就睡熟了呢。有天晚上，他的家人听到了屋顶上传来的声音。他们都想知道那是什么声音，便提了一盏灯，悄悄地沿着梯子爬上阁楼，突然打开了阁楼的小门；他们看到的，是穿着睡

Wondering what it could be, they took a lantern, and, quietly climbing the attic stairs, they suddenly opened the door, and there sat little Handel in his nightclothes on a chair with his feet reaching only half way to the floor, playing on the clavichord.

After that, Handel's father saw it was no use trying to make his son a lawyer. He got teachers for him, and before long the boy amazed the world with his playing. He went to England, lived there, became an Englishman, and when he died the English people buried him in Westminster Abbey, a church in which famous Englishmen were buried.

Handel set parts of the Bible to music. These songs with the Bible words to be sung by a chorus of voices were called *oratorios*, and one of these oratorios named The *Messiah* is sung almost everywhere at Christmas time. In addition to his religious music, Handel wrote forty-six operas!

Living at the same time as Handel was another German musician named Bach. Bach played divinely on the organ as Handel did on the clavichord and wrote some of the finest music for the organ that ever had been written. Strange that both Handel and Bach went blind in their old age, but to them it was sound, not sight, that counted most. Which do you think "counts more"?

Almost all musical geniuses have been musical wonders when they were still babies. They have been great musicians even before learning to read and write.

One such genius was born just before Bach and Handel died. He was an Austrian named Mozart.

Handel is found in the attic
在阁楼上练习翼琴的汉德尔被家人发现了

衣的小汉德尔正坐在椅子上，双脚在地板上方垂着，正在弹奏那架翼琴呢。

从那以后，汉德尔的父亲就明白，想要自己的儿子成为律师是不可能的事情了。于是，他给儿子请了老师；不久之后，这个小男孩便用自己的演奏，让全世界都惊讶不已了。后来他前往英国，在那里定居下来，变成了英国人，而他去世后，英国人还把他安葬在威斯敏斯特大教堂里；那座教堂里，安葬的可都是英国的名人呢。

汉德尔还给《圣经》中的一部分谱上了乐曲。这些以《圣经》经文为歌词且用于合唱的歌曲，被称为"神曲"；其中还有一首叫作《弥赛亚》的神曲，如今在圣诞期间，几乎各地都会诵唱呢。除了宗教音乐，汉德尔甚至还写了46部歌剧！

与汉德尔同一时期的，还有一位名叫巴赫的德国音乐家。巴赫演奏起风琴来，就像汉德尔演奏翼琴那样美妙；他还写出了有史以来最精美的一些风琴曲。奇怪的是，汉德尔和巴赫两人年老之后都双目失明了；可对他们而言，最重要的是声音，而不是视觉。你们觉得，声音和视觉对你们来说，哪一种"更重要"呢？

几乎所有的音乐天才还在襁褓中的时候，就已经是音乐奇迹了。甚至在学会读

Mozart, when only four years old, played the piano wonderfully. He also wrote music — composing, it is called — for others to play.

Mozart's father and sister played very well, so the three went on a concert tour. Mozart, the boy wonder, played before the empress, and everywhere he went he was treated like a prince, petted and praised and given parties and presents.

He grew up and married, and ever after he had the hardest kind of time trying to make a living. He composed all sorts of things, plays with music called *operas*, and *symphonies*, which are written for whole orchestras to play; but he made so little money that when he died he had to be buried where they put people who were too poor to have a grave for themselves alone. People afterward thought it a shame that such a great composer should have no monument over his grave, but then it was too late to find where he was buried. A monument was put up, but to this day no one knows where Mozart's body lies.

A German named Beethoven had read the stories of the boy wonder, Mozart, and he thought he, too, would like to have a boy wonder to play before kings and queens. When his son was only five years old, he kept the boy practicing long hours at the piano until he became so tired that the tears ran down his cheeks. But Ludwig Beethoven, as he was named, finally came to be one of the greatest musicians who have ever lived. He could sit at the piano and make up the most beautiful music as he went along — *improvise*, as it is called — but he was never satisfied with it when written down. Time and time again he would scratch out and rewrite his music until it had been rewritten often a dozen times.

写之前，他们往往就已经成为音乐大师。

巴赫和汉德尔去世之前，世界上就诞生了这样一位天才。这位天才是奥地利人，名叫莫扎特。

莫扎特只有四岁的时候，就已经弹得一手好钢琴了。他还写作音乐供别人去演奏；这叫作曲。

莫扎特的父亲和姐姐也弹得一手好钢琴，因此父子三人便去各地巡回演奏。莫扎特这位神童曾在皇后面前演奏过，并且每到一处，人们待他都像王子一样，宠他、称赞他，还给他举办晚会，送礼物给他。

他长大后，结了婚；而自此以后，他便一直过着最为艰难、千方百计养家糊口的生活。他创作过各种各样的作品，其中有称为歌剧的那种带有音乐的戏剧，以及供整个管弦乐队演奏的交响乐；可他挣的钱实在太少，以至于死后只能与那些生前太穷、无法自己购置墓地的穷人葬在一起。后来，人们认为这样一位伟大作曲家的坟墓上竟然没有纪念碑是一件憾事，可那时却已太迟，连他所葬之地也找不到了。虽然人们为他修建了一座纪念碑，但直至今日，依然没人知道莫扎特究竟安葬在哪里。

一位名叫贝多芬的德国人读到了莫扎特这位神童的故事后，也希望自己有这样一个能够在国王和王后们面前演奏的神童儿子。因此，在儿子刚到五岁的时候，他便让儿子每天都长时间地练习弹钢琴，直到儿子疲惫不堪、眼泪顺着脸颊滚滚而下才罢手。不过，这个叫作路德维希·贝多芬的儿子，最终还是成了有史以来最伟大的音乐家之一。他可以坐在一架钢琴前，一边弹奏，一边创作出最美妙的音乐来；这一过程，被称为即兴创作。可是，把乐曲记录下来之后，他却从未满意过。他会

But Beethoven's hearing began to grow dull. He was worried that he might lose it entirely — a terrible thing to happen to anyone, but to one whose hearing was his fortune, nothing could be worse. At last he did become deaf. This loss of his hearing made Beethoven hopelessly sad and bad-tempered, cross with everything and everybody. Nevertheless, he didn't give up; he kept on composing just the same, even after he could no longer hear what he had written.

Another great and unusual German musician named Wagner lived until 1883. Though he practiced all his life, he never could play very well. But he composed wonderful operas, and he wrote not only the music but the words, too. He took old Germanic myths and fairy tales and made them into plays to be sung to music. At first some people made fun of his music, for it seemed to them so noisy and "slam-bangy" and without tune. Now people make fun of those people who don't like it!

I have told you in other places of painters and poets, or architects and wise men, of kings and heroes, of wars and troubles. I have put this story of music of all ages in one chapter, which I have tucked in here between the acts, to give you a rest for a moment from wars and rumors of wars.

When I was a boy I never heard any great musicians play. Now you and I can turn on the record, tape, or CD player anytime and hear the music of Palestrina or Mozart, of Beethoven or Wagner, of dozens of other masters, played or sung to us whenever we wish. No caliph in the *Arabian Nights* could command such service for his pleasure!

一遍又一遍地将记下的乐曲划掉重写，并且经常会重写上十几次才作罢。

但是，后来贝多芬的听力开始慢慢变得迟钝了。他很担心，自己最终会完全失去听觉；这对任何一个人来说都是一件可怕的事情，而对于一个听力就是命根子的音乐家来说，更是没有什么会比丧失听力更糟糕的了。最后，他的确聋了。失去听力让贝多芬变得非常绝望，脾气也变得非常暴躁，对任何事情和任何人都极其乖戾。尽管如此，他还是没有放弃音乐；即便是根本听不到自己创作出来的乐曲演奏起来是个什么样子，他还是一如既往地作曲。

还有一位了不起的、非同寻常的德国音乐家，名叫瓦格纳，他直到1883年才去世。尽管终生都在练习，可他的演奏始终都不是很好。不过，他却创作出了许多精彩的歌剧作品；并且，他不但作曲，还会作词呢。他采用古老的日耳曼神话传说为题材，将它们编入戏剧当中，合着音乐诵唱。起初，有些人嘲笑他的这种音乐，因为在那些人看来，瓦格纳的音乐太过嘈杂、"喧闹"，很不成调。可如今，人们却是嘲笑那些不喜欢瓦格纳音乐的人了！

在其他章节中，我已经跟你们介绍过一些画家和诗人、建筑师和智者、国王和英雄人物，以及战争和问题了。而我之所以把各个时代的音乐故事集中于一章，并穿插在这里，目的就是让你们休息休息，不要再去想战争和关于战争的种种说法。

小的时候，我从来没有聆听过哪个伟大音乐家的演奏。如今，你们和我一样，任何时候都可以打开唱机，播放唱片、磁带或者光盘了；只要我们愿意，随时都可以聆听到帕莱斯特纳、莫扎特、贝多芬、瓦格纳以及其他数十位音乐大师的作品了。《一千零一夜》里，可没有哪个哈里发能够下令提供此种服务来供他享受呢！

80 The Daily Papers of 1854—1865

If you could go up into your grandmother's attic or the attic of somebody else's grandmother, or could dig down into some old trunk, you might find some of the newspapers that were printed during the years from 1854 to 1865. You might actually read in these daily papers the happenings that I am now going to tell you about. Under the heading, *Foreign News*, you would probably find some of the following things told about:

English News. At this time the queen of England was named Victoria. She was much beloved by her people because she had such a kindly nature. You may have seen a picture of her surrounded by her many children. Victoria had five daughters and four sons. So you can see that she was a mother as well as a queen. She was more like a mother to her people than a queen. She ruled for more than half a century, and the time when she ruled is called the Victorian Age.

The English news of 1854 would tell about a war that the English were then fighting with Russia. Russia was a long way off, and so the English had to send their soldiers in boats through the Mediterranean Sea to the end, then past Constantinople into the Black Sea. There, in a little spot of land that jutted out from Russia into the Black Sea, most of

80   1854—1865年间的日报

假如你们能够爬到自己奶奶的阁楼或别人奶奶的阁楼上去，或者能够到某个很古老的箱子里去翻一翻，没准就能找到一些印刷于1854年至1865年间的报纸来。在这些报纸上，你们可以实实在在地读到我现在正打算给你们介绍的这些事情。在"国外新闻"这一栏里，你们很可能会看到下面这样一些东西：

英国新闻。此时，英国女王名叫维多利亚。她深受英国人民爱戴，因为她的性格非常和善。你们可能会看到一张照片，照片中她的许多孩子都围在她的身边。维多利亚女王有五个女儿和四个儿子。因此，你们就会明白，她既是女王，同时也是一位母亲。对她的臣民们来说，她更像是一位母亲，而不像是一位女王。她在位达半个多世纪，而她统治英国的那一段时间，就被称为"维多利亚时代"。

1854年的英国新闻里会提到一场战争，因为当时英国正在与俄罗斯打仗。俄罗斯距英国非常遥远，因此英国必须派士兵乘船渡海至地中海的东端，然后经由君士坦丁堡进入黑海。在那里，有一个小小的地方，从俄罗斯的领土伸进了黑海之中；双方之间的战斗，也主要是在这里进行的。这个小地方，叫作克里米亚；而这场战争，也因此而被称为"克里米亚战争"。在遥远的克里米亚进行的这场战争中，有成千上万的英军士兵因受伤或者染病而死去。

the fighting was done. This little spot of land was called the Crimea, and the war therefore was called the Crimean War. In this war in that far-off land, thousands of English soldiers died from wounds and disease.

Now, there was living in England at the time of this war a lady named Florence Nightingale. She was very tender-hearted and always looking out for and taking care of those who were sick. Even as a little girl, she had played that her dolls were sick with a headache or a broken leg, and she would bandage the aching head or broken leg and pretend to take care of her sick patient. When her dog was ill, she nursed him as carefully as if he were a human being.

Florence Nightingale heard that English soldiers were dying by the thousands in that distant land far away from home and that there were no nurses to take care of the wounded. She got together a number of women, and they went out to the Crimea. Before she arrived, almost half the soldiers who were wounded died — fifty soldiers out of a hundred; after she and her nurses came, only two in a hundred died. She went about through the camps and over the battlefields at night carrying a lamp, looking for the wounded. The soldiers called her the Lady of the Lamp, and they all loved her.

When at last the war was over and she returned to England, the government voted to give her a large sum of money for what

Florence Nightingale searching out the wounded
弗洛伦斯·南丁格尔正在搜寻伤员

　　注意，在克里米亚战争期间，英国有一位女士，叫作弗洛伦斯·南丁格尔。她的心肠非常善良，经常留意和照料那些生了病的人。还是个小姑娘的时候，她在玩布娃娃时就会假装布娃娃生了病，或是头疼，或是腿上骨折了，而她自己则假装很耐心地照料着病人。小狗生病时，她也会把它当成病人一样悉心地进行照料呢。

　　弗洛伦斯·南丁格尔听说成千上万的英国士兵正在遥远的海外战场上死去，而且也没有护士来照料伤员。于是，她组织了一批妇女，带着她们出国前往克里米亚。在她到达之前，受伤的士兵差不多有一半会死去，也就是说，一百名伤员中就有约五十人会死；而她和手下的护士来到这里以后，每一百名伤员中就只会死上两个了。她在军营里四处查看，晚上则提着一盏油灯到战场上去搜寻伤员。因此，英军士兵们都称她"油灯女士"，并且都很爱戴她。

　　战争终于结束后，她回到了英国；英国政府决定奖给她一大笔钱，以表彰她所

she had done. She, however, refused the money for herself but took it to found a home for training nurses. Nowadays professional nurses are thought almost as necessary as doctors, and anyone who is sick can call in a trained nurse to take care of him, but at that time there were no professional nurses. Florence Nightingale was the first to start teaching nursing, and she is looked upon almost as a saint today.

In one battle in the Crimea, a company of soldiers mounted on horseback were given by mistake an order to attack the enemy. Though they knew it meant certain death, they never hesitated but charged, and two-thirds of them were killed or wounded in less than half an hour. Lord Tennyson, the English poet, has told this story in verse which you may know. It is called *The Charge of the Light Brigade*.

Japanese News. Japan is a group of islands near China. Although I have not told you about it before, it was an old country. In Europe there have been constant changes of kings and rulers and people and countries. But in Japan they have had the same line of kings since before Christ.

Japan was very lucky in one way. In all the years, the Japanese islands were never occupied by a foreign army. But in 1853, the year before England began the Crimean War, an American naval officer named Commodore Perry sailed into Tokyo Bay, an important Japanese harbor, with American warships. The Japanese emperor then allowed Americans to come in and do business in Japan.

These are some of the things you might read about in those old newspapers. Such news

做的贡献。然而，她自己并没有要这笔钱，而是将这笔钱用来成立了一个护士培训基地。如今人们认为，除了医生，专业护士同样是不可或缺的，病人也可以随时要求一名训练有素的护士前来照料自己；可在当时，世界上还没有专业护士呢。弗洛伦斯·南丁格尔是第一个开始教授护理学的人，因此如今差不多被人们看成是一位圣人了。

在克里米亚进行的一场战斗中，一个连队的骑兵阴差阳错地接到了命令，要他们去进攻敌人。尽管明白进攻就会有伤亡，但他们毫不犹豫，立即发动了进攻；结果，不到半个小时，就有三分之二的士兵要么阵亡、要么受伤。英国诗人丁尼生勋爵曾经写过一首诗，来记述这一过程，你们可能听说过。这首诗的名字，就叫《轻骑队之战歌》。

日本新闻。日本是一个群岛国家，距中国很近。尽管以前我并没有向你们介绍过，但日本也是一个历史悠久的国家；在欧洲，各国的国王、君主、民族和国家都在不停地发生着变化。但在日本，自公元前以来，历任国王却一直属于同一血统。

有一个方面，日本非常幸运。在整个历史上，日本群岛从来都没有被外国军队占领过。不过，在1853年，也就是英国发动克里米亚战争的前一年，有位名叫佩里准将的美国海军军官，率领着手下的美国军舰，驶入了日本的重要港口东京湾。接下来，日本天皇便允许美国人进入日本，并且与日本进行贸易了。

在那个时候的旧报纸上，你们可能会看到下面一些内容。这些新闻，很可能所占版面不大。如果是美国报纸的话，它们或许会位于某一栏的底部。不过，倘若这

would probably have taken up little space. Perhaps they would have been found down at the bottom of a column if the newspaper were American. But if the paper were printed between 1861 and 1864, the greater part of it would be about a war that was going on in our country at that time. This was a war between our own people, a family quarrel, which we call the Civil War, or the War between the States.

Two parts of our country, the North and the South, did not agree on several matters, chief of which was the question whether southerners could own slaves. So they went to war with each other. Thousands upon thousands of Americans died in this war. The war lasted for four years, from 1861 to 1865, before it was decided that no one could ever again own slaves in the United States.

Some of you who read these pages may be descended from men who fought in this Civil War. Some of these fought for the South; some fought for the North. Black men and white men and even some women fought. You should ask your parents or grandparents if any of your ancestors fought in the Civil War.

The president of the United States at that time was a man named Abraham Lincoln.

Lincoln visiting camp and shaking hands with the soldiers
林肯视察军营并与士兵们握手

份报纸出版于1861年至1864年间，那么其中的绝大部分内容，涉及的可能都是美国当时正在进行的一场战争。这是美国人民内部之间的一场战争，我们称之为"内战"，或者"南北战争"。

当时，美国的南方和北方这两个地区，在一些问题上的意见并不统一；其中最主要的，就是南方人能否蓄奴的问题。因此，他们之间便打了一场战争。有成千上万的美国人死于这场战争。从1861年至1865年，这场战争持续打了四年，最终才确定，美国国内任何人都不得再拥有奴隶。

你们当中一些看过这些报纸的小朋友，可能就是那些在这场内战中打过仗的人的后代呢。这些打过仗的人当中，有些人是替南方而战，有些人则是替北方而战。当时打仗的，不但有黑人、白人，甚至还有一些妇女。你们可以回去问问父母或者爷爷奶奶，你们的祖先有没有人曾经在这场"内战"中打过仗。

当时的美国总统，是一个叫作亚伯拉罕·林肯的人。林肯小的时候家里很穷，

Lincoln was a very poor boy who had been born in a log cabin. He had taught himself to read by the light of a blazing knot of wood at night after his day's work on his father's farm was done. As he was very poor, he had only a few books, and these he read over and over again. One of these books was the same *Aesop's Fables* that you read. When Lincoln was a young man, he became a storekeeper. One day he found that he had given a poor woman a smaller package of tea than she had paid for, and he closed the store and walked many miles to her house in order to return the change. People began to call him Honest Abe after that, for he was always very honest and kind-hearted.

He studied hard and became a lawyer and at last was elected president of the United States. While he was president, he declared that slavery should be abolished. One evening, Lincoln was watching a play from a private box at Fords Theater. Suddenly, John Wilkes Booth, who thought Lincoln had not done right in freeing the slaves, broke into the president's box and shot Lincoln, who died the next day.

Lincoln was one of our greatest presidents. Washington started our country; Lincoln prevented its splitting into two parts and kept it together as one big united land to grow into the great country it now is.

只有一座小木屋。他白天在父亲的农场上干完活后，晚上便借着木头疙瘩燃烧时的微弱光线自学识字。由于很穷，他只有寥寥的几本书，所以翻来覆去地读了一遍又一遍。其中有一本书，就是你们如今所看的《伊索寓言》。林肯长大后，开了一家小杂货店。有一天，一位贫穷的妇女前来买茶叶；他发现自己给那位妇女的茶叶分量不够之后，便把商店关上，走了好几英里的路，去那位妇女的家里，把钱找给她。此后，人们便称他为"正直的亚伯"，因为他一向都非常诚实正直、心地善良。

后来，他通过刻苦学习，成了一名律师，最终又被选举为美国总统。他就任总统之后，宣布美国应当废除奴隶制度。有天晚上，林肯正在福特剧院的一个包厢里看戏。突然之间，认为林肯解放奴隶这一做法不对的约翰·威尔克斯·布斯闯入了总统的包厢，开枪击中了林肯；第二天，林肯就重伤去世了。

林肯是美国最伟大的总统之一。华盛顿是美国的开国元勋；而林肯则阻止了美国分裂成南北两个部分，保持了美国的统一，使之作为一个统一的大国，一直发展到了今天这样一个强国。

81 Three New Postage Stamps

Let us look backward a minute to see what had been going on in Europe since the time of Napoleon.

After Napoleon was sent to Elba, the French had to have another ruler. They wanted their old kings back again. The family name of their old kings was Bourbon, and the French thought they ought to have a Bourbon ruler over them. Accordingly they tried out three Bourbons — one after the other — all relatives of their last king, whom they had beheaded.

All of them proved no good. The French people had given the Bourbon family a good tryout, and so at last they stopped worrying with kings and started another republic.

Now, a republic has a president instead of a king, so the people had to choose a president; and whom do you suppose they picked out? Why, the nephew of Napoleon. The nephew of Napoleon was named Louis Napoleon. He had planned and plotted again and again to make himself king of France, but again and again he had failed. And now he was elected president! But Louis Napoleon didn't want to be *only* president. He wanted to be like his uncle the great Napoleon. He dreamed of being emperor and conquering Europe, and so it was not long after this before he had himself made emperor, and called himself

81　三枚新邮票

我们暂时再回过头去，看一看自拿破仑时代以来，欧洲的情况吧。

拿破仑被流放到厄尔巴岛去了之后，法国人便不得不另找一位君主了。他们希望迎回原来的那个王室。原来那个王室叫作波旁王朝，因此法国人觉得，他们应当拥立一位波旁君主来统治法国。于是，他们先后拥立了三位波旁国王；而这三位国王，也都是法国人曾经将其砍了头的上一任国王的亲戚。

最终表明，这三位国王都不是善良之辈。法国人民已经给了波旁王室充分的机会，因此他们最后不再想要国王了，便成立了另一个共和国。

注意，一个共和国的最高统治者是总统，而不是国王，因此人民必须通过选举来产生一位总统；你们觉得，法国人民会选择谁来当总统呢？哎呀，他们选的，竟然是拿破仑的侄子。拿破仑的这个侄子，名叫路易·拿破仑。他曾一次又一次地计划，想要阴谋自立为法国国王，可一次又一次地失败了。如今，他竟然当选成了总统！可是，路易·拿破仑并不满足于只当总统。他希望自己成为老拿破仑叔父那样的人。他梦想着成为皇帝，梦想着征服整个欧洲；因此没过多久，他便自封皇帝，

Napoleon III[1].

Napoleon III was jealous of the neighboring country of Prussia. It was getting to be too strong, he thought. Prussia had a king at this time named William who was very able himself, and he had an able assistant or prime minister named Bismarck,3 who was looking for an excuse to fight France. Presently a war was started between the two countries in 1870. Napoleon soon found he had made a bad mistake in picking the war with Prussia. Prussia was not *getting* too strong; it was already too strong.

Napoleon III was completely beaten by Prussia, and he with a large army had to surrender. Then in disgrace he went to live in England.

The Prussians marched into Paris and made the French agree to pay them a billion dollars. When some of the French towns said they couldn't pay, Bismarck lined up the leading citizens of the place and told them they would be shot if they didn't raise the money that was demanded. France paid, and, to the wonder and amazement of everybody, they paid this immense sum in two years' time. But it took France a long time to forget the way they were made to pay and the way they were treated by the Prussians, and for a long time there was deadly enmity between these two countries. This war was called the Franco-Prussian War, as it was between France and Prussia.

---

[1]　Napoleon I had a young son who might have been Napoleon II if he had lived. The story is, that when Napoleon III was made emperor his name was printed simply with three exclamation marks after it — Napoleon!!! — and this was by mistake read Napoleon III.

自称拿破仑三世[1]了。

拿破仑三世对邻国普鲁士很是忌妒。他认为，普鲁士的实力正在变得太过强大。此时，普鲁士的国王名叫威廉；他非但自身非常能干，还有一位能力超群的助手或者首相，叫作俾斯麦，而俾斯麦也正在寻找借口，要与法国打上一仗。于是，两国很快便在1870年开战了。拿破仑三世不久便发现，他选择与普鲁士开战是一个巨大的错误。普鲁士并不是正在变得太过强大，而是实力已经太过强大了。

拿破仑三世完全被普鲁士打败了，因此他和手下的大军都不得不向普鲁士投降。接下来，他便带着耻辱，住到英国去了。

普鲁士军队挺进巴黎，迫使法国同意赔偿他们十亿美元。法国的一些城市拒绝支付赔款；俾斯麦便下令，将这些城市里领头拒交赔款的那些市民排成一行，并对他们说，如果筹不起所需的赔款，就要枪决他们。于是，法国不得不支付了这笔赔款；而令人稀奇和惊讶的是，该国竟然在两年之内，就支付了这笔巨额赔款。不过，法国人很久都无法忘记普鲁士人强迫他们支付赔款和压制他们的做法，因此两国之间很久都是死敌。这场战争，史称"普法战争"，因为它是在法国和普鲁士两国间进行的。

---

[1]　拿破仑一世原本有个年纪不大的儿子；这个儿子要是活着的话，可能会叫拿破仑二世的。据说，拿破仑三世当上皇帝的时候，报纸上只是在他的名字后面印了三个惊叹号，即"拿破仑!!!"，却被人们误读成"拿破仑三世"了。

There were a number of little countries near Prussia. They were called German states. But though their people were related and spoke the same language, the countries or states were separate. As a result of the war, Prussia was able to join all these German states together and to make for the first time one big, strong, powerful nation called Germany, feared by other countries on account of its great army of fighting men. William was made emperor of all Germany and called kaiser. He was crowned in the French palace that Louis XIV had built at Versailles.

The French thought the Germans had been able to win this war because they had public schools in which all their children were trained and because of the way their soldiers were drilled. So France set to work and started public schools everywhere in France and imitated the German way of drilling their army so that they would be prepared in the next war.

France became a republic with a president and an assembly chosen by the people. The French wanted no more emperors.

At that time Italy was not a single country as it is now. It was a collection of small states, as Germany had been. Some of these were independent; some were owned by France; some were owned by Austria. The king of one of these Italian states was Victor Emmanuel. He wanted all the Italian states to unite and become one single country like our United States. He was helped by his prime minister, a very able man named Cavour, and by a rough but romantic popular hero named Garibaldi, who was called the Hero of the Red Shirt.

普鲁士的附近，还有许多的小国家。当时，它们被称为德意志各邦。不过，尽管这些国家中的人民都关系密切，说的也是同一种语言，但这些国家或者邦国都是各自独立的。普法战争之后，普鲁士便有实力将这些德意志邦国全都统一起来，第一次形成一个疆域广阔、牢固无比、实力强大的国家了；这个国家，就叫德意志。由于军队庞大、骁勇善战，所以其他国家都很惧怕德国。于是，威廉便被加封为整个德意志的皇帝，称为德皇。他加冕称帝的地方，竟然是在路易十四于凡尔赛所建的那座法国王宫之内！

法国人认为，德国人之所以能够打赢这场战争，一方面在于德国开设了许多公立学校，所有孩子都能够在这些公立学校里接受教育；另一方面则在于德国训练士兵的方式很高明。于是，法国也开始在全国各地开设公立学校，并且模仿德国训练军队的做法，以便让军队为下一场战争做好准备。

此时，法国已经变成了一个共和国，有了民选的总统和议会。法国人再也不想要什么皇帝了。

当时，意大利跟如今不一样，还不是一个单一的国家。它像德国以前那样，是由许多小邦组成的。其中有些小邦是独立的国家，有些被法国占领了，还有一些则隶属于奥地利。这些意大利小邦中，有一个邦的国王叫作维克多·伊曼纽尔。他希望将意大利的这些小邦全都统一起来，成为像我们美国这样的一个单一国家。协助他来实现这一目标的，有两个人。一是他的首相，那是一个非常能干的人，叫作加

Garibaldi, who had been a candlemaker in New York City, was always poor and seemed not to care for money. He was so popular that whenever he called for soldiers to fight with him for his beloved Italy, they at once flocked around him, ready to fight to the death.

At last these three, Victor Emmanuel, Cavour, and Garibaldi, succeeded in making their country one big nation. The Italians erected monuments to them and named streets after them. To honor Victor Emmanuel, they built a magnificent building on a hill in Rome overlooking the city, a building that was intended to be more beautiful than anything built in Athens during the time of Pericles, or in Italy during the Renaissance.

If you collect postage stamps it would be interesting for you to get, if you can, stamps of these countries at that time, the New French Republic, United Germany, and United Italy.

富尔；一是一位粗野却又富有传奇色彩、广受民众爱戴的英雄人物加里波第，人们称他为"红衫军勇士"。

加里波第曾经是纽约市的一名蜡烛制造工，一向都穷得很，可他似乎不怎么在意钱财。由于深受人民爱戴，因此无论何时，只要他振臂一呼，要求士兵们为他深爱的意大利而战，士兵们马上都会聚集到他麾下，准备好投入战斗，视死如归。

最后，维克多·伊曼纽尔、加富尔和加里波第这三个人，成功地将意大利统一成一个疆域辽阔的国家。意大利人为他们修建了纪念碑，并且用他们的名字为街道命名。为了纪念维克多·伊曼纽尔，他们还在罗马城的一座小山上修建了一栋辉煌的建筑，让它俯瞰着整个罗马城；人们挖空心思，要让这座建筑比伯里克利时代雅典所建的，或者文艺复兴时期意大利所建的任何建筑都更加漂亮呢。

如果你们集邮，那么收集当时这些国家的邮票会是很有意思的一件事情；当然，要能够收集到才行。这些国家就是：新的法兰西共和国、统一的德国和统一的意大利。

82 The Age of Miracles

You may think the Age of Miracles was in Biblical days.

But if a man who lived at that time should come back to earth *now* he would think this the Age of Miracles.

If he heard you talk on a telephone to a person thousands of miles away, or even a hundred feet away, he would think you a magician.

If you showed him people moving and talking on a movie screen or a television screen, he would think you a witch.

If he heard you start a band playing by turning on a tape player or a radio, he would think you a devil.

If he saw you fly through me air in an airplane, he would think you a god.

We are so used to the telephone, television, and tape recorders, to automobiles and huge trucks and jet planes, to electric lights and moving pictures and radios and marvelous cameras that it is hard to imagine a world in which none of these things existed — absolutely none of these things. Yet in the year 1800, not a single one of these inventions was known.

Neither George Washington nor Napoleon ever saw an airplane or an automobile. They

82 奇迹时代

你们可能会觉得，"奇迹时代"是指《圣经》中的那个时代。

不过，假如生活在那个时代的一个人现在可以复活的话，那他可能就会认为，如今才是"奇迹时代"哩。

假如他听到你们在电话里跟相隔几千英里，甚至是几百英尺之外的人交谈的话，他可能会认为你们都是魔法师。

如果让他看到人们在电影或电视屏幕上来来去去、说着话，那么他可能会认为你们都是巫婆。

倘若他听到你们打开录音机或者收音机，便可以让一支乐队开始演奏的话，他可能会觉得你们都是魔鬼。

假若他看到你们坐在飞机里在空中飞行的话，他就会觉得你们都是神仙呢。

我们对电话、电视、录音机、汽车、重型卡车、飞机、电灯、电影、收音机、不可思议的照相机等等都已经习以为常了，因此很难想象一个没有这些东西的世界、一个完全没有这些东西的世界是个什么样子。然而，公元1800年的时候，这些发明却一个都不为人知呢。

乔治·华盛顿和拿破仑两人，都没有见过飞机或者汽车。他们从来没用过电话、

never used a telephone or a radio or even a bicycle. They never heard of a gasoline engine or a diesel engine or an electric light. They never even imagined men walking on the moon, or close-up photographs of Mars, or television sets, or even typewriters. And as for computers and radar and X-rays — well!

More wonders have been made in the last hundred years than in all the previous centuries of the world put together.

A Scotsman named James Watt was one of the first of these magicians whom we call inventors. Watt had watched a boiling kettle on the stove and noticed that the steam lifted the lid. This gave him an idea that steam might lift other things as well as the lid of a teakettle. So he made a machine in which steam lifted a lid called a piston in such a way as to turn a wheel. This was the first steam engine.

Watt's steam engine moved wheels and other things, but it didn't move itself. An Englishman named Stephenson put Watt's engine on wheels and made the engine move its own wheels. This was the first locomotive. Soon funny-looking carriages drawn by funny-looking engines were made to run on tracks in America. At first these trains ran only a few miles out, from such cities as Baltimore and Philadelphia.

Then a young fellow named Robert Fulton thought he could make a boat go by putting Watt's engine on board and making it turn paddle wheels. People laughed at him and called the boat he was building *Fulton's Folly*, which means *Fulton's foolishness*. But the boat worked, and Fulton had the laugh on those who had laughed at him. He called his

收音机，甚至也没有骑过自行车。他们从来没有听说过汽油发动机、柴油发动机或者电灯。他们甚至从来没有想象过人类能够在月球上行走，能够近距离地拍摄到火星的照片，能够拥有电视机，甚至还有打字机。至于电脑、雷达和X射线，就更是如此了！

过去一百年来人类所创造的奇迹，比整个世界过去那么多个世纪以来所创造的奇迹总和还要多哩。

苏格兰人詹姆斯·瓦特，便是最初的这种魔法师之一，我们称之为发明家。瓦特曾经观察过火炉上一只开着的水壶，注意到蒸汽把水壶的盖子顶了起来。这一现象让他想到，蒸汽既然能够顶起水壶的盖子，那它也有可能顶得起其他的东西。于是，他便发明了一种机器，用蒸汽顶起一个叫作活塞的"盖子"，然后再带动一只轮子。这就是世界上的第一台蒸汽发动机。

虽说瓦特发明的蒸汽发动机能够推动轮子和其他东西，但发动机本身却不会移动。有位名叫史蒂芬孙的英国人，他将瓦特的蒸汽发动机装上轮子，使得发动机能够推动自身的轮子而前进。这就是世界上的第一台机车。很快，由样子可笑的发动机牵引着的那些样子可笑的火车车厢，便在美国的铁路轨道上跑来跑去了。起初，这些火车只能跑数英里远，只能在巴尔的摩和费城这样的城市之间往返。

接下来，一个名叫富尔顿的年轻人心想，他可以将瓦特发明的发动机装到船上，让发动机转动桨轮，从而驱动船只前进。人们都嘲笑他，称他建造的那艘船为"富尔顿傻瓜号"，也就是嘲笑富尔顿很傻的意思。不过，这艘船却成功了；于是，富尔顿把嘲笑还给了那些曾经嘲笑过他的人。他将这艘船命名为"克莱蒙特

boat the *Clermont*, and it made regular trips up and down the Hudson River.

No one had ever before been able to talk to another far off until the telegraph was invented. The telegraph makes a clicking sound. Electricity flows through a wire from one place to another place which may be a long distance off. If you press a button at one end of the wire, you stop the electricity flowing through the wire, and the instrument at the other end makes a click. A short click is called a dot, and a long click is called a dash. These dots and dashes stand for letters of the alphabet so you can spell out a message by dots and dashes.

A is ·— dot-dash
B is —··· dash-dot-dot-dot
E is · dot
H is ···· dot-dot-dot-dot
T is — dash

An American painter named Morse invented this wonderful little instrument. He built the first telegraph line in America between Baltimore and Washington, and this was the first message he clicked across it: "What hath God wrought!"

A schoolteacher named Bell was trying to find some way of making deaf children hear, and in doing so he invented the telephone. The telephone carries words as the telegraph carries clicks. You do not have to know a special alphabet or spell out words by dots and

号"，后来它便定期往返于哈德逊河上下游。

在电报发明之前，没有人能够与一个相距很远的人进行交谈。电报会发出滴答滴答的声音。电流则会通过电线，从一个地方传输到距离可以相当远的另一个地方。假如在线路的一端按下一个按钮，就会切断线路中的电流，而线路另一端的设备就会发出一声嘀嗒声。一声短促的嘀嗒声称为"点"，而一声较长的嘀嗒声则称为"划"。这些点和划都代表着字母表中的字母，因此你们可以通过点和划的不同组合，来拼出一条消息。例如：

A用"·—"表示，即"点-划"
B用"—···"表示，即"划-点-点-点"
E用"·"表示，即"点"
H用"····"表示，即"点-点-点-点"
T用"—"表示，即"划"

这种神奇的小设备，是由一个叫作摩尔斯的美国画家发明的。他还在美国铺设了世界上的第一条电报线路，从巴尔的摩通到华盛顿；而他通过这条线路所拍的第一份电报，就是："上帝创造了什么！"

当时，一位叫作贝尔的教师，正在试图找出一种让聋哑儿童能够听到声音的方法；而在这一过程中，他发明了电话。电话传递话语的方式，与电报传递滴答声的

dashes as you do on the telegraph. With the telephone, anyone can talk from one side of the world to the other, and with ships at sea and planes in the air.

Many inventions now in everyday use have been partly invented by several people, so that it is hard to say just which one thought of the invention first. Several people thought of a way to run a machine by feeding it electricity. This was the electric motor. Then others thought of a way to run a machine by exploding gas. This was the motor used in automobiles.

Automobiles, as you know, became very popular. At first, people didn't need a license to drive and there were no traffic controls — like stop signs or traffic signals — on the streets. You can imagine some of the problems this caused. An African American named Garrett Morgan invented the three-color traffic signal and patented it in 1923. This helped make the streets safer for cars and for people walking too.

Electric lights were invented by Thomas Alva Edison. Edison was called a wizard, because in the Middle Ages, wizards were supposed to be able to do and to make all sorts of wonderful and impossible things, to turn lead into gold, to make people invisible, and that sort of thing. But Edison has done things that no wizard of a fairy tale had ever even thought of. Edison was a poor boy who sold newspapers and magazines on a train. He was interested in all sorts of experiments and fitted up a place in the baggage car where he could make experiments. But he made so much of a mess in the car that at last the baggageman kicked Edison's whole outfit off the train. Edison invented many things connected with the phonograph and the movies, and he has probably made more useful

方式一样。打电话时，人们不用像拍电报那样，必须了解一种特殊的字母表，并用点和划将语句拼写出来。有了电话之后，任何人都可以从世界的这一端与世界的另一端通话，并且还可以与大海上的轮船和空中的飞机通话呢。

如今我们日常所用的许多发明，都是由好几个人共同发明的，因此很难说是哪一个人首先想出了某种发明。用电力来驱动机器的方法，就是由好几个人共同想出来的。这种机器，就是电动机。接下来，其他的人又想出了用爆炸性气体来驱动一台机器的方法。这种机器，就是汽车上所用的发动机。

你们都知道，汽车如今已经变得非常普遍了。起初的时候，人们开车并不需要驾驶执照，街道上也没有像禁行、红绿灯这样的交通控制标志。你们可以想见，这种情况肯定会造成一些问题的。一位名叫加内特·摩根的非洲裔美国人发明了三色交通信号灯，并在1923年申请了专利。这种信号灯，让大街上行驶的汽车和步行的行人都安全一些了。

电灯是由托马斯·阿尔瓦·爱迪生发明出来的。爱迪生被人称为男巫；因为在中世纪，人们认为巫师能够做到各种奇妙的不可能之事，能够创造出各种奇妙的不可能之物，比如将铅变成黄金、让人们隐身，如此等等。不过，爱迪生所做的事情，却是任何神话传说中的巫师都没有想过的。爱迪生小的时候，家里很穷；因此，他靠在火车上售卖报纸和杂志为生。他对各种各样的实验都非常感兴趣，并在行李车厢里布置了一个能做实验的地方。可是，由于他将行李车厢里弄得一塌糊涂，因此行李收发员气得将爱迪生的所有装置全都踢下了火车。爱迪生发明了许多与照相和

and important inventions than any other man who has ever lived, so that he is much greater than those mere kings who have done nothing but quarrel and destroy — without whom the world would have been much better off if they had never lived!

Thousands of people who lived in the past ages tried to fly and failed. Millions of people have said it was impossible to fly and foolish to try. Some have even said it was wicked to try, that God meant that only birds and angels should fly. At last, after long years of work and thousands of trials, two American brothers named Wright did the impossible. They invented the airplane and, in 1905, the plane flew 24.2 miles in 38 minutes 3 seconds!

An Italian named Marconi invented the radio, and others every day are still making wonderful inventions, but you will have to read about these yourself, for this book isn't big enough for me to tell you all about them.

Here is a good subject for an argument or debate: Are we any happier *with* all these inventions than people were a thousand years ago *without* them?

Life is faster and more exciting; but it is more difficult and more dangerous. Instead of singing or playing the violin, or piano, we turn on the stereo or the radio and miss the chief joy in music, the joy of making it ourselves. Instead of the jogging drive in an old buggy behind a horse that goes along through the countryside almost by himself, we speed on in dangerous autos, to which we must pay constant, undivided attention or be wrecked. Instead of pure air, we often have pollution.

电影相关的东西。他的发明，很可能比有史以来任何人的发明都更加有用、更加重要；因此，与那些什么也不干、只会打仗和破坏的国王相比，他也要伟大得多。要是没有这些国王，要是他们从来没有存在过，那么整个世界的情况一定会好得多哩！

在过去的几个世代里，有成千上万的人曾经尝试过飞行，却无一成功。千百万人都曾说过，人类不可能飞起来，还说想要飞起来也是很愚蠢的。有些人甚至还说，连飞起来的想法也是很邪恶的，因为上帝规定，只有鸟儿和天使才能飞行。最终，经过漫长的努力和千百次尝试之后，美国有一对名叫莱特的兄弟，终于做出了不可能做到的事情。他们发明了飞机；1905年，他们发明的飞机竟然在38分3秒的时间内，飞行了24.2英里！

一位名叫马可尼的意大利人发明了收音机；而且，如今每天也仍然有其他人在做出一些不可思议的发明创造来。不过，这些方面都得你们自己去阅读和了解才行；因为这本书不大，我无法一一来向你们说明。

下面，有一个很不错的讨论或辩论主题：有了这些发明创造之后，与一千年前还没有这些发明创造的古人比起来，我们是不是更幸福呢？

如今人类的生活节奏更快、更令人激动了；不过，如今人类的生活也更艰难、更危险了。如今我们不是去唱歌、去拉小提琴，而是打开音响或者收音机，从而失去了音乐的主要乐趣，即自己演唱或演奏所带来的乐趣。如今我们不再坐上一辆古老的马车，在乡间几乎孤身一人地慢慢前行，而是开着危险的汽车飞快地来去；开车时，我们必须时刻集中注意力，否则就会出事故。如今我们也不再有纯净的空气，而是经常碰到污染问题了。

83 A Different Kind of Revolution

James Watt's steam engine and Robert Fulton's steam powered ship were part of a revolution — a different kind of revolution. Usually we think of a revolution as being like the American Revolution or the French Revolution when people fought a war against a government. But this revolution took place slowly and without any armies. Yet it certainly did change the world. It is called the Industrial Revolution.

In the last chapter, I told you about some of the wonderful inventions like cars, airplanes, radios, and televisions that we have because of the Industrial Revolution. That's the fun part. But a lot of other things happened, too. This peaceful revolution changed the world every bit as much as the big wars — maybe more! Here's how.

All those wonderful new things were made in factories. The first factories were built in England. They made cloth and then clothing. Later they made railroad cars and tracks. Soon English factories were making all sorts of good things, and England began to grow very rich and powerful.

In some ways countries are just like boys and girls. You know that sometimes, when one student in a class brings in a new toy or wears a new jacket, everybody else wants

83　另类革命

詹姆斯·瓦特发明的蒸汽发动机和罗伯特·富尔顿发明的汽轮，都是一场革命中的一部分；但这场革命，却是一种不同的革命。通常来说，我们都会觉得，所谓的"革命"，就是和美国革命或者法国大革命一样，是人们通过打仗来对抗政府的革命。可这里所说的革命，发生得却很缓慢，其中也没有军队的参与。不过，这种革命当然也确确实实地改变了整个世界。这场革命，史称"工业革命"。

在上一章，我已经给你们介绍了诸如汽车、飞机、收音机、电视之类的奇妙发明；正是因为工业革命，我们才拥有了这些发明创造。它们是工业革命中有趣的一个方面。可是，工业革命中还出现了许多其他的东西。这场平静的革命，就像一场场大规模的战争那样，改变了世界的每一个方面，没准比大战还要厉害！为什么这么说呢？

所有这些不可思议的东西，全都是在工厂里生产出来的。世界上最初的一批工厂，是在英国开设起来的。它们先是织布，然后开始生产服装。后来，它们又开始生产火车车厢和铁轨。不久之后，英国的工厂里便生产出了各种各样的东西，而整个英国也开始变得非常富裕和强大起来了。

从某些方面来看，各个国家其实就跟小朋友们没什么两样。你们都知道，有的

one, too. Well, soon other countries wanted to be like England and they began building factories so they would be rich and powerful, too. A lot of European countries like France, Germany, and Italy did this. So did the United States and Japan. Soon all these places were making lots of things in their factories. They made clothes and furniture. They made cars and even candy. This was called the Industrial Revolution.

We all know that now we can go to the store and buy these things that are made in factories. But would that be enough of a change to call it a REVOLUTION? Well, maybe yes, maybe no. But there were other things that began happening as soon as the factories were built. All of these things together really were a revolution.

One big change happened like this. A lot of people came to work in the new factories. You wouldn't have much of a factory if nobody worked there, would you? It took a lot of men and women to work in the factories. Families left the countryside. They stopped farming and became factory workers. The men who built the factories wanted so many workers that they even paid children to work there. This wasn't very good for the children, though, because they didn't get to go to school. It also wasn't very good because those early factories had a lot of unsafe machines and sometimes the children and the grownups, too, got hurt. Despite all that, lots of men, women, and children came to work. So one big change is that many people stopped farming and became factory workers. Which would you rather do? Why?

Some people had been making things at home — like candles or soap or sweaters to

时候，倘若某个班里的一个学生带来了一件新玩具，或者穿了一件新上衣，那么其他同学也都会想要一件这样的玩具或者一身这样的新衣。所以不久后，其他国家也都想变得跟英国一样，于是它们也开始修建工厂，以便本国也能够变得富裕和强大起来。许多的欧洲国家，比如法国、德国和意大利，就是这样。而美国和日本也是这样。很快，这些国家全都开始在本国的工厂生产各种各样的物品。它们制造服装和家具。它们生产汽车，甚至是糖果。这一过程，就被称为"工业革命"。

我们都知道，如今我们可以到商店里去，买到工厂生产出来的这些东西。但是，这种变革，是不是足以称为一场"革命"呢？好吧，也许是，也许不是。不过，工厂修建起来之后，随即还出现了另外一些情况。所有这些情况总括起来，确实就是一场革命了。

其中一个重大的变革，是这样发生的。许多人来到新建的这些工厂里一起工作。如果没人在工厂里工作，那就不能称为工厂了，对不对？工厂里需要很多的男工和女工一起工作。于是，一家家人全都离开了乡下。他们不再务农，而是变成了工厂里的工人。那些建立工厂的人需要的工人数量太多，因此甚至还给儿童支付工资，让他们也来工厂里工作哩。但这对儿童来说，并不是一件很好的事情；因为这样一来，他们就不会被父母送去上学了。之所以说不好，还因为早期的那些工厂里有很多并不安全的机器，有的时候儿童会受伤，连成年人也会受伤。尽管有这些不利之处，但还是有很多很多的男人、女人和儿童去工作。因此，一个重大的变革就是，许多人不再务农，变成了工厂里的工人。你们是更愿意务农呢，还是去当工

sell. When a family does this, it's called a *cottage industry* because they work in their cottage. After the Industrial Revolution, factories made many of the same things. Since a factory made so many sweaters, for example, so fast, it could sell them for less money than an individual could. Because of this, many people who had worked at home had to go to work in factories.

Most of the factories were built in cities. Coming to work in the factory meant coming to live in a city. Soon the cities got very crowded. In those early days people had to live close together, because they had to live near their jobs so they could walk to work.

How far would you be willing to walk to work or school? People often walked a mile or two each way. After trolley cars were invented, people could live farther away from work. At first, trolleys were pulled along tracks on city streets by horses, and they were slow. By the end of the nineteenth century, electric trolleys became common, and people could live even farther away. So the cities grew larger. Here's a second big change then. Cities grew big like the ones we know today.

Way around the world, even in countries where there weren't any factories yet, people's lives changed, too. You have to stop and think about this for a minute. It may seem hard to believe that the life of a child in Africa, India, Korea, or Hawaii could change just because men in England, America, or Japan built factories. But that's what happened. Here's how.

You know that when you make anything, you have to make it out of *something*. So the factories that made clothes and furniture, cars and candy had to make these out of

人？为什么？

有些人在家里生产东西，比如蜡烛、肥皂、毛衣等，然后拿来出售。假如一个家庭是这种情况的话，那就称之为"家庭作坊"，因为这些人都是在家里工作呀。工业革命之后，各家工厂都生产出了许多相同的产品。比如说，由于一家工厂生产出了大量的毛衣，可以用低于个人所售的价格来出售这些毛衣，所以许多曾经在家里工作的人，就不得不到工厂里去上班了。

绝大多数工厂，都是建在城市里。来到工厂里当工人，就意味着来到城市里面生活。很快，各大城市里的人口便变得非常拥挤了。在初期，人们必须彼此紧挨着居住在一起才行；因为他们住的地方必须离上班的地方很近，使得他们能够步行去上班。

你们各位，又愿意步行多远去上班或者上学呢？以前，人们经常单程就要走上一两英里路呢。发明有轨电车之后，人们便可以住得离上班的地方很远了。起初，电车是用马拉着在城市街道里的铁轨上行走，速度很慢。到了十九世纪末，用电力驱动的有轨电车变得很常见，人们也可以住得离上班的地方更远了。于是，城市的规模越来越大。这样一来，就出现了第二大变革。那就是城市变大，变得就像如今我们所知的那些大城市一样了。

在世界各地，甚至是在那些还没有任何工厂的国家里，人们的生活也发生了变化。你们必须停下来，仔细想一想这个问题才是。一个住在非洲、印度、朝鲜半岛或者夏威夷的孩子，他的生活会仅仅因为英国、美国或日本的人在国内建立了工

something. Some factories made clothes out of cotton that grew in India. Other factories made furniture out of the wood from trees that grew in forests in Africa, Asia, and the countries around the Caribbean Sea. Cars have to have tires, and they are made out of rubber that comes from rubber trees that grow in forests in Africa, Asia, and South America. To make candy, you use sugar that comes from plants that grow in places like Hawaii and Cuba. Now you can begin to see why the Industrial Revolution was felt around the world.

The countries that built the factories needed supplies from all around the world. Those countries were strong and had the advantage of modern ships and weapons built in their factories, so the *industrialized* countries soon moved in and took over a lot of places that had the supplies they wanted — the places where cotton grew, where trees like mahogany and rubber grew, where sugar cane grew. England, France, Germany, and other European countries made colonies of most of Africa and a lot of Asia as well. Japan conquered Korea and some other places nearby. Even the United States came to own places like Hawaii and the Philippines although we didn't call these our colonies.

Now the people who lived in all these places weren't very happy to have foreigners coming in and taking over. They felt the same way about them that you might feel about a bully at school. They didn't like that big guy who wanted to push all the little guys around. Sometimes the conquerors brought good things, like modern medical care. But, still, nobody really wants to be bossed around by somebody else. So, less than a hundred

厂，就可能发生改变；这一点，看起来似乎难以置信呢。可事实就是如此。下面就来说一说原因。

你们都知道，在制造一种东西的时候，人们必须用到某种别的东西，才能制造出这种东西来。因此，生产服装、家具、汽车和糖果的工厂，都必须用某种别的东西，才能制造出这些产品来。有些工厂，是用印度种植的棉花来生产衣服。其他一些工厂，则是用生长在非洲、亚洲及加勒比海周边国家的森林中的树木来制造家具。汽车必须用到轮胎，而轮胎则是用生长于非洲、亚洲和南美洲的橡胶树所生产的橡胶制成的。要想生产糖果，必须用到源自像夏威夷、古巴等地种植的糖料作物所制成的食糖。现在，你们就开始能够明白，工业革命为什么影响到了整个世界吧。

建有工厂的那些国家，需要世界各地的物资供应。那些国家都实力强大，拥有在工厂里制造出来的现代化坚船利炮的优势，所以这些实现了工业化的国家，很快便步步进逼，占领了许多拥有自己想要之物资的地区，即种植棉花的地区、生长着像红木和橡胶树这种树木的地区、种植甘蔗的地区，等等。英国、法国、德国以及其他的欧洲国家，将非洲的大部分地区和亚洲的许多地区，全都变成了它们的殖民地。日本则征服了朝鲜半岛和附近的其他一些地区。连美国也开始占有了像夏威夷、菲律宾群岛这样的地区，只是我们并没有将它们称作是美国的殖民地罢了。

注意，生活在这些地区的人，是不乐意让外国人进入并占领这些地方的。他们的感受，跟你们在学校里对一名横行霸道的同学的感受是一样的。他们不喜欢那种想要欺负所有小个子的大块头。有的时候，征服者会带来一些不错的东西，比如现

years later, the colonies around the world rose up, just as we did during the American Revolution, and fought to become independent. You'll read more about this later.

You know that sometimes changes aren't always all good. One bad thing that happened because of the Industrial Revolution was the taking of colonies by the rich industrialized countries. Another bad result of the Industrial Revolution is still troubling us today. That is pollution. Also, many natural resources are being used up or destroyed. Pollution and the loss of natural resources are called environmental problems.

We know that factories that make wonderful things sometimes discharge poisons into the air that we breathe and the water we drink. That is pollution. People can get sick from breathing polluted air and drinking polluted water.

We know that over the years, many of the earth's forests have been cut down so the wood from the trees could be used for building houses and furniture and for making paper. When a forest is destroyed or an ocean is polluted, then the animals that live there have no place to live any more, and so they die out. When there are no more animals Of any given kind, we say that they are

Urban factories spewing smoke
城市里的工厂正在向外喷出烟雾

代化的医疗服务。但尽管如此，也没有人真正希望被别人呼来喝去。因此，不到一百年后，世界各地的殖民地便都揭竿而起，就像我们美国人在美国革命中所做的那样，通过战斗来获得独立了。日后，你们还会了解到这方面更多内容的。

你们都知道，有的时候，变化并非始终都是好的。工业革命所导致的一个不好的方面，就是富裕的工业化国家纷纷掠夺殖民地。而工业革命的另一个恶果，直到今天还在给我们带来麻烦；那就是污染问题。还有，许多的自然资源正在被人类用光或者破坏。污染和浪费自然资源，都被称为环境问题。

我们都知道，一些制造奇妙产品的工厂，有时会将有毒物质排进我们呼吸的空气和饮用的水源当中。那就是污染。人们吸入受到了污染的空气、饮用受到了污染的淡水之后，可能就会生病。

我们都知道，多年以来，地球上的许多森林都被砍伐，由此得来的木材则被用于建造房屋、制造家具和造纸。一处森林被砍伐、一处海洋遭到污染之后，原本生活在那里的动物就没有地方可以生存了，因此会逐渐消失。倘若某一种动物再也没

extinct. Today, a number of animals are in danger of becoming extinct, either because they are being killed or because their homes are being destroyed. Can you name any of these animals?

These are some of the problems caused by the Industrial Revolution that we have not yet solved. Do you have any ideas how they could be solved? There's something for you to talk about.

There are four big things to remember about the Industrial Revolution. A lot of people worked in factories instead of on farms. The towns grew into the large cities that we know today. The industrialized nations became so rich and powerful that they could control most of the rest of the world. And we still have to solve environmental problems that were caused by the Industrial Revolution.

有了，我们就称它们"灭绝"了。如今，有许多的动物都面临着灭绝的危险；要么是因为它们正在被人类杀戮，要么就是因为它们生存的家园正在遭到人类的破坏。你们能够举出一些这样的动物来吗？

这些方面，就是工业革命所导致的、如今我们依然还没有解决的一些问题。你们有没有解决这些问题的什么好办法呢？大家不妨就此讨论讨论。

关于工业革命，有四个大的方面需要记住。一是许多人不再务农，而是进入工厂里去上班了。二是小城镇逐渐扩大，变成了如今我们所知的大城市。三是实现了工业化的国家变得非常富有和强大，从而能够掌控世界上其他绝大多数地区了。四是如今我们仍然要去解决工业革命所导致的环境问题。

84 A World at War

Now, I must tell you about a fight so big that the world was at war.

There was a little country in Europe called Serbia. It was next door to the big country of Austria. But though little Serbia and big Austria were next-door neighbors, they were not good neighbors. Each was always saying mean things about the other. This was because Austria ruled over several other kinds of people besides Austrians, and some of these people were related to the Serbians. The Serbians used to say that Austria treated these people unfairly. But the Serbians did more than say things. They formed secret societies to send people into Austria to stir up trouble. Austria said that Serbia was trying to break up the kingdom of Austria by making the people discontented and unwilling to be ruled by Austria.

Then a young man who lived in Serbia shot an Austrian prince, the prince who was to have been the next king of Austria.

Of course Austria was furious and blamed Serbia. The Serbians said they were very sorry but they had nothing to do with the death of the prince. However, Austria wouldn't accept Serbia's apology. Austria thought the time had come to punish Serbia for all the

84 战火蔓延的世界

现在，我必须跟你们说一说一场战争的情况了；这场战争，规模空前巨大，使得整个世界都陷入了战火纷飞的深渊。

欧洲有个小国家，叫作塞尔维亚。它与奥地利这个大国接壤。不过，尽管小国塞尔维亚和大国奥地利是近邻，可它们之间的关系却很不好。两国都经常说对方的坏话。个中原因，是因为奥地利除了统治着奥地利人，还统治着其他几个民族，其中有些民族与塞尔维亚人关系非常密切。塞尔维亚人说奥地利对这些民族很不公正。不过，塞尔维亚人可并非仅仅是口头上说一说就罢了。他们还组建了一些秘密的社团，并将这些社团派到奥地利去煽风点火。奥地利则说，塞尔维亚试图通过煽动民众的不满情绪，使得他们不愿受到奥地利统治，从而分裂奥地利王国。

接下来，一位塞尔维亚年轻人开枪刺杀了一位奥地利亲王；这位亲王同时也是王储，将是下一任奥地利国王。

自然，奥地利愤慨不已，谴责了塞尔维亚。塞尔维亚人说遗憾得很，但王储的遇刺与他们毫无关系。然而，奥地利并不接受塞尔维亚的道歉。奥地利觉得，惩罚塞尔维亚、让塞尔维亚为奥地利正在遭受的种种麻烦而付出代价的时机已经到来。于是，奥地利毫不理会其他欧洲国家为阻止战争所做的一切，向塞尔维亚宣战了。

trouble Austria was having. In spite of everything the other countries in Europe could do to stop this, Austria declared war on Serbia.

The trouble started to spread just like fire in a field of grass. Russia took the side of Serbia and ordered its army to get ready to fight. Germany took the side of Austria. Ever since the time of the Franco-Prussian War and Bismarck and William, the big countries of Europe had been training for a fight. Nearly all these countries had been getting together in two groups, one made up of the friends of Germany; the other, friends of France.

Russia was a friend of France and so when Russia got ready to fight, France ordered its armies to get ready to help Russia. That meant Germany would be between two big enemies, France on one side and Russia on the other. Germany decided to strike quickly and destroy France before Russia could hit hard from the other side.

To get at France quickly, Germany had to go through the little country of Belgium. Germany and France had agreed that neither would march armies through Belgium but when the war began German armies marched in anyway and pushed aside the Belgians, who tried to stop them. Germany's armies rushed on toward the capital of

Europe in 1914
1914年的欧洲

（图中文字：ATLANTIC OCEAN：大西洋；GREAT BRITAIN：大不列颠；NORTH SEA：北海；NORWAY：挪威；SWEDEN：瑞典；BALTIC SEA：波罗的海；RUSSIA：俄罗斯；NETH.：荷兰；BEL.：比利时；GERMANY：德国；PARIS：巴黎；FRANCE：法国；SWITZ.：瑞士；AUSTRIA-HUNGARY：奥匈帝国；PORTUGAL：葡萄牙；SPAIN：西班牙；MEDITERRANEAN SEA：地中海；AFRICA：非洲；ITALY：意大利；SERBIA：塞尔维亚；GREECE：希腊；RUMANIA：罗马尼亚；BULGARIA：保加利亚；BLACK SEA：黑海；OTTOMAN EMPIRE：奥斯曼帝国）

战争就像是草地上的星星之火一样，开始蔓延。俄罗斯站在塞尔维亚一边，下令本国军队做好了作战准备。德国则站在奥地利一边。自普法战争和俾斯麦、德皇威廉那个时代以来，欧洲各个大国始终都在进行训练，准备打上一仗。几乎所有大国全都加入进来，形成了两大阵营：一方由德国及其盟友组成，另一方则由法国及其盟友组成。

俄罗斯是法国的盟友，因此俄罗斯准备开战后，法国便下令本国军队做好准备，去支援俄罗斯。这就意味着德国会受到两个强大敌国的夹击：一侧是法国，另一侧则是俄罗斯。于是，德国决定速战速决，赶在俄国能够在另一侧发动猛击之前迅速出击，消灭法国。

要想迅速进击至法国，德国必须穿过比利时这个小国才行。德国和法国之间本来已经议定，两国军队都不得穿越比利时进击；可战争开始之后，德军却不管不顾，直取比利时，并将试图阻挡他们的比利时军队甩在了一边。然后，德军便迅速

France, Paris. They got as far as a river called the Marne, only twenty miles from Paris. There, the French under General Joffre stopped the German army. This battle of the Marne is probably one of the most famous of all the battles you have heard about so far in this history, for though the war went on for four years after this battle, if the Germans had won at the Marne, they would have captured Paris and probably made France a German country.

By this time, England had come into the war on the side of France and Belgium and Russia. England had the strongest navy in the world. The German navy wasn't strong enough to beat the English navy, so Germany kept its battleships at home. Germany had to fight from under the sea with submarines, which were hard for the English ships to catch. It was the first war in history in which battles were fought not only on land and on sea but up in the air and down under the water.

The German submarines sometimes sank ships belonging to countries that weren't in the war. That, of course, made these countries very angry with Germany, and so before the war was over, almost all the countries of the world were in the fight. That is why we call it a World War. Later there was another World War, so we call this World War I just as we call a king George I so as not to confuse him with George II.

Millions of people had been killed, millions of soldiers had been wounded, billions of dollars had been spent, and still the war went on, with neither side able to win. All of a sudden Russia had a revolution. Russia was so poor that some of its soldiers received no

朝着法国首都巴黎攻去。德军长驱直入，抵达了距巴黎仅仅20英里的马恩河地区。若弗尔将军所率的法军，在此挡住了德军的去路。在马恩河地区进行的这场战役，很可能是你们迄今为止在这本历史书中所了解到的最著名的战役之一；因为尽管战争在此次战役之后又持续打了四年，但倘若德军打赢了马恩河之战，他们可能就会攻陷巴黎，并且很可能会让法国变成德国的一个属国了。

此时，英国也已参战，它支持的是法国、比利时和俄国这一方。当时，英国拥有世界上实力最强大的海军。德国海军的实力并未强大到足以打败英国海军，因此德国便让战舰全都停在港内，闭门不战。德国只能用潜艇在水下作战，而英军的舰船则很难发现这些潜艇。因此，这是有史以来的第一场立体战争，不但陆地、海上是战场，而且战场还延伸到了空中和水下。

德军的潜艇有时会将一些不属于交战国的船只击沉。自然，这种做法使得那些国家全都对德国愤慨不已；所以，在战争结束之前，几乎世界各国全都参战了。这就是我们将这场战争称为"世界大战"的原因。由于后来又爆发了另一场世界大战，所以我们称此次战争为"第一次世界大战"，就像我们称一位国王为"乔治一世"，以便不把他与"乔治二世"混淆起来那样。

在这场战争中，有数百万人丧生，有数百万名战士受伤，并且耗费了数十亿美元；尽管如此，战争还是在继续，双方都无法获胜。就在此时，俄国突如其来地爆发了一场革命。当时的俄国还很贫穷，一些士兵连弹药和医药用品都没有。俄国人民处死了他们的君主，即沙皇，以及沙皇的家人，并且拒绝再战。形势看上去开始

ammunition and no medical supplies. The Russian people killed their ruler, the czar, and his family, and refused to fight any longer. Things began to look pretty bad for the Allies.

The United States did not enter the war until 1917, almost three years after it had begun; it did so after German submarines began sinking American ships and killing Americans.

America was so far off — three thousand miles away and across an ocean — that it seemed impossible that we could do much in the war. However, in a very short time, the United States had sent two million soldiers across in ships. Under General Pershing they fought great battles.

At last, Germany and its friends surrendered and on November 11, 1918, Germany signed a paper agreeing to do everything the Allies asked. The first World War in history was ended. The kaiser went to live in Holland, and Germany became a republic. Big Austria became little Austria, for all its lands and many of its people were taken away and made into independent countries. Little Serbia disappeared altogether. In its place was formed the new country of Yugoslavia, which included Serbia and several other small states.

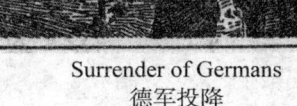

Surrender of Germans
德军投降

变得对协约国[1]极为不利了。

美国直至1917年才参战，此时差不多已是大战爆发的三年之后了；该国是在德国的潜艇击沉了美国船只并且杀死了一些美国人之后，才决定参战的。

美国距欧洲极其遥远，其间相距三千英里，还隔着一个大西洋，因此我们似乎在此次战争中发挥不了什么太大的作用。然而，在很短的时间内，美国便派出了200万士兵，乘船过海去参战。在潘兴[2]将军的率领下，美军打了好几场了不起的战役呢。

最后，德国及其盟友便投降了；而在1918年11月11日，德国还签署了一份文件，同意一切按照协约国的要求去做。人类历史上的第一次世界大战便告结束了。德皇前往荷兰去生活，而德国也变成了一个共和国。奥地利从一个大国变成了小国，因为该国管辖的所有国土和许多民众都脱离出去，组成了一个个独立的国家。小国塞尔维亚则完全不复存在了。在它原来所处的那个地方，建立了南斯拉夫这样一个新兴的国家，其中包括了塞尔维亚和其他几个小邦。

----

[1]　协约国（the Allies），第一次世界大战中由英、法、俄等国组成的一个同盟，后来美、意、日等国也加入进来。与之相对的是由德国、奥匈帝国、奥斯曼帝国和保加利亚王国等组成的同盟国。

[2]　潘兴（John Joseph Pershing，1860—1948），美国陆军上将，第一次世界大战期间美国远征军的统帅。

85 A Short Twenty Years

How long is a piece of string? That's a silly question and probably would get a silly answer.

How long is twenty years? That sounds like a silly question too, but it's not as silly as it sounds. To a dog twenty years is a long time, more than a lifetime. To a man, twenty years is not so long. In the history of the world, twenty years is just a tiny moment.

It was twenty years — twenty years and a few months — between the end of World War I and the start of World War II. Now, twenty years between two huge world wars is a very short time. Most countries had not fully recovered from World War I before World War II began. This chapter is about those twenty years of peace.

When World War I ended, people everywhere hoped and prayed that there would be no more wars. World War I was even called the "War to End All Wars". When World War I ended, the leaders of the Allied governments met at Versailles in France and drew up a peace treaty known as the Treaty of Versailles.

The treaty said that Germany should have a little army big enough to keep order in Germany but not big enough to make war with. There were to be no army or navy

85 二十年，弹指一挥间

一根绳子有多长呢？这是一个很傻的问题，很可能还会得出一个很傻的答案来。

二十年的时间究竟又有多久呢？这听上去也是一个很傻的问题，可实际上这个问题并不像乍听起来那么傻。对于小狗来说，二十年是一段很长的光阴，比它的一生都还要长呢。对于一个人来说，二十年则没有那么久。而在整个世界历史的长河中，二十年不过就是弹指一挥间，短短的一个瞬间罢了。

第一次世界大战结束到第二次世界大战爆发，中间正好相隔二十年；准确一点来说，是相隔二十年零几个月。注意，在两次规模空前的世界大战之间，这二十年是一段很短的时间。绝大多数国家都还没有从第一次世界大战的重创中恢复过来，第二次世界大战便爆发了。本章讲述的，就是这二十年和平时期的情况。

第一次世界大战结束后，世界各国人民都希望并祈祷日后不要再有战争了。人们甚至还将第一次世界大战称为"结束一切战争的战争"呢。第一次世界大战结束后，协约国各国政府的领导人便在法国的凡尔赛举行会议，制定了一份和约，即我们所称的《凡尔赛和约》。

和约规定，德国只能拥有一支规模不大的军队用于维持国内秩序，而不得拥有可以发动战争的大规模兵力。德国不得拥有陆军航空武器和海军航空武器，不得拥

airplanes in Germany, no army tanks, and no submarines. The treaty also said that Germany would have to pay large sums of money to the Allied nations to help pay for what it had destroyed in the war.

Then to try to keep the peace, a League of Nations was set up with headquarters in Switzerland. The greatest invention I can think of would be some thing or some way to keep wars from starting. People hoped the League of Nations would be the great invention that would keep wars from breaking out. Each country was to send men to act for that country at the meetings of the League. When war threatened, the League would warn the warlike country and ask it to bring its case before the judges of a World Court and let them settle the trouble there instead of having the question decided by war.

The League of Nations tried, but it didn't succeed. There were several reasons for this. One was that the United States decided not to join the League. The United States did not want the League to be able to say when the United States would have to send soldiers to help stop another country from making war, in case war started in spite of the World Court's decision.

Another reason that the League didn't work was that there was no way it could make nations do what it told them. It could only ask that the nations do what it wanted them to do. It could not make them do it.

A sign may say "Keep Off The Grass". If you walk on the grass in spite of the sign, the sign can't stop you, but a nearby policeman can. The League of Nations was like a "Keep

有陆军装甲坦克，不得拥有潜艇。《和约》还规定，德国必须向协约国各国支付大笔赔款，以赔偿该国在战争中所造成的破坏。

接下来，为了维护世界和平，还成立了一个国际联盟，其总部设在瑞士。我能想到的最伟大的发明创造，就是某种能够防止战争爆发的东西或者办法。人们都希望，国际联盟就是这样一种能够阻止战争爆发的伟大创举。每个国家都应当派出人员，代表本国在国际联盟举行的大会上行事。倘若有了爆发战争的危险，国际联盟就会警告那个想要开战的国家，要求该国将情况提交给一个国际法庭的法官们，由法官来进行裁决，而不是用战争去解决问题。

虽说国际联盟尽了自己的力，可它并没有成功地实现自己的目标。之所以如此，有几个原因。一是美国决定不参加国际联盟。美国并不希望国际联盟能够对本国指手画脚，因为万一有国家不顾国际法庭的裁决而发动战争，美国就必须派出军队去帮助阻止该国发动战争才行。

国际联盟并未发挥出作用的另一个原因，在于它没有办法强制各国按照国际联盟的意愿去行事。它只能要求各国按照它的意愿去行事，而无法强制各国去行事。

有一种标志，上面可能写着"请勿践踏草坪"。假如你们不顾标语而在草地上行走的话，这种标志并不能阻止你们，只有附近的警察才能阻止你们这样做。国际联盟则正像是这样一种"请勿"标志，而没有警察这样的强制力。

我觉得，以前从来没有过这么多的人如此希望并祈祷能够阻止战争。因此，除了国际联盟，人们还尝试了其他许多阻止战争的办法呢。

Off" sign without a policeman.

Never before, I suppose, did so many people hope and pray that wars could be stopped. Other ways to stop wars, besides the League of Nations, were tried, too.

People thought that if nations were not so heavily armed, it might help. The countries with the biggest navies held a conference in Washington and agreed to limit the size of their navies. People thought, too, that if all the countries of the world solemnly promised not to make war, it might help. So an anti-war treaty was made. More than fifty countries signed this treaty and promised to give up war.

Yet wars did break out again, in spite of the League of Nations, in spite of limiting the navies, in spite of the anti-war treaty. There was no force in the world that could be used to stop a war when one started. When a building catches fire in a city, someone calls the fire department. Firemen come rushing with their fire engines and put the fire out. When a fist fight starts in a city, someone calls the police department, and policemen are sent to stop the fight.

But there was no fire department or police department to put out a war when it started. Before long, wars started again. Even the twenty years of peace between world wars were not free from wars. The first new war was in Asia.

After Commodore Perry had opened Japan to foreign trade, Japan had quickly become an industrial nation. Japan had learned the bad things as well as the good things of our civilization. It had built a large war-making modern army and navy. In 1931, Japan used that army to take the northern part of China, called Manchuria, away from China. Later the Japanese started to take over all of China. Of course the Chinese fought to keep the

人们认为，假如各国不装备那么多武器的话，可能会有助于阻止战争。于是，海军规模最大的那些国家，便在华盛顿召开了一次会议，同意限制各国的海军规模。人们还认为，假如世界各国全都庄严承诺不开战的话，可能也有助于阻止战争。于是，各国间又签署了一份反战条约。有五十多个国家都在这份条约上签了字，承诺不用战争来解决争端。

可事实上，尽管有国际联盟，尽管有限制海军规模的措施，尽管有反战条约，战争还是再次爆发了。一旦战争爆发，世界上就没有任何一种力量能够用于阻止战争进行下去了。倘若是一座城市里的某栋建筑失了火，人们就会给消防队打电话。消防员们开着消防车匆匆赶来后，就会把火灭了。倘若一座城市里有人打架斗殴，人们就会打电话给警察局，而警局则会派警察前来阻止这场斗殴。

可是，一场战争爆发后，却是既没有消防队，也没有警察局能将战争平息下去的。不久之后，战争便再次爆发了。即便是两次世界大战之间那二十年的和平时期，也不是没有发生过战争。其中第一场新的战争，是在亚洲爆发的。

佩里准将打开日本的门户，使该国开放了对外贸易之后，日本很快就变成了一个工业国家。日本不但学到了我们的文明中那些好的东西，同时也学到了其中一些不好的东西。该国组建起了一支庞大的、用于战争的现代化陆军与海军。1931年，日本便用这支陆军，侵占了中国时称"满洲"的东北地区。后来，日本又开始去侵占整个中国。中国人自然会起来战斗，以阻止日本这样做。其他国家也都纷纷写信

Japanese from doing this. Other countries wrote letters to the Japanese government saying they did not like to see Japan using its armies against China.

"What about that anti-war treaty you signed?" these other countries said to Japan.

But as no other country tried to stop the Japanese by force, the war continued. The Chinese fought hard, but they had very few army supplies and soon Japan had taken all the eastern coast of China and driven the Chinese government into western China. The League of Nations didn't know how to stop the war, and this war was still going on when World War II started.

While this was going on in Asia, another war had started in Africa. The Italian army marched into the ancient country of Ethiopia. Ethiopia was the same country as the ancient Axum. Do you remember Axum's famous king, who became a Christian in 350 A.D.? That's right. His name was Ezana.

Since the time of King Ezana, Ethiopia had always been independent and ruled by a king. Italy had tried to conquer Ethiopia fifty years earlier and had failed. Now the Ethiopian king's army had a few guns, but his soldiers were mostly armed with spears. The Italian army used airplanes, bombs, artillery, and even poison gas, and so it soon conquered the Ethiopians.

Then a civil war broke out in Spain, in Europe. One set of Spaniards fought another set of Spaniards about which group would govern Spain. Instead of trying to stop the war, Russia sent soldiers to help one side, and Germany and Italy sent soldiers to help the other side.

One, two, three — war, war, war — China, Ethiopia, Spain. The League of Nations

给日本政府，说它们都不愿看到日本对中国用兵。

"贵国签署过反战条约，如今又是怎么回事呢？"其他的国家都如此质问日本。

不过，由于没有一个国家想要通过武力阻止日本，所以这场战争就继续进行下去了。虽说中国人民一直浴血奋战，可由于他们的战争物资很少，因此日本很快便占领了中国的整个东部沿海地区，并将中国政府赶到西部地区去了。国际联盟不知道如何来阻止这场战争，所以此战一直持续到了第二次世界大战爆发的时候。

就在亚洲正在打这场战争的时候，另一场战争又在非洲爆发了。当时，意大利军队进军到了埃塞俄比亚这个历史悠久的古国境内。埃塞俄比亚就是古时的阿克苏姆。你们都还记得阿克苏姆那位赫赫有名的、在公元前350年皈依了基督教的国王吧？那就好。那位国王，名叫埃扎那。 ．

自埃扎那国王那时起，埃塞俄比亚一直都是一个独立的国家，由一位国王统治着。五十年前，意大利曾经想要征服埃塞俄比亚，可没有成功。到了此时，埃塞俄比亚国王手下的军队仍然没有多少枪支，士兵们的主要装备仍然还是长矛。而意大利军队却动用了飞机、炸弹、大炮甚至毒气，因此很快便征服了埃塞俄比亚人。

接下来，欧洲的西班牙又爆发了内战。这是一帮西班牙人打另一帮西班牙人，以决定究竟由哪一帮人来统治西班牙。俄国没有设法制止这场内战，而是派军队去支援其中的一方；而德国和意大利也派出军队，去支援另一方。

一、二、三，战争、战争、战争，中国、埃塞俄比亚、西班牙。国际联盟无力

hadn't been able to stop the Japanese from attacking China. It couldn't keep Italy from taking Ethiopia though it tried to punish Italy by stopping other countries from sending supplies to Italy. But Italy took Ethiopia anyway. The League had not stopped the war in Spain. As an invention for stopping wars, the League of Nations hadn't worked.

There were other important happenings besides wars in this twenty years of peace. For the first ten years of the peace, people were busy making and selling and buying and using the peacetime things that they could not enjoy while World War I was going on. In the United States, almost everyone who wanted to work could get a job. Factories were busy turning out everything from automobiles to clothespins. Business was booming. People were making money and spending it. Many people thought these booming times would go on forever. But they were wrong. The boom didn't last. What businessmen call a *depression* followed the boom. Good jobs became scarce. Millions of people could not get jobs at all. Factories could not sell as many things as they could make. Many factories had to close. This caused more people to be without jobs. How can a man or woman get money to buy food or clothes or anything if he or she can't find a job? Thus the last ten years of the peace were a troubled time of depression.

The depression had been going on for several years and people were getting desperate when a new president, Franklin Delano Roosevelt, was elected. He became president just when the depression seemed hopeless, when everything looked black and gloomy. People were afraid of what would happen to them. The first day he was president, Roosevelt said,

阻止日本进攻中国。国际联盟无法阻止西班牙占领埃塞俄比亚；尽管国联曾经试图通过禁止其他国家给意大利运送军备给养来惩处该国，可最终西班牙还是占领了埃塞俄比亚。国际联盟也没有制止西班牙的内战。作为一种阻止战争的创举，国际联盟并没有发挥出它应有的作用。

在这二十年的和平时期里，除了战争，还发生了其他一些大事。这一和平时期的前十年里，人们都在忙着制造、买卖和使用和平时期的商品；在打第一次世界大战的过程中，他们是享受不到这些商品的。在美国，几乎每个希望去工作的人都可以找到工作岗位。工厂忙着生产，产品从汽车到晒衣夹，应有尽有。贸易业正在蓬勃发展。人们都在赚钱、花钱。许多人都以为，这种蓬勃发展的局面会永远持续下去。可他们错了。这种蓬勃发展的局面，并没有持续多久。繁荣过后，生意人所称的"经济萧条"便接踵而来。好工作变得很稀有了。数百万人根本就找不到工作。工厂生产出来的产品，无法全都卖出去了。许多工厂不得不关门大吉。这使得更多的人失去了工作。如果连工作都找不到，一个人又哪来的钱去买食品、衣物和其他东西呢？因此，这段和平时期的后十年，就是一个经济萧条、混乱不堪的时期。

这次大萧条持续了几年的时间，因此到了富兰克林·德拉诺·罗斯福当选为美国新一任总统的时候，美国人民都已经变得非常绝望了。富兰克林·德拉诺·罗斯福是在此次大萧条似乎到了无可救药的地步、一切看上去似乎都非常阴郁悲观的时候当选为美国总统的。当时人们都在担心，他们接下来会落得个什么样的结局。当选总统后的第一天，罗斯福曾说："我们唯一不得不害怕的，就是害怕本身。"罗

"The only thing we have to fear is fear itself." Roosevelt seemed to know what to do. He asked that laws be passed so money could be given to people who could not find work.

Then the government hired thousands of people to work in any way they could. Artists painted pictures, musicians gave concerts, writers wrote books, laborers raked leaves, dug ditches, built parks, and did many other kinds of work; and all these people were paid for their work by the government. Roosevelt tried out many new ways of running the country. His way of being president became known as the New Deal.

Roosevelt helped the poor people at the expense of the rich people. And yet Roosevelt's family had always been rich, and Roosevelt himself was a rich man. When he was thirty nine years old, he had become ill with polio that left him with his legs paralyzed. After that he could stand only with the help of canes and with steel braces on his legs. He couldn't walk at all but could take a few steps leaning on someone's arm. But in spite of such a handicap, Roosevelt twice became governor of the state of New York and at last president of the United States.

A president of the United States is elected for four years. Every four years the people vote for their next president. Roosevelt was elected for a second four years. The Father of his Country, George Washington, had been made president for two terms of four years each. Washington had refused to be elected for three terms.

President Roosevelt about to address the nation on the radio
罗斯福总统准备通过收音机向全国发表讲话

斯福似乎知道该怎么做。他要求国会制定了法律，从而可以给那些找不到工作的人提供补贴。

接下来，美国政府又雇用了成千上万的人，去干他们力所能及的一切工作。画家画画，音乐家举办音乐会，作家写书，工人则去扫落叶、挖沟渠、建公园以及其他许多的工作；而这些人，全都由政府支付工资。罗斯福还尝试过许多新的办法来治理整个国家。他在总统任期内的这些措施，人称"新政"。

罗斯福还通过牺牲富人的利益，来救济穷人。不过，罗斯福家族一直都很富有，而罗斯福本人也是一个富人。他三十九岁的时候得了脊髓灰质炎，使得他的双腿都瘫痪了。此后，他只能依靠拐杖才能站立起来，腿上还绑有钢质的支架。他根本无法行走，只能靠着别人的胳膊挪上几步。但是，尽管有这样一种缺陷，罗斯福还是两次当选为纽约州州长，并且最终登上了美国总统的宝座。

美国的总统选举每四年举行一次。就是说，人们每四年便会进行一次选举，选出下一任总统。罗斯福后来再次当选，又担任了四年的总统。美国的国父乔治·华盛顿也曾连任了两届总统，每届的任期都是四年。华盛顿拒绝连任第三届。由于乔治·华盛顿都拒绝连任三届总统，因此后来就没有哪位美国总统连续三次当选了。

Since George Washington had refused a third term, no president had ever been elected three times. But when Franklin D. Roosevelt's eight years were up, he became president a third time — for four more years, four years longer than any president had been before. And when twelve years were up, Franklin D. Roosevelt was elected president a fourth time. That would have made sixteen years as president for Roosevelt if he had not died before his fourth term was over. Roosevelt was president from 1933 to 1945. No other man had been president more than eight years, nor been elected more than twice. Roosevelt had been elected four times in a row.

Roosevelt wasn't able to stop the depression right away. He did show people that everything wasn't hopeless, and he did keep people from going hungry and perhaps starving. But it cost the American people millions and millions of dollars.

Before Roosevelt's third term had begun, the twenty years of peace were over. World War II had started in Europe. The people of the United States hoped their country could keep out of this war. But Roosevelt felt that America might be attacked even though the war was far away across the ocean. He led the country into getting ready for war in case it came to us. And when we were attacked, Roosevelt led the country through the war to victory against Germany, Japan, and Italy. He died a month before the Germans surrendered.

Twenty years of peace — twenty years of an invention-to-stop-wars that didn't work — a boom and depression, and then the biggest and worst war of all. How long is twenty years? It was a short time indeed between two world wars.

不过，到了德拉诺·罗斯福的八年任期届满之时，他却第三次当选为美国总统；也就是说，他可以再担任四年的总统，比以前历届总统的任期都多了四年。并且，在他的十二年任期届满后，他又第四次当选为美国总统。要不是他在第四个任期还没有届满的时候就去世了的话，罗斯福就会当上十六年的美国总统呢。罗斯福的总统任期，是从1933年至1945年。以前还从来没有哪位总统的任期超过了八年，也没有哪位总统曾经当选过两次以上呢。可罗斯福却连续当选了四次！

当时，罗斯福无法马上结束经济萧条的局面。但他向人民表明，一切都并非毫无希望，并且他也确实使得美国人民不再饿肚子、不再饿死了。不过，这也让美国人民付出了数百万美元的代价。

罗斯福第三届总统任期开始之前，那二十年的和平时光便结束了。第二次世界大战已经在欧洲开始打起来了。美国人民都希望，他们能够不卷入这场战争之中。但罗斯福认为，即便这场战争是在遥远的大西洋彼岸进行的，美国也有可能受到别国的攻击。于是，他带领整个国家开始备战，以防战争真的降临到美国人民的头上。而在美国真的遭到攻击之后，罗斯福又带领整个国家抗击德国、日本和意大利，在这场战争中走向了胜利。不过，距德国投降还有一个月的时候，他便与世长辞了。

这二十年的和平时期，就是国际联盟这一阻止战争的创举并未发挥出作用的二十年，其间经历了经济繁荣与大萧条，然后又爆发了有史以来规模最大、最可怕的一场战争。二十年又有多久呢？夹在两次世界大战当中，这段时间确实是弹指一挥间，短暂得很哪。

86 Modern Barbarians

Italy had a king, but the real ruler of the country was not the king but a dictator named Mussolini. He became dictator some years after the end of World War I. It was Mussolini who led Italy into war with Ethiopia.

Do you remember the story of Cincinnatus in the days of ancient Rome, and how he was made a dictator and saved Rome? And after the enemy was defeated how he gave up being a dictator and went back to being a simple farmer again?

Well, Mussolini was a dictator quite different from Cincinnatus. He did not give up being a dictator. Mussolini made himself more and more powerful all the time.

Now, the people of a country run by a dictator are seldom really happy because they have to do whatever the dictator tells them to do whether they like it or not. What the people think, they must not say for fear of saying something the dictator might not like. People may be imprisoned without a trial. They cannot read about both sides of a question in their newspapers, for the newspapers only print what the dictator wants them to print. People are always afraid in a dictatorship, for the dictator's spies are always listening and watching and waiting for someone to make a slip — to say something against the dictator

86 现代 "蛮子"

意大利虽说有一位国王，但该国真正的统治者却并非国王，而是一个叫作墨索里尼的独裁者。他是第一次世界大战结束几年之后，成为意大利的独裁者。而带领意大利与埃塞俄比亚开战的，也正是这个墨索里尼。

你们还记得古罗马时期那个辛辛纳图斯的故事，以及他是如何被推举为独裁官并拯救了罗马的过程吗？并且，等打败敌人之后，他又是如何不做独裁官，重新回去做了一名简单的农夫呢？

可是，墨索里尼这位独裁者，却与辛辛纳图斯完全不同。他并没有不做独裁者。墨索里尼始终都在让自己的权势变得越来越强大起来。

注意，凡是由独裁者统治的国家，国民很少有生活得真正幸福的；因为无论喜欢与否，他们都必须遵照独裁者的命令去行事。人民不能将心中所想的东西说出来，以免说出独裁者可能不喜欢的话语。人们可能不经过审判便被关押起来。在他们的报纸上，看不到对一个问题的两个方面进行分析的内容，因为这些国家的报纸都只能发表独裁者希望它们发表的内容。在独裁统治下，人们的心中总是担惊受怕，因为独裁者手下的特务始终都在监听、监视，等待着某个人犯错，比如说出一些反对独裁者的话语，或者做出一些独裁者可能不喜欢的事情来。然后，那个人就

or do something he might not like. It's then goodbye to that person.

The short twenty years of peace after World War I were long enough for several dictators to come to power in Europe.

Mussolini was bad enough. He took away the liberties of the people in Italy. He made war on the Ethiopians just because he wanted their country.

But Mussolini was "small potatoes" to another dictator who also came to power in Europe. This was Adolf Hitler, who became the dictator of Germany. Hitler's gang called themselves Nazis. The word NAZI was made up of the initial letters of the German words for National Socialist German Workers' *Party*, but most people think NASTY would be a better way to spell it. You might think when you hear the word party that it had something to do with a good time like a birthday party. But the party of the Nazis meant a society or group of people who were the followers of Hitler, Hitler's gang.

The Nazis were brutal and cruel. They did horrible things that even Alaric and his Goths, or Attila and his Huns, would not have done. I think the Nazi gang was worse than the Goths or the Huns because the Goths and the Huns were living at a time in history when almost the whole world was ignorant and more primitive. The Nazis lived in a civilized Christian country, with schools and universities and churches, amid the science and knowledge and rules of good behavior of the twentieth century.

The Nazis were against all Jews. They began to persecute the Jews of Germany. Some of the Jews escaped to other countries, but those who could not get away were put in

会跟这个世界说再见了。

第一次世界大战结束后那短暂的二十年和平时期已经够久，足以让欧洲的几位独裁者上台掌权了。

墨索里尼简直坏透了顶。他剥夺了意大利人民的自由。他之所以向埃塞俄比亚人开战，只是因为他想攫取埃塞俄比亚这个国家。

不过，跟欧洲另一位大权在握的独裁者比较起来，墨索里尼不过是"小巫见大巫"罢了。这个独裁者便是阿道夫·希特勒，他是德国的独裁者。希特勒的党徒自称为"纳粹党人"。"纳粹"（NAZI）这个英文单词，本是德语"德国社会主义国家工人党"首字母的缩写；不过大多数人都觉得，把"德国社会主义国家工人党"缩写成"恶毒"（NASTY）要更好呢。你们在听到party这个英语单词的时候，可能都觉得它与某种美好的时光有关，比如一次生日party。不过，纳粹party却是指一个由希特勒的追随者所组成的社团或群体，即希特勒的党徒；这里的party，就是"党派"的意思。

纳粹党人既残忍嗜杀，又冷酷无情。他们干出的那些令人发指的事情，连阿拉里克及其手下的哥特人、阿提拉及其手下的匈奴人也不会去干。我觉得，纳粹党人之所以比哥特人或匈奴人更坏，是因为在哥特人和匈奴人所生活的那个历史时代，整个世界都很愚昧，也更加原始。可纳粹分子则生活在一个文明的基督教国家里，该国既有中小学、大学和教堂，也有20世纪的科学、知识和种种良好行为的准则呢。

纳粹分子敌视所有的犹太人。他们开始处死德国境内的犹太人。有些犹太人逃

concentration camps where most of them were tortured and killed. The Nazis built large gas chambers, which were big rooms into which poison gas could be piped. They would crowd the Jews — men, women, and children — into these chambers and turn on the gas. In this way the Nazis murdered millions of Jews.

Not only Jews but thousands of other people in Germany who were thought to be against the Nazis were put in the concentration camps, where many of them died.

Hitler became chancellor and dictator of Germany in 1933. He was a powerful speaker and by his speeches he could move his listeners to do anything he wanted. He did not depend only on his speeches. His Nazi spies were everywhere and whoever said a word against him was apt to be arrested by the Nazi secret police.

Hitler planned to make Germany the most powerful nation in the world. To do this he started to build a huge army. Everyone in Germany was supposed to help make the Germans a warlike nation. Even boys and girls belonged to Nazi clubs and learned to drill and work for the nation. Those men who weren't in the army or navy or air force were put in labor battalions to build forts and military roads and fighting equipment.

I told you that the Treaty of Versailles did not allow the Germans to have a big army or an air force. How about that? But Hitler said that Germany was not bound by the Treaty of Versailles, even though it had been signed by the German government. Before long the Germans had a huge army and air force. Then the Germans started to take lands that were not theirs. Their army marched into Austria and made Austria a part of Germany. Then

到了其他国家，而那些没法逃走的犹太人则被关进了集中营；在集中营里，绝大多数犹太人都受到了折磨，然后再被杀死。纳粹分子修建了一座座巨大的毒气室，也就是一间间可以将毒气通过管道输入进去的大房间。他们不管男女老幼，把犹太人全都关进这些毒气室，然后打开毒气开关，将他们毒死。用这种方式，纳粹分子杀害了数百万名犹太人呢。

不只是犹太人，德国还有成千上万被认为是反对纳粹党的人也被关进了集中营，其中的许多人都死在了集中营里。

1933年，希特勒成了德国的总理和独裁者。他是一位很有影响力的演说大师；通过演讲，他可以鼓动听众去做他所希望的任何事情。当然，他也并非全然依靠自己的演讲。他手下的纳粹特务无所不在；只要有人说上一句反对他的话语，很可能就会被纳粹的秘密警察逮捕起来。

希特勒打算让德国变成世界上实力最强大的国家。为此，他开始组建一支规模极其庞大的军队。德国的每位公民，都应当有助于让德国人变成一个好战的民族。连儿童们也都加入了纳粹分子的社团，学会操练和为国家工作。那些没有加入陆军、海军或者空军的人，则被编入劳工营，去修筑要塞、军用道路和作战设施。

前面我已经跟你们说过，《凡尔赛和约》不允许德国拥有一支庞大的陆军或空军。那又怎么样呢？希特勒称，即便是以前的德国政府签了字，德国也不受《凡尔赛和约》的约束。不久以后，德国便拥有了一支规模极其庞大的陆军和空军。接下来，德国人又开始占领其他国家的领土。德军侵入奥地利，把奥地利变成了德国领

they began seizing other pieces of land around them.

Now, England had a treaty or agreement with Poland, which was the next country to Germany on the east. This treaty with Poland said that England would protect the independence of Poland. When Germany threatened to attack Poland, England warned Germany about the treaty and said it was England's duty under the treaty to protect Poland. Hitler went ahead anyway and attacked Poland. First he sent his airplanes over Poland and bombed the Poles. Then came the German army, and in a few days it was all over for the Polish army. So England declared war on Germany. It was in 1939 when this happened and World War II began.

Russia was on the other side of Poland, and Russia marched into Poland from the eastern side. There wasn't any Poland left.

Next Germany attacked Norway and Denmark. Norway was seized by German soldiers,

Europe in World War II
第二次世界大战期间的欧洲

（图中文字：ATLANTIC OCEAN：大西洋；GREAT BRITAIN：大不列颠；NORTH SEA：北海；NORWAY：挪威；SWEDEN：瑞典；DENMARK：丹麦；BALTIC SEA：波罗的海；U.S.S.R.：苏维埃社会主义共和国联盟（苏联）；London：伦敦；NETH.：荷兰；BEL.：比利时；GERMANY：德国；POLAND：波兰；PARIS：巴黎；FRANCE：法国；SWITZ.：瑞士；AUSTRIA：奥地利；CZECHOSLOVAKIA：捷克斯洛伐克；HUNGARY：匈牙利；RUMANIA：罗马尼亚；PORTUGAL：葡萄牙；SPAIN：西班牙；MEDITERRANEAN SEA：地中海；AFRICA：非洲；ITALY：意大利；YUGOSLAVIA：南斯拉夫；ALBANIA：阿尔巴尼亚；GREECE：希腊；BULGARIA：保加利亚；BLACK SEA：黑海；TURKEY：土耳其）

土的一部分。然后，德军又开始不断地攫取周围邻国的领土。

注意，当时英国与德国东边的邻国波兰签署了一份条约或者协定。英、波之间的这份条约规定，英国应当保护波兰的独立自主。德国威胁说要进攻波兰后，英国就以这份条约为由，警告德国说，根据这份条约，英国有义务保护波兰。可希特勒依然我行我素，前去进攻波兰。他首先派战机飞到波兰的领空，对波兰人实施了轰炸。接下来，德国陆军又向东挺进；几天之后，波兰陆军便全军覆灭了。于是，英国便向德国宣战。此时正是1939年，第二次世界大战由此拉开了序幕。

由于俄国位于波兰的东边，俄军便从东部开进了波兰。这样一来，波兰这个国家便不复存在了。

接下来，德国又袭击了挪威和丹麦。德国用飞机运送军队，并在挪威一些叛徒的协助下，攻陷了该国。

who were carried by airplanes and were helped by a few traitors in Norway.

Then Germany attacked France and Belgium and Holland. The German airplanes and tanks were too much for the French, Belgian, and Dutch armies and for the English army that had been sent to France to help them. As soon as Mussolini saw the Germans were winning, he brought Italy into the war on the side of Germany. Soon Holland and Belgium and most of France were taken by the Germans. The German army marched into Paris. Thousands of Frenchmen were sent to work as slaves in Germany, and only England was left to fight the Nazis.

You remember I told you that Parliament was the real ruler of England and not the king. The leader of Parliament, and the man who carries out the laws Parliament makes, is called the prime minister. The prime minister at this time of great danger for England was Winston Churchill. Winston Churchill was a brave and stubborn man. Although England's army had lost its weapons in France, and there were fewer than one hundred tanks in all England and the English had fewer airplanes and a much smaller army than the Germans, Churchill refused to give up. Churchill made speeches over the radio to the people to encourage them to fight on in spite of all the odds against them. Churchill said, "We shall defend our island, whatever the cost may be. We shall fight on the beaches, we shall fight on the landing grounds, we shall fight in the fields and in the streets, we shall fight in the hills: we shall never surrender."

Does that remind you of the answer Leonidas gave to the Persians before the battle

然后，德国又去进攻法国、比利时与荷兰三国了。德军的战机和坦克数量庞大，法、比、荷三国的陆军以及派往法国去支援他们的英国陆军根本抵挡不住。墨索里尼一见德军快要打赢了，便下令意大利参战，支持德国。很快，德军便攻占了荷兰、比利时两国，以及法国的绝大部分领土。成千上万的法国人被送往德国，像奴隶一样去干苦力，只剩下英国仍然在与纳粹分子苦战了。

你们应该都还记得，我曾经告诉过你们，真正统治英国的是议会而不是国王。英国议会的议长兼实施议会所制法律的人，被称为首相。在这个面临着巨大危险的时期，担任英国首相的正是温斯顿·丘吉尔。温斯顿·丘吉尔是一个勇敢无畏、不屈不挠的人。尽管英国的陆军在法国境内被德军打得丢盔弃甲，整个英国装备的坦克还不到一百辆，并且英军的战机数量比德军少，总兵力也要比德军少得多，但丘吉尔却拒绝投降。虽然形势对英国很不利，但丘吉尔还是通过广播电台向英国人民讲话，鼓励他们继续战斗。丘吉尔说："无论可能付出什么样的代价，我们都应当保卫这个岛屿。我们应当在海滩上战斗，我们应当在着陆场地上战斗，我们将在田野上和街道中战斗，我们将在群山之中战斗：我们决不投降。"

这些话，有没有让你们想起两千多年前，温泉关之战打响前列奥尼达给波斯大军的答复呢？列奥尼达说："来打败我们吧。"虽然丘吉尔的讲话并不简短，不是拉科尼亚式的讲话，但意思却是一样的。

纳粹分子做好了侵入英国的准备。

他们在正对着英国的欧洲沿海集结了三千多艘驳船。他们准备用这些驳船来运

of Thermopylae over two thousand years ago? Leonidas said, "Come and take us." Churchill's speech was not short and laconic but it meant the same thing.

The Nazis got ready to invade England.

They brought more than three thousand barges to the coast of Europe opposite England. These were to carry the Nazi soldiers across the English Channel. But first Hitler wanted to defeat the English air force, so his troops could land in England more easily. Nazi planes were sent over in great fleets to bomb the English airfields and seaports.

Then Hitler met his first defeat. The English had many fewer planes, but they were able to outfight the Nazi planes. This was called the Battle of Britain. In the first ten days of this air battle, the English shot down 697 planes and lost only 153 themselves!

When Hitler found his planes could not destroy the English air force, he sent fleets of airplanes day and night to bomb London. Thousands and thousands of London civilians were killed by these German bombs. However, the English pilots of the Royal Air Force kept shooting down so many German planes that at last the Germans were afraid to send planes over England except at night. All during the war these night raids on English cities kept up, but Hitler had lost his best chance to invade England. The English had had a few more months to get some weapons and build up their army. Prime Minister Churchill said of the English airplane pilots, "Never in the field of human conflict was so much owed by so many to so few."

送纳粹军队渡过英吉利海峡。不过，希特勒首先想要打败英国的空军；这样的话，德军就可以比较轻松地登陆英国了。因此，纳粹德国派了一批又一批战机，前去轰炸英国的机场和海港。

接下来，希特勒便遇到了自己的首次失败。英军的战机虽然数量少得多，但那些战机全都本领高强，能够打败纳粹分子的飞机。此次战役，被称为"不列颠之战"。在这场空战的前十天里，英军便击落了697架敌机，己方却只损失了153架！

希特勒发现德军的战机无法消灭英国空军后，便派遣一批批战机对伦敦进行了日夜不停的轰炸。成千上万的伦敦市民纷纷丧生于德军的炸弹之下。然而，英国皇家空军的飞行员们，却不停地击落了一架又一架敌机，打得德军胆战心惊，最终只有在夜里才敢派战机进入英国领空了。在整个战争期间，对英国城市进行的此种夜间轰炸一直没有间断，可希特勒已经失去了入侵英国的最佳战机。英军争取到了几个月的时间，来获取武器并加强自己的陆军力量。丘吉尔首相曾经如此评价英国的那些战斗机飞行员："在人类战争史上，从来没有一次像这样，以如此之少的兵力取得如此之大的成功，保护了如此之多的众生。"

87 Fighting the Dictators

The story of the biggest war that ever was cannot be told all in one chapter.

So this chapter is about World War II, too.

After France was taken, only the British Empire was left unconquered of all those countries that Germany had attacked. Even after the Battle of Britain, no one was sure that the Nazis would not try to invade England. But just keeping the Germans out of England would not win the war. No one believed that the English by themselves could beat the Germans. That is, no one believed it except the English. They refused to give up and they kept right on trying to beat the most powerful, the best trained, and best equipped army in the world.

Other parts of the British Empire sent soldiers to help England. But these other countries (Canada, Australia, South Africa, New Zealand, and India) were far away across seas in which German submarines hunted for ships to torpedo.

Mussolini had brought Italy into the war on the side of Germany. Japan was burning, killing, and bombing in China, and Japan was friendly to Germany.

No country could be sure it would be safe from attack. Who would be next on the list?

Even the United States, three thousand miles across the ocean from Europe, felt its

87　对抗独裁者

这场有史以来规模最大战争的经过，是不可能在一章里全部讲完的。

所以，这一章讲述的也是第二次世界大战的情况。

法国被德国占领之后，所有受到德国进攻的那些国家里，只剩下大英帝国没有被德国征服。即便是在"不列颠之战"过后，也没有人敢肯定地说，纳粹德国日后不会再试图入侵英国了。不过，仅仅将德军挡在英国境外，并不会让英国打赢此次战争。其他国家没有人认为，仅凭英国人自己就能打败德军。也就是说，只有英国人这样认为。他们拒绝投降，继续全力以赴，想要打败世界上这支实力最强大、训练最有素、装备最精良的军队。

大英帝国的其他属国和地区，也纷纷派遣军队来帮助英国本土。但这些属国（加拿大、澳大利亚、南非、新西兰以及印度）都远在万里重洋之外，而德国潜艇却在大洋中四处搜寻，准备用鱼雷袭击这些属国的船只。

墨索里尼已经让意大利站在德国一边参战了。同时，日本正在中国境内四处烧杀掳掠和轰炸，而日本跟德国的关系也很友好。

此时，世界上没有哪个国家敢肯定地说，本国不会有遭到攻击的危险。谁将是下一个遭到袭击的国家呢？

即便是与欧洲远隔重洋、相距三千英里的美国，也觉得本国的防御力量必须加

defenses should be strengthened. The very small American army was made into a very large army and American factories were put to work making tanks and airplanes and other war supplies. New ships began to be built for the navy. A large modern army, however, cannot be raised and trained and equipped in just a few days. It takes not a few days, nor months, but years. Warships take even longer than an army. Luckily for us the president, Franklin D. Roosevelt, led the country to prepare itself for war when he did, for just about a year later we were attacked. Even then we weren't ready. But that comes later in the story.

Now, while the Germans were still busy setting up their rule in France and Denmark and Norway and trying to subdue England with their airplanes, Italy tried to capture Greece and Egypt. But the Italians were not as good fighters as the Germans. A brave little Greek army held off the Italians there while an English general in North Africa, using soldiers from all parts of the British Empire, beat two Italian armies that had five times as many soldiers as he had. This freed Ethiopia from the Italians.

But then the Germans sent an army that conquered Greece in three weeks. They sent an army also to North Africa, which fought the British there for the next three years.

Suddenly Hitler attacked Russia. Now, you might think this was a foolish thing for Hitler to do. Russia was a huge country with a large army. Even Napoleon had been unable to take Russia. But Hitler knew that if he conquered Russia, Germany would gain great quantities of oil, wheat, lumber, and minerals. Besides, he thought Russia might attack Germany, for Russia had been building up a big army ever since the Nazis had started their conquests.

强才行了。于是，规模本来很小的美国陆军，被扩充成了一支规模庞大的陆军；而美国国内的工厂，也纷纷转而生产坦克、飞机以及其他的军需装备了。海军也开始建造新的舰船。然而，一支大型的现代化陆军，可不是短短几天就能组建、训练和装备起来的。做到这一点，需要的不是几天，也不是几个月，而是需要几年的时间。建造军舰所需的时间，甚至比组建一支陆军更久。但幸运的是，美国总统富兰克林·罗斯福一直致力领导着美国备战，因为仅仅过了一年左右，美国便遭到了攻击。而就算是到了那个时候，我们也还没有做好准备呢。不过，这一点我们要到后面再来说明。

注意，正当德国人忙着在法国、丹麦、挪威等国稳固统治，并且试图用战机征服英国的时候，意大利则在想方设法地要占领希腊和埃及。但是，意军可没有德军那样勇猛善战。一小支英勇顽强的希腊军队，便挡住了意军的去路；而在北非，一名英国将领指挥着一支来自大英帝国各地的杂牌军，也打败了两支兵力达其五倍之多的意大利陆军。这场战役，将埃塞俄比亚从意大利的统治下解放出来了。

不过，接下来德国派出了一支军队，三个星期后就打败了希腊。德国还向北非地区派出了一支陆军；而在接下来的三年里，这支陆军一直都在北非地区同英军作战。

后来，希特勒对俄国发动了突袭。注意，你们可能觉得希特勒这样做非常愚蠢。俄国国土广袤，并且拥有一支规模庞大的军队。连拿破仑也没能打败俄国呢。可希特勒很清楚，如果他能征服俄国，德国就能获得大量的石油、小麦、木材和矿产。除此之外，他还认为俄国可能会进攻德国；因为自纳粹德国开始实施征服以来，俄国一直都在组建一支规模庞大的陆军。到目前为止，希特勒已经征服了十五

Hitler had by now brought fifteen European countries under Nazi rule and his armies had never been beaten, though his air force had not been able to make England surrender.

Into Russia rushed the Nazis. They hoped to destroy the Russian armies quickly. Far into Russia the Nazis fought, but the Russian armies, though driven back, were not destroyed. Finally the Nazis reached Moscow and attacked the city on three sides at once. Hitler announced that the battle of Moscow would be the death blow of the Russian armies. But he spoke too soon. The Russians held Moscow for weeks against Germans, who were attacking with thousands of tanks and airplanes. Russian soldiers and the civilians of the city fought side by side to defend it. Finally the Russians pushed back the German army. Moscow was saved.

However, keeping the Germans from taking Moscow would not win the war, just as keeping them out of England wouldn't win the war. Germany and Italy still held almost all of Europe.

Then just as the Russians were driving back the Nazis from Moscow, Japan struck. Japanese airplanes without warning bombed the American fleet at Pearl Harbor in Hawaii. This was on December 7, 1941. All the American warships there were sunk or damaged and more than two thousand Americans were killed. The next day Britain and the United States declared war on Japan. Four days later, Germany and Italy declared war on the United States.

The United States was still not ready to fight both Germany and Japan at the same time.

个欧洲国家，并将它们全都置于纳粹的统治之下；而且，尽管德国空军未能让英国投降，可德国陆军还从未打过败仗哩。

纳粹军队迅速攻入了俄国领土。他们希望迅速消灭俄军。纳粹军队深入攻打到了俄国的腹地；可俄国陆军虽说节节败退，却没有被德军消灭。最后，纳粹军队打到了莫斯科城下，并且随即对该市发动了三面夹击。希特勒曾经声称，莫斯科之战将会给俄军以致命一击。可他的结论下得太早了。尽管德军用成千上万辆坦克和战机轮番进攻，可俄军却在莫斯科坚守了好几个星期，顽强地抵抗着德军。俄国的士兵和莫斯科市民并肩战斗，捍卫着这座城市。最终，俄军击退了德军。莫斯科守住了。

然而，正如仅仅将德军挡在英国境外并不会让英国打赢战争一样，仅仅阻止德军占领莫斯科，也不会让俄国赢得这场战争的胜利。当时，德国和意大利两国，仍然还控制着几乎整个欧洲呢。

接下来，正当俄罗斯人在莫斯科击退纳粹德军的时候，日本又发动了进攻。在毫无征兆的情况下，日本战机突然轰炸了位于夏威夷珍珠港的美国舰队。这一事件，发生在1941年12月7日。停泊在那里的美国军舰，全都被日军击沉或者损毁了，并且还有两千多名美国人被炸死。第二天，英国和美国便向日本宣战。四天之后，德国和意大利两国则向美国宣战。

此时，美国还没有做好同时与德国和日本作战的准备。美国组建起来的那一支支新的陆军，都还没有完成训练；而珍珠港被炸毁的舰船，也还来不及用一支新的舰队去取代。幸亏当时俄军正在欧洲与德军鏖战；因为这样一来，就拖住了数百万的纳粹军

Our new armies were not yet trained, and a new fleet was not yet ready to take the place of the ships bombed at Pearl Harbor. It was lucky that Russia was fighting so fiercely in Europe, for this kept millions of Nazis occupied there and gave us another year to get ready. As fast as our factories could make them and ships could carry them, we sent tanks and trucks and other supplies to Russia and to the British army in Egypt.

Japan, however, could not be stopped at first. The Japanese captured the Philippine Islands, which belonged to the United States. They captured the great British naval base of Singapore in Asia. They captured the islands of the East Indies, which belonged to Holland. They captured Siam and Burma and pushed on toward India. They captured the Malay Peninsula. They had already seized French Indo-China and a lot of China.

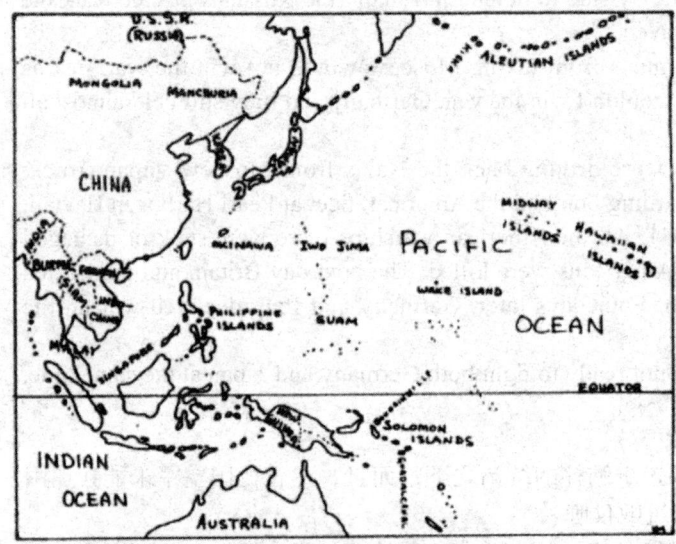

You probably have a map of Asia in your atlas or geography book. If you look these places up on the map, you'll see how far Japan's armies went

Pacific areas in World War II
第二次世界大战中的太平洋地区示意图

（图中文字：U.S.S.R：苏联；RUSSIA：俄国；MONGOLIA：蒙古；MANCHURIA：满洲；CHINA：中国；KOREA：朝鲜半岛；JAPAN：日本；KISKA：吉斯卡岛；ALEUTIAN ISLANDS：阿留申群岛；INDIA：印度；BURMA：缅甸；SIAM：暹罗；FRENCH INDO-CHINA：法属印度支那；MALAY：马来半岛；SINGAPORE：新加坡；OKINAWA：冲绳岛；IWO JIMA：硫黄岛；PHILIPPINE ISLANDS：菲律宾群岛；GUAM：关岛；PACIFIC OCEAN：太平洋；MIDWAY ISLANDS：中途岛群岛；HAWAIIAN ISLANDS：夏威夷群岛；EQUATOR：赤道；INDIAN OCEAN：印度洋；AUSTRALIA：澳大利亚；NEW GUINEA：新几内亚；BOUGAINVILLE：布干维尔岛；SOLOMON ISLANDS：所罗门群岛；GUADALCANAL：瓜达尔卡纳尔岛）

队，从而又给了美国一年的备战时间。美国的工厂以最快的速度生产，船只则以最快的速度运送，将坦克、卡车以及其他的军需装备，源源不断地运送给俄罗斯，运送给埃及境内的英军。

然而，日本起初可以说是所向披靡。日军占领了原本属于美国的菲律宾群岛。他们占领

了新加坡，那里原本是英国在亚洲的海军基地。他们占领了原本属于荷兰的东印度群岛。他们占领了暹罗[1]和缅甸，并且还在向印度推进。他们占领了马来半岛。他们还攻占了法属印度支那以及中国的许多地方。

你们的地图集或者地理书上，很可能会有一张亚洲地图。如果到地图上去看一看这些地方，你们就会明白，日军深入到了亚洲多远的地方。在一幅太平洋的地图

----

[1] 暹罗（Siam），是泰国（Thailand）的旧称。

in Asia. On a map of the Pacific Ocean, you can find the islands they captured far from Japan, islands with strange names you would never hear about in a history book except for the battles that were fought there in World War II:

Guam and Wake
New Guinea
Bougainville and Guadalcanal
Kiska in the Aleutians

Many of the places the Japanese captured were defended bravely. The Philippines were taken only after the American and Philippine soldiers were all either killed or captured, except the few that escaped to the hills, where little bands of men kept on doing what damage they could to the Japanese conquerors.

President Roosevelt and Prime Minister Churchill had decided to try to beat Hitler first and then clean up the Japanese. So American and British soldiers were sent to North Africa and fought and beat the German army there. Then they attacked Italy.

Great numbers of American and British soldiers were assembled in England. From England their airplanes bombed the Germans and fought the German airplanes. Finally, in June, 1944, all was ready for the attack on the main German armies. A huge force of American and British soldiers, under the command of General Dwight Eisenhower,

上，你们可以找到他们占领的、一些距日本本土非常遥远的岛屿；那些岛屿的名称都很陌生，要不是第二次世界大战期间在这些地方打了数场战役，你们在历史书上绝不可能听到这些岛屿的情况呢：

关岛和威克岛
新几内亚岛
布干维尔岛和瓜达尔卡纳尔岛
阿留申群岛的吉斯卡岛

许多被日军攻占的地方，都进行了英勇顽强的抵抗。菲律宾群岛只是在所有美军和菲律宾士兵要么阵亡、要么被俘之后，才被日军占领；只有少量军人逃进了山里，并且这一小部分兵力仍然在竭尽全力地对日本侵略者进行袭扰呢。

罗斯福总统和丘吉尔首相决定，首先应当全力打败希特勒，然后再去收拾日本人。于是，美国和英国都派军队前往北非，去与德军作战，并且最终打败了那里的德军。接下来，美、英两军又向意大利发动了进攻。

在英国，集结了大批美军和英军。他们的战机从英国起飞，对德军进行轰炸，并与德国战机进行空战。最后，1944年6月，两国做好了对德国主力部队发动进攻的一切准备。在德怀特·艾森豪威尔将军的指挥下，一支由美军和英军组成的庞大陆军渡过了英吉利海峡，在法国的诺曼底海岸成功登陆。他们猛击德军，打了一场

crossed the English Channel and landed on the coast of Normandy in France. They fought the Germans in fierce and bloody battles and chased them back across France to Germany. France and Belgium and Holland were made free and became again independent countries.

Meanwhile, the Russians who had been fighting the Germans all this time on the other side of Germany, put on a tremendous drive and pushed the Germans back into Germany. They captured Berlin, the capital. Mussolini had been caught and shot by the Italians themselves in Italy, and now Hitler, with his armies defeated, committed suicide. He could not stand the thought of defeat.

The terrible Nazis were at last beaten, but thousands of people were still homeless and hungry and had to be fed with food shipped in from other countries.

On the other side of the world, the war against Japan was still going on. Many battles had been fought against the Japanese — airplane battles, sea battles, and land battles. One after another, the islands Japan had overrun were recaptured, not easily but by fierce and bloody fights often with the heat and diseases of tropical jungles to add to the difficulties of our soldiers. In the Pacific war, General Douglas MacArthur was the commanding general. His armies with the help of the navy recaptured the Philippines. They were ready to invade Japan itself, when a terrible new weapon was used against the Japanese, and Japan surrendered.

This new weapon was the atomic bomb. Just two of them were dropped from American airplanes onto two Japanese cities. They caused such awful destruction that only two were needed.

Germany surrendered in May, Japan in August of 1945. The biggest and most terrible war in the history of the world was over

又一场惨烈血腥的战役，将德军赶出了法国，并且一路追击，攻入了德国境内。法国、比利时与荷兰相继获得解放，重新成了独立自主的国家。

与此同时，一直都在德国的另一侧与德军浴血奋战的俄军，也发动了猛烈的驱逐行动，将德军赶回了德国境内。俄军还占领了德国的首都柏林。在意大利，墨索里尼已经被意大利人自己抓起来枪决了；而到了这时，希特勒也由于手下的军队被打败而自杀了。因为他一想到失败，就完全无法承受。

可怕的纳粹分子终于被打败了；可是，依然有成千上万的民众无家可归、饥肠辘辘，不得不依靠别的国家运送的粮食来维持生计。

而在地球的另一边，抗击日本的战争仍在继续。各国为了抗击日本，已经打了多场战役，既有空战，有海战，也有陆上战役。日本占领的那些岛屿，被一个又一个地重新夺了回来；每次胜利都来之不易，因为我们的战士除了要与敌人进行激烈残酷的战斗，热带丛林的高温与疾病也给他们带来了巨大的困难。在太平洋战场上，道格拉斯·麦克阿瑟将军是总司令。他手下的陆军在海军的协助下，已重新夺取了菲律宾群岛。他们已经做好了侵入日本本土的准备；可就在此时，美国对日本使用了一种可怕的新式武器，于是日本就投降了。

这种新式武器，就是原子弹。当时，美国的战机仅仅向日本的两个城市分别投下了一颗原子弹。它们造成了如此巨大的杀伤力，因此只需要两颗就够了。

1945年5月，德国投降；同一年的8月，日本也投降了。于是，这场世界历史上规模最大、最可怕的战争，便告结束了。

88 A New Spirit in the World

After World War II was over, a lot of people everywhere were talking about making the world a better place. After World War I you remember, most countries of the world joined in a League of Nations to keep new wars from starting; but wars kept right on happening anyway.

After World War II, the countries of the world decided to try again to provide a way for countries to talk with each other to try to solve their differences peacefully rather than by fighting. So they formed the United Nations. The headquarters of the United Nations is right here in the United States, in New York City. Have you ever visited the U.N. headquarters? If you go to New York, you can take a tour of the building and meet people from all over the world who work there.

The United Nations has been more successful than the League of Nations was. Still, there have been a lot of problems that the world has had to face since the end of World War II. I guess it would be too much to expect that the world could get by for very long without any problems. But we can always hope.

Here is one problem that did get solved, at least partly solved, after World War II. The

88　全球新精神

第二次世界大战结束后，世界各国都有许多人在讨论，要让世界变得更加美好起来。你们都还记得吧，第一次世界大战后，世界上的绝大多数国家都曾加入一个国际联盟，想要防止爆发新的战争；可尽管如此，战争却还是继续爆发了。

第二次世界大战后，世界各国决定再努力一次，制定出一种国家间的协商机制，从而尽量让各国和平地而不是通过战争来解决争端。于是，它们便成立了联合国。联合国的总部，就设在美国的纽约。你们有没有参观过联合国总部呢？如果以后去纽约的话，你们不妨游览一下联合国大楼，还能碰到来自世界各国并在那里工作的人呢。

联合国已经取得了比国际联盟更大的成就。尽管如此，自第二次世界大战结束以来，全世界仍然面临着一大堆的问题。我倒觉得，指望全世界在很长一段时间里不出现任何问题，完全就是一种痴心妄想呢。不过，我们还是可以始终抱有这种希望的。

第二次世界大战后，有一个问题的确已经解决，起码也可以说是部分地得到了解决。而联合国在解决这一问题的过程中，则发挥出了作用。第二次世界大战结束后，世界各国都有许多人在讨论，要让世界变得更加美好。"二战"期间，人们曾

United Nations helped. After the war was over, a lot of people everywhere were talking about making the world a better place. During the war, people had said that it was wrong for Germany and Japan to conquer and rule other countries and their people. After the war was over, some men and women began to ask why some other nations still had the right to rule countries they had conquered earlier. Remember how the industrialized nations had taken colonies to provide their factories with supplies like wood, rubber, cotton, and sugar? Well, after World War II they still had those colonies. In fact, the British colonies were so widespread that the English bragged that, "The sun never sets on the British Empire." Do you know what this means?

Imagine owning so much of the rest of the world that the sun was always shining on a part of the world you owned. The British owned countries like Ghana and Kenya in Africa, big countries like India, and small islands like the Bahamas and Jamaica. The British were very proud of their big empire. But a lot of people in Africa, India, and the islands of the Caribbean weren't so happy about the British. In fact, they had been talking for a long time about getting rid of those foreigners! And after World War II the British were tired from having fought so hard against the Germans and the Japanese. Besides that, people all over the world were saying that every nation should be able to choose its own government. In this discussion, it was hard for the Americans to take the side of their old ally, the English. Why do you suppose this was true? Do you suppose it's because we remembered our own American Revolution?

说，德、日两国去征服并统治别的国家及其人民的做法是不对的。而"二战"结束后，一些人则开始质疑，为什么其他一些国家仍然有权统治着它们早前征服的那些国家呢？你们是否还记得，工业化国家是如何占领殖民地，以便为国内的工厂提供诸如木材、橡胶、棉花以及食糖等原料的呢？好吧，第二次世界大战结束后，它们却依然统治着那些殖民地。事实上，由于英国的殖民地遍布全球，因此英国人还曾夸口说："大英帝国的太阳永远不会落下。"你们明白这是什么意思吗？

大家不妨想象一下，假如你们拥有世界上其他那么多的地方，以至于太阳总会照耀着你们所拥有的那个世界里的某个地方，将是一种什么样的情形啊。英国人既掌控着像加纳和肯尼亚这样的非洲国家，掌控着像印度这样的大国，还统治着像巴哈马群岛和牙买加那样的小小岛国。英国人对他们那个广袤的帝国感到非常自豪。但是，在非洲、印度和加勒比海地区的那些岛国上，许多人却不是那么喜欢英国人。事实上，他们长期以来还在讨论，要摆脱这些外国人呢！而由于在战争期间曾与德、日两国进行了殊死搏斗，因此第二次世界大战后，英国人全都精疲力竭了。除此之外，当时世界各国人民也都在说，所有国家都应该有权选择自己的政治体制。在这场讨论中，美国也很难站在英国一方，很难再去支持这个老盟友。你们觉得，为什么会是这样呢？你们认为，原因是不是在于我们都还记得本国曾经经历过的那场"美国革命"呢？

不同殖民地的领袖人物，都曾努力用不同的方式来为本国人民赢得独立。在有些地方，人们组建起了军队，就像乔治·华盛顿组建起了美国军队一样。在其他一

Leaders in different colonies worked in different ways to win independence for their people. In some places, men organized armies just as George Washington had organized the American army. In other places, men and women organized less violent protests, like marches and speeches. One of the best known heroes of this time was a man in India named Gandhi.

Mohandas Gandhi didn't look much like the hero of a revolution! He was small and thin. He didn't talk much like a revolutionary leader. He said that people should not be violent in their protests. Now, India was a British colony. Gandhi had decided that the British were, at heart, a moral people, so he felt that he just needed to make them, as well as the rest of the world, see what was right. Then they would grant India its independence without a lot of people being killed.

Gandhi was very clever in thinking up things to do to draw attention to India's desire to become independent. He knew that England kept India to make money from the resources that India provided for England's factories and from the taxes that Indians paid. So he decided to make it harder for England to make money from India.

You know that the English in India had been buying cotton to ship to factories in England. This cotton was made into cloth and clothing. Some of the clothing was then shipped back to India and sold at very high prices. The English, of course, kept the profits. Now, before I tell you what Gandhi

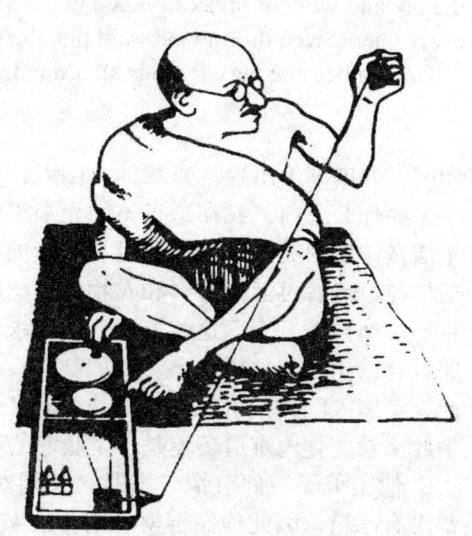

Gandhi spinning
甘地正在纺纱

些地方，人们则组织起来，进行不那么暴力的抵抗，比如游行啦，演讲啦。这一时期最著名的英雄人物之一，就是印度一个名叫甘地的人。

莫罕达斯·甘地的样子，可不太像是革命英雄呢！他的身材，既矮又瘦。他寡言少语，不太像革命领袖。他说，人们在进行抗议时，不应该使用暴力。注意，印度当时还是英国的一个殖民地。甘地判断，英国人本质上还是一个拥有道德观念的民族，因此他认为，只需让英国人和其他各国人民都明白什么东西是正确的就行了。然后，英国人就会同意印度独立，而无须让许多的人在暴力行动中丧生。

甘地非常聪明；他想出了许多的行动，来引起世人对印度渴望独立的关注。他清楚，英国之所以控制印度不放，是因为该国要通过印度给英国工厂提供的资源和印度人缴纳的税金来赚钱。所以，他决定要让英国难以从印度赚到钱。

你们都知道，英国人一直都在印度收购棉花，然后将棉花运回英国本土的工厂。这些棉花在工厂里被加工成布料和衣服。接下来，其中的一部分衣物又被运回

did, let me tell you what he *didn't* do. He didn't shoot the English living in India. He didn't burn the fields of cotton. He didn't try to sink the English ships that carried the cotton and later the cloth and clothing. He didn't do any of those violent things to drive the English away. What he did do was this. He asked all Indians to spend several hours a day spinning and weaving their own cloth. This way, they would have plenty of cloth without ever having to buy any more from England. So the English wouldn't be making money, but they also wouldn't have any excuse to come and shoot the Indian protesters either. Wasn't Gandhi a clever revolutionary?

Here's another thing he did. The English collected a big tax on salt. Indians had to have salt to preserve their food because most of them had no refrigerator. So the English had a sure source of tax money. Remember how Americans felt about the taxes they paid to England before the American Revolution? Well, the Indians felt the same way about the taxes they had to pay to England. Gandhi figured out a way to avoid paying the tax on salt without breaking the law. He led a great march to the sea. We all know that ocean water is very salty. Gandhi knew this too. So he led thousands of Indians to the edge of the sea. Once there, he taught them how to make the sea water evaporate. This would leave them lots of salt. This way his people could have all the salt they needed — without paying the tax and without breaking any law! When soldiers beat the people making salt, people everywhere, even in England, said that the soldiers were wrong.

Gandhi became very famous all around the world. People thought that it was marvelous

印度，并以高价出售。当然，英国人在这一过程中获得了利润。在告诉大家甘地都干了些什么之前，我在这里不妨先来跟大家说一说他没有干过什么。他并没有枪杀生活在印度的英国人。他并没有焚毁棉田。他并没有想方设法地去弄沉那些用于运送棉花、然后再运回布料和衣物的英国船只。他并没有实施暴力驱赶英国人的任何行动。他只做了下面这些事情：他要求所有的印度人每天都花上几个小时来纺纱，并且自己织布。这样一来，他们就会有足够多的布料，再也不需要从英国购买。因此，英国人既无钱可赚，也就找不到任何借口前来枪杀那些进行抗议的印度人了。由此来看，甘地难道还不是一个聪明的革命者吗？

他还干了一件事情。当时，英国对食盐征收巨额的税金。由于大多数印度人都没有冰箱，因此他们不得不用食盐来储存食物。于是，英国人就有了一种稳定的税收来源。你们还记得吗，在美国革命之前，美国人对他们要给英国交税又是一种什么样的感受呢？好吧，印度人对他们不得不向英国交税这一点，也有着同样的感受。甘地想出了一个既能逃避交税，同时又并不违法的办法。他向海洋发动了一场伟大的进军。我们都知道，海水是很咸的。甘地也清楚这一点。因此，他带领着成千上万的印度人来到了海边。一到那里，他就把蒸发海水的方法教给了他们。海水蒸发掉之后，就会给他们留下大量的食盐。这样，印度人民就能获得他们所需的全部食盐了，并且既不需要交税，也没有违法！英军前去搜捕那些制盐的民众后，世界各国的人们，甚至包括英国国内的人，都说英军的做法不对呢。

甘地变成了全世界家喻户晓的人物。人们觉得，不使用暴力就能进行如此强有

that he could make such a strong protest without using violence. Finally the pressure on England became too great, and England gave up. Soon after World War II was over, Indians had won their independence.

Once India was independent, other countries followed quickly. Leaders in Africa, like Kwame Nkrumah in Ghana and Jomo Kenyatta of Kenya, won independence for their countries. Algeria became independent from France, but only after a long war. The United States agreed to give the Philippines independence . . . and so it went all over the world. Country after country in Africa and Asia became independent. Large and small islands in the Pacific and Caribbean became independent. Many of these countries were poor and really had to struggle. Many of them are still struggling, but at least they are no longer ruled by foreigners. Do you know what? They almost all celebrate their Independence Day just as we celebrate the Fourth of July. Wouldn't it be fun to travel all around the world and visit every country on its national holiday? Now that almost every country is independent, that would make a very long trip! Do you suppose they all have fireworks?

力的反抗，简直就是一种奇迹。最终，由于承受的压力变得太过巨大，英国便妥协了。第二次世界大战结束后不久，印度人便赢得了独立。

印度一独立，其他国家便马上效仿起该国的做法来。非洲的一些领导人，比如加纳的夸梅·恩克鲁玛和肯尼亚的乔莫·肯雅塔，都为本国赢得了独立。阿尔及利亚摆脱了法国的统治，获得了独立，只是该国还经历了一场旷日持久的战争，才最终获得独立。美国也同意，让菲律宾获得独立……所以，独立运动席卷了全世界。亚洲和非洲各国一个接着一个地获得了独立。太平洋和加勒比海上大大小小的岛国，也纷纷获得了独立。在这些国家当中，许多都非常贫穷，确实不得不努力奋斗。虽说其中的许多国家如今依然在努力奋斗，但起码它们不再由外国人统治了。你们知道后来怎么样了吗？它们几乎都把自己的独立日当成国庆节，就像我们美国把7月4日当成国庆节一样呢。要是能够周游全世界，并在每个国家的国庆节那天去访问该国的话，不是很有意思的一件事情吗？既然差不多所有国家全都获得了独立，那么这会是一场旷日持久的旅行呢！你们觉得，这些国家会不会在国庆节里放焰火呢？

89 A New BIG POWER in the World

After World War II and all its killing and destruction, only two really strong countries were left in the world. These were both very

BIG COUNTRIES.

One of the reasons these two countries were strong is that they were

SO BIG.

On all that land they had lots of the resources a country needs to make it strong: land to grow food; lots of water; wood to build things; and minerals like iron, coal, and oil. These all help make a country strong.

Have you guessed which two big countries I'm talking about? One is very easy to guess. It's the United States. The other is Russia.

During World War II, you remember, these two giants were friends. They were allies. They fought on the same side. After the war was over, they became rivals. They competed to see which would be the stronger. This made for a lot of trouble in the world.

Let me tell you what had been happening in Russia since you last read about that country.

89　一个新的世界大国

经历了第二次世界大战，经历了其间的所有杀戮和毁灭之后，世界上便只剩下两个真正的强国了。这两个国家，都是国土非常广袤的

大国。

而这两个国家实力强大的原因之一，就在于它们的疆域都

非常广袤。

它们的国土上，都具有让一个国家强大起来所必需的诸多资源：种植粮食的土地；丰富的水资源；建筑所用的木材；以及诸如钢铁、煤炭和石油之类的矿产。所有这些，全都有助于一个国家变得强大起来。

你们有没有猜到，我现在所讲的是哪两个大国呢？其中一个国家很容易猜到。那就是美国。而另一个国家，就是俄国。

你们都还记得吧，在第二次世界大战期间，这两个大国还是友邦呢。它们结成了同盟。它们站在同一边战斗。可大战一结束，它们却变成了对手。它们相互竞争，看谁会变得更加强大。这就给世界带来了严重的问题。

现在我就来跟大家说一说，自上一次你们听到这个国家的情况之后，俄国发生了一些什么样的事情吧。

Peter the Great was a ruler of Russia called a czar or emperor. Russia was ruled by a czar or czarina (as a Russian queen was called) for almost two hundred years after Peter the Great. Then the Russians had a big and bloody revolution. This began in 1917. The czar who was ruling then and all of his family were shot.

The reason for the Russian Revolution was about the same as for the French Revolution. The czar and his nobles had great riches and power, but most of the people were very poor and they had no hope of life ever getting better for them.

In 1917 Russia had been fighting in World War I for three hard years. The war had made the misery of the people even more hopeless. When the revolution started, the soldiers stopped fighting and came home to help overthrow the rulers.

A Russian named Lenin had been working and plotting for many years to start the revolution, and he and his friends took charge. Soon Lenin was the head of the revolutionary government and the ruler of Russia.

In 1922, after the revolution, Russia was called the Union of Soviet Socialist Republics, shortened to U.S.S.R., the Soviet Union, or the Soviets. The U.S.S.R. included not only Russia, but eventually fourteen other republics in Europe and in Asia that had been conquered by Russia.

Lenin believed in a kind of government called communism. In communism everything was supposed to belong to the state for the good of all the poor people. Most of the big farms, for instance, were taken away from their rich owners and made into collective

彼得大帝是俄国的一位君主，称为沙皇或者皇帝。彼得大帝之后，在近两百年的时间里，俄国一直都是由一位沙皇或者女沙皇（这是俄国女皇的称谓）统治着。接下来，俄国人发动了一次大规模的血腥革命。此次革命，始于1917年。当时统治着俄国的那位沙皇，以及所有的皇室成员，全部被枪决了。

俄国革命的原因，与法国革命的原因差不多相同。沙皇及其手下的贵族掌握着巨大的财富和权力，但绝大部分人民却非常贫穷，没有改善自身生活的任何希望。

到了1917年的时候，俄国已经在第一次世界大战中艰难无比地打了三年的仗。这场战争，使得本已悲苦的人民更加没有了指望。革命爆发后，俄国士兵们都停止作战，回去帮助人民推翻本国的统治者了。

一位名叫列宁的俄国人，多年以来一直都在为发动这场革命而工作与谋划，并且是由他和他的朋友们负责来发动革命。不久后，列宁便成了革命政府的领袖和俄国的统治者。

革命之后，俄国在1922年更名为苏维埃社会主义共和国联盟，缩写为U.S.S.R.，简称"苏联"。苏维埃社会主义共和国联盟不只是由俄罗斯组成，其加盟共和国最终还包括了其他十四个被俄国征服了的欧、亚共和国。

列宁信仰一种叫作共产主义的政治制度。在共产主义的制度中，为了所有劳苦大众的利益，一切都应当属于国有。例如，人们从富有的地主手中收缴了绝大部分大型的农庄，将它们变成了集体农场。集体农场就是一个大型农庄；在那里，大家都在一起工作，种植庄稼，而所获利润的一部分，也由这个集体农场里的人共享。

farms. A collective farm is a large farm where everybody works together to raise the crops and the profit goes partly to all the people on the collective farm.

All the factories and stores in a communist country are owned not by private people, as they mostly are in our country, but by the state. The communist state itself is supposed to be owned by all the people together. This was a great change from the rule of the czars where most of the wealth and power was in the hands of the czar and his nobles. The communists felt they had to be sure that the new government would work, so they gave a great deal of power to the head of the Communist party. He became as powerful as a dictator.

After the revolution there was much suffering at first. Many people even starved to death, and many who were not in favor of communism were shot. But more and more schools were built, and this was good, for few people had been able to go to school when the czars had ruled. The poor people were still poor, but they felt now that there was a great difference from being poor under the czar with no hope of life ever becoming better for them. Now there was hope of better things to come. Great dams were built across the rivers to supply electricity for steel plants and tractor factories. The nobles' palaces were turned into museums for the people. Subways were built in Moscow. The army was given good leaders and was well trained.

The communists did two things that worried other countries a great deal. They made religious practice unlawful so that all houses of worship were closed. And they believed that communism should be spread all over the world. Even in countries where the people were not ill-treated and were satisfied with their own kinds of government, the communists

共产主义国家里的所有工厂和商店，也不是像我们美国常见的那样归私人所有，而是归国家所有。共产主义国家本身应当属于全体人民。与沙皇统治时期相比，这是一种翻天覆地的改变；因为在沙皇时期，财富和权力都是掌握在沙皇和贵族们的手中。共产主义者认为，他们必须确保新政府正常运作才行，因此将大量权力授予了共产党的领袖。

革命之后，苏联国内起初存在着一大堆困难。许多人甚至饿死了，还有许多不赞同共产主义的人则被枪杀了。不过，该国开设了越来越多的学校；而这是一件好事，因为在沙皇统治时期，很少有人上得起学。虽然贫苦的人依然贫苦，可他们觉得，如今这种贫苦，与沙皇统治时期他们毫无改善生活的指望那种贫苦相比，可是有了天渊之别呢。因为如今至少有了出现更加美好的事物的希望啊。该国在河流上修建了一座座大坝，为钢铁厂和拖拉机工厂提供电力。贵族们的宫殿，都被改造成了供人民参观的博物馆。莫斯科修建了地铁。军队也指派了优秀的领导，并且进行了很好的训练。

共产党人做了两件事情，让其他一些国家都大感担忧。他们把宗教仪式定为非法活动，因而关闭了所有的礼拜场所。同时他们还认为，应该将共产主义传播到全世界。即便是在人民没有受到压迫并对本国政体感到满意的那些国家里，共产党人也希望发动革命，从而让共产主义成为世界各国的政体形式。

hoped to get revolutions going so that communism could be made the form of government everywhere.

When Lenin died, the man who took his place as the ruler of the Soviet Union had a long name which would be very hard for you or me to pronounce because we are not used to the Russian language. But luckily he was called by his nickname, Stalin, which is quite easy and means "man of steel". Stalin[1] had first studied as a young man to be a priest. But then, instead of becoming a priest he had become a communist. It was of course very dangerous to be a communist under the czar's government, and Stalin had been put in prison and had often had to hide from the czar's men for trying to stir up a revolution. His experiences had made him hard and tough and that's why he was nicknamed Stalin.

Under Stalin, the Soviets built more factories and large new cities. When Germany suddenly attacked the U.S.S.R. in World War II, the Soviet armies under Stalin fought desperately against the Germans. Finally, as you know, the Soviet armies drove the Germans out of the Soviet Union and entered Germany from the Soviet Union, while the American and British armies were coming in from France.

After World War II, other countries found it hard to get along with the U.S.S.R. because the Soviets had ideas about government and freedom so very different from the ideas of democracies like the United States and England.

The biggest country in Europe, and the biggest country in Asia, and the biggest country

---

[1]　His real name was Iosif Vissarionovich Dzugashvili.

　　列宁去世后，继任苏联领导人职位的那个人有一个长长的名字，你们和我都很难念出来，因为我们都不熟悉俄语。但幸运的是，人们都用他的昵称"斯大林"来称呼他；这个昵称很容易念，意思则是指"钢铁一般的人"。斯大林[1]年轻的时候，起初学的是当一名牧师。但后来，他并没有变成一位牧师，而是变成了一名共产党人。在沙皇的统治下，成为一名共产党人当然是非常危险的；所以，斯大林曾经因为煽动革命未遂而被捕入狱，并且经常得躲避沙皇手下人的追捕。这些经历，让他变成了一个强硬坚韧的人；而他的昵称之所以是"斯大林"，原因也在于此。

　　在斯大林的统治下，苏联建立了更多的工厂、更多新的大城市。德国在第二次世界大战中向苏联发起突然袭击后，苏联军队在斯大林的指挥下，与德军进行了殊死搏斗。你们都知道，最后苏军将德军赶出了苏联，并从苏联攻入了德国本土；当时，美、英两国的军队也正在从法国攻入德国境内。

　　第二次世界大战结束后，其他国家都发现，它们很难与苏联打交道；因为苏联人在政体、自由等方面的观念，与美、英等国的民主观念都大相径庭。

---

　　[1]　斯大林（Stalin）的真名叫作约瑟夫·维萨里奥诺维奇·朱加什维利（Iosif Vissarionovich Dzugashvili）。

in the whole world had now become also one of the most important and powerful countries in the whole world. It also soon became the most dangerous country in the world. I'll tell you why in the next chapter.

　　这个属于欧洲最大、亚洲最大以及全世界最大的国家，此时也已变成了全世界最具影响力、实力最强大的国家之一。不久之后，它又变成了世界上最危险的一个国家。在下一章里，我将跟你们来说一说其中的原因。

90 Yesterday, Today, and Tomorrow

There is a candy shop near where I live. On its sign it says, "Made Fresh Every Hour." History is being made every day. It is being made fresh every hour. We read about it in the newspapers and the magazines, or hear about it on the radio or television.

Up to this time, history has been marked by the story of one war after another — some big, some small, some short, some long. Almost always a fight has been going on somewhere. It has been War, War, War — Fight, Fight, Fight. Children scratch, kick, and bite. But the older we get, the less do we use our fists and feet to settle quarrels. Fighting seems to be a sign of childhood — that we are *kids* — and our fights, that we call wars, a sign of how young the world really is and we really are — a sign that the world is still but a minute or two old.

Now we admire and praise as heroes Horatius, Leonidas, Joan of Arc, General Eisenhower, and those who have defended their countries against the attacks of the enemy, as we would admire a man who stops a burglar or a murderer who attacks his family in the night. But those, whether kings, generals, or princes, who do the attacking and take

90 昨天、今天和明天

我家的附近，有一家糖果商店。商店的招牌上，写着这样一句话："时时新鲜。"历史是由一天一天组成的。因此，历史就是"时时新鲜"的。我们既可以在报纸、杂志上看到历史，也可以在收音机或者电视上收听、收看到历史。

迄今为止，历史是以打了一场又一场战争为特征的；有些战争的规模很大，有些战争的规模很小；有些战争打得时间很短，有些战争则打得旷日持久。战争几乎总是在某个地方进行着。整个历史，始终都是战争、战争、再战争，打仗、打仗、再打仗。小朋友在打架的时候，都会抓呀、踢呀、咬呀。但我们年纪越大，就越会不常用拳脚和牙齿去解决争执了。打架似乎是孩子气的一种表现，即打架表明我们还是孩子；而各国之间、我们称之为战争的那种打架，则表明整个世界实际上还非常年轻，表明我们实际上还非常不懂事，表明整个世界仍然只有刚出生一两分钟那么大哩。

如今，我们都很崇拜、很赞赏像贺雷修斯、列奥尼达、圣女贞德、艾森豪威尔将军这样的英雄人物，以及那些抵抗来犯之敌并捍卫祖国的人，就像我们崇拜一个阻止了小偷或者凶徒在晚上袭击其家人的男人那样。而那些无缘无故，只是为了攫取更多权力、财富或者荣耀就发动袭击、夺走生命的人，无论身为国王、将军或

life with no other excuse than to add to their power or wealth or glory, are no better than burglars, who go forth with a gun and a blackjack to waylay, rob, and murder for the same purpose. War kills, war destroys, war costs millions of lives and billions of dollars — money that could be used to make us happy, to make the world a better place, instead of causing bitterness, suffering, misery, and unhappiness, widows, and orphans. No one is better off, not even the winner. War is a terrible game, in which even the winner loses.

This is certain: If wars do not end, they will be fought with weapons so deadly that all the people of a country or even of a continent may be killed. Already atomic bombs explode with such a blast that one bomb can blow a whole city to smithereens. Perhaps, if wars continue, there won't be anyone left alive in the whole wide world; and that will be the end of human history.

Perhaps wars can be stopped. Many people everywhere go on trying and hoping to end the danger of another war. It isn't easy to prevent wars, but if the United Nations can act like a fire department to put out wars like fires before they get burning too fiercely, then the world can go on with years of peace. New inventions will be used for peace instead of war.

Already man's inventions seem more magical than magic itself. Airplanes and helicopters and spaceships take the place of flying carpets. They're much better, too, than flying carpets for there really are airplanes, but magic carpets never flew except in man's imagination. Whatever you can imagine, no matter how wild your imagination is, will

者王子，与那些为了同样目的而带着枪棒前去拦路抢劫、劫掠财物或谋杀他人的盗贼比起来，却好不到哪里去。战争会杀人，战争会破坏，战争会夺走数百万人的性命，耗费数十亿美元的资金；这些资金，本来是可以用于让我们生活得很幸福、让世界变得更美好，而不是用于去制造痛苦、磨难、悲剧和不幸，不用于去导致寡妇成群、孤儿遍地的。战争过后，没有哪一方会变得更好，连获胜方也是如此。战争是一种可怕的游戏；即便是获胜者，最终也会损失惨重。

我们可以肯定的是：假如战争没有结果，双方都会使用致命武器来进行厮杀，使得一个国家，甚至是一个大陆上的人都有可能丧生。原子弹爆炸已经显示出了如此巨大的威力，因此只需一颗原子弹，就可以将整座城市夷为平地。假如战争继续下去的话，没准整个世界都不会再有活人幸存下来呢；到了那时，人类历史的末日就将到来。

或许，我们是可以防止战争爆发的。在世界各国，有许多的人都正在努力并希望消除再次爆发战争的隐患。虽说要阻止战争爆发并不容易，但如果联合国能够像一支消防队在火势变得猛烈之前将火扑灭那样，去扑灭战火的话，那么整个世界就可以保持长久的和平了。我们的新发明，就会用于和平目的，而不会用于战争了。

人类业已做出的发明，如今似乎比魔法本身更加神奇了。飞机、直升机和宇宙飞船，已经取代了飞毯。它们也比飞毯要好得多，因为飞机的的确确存在，而魔毯却只有在人们的想象之中才能飞起来。要是我们能够阻止战争爆发的话，那么不管什么东西，只要你们想得出，不管你们的想象有多么荒唐，有朝一日它们都很有可能发明出来。你们可以想出一种能够阻止所有战争的发明，并且你们也完全可以肯

probably someday be invented — if wars can be prevented. You can imagine an invention to prevent all wars and you can be pretty sure it will someday be in use — if another war doesn't spoil everything first.

Inventions are not quite the same as discoveries. If a thing was there all the time but people didn't know about it, it became a discovery, not an invention.

Discoveries and inventions! Discoveries have been just as important as inventions in the last hundred years and seem just as magical. Of course there are no more continents to discover, but there are still wonderful discoveries being made all the time.

Some of the most important discoveries have been about diseases and how to prevent them. These discoveries have long names like:

Vaccination! Smallpox used to be everywhere. It was a deadly disease. The discovery of how to prevent it by vaccination has saved maybe as many lives as war has taken.

Pasteurization of milk! Do you know what that is? It was named for the Frenchman who discovered how to kill deadly germs. You can guess his name. Yes, it was Pasteur.

Inoculation! Do you know what that is? Has the doctor ever given you an injection from a needle to protect you from tetanus or typhoid?

Anesthetics! Do you know what that is? Anesthetics put you to sleep if you have to have an operation. Think of the suffering the discovery of anesthetics has prevented.

Penicillin! Do you know what this is? It was discovered just in time to save the lives of

定，如果没有下一场战争先把一切全都毁灭掉的话，那么这种发明总有一天会被人类利用起来呢。

发明并非等同于发现。假如某种东西一直存在，只是人们过去并不了解，那么找到这种东西就是一种发现，而不是一种发明。

发现和发明！在过去的一百年里[1]，发现一直都与发明有着同等的重要性，并且似乎非常神奇。当然，尽管人类不会再发现更多的新大陆，但各种奇妙的发现却一直都在层出不穷呢。

人类最重要的发现当中，有一些是关于疾病和预防疾病的。这些发现的叫法都有很长的名字，比如：

疫苗接种！过去，世界各地都有天花。这是一种致命的疾病。通过接种疫苗来预防天花这一发现，挽救了许许多多的生命，数量没准与战争夺走的生命一样多呢。

巴氏灭菌奶！你们知道这是什么吗？有一个法国人，他发现了杀灭致命细菌的办法；这种办法，就是以他的名字命名的。你们可能已经猜到了他的名字。对，他就是巴斯德。

预防注射！你们知道这是什么东西吗？医生有没有给你们打过那种预防破伤风或者伤寒的针呢？

麻醉剂！你们知道这是什么东西吗？如果要动手术的话，麻醉剂就能让你们在

---

[1]　作者编著本书的时间是二十世纪五十年代，所以此处所说的"过去的一百年里（in the last hundred years）"，指的就是十八世纪。

many wounded men in World War II.

I wish I could tell you about inventions like the electric eye and radar and jet propulsion. I wish I could tell you about famous scientists like Charles Steinmetz and Albert Einstein. I wish I could tell you about all the inventions and discoveries — from vacuum cleaners to cyclotrons, from air conditioners to electron microscopes, from dynamos to lasers and quasars and human-heart transplants. And blood plasma — an African American, Charles Drew, figured out how to store this in blood banks so it, too, could be used to save the wounded fighting men. You see, scientists can be war heroes just as much as the soldiers! I wish I could tell you about all of them, but I can't. There isn't room in this book for the story of these and dozens of other wonderful things; and besides, I'd never catch up, for new discoveries and inventions are being made all the time — "Made Fresh Every Hour."

This story ends here, but only for the moment, for history is a continuing story and keeps going on and on. Even while you are reading this line, scientists are working on inventions and discoveries that may be in the history books of the future.

If you were living in the year 10,000 A.D., as some boy or girl will be, your history would only be just begun when you had reached where we are now. Even World War II would then seem as long ago as the fights of the Stone Age men seem to us. You might think of us and all our wonderful inventions in the same way that we now think of the

手术的过程中昏睡过去。想一想吧，麻醉剂这种发现，减少了多少痛苦啊。

盘尼西林[1]！你们知道这是什么东西吗？它的及时发现，在第二次世界大战中可拯救了无数伤员的性命哩。

我希望，还能给你们说一说像光电管、雷达以及喷气动力这样的发明。我希望，还能给你们讲一讲像查尔斯·施泰因梅茨和阿尔伯特·爱因斯坦这些知名科学家的情况。我希望，还能给你们介绍所有的发明与发现，从吸尘器到回旋加速器，从空调到电子显微镜，从发电机到激光、类星体，再到人类心脏的移植，一一说给你们听。还有血浆；一位名叫查尔斯·德鲁的非洲裔美国人，想出了把血浆储藏在血库里的办法，从而使之可以用于挽救伤员。你们看到了吧，科学家完全可以像士兵一样，成为战争中的英雄呢！我希望能够把这一切都介绍给大家，可我做不到。本书已经没有足够多的篇幅，来装下这些故事，以及其他诸多的精彩内容了；此外，我也跟不上时代的发展，因为时时刻刻都有新的发现和发明出现：它们的确是"时时新鲜"啊。

本书所讲述的故事，到此就算结束了；但这只是暂时的，因为历史是一个讲不完的故事，而历史的脚步也永远不会停下来。即便就在你们读到这句话的时候，科学家们也正在刻苦钻研那些可能会出现在未来的历史书中的发明和发现呢。

假若你们像将来的某个小朋友那样，生活在公元10000年的话，那么当你们读到我们现在所处的这个时代后，你们的历史可能刚刚开始呢。到了那时，就算是第

---

[1] 盘尼西林（Penicillin），即青霉素。它是从青霉菌中提取出来的一种常用抗生素。

discovery of copper and bronze.

Perhaps then people will no longer use trains, boats, automobiles, or even airplanes, but go from place to place as on some magic carpet, simply by wishing. Perhaps then they will no longer use letters, telephones, radio, television, or even computers, but read each other's thoughts at any distance.

Perhaps by then people will know how to build factories that don't poison the air and water and to use earth's resources wisely so we don't run out. And perhaps people will have learned to share, so that everyone in the whole wide world has enough food to eat and a decent place to live. Perhaps, best of all, people by then will know how to settle their problems without fighting wars.

And so on — World without end — Amen!

二次世界大战，似乎也发生在很久以前，就像石器时代的战争给我们的感受一样。那时，你们在看待我们、看待我们做出的所有奇妙发明时，可能就会跟我们如今看待古人发现铜和青铜的过程一样呢。

到了那时，人们或许会不再使用火车、轮船、汽车，甚至不再使用飞机，而是只需动动念头，就会像是坐着某种魔毯那样，从一个地方飞到另一个地方了。到了那时，人们或许会不再使用书信、电话、收音机、电视机，甚至不再使用电脑，而是不管相隔多远，都能读取彼此的想法呢。

到了那时，人们或许会知道如何建造一座座不再污染空气和水源的工厂，知道如何审慎地使用地球上的资源，从而使得我们不会耗尽这些资源了。到了那时，人们或许会不得不学会共享，从而让世界所有的人都有足够多的粮食可吃，都有像样的地方可住。而最重要的则是，到了那时，人们或许就会懂得不用诉诸战争便可以解决彼此之间争端的窍门了。

如此等等——世界便会生生不息，永无尽头！